Sons of Sarasvatī

Late Exemplars of the Indian Intellectual Tradition

HEDGEHOG AND FOX

ashoka UNIVERSITY
HISTORY SERIES

GENERAL EDITOR RUDRANGSHU MUKHERJEE
"The fox knows many things, but the hedgehog knows one big thing"

Steven I. Wilkinson ARMY AND NATION
Thomas R. Trautmann ELEPHANTS AND KINGS
Partha Chatterjee, Sudipta Kaviraj, Nivedita Menon THE INDIAN IDEOLOGY
Nayanjot Lahiri ASHOKA IN ANCIENT INDIA
Nicholas B. Dirks AUTOBIOGRAPHY OF AN ARCHIVE
Vasudha Dalmia HINDU PASTS
Dipesh Chakrabarty THE CALLING OF HISTORY
Sunil Agnani HATING EMPIRE PROPERLY
Mahesh Rangarajan NATURE AND NATION
Bhavani Raman DOCUMENT RAJ
Sumit Guha BEYOND CASTE
Iqtidar Alam Khan INDIA'S POLITY IN THE AGE OF AKBAR
Linda Hess BODIES OF SONG
Charu Gupta THE GENDER OF CASTE
Ajay Skaria UNCONDITIONAL EQUALITY
Velcheru Narayana Rao TEXT AND TRADITION IN SOUTH INDIA
Uday Kumar WRITING THE FIRST PERSON
Chinya V. Ravishankar SONS OF SARASVATI
Christian Lee Novetzke THE QUOTIDIAN REVOLUTION

INDIAN HISTORY CLASSICS
Ranajit Guha A RULE OF PROPERTY FOR BENGAL
Ranajit Guha THE SMALL VOICE OF HISTORY
Romila Thapar THE PAST BEFORE US
Muzaffar Alam THE LANGUAGES OF POLITICAL ISLAM IN INDIA *c.*1200–1800
Asok Sen ISWAR CHANDRA VIDYASAGAR AND HIS ELUSIVE MILESTONES
Rosalind O'Hanlon CASTE CONFLICT AND IDEOLOGY
Arvind Krishna Mehrotra, ed. A CONCISE HISTORY OF INDIAN LITERATURE IN ENGLISH
Ramachandra Guha AN ANTHROPOLOGIST AMONG THE MARXISTS AND OTHER ESSAYS
Partha Chatterjee DEAD MAN WANDERING
Partha Chatterjee EMPIRE AND NATION
Partha Chatterjee THE BLACK HOLE OF EMPIRE
M.S.S. Pandian BRAHMIN AND NON-BRAHMIN
Nayanjot Lahiri FINDING FORGOTTEN CITIES
Iqtidar Alam Khan THE MUGHAL NOBILITY
Srinath Raghavan WAR AND PEACE IN MODERN INDIA

HISTORICAL SOURCEBOOKS IN CLASSICAL INDIAN THOUGHT
Patrick Olivelle, ed. A DHARMA READER

Sons of Sarasvatī

Late Exemplars of the Indian Intellectual Tradition

By

Chinya V. Ravishankar

Translations of Biographies in Kannaḍa by

Çāmarājanagara Veṅkaṭaramaṇa Śāstri

and

Maisūru Sūryanārāyaṇabhaṭṭa Puṭṭaṇṇa

permanent black

in association with

ashoka UNIVERSITY

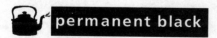

Published by
PERMANENT BLACK
'Himalayana', Mall Road, Ranikhet Cantt,
Ranikhet 263645
Email: perblack@gmail.com

in association with

ashoka
UNIVERSITY

Distributed by
ORIENT BLACKSWAN PRIVATE LIMITED
Bangalore Bhopal Bhubaneshwar Chandigarh Chennai
Ernakulam Guwahati Hyderabad Jaipur Kolkata
Lucknow Mumbai New Delhi Patna
www.orientblackswan.com

ISBN 978-81-7824-496-9

Printed and bound by Sapra Brothers, New Delhi 110092

To my mother
and the memory of my father

ಹೊತ್ತು ಹೋಗುವುದೆನಗೆ ಸತ್ತವರ ಸಂಗದಲಿ
ಬಳಸಿನಲಿ ಬಂದಿಹರ ಕಾಣುತಿಹೆನು
ಎತ್ತೆತ್ತ ಸುಳಿಸುವೆನೋ ಈ ಕಣ್ಣನತ್ತತ್ತ
ಹಳಮೆಯ ಮಹಾತ್ಮರನು ಪರಮಕವಿಗಳನು
ನನಗವರೆ ಕೈಬಿಡದ ಕೆಳೆಯರಾದವರು
ದಿನದಿನದ ಮಾತುಕಥೆಗೆನಗಿರುವರು

⋮

ನನ್ನ ಯೋಚನೆಯೆಲ್ಲ ಸತ್ತವರ ಸೇರಿದುವು
ಅವರೊಡನೆ ಬಾಳುವೆ ಪುರಾತನದಲಿ
ಅವರ ಗುಣಗಳನೊಲಿವೆ, ಅವರ ದೋಷವ ಸುಲಿವೆ
ಅವರಾಶೆಭಯಗಳಲಿ ಪಾಲ ಕೊಳುವೆ
ವಿನಯಭಾವದವರ ಮನವನಾರಯ್ವೆ
ಒನೆದ ಶಿಕ್ಷಣದೆಡೆಗೆ ಬಗೆಯನೆಳೆದೊಯ್ವೆ

⋮

From *Kaviśiṣya*, B.M. Srikantaiah's Kannaḍa translation of Robert Southey's poem *The Scholar*.

CONTENTS

LIST OF PLATES

ACKNOWLEDGEMENTS

ACKNOWLEDGEMENTS are due, first and foremost, to my mother, who has long been an understated and subtle force shaping my intellectual and personal development. She surely deserves the most direct credit for my having undertaken this work. My numerous discussions with her, even in childhood, have piqued and maintained my interest in a variety of matters, including such as form the substance of this work. She has also played a direct role in this work, collecting material for me, and helping me clarify my thinking on numerous points. She has always been, and continues to be an inspiration.

Thanks are due next to Professor T.V. Venkatachala Sastry of Mysore, with whom I have had the privilege of discussing this work on several occasions. Each time, I was enriched by copies of relevant material as well as engaging conversation. The breadth and depth of his scholarship, his generosity, and his encouragment were all reasons for me to look forward to our meetings with anticipation. Half a world happens to intervene between our locations, making our meetings rare but precious. I am grateful that no such distance has existed between his enthusiasm and mine for the substance of these efforts.

Many of the Sanskrit verses in this volume were of such quality and subtlety that I did not feel I could do them justice. I am indebted to several individuals who have helped me with this task. *Vidvān* H.V. Nagaraja Rao, formerly of the Oriental Research Institute of Mysore, and a well-known scholar of Sanskrit literature and grammar, translated the verses appearing on pages 45–51. Dr Shankar Rajaraman of Bangalore undertook to translate many other verses, including the *citrakāvya* in this volume. Apart from being a psychiatrist with a busy practice, he is also a researcher at the National Institute of Advanced Studies, an accomplished Sanskrit poet who composes and publishes *citrakāvya,* and among the handful of individuals today who are up to the challenges of the classical art of *aṣṭāvadhāna.* Mr Naresh Keerti of the National Institute of Advanced Studies, Bangalore, has also been of great assistance. He undertook a reading of the full manuscript, made various suggestions for improvement, and checked and recast my original transliterations in punctuated form.

I am grateful to Professor Sheldon Pollock of Columbia University for his encouragement and for his early affirmation of the value of this effort. It was at his suggestion that I began to enlarge this work beyond the parameters I had originally envisioned. I found his support especially valuable as this work neared publication.

Finally, I want to thank my wife Aruna for her patience, understanding, and support; the list of things deferred on account of this work is not inconsiderable. My daughters Tara and Leena, both sources of unending delight for me, have long been bemused by the sight of their father's poring over books and manuscripts in strange scripts. They deserve my thanks for periodically enquiring how the work was coming along, and suggesting that I get it done. Now, they might see the results of those efforts, and perhaps some day, even read it.

TRANSLATOR'S INTRODUCTION

TRADITIONAL *pāṇḍitya,* or scholarship acquired in the traditional Indian fashion, through intense study under the academic tutelage and personal nurture of an accomplished guru, is an ancient institution with a distinguished history. Sadly, it is practically extinct in modern India. Its decline is remarkably recent; it flourished in its full glory even in the 19th century, and traditionally trained scholars were numerous well into the 20th century. To a degree, the political changes that occurred in India during and after the 19th century contributed to this decline. Such changes caused the loss of many traditional sources of scholarly patronage, such as the numerous kings, princes, and feudal lords who had long been primary centers of political and economic power in India. These notables generally upheld the traditions of *rājadharma,* or princely duties, which valued scholarly patronage highly. This subtlety was entirely lost on the British overlords of India, who disdained such patronage as wasteful indulgence [Ikegame 2007], and focused instead on ensuring peace in their empire and on its efficient administration. To this end, they instituted a system of indirect rule, keeping in power numerous kings and princes to serve as the nominal rulers of their respective states [Ramusack 2004]. Happily, such rulers often continued their traditions of patronage. As these traditional institutions diminished, however, scholars were increasingly forced to depend on erratic support from indifferent government institutions.

While the decline of traditional *pāṇḍitya* is a complex phenomenon, its proximal cause is surely the move to Western education, and away from traditional learning, by the last three generations of brāhmaṇa families.[1] These

[1] This trend owes much to Thomas Babbington Macaulay's infamous Minute on Education persuading William Bentinck, then Governor General, to establish English as the sole medium of higher education in India [Sharp and Richey 1920]. Sadly, it need not have been thus. Bentinck's action reversed the policies of his predecessor Warren Hastings, who saw far greater value in British administrators becoming familiar with Indian scholarship and traditions. Outstanding scholars like James Prinsep and Horace Wilson, themselves products of Hastings's policies, strongly opposed Macaulay, but to no avail. As Cutts [1953] shows, Macaulay's evangelical background had much to do with his antipathy to Indian scholarship and tradition. In his Minute, Macaulay derides Hinduism as a "false religion", Indian scholarship as "an incumbrance and blemish", and "useless", and proudly proclaims his ignorance of Sanskrit and Arabic. The irony of the contrast between this declared ignorance

latest heirs to an unbroken line of tradition reaching back five or more millennia would otherwise have been the standard bearers for this rich and venerable heritage of scholarship. Sadly, this break has inevitably resulted in the loss of connection not just with Sanskrit, in which are firmly embedded the roots of the rich scholarly values and traditions of India, but also with many subtle aspects and insights of Indian culture. Pollock argues urgently that several millennia of accumulated scholarly heritage is at risk of becoming irrecoverably lost in the next generation or two [Pollock 2009, 2008]. Entire fields of Indian scholarship may already be defunct, or at best represented by one or two octagenarians.[2] Compounding this decline are the many dominant actors in modern Indian politics who associate such scholarship with Brahminic traditions, with which they neither identify nor empathize. There is little immediate prospect of any initiatives by the Indian government aimed at buttressing the walls of this crumbling edifice.

Dimmer still, are the prospects for such initiatives by Indian society at large, or by the brāhmaṇa community, whose members stand justly accused of having frittered away their scholarly patrimony through utter neglect. Indifference to scholarship is widespread, whether in India or elsewhere, and such indifference would be no surprise in the absence of an intellectual tradition.[3] Yet, among the brāhmaṇas, erstwhile custodians of the Indian scholarly tradition, it is common today for even the best-educated descendants of the finest scholars of just two generations ago to be entirely ignorant of their own scholarly heritage.[4]

---

and the certitude of his judgments on the value of Indian learning appears to have been lost on him and his superiors.

[2]Aklujkar makes this same point [in Michaels 2001, p. 43]: "In 1992 Professor Robert O. Goldman came to India with a video camera with the intention of filming the pandits in action. When he asked me if I could suggest the names of some truly impressive pandits whom he could interview and capture on film, I could not come up with more than two or three names, all of them belonging to pandits close to or beyond their seventies! This may be due to my limited knowledge of traditional scholarship in India… It is also possible that the standard I was applying was too high… However, in view of what I hear from many of my knowledgeable colleagues, I am inclined to discount these possibilities. I consider it almost certain that a true pandit is now an extremely endangered species."

[3]There is a long-established and politically powerful tradition of anti-intellectualism in America, for example. Also see AAAS [2013], where the Humanities and Social Sciences Commission of the AAAS, the leading academy for these disciplines in the nation with the strongest economy in history, is obliged to make the case for a liberal education in economic terms, the only language that contemporary American society readily relates to.

[4]This is an unfortunate but common impediment to scholarship. For instance, Sharma

This sudden decline in traditional Sanskrit scholarship presents a stark contrast to the remarkable flowering it witnessed between the 15th and 18th centuries C.E. This efflorescence brought about major innovations across a diverse collection of fields, including grammar, logic, literary theory, philosophy, and mathematics. The ideas and theories produced during this period are judged as having been unprecedented in their quality and quantity (see, for example, Pollock [2001]).[5]

The precipitous decline of traditional *pāṇḍitya* that immediately followed hence presents a major paradox, and is the subject of much ongoing research.[6] This institution, after all, had remained robust in the face of very adverse circumstances, such as a full millennium of Muslim rule. We can, however, point to some factors in the waning of traditional scholarship.

The 19th century is of exceptional significance in the intellectual history of India. During this time can clearly be seen the decline of traditional ways, and the wholesale intrusion of Western-style modernity into Indian society, and thence into the domain of scholarship. If we look specifically at the example of Maisūru, we see the classical traditions of *rājadharma* surviving more or less intact till 1868, the year of Kṛṣṇarāja Voḍeyar III's death. The British had allowed him free rein in such matters, but undertook a reorganization of his practices of scholarly and religious patronage upon his death. Perhaps for the first time, economic considerations overrode traditional criteria for royal patronage. Çāmarāja Voḍeyar X, the successor, was given a Western-style education, and while he continued traditional patronage, under him began a process of economic and social transformation that reached its zenith under his son and successor Kṛṣṇarāja Voḍeyar IV. By the first quarter of the 20th century, Maisūru's social and economic fabric had been transformed, and with it, the traditions of learning and scholarship.

[1981, p. 545] laments after listing numerous scholars of *Navya Nyāya* logic: "The lack of historical material, for which the indifference of their descendants is not a little to blame, prevents a fuller account of these celebrities." Also see the preface to Gundappa [1970, v. 1].

[5] A small sample of the luminaries it produced would include Raghunātha Śiromaṇi and Gadādhara Bhaṭṭāçārya in logic, Jagannātha Paṇḍita in literary theory, Bhaṭṭoji Dīkṣita in grammar, Madhusūdana Sarasvatī in philosophy, and the astonishingly prolific Appayya Dīkṣita. In mathematics, this efflorescence may have begun nearer the earlier part of this period, as the dates ascribed to the Keralite mathematician Mādhava of Saṅgamagrāma suggest, but this was a tradition of true excellence. It had, for example, obtained infinite series expansions of circular functions two centuries before the calculus was invented.

[6] See, for example, the *Sanskrit Knowledge Systems on the Eve of Colonialism* project at Columbia University (`http://www.columbia.edu/itc/mealac/pollock/sks`).

As the traditions of *rājadharma* declined, scholars lost not just their traditional sources of economic support, but more significantly, a major source of social status and prestige. Support of *pāṇḍitya* was a deeply held societal value, but high regard from the monarch for scholarship affirmed this value through his high-profile example.[7] Patronage of *paṇḍitas*, whose lives were dedicated to learning and *dhārmic* observances, flowed from the universal obligation to sustain *dharma*, which in turn sustained order and well-being in kingdom and society. This relationship between patron and *paṇḍita*, however, was never transactional, since the *paṇḍita's* devotion to learning and observance arose from his own *dharma*, whose obligations he discharged regardless of patronage.[8]

In contrast, this relationship became entirely transactional with the British, who saw the *paṇḍita* as economically unproductive, unless as teacher. Sustenance of *dharma* transformed into wages for work, and with the devaluation of traditional learning that was official policy, such wages were always meagre. The result was a loss of both economic and social status for traditional scholars. Social status and prestige were now to be attained mainly through such means as Western education, knowledge of English, and government employment.[9]

Paradoxically, their very devotion to learning may have nudged brāhmaṇas away from traditional *pāṇḍitya*. Modern European thought came to India mature, its transition to scientific empiricism complete, and the technical prowess it engendered on full display. Earlier invaders, such as Muslims, had learned more from Indian *paṇḍitas* than they had taught them. In contrast, Western education offered new, secular, and practical knowledge. There was no equivalent in traditional *pāṇḍitya*, and no doctrinal

---

[7] The greatest scholars were granted even the insignia of royalty (see footnote 547).

[8] See page 165 and footnote 443 for an extraordinary instance of dedication to observance.

[9] The modern cash-based economy increased the pressure to seek salaried employment. Western-educated Indians quickly gained wealth and prestige, and traditionalists fell behind in both respects. Conflicts such as that recounted on page 292 play out even to this day.

prohibitions standing in the way.[10] Their scholarly traditions led brāhmaṇas inevitably to Western education.[11]

What they gained in the process is clear, but what they lost is less obvious. The loss of the traditions of debate and innovation integral to traditional scholarship, for instance, has resulted in a broad decline in the standards of all scholarly activity in contemporary India.[12] This loss, sadly, is not just intellectual, but also deeply cultural. Indian tradition reveres scholars not merely as learned men, but as embodiments of certain moral and human ideals. The ascetic practices of the traditional Brahminic way of life and the strict discipline required for extensive mastery of a subject intersected in a traditional scholar, each complementing and contributing to the other's intensity.[13] The highest measure of respect was thus paid to *vaidika* brāhmaṇas, who devoted themselves to scholarship and to upholding traditions, relying for sustenance on societal patronage or honoraria from students upon completing their studies.[14]

Such lives are lived even now in India, but far less commonly than they were even fifty years ago. Practices, norms, and attitudes that were prevalent and widespread are now uncommon and unappreciated.[15] The intellectual output of traditional scholars continues to be studied, and has indeed become more available than previously. However, relatively little material

---

[10] Even taboos on associating with those without caste were observed mostly in the personal and ritual spheres. High-caste Hindus had even served in Muslim courts and armies for a long time. Dilemmas did arise, however. See, for example, the incident involving J.G. Tait and Rāmaśēśa Śāstri on page 289.

[11] The value of modern education was readily recognized even by some of the most traditional scholars. See the views expressed by Viśvēśvara Śāstri on page 291.

[12] Scholarly debates also had social and cultural impact. Debates had prominent sponsors, and the laity often attended, drawn by interest, the audience, or the event's significance.

[13] This point is elaborated by Michaels [2001, p. 3]: "The functions of a pandit in the traditional sense are manifold. He is a scholar, teacher, adviser, spiritual master, specialist, and legal expert. He is a symbol of purity and identity for Sanskrit scholarship... In India, it is believed that a traditional pandit should have a deep commitment to learning and teaching, a special charisma, and sometimes even a sectarian initiation (*dīkṣa*...) ...a pandit quite often has an ascetic way of life, with restraints on food or sexual relations aiming at a balance between knowledge and personality similar to the life of holy men..."

[14] An illustration of societal commitment to such patronage appears on page 294.

[15] For instance, Sanskrit quotations from a variety of sources appear frequently in these biographies. The educated reader of the time was clearly assumed to be capable of understanding them in their original context, and appreciating the various associated subtleties. That assumption would not be valid today.

exists on the personal lives of such individuals, who were the very embodiments of scholarly, cultural, and societal traditions. Their lives are rich in reference markers that help understand transformations in these traditions.

The biographies in this volume are about a century old, and were written precisely to provide such signposts. Their subjects are three of the finest scholars of the time, representing exceptional examples of traditional *pāṇḍitya.* These works also yield valuable insights into contemporary society and into the traditions of royal patronage in 19th-century Mysore, whose kings emerged as the greatest patrons of the arts and scholarship in India following the decline of the Marāṭhas, and after four decades of diminished patronage during the usurpation by Haider 'Ali and his son Ṭippu.

If an understanding of scholarly lives was important a hundred years ago, it is surely even more so today, given our greater remove from the tradition. Scholarly activity is a cultural process; its vitality derives from cultural and societal context. The dynamics of scholarly activity, however, are not discernible in its end products. There are even fields (grammar and logic, say, in our context), where the scholarly end product must be cast in culturally inert terms. A scholar's legacy can hence be impersonal and static, and open to imputations of cause long after the fact. Motivations aside, such imputations are dangerous to make in the absence of proper context, which of course, our modern sensibilites and perspectives could never provide.

For instance, the lively ongoing debate in India on its cultural and scholarly heritage and what it means to be Indian is not always well-informed by historical context, not least because Indian tradition has long been oblivious to its value, and indifferent to its preservation. Both the Indian and Western intellectual traditions are deeply indebted to classical thought.[16] The intellectual self-confidence of the West, however, does not obtain from an effort to reach back to these ancients, but from a sense of connection to intellectual antecedents of the proximate past, a recognition among intellectuals that many of the greatest figures of their tradition lived within just the last six hundred years, and a sense of pride and privilege in keeping this tradition alive. The tradition is within reach. There is sufficient context when seeking to understand it.[17]

---

[16] See, for instance, the famous quote from Whitehead [1978]: "The safest general characterization of the European philosophical tradition is that it consists of a series of footnotes to Plato." The high regard for ancient traditions in India, is of course, well known.

[17] Whitehead [1925] observes the following of the 17th century, a remarkable epoch in the

Some of the very greatest figures in the Indian intellectual tradition too, flourished in the immediate past. Just a couple of generations ago, Indian scholars enjoyed the same sense of connection to their intellectual forebears as do modern Western scholars. Moreover, the Indian tradition, unlike that of the West, represented a continuum of intellectual heritage, reaching back to the most ancient of times. Recent forebears of the tradition embodied ancient traditions not just in spirit, but even in the specifics. Scholars surely derived great intellectual assurance from being rooted in an ancient tradition whose scholarly acomplishments were on par with those of any other.

Today, this sense of connection or proximity to this tradition seems to have been lost. We live, as it were, on the wrong side of a high wall dividing us from this precious intellectual heritage. Over the top of this wall, we may catch glimpses of towering but distant peaks, the presumed abode of the mighty ancients. Nothing is visible of what lies just across the wall, however, except to those who would exert themselves to scale it.

Many do succeed in this effort, but the loudest and most strident voices in the debate alluded to above, so full of sound and fury, often belong to those who appear to just discount the possibility of much value lying across this metaphorical wall, and to others who make extravagant claims based on fanciful reconstructions of a venerable but inaccessible past atop those remote peaks. One side may suffer from a lack of imagination and the other from a surfeit of it, but more information would surely be helpful everywhere.[18] Fortunately, just across the wall lies a wealth of textual artifacts, whose exploration can reveal much about who we are and how we got here.

Such philological explorations are most meaningful if done by the light of proper historical, social, and intellectual context. Well-documented biographies of individuals defining historical, social, and intellectual traditions can provide some of this missing context. Their importance goes far

---

intellectual history of the West: "A brief, and sufficiently accurate, description of the intellectual life of the European races during the succeeding two centuries and a quarter up to our own times is that they have been living on the accumulated capital of ideas provided for them by the genius of the seventeenth century."

[18] We note in this context that the European Rennaisance was characterized by a nostalgia, even reverence, for classical antiquity. Later thinkers, such as Bacon and Descartes, helped clarify the role of empiricism in modern scientific thought, and set modern science apart from traditional philosophy. The point here is not that such processes should be unique to the West. It is, rather, that the Indian intellectual tradition is likely guilty of having squandered precisely the sort of intellectual capital that Whitehead alludes to in footnote 17.

beyond their value to scholars. They can contribute to the evolution of a nation's self-image.

Such considerations apply beyond societal discourse; indeed, our argument elicits resonant echoes within the domain of scholarship. Humanist scholarship is centrally the project of placing ideas into context to foster their fuller understanding.[19] Theory defines the terms of discourse, methods, and vocabulary. When scholarship applies these tools, it is always with context as backdrop, the frame of reference within which all is measured and all meaning construed.

The value of such context is well illustrated for the domain of political philosophy by work such as that of Skinner [2002], which approaches textual artifacts as illocutory interventions in a contemporaneous debate or polemic. This approach is difficult to apply to Indian texts, however, since individual and societal context are entirely absent from Indian texts [Pollock 2001]. Not only is biographical information uniformly lacking in the original texts, it is missing even from the extensive corpus of commentaries. Some have therefore suggested a shift of focus to the extraordinary wealth of available textual material [Ganeri 2008], arguing that when authors deliberately omit autobiographical, social, and political context to avoid distracting from their intended illocutionary acts, conclusions drawn from these omissions are valid even in Skinnerian terms, and suggest inter-textual analysis as a partial solution to these difficulties. Such alternatives, however, are no substitutes for context derived from primary source material. Others have thus called for more biographies of Indian scholars to be brought to light, perhaps as translations from vernaculars [Minkowski 2014].

The needs of scholars aside, a greater availability of such biographies in languages other than those of the originals would be of value to Indian society, and even to the descendants of these scholars. M.S. Puṭṭaṇṇa, even in his 1910 biography of Kuṇigala Rāmaśāstri (see page 161) laments the lack of such biographies, and the consequent inability of Indian society to view itself in the context of its own accomplishments.

I was therefore excited to receive a copy of a biography of Sōsale Garaḷapurī Śāstri, a leading 19th-century scholar of literature in the kingdom of Maisūru, from his great-granddaughter, Smt. Sarōjā Veṅkaṭarām, who had

[19] At least, so it seems to me. I trust this will not be seen as a controversial position.

obtained it from her brother, S.R. Śivasvāmi. This work is a detailed narrative of Garaḷapurī Śāstri's life and contains the family's own account of its antecedents and history. Its information comes directly from Garaḷapurī Śāstri's son Ayyā Śāstri, a great scholar in his own right, and the last family member to have had close associations with Sōsale, home to his ancestors for four generations.

I spent four very fulfilling days in Mysore (Dec. 24–Dec. 27, 2008), two of them sorting through a disorganized and musty pile of manuscripts and books belonging to Garaḷapurī Śāstri and Ayyā Śāstri, restoring some order to the collection.[20] As far as I know, these materials had lain in neglect for around seven or eight decades. Kavitāvilāsa, the house Ayyā Śāstri and his descendants had lived in since 1894, had recently been demolished and replaced with commercial property. Ayyā Śāstri's books and manuscripts had been put away in a steel closet. Time and neglect had taken their toll, but I was able to locate and identify many manuscripts in Garaḷapurī Śāstri's meticulous, calligraphic hand. I was unable to complete my task of cataloguing the manuscripts, but they were stored in plastic bags, preliminary to their fuller rehabilitation.

Immediately thereafter, they entered into the possession of Ayyā Śāstri's great-grandson Mr Sandeep Sastry, whose father Mr S.K. Dwarki inherited Kavitāvilāsa. Access to these materials has since not been possible. At the time, Mr Sandeep Sastry indicated that he intended to digitize all these documents. It is to be hoped that efforts in this direction will proceed before the passage of too many more years, to ensure both the preservation as well as accessibility of these precious documents.

I was also fortunate to have obtained manuscripts of Ayyā Śāstri's will and a genealogy, both in Ayyā Śāstri's own hand, from his grandson Mr S.R. Śivasvāmi. In his will, Ayyā Śāstri made the care, maintenance, and propagation of the books and manuscripts he left behind in Kavitāvilāsa, and the body of work they represent, a common charge for the family, not designating any one person as their custodian. I see my work as constituting substantial headway in this direction. I have found immense satisfaction in having rendered this small service in fulfillment of the intentions of a great scholar, a simple act that had sadly been overdue for three generations.

[20] This possible due to the help of Mr S.K. Dwarki, the son of Sōsale Kṛṣṇasvāmi Śāstri, who was himself the son of Ayyā Śāstri.

My original purpose had been to undertake a straightforward translation of Garaḷapurī Śāstri's biography, to make it more widely available as a record of a scholarly life, and provide some insight into the ways of those times, including a glimpse of life at the Mysore Royal Court. I later added the biographies of Śrīkaṇṭha Śāstri and Kuṇigala Rāmaśāstri, which have have served to round out the original biography of Garaḷapurī Śāstri. This trilogy covers three of the leading scholarly disciplines of the time, namely, literature, grammar, and logic.

I also included a handful of excerpts from D.V. Guṇḍappa's *Jñāpaka Ҫitraśāle*, a priceless collection of short biographies and reminiscences by an outstanding *littérateur* who seemed to know everyone who mattered in the nearly nine decades of his life. These excerpts bring us into the first half of the 20th century, a time when traditional and modern mores coexisted, and highlight some contradictions and challenges traditional scholars confronted in a society looking increasingly to Western education and norms.

The biographies in this volume are also works of literary significance. M.S. Puṭṭaṇṇa's biography of Kuṇigala Rāmaśāstri was the first major biographical work in Kannaḍa, and became the model for many later works, including the two by Veṅkaṭaramaṇa Śāstri that appear here. These three works have served as primary source material for almost everything that has since been written about their subjects, and about many topics relating to the period. Puṭṭaṇṇa was a major literary figure of the time, and the author of numerous literary and historical works. He had excellent facility in Kannaḍa, English, Marāṭhi, Hindi, Urdu, Telugu, and Sanskrit. His deep knowledge of and respect for Indian tradition clearly shows through in his work. Yet, his outlook was thoroughly modern. He held a B.A. in logic and political science earned in 1885, and brought a Western analytical sensibility to his work.[21]

[21] Puṭṭaṇṇa also had enormous administrative experience, having served a *Amaldār* in the *tālūks* of Nelamaṅgala, Bāgēpalli, Ҫāmarājanagara, Muḷabāgilu, and Hosadurga. He was notoriously independent-minded, and insisted that he himself and others around him observe strict norms of propriety and rectitude in all matters, meticulously avoiding even the appearance of wrongdoing. See Sujātā [2001] for a list of episodes illustrating this point. In one case, as *Amaldār*, he summoned to court and levied a fine of Re. 1 on his own wife for taking a few curry leaves (*Murraya koenigii*) from a tree in an adjacent yard to season her cooking. The neighbouring house had been vacant, but had belonged to the government, so she was technically guilty of misappropriating public property. Since the summons had

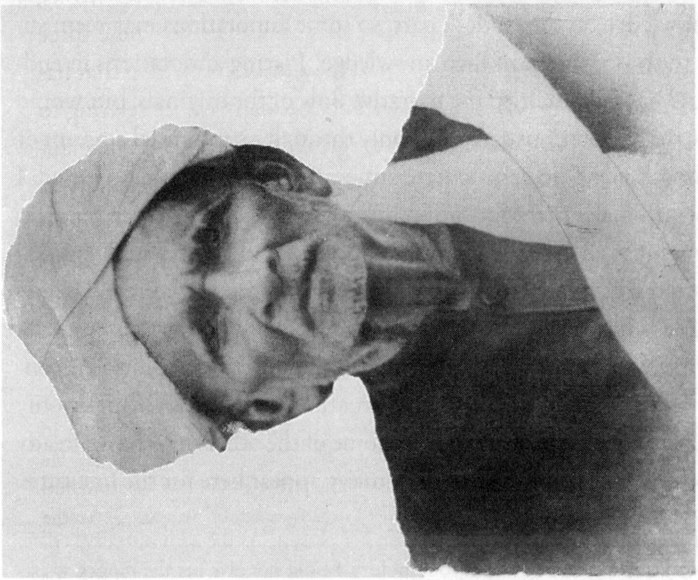

(a) Maisūru Sūryanārāyaṇabhaṭṭa Puṭṭaṇṇa. (1854–1930).

(b) Cāmarājanagara Veṅkaṭaramaṇa Śāstri (1888–1945).
Image courtesy Mr C.R. Venkataramu.

Plate 1: Portraits of M.S. Puṭṭaṇṇa and Cāmarājanagara Veṅkaṭaramaṇa Śāstri

Veṅkaṭaramaṇa Śāstri's literary stature may be lower, but his contributions to the cause of Kannaḍa are substantial. Even in the face of crippling adversity, he maintained publication of his *Kādambarī Saṅgraha Granthamālā* series, in which appeared many novels, literary works, and biographies, much of which was his own work. He is also known to have often printed material himself, page by grueling page, on a manual press he maintained at home.[22] Sadly, the *Kādambarī Saṅgraha* series survives only in fragments. What survives, however, is now invaluable.

My work has gone considerably beyond my original purpose. In its course, I have interpolated many details missing from the source texts, and supplied footnotes to help readers relate to these events of a long time ago. What was evident to the educated reader a hundred years ago may not be so evident today. Some footnotes provide dates for the events described, as reliable dates are sparse in the original biographies. Other footnotes of mine provide cultural, geographic, and historical context, or correct errors in the original, of which there are a few. The footnotes are almost exclusively mine, but I have been careful to distinguish between my footnotes and those appearing in the source texts. I have presumed little cultural or contextual knowledge on the reader's part, so some annotations may seem superfluous to those who have such knowledge. Placing annotations in endnotes would have maintained the narrative flow of the originals, but would have made the annotations accessible only through a substantial amount of page-turning. Since I do expect these annotations to be frequently used, I have chosen to make them footnotes intead. Whimsically, I note that this approach is not so alien to the Indian tradition. A traditional Indian *vyākhā* or gloss also tracks its source page by page, and is presented directly below it, precisely as I have done with my footnotes.

The images appearing in this volume should provide additional context with regard to the individuals and situations described. Of these, only Plates 10 and 34 appear in the originals. Some of the others may have already appeared elsewhere, but it is likely that many appear here for the first time.

been urgent, she had arrived with no money on her person. As the administrative officer who had levied the fine, and who was still on duty, he did not give her the money to pay the fine. She was obliged to borrow money from her household servants, who were later reimbursed by Puṭṭaṇṇa.

[22] See the reference to "our own" Bhuvanēśvarī Press on page 73. A press by the name of Srīkaṇṭhēśvara Press still operates out of the home where he lived.

I have supplied dates for most of the significant events described in the source texts, placing them within boxes inset next to margins. Some of these dates are derived from the source texts, but most are reconstructions based on inferences from contextual material I have discovered inside and outside the source texts.

The genealogical document by Ayyā Śāstri was of special interest, since it records the memory of the migration of a scholarly family after a watershed event in South Indian history. I have looked into Ayyā Śāstri's account in some detail, as such migrations are of intrinsic interest to intellectual historians as means and markers for the flow of ideas (see Datta [1989], for example). The stories of many such migrations are preserved in family folklore, but are hard to verify. I have found, not surprisingly, that the context for this family's move was likely different from that handed down by its oral history.

I have tried to preserve the style, sentence structure, and wherever possible, word meanings of the Kannaḍa sources. Such fidelity to the original is atypical in translations, but I have chosen to respect the originals as source material. These are almost contemporaneous accounts; Śrīkaṇṭha Śāstri's biography is a first-hand account by the biographer, and in the other cases, the informants had intimate and first-hand knowledge of the subjects of the biographies.

From a literary standpoint as well, I hope such fidelity will convey to the modern reader a sense of the sometimes archaic style of the Kannaḍa originals. Puṭṭaṇṇa's is the easier and more direct style; despite the breadth of his erudition, he valued simplicity. He was also an independent thinker, and among the first Kannaḍa authors to make contemporary issues central to his novels and other works. Veṅkaṭaramaṇa Śāstri's skills as a writer are evident from his fluent and moving biography of Çāmarājanagara Śrīkaṇṭha Śāstri. His biography of Garaḷapurī Śāstri, however, is in a less even style, often switching its thematic horses midstream, and mixing short sentences with others running the entire length of a paragraph. These elaborate sentences are strung out across a scaffolding of gerunds, a style that creates a certain sense of flow in the formal, highly inflected and Sanskritized Kannaḍa of the original. In English, sadly, it comes across as stilted and ungainly. My attempts to preserve the textures of the originals have no doubt come at the cost of readability.

Preserving the character of the original has also meant retaining inconsistencies that arise naturally in the source texts, which were composed at various times by various individuals. While consistency is desirable, I have chosen to pay more regard to the voice of the source than to the stylistic sensibilities of the modern reader. Imposing an artificial uniformity also risks censoring the source writer's intent. For instance, one sees "Maisūru" and "Mahisūru" within a single original biography. "Mahisūru" is correct but more archaic, but the speaker in this case being an older person, this usage may reflect a generational variant that the source was trying to preserve. English sources frequently use anglicized forms ("Bangalore") that are inconsistent with the forms appearing in Kannaḍa sources ("Beṅgaḷūru"). Differences between Kannaḍa and Sanskrit phonology (see page xxxiii) also result in variant transliterations for the same word. Thus, we see *ēkō* and *eko*, *ślōka* and *śloka*, *maṅgaḷa* and *maṅgala*, and so on. Indian proper names may also have context-dependent spellings. The Kannaḍa original, for instance, refers to a *Dīvān* Sūrappa, but a footnote references a street in Bangalore, surely named for this same individual, but spelled "Dewan Surappa Street", causing an apparent inconsistency. When quoting sources in the footnotes, I have preserved the original spellings. For example, while I use "Rāv" in both the main text and the footnotes, variants spellings, such as "Rao", "Rāo", or "Ráo" may appear within a quote, depending on the source quoted. In some cases, imposing uniformity may even risk altering meanings. For instance, variants such as *tāluk, tāluka,* and *tāllūk* appear in the source to refer to administrative zones, reflecting local usage. Insisting on uniformity would require me to decree a standard. But what standard? The term had different connotations at different times and places. Substituting some modern equivalent would be as misleading as reverting to the Arabic original *ta'alluqa,* which referred in Mughal times to a certain type of land tenure.

With me rests the blame for any shortcomings in the typesetting of this book and the compilation of the index; both have been the result of my own modest efforts, with the versatile yet inconstant LaTeX at my side.[23] I have relished the pleasure of its company when it has been compliant, as well as the triumph of bending it to my will when it has chosen intransigence. The index, especially, falls well short of the standards I had hoped to achieve,

[23] Subject, of course, to the publisher's specifications and requirements.

but I hope readers will at least find it serviceable. Building a better index is a task I have chosen to defer to the future.

Finding a humanist font suitable for this work turned out to be harder than I had expected; commercial fonts do not typically support the profusion of diacritical signs needed to accommodate the several languages encontered herein. I finally compromised on Georg Duffner's EB Garamond interpretation of the classic Garamond font. Although this font is still under development, it is based on the Egenolff-Berner typography specimen, and at least to my eye, has succeeded in retaining an old-world feel that suits the archaic feel of the language of the originals.

Overall, the effort involved in this work has been rather greater than I had originally anticipated, and not merely due to my professional responsibilities. I have lacked access to much of the material I have required, whether manuscripts in the family's possession, government records, authoritative historical sources, or frequently, standard bibliographic material. These and other frustrations notwithstanding, I have greatly enjoyed this modest foray into new territory.

Despite all efforts to correct mistakes in this book, many surely remain. I am responsible for all errors. I would be grateful to all who trouble themselves to bring these errors to my notice.

Irvine, CA, U.S.A. January 9, 2017

a	*ā*	*i*	*ī*	*u*	*ū*	*ṛ*	*ṝ*	*l̈*	*l̋*
അ	ആ	ഇ	ഈ	ഉ	ഊ	ഋ	ൠ	ഌ	ൡ
अ	आ	इ	ई	उ	ऊ	ऋ	ॠ	ऌ	ॡ

e	*ē*	*ai*	*o*	*ō*	*au*	*ṁ*	*ḥ*	–
എ	ഏ	ഐ	ഒ	ഓ	ഔ	അം	അഃ	ഽ
ए		ऐ	ओ		औ	अं	अः	ऽ

k	*kh*	*g*	*gh*	*ṅ*
ക	ഖ	ഗ	ഘ	ങ
क	ख	ग	घ	ङ

ç	*çh*	*j*	*jh*	*ñ*
ച	ഛ	ജ	ഝ	ഞ
च	छ	ज	झ	ञ

ṭ	*ṭh*	*ḍ*	*ḍh*	*ṇ*
ട	ഠ	ഡ	ഢ	ണ
ट	ठ	ड	ढ	ण

t	*th*	*d*	*dh*	*n*
ത	ഥ	ദ	ധ	ന
त	थ	द	ध	न

p	*ph*	*b*	*bh*	*m*
പ	ഫ	ബ	ഭ	മ
प	फ	ब	भ	म

y	*r*	*r̂*	*l*	*v*	*ś*	*ṣ*	*s*	*h*	*ḷ*	*l̂*
യ	ര	റ	ല	വ	ശ	ഷ	സ	ഹ	ള	ഴ
य	र		ल	व	श	ष	स	ह	ळ	

q	*ḳh*	*z*	*z*	*'a*
ق	خ	ز	ض	ع
क़	ख़	ज़	ज़	अ

Plate 2: Transliteration equivalents in Roman, Indic and Arabic scripts.

TRANSLITERATION AND PUNCTUATION CONVENTIONS

THE transliterations in this volume use a variant of IAST, as shown in Plate 2. The language of the source biographies is modern Kannaḍa, whose phonology includes the long vowels *ē* and *ō* and the retroflex consonant *ḷ*, all absent in *Saṁskṛta.* Old Kannaḍa also had two other consonants, appearing as *r̂* and *l̂* in Plate 2, which have disappeared entirely from Kannaḍa speech, but survived in the written language till recently. Words in which they appeared are now written using *r* or *ḷ*, and pronounced accordingly.[24] The Kannaḍa of these biographies does not use them, but *r̂* makes an appearance on page 333 within a quotation from an archaic source. Both *l̈* and *l̋* are *Saṁskṛta* borrowings, and appear as diacritics when strict adherence to the original *Saṁskṛta* is required. They are rare (indeed, even in *Saṁskṛta*), and needed in only a couple of places within this volume.[25] *Varṇamālā* charts such as that shown in Plate 2 customarily omit the proliferation of conjunct digraphs and trigraphs commonly seen in Indic scripts.

Saṁskṛta words are pronounced, and by convention, written to match Kannaḍa phonology, distinguishing *e* from *ē*, *o* from *ō*, and often changing the alveolar *l* to the retroflex *ḷ* (thus, *naḷinīdaḷa*, not *nalinīdala*). I have hence tried to stay faithful to the originals in my transliterations.

My use of *ç* in place of *c* for the first of the palatal consonants is nonstandard, but is motivated by my observation that non-specialists had difficulty reading *c* correctly, tending from habit to associate it with either the *k* sound or the *s* sound. The eye does not read letter by letter, but takes in entire words at a time, particularly in the case of Roman orthography. I was persuaded that *cāmara* was rather more likely to evoke photographic associations than *çāmara*, and *caṇḍī* more likely to evoke confectionery than *çaṇḍī*. I will regard this liberty as justified if it spares the reader a moment's perplexity upon reading that Kuṇigala Rāmaśāstri took along on his travels in 1840 a *cāmara* he was given by Kṛṣṇarāja Voḍeyar III (see page 210).

[24]The common Kannaḍa words *hēru* ("carry, raise up") and *hēḷu* ("speak, narrate"), for example, are in fact *hēr̂u* and *hēl̂u*, respectively.

[25]In one case, the Kannaḍa source is content to simply write *klupta* in place of *kl̈pta*. I have chosen to revert to the original *Saṁskṛta* form since the phrase in question is a definition from *Navya Nyāya*. I saw fidelity to the original as important in this context.

In the translated text, I follow the English convention of using initial capitals for proper nouns, regardless of their source language. I do not use capitals in sentences or phrases quoted in the original Sanskrit or vernacular. I italicise Sanskrit and vernacular words and expressions which are not typically used in English, the names of books and other works, as well as formal titles or ranks. I do not italicize Anglicised versions of Indian words, such as "Sanskrit" (but would italicise *Saṁskṛta*), or proper nouns constituted from Sanskrit or vernacular words. Thus, I write "Parakāla Maṭha", since this is the actual name of the institution, making it identifiable without the constituent words having to be interpreted, but would write "Sōsale *maṭha*", since this is a reference to a *maṭha* qualified by its location in Sōsale. Its actual name, of course, would be written as "Sōsale Vyāsarāya Maṭha". Apparent anomalies should resolve upon further analysis. The proper name Śrīnivāsāçārya, for instance, would appear in Roman with an initial capital, but this individual may also be referenced as *Āçārya*, where the first part of the name has been elided. This form would take both italics and an initial capital, since Śrīnivāsāçārya is just the compound Śrīnivāsa-Āçārya, which is the semantic equivalent of *Āçārya* Śrīnivāsa, in English. It is now apparent that the word *Āçārya* is a title or honorific.

The following honorifics commonly used in Karṇāṭaka appear in abbreviated form in the original sources; I have retained their abbreviated forms in the translations: *Ma*|| abbreviates *Mahārājaśrī*, *Vē*|| abbreviates *Vēdabrahma* (or *Vēdamūrti*), *Br*|| abbreviates *Brahmaśrī*, *Gau*|| abbreviates *Gauravānvita*, and *Sau*|| abbreviates *Saubhāgyavatī*.

Punctuation Conventions

Most (but not all) Sanskrit verses in this volume have been punctuated as an aid to the non-expert but interested reader. Sanskrit is traditionally written not as a sequence of words, but as a euphonic cascade of the syllables constituting these words. The language has mandatory *saṁdhi* and *saṁyoga* rules of euphony which may conjoin adjacent words and transmute the syllables at their boundaries, making it hard to identify the words. A framework of *samāsa* compounds commonly overlays this substructure, whether in prose or poetry.[26] Parsing Sanskrit requires practice and sound knowledge of the language.

[26] *Saṁskṛta* poetry, especially, revels in constructions that permit multiple meanings to

Our punctuation conventions are as follows. An apostrophe appearing in a Sanskrit phrase marks either a *saṁdhi* that has caused a phonological transformation of adjacent syllables, or a *saṁyoga* that has merged adjacent words with no concomitant phonological changes. Interpuncts (centered dots) separate the words within *samāsa* compounds. An en-dash – marks an *avagraha*, the euphonic elision of an initial *a* sound. As an example, what might have conventionally been written as

nalinīdalagatajalamatitaralaṁ tadvajjīvitamatiśayaçapalaṁ

would appear with punctuation as

nalinī·dala·gata·jalam'ati·taralaṁ tadvaj'jīvitam'atiśaya·çapalaṁ

Here, the words constituting the two *samāsas* *"nalinī·dala·gata·jalam"* and *"ati·taralaṁ"* are separated by interpuncts, the first apostrophe marking a *saṁyoga* between these *samāsas.* The second apostrophe marks the *saṁdhi* between *"tadvat"* and *"jīvitam"*, which has changed the final *t* of *"tadvat"* to *j*.

A *saṁdhi* between the words *saḥ* and *aham* would change *saḥ* to *so* and elide the initial *a* of *aham*, thereby introducing an *avagraha*, so that this *saṁdhi* would be rendered as *so–ham*.

---

be construed by grouping or associating syllabic sequences in different ways. This is not mere gimmickry but subtle art; skilled practitioners use this device in very sophisticated ways to add depth and dimension to their compositions. A rather playful example appears on page 61: *"pramadōrasikaśśētē"*. By *saṁdhi* rules, this may be parsed either as *"pramadā·urasi kaḥ śētē"* or as *"pramadaḥ rasikaḥ śētē"*, to get two meanings, the first of which is a question, and the other its answer. A number of poetic examples appear following page 55.

|| ŚRĪ ||

BIOGRAPHY OF SŌSALE GARAḶAPURĪ ŚĀSTRI

ÇĀMARĀJANAGARA VEṄKAṬARAMAṆA ŚĀSTRI

ŚUBHAMASTU

Kādambarī Saṅgraha Granthamāla No. 43
Madhuravāṇī Press
Maisūru, 1919

Plate 3: Portrait believed to be that of *Āsthāna Mahāvidvān* Sōsale Garaḷapurī Śāstri (1822–1877). The original colour painting is in the possession of Mr Sandeep Sastry, great-great-grandson of Garaḷapurī Śāstri.

Preface

Biographies are certainly rare in Kannaḍa literature. M.S. Puṭṭaṇṇa's biography of Kuṇigala Rāmaśastri made clear to me the desirability of more such works in Kannaḍa, and I began by writing a biography of my grandfather, Srīkanṭha Śāstri of Çāmarājanagara.[27] I then determined to write a biography of his in-law Sōsale Garaḷapurī Śāstri, and as I collected the relevant material, I approached his second son Sōsale Ayyā Śāstri for assistance. He provided much information, placing great faith and confidence in me. I have been able to publish this book only with his help. I plan to follow up with a biography of Rāmaśāstri of Çāmarājanagara.[28] I hope to continue these efforts, publishing the biography of a great (Kannaḍa) scholar each year in the *Kādambarī Saṅgraha* monthly. Readers supportive of my intentions may send me other biographies they may come across of scholars. I plan to begin work soon on the biographies of *Aḷiya* Liṅgarāja Arasu, who was a student of Garaḷapurī Śāstri, and of the well-known Basappa Śāstri.[29] There is no doubt that the number of such works of significance will grow in proportion to encouragement by Kannaḍigas.

April 17, 1919 — Publisher
Çāmarājanagara

---

[27] This biography of Çāmarājanagara Śrīkaṇṭha Śāstri is the second biography incuded in this volume, and Puṭṭaṇṇa's biography of Kuṇigala Rāmaśāstri, first published in 1910 C.E., is the third. M.S. Puṭṭaṇṇa (1854–1930 C.E.) and Garaḷapurī Śāstri's second son Ayyā Śāstri (1855–1934 C.E.) were both noted literary figures of the time. The families were connectẹd by marriage, Puṭṭaṇṇa's daughter Sītammā being married to Ayyā Śāstri's third son Rāmasvāmi Śāstri.

[28] Çāmarājanagara Rāmaśāstri's biography appeared in Śāstri [1925b]. Though this work is substantial, it is far from being a succint account of Rāmaśāstri's life and work, and contains a great deal of incidental and supplementary material.

[29] These biographies, assuming they were published, do not appear to have survived. The two individuals named, however, figure in the biography of Garaḷapurī Śāstri that appears in this volume.

The Narrative of Vijayanagara

nāgēṣvarkē niyamita·śakē śālivāhasya yātē
dhātary'abdhē suguṇa·sahitē māsi vaiśākha·nāmni |
śuklē pakṣē suraguru·yutē saumya·vārē sulagnē
saptamyām śrī·vijayanagaram nirmamē dēṣikēndraḥ [30] ‖

Vidyāraṇya *Svāmi* founded Vijayanagara on Wednesday, the seventh day of the *śuddha* fortnight in the month of Vaiśākha, in the Dhātu year 1258 of the Śālivāhana era, corresponding to the year 1336 of the Christian era.[31]

[30] The translator has found several sources for this verse, which is clearly of importance. Row [1905, p. 10] claims that this verse is a temple inscription in Hampi. It has not been possible to trace the original inscription. A version also appears in the *Guruvaṁśakāvya* [Śāstri 1928], dated to c. 1735 C.E.: *"nāgeṣvarkairmita iha śake śālivāhasya yāte dhātaryabde śubhasamuçite māsi vaiśākhanāmni | śukle pakśe suguṇapitṛbhe sūryavāre sulagne saptamyām śrīvijayanagarīm nirmane nirmamendraḥ* ‖*"* This verse appears to have been traditionally known, and appears in a document dating to 1809 C.E., called the *Kaifiyattu Kurugōḍu* [Kalburgi 1994, p. 449], part of the Mackenzie collection of *Kaifiyats*. The Archeological Department of Maisūru [1932, p. 111] references this verse via Row [1905]. This chronology is also referenced by Sastry and Venkataramanayya [1946, p. 15]. The version in this biography is a variation of the version in the Introduction and Chapter 1 of Row [1905].

> "Nagashwarkay, Namitasakay, Salivahasyayata, Dhaturyabday, Sugunasahitay Masa Visaki Namny Suklay Pakshay Suraguruyutay Soumya Varay Sulagnay Saptamyam Sri Vijayanagaray Nirmamay Nerinamendra."

The following chronogram is critical to this verse. *Nāgeṣvarke: dvandva* compound of the masculine locative singulars *nāge+iṣau+arke*, encoding the date. Row [1905] uses the encoding *nāga=8, iṣu=5, arka=12*, matching those of Sircar [1996, p. 230], and Monier-Williams [1899], who gives *nāga=7 or 8, iṣu=5, and arka=12*. The "reversal" formula *aṅkānaṁ vāmato gatiḥ* [Sircar 1996] leads to the date Śālivāhana 1258, or 1336 C.E. The following translation (after Row [1905]) is adequate for our purposes.

> "On Wednesday, the seventh lunar day of the bright half of Vaiśakha, in the year Dhātu, Śālivāhana śaka 1258, in an auspicious time with Guru (Jupiter) in the rising sign (lagna), I, the prince of ascetics, have constructed this city in Vijayanagar."

[31] Vidyāraṇya is a deeply revered figure for his scholarly and political accomplishments. He helped the brothers Hakka (Harihara I, 1346–1357 C.E.) and Bukka (Bukka Rāya I, 1357–1377 C.E.) establish the Vijayanagara kingdom, and served as mentor and inspiration for its

A Muslim torrent had raged uncontrolled through our Bhārata before the founding of Vijayanagara. Tossed about in this flow, now sinking, now rising, undefended, at imminent risk of extinction, were pious sects, ancient temples, and great repositories of learning.[32] At such a time it was that a titan named Vidyāraṇya checked this torrent, founded Vijayanagara, and restored *sanātana dharma*.[33] Vijayanagara, indeed, was the kingdom that protected all Hindus of the south when the Muslims had grown strong, and threatened their *āryan* ways and freedoms. Vidyāraṇya, indeed, was the august figure who delivered such succour by halting the spread of impious ways. But for his founding of this kingdom, all peoples of the South would have become Muslims, ceding to them this Bhārata of ours, and wiping out all traces of the great *āryan* people they once were.

The celebrated kingdom of Vijayanagara occupied a vast expanse on the southern bank of the Tuṅgabhadrā river, near the city of Hosapēṭe in the region of Baḷḷāri. On the northern bank of this river is the city of Ānēgondi. According to tradition, this is the renowned city of Kiṣkindha,[34] dating to the times of Śrī Rāma. It had been ruled by great kings from *āryan* dynasties for seven hundred years.[35]

---

early kings. The kingdom even appears to have been called Vidyānagara, in his honour. He was also a profound scholar, and with his brother Sāyaṇa, ranks among the most authoritative *Vēdic* commentators, especially on *Advaita* philosophy. Vidyāraṇya is believed to have become pontiff of the Śṛṅgēri Maṭha around 1375 C.E.

[32] A reference to the extensive destruction of temples and libraries by the Muslims, and forced conversions to Islam.

[33] "Eternal/ancient *dharma*", the traditional and correct name for "Hinduism". It is certainly true that Vijayanagara's existence helped preserve Hindu traditions and culture. While we have no insights into the minds of its founders, Vijayanagara's later kings and their Muslim rivals appear not to have been motivated purely by religious considerations. See page 335.

[34] The kingdom of the *vānara* king Vāli. En route to Rāvaṇa's capital Laṅkā, Rāma slew Vāli, and forged an alliance with his brother Sugrīva.

[35] This statement is initially baffling, given the preceding allusion to Kiṣkindha's great antiquity. The present author, however, is merely echoing a line from Farishta [Briggs 1829], which is also quoted by Row [1905, p. 4]: "Chiefs of Anagondi had existed as a ruling family for seven hundred years prior to the year 1350." Farishta saw Vijayanagara as a continuation of the Çāḷukyan empire, which spanned seven centuries, and included three dynasties which, albeit unrelated, shared a name. The first, based in Bādāmi, was founded in 543 C.E.; the others, based in Veṅgi and Kalyāṇa, lasted till around 1189 C.E. Farishta's error, however, is understandable. The Āraviḍus, Vijayanagara's last dynasty, and usurpers of the throne from the Tuḷuvas, had promoted this theory to claim illustrious descent. Sources such as

Vidyāraṇya, ascending the throne of Vijayanagara, ruled it with great devotion for twenty years, creating prosperity akin to that of *Rāmarājya* by the grace of the goddess Bhuvanēśvarī,[36] and handing it over to Bukkarāya in the year 1363 of the Christian era,[37] corresponding to the Śubhakṛtu year 1284 of the Śālīvāhana era, attained transcendence after 32 years of deep contemplation. *Svāmi* Vidyāraṇya is known to have been a *Smārta* brāhmaṇa belonging to the *Hoysaḷa Karṇāṭaka* sect.[38] A poet has had this to say about how he imbued our world with virtue:[39]

Kōnērinātha's *Bālabhāgavatam*, the *Basava Purāṇa*, and an inscription from Dēvanahaḷḷi [Rice 1879, p. 252] claim that the Āravīḍus were descendants of Vijjala, the *Kaḷaçūri* prince who usurped the Çāḷukyan throne (see Plate 39). These works use titles such as as *Çāḷukya Çakravarti* (Çāḷukya emperor), *Çāḷukya Anvaya Bhava* (Çāḷukya by descent), and *Çālikki Nārāyaṇa* (Çāḷukya Nārāyaṇa) for members of this family, including the regent Rāma Rāya (1484–1565 C.E.) and his grandfather Tirumala. This Çāḷukya connection is dismissed by Eaton [2005, p. 94], but a deeper irony arises from this claim. The Muslim Deccan Sultanates and Vijayanagara had been engaged in a complex dance of warfare and shifting alliances. Kalyāṇa had been under Muslim rule for at least two centuries before Rāma Rāya's time, but his preoccupation with it caused him to ensure that the city always remained under the control of the Muslim kingdom currently allied with him. Such moves likely caused frustration among the four Sultanates, as well as the perception of treachery, strengthening their resolve to join forces against Rāma Rāya, ultimately causing Vijayanagara's fall in 1565 C.E. See the prelude to Tāḷikōṭe starting page 335.

[36] Bhuvanēśvarī is a manifestation of Durgā or Pārvatī, and the patroness of Vijayanagara. Vidyāraṇya was a devotee of this deity. *Rāmarājya* is 10,000-year reign of Rāma after his return to Ayodhyā following his victory over Rāvaṇa, as described in the *Rāmāyaṇa* (Yuddhakāṇḍa 128:99–106). Rāmarājya represents the Utopian ideal not merely of good and just governance, but also of the action of *dharma* in sustaining order in the world, where everything in the personal, societal, and natural realms functions in perfect mutual harmony, and in consonance with the order of *ṛta*.

[37] See footnote 547 for clarification on Vidyāraṇya's role as ruler of Vijayanagara. The dates and many particulars pertaining to Hakka and Bukka are unresolved. See page 358.

[38] *Smārta* brāhmaṇas are devoted to the study and preservation of the *smṛtis* (the "remembered" corpus). The *smṛtis* include the six *Vedāṅgas*, the *Itihāsas*, the *Purāṇas*, the *Dharmaśāstras*, the *Sūtras*, the *Kāvyas*, and the extensive corpus of commentaries. The *śmṛti* corpus is regarded as *pauruṣeya*, or of human creation, in contrast with the *śruti*, the "heard" or revealed corpus of ancient Indian oral tradition, seen as *apauruṣeya*, not of human creation. The *śrutis* include the *Vēdas*, the *Brāhmaṇas*, the *Āraṇyakas*, and the *Upaniṣads*.

[39] The metre is *Śārdūlavikrīḍitā*. See page 362 for a translation. The suggestion is that the kingdom flourishes because of *mādhava*. There is wordplay here on *mādhava*, which refers to Vidyāraṇya, but also connotes the season of spring. If the word is taken to mean spring, the verse treats the kingdom metaphorically as a tree, which puts out branches, shoots, and flowers, and thrives in the season of spring. If taken to mean Vidyāraṇya, the kingdom flourishes because of his skills in statecraft. A series of metaphors reference the classical

prajñā·mūla·mahī vivēka·salilaiḥ siktā balopaghnikā
mantraiḥ pallavitā viśāla·viṭapā sandhy'ādibhiṣ'ṣaḍguṇaiḥ |
śaktyā korakitā yaśas'surabhitā siddhyā samudyat'phalā
samprāptā bhuvi bhāti nīti·latikā sarvottaraṁ mādhavaṁ ‖

In this verse is described how the vine Statecraft, using the most excellent and omniscient Mādhava (Vidyāraṇya) as support, grows to bear finest fruit.

Early–mid 1400s

In the period after the departure of this august figure from Vijayanagara, there was at the court of Ānēgondi, a capable minister engaged in the duties of governance. His descendants, over the generations, continued in this ministerial role. Minister in the fifth generation of his heirs was the famous Tammaṇṇa Śāstri.[40]

techniques of statecraft. These techniques are a set of six *guṇas* enumerated as follows in Kauṭilya's *Arthaśāstra* VII.1: *"saṁdhi vigrahāsanayānasaṁśrayadvaidhībhāva ṣāḍguṇyam ityāçāryāḥ |"*, and elaborated further as *"tatra paṇabandhaḥ saṁdhiḥ | apakāro vigrahaḥ | upekṣaṇamāsanam | abhyuççayo yānam | parārpaṇam saṁśrayam | saṁdhivigrahopādanam dvaidhībhāvaḥ |"* The first statement, in light of the second, translates to: "The learned teachers say that the six forms of state policy are are *saṁdhi* (treaty, or rapprochement), *vigraha* (warfare), *āsana* (forbearance, or neutrality), *yāna* (expedition), *saṁśraya* (asylum), and *dvaidhībhāva* (sowing dissention)."

[40]The translator has located a manuscript in the hand of Garaḷapurī Śāstri's son Ayyā Śāstri, giving a genealogy identical to that in this biography. See page 312. The genealogical account that has come down to us lacks dates, but the translator's analysis suggests that Tammaṇṇa Śāstri was born around 1600 C.E. (see page 67). If we reckon 30–40 years per generation, the first of his ministerial ancestors would have been born about 150–200 years before this date, that is, in the early-to-mid 1400s C.E. This date is later than that assigned to Vidyāraṇya, and is consistent with the narrative in the biography, which places this person after Vidyāraṇya's departure from Ānēgondi. Tammaṇṇa Śāstri's remote ancestors likely came to Ānēgondi from the Hoysaḷa regions during Vidyāraṇya's time, and assumed ministerial roles a little later. See footnote 41.

Chapter Two

Tammaṇṇa Śāstri was a *Smārta* brāhmaṇa of the *Hoysaḷa Karṇāṭaka* sect.[41] He was born into the Kāśyapa *gōtra* and belonged to the *Drāhyāyaṇa* school of the *Sāmavēdic* tradition.[42] This distinguished administrator was also a great *Vēdic* scholar. Tammaṇṇa Śāstri had two sons: Śaṅkara Śāstri and Paṭṭābhirāma Śāstri.[43] The king held the illustrious Śāstri in high esteem, and relied on his able counsel in all matters.

The paths of history are indeed tortuous; Vijayanagara now entered a decline as remarkable as its glorious ascent. The strength of the Muslims began growing by the day all over Hindustan. Confirmation appeared to be at hand of the impermanence of all creation. The Muslims of Haiderābād now cast their cruel sights in Vijayanagara's direction. Not contented thereby, they besieged Vijayanagara with huge armies.[44] How long indeed, could small numbers of Hindū soldiers, mere water droplets, hold out against the Muslim hordes that surged on like ocean waves? Yet, could these *āryan* offspring ever yield? Each Hindū hero killed Muslims by the hundred as he won his place in the heaven for heroes. In the end, the Muslims, with their far more numerous armies, were the ones to find favour with Jayalakṣmī.[45]

---

[41] See footnotes 38 and 521. The family's oral history holds, according to Garaḷapurī Śāstri's great-grandson S.R. Śivasvāmi, that Tammaṇṇa Śāstri's remote ancestors migrated to Ānēgondi from Dōrasamudra, the Hoysaḷa capital, where also they held ministerial positions.

[42] *"kāśyapasagōtrōtpanna"* in the source. The *gōtra* is often taken to be *kāśyapasa*. But by Pāṇini (*4.1.162*): *"apatyam pautraprabhṛti gotram"*, the grandson's name defines the *gōtra*. The progenitor *ṛṣi* Kaśyapa's grandson being Kāśyapa, the *gōtra* name should be *kāśyapa*, not *kāśyapasa*. Either *"kāśyapa·gōtrō'tpannaḥ"*, or *"kāśyapa·sagōtraḥ"* may have been better.

[43] The name appears as Śaṅkarabhaṭṭa, rather than as Śaṅkaraśāstri, in the genealogical manuscript by Ayyā Śāstri. *Śāstri, bhaṭṭa,* and *śarma* are equivalent qualifiers, all connoting brahminhood. Members of the *Liṅgāyata* or *Vīraśaiva* community do also adopt the qualifier Śāstri. An excellent example would be Basappa Śāstri (see footnote 123).

[44] Vijayanagara was destroyed in the aftermath of the Battle of Rakkasa-Taṅgaḍi (also referred to as Tāḷikōte), January 26, 1565 C.E. Contemporary writers give various reasons for the defeat, including betrayal by the Gilani brothers, Muslim defectors from 'Ali 'Ādil Śāh I, who commanded large Vijayanagara forces. The city was sacked by the combined forces of the Deccan Sultanates. In the present account, however, the attackers are specifically identified as Haiderābādī Muslims. The battle being referenced here is almost surely different from Tāḷikōṭe. See pages 335 and 348 for further discussion.

[45] The godess Lakṣmī has the following eight manifestations, representing various aspects of wealth or well-being: *Ādi* Lakṣmī (primæval form), *Dhana* Lakṣmī (wealth), *Dhānya*

Vijayanagara fell to the Muslims. They now proceeded to exact vengeance for their many long-standing envies of the Hindūs. They began to enter and loot every home, directly after having gained the kingdom. Boundless wealth fell into Muslim hands. Many began to flee in the face of
this calamity. Cries of distress everywhere! Dreadful sights every- 1565
where! Many Hindū residents, abandoning all they had, fled to foreign lands. Nobody knew what became of the king.[46]

We are drawn to describe the state of mind of Tammaṇṇa Śāstri at this time of anguish. This noble, gentle figure remained composed even at the loss of all his material possessions. The Muslims had spared his palm-leaf manuscripts, more precious to him than his own life, thinking them to be kindling, or otherwise worthless. Rejoicing at this, the Śāstri loaded them on to buffaloes, the popular transport of the time, and departed with his family for the province of Anantaśayana.[47]

En route, he arrived at a town called Ānēkallu, part of Maisūru, our realm.[48] The local *paḷeyagāra* was engaged in building a strong fort around this town.[49] Astonished at the arrival of Tammaṇṇa Śāstri, who
was traveling with eight buffaloes, and deeply anguished by his nar- 1639
rative, he conducted the Śāstri with great respect to his home, and urged him to settle in his domain. Unable to decline his entreaties, the Śāstri graciously accepted his gift of ten *vṛttis* and a house, and settled down

---

Lakṣmī (grain), *Gaja* Lakṣmī (sovereignty), *Santāna* Lakṣmī (progeny), *Vīra* Lakṣmī (valour), *Jaya* Lakṣmī (victory), and *Vidyā* Lakṣmī (learning).

[46] If we grant the erroneous suggestion that this was the battle of Tāḷikōṭe, which led to the fall of Vijayanagara (see footnote 44), the reference to the king's disappearance becomes meaningful. Sadāśiva Rāya was nominally king, but his regent *Aḷiya* Rāma Rāya, a distinguished general, held the reins of power, and led the Vijayanagara forces, despite being 80 years old. Rāmarāya was captured and beheaded at Tāḷikōṭe, causing the Vijayanagara army to fall apart. Rāmarāya's brother Tirumala is known to have rushed back to Vijayanagara after the battle was lost, and immediately fled to Pēnukōṇḍa with enormous treasure. See pages 335–342 for further details.

[47] Anantaśayana is identified with modern-day Tiruvanantapuram, Kerala [Sircar 1971, p. 92].

[48] That is, Ānēkallu was part of Maisūru in 1919 C.E., rather than at Tammaṇṇa Śāstri's time.

[49] This allusion to the fort's construction allows us to date Tammaṇṇa Śāstri's arrival in Ānēkallu to after 1638 C.E., much later than Vijayanagara's fall in 1565 C.E. See footnote 56 and page 312.

there.[50] He lived there contentedly for some time, and passed on into the next world.

After Tammaṇṇa Śāstri's passing, his son Śaṅkara Śāstri remained in Ānēkallu for some time, then moved to Māgaḍi, where he settled down. The second son continued in Ānēkallu. Śaṅkara Śāstri had two children, Veṅkaṭarāmābhaṭṭa and Tammaṇṇabhaṭṭa by name. Veṅkaṭarāmābhaṭṭa came to the village of Sōsale in the province of Tirumakūḍalu-Narasīpura, and remained, finding support from many families there.[51] Veṅkaṭarāmābhaṭṭa's son was Timmappa Śāstri, whose son Veṅkaṭadāsappa was well known by the name of Sōsale Aṇṇayya Śāstri.

Even from childhood, Aṇṇayya Śāstri immersed himself in our ancient learning, and after his *upanayana,* devoted himself to *Vēdic* and literary studies. Those times were indeed unlike our own. Each person preserved his own traditions with great solicitude. Even when brāhmaṇas pursued occupations for their livelihoods, they never neglected their daily devotions, even by oversight. The *pañçamahāyajñas* sanctified the residence of every householder. Our *śāstric* traditions require every married brāhmaṇa to perform the *pançamahāyajñas.* The *pançayajñas* are: worship of the *dēvas,* worship of the *ṛṣis,* compassion for all creatures, rituals for departed ancestors, and solicitude for guests. Knowing these to be important to well-being in both worlds, ancient sages codified them as *nitya* rituals, and enjoined their daily performance on all brāhmaṇas.[52] Our ancestors performed them with devotion, and ensured the continuance of this tradition.[53]

Late 1700s–early 1800s.

---

[50] A *vṛtti* ("living") is a unit of largesse or endowment to a brāhmaṇa, typically comprising land, a home in an *agrahāra,* and means of sustenance, such as a well and cattle. The grant of as many as ten *vṛttis* to Tammaṇṇa Śāstri indicates high esteem.

[51] Ānēkallu is at 12.7°N, 77.7°E, Māgaḍi at 12.97°N, 77.23°E, and Sōsale at 12.23°N, 76.92°E.

[52] These are *nitya* or mandatory daily rituals. We see in *Manusmṛti* 3 (69–71): *"tāsām krameṇa sarvāsām niṣkṛtyartham maharṣibhiḥ | pañça klṗtā mahāyajñāḥ pratyaham gṛhamedhinām ‖ adhyāpanam brahmayajñaḥ pitṛyajñam tu tarpaṇam | homo daivo balir bhauto nṛyajño atithipūjanam ‖ pañça etān yo mahāyajñān na hāpayati śaktitaḥ | sa gṛhe api vasan nityaṁ sūnādoṣair na lipyate ‖"*

[53] See page 295 for an example from the early 20th century of solicitude for guests. Indeed, *atithi,* the word for guest, literally refers to one who arrives without warning. Well into the 20th century, such hospitality was the norm, and mandatory. See *Yājñavalkyasmṛti* (105): *"bālasavavāsinīvṛddhagarbhiṇyāturakanyakā | sambhojyātithibhṛtyāṁṣça dampatyoḥ śeṣa-*

In Aṇṇayya Śāstri's time, 120 years before the present, brāhmaṇic traditions flourished everywhere in forms tangible and incarnate. As a householder, Aṇṇayya Śāstri rose at dawn each morning, and after bathing and finishing his daily rituals, engaged himself in acts of service. He was skilled in practical matters. He founded a large *agrahāra* in Sōsale, which was home to many brāhmaṇas.[54] This was known as Aṇṇayya Śāstri's Agrahāra.[55]

His home was well attended by servants. Guests were always welcome and well-served. He was kindly and generous, always treating everyone as his own.

---

bhojanam ‖" meaning: "Having fed children, married damsels, the old, the pregnant, the ill, unmarried girls, guests, and servants, the couple may then partake of what remains." Similarly, see *Yājñavalkyasmṛti* (111): *adhvanīno-tithidjñeyaḥ śrotriyovedapāragaḥ | mānyāvetau gṛhastasya brahmalokamabhīpsitaḥ* ‖" meaning: "Travellers are to be seen as guests. The *śrotrīya* and the one learned in the *Vēdas* are both to be honoured by the householder who wishes to attain the regions of Brahma."

[54] An *agrahāra* is a settlement of brāhmaṇas, usually resulting from a charter or a grant of land. The granting of *agrahāras* is an ancient tradition, as *Mahābhārata* III 65.3 illustrates: *"asmin karmaṇi niṣpanne vijñāte niṣadhādhipe | gavāṁ sahasraṁ dāsyāmi yo vas tāv ānayiṣyati | agrahāraṁ ça dāsyāmi grāmaṁ nagarasammitaṁ |"*

[55] Aṇṇayya Śāstri's Agrahāra no longer exists. As of August 2010, only a handful of brāhmaṇa households remained in Sōsale. Apart from three or four *Ayyangār* families, there is the family of Mr V. Narasiṁha Mūrti, the resident priest at the old location of Sōsale's Vyāsarāya Maṭha, and that of Mr Narendra Bābu, a *Baḍaganāḍu* brāhmaṇa of the Ātreya *gōtra.* Aṇṇayya Śāstri was a *Hoysaḷa Karṇāṭaka* brāhmaṇa of the Kāśyapa *gōtra,* so it appears that none of his male descendents remain in Sōsale. Such migrations of brāhmaṇas to larger urban centers in search of opportunities is not unusual. According to the Indian Census of 2011, over 63% of the 7,260 residents of Sōsale were engaged in marginal occupations providing livelihood for at least six months of the year, and 80% were from the Scheduled Castes or Tribes of India.

Chapter Three

Aṇṇayya Śāstri had two sons, Veṅkaṭarāmā Śāstri and Timmappa Śāstri by name. They were both excellent *Vēdic* scholars and kind-hearted. Even from an early age, they were erudite and righteous, and benefited from the good advice of their parents, always treating them with godlike respect.

Another son was born to Aṇṇayya Śāstri in the Çitrabhānu *saṁvatsara* (1822 C.E.).[56] This was the renowned Garaḷapurī Śāstri.[57] It is from this luminary that we have learned of the positions of high esteem held by his ancestors. This son was the object of special affection on the part of Aṇṇayya Śāstri. Even from the age of three, he called him to his side every
1822 day, teaching him words from the *Amara Kōśa*,[58] as well as grammatical formulæ. Garaḷapurī Śāstri quickly learned everything he was taught. By the age of eight, the Śāstri had already attained proficiency in poetry, and was ready for more advanced study. He had also completed his *upanayana* by this time.[59]

Recognizing the brilliance of this child, and wishing to further his learning at the hands of a great scholar, his father and older brother took him to Rāmāśāstri, an eminent scholar in the town of Tirumakūḍalu. Welcoming them with respect, and learning of their intentions, Rāmāśāstri evaluated the boy, and accepting him with great enthusiasm, said "Let Garaḷapurī remain here, studying while living with us"; Aṇṇayya Śāstri responded: "He will arrive from Sōsale every day for his lessons," and returned with his son

---

[56] This date comes from Garaḷapurī Śāstri's son Ayyā Śāstri. As the only reliable date in this biography, it is one of our anchors for dating the rest of the genealogy. See the discussion following page 312.

[57] The correct form is Garaḷapurīśa, meaning Śiva, the lord of Garaḷapurī, a town better known as Nañjanagūḍu, and famous for its Śiva temple. The final *śa* of *Garaḷapurīśa* becomes assimilated into the initial syllable of *Śāstri* upon vocalization, and the name is articulated as *Garaḷapurī Śāstri*. *Sandhi* rules require *Garaḷapurīśśāstri*, but the doubled *śa* would be hard to discern in speech.

[58] A thesaurus, by Amara Siṁha of the 4th century. It is written in verse in the *Anuṣṭhubh* metre, and comprises 10,000 words arranged in categories. It is traditionally memorized by children.

[59] The *upanayana* ("taking near") is the ceremonial initiation of a boy into Brāhminhood, and is a traditional ritual prerequisite to starting one's formal tutelage under a guru.

to Sōsale.[60] Aṇṇayya Śāstri possessed the great virtue that while lavish in his generosity and hospitality to all, he did not accept unwarranted favours from others. He paid no heed to the strain of physical exertion. That he too should adopt and practice this ideal, going back and forth each day between Sōsale and Tirumakūḍalu, was agreeable to Garaḷapurī Śāstri. He never acted against the wishes of his father or brother. *1830*

The idea of going to Tirumakūḍalu for advanced study with his brother now also occurred to Timmappa Śāstri. Aṇṇayya Śāstri and Veṅkaṭarāmā Śāstri approved of the idea, and bade Timmappa Śāstri do so, feeling that the brothers would be mutually supportive; the two now began to travel back and forth enthusiastically to Tirumakūḍalu each day.

The river Kāvērī flows between Sōsale and Tirumakūḍalu. Tirumakūḍalu is a noted place of pilgrimage in the South, akin to Kāśī in the North. The temple of Agastyēśvara here is well renowned, just as the temple of Viśveśvara is in Kāśī. The holy Gaṅgā is ever present in Agastyēśvara's hair.[61] This is a place of pilgrimage of infinite sanctity and beneficience. Tirumakūḍalu is ringed by the Kapilā and Kāvērī rivers. "Tirumakūḍalu" means the confluence of three holy bodies of water. *Saṁskṛta* works refer to it as Trimakuṭa or Trimakuṭi.

Prayāga is the site of the confluence of the Gaṅgā, Yamunā, and Sarasvatī rivers. Here is the site of the confluence of the Kapilā and Kāvērī rivers, and the Sphaṭika lake. The Sphaṭika is invisible to our eyes. A stone pillar stands in the middle of the Kāvērī. This pillar is said to mark the middle of the Sphaṭika lake, which is the region around it. Tradition enjoins us not to question the origins of gods, of rivers, or of *ṛsis*.[62] Indeed, the *Purāṇas* hold that nobody has apprehended the origins of this lake, and we are obliged to take this as the truth.[63] At the site of confluence in Tirumakūḍalu is a stone staircase. Sitting on these stairs, we may behold the Kapilā flowing to our right and the Kāvērī to our left. Wherever we may sit, the meeting of these great rivers is a thrilling sight.

---

[60] In the traditional *gurukula* system, the student lived with the guru during his education. Garaḷapurī Śāstri would have likely traveled 3–4 km each way to Rāmāśāstri's house.

[61] A hollow atop of the Śiva *liṅga* in the Agastyēśvara temple is said to collect water, an effect that the faithful attribute to the waters of the Gaṅgā, which Śiva is represented as bearing in his hair.

[62] See *Garuḍapurāṇa* 1.115.57: *"nadīnāmagnihōtrāṇāṁ bhāratasya kulasya ca | mūlānvēṣō na kartavyō mūlāddoṣēṇa hīyate ‖"*

[63] The possibility of the Kāvērī having subsumed a lake in early times is an obvious one.

Casting our sights on the banks of the Kapilā, we behold the Guñjā-narasimhasvāmi temple. If we extend our gaze farther along the bank, we perceive a *ghāt*. This is called the Jñānavāpī Tīrtha. At the edge of this *ghāt* is the temple of Anādi Mūlasthāneśvara. If we cross the stream and proceed to Narasīpura, we may visit the deities of Narasiṁhasvāmi and Mūlasthāneśvara. Our eyes and hearts long for more, no matter how long we remain at this *saṅgama*. If we now tear ourselves away, and ascend the steps, we behold a giant *aśvattha* tree. All around this *aśvattha* tree are consecrated innumerable *nāgaśilas*.[64] Upon circumambulating this *aśvattha* tree and proceeding further, our eyes are gratified by an image of Agastyēśvara with Pūrṇamaṅgaḷa Kāmākṣi.

This town is thick with the residences of *śrōtri* brāhmaṇas.[65] The *Purāṇas* hold this place as no less than Kailāsa on earth, with its five *liṅgas* Sōmēśvara, Hanumantēśvara, Pātāḷēśvara, Agastyēśvara, and Mūlasthānēśvara, representing the five aspects of Īśvara. This is regarded as an important place of pilgrimage in our country of Maisūru.[66] One may reach this place by an overnight journey by cart from Maisūru. The distance between Maisūru and here is eighteen miles.

Rāmāśāstri lived here, a pure *vaidika* brāhmaṇa, ever observant of tradition, and ever engaged in worship and devotion.[67] His scholarship in literature and grammar was unequalled. Garaḷapurī Śāstri now began his tutelage under him. A proverb says "The tender shoot foreshadows the full-grown crop";[68] delighting in the brilliance of Garaḷapurī Śāstri, Rāmāśāstri was

---

[64] The *aśvattha* tree is *Ficus religiosa*, sometimes called the *pippala* (peepal) tree. It holds great religious significance. *Nāgaśilās* are granite plaques with carved images of the snake god *Nāgēśvara*, and are quite commonly seen in South India.

[65] *Śrōtris (śrōtrīyas)* are *Vēdic* scholars, and preservers of the *śrutis*, or the "revealed" oral traditions. The following verse from Śaṅkara's commentary on Kālidāsa's *Śakuntala* shows the high regard they command: *"janmanā brāhmaṇo jñeyaḥ saṁskārair dvija uçyate | vidyayā yāti vipratvam tribhiḥ śrotriya uçyate ‖"* (By birth is derived the status of brāhmaṇa, by sacrament that of the twice-born. By learning comes the status of *vipra*, and by all three that of *śrōtrīya*.)

[66] Maisūru was still a kingdom in 1919 C.E., with the city of Maisūru as its capital. This kingdom formed the basis for the state of Karnāṭaka, which was called Mysore till 1973 C.E.

[67] In contrast to *laukika* (worldly) brāhmaṇas, *vaidika* brāhmaṇas devoted themselves to *Vēdic* studies and traditional learning, eschewing other more lucrative occupations. *Vaidikas* are especially respected. See the episode recounted on page 294.

[68] This is a literal translation. This proverb has equivalents in many Indian languages, but there appears to be none in English.

content that his great learning had found fulfillment in the instruction of a student of such merit.

The flow in the river being greatly diminished between the months of Mārgaśira and Vaiśakha, Garaḷapurī Śāstri and Timmappa Śāstri waded through it each day en route to Tirumakūḍalu.[69] When the river was in flood, they would cross it by boat, returning to Sōsale after their lessons.[70] The rain, wind, cold, or the sun would frequently be cruel and merciless, but they continued their studies with dedication and enthusiasm, heedless of these discomforts, recognizing that the cycle of the seasons followed the patterns of Nature.

---

[69]The shallow Kāvērī crossing at Sōsale has played a pivotal role in shaping the history of Maisūru, through events that Aṇṇayya Śāstri is sure to have witnessed. In its advance on Śrīraṅgapaṭṭaṇa during the Fourth Mysore War, the campaign that led to Ṭippu Sultān's death, the British army under Major General George Harris abruptly turned south after an engagement with Ṭippu's troops at Maḷavaḷḷi, and forded the Kāvērī at Sōsale on March 30, 1799 C.E., in a manœuvre that outflanked the Sultān's forces, which were deployed in anticipation of a crossing at Arakere. Intending to use Sōsale as a supply depot, Ṭippu had stockpiled vast stocks of provisions at the village, which all fell into British hands. A ruined brick hut, which the locals attribute to Ṭippu, still stands on the Kāvērī's banks directly to the west of Sōsale. The river was about three feet deep and three hundred yards wide at the Sōsale crossing [Groves 1887, Hook 1832], and the place had 15,000 head of cattle and large stocks of fodder and grain, which the British commandeered. The attacking forces, the largest British army ever assembled in India, must have presented quite a spectacle at Sōsale, consisting of 15,076 infantry, 2635 cavalry, 608 gunners, 104 pieces of artillery, joined by 10,157 infantry and 6000 horse belonging to the *Nizām* [Murray 1853]. The supply train included 60,000 oxen, carrying sufficient supplies for several months. Sōsale's economy must have been devastated by the passage of such a large force, since the British armies tended to preserve their supplies, living off the land in their conquest of South India. Nonetheless, Sōsale benefited greatly from Ṭippu's miscalculation. Had he expected the Sōsale crossing, he would have devastated the surrounding countryside to deny the British forage and shelter, as he did the countryside between Maḷavaḷḷi and the expected crossing near Arakere. Every dwelling there was torched, and not a blade of grass left intact. The supplies secured at Sōsale were vital to the British success, since the march was rigorous and the cattle, used as draft and pack animals, were driven mercilessly. In fact, the assault on Śrīraṅgapaṭṭaṇa was forced on May 4 by impending starvation in the British camp, and the death of almost all its cattle [Dundas 1800, p. 279].

[70]Coracles, called *teppas* in Kannaḍa, are widely used for crossing rivers and streams in the region. *Teppas* are circular baskets of bamboo and reed, measuring 5–8 feet in diameter and often covered on the outside with hide and tar. They are propelled and steered with a single paddle, and accommodate about six passengers. Steel *teppas* are now commonly used for transportation, since these accommodate up to a dozen people (or goods), and are more robust to bottom scraping in shallow water. Bamboo *teppas* are still used by fishermen, being cheaper, lighter, and more manœuvrable.

By the age of sixteen, Garaḷapurī Śāstri had attained proficiency in the subjects of *çampū*,[71] dramaturgy, poetics,[72] and grammar. Upon hearing of Garaḷapurī Śāstri's scholarly achievements, his great virtues, and his *śrōtric* heritage, Veṅkaṭasubbayya of Hulluhaḷḷi[73] in Nañjanagūḍu district
1838 approached Aṇṇayya Śāstri with a proposal for marriage with his eight-year-old daughter Subbamma.[74] Veṅkaṭasubbayya's also being an illustrious heritage, this alliance met with mutual approval. Garaḷapurī Śāstri accepted the duties of a householder at an auspicious time. Aṇṇayya Śāstri had a son before Garaḷapurī Śāstri, whom everyone called Rāmappa. Having an unusually sluggish intellect, he had been unreceptive to learning as a child. The father and older brothers had made great efforts to ensure an education for this brother, but had remained unsuccessful. They were finally resigned for this to remain his fate in this birth. Though Rāmappa was not learned, he was extremely virtuous. Everyone had great compassion for him. In his case too, Aṇṇayya Śāstri ensured the timely completion of all such rituals as *upanayana* and marriage.

[71] A complex literary form, which treats a subject in both rhythmic prose and poetry.

[72] The word used is *alaṅkāra*, which literally means tropology. As will become clear shortly, he was also a proficient poet.

[73] This name appears inconsistently as Veṅkaṭarāmayya in subsequent references.

[74] Subbamma, eight years Garaḷapurī Śāstri's junior, must have been born in 1830 C.E.

Chapter Four

Garaḷapuri Śāstri remained in Sōsale after his marriage. At the time, Sōsale too, was home to great scholars. The grand *maṭha* of the great *Mādhva* guru Vyāsarāyasvāmi is in Sōsale.[75] Many scholars were attached to this *maṭha*. Among them was the great scholar Tammayyāçārya.[76] This stalwart possessed a deep mastery of logic. Wishing to study logic with him, Garaḷapurī Śāstri ventured to approach Tammayyāçārya to make his wishes known. The *Āçārya* accepted him gladly. Applying himself assiduously to the study of logic, the Śāstri attained great proficiency in this field as well.[77]

---

[75]This *maṭha,* originally called the Pūrvādi Maṭha, is named after *Śrī* Vyāsarāya (1460–1539 C.E.), who became its head in 1476 C.E. This *Mādhva* saint was guru to Vijayanagara kings such as Kṛṣṇadēvarāya, and is often held as being second only to Madhvāçārya, the founder of the *Dvaita* branch of *Vēdantic* philosophy. The poet-composers Purandaradāsa and Kanakadāsa were his students. After being damaged by the Kāvērī floods of 1924 C.E., this *maṭha* was relocated to Vyāsarājapura, just north of Sōsale, and again in 1981 C.E. to a new site at the *saṅgama* in Tirumakūḍalu, next to the temple of Agastyēśvara. Thereafter, the old *maṭha* location remained shuttered for many years, but was reopened in 2008, with Mr V. Narasiṁha Mūrti of Baḷḷāri as its resident priest. Activity at this *maṭha* remains limited, but it is accessible to visiting devotees.

[76]The records of the Parakāla Maṭha in Maisūru indicate that Tammayyāçārya of Sōsale's Vyāsarāya Maṭha welcomed *Śrī* Śrīnivāsa Parakālasvāmi with *kāṇikas,* fruit trays, and shawls upon the *Svāmi's* return on May 24, 1859 C.E. from a trip away from Maisūru, and that he received *phalamantrākṣate* from the *Svāmi* [Desikāchārya 1949, p. cxxxvii]. Garaḷapurī Śāstri appears to have moved to Maisūru around this time, and may have been by his guru's side on this occasion.

[77]According to the information on page 302, it appears that Garaḷapurī Śāstri also taught logic to his students. A *Dēvanāgari* manuscript the translator has discovered in Kavitāvilāsa is an extensive *krōḍapatra* (scholium) on the *Sāmānyanirukta,* a treatise on *Navya Nyāya* logic by the well-known Gadādhara Bhaṭṭāçārya. The colophon credits it to a Śrīpurīśa in the *saṁvatsara Krōdhin,* or 1844 C.E., when Garaḷapurī Śāstri would have been 22 years old. We can be confident that this Śrīpurīśa is none other than Garaḷapurī Śāstri from the final colophon in his *Kṛṣṇabhūpālīyam: "iti śrīpurīśakṛtau kṛṣṇabhūpālīye alaṅkāraśāstre śabdālaṅkāra prakaraṇaṁ saṁpūrṇaṁ".* His proficiency in *Navya Nyāya* is clearly evident in his definition of *alaṅkāra* in his *Kṛṣṇabhūpālīyam: "... śabdārthaçārutvātiśayahētutvam ça śabdārthānyataraniṣṭhā yā viṣayitāsaṁbandhāvaççhinnāçamatkṛtijanakatā tadavaççhēdakatvam".* This technical and precise definition uses a cascade of formal constructions and technical concepts from *Navya Nyāya,* such as *hētutvam, viṣayitā, avaççhinna,* and *avaççhedakatvam.* The use of *Navya Nyāya* concepts in defining *alaṅkāras* was pioneered by the well-known Jagannātha Paṇḍita in works such as the *Rasagaṅgādhara.* The *Kṛṣṇabhūpālīyam* follows Appayya Dīkṣita's treatment of *alaṅkāras,* but Garaḷapurī Śāstri was clearly familiar with the work of Dīkṣita's rival Jagannātha.

Timmappa Śāstri had trained, with his brother, to the extent of dramaturgy under Rāmāśāstri, but no further in literary fields. Nonetheless, like his brother, he was accomplished in literature, and tutored many students in his home.

Garaḷapurī Śāstri had a natural and innate talent for poetry. This is not an ability that can be taught. Following the example of his illustrious guru Rāmāśāstri, an exceptional poet, who would frequently compose exquisite verses on Agastyēśvara and other deities, he too would often compose splendid *ślokās* on various topics. Shortly after his marriage, according to an anecdote of his childhood that has survived, his father-in-law Hulluhaḷḷi Veṅkaṭarāmayya,[78] reciting the following *ślōka* in praise of Rāma[79]

vāme bhūmi·sutā puras'ca hanumān paścāt sumitrā·sutaḥ
śatrughno bharataś'ca pārśva·dalayor vāyvādi·koṇeṣu ca |
sugrīvaś'ca vibhīṣaṇaś'ca yuvarāṭ tārā·suto jāmbavān
madhye nīla·saroja·komala·ruciṁ rāmaṁ bhaje śyāmalam ‖

before his household deity, asked: "Garaḷapurī, what do you think of this *ślōka?* Do you happen to know it?" The Śāstri, listening with great respect and devotion, answered that it was a mere prayer *ślōka.* His father-in-law then asked: "Could you compose a similar *ślōka* on Īśvara?"[80] Rising to the challenge, the Śāstri promptly composed the *ślōka*[81]

vāmāṅke girijā puras'tricaraṇaḥ paścāc'ca nandīśvarō
herambaś'ça guhaś'ça pārśva·dalayōr vāyvādi·koṇeṣu ça |
çaṇḍīśo'pi ça bhairavas'savinayo bāṇas'tathā rāvaṇaḥ
tan'madhye sphuṭa·puṇḍārīka·ruciraṁ śrī·nīlakanthaṁ bhaje ‖

---

[78]This name appeared inconsistently as Hulluhaḷḷi Veṅkaṭasubbayya on page 16.

[79]This is a well-known *ślōka* in the *Śārdūlavikrīḍitā* metre. Many South Indian household shrines include paintings or pictures depicting deities surrounded in this fashion by attendants and devotees. The image described in this *ślōka* is a common image, and generally referred to as *Srīrāma paṭṭābhiṣekaṁ*, or Śrīrāma's coronation. The imagery reflects the description of Rāma's coronation in the *Yuddhakāṇḍa:128* of the *Rāmāyana.* See page 362 for a translation.

[80]Given the imagery in the *ślōka,* the challenge was likely not simply to compose any Śiva *ślōka* similar to the Rāma *ślōka,* but to compose one describing an image of Īśvara in Hulluhaḷḷi Veṅkaṭarāmayya's household shrine.

[81]See page 363 for a translation.

Overjoyed at hearing this, Veṅkaṭarāmayya declared, "Garaḷapurī, you are destined for great fame!" to which the Śāstri respectfully responded, "These are merely the fruits of your blessings."[82] The poetic muse had favored him even as a student. The meaning of the saying *"kavitāvanitāçaivasvayamēvāgatāvarā"*[83] was exemplified in him. His poetic abilities were well known to his fellow-students, but not to either Tammayyāçārya or the *Śrī Svāmi.*[84] These came to light through a remarkable episode.

A scholar of ordinary merit and without poetic talent once arrived in Sōsale from elsewhere, craving to be rewarded for a *ślōka* of his own composition, though it lacked integrity of meaning or structure. He met the *Śrī Svāmi* with the help of officials from the Maṭha. Upon his indicating that he had composed poetry, which he would gladly present at the *Svāmi's* behest, the *Svāmi* arranged for a large audience.[85] The poem was recited. In the audience that day were Tammayyāçārya, his student Garaḷapurī Śāstri, as well as many other scholars. Out of politeness, and a sense that criticism would amount to rudeness, everyone was content to merely acknowledge the work. Sensing this, the *Śrī Svāmi* remained silent, and respecting all mutual courtesies between scholars, saw off the scholar with proper deference.

Garaḷapurī Śāstri, who was in the audience, was greatly saddened at the lack of criticism of a work so shoddy and lacking in poetic merit. He sat silently, however, out of regard for his guru Tammayyāçārya, not wanting to anger him. The sadness, however, remained with him, even after he returned home and went to bed. He did not sleep well. Rising before dawn the next morning, he went to the river for his ablutions. A stone *maṇṭapa* stands en route to the river from the Maṭha.[86] While returning

---

[82]The traditional response to a compliment from an elder.

[83]"Of maidens and verses, they alone are most excellent, who come of their own accord." A couplet expressing a similar sentiment says: *"kavitā vanitā çaiva svayātā rasadāyinī | balādākṛṣyamāṇā çet sarasā nirasā bhavet ‖"*

[84]The honorific title of the head of the Vyāsarāyasvāmi Maṭha. *Śrī* Vidyāpūrṇa Tīrtha was the head of this *maṭha* 1824–1872 C.E. These events date to 1842 C.E. See footnote 90.

[85]Footnote in original: "These verses do not appear here, having been lost. Likewise, many poems of Garaḷapurī Śāstri's childhood have been lost with him."

[86]This *maṇṭapa* no longer exists. Mr V. Narasiṁha Mūrti, the resident priest at the Sōsale *maṭha* in 2010 C.E., was aware of a *maṇṭapa* gurus had used for meditation in the past.

from the river, he wrote the following *ślōka* on the walls of the *maṇṭapa* in Dēvanāgari script, reflecting the sadness within him.[87]

anāghrāta·vyaṅgyair aparicita·śabdārtha·racanair
abuddhā'laṅkārair'anavagata·bhāvojjvala·rasaiḥ |
yaśo·mātr'āṅkūrān'nava·nava·durāśaiḥ kukavibhiḥ
duradhvē vyākṛṣṭā bhagavati vipannāsi kavitē ‖

The meaning of this *ślōka* is as follows: O beautiful muse of poetry, how tragically have you been drawn down the path of ruin by base poets, who are unacquainted with *vyaṅgya*, unskilled in poetic composition, and ignorant of poetic tropes and devices![88]

---

[87] The metre is *Śikhariṇī*. See page 363 for a translation.

[88] *Vyaṅgya* is the poetic device where subtle meaning is revealed through suggestion, inference, or implication in context, rather than from the overt meanings of the words. Poetic meaning can be construed at three levels: *vācyārtha, lakṣyārtha*, and the *vyaṅgyārtha*, corresponding to the word-meaning, metaphorical meaning, and suggested meaning. Effective use of *vyaṅgya* requires great subtlety, and represents the highest form of accomplishment in Indian poetics. A good example is the following verse from Kālidāsa (*Kumārasambhava,* 6:84)*:*

evaṁ vādini devarṣau pārśve pituradhomukhī | *līlākamalapatrāṇi gaṇayāmāsa pārvatī* ‖,

which translates to "As the divine sage (Aṅgīrasa) spoke thus, Pārvatī, by her father's (Himālaya's) side, lowered her gaze and began counting the petals of the lotus she was playing with." Aṅgīrasa has just asked Himālaya to give his daughter Pārvatī in marriage to Śiva. Kālidāsa paints a picture of a bashful but willing Pārvatī, without ever explicitly using words suggesting these sentiments. *Vyaṅgya* can operate in very subtle ways in the hands of accomplished master. Consider, for example, Kālidāsa's invocation of Śiva and Pārvatī in the justly celebrated first verse of his *Raghuvaṁśa*:

vāgarthāviva saṁpṛktau vāgārtha pratipattaye |
jagataḥ pitarau vande pārvatīparameśvarau ‖

Kālidāsa never explicitly mentions the conjoined *Ardhanārīśvara* form of Śiva and Pārvatī, but readily reveals his intention by using the word *saṁpraktau* (commingled) to describe the pair. Having thus prepared the reader's mind, he deploys such an astonishing variety of subtle grammatical, philosophical, and poetical devices to reinforce this image as to leave one breathless. Thus, at the grammatical level, Kālidāsa is implicitly invoking the *vārtika "ivena nityasamāso vibhaktyalopaḥ purvapadaprakṛtisvaratvaṁ ca"*, which declares *vāgārthāviva* ("as are word and meaning") to be a *nityasamāsa* or inseparable compound, which we cannot separate into *vāk* (word) + *artha* (meaning) + *iva* (as are), though these components are clearly apparent. This evokes the inseparability of the couple in their *Ardhanārīśvara* form. In his commentary, Mallinātha takes note of an even subtler evocation of this inseparability at the semantic level, through the *vārtika "siddhe śabdārtha sambandhe"* ("eternal are

The Śāstri returned home after having written this *ślōka.* Now, it was the *Śrī Svāmi's* practice to perform *japa* at this *maṇṭapa* after bathing in the river each morning.[89] When the *Svāmi* arrived at the *manṭapa* as usual for his *japa,* his eyes fell upon the *ślōka* written on the wall. When the *Svāmi* read it, he wondered who could have composed a *ślōka* of such delicacy, surmising that it had to be the work of some great poet from times past. While the other scholars accompanying the *Svāmi* were tending to the same opinion upon reading it, the *Svāmi* called out to Tammayyāçārya, and asked, "*Āçārya,* where is the *ślōka* on the wall from?" A number of Garaḷapurī Śāstri's fellow-students, who were around, now suggested to the *Svāmi* that this was very likely to have been the work of Garaḷapurī Śāstri. At this, the *Svāmi* and Tammayyāçārya, summoning Garaḷapurī Śāstri, asked him "Garaḷapurī, do tell us, who from the *maṭha* is likely to have composed this *ślōka*?". The Śāstri, unwilling to speak anything but the full truth in the presence of his guru, acknowledged that he had composed and written the *ślōka,* and explained his reasons. The *Svāmi* and 1842 the scholars present were full of praise for his abilities. The *Svāmi* blessed the Śāstri, saying "Śāstri, you will go on to be a great poet; this is truly the result of divine favour." Such was the extraordinary extent of the Śāstri's accomplishments, even by the age of twenty.[90]

Garaḷapurī Śāstri knew all five of the Nāgara, Dēvanāgara, Grantha, Telugu, and Kannaḍa scripts. He could write in an elegant hand in each of these scripts, and used them all as he wrote in his books.[91]

When Aṇṇayya Śāstri passed on, his sons completed his last rites, and divided their paternal property amongst themselves. Since the youngest brother Rāmappa was the least intellectually accomplished, the three eldest brothers gave him the largest share.

---

word, meaning, and their relationship"), the very first commented upon by Patañjali in his *Mahābhāṣya.* Similarly, *pitarau* (*mātā ça pitā ça pitarau*) is an *ekaśeṣa dvandva* compound, in which only *pitā* remains when *mātā* and *pitā* are compounded, again evoking the oneness of the conjoined form. And so on. This is *vyaṅgya,* indeed, for the profoundly erudite.

[89] *Japa* is a form of meditation involving repetition of a word, phrase, or idea.

[90] Making 1842 C.E. the date of this episode.

[91] Garaḷapurī Śāstri's surviving manuscripts are indeed in a beautiful calligraphic hand.

Chapter Five

After this time, Timmappa Śāstri and Ramappa looked after their respective lands, living on different sides of the courtyard of the large house in Sōsale they had divided between themselves. Veṅkaṭarāmāśāstri, the eldest, having always had a knack for practical affairs, enjoyed the confidence of people in surrounding villages, and was frequently called upon to adjudicate various matters arising between them. As head of the joint family, he made his residence in the great hall upstairs in the Sōsale house, and continued looking after his lands.

Now, when his father-in-law Giribhaṭṭa, royal *ṛtvik* at the Palace,[92] impressed by his great skill in practical matters, appointed him head of his *jōḍi* village of Duddagere,[93] he brought about great improvements in this village, and receiving particular assistance and resources from his father-in-law, built a large house just north of the temple of Gargēśvara Svāmi.[94] This house still stands.

In the month of Māgha each year, as a mark of deep devotion, his father Aṇṇayya Śāstri conducted a generous *santarpaṇa* for a thousand brāhmaṇas and a thousand of their womenfolk, in a grove near the river in Sōsale.[95] It was quite difficult to accommodate so many brahmaṇas and their womenfolk in the village in a single day.[96] Arrangements had therefore been made for brahmaṇas and their wives to arrive from various places, such as Tirumakūḍalu and Narasīpura, on different days. Brahmaṇas and their wives would continue to arrive from all over, for as many as five or six days,

[92] Officiating priest at *Vēdic* rituals. It is unclear who this Giribhaṭṭa is. A reference to the work *Saṁskāra Kaumudi* by a Giribhaṭṭa appears in Pandey [1998, p. 288] without a date or publisher.

[93] Duddagere is about 16 km east of Maisūru. A *jōḍi* village is a freehold or leasehold grant by royal decree, obligating the recipient only to some nominal taxes. The types of land grants in Kṛṣṇarāja Voḍeyar III's reign were *sarvamānya, ardhamānya, jōḍi grāma, jōḍi agrahāra, bhaṭamānya, dēvādāya, dharmādāya, koḍagi inām*, and *kere bandi* [Arasu 1993, p. 151]. See George [1970] for a discussion of the land revenue system in Maisūru.

[94] The temple referenced appears to be in the village of Gargēśvarī, not in Duddagere.

[95] Technically, this would be an *anna santarpaṇa*, or a feast for brāhmaṇas, from which great merit is believed to accrue. *Santarpaṇa* literally means "satiating".

[96] In 1876 C.E., Sōsale had 536 houses and 2,716 people, Narasīpura had 82 houses and 444 people (Tirumakuḍalu-Narasīpura had 1,650 people in 1891 C.E.), Hulluhaḷḷi had a population of 1,277, and Maisūru itself had 11,618 houses with 57,815 people [Rice 1877a].

until their count reached a thousand. Many relatives of theirs would come along as well. Cooks and servants were not readily available in those times. Family members and relatives helped out, participating enthusiastically in cooking and other such activities. As a result, the *santarpaṇas* proceeded with grandeur. Well pleased, brahmaṇas from the neighbouring villages and their wives bestowed their blessings on Aṇṇayya Śāstri's household.[97]

After Aṇṇayya Śāstri's time, Veṅkaṭarāmāśāstri continued this tradition with great devotion. Since the country was prosperous in those times, the essentials for *santarpaṇas,* such as grain, flowers, fruit, milk, yoghurt, ghee, and vegetables were readily and cheaply available; it was also usual for the residents of one village to send such essentials to the residents of another village, when the need arose. Consequently, *santarpaṇas* proceeded with great splendour.

From time to time, Garaḷapurī Śāstri accompanied his guru Tammayyāçārya, *paṇḍita* at the court, on his trips to Maisūru to see His Highness regarding matters concerning the *maṭha.* On one such occasion, Tammayyāçārya took his student Garaḷapurī Śāstri to the court with him.[98] His Highness always treated Tammayyāçārya, great scholar that he was, with enormous respect. Such pillars of scholarship as Dādāśāstri,[99] Rāmaśēṣāśāstri,[100] Kavi Varadāçārya, Sajjayyāçārya, Kuṇigala Rāmaśāstri, *Vyākaraṇa* Narasimhaśāstri, Kāśī Timmaṇṇāçārya,[101] and Kumbhakōṇa Śēṣāçārya[102] graced the court. Garaḷapurī Śāstri decided to move to Maisūru upon witnessing this

---

[97] See footnote 266. The *āśirvāda* or blessing is an essential and integral component of any ritual, and occurs at the end.

[98] See footnote 76.

[99] From the Kannaḍa caption in the painting shown in Plate 25b, it appears that Dādāśāstri was in fact none other than Tryambakaśāstri, who figures prominently in Kuṇigala Rāmaśāstri's biography.

[100] It has been argued [in Lakshminarasimhaiya *et al.,* 1970, p. 140] that the Rāmaśēṣāśāstri appearing in M.S. Puṭṭaṇṇa's biography of Kuṇigala Rāmaśāstri should be identified with Kaśi Śēṣa Śāstri. These authors also note [on p. 22] that Kaśi Śēṣa Śāstri established a school of *Saṁskṛta* grammar in Maisūru, and list a number of famous scholars of the time, who are claimed to have become eminent professors under his "guidance". This list, however, is excessively broad, and includes several great scholars, such as Garaḷapurī Śāstri and Kumbhakōṇa Śēṣāçārya, who definitely *were not* his students. (See footnote 102.) This erroneous information has been reproduced, as by Naidu [1996]. In fact, when Śēṣa Śāstri died on April 26, 1860 C.E., Garaḷapurī Śāstri, himself a mature thirty-eight, had likely just moved to Maisūru. See page 176 for an illustration of Rāmaśeṣaśāstri's prodigious intellect.

[101] See footnote 579.

[102] Kumbhakōṇa Śēṣāçārya lived in the Ramāvilāsa *agrahāra,* and was a guru of Garaḷapurī

constellation of scholars, the great regard they were held in by His Highness, and the grandeur of the capital city, and with support from Kempu Rāmāśāstri, who was his sister's father-in-law and physician at the court, he moved with his family from Sōsale to Maisūru, and took
1859 up temporary residence in Kempu Rāmāśāstri's home.[103] The Śāstri's brother-in-law Subbaṇṇa was studying medicine at this time. Kempu Rāmāpaṇḍita, who later became principal of the Maisūru Āyurvēdic College, was none other than his son.[104] Kempu Rāmāśāstri arranged to have his eldest son Subbaṇṇa receive instruction from Garaḷapurī Śāstri on the *Vāgbhaṭa*, a book on medicine.[105]

Śāstri's son *Kavitilaka* Ayyā Śāstri. In December 2010, the translator had the great privilege of meeting Śēṣāçārya's grandson, Kaulagi Śēṣāçārya, then a hundred years of age, living at 5/1 Sītāvilāsa Road, opposite Marimallappa's Junior College. Despite his advanced age, he remained astonishingly robust, and in full possession of his mental faculties. Not only was he able to recount his various memories of Ayyā Śāstri from over eighty years past, he instantly remembered all of Ayyā Śāstri's children in birth order. He also correctly pointed out that the name was properly "Ayya" Śāstri, not "Ayyā" Śāstri, as it is pronounced by Ayya Śāstri's surviving relatives. The present work uses the form "Ayyā" Śāstri, so this pronounciation was clearly acceptable to Ayyā Śāstri himself, although it appears as "Ayya" in his own works. Kaulagi Śēṣāçārya also strongly refuted the claim [in Lakshminarasimhaiya *et al.*, 1970] that his grandfather Kumbhakōṇa Śēṣāçārya had been one of Kāśī Śēṣa Śāstri's students. Incidentally, the "Kumbhakōṇa" in his name can mislead. Śēṣāçārya's ancestors were in fact Marāṭhi-speaking immigrants. The family still speaks an archaic form of the language. Regrettably, Kaulagi Śēṣāçārya passed away in 2011.

[103] No date is given for Garaḷapurī Śāstri's move to Maisūru. However, a biography of Garaḷapurī Śāstri's son Ayyā Śāstri (b. 1855 C.E.) written by his son Kṛṣṇasvāmi Śāstri (see page 301) indicates that Ayyā Śāstri moved to Maisūru with his father and his family at the age of about six or seven. This account places the year of his move to around 1861–1862 C.E. Among Ayyā Śāstri's papers, the translator found an anonymous manuscript biography [Sāstri 2012], likely also to have been by this biography's author, of Perisvāmi Tirumalāçārya (b. 1847 C.E.), which states that he was 12 when he became Garaḷapurī Śāstri's student, placing Garaḷapurī Śāstri in Maisūru by 1859 C.E. Perhaps Garaḷapurī Śāstri moved to Maisūru first, and his family followed a few years later.

[104] See Plate 17c for a portrait of Kempu Śāstri. The following depicts the family's known genealogy.

Rāmā Śāstri → Kempu Śāstri (Kempu Nārāyaṇa Kavi), born 1773, author of *Mudrāmañjūṣa* → Kempu Rāmā Śāstri → Subbaṇṇa (married Garaḷapurī Śāstri's sister) → Kempu Rāmāpaṇḍita (married Garaḷapurī Śāstri's 2nd daughter Sītamma)

A more complete genealogy of Kempu Rāmāpaṇḍita's descendents has been prepared by Professor T.V. Venkatachala Sastry of Maisūru.

[105] The adjectival form *Vāgbhāṭīya* would be more grammatical, but the author's name is

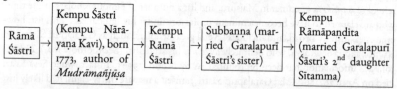

The father of this Kempu Rāmāśāstri was Kempu Śāstri, also known as Kempu Nārāyaṇakavi, the author of the *Mudrāmañjūṣa*,[106] a Kannaḍa literary work. After some time, Garaḷapurī Śāstri decided to move into a house of his own, and made his intentions known to Kānkānhaḷḷi Subrahmaṇyāçārya,[107] *paurāṇika* at the royal court, who lived in the *vaṭhāra* of *Vīṇe* Veṅkaṭasubbayya's house,[108] close to Kempu Rāmāśāstri's home in Maisūru's Old Agrahāra, and to his younger brother Guṇḍāçārya. These brothers approached *Vīṇe* Veṅkaṭasubbayya's son *Vīṇe* Śēṣaṇṇa, *Vīṇā Bakṣi* at the court, who then arranged to have Garaḷapurī Śāstri occupy a house that had become vacant in the *vaṭhāra* where he himself resided.[109] It was generally not the practice at that time to charge rent. Garaḷapurī Śāstri and his family lived contentedly in this house, which, by *> 1864*

being used here as a metonym. Garaḷapurī Śāstri, though not trained in medicine, clearly had the scholarship in *Saṁskṛta* to interpret the text. Indian scientific treatises were generally written in poetry or as terse aphorisms, requiring facility in *Saṁskṛta*. The *Aṣṭāṅgahṛdaya* and *Aṣṭāṅgasaṁhita (Vāgbhaṭa)* are attributed to Vāgbhaṭa. Çaraka, Suśruta, and Vāgbhaṭa were the three classical writers on Āyurvēda.

[106] This landmark work of Kannaḍa literature dates to 1823 C.E., and is based on a study of Viśākhadatta's *Mudrārākṣasa* (a play of the 9th century C.E. on Çandragupta Maurya), the *Mudrārākṣasa Kathā* by Mahādēva Tirtha and *Mudrārākṣasa Kathāsāra* by Ravikartana (both 16th century C.E.). Professor T.V. Venkatachala Sastry has prepared a modern critical edition of this work [Śāstri 1999].

[107] Kānkānhaḷḷi Subrahmaṇyāçārya was the father of the celebrated vocalist Mysore Vāsudevāçārya (1865–1961 C.E.), to whom we owe *Nā Kaṇḍa Kalāvidaru*, a treasury of first-hand accounts of musicians of the period [Vasudevaçārya 1994]. In childhood, Vāsudēvāçārya would have known Garaḷapurī Śāstri.

[108] A *vaṭhāra* is a community of families living in a cluster of houses within a walled enclosure. *Vīṇe* Veṅkaṭasubbayya (1750–1838 C.E.) was a well-known *vīṇā* player who wielded enormous political influence. See Plate 18a. Contemporary British accounts pillory him as a corrupt official who was *qāzi* at the court when Liṅga Raj Arasu (not *Aḷiya* Liṅgarajē Arasu) was *Dīvān*, and who was even convicted of corruption [Gopal 1993]. Veṅkaṭasubbayya's residence was a palatial mansion within the Maisūru fort, protected by seven guards with swords drawn [Vasudevaçārya 1994, p. 6]. The house referred to here was clearly among his other properties.

[109] *Bakṣi* (properly *bakhśi*, from the Persian *bakhśidan*, "to bestow", but often encountered as the droll variant *bhakṣi*, related to *bhakṣa*, "to consume") was a title derived from Mughal administration, where it referred to an executive position, including the function of paymaster. In Maisūru of the time, however, it was an honorary administrative title given to heads of departments at the Palace, with status equivalent to that of Assistant Commissioners in the State Government [Ikegame 2007, p. 24]. The Śēṣaṇṇa referred to would be *Doḍḍa* (the elder) *Vīṇe* Śēṣaṇṇa, *Vīṇe* Veṅkaṭasubbayya's adopted son [Subramanian 1985, p. 71; Vedavalli 1992, p. 55]. *Doḍḍa Vīṇe* Śēṣaṇṇa became *Vīṇā Bakṣi* at the Palace after the death of *Çikka* Rāmappa in 1864 C.E., who had himself been appointed to the post after the

providence, they were able to obtain so quickly. This *vaṭhara,* and the mansion in it, survives to this day.[110] The lower floor of this mansion contains a large hall. This hall served as Garaḷapurī Śāstri's classroom. Schools, by themselves, did not exist in those times. The homes of great scholars served as schools.

At this time, some ten or twelve students, some local, some from elsewhere, came to study with the Śāstri. Some studied poetics, while others studied *çampū.* The Śāstri would include newly arriving students in these same classes. His students numbered about twenty, after a year or so. Gradually, the number of students studying subjects such as poetics, *çampū,* and dramaturgy with the Śāstri reached thirty or thirty-five. Among them were many advanced students, such as Perīsvāmi Tirumalāçārya, the principal of Maisūru's Sadvidyāśāla,[111] Narasiṁhasvāmi of Mahādēvapura, Nārāyaṇa Sōmayāji, and Kūḍli Subbarāya Śāstri. That three-fourths of these students became great scholars in their own right is even now well known to many.

Over time, the Śāstri's great scholarship, poetic abilities, nobility of nature, reputation, and generosity with learning came to the attention of His Highness Kṛṣṇarāja Voḍeyar III,[112] who called him to court through *Bakṣi*

death of his guru *Vīṇe* Veṅkaṭasubbayya in 1838 C.E. Interestingly, *Çikka* Rāmappa's son was *Çikka* (the younger) *Vīṇe* Śēṣaṇṇa (1852–1926 C.E.), himself a celebrated *vīṇā* player, and a student of *Doḍḍa* Śēṣaṇṇa and the vocalist Sadāśiva Rāv. *Doḍḍa* Śēṣaṇṇa's son was the equally celebrated *Vīṇe* Subbaṇṇa (1854–1939 C.E.). At any rate, the text's allusion to *Vīṇe* Śēṣaṇṇa as *Bakṣi* allows us to date Garaḷapurī Śāstri's move to *Vīṇe* Śēṣaṇṇa's *vaṭhāra* to after 1864 C.E.

[110] Subrahmaṇyāçārya's son Vāsudēvāçārya (1865–1961 C.E.) has recorded his clear memories of Garaḷapurī Śāstri's house having been within the walls of the Maisūru fort, in apparent conflict with the information here [Vāsudevāçārya 1962, p. 39]. Kempu Rāmāśāstri's house, Garaḷapurī Śāstri's initial residence in Maisūru, is stated above to have been close to Veṅkaṭasubbayya's *vaṭhāra* in the Old Agrahāra, which is itself outside and to the south of the fort. Subrahmaṇyāçārya died in 1868 C.E., so Garaḷapurī Śāstri must have moved into his own residence in the *vaṭhāra* before this date. He appears to have continued living here till around 1873 C.E. (see footnote 129), so it is unclear when exactly he would have lived within the fort.

[111] Tirumalaçārya was only 12 when he became Garaḷapurī Śāstri's student (see footnote 103). The Sadvidyāśāla, founded in 1870 C.E. by Tirumalāçārya, still flourishes in Maisūru. Garaḷapurī Śāstri's son Ayyā Śāstri (b. 1855 C.E.) a student of Tirumalāçārya, was the school's vice-principal in 1871 C.E.

[112] Reigned 1799–1868 C.E. He was a child of five when installed king by the British, with Pūrṇayya as *Dīvān,* after the defeat and death in 1799 C.E. of Ṭippu Sultān, whose father Haidar 'Ali had usurped the Maisūru throne from the Voḍeyars. Kṛṣṇarāja Voḍeyar III held

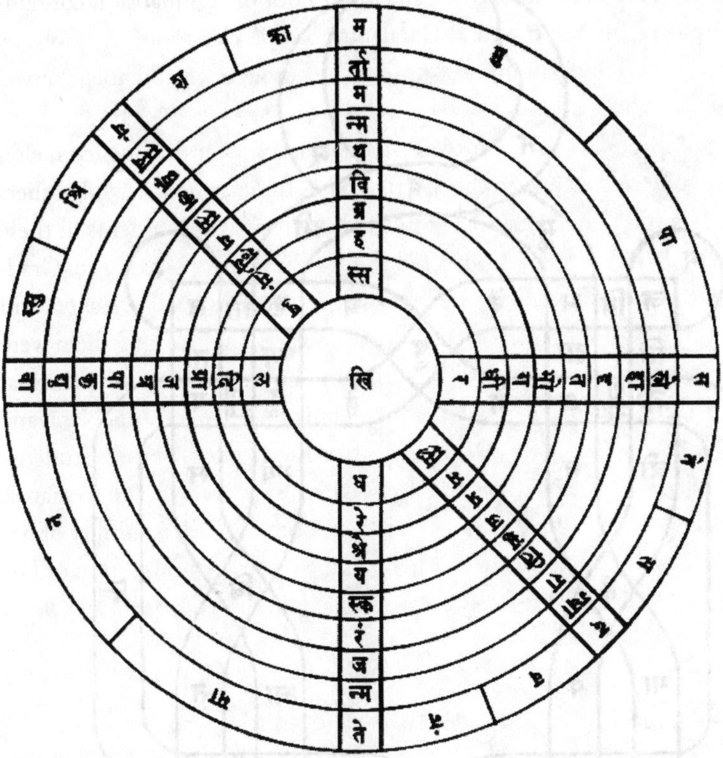

Plate 4: *Ṣaḍaraçakrabandha* (six-spoked wheel scheme) *çitrakāvya* composition from Garaḷapurī Śāstri's *Kṛṣṇabhūpālīyam*. Ten concentric circles are each divided into six equal sectors by the three diameters. The wheel's hub houses the single *akṣara "khi"*, its rim houses 18 *akṣaras* distributed in radially symmetric positions, and the segment of each spoke between the rim and the hub holds 8 *akṣaras*, the outermost always being a conjunct consonant. Traversing the vertical, horizontal, and diagonal diameters, and the rim, in that order, yields the following verse in praise of Kṛṣṇarāja Voḍeyar III:

bhartā manmathavigrahassakhidhare śreyaskaram janma te
sasnehādṛtabhogadhīrakhiladigrājatrapākṛdyuvā |
dagdhārātibhujaprabhassukhiṣu saṅkhyeyassakṛṣṇassvayam
yam śakrābhamupāsate sadavanam te mānavāssuśriyam ||

Further, going clockwise around the third and sixth rings yields the benediction *mahārāja kṛṣṇavibho jayajaya.*

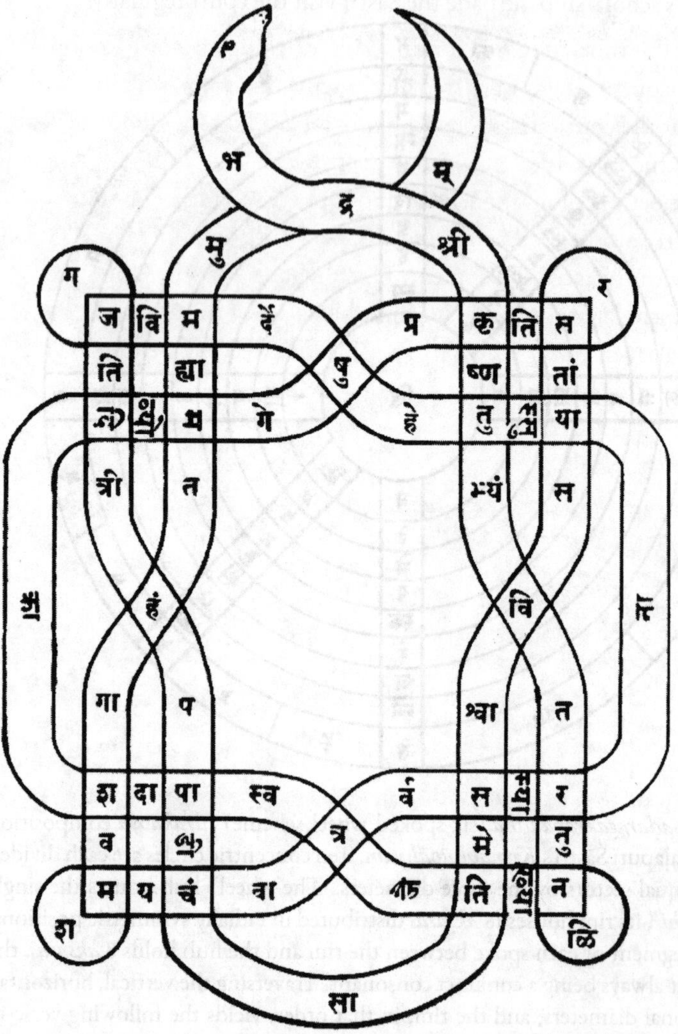

Plate 5: *Nāgabandha* (serpentine scheme) composition from Garaḷapurī Śāstri's *Kṛṣṇabhūpālīyam.* Tracing the coils of the "snake", starting at top left, we obtain the following verse in praise of Kṛṣṇarāja Voḍeyar III:

bhadram śrikṛṣṇa tubhyam vitaratu naḷinakhyātijaitrasvapādā
śakrādi vyomageṣu prakṛtisarasatām yā saviśvāsameti |
sā çaṇḍī pāpahantrī ditijagajavimardeṣu hetussuyānā
ramyā sarvatra vāçamyamaśamavaśagā hanta mahyāmamudram ||

Narasappa,[113] and pleased with the acclaim of the scholars at his court for the Śāstri's scholarship, he bade the Śāstri visit the court regularly.

After this time, the Śāstri continued his teaching, paying occasional visits to the court. There were frequent discussions among the scholars assembled at the court on various scholarly topics. Poetics and poetic tropes would be the topic of discussion on some occasions. Wishing to demonstrate his poetic abilities and scholarship in poetics to His Highness, Garaḷapurī Śāstri composed the *Kṛṣṇabhūpālīyam,* a work on tropology.[114] Greatly pleased with this accomplishment, His Highness formally appointed the Śāstri as a scholar at the court, at a monthly salary of thirty *Haṇas.* In those times, a salary of thirty *Haṇas* had a value far exceeding that of a salary of even thirty *Rūpīs* today.[115]

---

the title of Mahārāja, was entitled to the style "His Highness", and as of the 1861 darbar at Allāhābād by Lord Canning, was entitled to a 19-gun salute. At the time, only the Nizām of Haiderābād had higher status, with the style "His Exalted Highness", and a 21-gun salute. In 1867, Mysore was elevated to the status of a 21-gun salute state.

[113] A distinguished public servant who was effectively the chief executive officer to both Kṛṣṇarāja Voḍeyar III and his successor Çāmarāja Voḍeyar X. He died on or around August 27, 1878 [Venkataramayya 1905, p. 270], but had played an important role in Kṛṣṇarāja Voḍeyar III's attempts to secure the succesion of his adopted son, as well as the restoration of his rule, which ultimately occurred in 1881 C.E. Despite the central role he had in the administration, surprisingly little information is available about him. He received the title *Rāi Bahādūr* on January 1, 1877 at the Delhi Darbār.

[114] Meaning "Of the Emperor Kṛṣṇa", a reference to Kṛṣṇarāja Voḍeyar III, his patron. This work deals with 107 different *alaṅkāras* (generally mirroring their treatment in Appayya Dīkṣita's *Kuvalayānanda*), but illustrating them with 187 verses of Garaḷapurī Śāstri's own composition, all in praise of Kṛṣṇarāja Voḍeyar III. The three final verses illustrate the *çitrakāvya* forms *padmabandha, çakrabandha,* and *nāgabandha* (see Plates 4 and 5). Garaḷapurī Śāstri's son Ayyā Śāstri had the work published in 1931 C.E., with the help of a royal grant of Rs. 310. No date is given for the manuscript, but in 2008, the translator was able to identify and rescue the original manuscript, which is in Kannaḍa script. The paper is watermarked 1850, so the manuscript is subsequent to this date, matching the dates given in footnote 103. The manuscript remains in the custody of Mr Sandeep Sastry, son of Mr S.K. Dwarki.

[115] All Palace employees were paid in *Kaṇṭhīrava Haṇas* and *Pagōḍas* during Kṛṣṇarāja Voḍeyar III's reign, and in British-issued currency after his demise [Rao 1936b, p. 16]. A *Kaṇṭhīrava Haṇa* was a gold coin weighing an eightieth of a Troy ounce [Sircar 1966, p. 74], and valued at 7.489 Pence [in Buchanan 1807, p. 88]. Thirty *Haṇas* would have contained 3/8 ounces of gold, and at the time of Buchanan's travels in 1800 C.E., would have been worth just under £ 1. After 1868 C.E., a *Haṇa* was worth 4 *Annas* and 8 *Pais,* so that 30 *Haṇas* were worth about 9 *Rūpīs,* or just under £ 1, using the 1868 C.E. valuation of the Mysore crown jewels [in Bell 1882, p. vi] as a benchmark.

Chapter Six

His Highness Kṛṣṇarāja Voḍeyar III, who was himself very learned, convened daily discussions among the scholars at his court on matters such as the *Vēdas,* the *Purāṇas,* the *Itihāsas,* and poetics.[116] On one such occasion, the scholar *Vyākaraṇa* Narasiṁhaśāstri recited a *ślōka* he had composed in praise of the king, which had four metrically identical quarters in an unusual metre. His Highness was very appreciative. At once, the scholar Kavi Varadāçārya declared loudly: "Your Majesty, the structure of this verse is entirely opaque, and does not correspond to any known poetic metre."

At this, His Highness turned to Garaḷapurī Śāstri, and bade him examine this matter and judge the soundness of the verse. Accordingly, the Śāstri analyzed the verse closely, and having determined, by the rules of prosody, which subclass of which poetic metre it belonged to, presented a manuscript on the matter to His Highness. When it was read, the assembled scholars all concurred on the correctness of the verse, whereupon *Vyākaraṇa* Narasiṁhaśāstri promptly composed the following verse, rose to his feet, and loudly declaimed:[117]

nṛsimhākhyē gaṇḍa-sailē varadākhyo mahāmaṇiḥ |
nipatya khalu tatraiva vyaśīryata sahasradhā ‖

Meaning: The great jewel Varadāçārya, falling down upon the rock Narasiṁha Śāstri, was broken asunder into a thousand pieces.

---

[116] Kṛṣṇarāja Voḍeyar III was well versed in Kannaḍa, Marāṭhi, and Hindustāni, which were all languages current in Maisūru, as well as knowledgeable in Persian and *Saṁskṛta.* He also knew some English [Rao 1936a, p. 605]. After having been relieved of administrative responsibilities for his dominions in 1831 C.E., he was able to devote himself to scholarly and cultural pursuits. In Ayyāśāstri [1916], we see the following works attributed to him: *Śrītatvanidhi, Gaṇitasaṅgraha, Svaraçūḍāmaṇi, Saṅkhyāratnakōśa, Saugandhikāpariṇaya, Śrīkṛṣṇakathāsārasaṅgraha, Āryārāmāyaṇa, Mahākōśasudhākara, Çāmuṇḍēśvarītriśati, Śrīkaṇṭhēśvaratriśati, Mahāviṣṇutrisati,* and *Gaṇapatitriśati.* He is also credited with the *Sūryaçandrādivaṁśāvataraṇa, Daśarathanandanaçaritra, Grahaṇadarpaṇa,* and the *Çaturaṅgasārasarvasa.* Many of these works, of course, may have been composed in his name by scholars at his court.

[117] The original reads *saharsrathā* in the last line, but *sahasradhā* would be more correct. The Kannaḍa *thā* and *dhā* are orthographically close. The metre used is *Anuṣṭhubh.* See page 363 for a translation.

Upon hearing this, His Highness, with great composure, declared: "It was altogether proper for Varadāçārya to critique a verse of obscure structure, as it was for Garaḷapurī Śāstri to research the issue and determine the soundness of the verse, as it was for Narasiṁha Śāstri to compose the second *ślōka* for satisfaction that his first composition was judged sound," and by gifting expensive shawls to all three,[118] ensured that no ill feelings developed between them.

Garaḷapurī Śāstri was held in ever greater regard after this episode. At this time, Liṅgarāje Arasu,[119] who was son-in-law to His Highness, and had himself been born into great wealth, used to engage himself in the melodious recitation of works such as the Kannaḍa *Bhārata Jaimini*,[120] as well as in the study of *Saṁskṛta* works such as *Raghuvaṁśa* and that of Māgha,[121] and having a talent for poetry, in creating new compositions, such as short *yakṣagānas*.[122] Impressed with the scholarship and poetic skills of Garaḷapurī Śāstri, and wishing to study *Saṁskṛta çampū* works under his guidance, he received the Śāstri with great respect, and made his wishes known. The Śāstri agreed, and began visiting the Palace in the evenings, systematically tutoring him in *çampū* works.

Basappa Śāstri,[123] under Liṅgarāje Arasu's care from childhood, also participated in these lessons. He made excellent progress, absorbing even

---

[118] A traditional way of honoring scholars.

[119] A noted literary and musical figure (1823–1874 C.E.). See Plate 20. Since he was born posthumously to *Doḍḍa* (senior) Liṅgarāje Arasu, Kṛṣṇarāja Voḍeyar III himself performed all neonatal ceremonies, named him after his deceased father, and subsequently ensured his proper education and nurture. His sobriquet *Aḷiya* (son-in-law) derives from his marriages to the princesses Kempunañjammaṇṇi and Kempadēvājamaṇṇi [Arasu 1993, p. 75]. *Aḷiya* Liṅgarāje Arasu's three-story mansion was located on "Hūvina Bīdi" street within the old Maisūru fort [Arasu 1993, p. 77]. Also see footnote 176 for the precise date of his death.

[120] Poetry has traditionally been sung in India. Rabindrasangīt serves as a good contemporary example of this tradition. The *Jaimini Bhārata* is a work based on the *Mahābhārata* by the Kannaḍa poet Lakṣmīśa (16th or 17th century).

[121] The *Raghuvaṁśa* is an epic poem by Kālidāsa on the dynasty of Raghu, to which Rāma belonged. Māgha is the author of the celebrated *Saṁskṛta* work *Śiśupālavadha,* and is held in very high regard for his well-rounded poetic abilities. A measure of this regard is indicated by the well-known *ślōka: "upamā kalidāsasya bhāravairarthagauravam | daṇḍinaḥ padalālityam māghe santi trayoguṇāḥ ‖"*

[122] An operatic folk art prevalent in Karnāṭaka.

[123] Also called Basavappa Śāstri (1843–1891 C.E.), he became a dominant literary figure, with extraordinary facility in both *Saṁskṛta* and Kannaḍa. Śāstri [1949] provides the following information: "He belonged to the Vīraśaiva community. His ancestor was Muruḍu Basavasvāmi, *maṭhādhikāri* of the Rudrākṣi Maṭha Vīramāhēśvara sect, located in the

(a) Old Maisūru Palace, before its destruction by fire in 1897 C.E.

(b) Parade on ceremonial occasion before the old Maisūru Palace.

Plate 6: Views of the Old Palace at Maisūru as Garaḷapurī Śāstri would have seen it. By permission of the British Library.

more of Garaḷapurī Śāstri's instruction than Liṅgarāje Arasu did. Towards the end of his studies in dramaturgy and poetics, Liṅgarāje Arasu had also attained sufficient expertise in music and *Saṁskṛta* to put them to good use in his works in Kannaḍa. He had, in fact, become a substantial scholar.

Basappa Śāstri and he were both strong Kannaḍa scholars. Liṅgarāje Arasu continued his cordial and selfless patronage of Garaḷapurī Śāstri and Basappa, his ward from childhood; with their encouragement, he also composed many excellent *yakṣagānas* in Kannaḍa, and arranged for their performance on a stage built at his residence, with many children and youths under his patronage serving as actors. He also authored many excellent musical compositions in Kannaḍa and *Saṁskṛta*. Garaḷapurī Śāstri too, gained considerable scholarship in Kannaḍa through this association, and from his resulting contact with classical and contemporary Kannaḍa literature.

In poetic matters, Garaḷapurī Śāstri and Basappa were as the right and left arms of Liṅgarāje Arasu. They critiqued all his poetic compositions, pointing out shortcomings, and editing them to make them more generally accessible.[124] Over time, Liṅgarāje Arasu matured as a poet. Resolving

Nārusandra village of Beṅgaḷūru district. His son was the well-known *Vēdic* scholar Mahādevaśāstri, who had been named chief priest in the Sammukha division of the Palace by the great patron of scholarship Kṛṣṇarāja Voḍeyar III. Basavappa Śāstri was born to him in the Śubhakṛt *saṁvatsara*, that is, in 1843 C.E. Having lost his father in infancy, he grew up under the care of the well-known poet *Aḷiya* Liṅgarāja Arasu, and attained great scholarship in *Saṁskṛta*, Kannaḍa, and various arts, including music, under the tutelage of great scholars. As an accomplished scholar even by the age of eighteen, he composed the *Bilvavṛkṣapūjāvidhi* in *Saṁskṛta* and the *çampū* work *Kṛṣṇarājābhyudaya* in Kannaḍa, upon Her Highness's bidding. Subsequently, he became teacher to Śrī Çāmarāja Voḍeyar, and later, a poet at his court. He acquired the title *Abhinavakāḷidāsa* owing to his poetic skills. His works include the plays *Śākuntala, Ratnāvaḷi, Vikramōrvaśīya, Mālatīmādhava, Çaṇḍakauśika,* and *Śūrasēnaçaritre*, a translation of Shakespeare's Othello. His works include many for children in simple style, such as Bhartṛhari's *Nītiśataka, Śṛṅgāraśataka, Vairāgyaśataka, Śaṁkaraśataka, Nītisārasaṅgraha, Sāvitriçaritre*, and works for scholars, such as the *çampū Damayantīsvayaṁvara, Śrīharṣaçarite, Rēṇukāvijaya*, and in *Saṁskṛta*, *Śivabhakti Sudhātraṅgiṇī, Āryāśataka, Nakṣatramālikā, Ambāṣōḍaśamañjarī, Aṣṭamūrti Tanayāṣṭaka, Dakṣiṇāmūrtyaṣṭaka, Śivāṣṭaka, Sadāśivāṣṭaka*. He passed away in the Vikṛti *saṁvatsara* on Saturday, the thirteenth *śuddha tithi* of Māgha." The *tithi* of his passing corresponds to February 21, 1891 C.E.

[124] Sarōjā Veṅkaṭarām, the only daughter of Rāmasvāmi Śāstri (1894–1973 C.E., Ayyā Śāstri's third son) recalls the statement of her mother Sītamma (1904–1993 C.E, the daughter of M.S. Puṭṭaṇṇa), that the well-known composition *Śṛṅgāralaharī* in rāga *Nīlāmbarī*, though generally attributed to Liṅgarāje Arasu, was actually the work of Garaḷapurī Śāstri. The two may well have collaborated, especially on the *Saṁskṛta* lyrics.

to undertake a major poetic work, similar to the *Jaimini,* in the *Vārdhaka Ṣaṭpadi* metre, he began the *Prabhāvatīsvayamvara,* completing a chapter a month. The work progressed rapidly to a stage where it lacked no more than two or three chapters; it was then already larger than the Karnāṭaka *Jaimini.* Here, the Arasu stopped his work, intending to hold a grand *maṅgaḷa,* and a celebration.[125] The poetic flow, the richness of sentiment, and the rhetorical ornamentation in this work are especially praiseworthy.

Liṅgarāje Arasu treated his guru Garaḷapurī Śāstri with the greatest respect, always rising to his feet to lead him to his seat as he welcomed him to his home every day.[126] His gifts to the Śāstri were bestowed without his ever being asked. Thus freed from material concerns, the Śāstri could devote himself to gifting his knowledge to others at home, and sometimes visiting the Palace, and sometimes Liṅgarāje Arasu's home. Garaḷapurī Śāstri's small house became inadequate as his own family grew;[127] determining that he needed a larger residence, he composed a *ślōka,* and recited it to Liṅgarāje Arasu, when he went to his house, as usual. The Arasu wrote it down respectfully. The *ślōka* was as follows:[128]

tvam'asi rasika·madhye <u>maṅ</u>gaḷa·svāna·ramya·
s'samara·mṛ<u>di</u>ta·śatruḥ kiñça <u>ram</u>bhā·ratī'ççhuḥ |
dara·dhara·hṛdayō'ham nēśvara·śrīr jitō'nyaih
mama vitara samṛddhyai mandiram kā kṣatis'tē ‖

[125] A *maṅgaḷa* is a ceremony of benediction. Professor T.V. Venkatachala Sastry of Maisūru indicates that a boxed Royal Edition of the *Prabhāvatisvayamvara* exists in the library of the Kuvempu Institute of Kannaḍa Studies, University of Maisūru.

[126] There appears to have been a warm friendship between Garaḷapurī Śāstri and Liṅgarāje Arasu. According to the biographical manuscript referenced in footnote 103, they were both great chess afficionados, and spent a great deal of time playing chess.

[127] His eldest son was Aṇṇayya Śāstri (see the front matter for Śāstri 1891), his second son Ayya Śāstri ("Ayya" was a term of endearment, his real name being Veṅkaṭasubbaśarma), and his third son Rāmasvāmi Śāstri (referred to in Ayya Śāstri's will). Garaḷapurī Śāstri's first daughter was Nañjamma, and his second was Sītamma. Nañjamma married Hemmanahalli Kṛṣṇabhaṭṭa [Śāstri 1925a], and Sītamma married Kempu Rāmāpaṇḍita (footnote 104). Attiguppe Kṛṣṇaśāstri (1873–1924 C.E.), a well-known member of the Maisūru Representative Assembly, was Nañjamma's son. As a child, he lived and studied in Garaḷapurī Śāstri's house. His biography has been published by Veṅkaṭaramaṇa Śāstri [Śāstri 1925a].

[128] The metre is *Mālini.* This *slōka* apparently gained some renown at the time. Attiguppe Kṛṣṇaśāstri reports that he had accompanied Garaḷapurī Śāstri to the Palace on one occasion (he was less than four when Garaḷapurī Śāstri died), and greatly impressed Çāmarāja Vodeyar X by reciting this *slōka* [Śāstri 1925a]. The king, barely into his teens at the time, appears to have been acquainted with the composition.

Meaning: (My lord, inferred address) *tvamasirasikamadhyē maṅgaḷasvānaramyaḥ*—with melodious voice are you resplendent amidst connoisseurs, and *samaramṛditaśatruḥ*—you are he whose foes have been crushed in battle; *kiñçarambhāratīçchuḥ*—moreover, your righteousness makes you properly deserving of heaven and desirous of amorous sport with the heavenly nymph Rambhā; *daradharahṛdayōham*—my heart is fearful since I live in someone else's house; *nēśvaraśrīḥ*—and I am penurious; *jitōnyaiḥ*—I am scorned by all, having no house of my own, and hence— *mamavitarasamṛddhyai mandiraṁ*—give me prosperity by bestowing upon me the syllables *man, di,* and *ram*; *kākṣatistē*—what indeed, do you lack?

You lack nothing, and I will gain respect because of you. Transfer to me the syllable *man*, for you, who are *maṅ-gaḷasvānaramyaḥ* will then become *gaḷasvānaramyaḥ,* that is, resplendent through melodious speech, meaning that the euphony of scholarship will manifest itself in your speech. By the syllable *man*, I, who am now *daradharahṛdayaḥ,* will become *man-daradharahṛdayaḥ,* the one who holds Narayaṇa in his heart. That is, I will attain peace meditating upon Narayaṇa. Give me *di*, for then you, who are *samaramṛ-di-taśatruḥ* will become *samaramṛtaśatruḥ,* the one whose foes have died in battle; that is, your foes will die when you take to battle. I, who am now *nēśvaraśrīḥ* will become *di-nēśvaraśrīḥ,* or luminous like the sun, meaning I will shine with happiness. When you give me *ram*, you, who are *ram-bhāratīçchuḥ* will become *bhāratīçchuḥ,* or the one who seeks Sarasvatī, that is, a scholar. I, who am *jita* on the part of others will become *rañ-jita* on their part, meaning I will be liked by everyone.

The main but cleverly concealed message calls for the gift of *mandiram*, a dwelling. Grasping the ingenious construction of the *ślōka,* the Arasu exclaimed joyously to the Śāstri, "Truly, the gift of a house is unbefitting of this feat of poetry! This merits the gift of a kingdom!" He then summoned the steward of his estates, and ordered that all resources be made available towards the construction of a house for the Śāstri, as and where he pleased. The Śāstri had a house constructed on a site he purchased in the row of houses in the Katvāḍipura Agrahāra.[129]

c. 1873

[129] In 2008 C.E., the translator located the Katvāḍipura Agrahāra as the 2nd Cross Road behind Lakṣmi movie theatre, passing through 12.3008°N, 76.651°E. See footnote 230 for the origins of this *agrahāra.* We can date the episode referenced. Garaḷapurī Śāstri

At this time, His Highness Kṛṣṇarāja Voḍeyar III made arrangements for the housing, board, and education of *Saṁskṛta* students from elsewhere in the stables belonging to Sañjīvarajē Arasu, and through *Bakṣi* Narasappa, established a school to promote *Saṁskṛta* learning in the realm.[130] *Bakṣi* Narasappa appointed Garaḷapurī Śāstri as the instructor in this school for dramaturgy and poetry. Garaḷapurī Śāstri had his current pupils join this school; they continued their advanced studies with him, along with the other pupils there.

A *vaidika* scholar of unsound intellect, who went by the name of Āśukavi, arrived at around this time from the village of Gargēśvarī, and being an acquaintance, lodged in Garaḷapurī Śāstri's house.[131] Knowing his temperament all too well, the Śāstri welcomed him tactfully, upon which the Āśukavi intimated that he had composed poetry in praise of the Mahārāja, and requested help in obtaining an audience.[132] The Śāstri heard the fatuous and awkward poem, and seeing much humour in it, and thinking it worthwhile to arrange an audience, composed a *ślōka* of his own, and placing it into an envelope, suggested that an audience might be arranged were it conveyed to Kavi Varadāçārya, whereupon the Āśukavi delivered it to Kavi Varadāçārya. The envelope contained a single *ślōka*. It held no other intimations or names. Kavi Varadāçārya read it, and tactfully inquiring after the well-being and intentions of the Āśukavi, asked where he was lodged, to which the Āśukavi carelessly replied that he was staying with Garaḷapurī Śāstri. Kavi Varadāçārya, thinking amusedly, "Who else but Garaḷapurī Śāstri could have composed such a delicious *ślōka* for a recommendation?", and seeing the Āśukavi off courteously, saying that he had been pleased to

still lived in *Viṇe* Veṅkaṭasubbayya's *vaṭhāra* in 1873 C.E., the year his grandson Attiguppe Kṛṣṇasvāmi Śāstri was born [Śāstri 1925a]. *Aḷiya* Liṅgarāje Arasu died in December 1874 C.E., so the verse was likely composed in 1873 C.E. Garaḷapurī Śāstri must have moved to his new home in the Katvādipura Agrahāra in 1873 or 1874 C.E. An old home, perhaps dating to the time, still exists at #721 on this street. In 2008 C.E., this house was owned by Gōpayya, a brāhmaṇa who was then 84 years old. See Plate 16.

[130] This appears to be the Śaradāvilāsa Pāṭhaśāla, established by *Bakṣi* Narasappa in 1861 C.E. It started as a *Saṁskrta* school, became a general primary school in 1870 C.E., and is now a large organization running a range of institutions from the elementary to the university levels.

[131] *Āśu* means "quick" in *Saṁskṛta*, so an *āśukavi* is a poet skilled in composing verses impromptu, either spontaneously or in response to a challenge. Gargēśvarī is on the Kāvērī's west bank, across from Sōsale, which is on its eastern bank.

[132] Footnote in original: "This poem has not come to hand."

meet him and would try to arrange a Royal audience, acquainted His Highness with the episode, and upon his command, conducted the Āśukavi to the Royal court, and after an audience, made reference to the *ślōka* he had received. The *ślōka* was as follows:[133]

nihsvatā·yuvati·cumbana·jany'onmāda·mūla·kavitā·kṛti·dakṣaṁ |
sarva·loka·parihāsa·padaṁ māṁ ko nirīkṣya na bhavet karunārdraḥ ‖

Meaning: I am adept at composing fatuous *ślokās*, distracted as I am from keeping company with the maiden Poverty. Who would not feel compassion for me, the object of universal ridicule? (That is, please help me.)

At this, His Highness and the scholars at the court, greatly amused, inquired after the well-being of the Āśukavi, and had him recite the *ślōka* he had composed in praise of His Highness. When the entire court laughed out loudly at the silly and awkward composition, His Highness, seeking to allay the Āśukavi's discomfiture, declared that there was no one else capable of such compositions, that he had derived great pleasure from his poetry, and bade him visit the court regularly.

When, after a few days of the Āśukavi's attendance at the court, a reference again arose to the *ślōka "nisvatāyuvati"*, and the Āśukavi arrived home unhappy, having seen everyone laughing to themselves, the Śāstri asked why he seemed so distracted. The Āśukavi responded unhappily: "Whatever was it that you sent Kavi Varadāçārya! As you well know, he recites this *ślōka* over and over again at court, his manner suggesting that I am the speaker. I appear to have become an object of ridicule at the court! All this seems to have been on your account!" The Śāstri comforted him, saying, "It is really not as you suppose. You should not feel troubled by levity on the part of anyone. The Mahārāja has great regard for you", but the Āśukavi insisted on moving into Kempuśāstri's house, and in court the following day, recited the following *ślōka* before His Highness:

garaḷapuri·śāstrī rāja·pāṇḍitya·mānī
budha·jana·parihartrī khpitāṇṇayya·nāmā |
kavi·jana·karuṇārī kāśyapī drāhyasūtrī
kisalaya·salilāyām sosalē'ghrāra·vāsī ‖

[133]The metre is *Svāgatā*. See page 364 for a translation.

When the Mahārāja, remarking that this appeared to be a new composition, bade the Āśukavi explain its meaning, the Āśukavi submitted: "Your Highness, anything I say appears to become cause for merriment at this court. This *ślōka* is merely a composition arising from my anger at Garaḷapurī Śāstri, who appears to have been responsible for this situation. I refuse to be intimidated by these scholars." When His Highness said: "The course you have chosen in the case of Garaḷapurī Śāstri is surely proper, but we would like to hear the meaning of this *ślōka* in your own words", the Āśukavi responded: "I am incapable of difficult poetic compositions, and even a child would understand my poetry. The meaning of this *ślōka* is as follows—This Garaḷapurī Śāstri fancies himself a great royal scholar, and has little respect for scholars like me. His father's name was Aṇṇayya. However, there remains some intrigue in this poem."

With everyone urging him to reveal this intrigue, the Āśukavi said: "Everyone calls him Aṇṇayya Śāstri. But even he, surely, is not as great a *śāstri* as Garaḷapurī Śāstri, so I have left out the word *śāstri,* and said 'Aṇṇayya *nāmā*' instead, thereby marking him with a *nāmā.*"[134] Everyone laughed out loudly at this, and eagerly urged him to continue. The Āśukavi continued: "Having no regard for ordinary poets like us, he has sent Kavi Varadāçārya some secret intimation. He was born into the Kāśyapa *gōtra,* and follows the *Drāhyāyaṇa sūtra. Drāhya* being the same as *Drāhyāyaṇa,* there are no hidden allusions there. However, there is some intrigue in the final quarter of the verse."

With everyone again urging him to reveal this hidden intrigue, the Āśukavi continued: "He is a resident of the Sōsale *agrahāra.* His garden has a patch of *kīre* greens.[135] When visiting his house once, I have actually seen Garaḷapurī Śāstri, this great royal scholar, watering his *kīre* shoots. This is the hidden intrigue in my poem." As the court laughed at his poem, the Āśukavi laughed along, thinking they were laughing at the intrigue he had described. His Highness, smiling amusedly, congratulated the Āśukavi on such a diverting *ślōka.*

[134] *Aṇṇayya nāmā* means "named Aṇṇayya" in *Saṁskṛta.* In Kannaḍa, however, the word *nāma* also refers to a *tilaka,* or mark on the forehead, in the form of one, two, or three vertical lines, worn by *Vaiṣnava* brāhmaṇas. The exact form is specific to the sect. This type of *tilaka* is also called an *ūrdhva puṇḍra.* In colloquial Kannaḍa, to mark someone with a *nāma* is to play a trick on them, so this is a pun on the part of the Āśukavi. Also see footnote 427.

[135] The leaves of a member of the family *Amaranthus,* most likely *Amaranthus frumentaceus.*

The Āśukavi carried on thus every day, composing silly *ślōkas* on the spur of the moment, suffering, no doubt, the effects of his experiences and deeds in earlier births. On one occasion, he had returned from a visit to Çāmuṇḍī hill and Kārañjī lake. When someone at the court asked him how he had found Çāmuṇḍī hill and Kārañjī lake, the Āśukavi, intending to say that the breeze on Çāmuṇḍī hill was pleasant and that the water in Kārañjī lake was excellent to drink,[136] instantly responded *"çāmuṇḍī parvatōvatō kārañjīudakōpibō"*, causing great merriment among those present.[137]

Finally, His Highness, out of pity for this accomplished but mentally unsound brāhmaṇa, awarded him a pair of shawls and a hundred *Rūpīs*. This gift greatly pleased the Āśukavi, who learning from others that this had been on account of Garaḷapurī Śāstri and Kavi Varadāçārya, laid aside his anger, thanked them, and departed for home.

Subsequently, when His Highness Kṛṣṇarāja Voḍeyar III took Çāmarajēndra Voḍeyar as his adopted son, he appointed Garaḷapurī Śāstri as his *Saṁskṛta* instructor when the prince was formally initiated into learning.[138] After this time, Garaḷapurī Śāstri's day was spent teaching at the *Saṁskṛta* school in the mornings, tutoring the prince in the afternoons, and visiting Liṅgarāje Arasu in the evenings.

Around this time, His Highness determined to have competent scholars research and edit the medical work *Aṣṭāṅgahṛdaya* by Bāhaṭāçārya, all available versions of which were corrupt, intending to have it published through the lithographic press at the Palace.[139] After he appointed Garaḷapurī Śāstri and Hulluhaḷḷi Nallāṁ Gōpalakṛṣṇāçārya to this task, Garaḷapurī

[136] Footnote in original: "The fate of many of the Āśukavi's *ślōkas* remains unknown."

[137] This utterance translates roughly into "Çāmuṇḍi mountain (is) wind, and the Kārañjī lake (is) drink."

[138] Çāmarajēndra Voḍeyar (b. February 22, 1863 C.E.) was adopted on June 18, 1865 C.E., but the adoption received official sanction from the (British) Government of India only in April 1867 C.E. This adoption was triggered partly by the fear of the kingdom being usurped by the British under Lord Dalhousie's Doctrine of Lapse (see footnote 505). In a minute dated January 16, 1856, Dalhousie says: "The Raja of Mysore is now 62 years of age. He is the only Raja who for twenty generations past, as he himself informed me, has lived to the age of 60 years. It is probable therefore that his life will not be much further prolonged... I trust therefore that when the decease of the present Raja shall come to pass with no son or grandson or legitimate male heir of any description, the territory of Mysore, which will then have lapsed to the British Government will be resumed and that the good work which has been so well begun will be completed."

[139] Kṛṣṇarāja Voḍeyar III established the lithographic press in the Ambāvilāsa section of the Palace in 1841 C.E. [Kamath 1996, p. 42].

Śāstri reduced his tutoring of the young prince to a half-hour in the afternoons, and then worked till the evening on the premises of the Palace Press, researching Bāhaṭā's book with Gōpalakṛṣṇāçārya.[140]

Thus progressed things for some time, and when in the Vibhava *saṁvatsara,*[141] time in its course claimed the aged Kṛṣṇarāja Voḍeyar III Raṅgāçārya,[142] who had just become Palace Controller, had the work published[143]

[140]The front matter for Garaḷapurī Śāstri's edition (see footnote 143) attributes the work to Bāhaṭa, though a work called the *Aṣṭāṅgahṛdaya* is generally attributed to Vāgbhaṭa (see footnote 105). Hymavathi [1993, p. 49] suggests that Bāhaṭa was a Telugu author who composed the *Bāhaṭagrantha* and *Aṣṭāṅganighaṇṭu.* Rao [1985, p. 89] and Bendall [1886, p. 61] suggest that Bāhaṭa is a Prākṛtized version, popular in Southern India, of the *Saṁskṛta* name Vāgbhaṭa. A lithographed copy of the *Aṣṭāṅgahṛdaya* was presented to the Royal Asiatic Society of Bengal on June 1, 1870 by Colonel G.B. Malleson [Society 1870], who was guardian to H.H. Çamarājendra Voḍeyar, July 1869–June 1877 C.E. This was surely the work being referred to here.

[141]See footnote 157.

[142]Footnote in original: "He became *Dīvān* of Mysore after Śrī Çamarājēndra Voḍeyar was invested with ruling powers." Voḍeyar was recognized as the sovereign on March 28, 1868 C.E., and formally crowned on September 23, 1868 C.E., but was invested with ruling powers only upon the Rendition of Mysore on March 25, 1881 C.E. C.V. Raṅgāçārlu was appointed *Dīvān* of Mysore that same day. See Bowring [1872, p. 388] for Lady Bowring's delightful account of the coronation. Raṅgāçārlu had been appointed Palace Controller around May 1868, at a salary of Rs. 800 per month.

[143]Footnote in original: "Front matter for the Bāhaṭa volume: *"āryā ‖ karnātaka janapada jananātha śrī kṛṣṇarājatanayasya ‖ śrīmaççāmanṛpēndōranavaratam prājyamastusāmrājyam ‖ svastiśrī vijayābhyudaya śālivāhanaśakavatsarāḥ 1792 śukla saṁvatsarada śrāvaṇaśukla pançamyām śrimanmahiśūra mahārāja prāsāda samunnidramudrākṣara śālāyām śrī bāhaṭāçāryēṇa çarakasuśrutādyāyurvēda tantrakāramatānurōdhinātadīya mūlagranthasārabhūtārthāṅsaṅgrhya çikitsakānāmatyantōpakārāya ṣadbhissthānairudīritamidam aṣṭāṅgahṛdayamnāma vaidyaśāstraṁ naikavidhalēkhakapramāda vaśādayathābhūta śithilamapiprāgukta mahārājāśrita vidvajjanāntargatēna sōsale garaḷapurīśāstriṇā nallāṁ gōpālakṛṣṇāçāryēṇaça yathāmatisamyakpariśōdhya mahīśūra mahārāja çīpakamiṣanar bavaraṅgnāmakaprabhōranumatyāvimudritamāsīt. san 1869 nē isavi agīṣtu tā‖ 12."*

This is, of course, *Saṁskṛta*, but curiously, it includes words and phrases with Kannaḍa declensional endings, such as *"saṁvatsarada"*, and *"san 1869 nē isavi"*. We give the following translation:

"Ārya. May the reign of the moon Çāmarāja, the son of Kṛṣṇarāja, king of the Karṇāṭaka nation, be great and everlasting. In the saṁvatsara named Śukla, year 1792 of the Śālīvāhana era, on the day corresponding to the fifth tithi of the waxing phase of the lunar month Śrāvaṇa, in the printing press opened at the Palace of the Mahārāja of Maisūru, under the imprimatur of the Maisūru Royal Chief Commissioner Lord Bowring, has been published this medical work called Aṣṭāṅgahṛdaya, being a compendium in six divisions created for the great benefit of physicians by Bāhaṭāçārya, from the substance of original works by earlier followers of the system of Çaraka, Suśrūtha and others, but which, having become

by the lithographic press at the Palace with the permission of Mysore State Commissioner Bowring.[144] After its publication, Garaḷapurī Śāstri himself tutored his son-in-law Kempu Rāmāpaṇḍita as well as Puṭṭaśyāmapaṇḍita on the entirety of the material in this book. The two of them became very accomplished in medicine, and taught medicine at the *Saṁskṛta* College at Maisūru.[145] Later, Kempu Rāmāpandịta became principal of the Āyurvēda College. Garaḷapurī Śāstri taught not just literature, but also medicine to many students. *1869*

While he was still resident in the *vaṭhāra* of *Viṇe* Veṅkaṭasubbayya's mansion in the Old Agrahāra,[146] some of the Śāstri's advanced students, seeing that the *Yuddhakāṇḍa* addendum by Lakṣmaṇakavi was stylistically quite different from the first five cantos of the *Çampu Rāmāyaṇa* by Bhōja Rāja,[147] now urged him to compose a new *Yuddhakāṇḍa* in the style of Bhōja Rāja; the Śāstri, feeling that such an effort would be in fulfilment of Bhōja Rāja's own intentions, began work on a new *Yuddhakāṇḍa* at an auspicious time. The work was complete within a year. All students of his studying the *Çampu Rāmāyaṇa* now began studying this work.[148]

---

altered, confused, and inexact due to inconsistencies in writing styles, has been judiciously researched and edited by Sōsale Garaḷapurī Śāstri and Nallāṁ Gōpālakṛṣṇāçāryā, members of the community of scholars under the patronage of the monarch aforesaid. Dated August 12, 1869 C.E."

[144] This would be Lewin Bentham Bowring, Mysore Chief Commissioner, 1862–1870 C.E.

[145] Mahārāja's *Saṁskṛta* College was established in 1876 C.E. in a building called *Sarasvatī Prāsāda.* After moving to Sayyāji Road in 1883 C.E., it added subjects such as Āyurvēda, music, and astrology.

[146] The Katvāḍipura Agrahāra was also known as the Old Agrahāra. See footnote 158.

[147] The remarkable Bhoja of the Paramāra dynasty ruled Malwa *c.* 1000–1060 C.E., and was renowned both as a general and a literary figure. He is the Bhoja Rāja of legend. His substantial military accomplishments include victories over the Ghaznavid invaders. He also authored numerous distinguished literary works, including the first five cantos of the *Çampūrāmayaṇa*, though the colophons refer to him indirectly as *Vaidarbharāja.* A sixth canto (*Yuddhakāṇḍa*) was contributed by Lakṣmaṇa, who according to the colophon, was from Śanagara village (Śanigaram of modern-day Karīmnagar district in Āndhra Pradēśa) and the son of Gaṅgādhara and Gaṅgāmbikā. He is assigned to 12th–13th century C.E.

[148] The original date of this work is not given, but is likely to have been around 1869–1870 C.E. It was published in 1891 C.E. by Garaḷapurī Śāstri's son Ayyā Śāstri, some fourteen years after his father's demise. In the colophon, Garaḷapurī Śāstri alludes to himself as the first *Saṁskṛta* teacher of H.H. Çāmarājēndra Voḍeyar, who was born in 1863 C.E. It is unlikely that colophon was altered during publication, so the work was likely completed after 1869 C.E., in light of footnote 159, and the information on page 61 that Tirumalāçārya founded

In later years, Garaḷapurī Śāstri devoted himself entirely to teaching advanced students, and stopped teaching beginners. Even his own children were taught by his advanced students.[149] He also knew by heart every book he taught. His lessons were always lucid, enjoyable, and delivered with great facility. Many students were therefore eager to study with him. The Śāstri's conversations with his friends, students, and his children were often humorous, inventive, and witty. I will now recount a couple of incidents in this respect—It was Garaḷapurī Śāstri's practice to leave home after five every evening, and return at nine-thirty. A manservant by the name of Javara had been employed at the time to milk the cattle belonging to Kānkānhaḷḷi Subrahmaṇyāçārya and Guṇḍāçārya, who both lived in the same *vaṭhāra* as Garaḷapurī Śāstri.[150] On one occasion, Garaḷapurī Śāstri returned home after nine thirty, to find the main door to the *vaṭhāra* locked. The Śāstri called out loudly for the door to be opened. Hearing this, Subrahmaṇyāçārya, just settling down in front of his house after dinner, shouted back playfully: "Who are you fellow? Javara, surely?" Garaḷapurī Śāstri responded immediately: "Indeed not, fellow, it's I–*dvijavara!*"[151] Subrahmaṇyāçārya immediately opened the door, took Garaḷapurī Śāstri by the hand, and led him inside, saying: "Śāstri! How quickly you made your riposte! A *dvijavara* you truly are!"

On another occasion, when the Śāstri's second son returned after fetching some banana-flower *kari*[152] from the nearby garden of Narasē Arasu, the Śāstri interrupted his *çintana*[153] to ask him where he had been. When the

---

the Sadvidyāśālā (in 1870 C.E.) after he had written the commentary. Other information (see footnote 175) suggesting that the work may have been complete as early as 1866 C.E may be discounted. The prince would have been only three years old at that time, too young to have received *Saṁskṛta* instruction from Garaḷapurī Śāstri.

[149] His son Ayyā Śāstri was a student of both Perīsvāmi Tirumalāçārya and Basappa Śāstri.

[150] Subrahmaṇyāçārya and Guṇḍāçārya were brothers. See page 25.

[151] Footnote in original: "*dvijavara*—an excellent brāhmaṇa." "*Dvijavara*" can be parsed as *dvija·vara, dvija* meaning twice-born, a common reference to brāhmaṇas, and *vara* meaning excellent. Another parsing (not the one intended here) yields *dvi·javara,* translating roughly as *a double Javara.*

[152] Footnote in original: "*kari*—elephant in *Saṁskṛta.* In Kannaḍa, it refers to the petals of the banana flower, roasted and added to turmeric paste to give it reddish colour." Sarōjā Veṅkaṭarām, the great-granddaughter of Garaḷapurī Śāstri, recalls that her family would use roast banana peel to make *akṣate*, a pigment used to form a circular *tilaka* (itself also *akṣate*) in the middle of *vibhūti* on the forehead. Also see footnote 367.

[153] Footnote in original: "*çintana*—deliberation over some subject of recent study."

son responded that he had been to fetch (some) *kari,* the Śāstri asked him where he would tie (tether) it. When the son responded that he would tie it in the sunshine, the Śāstri chidingly asked him how tying it in the sunshine could be the right thing to do. When the son responded that he would tie it in the shade, the Śāstri smiled and asked him how he proposed to care for it. The son, realizing that the Śāstri's elaborate discussion *1868* of so simple a matter could not be without motive, immediately recalled the *nighaṇṭu "kuñjarō vāraṇaḥ karī"*,[154] and realizing the Śāstri's meaning, responded that he would take care of it somehow; the Śāstri too, was pleased that his son, then just thirteen,[155] had grasped his meaning. This second son of his is none other than *Kavitilaka* Ayyā Śāstri,[156] who is presently a *mahāvidvān* at the court. Garaḷapurī Śāstri's conversations were always full of wit and humour.

Now, some time after H.H. Kṛṣṇarāja Voḍeyar III passed away in the Vibhava *saṁvatsara,*[157] Garaḷapurī Śāstri, still resident in the Katvāḍipura Agrahāra,[158] tutored H.H. Çāmarāja Voḍeyar X in *Saṁskṛta* every day in the Royal School specially established in a mansion for His Highness's education;[159] Raṅgāçarya, who was Palace Controller at the time, witnessing first-hand the scholarship and virtues of Garaḷapurī Śāstri, would very respectfully invite Garaḷapurī Śāstri to his own home every day, and out of regard for him as among the most distinguished of the distinguished scholars at the court, would occasionally do him the honor of some reward.

[154] A *nighaṇṭu* is a thesaurus or glossary. The work being referred to is the *Amara Kōśa* (see footnote 58). *Kuñjaraḥ, vāraṇaḥ,* and *karī* are synonyms for elephant. See *Amara Kōśa* (kṣatriyavarga:35): *"dantī dantāvalō hastī dviradō'anēkapō dvipaḥ | mataṅgajō gajō nāgaḥ kuñjarō vāraṇaḥ karī ‖"*

[155] That makes 1868 C.E. the date of this episode. Ayyā Śāstri was born in 1855 C.E.

[156] Kṛṣṇarāja Voḍeyar IV bestowed the title *Kavitilaka* on Ayyā Śāstri in 1912 C.E.

[157] He died on March 27, 1868 C.E. at 10:45 pm, after a long illness [Desikāchārya 1949]. According to Bowring [1872], he had "...long sufferred from swellings in the legs and neck, accompanied by severe coughing, vomiting, and purging..."

[158] The dates in footnote 129 suggest that Garaḷapurī Śāstri still lived at the time in *Vīṇe* Veṅkaṭasubbayya's *vaṭhāra,* which must have been located in the Katvāḍipura Agrahāra.

[159] The Royal School was established by Colonel Malleson within two months of his arrival in Maisūru at the end of June 1869 C.E. to become guardian of the young Çāmarājēndra Voḍeyar. The school was situated in a building now known as the Lōkarañjana Mahal, and run by two English-educated brāhmaṇas named A. Narasiṁha Ayyaṅgār and Jayarām Rāv (the headmaster), both in their twenties. Jayarām Rāv could apparently read Kant and Goethe in the German original [Ikegame 2009]. Kṛṣṇarāja Voḍeyar III and the British had both wished to ensure a modern education for the young prince.

(a) Ceṭṭipuṇyam Vīravalli Raṅgāçārlu (1831–1883).

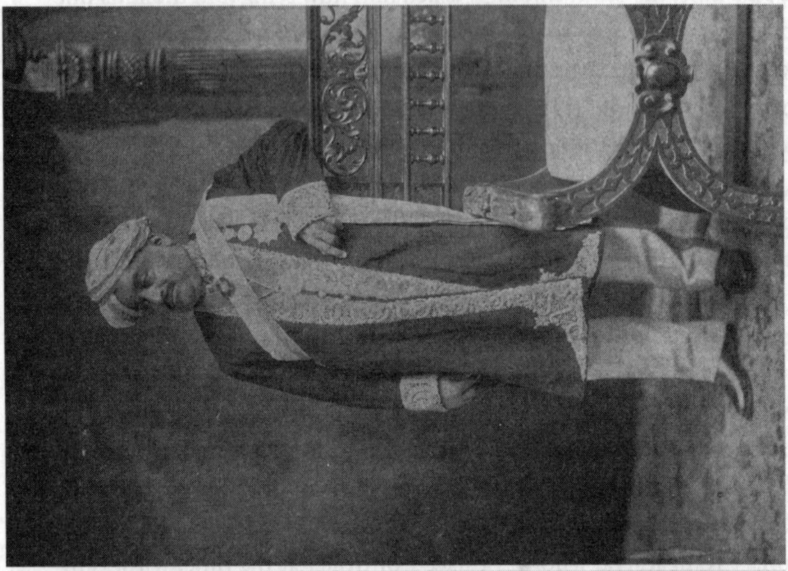

(b) Pūrṇayya Narasiṅgarāv Kṛṣṇamūrti (1849–1911).

Plate 7: C.V. Raṅgāçārlu (*Dīvān* of Maisūru, 1881–1883) and P.N. Kṛṣṇamūrti (*Dīvān* of Maisūru, 1901–1906).

At this time, the Śāstri composed a work called the *Hariharāṣṭōttara* that could be construed to have one meaning with respect to Īśvara and a different meaning with respect to Viṣṇu.[160] Raṅgāçārya, hearing of this work and his other works, developed a great regard for the Śāstri.

Around this same time, a missive arrived from Veṅkōbarāv and Rāmaçandrarāv, officials of a state in the region of Mahārāṣṭra,[161] announcing a *Bhāgavata Saptāha* celebration,[162] and forwarding an invitation to the distinguished scholars of the Maisūru court through Raṅgāçārya. The invitation comprised delicate verses in the *Āryā* metre. Raṅgāçārya forwarded the invitation to the Parakāla Svāmi.[163] The *Śrī Svāmi* gathered the scholars of the court around him, and acquainted them with its contents. Some verses at the beginning of the document have been lost. The rest are as follows.[164]

ati·ruçira·bhavana·sīmani
vāk·yajñō'yam sudurlabhō'timahān |
bhagavat'kṛp'aika·kāraṇam'
açirād'āvirbhaviṣyati mahārghaḥ ‖ 23

ētad'ati·maṅgaḷa·tamaṁ
pavitra·tamam'adbhutaṁ manōhāri |
brahma·sabhaṁ pārāyaṇa·
gabhīram'ālōkanīyam'iha sarvaiḥ ‖ 24

abhyarthayāvahē–tad
yuṣmān śirasā praṇamya śatakṛtvaḥ |
baddhāñjali bahu·kṛpayā
saptāh'ārthaṁ mudā samāyāta ‖ 25

bhavati mahatāṁ samājas'
saptāhaṁ parama·durlabhatamō'tra |
bhāgavatī ç'ātra kathā
gabhīra·bhāvā pravartatē madhurā ‖ 26

---

160 The translator has been unable to locate this work. Hopefully, it is among the currently inaccessible manuscripts of Garaḷapurī Śāstri that await digitization by Mr Sandeep Sastry.

161 Footnote in original: "The identity of this kingdom remains unclear."

162 A week-long festive reading of the *Bhāgavata Purāṇa*, and other associated rituals.

163 The *Śrīvaiṣṇavaite* Parakāla Maṭha held a position of great importance in the political and religious life of Maisūru at the time. Śrī Śrīnivāsa Deśikēndra Brahmatantra Swatantra Parakāla Mahā Dēśikan, head of the Maṭha (1860–1873 C.E.), was accorded a 21-gun salute by the Mahārāja, and was the *rājaguru* [Desikāchārya 1949]. Raṅgāçārlu, the Palace Controller, was himself a *Śrīvaiṣṇavaite*.

164 See page 378 for a translation.

śrī·bhāgavata·sudhā·rasa·
pāna·vilōlā bhavanta iha sarvē |
sa·parīvārāḥ prēmṇā
pada·kamala·parāgam'atra kurvantu ‖ 27

arvāg'ēv'ārambhāt[165]
saptāhasy'ādarād'upēty'ēha |
āsaptāhaṁ bhagavat·
kathā'mṛt'āsvāda·lōlupais'sthēyam ‖ 28

yadi jātu n'āvakāśō
dina·mātraṁ vā ksanaṁ ksan'ārdhaṁ vā |
āgantavyam'avaśyaṁ
nānyad'itaś'śrēyasāṁ padaṁ kiñcit ‖ 29

taduktaṁ śrī·bhāgavatē ‖

kiṁ pramattasya bahubhiḥ parōkṣair'hāyanair'iha |
varaṁ muhūrtaṁ viditaṁ ghaṭatē śrēyasē yataḥ ‖ 30

na hy'atō'nyaś'śivaḥ panthā viśatas'saṁsṛtāv'iha |
vāsudēvē bhagavati bhakti·yōgō yatō bhavēt ‖ 31

pibanti yē bhagavata ātmanas'satāṁ
kathāmṛtaṁ śravaṇa·puṭēṣu saṁbhṛtam |
punanti tē viṣaya·vidūṣit'āśayaṁ
vrajanti taç'çaraṇa·sarōruh'āntikam ‖ 32

āyur'harati vai puṁsāṁ'udyann'astaṁça yannasau |
tasyartē yaḥ kṣaṇō nīta uttama·ślōka·vārtayā ‖ 33

iti | kiṁ bahunā ‖ nigama·bhāvukāḥ ‖ 34

sarvē yūyaṁ sudhiyaś'
çikīrṣatōḥ kim'api durlabhaṁ kṛtyam |
kṛpayā'vayōr'udāraṁ
manōrath'āvaniruham kuruta saphalaṁ ‖ 35

yē yē'tra yad'yad'icchās'
tē tē…[166] *darās'tāstāḥ |*
bhāgavata·kalpavṛkṣāl'
labhanta ēv'āsti kō'tra sandēhaḥ ‖ 36

---

[165] The original shows *ārvāg…*

[166] Footnote in original: "A section of the page containing 7 mātras has deteriorated here due to mold. Upon inspection, Vē ‖ *Kavitilaka* Ayyāśastri conjectures the missing letters to be *'niśyaṅkamā'*. This appears likely."

kim pallavitēna ‖

āsmākīnaṁ prārthanam'
aṅgīkṛty'ādarēṇa pūrṇēna |
āgaççhata rasikatamā
yuṣmābhir'imē'tra vayaṁ'anugrāhyāḥ ‖ 37
duruktam vipratīpaṁ vā rabhasāç'çāpalād'api |
yad'asmal'likhitaṁ dhīrās'tat sarvaṁ kṣantum'arhatha ‖ 38

The great scholars assembled were unanimous in their appreciation of this missive, but with no one indicating the ability to travel abroad at the time, the *Śrī Svāmi,* in accordance with Raṅgāçārya's request to arrange for a response, asked Garaḷapurī Śāstri to compose a suitable reply in the *Āryā* metre; the Śāstri composed a response accordingly. It was as follows:[167]

śrī vallavī·jana·vallabhāya namaḥ

vaidarbhī·praṇay'ōpabṛṁhaṇa·paras'satyā·smar'ōddīpanaḥ
kṣībō jāmbavatī·nav'ādhara·rasād' rādhā·parādhīna·dhīḥ |
nīḷā·çōla·niviṣṭa·dṛṣṭir' amanāg'akrīta·dāsaḥ punar·
gōpīnām'atha yōginām'asulabhō mugdhō hariḥ pātu naḥ ‖[168] 1
svasty'astu sarva·jagatē
santas'santōṣa·danturās'santu |
bhuvi tatkriyāś'ça dharmyā
nispratyūhāḥ pravartantām ‖[169] 1
asti nanu rājadhānī
kāçana karṇāṭa·janapadā'bharaṇam |
mahiśūra·nāmadhēyā
sva·vibhūti·lav'āvadhīrita·tridivā ‖ 2

[167] The translator has located the original manuscript in Garaḷapurī Śāstri's hand, in Kannaḍa script, with the heading: *"śrī rāma | śrī vallavījana vallabhāya namōnamaḥ."* This title clearly echoes the first line of Vēdānta Dēśika's *Yādavābhyudaya: "vande vṛndāvanaçaram vallavījanavallabham | jayantīsambhavam dhāma vaijayantīvibhūṣaṇam ‖"* I am grateful to Mr Naresh Keerti for this observation. See page 380 for a translation.

[168] This first verse is in the *Śārdūlavikrīditā* metre. The following verses are in *Āryā*.

[169] The text numbers these verses sequentially, marking this the second verse. However, Garaḷapurī Śāstri's original manuscript correctly resets the numbering, marking this as the first verse of the *Āryā* series, the preceding being an invocatory verse in a different metre. The manuscript also shows hemistich cæsurae (such as the ‖ after *santu*) absent in the text.

tām'adhyāsta vitandras'
sadguṇa·sāndras'sa kṛṣṇa·bhūmī'ndraḥ |
vibudha·jan'āmbudhi·c̣andraḥ
kimanyad'anyō hariśc̣andraḥ ‖ 3

tēna dig'adhīśvar'āṁśa·
prabhavēn'ārthi·pradēya·vibhavēna |
pitr'ēva sapramōdaṁ
gōptrā sarvatra guptānām ‖ 4

adhunā tat'pratibimba
śrīmac̣'c̣āma·kṛmā·maghōnā'pi |[170]
tasmād'apy'aty'arghyaṁ
raksitrā rakṣyamāṇānām ‖ 5

upaniṣad'artha·rahasya·
śravaṇa·smaraṇādy'upāya·kalanēna |
vāṅ'manasāgōc̣aram'api
tattvam tat'kim'api kurvatāṁ sākṣāt ‖ 6

vidyāsv'aṣṭādaśasu
prāgalbhyaṁ pratibhaṭa·trapā·kṣētram |
api bibhratām'ajasraṁ
svapnē'py'aspṛṣṭa·vinaya·virahāṇām ‖ 7

śrī·kṛṣṇa·nṛpati·dattaṁ
muktāmayam'akhila·sugraha·guṇāḍhyam |
sadvṛttam'agrahāraṁ
dadhatām'atha vā tamāvasatām ‖ 8

pratiṣēdhē'pi spaṣṭaṁ
dhvani·bhaṅgyā vidadhatīṁ vidhiṁ kvac̣ana |
prauḍhām'iv'ānubhavatāṁ
vanitāṁ kavitāṁ manōjña·rasām ‖ 9

aṇu·mātram'api marandaṁ
sumanasa·dhūlīr vin'ēva puṣpa·lihām |
dōṣān'apāsya tanum'api
guṇam'abhyupajagmuṣāṁ viduṣām ‖ 10

śauri·purāri·pramukha
·svōpāsya·prārthanā·purassaryaḥ |
āmnāya·samāmnātāś'
śubha·bījāny'āśiṣaḥ phalē·grahayaḥ ‖ 11

---

[170] Garaḷapurī Śāstri's manuscript clearly shows *śrīmac̣c̣āmakṣamāmaghōnāpi* here.

āyuṣmatōr'analpaṁ
rājñāṁ mahatīṁ śriyaṁ samudvahatōḥ |
mēru·himāçalayōr'iva
krççhrēṣv'api niṣprakampa·nija·dhṛtyōḥ ‖ 12

padmā·pāda·payōruha·
lākṣā·mudrā'ṅka·bhadra·sadma·bhuvōḥ |
gōkṣīra·mākṣik'ēkṣu·
drākṣā'dhikṣēpa·sākṣi'vāg'rasayōḥ ‖ 13

ājagad'utpatti mithō·
vairiṇyōr'api bhṛśaṁ ramā·vāṇyōḥ |
sāmānādhikaraṇyaṁ
sampādayatōs'svanaipuṇyāt ‖ 14

nidrāṇa·paramapūruṣa·
tanu·ruçi·santāna·kavaçit'ābhōgam |
dugdh'āmbudhiṁ yaśōbhis'
svām'ēva ruçaṁ punar'nayatōḥ ‖ 15

gurum'api saçiva·pad'ōçitam'
anaghaṁ sva·svāmi·rājya·kārya·bharam |
aśramatō nirvahatōr'
akṣi·bhruva·vibhramair'ēva ‖ 16

āstīrya bhakti·talpaṁ
śraddhā·guṇa·bhāji çitta·ḍōḷāyām |
apitṛkam'amātṛkaṁ para·
m'anātham'ēkam kiśōram'upaçaratōḥ ‖ 17

vēṅkōba·rāmaçandrā·
bhidha·nāyakayōr' manīṣi·rañjakayōḥ |
śrēyaḥ·paramparāyai
kalpantāṁ dūra·dīrghāyai ‖ 18

vibhav'ābdha·pauṣa·mās'ā·
sita·daśamī·prātar'avadhikaṁ kālam [171] |
sarvē vayaṁ kuśalinaḥ
kōsala·nāth'ānukampayā gurvyā ‖ 19

bhavatōr'api bhāgyavatōs'
sa·kaḷatra·suputra·mitra·bāndhavayōḥ |
bhūyō nēyā patrī
yōgakṣēm'āvabōdhana·vidhātrī ‖ 20

[171] This hemistich yields a date. The *tithi* referenced is *Pauṣa śukla daśami* of the *Vibhava saṁvatsara*. This *tithi* corresponds to December 24, 1868 C.E.

saṁprati ‖

śrī·parakāla·svāmibhir’
āryair’āśçarya·kara·tapaś’çaryaiḥ |
sānugraham’arpitayā
patrikayā vāk’kratu·prabōdhinyā ‖ 21

pāpini kalāv’api yugē
vidhitsatōḥ karma kimapi kārta·yugam |
yuvayōr’hi sāhasikyaṁ
grāhaṁ grāhaṁ prahṛṣyāmaḥ ‖ 22

idaṁ’ēva hi janma·phalaṁ
prāṇa·phalaṁ vā dhanarddhi·phalam’atha vā |
puṁsām sva·dēvatābhir’
yadd’harir’ārādhyatē dvijais’sārdham ‖ [172] 23

tad’yuvayōs’satkulayōr’
anvayabhājāṁ purāṇa·puruṣāṇām |
vaktuṁ suçarita·niçayaṁ
kasya na jihrēti jihva’iva ‖ 24

tatr’ānāhūtair’apy
’asmābhir gantum’asti hi nyāyaḥ |
kiṁ punar’ētādṛśi vāṁ
praṇayē vinayē na sāram’ayē ‖ 25

kiṁ tu çir’āpariśīlita·
dūra·pathais’sthīyatē yad’asmābhiḥ |
atr’aiva tadd’hi satyaṁ
kāṣṭha·prāyēṇa kāya·mātrēṇa ‖ 26

sākaṁ samasta·bhāvaiś’
çētōbhis’tu prayātam’ēva javāt |
tasmāt kin’naḥ kṣuṇṇāt
kathitā khalu bhāvanā’pi phala·dātrī ‖ 27

prāripsita·vāg’adhvara·
ramy’āvabhṛtōtsa… [173] *nām |*
śravaṇa·sukhāya drāk’punar’
ēkō lēkhō vilēkhanīyas’syāt ‖ 28

---

[172] The partial manuscript the translator has located ends with the previous hemistich.

[173] Footnote in original: “7 *mātrās* are indecipherable in the worn-out sheet. *Vē ‖ Kavitilaka* Ayyāśāstri suggests that the missing characters are *‘vapravṛtti’*. This appears likely.”

svata ēva sarva viduṣōs'
sadguru·ċaraṇābja·sēvayā ċa ċiram |
vyapagata·duśśaṅkitayōḥ
kim'aparam'āśāsyam'astu tad'ap'īdam ‖ 29

tava ċa tava ċa prasādō
bhavatu strī·puṃsayōr'jagan·mātrōḥ |
yaś'ċa yuvayōs'sahāyas'
sa ċa rājā rāja·rājō'stu ‖ 30

‖ *ity'āśiṣaḥ* ‖

The Parakālasvāmi and Raṅgāċārya, very pleased with this response, forwarded it to those ministers.

At this time, when Perīsvāmi Tirumalāċārya, the Śāstri's student and principal of the Sadvidyāśāla,[174] wrote a commentary called the *Madhumañjari* on the *Ċampūrāmāyaṇa Yuddhakāṇḍa* that the Śāstri had composed in the past, the Śāstri delighted greatly in having it read to him in its entirety by his student, and approved of it as having done justice to the poet's intent. 1866 An edition of the Śāstri's *Campūrāmayaṇa* with this commentary is now available, having recently been published by the Śāstri's second son *Vē‖ Kavitilaka* Ayyā Śāstri.[175] Great poets capable

[174]Perīsvāmi Tirumalāċārya (b. March 8, 1848 C.E.) was Garaḷapuri Śāstri's most distinguished student. He was teacher to a large number of distinguished scholars, including Garaḷapurī Śāstri's son Ayyā Śāstri, the distinguished philosopher M. Hiriyaṇṇa, M.N. Kṛṣṇarāo (future *Dīvān* of Mysore), and the polymath *Rao Bahadur* M. Rangāċārya. His works include *Upāyaniśrēṇikā*, *Vigrahārādhana Vidhāyini*, *Prauḍhabodhinī*, and *Vṛddhasevinī*. In connection with his role as principal of the Sadvidya Pāṭhaśālā, Tirumalaċārya wrote the *Bālabōdhinī*, described in [Bendall 1893] as "A Sanskrit grammar for schools in Mysore, printed in the Devanāgarī character, with lithographed tables of other South Indian characters, and preceded by an English preface. Pt. 1. Mysore, 1880", and the *Sadvidyāsaṅgraha*, described as "…an elementary reading book…, Bangalore 1890."

[175]An anonymous manuscript biography of Tirumalāċārya that the translator discovered among Ayyā Śāstri's papers (and published recently [Sāstri 2012]) recounts lore that Tirumalāċārya wrote this commentary when he was 18 years of age, i.e., in 1866 C.E., suggesting that the *Yuddhakāṇḍa* had been finished by this time. This appears unlikely (see footnote 148). Ayyā Śāstri had the *Yuddhakāṇḍa* with the *Madhumajarī* published in 1891 C.E. The front matter for the work acknowledges the assistance of Garaḷapurī Śāstri's eldest son Sōsale Aṇṇayya Śāstri, the King's brother-in-law Kāntarājē Arasu, the commentator Perīsvāmi Tirumalāċārya, Puṭṭaśyāmāpaṇḍita of the Royal Hospital, and Ayyanayyaṅgār, the head of the printing press at the Sadvidyāmandira.

of producing original works of such calibre, and scholars capable of such excellent commentaries are rare indeed in our times.

December 5, 1874

When Liṅgarājē Arasu passed away, his in-law Nañjarāj Bahādūr took charge of managing his estate as well as the care of his son *Çikka* Liṅgarājē Arasu, who was then still a child. Many scholars under the patronage of Liṅgarājē Arasu accepted the patronage of Nañjarāj Bahādūr. One day, Garaḷapurī Śāstri composed the following *çarama ślōka*[176]

lakṣmī·śāradayōs'svayaṁ'gṛha·patir'dātā dayāluḥ kṣamī
jāmātā dharaṇīśa·kṛṣṇa·nṛpatēś'śrīliṅgarāja·prabhuḥ |
bhāvābdē sahasi dvipāsya·divasē vārē śanēr' viṣṇu·bhē
śrīkaṇṭh'āṅghri·sarōruha·bhramaratāṁ āpat'tapōbhir'nijaiḥ ||

and thereafter remained engaged in his appointed duties, desirous of no one else's patronage; by this time, the young *Mahārāja* had reached the end of his primary education in *Saṁskṛta*. To make more time for his education in English, Raṅgāçārya discontinued his *Saṁskṛta* lessons, and with the purpose of enhancing the *Saṁskṛta* school established by Kṛṣṇarāja Voḍeyar III, established a *Saṁskṛta* college in a new building called *Sarasvatī Prāsāda* constructed for the purpose, in which he appointed Garaḷapurī Śāstri a Professor of Literature.[177] Garaḷapurī Śāstri taught literature to a large number of students here.

1876

Now, after Sōsale Garaḷapurī Śāstri arranged for the marriage of his second son *Brahmaśrī Kavitilaka* Sōsale Ayyā Śāstri, now *Mahāvidvāṁsa* at

[176] A *çarama ślōka*, literally a "final *ślōka*", is a *ślōka* of eulogy. The metre used here is *Śārdūlavikrīditā*. See page 364 for a translation. The line *bhāvābdē sahasi dvipāsyadivasē vārēśanēḥ viṣṇubhē* turned out to be a challenging chronogram for the translator, but it yields the date of Liṅgarājē Arasu's death: *In the Bhāva saṁvatsara, on Saturday, the fourth day of Mārgaśira, under the nakṣatra Śravaṇa.* The key is as follows. *Bhāvē abdē:* in the *Bhāva saṁvatsara*; *sahasi:* in the month of *Sahas*, an ancient name for *Mārgaśira*; *dvipāsya divasē:* on the 4th day, since *dvipāsya = dvipa + āsya* means "elephant-faced one", or Gaṇeśa, whose number is 4; *vārē śanē:* on Saturday; *viṣṇu bhē*: *Viṣṇu's nakṣatra,* namely *Śravaṇa.* Saturday, December 5, 1874 C.E. matches the *māsa, nakṣatra, tithi*, and weekday specified. *Śravaṇa* was current from 11:30 am that day till 11:30 am on December 6, 1874 C.E.

[177] This institution was established in 1876 C.E. See footnote 145 for more information. Colonel G.B. Malleson's appointment as guardian of the prince Çāmarājendra having ended in June 1876 C.E., Raṅgāçārlu was placed in charge till August 1876, after which Major F.A. Wilson came to this position. This episode likely dates to this time.

the court, with the daughter of Çāmarājanagara Śrīkanṭhaśāstri,[178] who became *Dharmādhikāri* at the court, he would very affectionately host his in-law Ç.‖ Śrīkanṭhaśāstri and his younger brother Çāmarājanagara Rāmaśāstri, who became *Mahāvidvāṁsa* at the court and *Paṇḍita* at Mahārāja's *Saṁskṛta* College, during their trips to Maisūru, always delighing in erudite discussions with them, as well as in tutoring his many students.[179]

On such occasions, he and his younger in-law Rāmaśāstri would discuss poetry, and compose assorted *ślōkas,* sometimes together, sometimes by themselves. Most of these *ślōkas* have been lost with them. However, his son *Br.*‖ *Kavitilaka* Ayyā Śāstri happened to be present when a few were composed. We will now describe how and when these were composed.

Garaḷapurī Śāstri was resting one morning, after having just woken, when Rāmaśāstri, who had also just arisen nearby, recited the *ślōka "bālāyanīlavapruṣē...* " during his morning prayers.[180] On hearing this, Garaḷapurī Śāstri playfully challenged him, saying: "What! Must you recite such timeworn *ślōkas*? Couldn't we have something new, of your own composition?" He responded: "Indeed, tell me what sort of *ślōka* you would like, and I will compose one accordingly." Garaḷapurī Śāstri said: "In that case, I will compose a *pāda* in the *Āryā* metre, and we shall see how well you compose a second *pāda* to match mine," and started the first *pāda* as follows:[181]

GARAḶAPURĪ ŚĀSTRI: *badhnīmō vayam'añjali·*
    RĀMAŚĀSTRI: *sampuṭam'avanamritē mūrdhni |*
GARAḶAPURĪ ŚĀSTRI: *dadhnā sikta·kalēbaram*
    RĀMAŚĀSTRI: *arbhakam'ēkaṁ purāṇam'uddiśya ‖*

---

[178] Lakṣmīdevamma was married to Sōsale Ayyā Śāstri in her ninth year [Śāstri 1917]. According to a biography of Ayyā Śāstri by his son Kṛṣṇasvāmi Śāstri (see page 303) this marriage took place in the Kṣaya *saṁvatsara* of 1866–1867 C.E., when Ayyā Śāstri was fourteen. However, he was only twelve that year, so the *saṁvatsara* is likely incorrect, and the marriage took place in 1868 or 1869 C.E. Lakṣmīdevamma's brother Veṅkaṭakṛṣṇa Śāstri was, in fact, the father of Veṅkaṭaramaṇa Śāstri, the author of this biography.

[179] Śrīkanṭha Śāstri was made *Dhamādhikāri* in 1913 C.E. See page 119. Rāmaśāstri was made *Āsthānavidvān* in 1878 C.E., and later *Āsthānamahāvidvān* [Rāmaśāstri 1997].

[180] This should be *vapuṣe,* rather than *vapruṣe.* This *ślōka* in the *Vasantatilakā* metre appears in the second chapter of the *Śrīkṛṣṇa Karṇāmṛtam* by Līlāśuka Bilvamaṅgala. The full *ślōka* is: *"bālāya nīla vapuṣe navakiṅkiṇīka jālābhirāma jaghanāya digambarāya | śārdūla divya nakha bhūṣaṇa bhūṣitāya nandātmajāya navanītamuṣe namaste ‖"*

[181] See page 365 for a translation.

(a) *Abhinavakālidāsa* Basappa Śāstri (1843–1891).

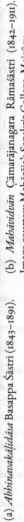

(b) *Mahāvidvan* Cāmarājanagara Rāmaśāstri (1842–1911).
Image courtesy Mahārāja's Sanskrit College, Maisūru.

Plate 8: Garalapurī Śāstri's student Basappa Śāstri and in-law Rāmaśāstri.

They proceeded to compose five such *ślōkas.* This *ślōka,* however, is the only to have remained in Ayyā Śāstri's memory.

When the topic of *yamaka ślōkas* arose on another occasion, Rāmaśāstri remarked how utterly devoid of poetic purpose a meaningless *yamaka ślōka* by a certain ancient poet had been, and recited it as follows:[182]

mukhañ'ca çandra·pratimaṁ timaṁ timam
kuçau ça pīnau kaṭhinau ṭhinau ṭhinau |
kaṭir'viśālā rabhasā bhasā bhasā
ahō viçitrā taruṇī ruṇī ruṇī ‖

Garaḷapurī Śāstri responded: "Well then, let me compose a *ślōka,* and you can see how it turns out," and composed the following verse right away:[183]

smara·śriyaṁ yaṁ tarasā rasā'rasā
nirīkṣya gōpyō mumuhur' muhurmuhuḥ |
anudravad'dhēnu·paramparaṁ param
tam'ēha jihvē vada nanda·nandanaṁ ‖

One is to interpolate as per *"ralayōrabhēdēnarasālasāḥ"* for *"rasārasāḥ".*[184] He composed the following structurally similar *ślōka* the next day:[185]

vṛṣā'py'upēkṣā·priyayā yayā yayā·
v'adhaşca bhikṣāñ'jagṛhē gṛhē gṛhē |
dayārdray'airāvata·yātayā tayā
vayaṅ'galad'dainya·may'āmayā mayā ‖

The following day, he composed two more *ślōkas:*[186]

[182] In the fourth *saṁdhi* of his *Kavikaṇṭhābharaṇa,* the 11th-century poet Kṣemendra of Kāśmīra criticises the following verse by the poet Çandraka for lack of poetic merit: *"stanau supīnau kaṭhinau ṭhinau ṭhinau | kaṭirviśālā rabhasābhasābhasā ‖ mukhaṅça çandrapratimaṁtimaṁtimaṁ | ahō surūpā taruṇiruṇiruṇiruṇi ‖"* The metre used is *Vaṁśasthavila.* See page 365 for a translation.

[183] The translator has found a manuscript, in more than one hand, with several of the ensuing verses. Garaḷapurī Śāstri's hand is readily recognizable. The other hand is presumably Rāmaśāstri's. The manuscript shows *tamēvajihvē* rather than *tamēhajihvē.* The metre used is *Vaṁśasthavila.* See page 366 for a translation.

[184] The grammatical formula *ralayōrabhedaḥ* declares the phonemes *ra* and *la* to be allophones in *Saṁskṛta.* We are therefore to read *rasālasāḥ* in place of *rasārasāḥ.*

[185] The metre used is *Vaṁśasthavila.* See page 366 for a translation.

[186] The metre used is *Vaṁśasthavila.* See pages 367 and 368 for translations.

tav'āmba kund'ōtkara·dāradā radāḥ
kuc'ābham'ētan'na tu kantu·kantukaṁ |
dṛśōs'sakhāyō'jina·yōnayō'nayōḥ
kaçō'rçitōñçan'nalinālinā'linā ||

pravāḷa·kānti·prakar'ākarā karāḥ
radaç'chada·śrīr'tarun'ārun'āruṇā |
iti sphuṭ'ōpāsanayā'nayā nayā·
my'ahāni sarva·kratavas'tava stavaḥ ||

Having thus composed five *ślōkas,* he turned to Rāmaśāstri and said "Now, shall we hear one from you?" Rāmaśastri composed the following *ślōka* that same day:[187]

bhavēt'tavā'nugraha·dōha·dōhadō
dayā·plutō'pāṅga·lav'ālavālavān
manōratha·drur'mama nāma nā'manā·
k'phalaḥ kathaṁ vā'bja·padē padē·padē ||

After having composed this *ślōka,* Rāmaśāstri declared: "I will now compose another for you," and remained deep in thought for some time. After a while, Garaḷapurī Śāstri asked: "It is now nearly afternoon. Do we have even a single *pāda* complete?" Rāmaśastri replied: "The first *pāda* is indeed complete. However, I had intended to incorporate both *ślēṣa* and *yamaka alaṅkāras* into the composition.[188] I am now considering how to complete the verse." Garaḷapurī Śāstri said: "Let's hear the *pāda,* then," and Rāmaśāstri responded:

budh'ālir'ēkā mahit'ēhitē hi tē

Garaḷapurī Śāstri replied to this *pāda* with

tav'ābhibhūtā sva·pad'āpadā padā

---

[187] The metre used is *Vaṁśasthavila.* See page 369 for a translation.

[188] A *ślēṣa* is a pun. A *yamaka* is the repetition of a set of syllables that can be parsed differently to yield different meanings in each case. In his *Kṛṣṇabhūpālīyam,* Garaḷapurī Śāstri defines a *yamaka* as *sasvaravyañjanasamudāyasyāvṛttiryamakaṁ,* or as the repetition of a group of syllables.

Rāmaśastri now said: "Very well, I will then compose the third *pāda;* let us see how fitting a fourth *pāda* you compose," and continued:

nirasta·kalpa·prasav'āsavā savā

By itself, the final *vā* in this *pāda* is devoid of meaning. Garaḷapurī Śāstri was now faced with the task of composing a fourth *pāda* whose initial letters would cause this final *vā* to become meaningful, and at the same time, would stand as a sentence with meaning fully consonant with Rāmaśāstri's poetic intent. After considering this challenge, Garaḷapurī Śāstri responded with

g'rasaiḥ par'ābhukta·savā sa·vāsavā[189]

Astonished by the manner in which Garaḷapurī Śāstri had not merely fulfilled his poetic intent, but had masterfully echoed *savāsavāsavā*, his *yamaka* from the third *pāda,* but with a different meaning in the fourth, Rāmaśāstri now exclaimed loudly: "Well done! Well done, dear Śāstri! How wonderfully you have framed this final *pāda*!", and praised his feat over and over again. He then remarked that the *ślōkas* they had composed all had *yamakas* of two syllables, and that it would likely be very difficult to compose *ślōkas* with three-syllable *yamakas.*

Garaḷapurī Śāstri composed the following *ślōka* the very next day:[190]

kamalā punātu bhava·śōka·malā·
n'avadhūya māṁ garuḍa·yāna·vadhūḥ |
sumanā natā'vana·kalāsu manā·
g'avanamra·mūrtir'agha·nāga·vanaṁ ||

On another occasion, Rāmaśāstri challenged Garaḷapurī Śāstri by saying: "Let's have a *ślōka* with a three-syllable *yamaka* at the start. I will begin by composing such a *pāda;* your task is to compose the next *pāda* that is consonant with my meaning," and started thus:[191]

---

[189] The metre used is *Vaṁśasthavila.* See page 369 for a translation.
[190] The metre used is *Pramitākṣara.* See page 370 for a translation.
[191] The metre used is *Indravajrā.* See page 371 for a translation.

RĀMAŚĀSTRI: vandē śivaṁ dēśikam'apy'udañça·
GARAḶAPURĪ ŚĀSTRI: d'āmōda·dāmōdara·padmayōnyōḥ |
RĀMAŚĀSTRI: mōhaṁ tamō hanta jighamsatāṁ svaṁ
GARAḶAPURĪ ŚĀSTRI: dīpam nadī·pannaga·çandra·bhūṣam ||

One yet another occasion, during a playful discussion of poetry, Rāmaśāstri remarked: "It would be quite novel if a *yamaka* at the start of a *pāda* in a *ślōka* were to repeat at the end of that *pāda* as well." Garaḷapurī Śāstri responded: "Well, we shall compose such a *ślōka,* then!" and composed the following *ślōka:*[192]

stainyēna praṇayēna vā bhuvi sakṛd yas'tē namas'stēnam'a·
py'amba tvaṁ paripāsi taṁ dalita·daurgatyā'hitā'tyāhitā |
padmē tvāṁ tu vayaṁ vaçaḥ·parimaḷair āmōdayamō dayā·
m'ady'āpadya na çēt prasīdasi numaś'śrī·kāmataḥ kām'ataḥ ||

The *ślōkas* composed subsequently by Rāmaśāstri were as follows.[193]

hṛdyas'suhṛd yas'sutarān'nidhīnāṁ
nētur'vinētur'viṣamāṁś'ça daityān |
jāyān'nijāyān'nidadhat'tanau sa
dēvō mudē vō munibhis'stutō'stu ||

vēdyā trivēdyā'tridiva·prasūna·
dhūlī·madhūlī·masṛṇā'ṅghri·padmā |
rakṣō·bhara·kṣōbhakarī śubhāni
tanvīta tanvī taruṇēndu·mauḷēḥ ||

kāma·prakāma·prahitaṁ kaṭākṣam
lōlamba·lōlaṁ bahudhā kirantī |
bhāvaṁ svabhāvaṁ sva·vaśaṁ nayantī
pāyād'apāyād'aniśaṁ bhavānī ||

The *ślōkas* composed by Garaḷapurī Śāstri were the following.[194]

---

[192] See page 372 for a translation.

[193] The metre used is *Indravajrā.* Translations appear, respectively, on pages 373, 373, and 374.

[194] The metre used is *Indravajrā.* Translations appear, respectively, on pages 375 and 375.

nānā'ṅganānāṁ gaṇanīya·śōbhā
dāyādadā yādava·puṅgavasya |
pāyād'apāyād'anaghā'cyutasya
jāy'ānujā yānuparōdham'indōḥ ||

mātā ramā tārakit'eva hāraiḥ
kaṇṭh'ōpakaṇṭhō'panata·pralambhaiḥ |
dīnān'nadīnāṁ na jahātu patyus'
tādṛk sutā dṛk·sudhayā'rthinō naḥ ||

Upon hearing this, Rāmaśāstri said: "A *ślōka* on Pārvatī would have the ending *'śrī kāḷikākāḷikā'*; let us see if you can compose a *ślōka* following my design." Garaḷapurī Śāstri then proceeded to compose the following *ślōka:*

śēṣasphāraphaṇāsahasravikasannānāpadānāpadā |
muççētrībhajatāñjitēnduśakala śrīkāḷikākāḷikā ||

It is most regrettable that the latter half this *ślōka* has not come to hand. On an earlier occasion, while starting out his students on a work on poetics called *Pratāparudrīya,*[195] which begins with the invocatory *ślōka*[196]

vidyā·kairava·kaumudīṁ śruti·śiras'sīmanta·muktāmaṇiṁ
dārān padmabhuvas'trilōka·jananīṁ vandē girāṁ dēvatām |
yat'pādabja·namaskriyās'sukṛtināṁ sārasvata·prakriyā
bīja·nyāsa·bhuvō bhavanti kavitā·nāṭy'aika·jīvātavaḥ ||

[195] An encyclopædic work on poetics, rhetoric, and dramaturgy by Vidyānātha, a scholar in the court of Pratāparudra II (1294–1325 C.E.), who ruled from Waraṅgal over the Kākaṭiya kingdom. All examples and illustrations in the work eulogize Pratāparudra, whence the work's name. In his own *Kṛṣṇabhūpālīyam*, Garaḷapurī Śāstri uses this same device to honour Kṛṣṇarāja Voḍeyar III.

[196] The metre is *Śārdūlavikrīditā*. See page 376.

Garaḷapurī Śāstri explained that the word *dārān*, which must always appear with masculine plural case endings as per the *nighaṇṭu* formula *dārāḥvuṁsiçabhūmnyēva*,[197] is an adjective qualifying the noun *girāṁ dēvataṁ*.[198] The students then asked: "If instead *dārāḥ* were to appear as a substantive, must its qualifier then appear in plural form?" Garaḷapurī Śāstri explained that adjectives must always appear in the same case and number as the nouns they qualify. However, poetry is better served on some occasions by using words that follow normal rules, and on other occasions by words that represent exceptions to these rules. When the students began to look for other such *ślōkas*, Garaḷapurī Śāstri said: "Do not trouble yourselves to search for other such *ślōkas*. I will compose such a *ślōka* for you myself," and immediately dictated the following *ślōka*:[199]

> *śrī·vatsa·kaustabh'ālaṅkāra·sadmānō gr̥hīta·padmānō* |
> *kāmita·mati·mandārāḥ paramōdārāḥ phalantu hari·dārāḥ* ||

The students were truly delighted by the Śāstri's work.

---

[197] This should be *dārāḥpuṁsiçabhūmnyēva. dārāh:* wife, *puṁsi:* in the masculine, *bhūmnyēva:* only in the plural. The singular noun *dāra* is always declined in the masculine plural, whence *dārāḥ*.

[198] *Dārāṅpadmabhuva* is fashioned as follows. We start with *padmabhuvadārāḥ*, a *bahuvrīhi* compound (*padmabhuvasya dārāḥ yā sā*), which, as a qualifier, must follow the inflectional endings of its external referent. Although the referent is abstractly Sarasvatī, it is necessary for grammatical purposes to identify and follow a substantive in the sentence. The logical and poetic flow leads to *girāṁ dēvataṁ*, declined in the feminine singular accusative. The *nighaṇṭu* rule for *dārāḥ* nonetheless forces the *bahuvrīhi* to be declined in the masculine plural accusative as *padmabhuvadārān*, falsely suggesting a grammatical anomaly. For poetical effect and metrical purposes, the components of this compound are transposed, yielding *dārāṅpadmabhuva*. We note how the *girāṁ* at the end of the quarter elegantly echoes and balances the initial *dārān*.

[199] In this verse, the *tatpuruṣa* compound *haridārāḥ* (*hareḥ dārāḥ*, Hari's wife, or Lakṣmī) is the referent for a series of *bahuvrīhi* compounds. The noun Lakṣmī itself would be declined as feminine singular, but the *nighaṇṭu* rule for *dāra* requires the compound *haridārāḥ* to be declined as masculine plural. The verb *phal*, which must agree with this substantive, is hence conjugated in the imperative plural as *phalantu*, rather in the singular, as *phalatu*. Now, the *nighaṇṭu* rule forces the *bahuvrīhi* compounds with Lakṣmī as their referent to have masculine plural declensions, as we see with *paramōdārāḥ*, say. In the first line of the verse, however, Garaḷapurī Śāstri violates this rule, using the masculine singular form *sadmānaḥ* rather than the masculine plural form *sadmānāḥ*. This allows him to create the *yamaka* consonance between *sadmānaḥ* and the *padmānaḥ*. Adding to the intrigue in the verse is the repeated appearance of *dārāḥ*, first in *mandārāḥ*, then in *udārāḥ*, and finally in *haridārāḥ*. The metre used is *Āryā*. See page 376 for a translation.

Chapter Seven

On another occasion, his younger in-law Rāmaśāstri, while on a visit from Çāmarājanagara, recited a palindromic *ślōka* in the course of some discussion, and playfully challenged Garaḷapurī Śāstri to compose a similar *ślōka.* Garaḷapurī Śāstri promised to have it done by dinner time the same day after he had completed his teaching and other duties, and spending the day in thought as he went about his normal routine, returned in the late evening, and calling for Rāmaśāstri's attention, recited[200]

draupad'īna·nadīpa·drau māra·bhē śuśubhē ramā |
sv'āparādha·dharā'pa·svā vēda·yānini yādavē ||

which Rāmaśāstri greatly applauded, enthusiastically shaking and nodding his head. This *ślōka* has survived only because we were able to find the piece of paper on which the Śāstri's second son had jotted it down after dinner. With this *ślōka* we discovered another moldy scrap of paper, on one corner of which was the following single quarter of a *praśṇōttarābhinna ślōka* the Śāstri had composed on some occasion: *"pramadōrasikaśśētē"*. Here, *"pramadōrasi, kaḥ, śētē"* is the question, to which the answer is *"pramadaḥ, rasikaḥ, śētē"*.[201] Unfortunately, a large number of the Śāstri's *ślōkas,* having remained unrecorded, have been lost with him.

Around that time, after he had written his commentary on the *Yuddhakāṇḍa,* Perīsvāmi Tirumalāçārya founded a *Saṁskṛta* school called the Sadvidyāśāla, along the lines of an English school, and became its principal. The school grew rapidly, and soon enrolled about two hundred students. Many of these students studied in an English school for a half-day, and studied *Saṁskṛta* at this school the other half-day. Some others attended this school alone, studying *Saṁskṛta* for a half-day. Many of the younger pupils

[200] The metre used is *Anuṣṭubh.* See page 377 for a translation.

[201] First, *pramadōrasi* is decomposed as *pramadā + urasi,* which yields the *tatpurusa* compound *pramadāyā urasi,* meaning "on the chest of a (wanton) woman". The sentence is now asking "Who sleeps on the chest of a (wanton) woman?" The answer is provided by the decompostion *pramadaḥ rasikaḥ sete,* meaning "the intoxicated libertine sleeps".

studied *Saṁskṛta* at this school for both half-days. There were four teachers at this school at the time, including its principal.[202] The subjects taught included literature, poetry, *çampū,* drama, *alaṅkāra,* logic, and grammar.

Now, as he was teaching the *Nīlakaṇṭhavijaya* to some of his students one day,[203] Perīsvāmi Tirumalāçārya thought of asking his guru Garaḷapurī Śāstri to write a commentary on this work, and accompanied by his fellow-student Noṇavinakere Tirumalāçārya, visited the Śāstri, and made this suggestion. Garaḷapurī Śāstri responded that he had indeed planned to write such a commentary, and in light of their suggestion, would start on it immediately. He began on this endeavour, working whenever he found time. Within a month, he had completed his commentary on half of the first canto of the *Nīlakaṇṭhavijaya.*

---

[202]See footnote 111. According to an anonymous manuscript the translator discovered in Kavitāvilāsa (and published recently [Sāstri 2012]), the instructors at the time included Perīsvāmi Tirumalāçārya, Sōsale Ayyā Śāstri, Āji Ayyanayyaṅgār, Sō‖ Śrīnivāsāçārya, and Guṇḍa Śāstri.

[203]This is a famous *çampū* work in five chapters written by Nīlakaṇṭha Dīkṣita around 1637–1638 C.E. A minister in the court of Tirumala *Nāyaka* of Madurai, he is from what is surely the most important family of scholars of the period. Nīlakaṇṭha's grandfather Aççhan Dīkṣita was the younger brother of the astonishingly prolific poet and scholar Appayya Dīkṣita, who was reportedly patronized by the Āravīḍu kings *Çinna* Timma and Veṅkaṭāpati, as well as *Çinna* Bomma Nāyaka of Vēlūr. As many as 104 works are attributed to Appayya Dīkṣita, many authoritative, in fields as diverse as poetry, grammar, and philosophy. Garaḷapurī Śāstri's *Kṛṣṇabhūpālīyam* follows the treatment of *alaṅkāras* in Appayya Dīkṣita's *Kuvalayānanda,* although the verses illustrating the *alaṅkāras* are Garaḷapurī Śāstri's own.

Chapter Eight

Just then, by some twist of fate, a mildly painful boil happened to erupt on the Śāstri's left cheek. Since it seemed to be a minor problem, little attention was paid to it for two or three days, beyond the application of some simple home remedies; it quickly swelled up and worsened, however, requiring the Śāstri to take a leave of absence from his teaching at the Pāṭhaśāla and the Royal School.[204] Upon becoming aware of this problem, Controller Raṅgāçārya promptly arranged for proper treatment for the Śāstri at the hands of Dr. Jagannātha Nāyaḍu of the Palace Hospital.

This doctor, who was then renowned as a skilled physician, exerted himself to the utmost, both from respect for the Śāstri as well as in deference to the directives of authority. However, the ailment failed to yield. Many of the Śāstri's students, relatives, and friends attended to the Śāstri day and night, helping to lighten his suffering. The Śāstri remained in high spirits, bantering in good humour with this company, and having his students read to him from the *Vēṇīsaṁhāra* and the *Bhagavadgīta*.[205]

However, having a premonition of his own passing, he called together his family and a group of his foremost students on the morning of the day of the tenth *bahuḷa tithi* in the Çaitra month of the Īśvara *saṁvatsara*,[206] and seating them by his side and speaking many words of advice to them, asked them to arrange for him to perform the *pañçagavya prāyaśçitta*,[207] bathed, attired himself in

April 8, 1877

[204] The Pāṭhaśāla is presumably the *Saṁskṛta* College referred to in footnotes 177 and 145. The Royal School is referred to in footnote 159.

[205] The *Vēṇīsaṁhāra* is a play by Bhaṭṭa Nārāyaṇa (8th century C.E.) centering on events occurring in the *Mahābhārata* between the return of the Pāṇḍavas from exile and Yudhiṣṭhira's coronation. *Vēṇīsaṁhāra* means "tying (braiding) of the hair", and is an allusion to Draupadī's vow not to tie her hair until it had been washed in Duśśāsana's blood, which task Bhīma performed.

[206] This date corresponds to Sunday, April 8, 1877 C.E.

[207] A rite of purification and penance involving the drinking of five products of the cow, seen as providing exculpation from all sins and ritual improprieties committed during one's life.

maḍi vestments,[208] donned the *vibhūti*,[209] seated himself on a *maṇe*,[210] and with a priest in attendance, completed the *pañçagavya prāyaśçitta* in the prescribed manner, and after making many gifts, including *gōdāna*,[211] declared his intent to remain in a state of ritual purity; he then prepared for himself a bed of *darbha* grass, spreading a grass mat on it and using only *maḍi* clothes, and bade farewell to the many dignitaries who visited him, speaking to them of his impending departure the next day; the following morning, he had his second son perform *arçana*,[212] partook of the *tīrtha*,[213] and his strength having left him by this time, gestured gently towards his right ear. Grasping his meaning, his son quickly wedged a *tuḷasi* stalk from the *arçana* behind his right ear. Within two or three minutes of his doing so, the Śāstri had attained the lotus feet of Śrī Veṅkaṭāçalapati.[214]

---

[208] *Maḍi* vestments are ritually pure, and in modern times connote freshly washed clothes, generally worn dripping wet to avoid any possible contamination. This echoes the ancient practice of wearing bark vestments, regarded as having intrinsic purity. More generally, to practice *maḍi* is to follow detailed norms of ritual conduct that ensure freedom from ritual pollution.

[209] Horizontal bands of ash across the forehead, indicative of the *Smārta* tradition. One dips the first three fingers in ash and draws them across the forehead horizontally.

[210] A platform of wood, a couple of inches high, used as a seat on formal and ritual occasions.

[211] The sacrifice of gifting away a cow, traditionally seen as the most meritorious of sacrifices. The *dānas* prescribed by the *Śuddhiprakāśa* at the time of death include cows, land, sesame, gold, grain, salt, ghee, jaggery, and silver, but only the first eight are mentioned in the *Garuḍa Purāṇa*. A good death is traditionally regarded as occurring in the presence of family and loved ones, after completing the specified *dānas* and other rituals, on the ground or on a bed of *darbha* or *kuśa* grass, and in the presence of a *tulasi* plant or in contact with *tulasi*.

[212] A ceremony of worship.

[213] Ritual sipping from the palm of the water used to bathe the deity during the *arçana*.

[214] It is impossible to accurately diagnose Garaḷapurī Śāstri's ailment at this point, but we can make some educated guesses. The account gives few specifics regarding the presentation of the ailment, but refers to the lesion using the Kannaḍa word *"guḷḷe"*, which suggests a boil, blister, or furuncle, most likely involving suppuration. This seems to exclude the possibility of neoplasm. The relatively rapid course of the illness is also highly suggestive of infection. Diabetes can increase the severity of any infections, and predispose the patient to skin and soft-tissue infections. However, diabetes is not known among current descendants of Garaḷapurī Śāstri. A likely scenario is that of a superficial infection leading to a furuncle that got out of hand, resulting in a systemic infection such as sepsis, or a secondary infection, such as endocarditis. An infection of the lymph nodes in the cheek is also a possibility. Furuncles are usually *Staphylococcus aureus* infections that generally heal in a couple of weeks, but can sometimes persist much longer, and lead to secondary infections. Once a

Chapter Nine

Following Garaḷapurī Śāstri's passing, *Jahgīrdār* Kṛṣṇamūrti,[215] who had been officiating as Controller for three months in Raṅgāçārya's absence,[216] appointed Garaḷapurī Śāstri's second son *Kavitilaka* Ayyā Śāstri as

furuncle forms, topical remedies, including anti-bacterial preparations, are generally of little value in pre-empting deeper abscesses or systemic infections. Topical preparations, herbal potions, dietary regimes, compresses, and surgical drainage were most likely the only treatment options available. Secondary infections and sepsis were likely much more common at the time than they are now, since antibiotics were unknown, and the infection had to be overcome by the body's own immune response. The location of the lesion and the lack of effective painkillers would have made it very difficult for Garaḷapurī Śāstri to eat or drink, increasing the likelihood that he had become malnourished, and that his immune response was depressed. He appears to have remained mentally alert as well as active on the eve of his death, reducing the likelihood that the cause of death was either secondary sepsis or meningitis, both of which cause extreme fatigue, prostration, and frequently, mental confusion. Secondary endocarditis remains a possibility, although the account makes no reference to fevers. Ayyā Śāstri (or the biographer) may simply have seen fever as a routine symptom, and not worth explicit mention. Garaḷapurī Śāstri also probably received much help from family members and friends in attendance during his ritual preparations on the eve of his passing. The deterioration of cardiac function in the final stages of endocarditis would have been debilitating and clearly perceptible to Garaḷapurī Śāstri; it may have served as an indication that his body was giving up, leading to his premonition of death. All of this, of course, is speculation, albeit somewhat informed by current understanding of disease processes, but he seems to have died of an infection that would likely be easily cured today.

[215] Sir Pūrṇayya Narasiṅgarāv Kṛṣṇamūrti, who went on to become *Dīvān* of Maisūru (1901–1906 C.E.), was the grandson of the famous Pūrṇayya, who was *Dīvān* under Ṭippu Sultān, and continued in this capacity after Kṛṣṇarāja Voḍeyar III came to the throne as a minor in 1799 C.E. Pūrṇayya was granted Yeḷandūr in Çamarājanagara district as a *jāhgīr* in 1807 C.E. Pūrṇayya died in 1812 C.E., but by 1835, the *jāhgīr* had been divided piecemeal among his descendants, and largely dissipated. Cubbon was forced to intervene, and cancelled the rights of all except P.N. Kṛṣṇamūrti's father Narasiṅga Rāo Kṛṣṇamūrti (he was the son of Śrīnivāsa Mūrti, himself the son of Pūrṇayya's son Narasiṅga Rāo). P.N. Kṛṣṇamūrti would have inherited the *jāhgīr*.

[216] There is significant inconsistency between the account in this biography and the historical record of Raṅgāçārlu's period of absence. The biography suggests that Raṅgāçārlu was present at the onset of Garaḷapurī Śāstri's illness (he arranged for Garaḷapurī Śāstri's treatment), but was absent at his death, and further, that he learned of his death only upon his return to his duties after an absence of three months. Garaḷapurī Śāstri died on April 9, 1877 C.E. However, Raṅgāçārlu testified during an inquiry into the theft of certain Palace jewels, that he proceeded on leave in July and returned in September of 1877 C.E., dates which are confirmed by Kṛṣṇamūrti's testimony [Stanhope 1878, pp. 171, 173]. (For an account of the theft and the resulting scandal, see [Bell 1882].) It is nearly impossible that the *tithi* given

a scholar at the court at a salary of three *Varāhas,* demonstrating regard for him as the son of a great scholar.[217] When Raṅgāçāri returned from his absence, he was greatly saddened by the news of Garaḷapurī Śāstri's passing, and considering a salary of three *Varāhas* inadequate for his second son Ayyā Śāstri, increased it to four *Varāhas,* and continued to maintain great regard for him. Since that time, *Kavitilaka* Ayyā Śāstri has attained great fame and stature, and has now come to be regarded by all as a truly fitting successor to Garaḷapurī Śāstri.[218]

for Garaḷapurī Śāstri's death is incorrect, since his son Ayyā Śāstri, the primary source of information for this biography, would have performed the obsequial ceremonies for his father each year on that *tithi.* One possibility is that Raṅgāçārlu was present in Maisūru at the time of Garaḷapurī Śāstri's passing, but that Ayyā Śāstri's appointment as a scholar at a salary of three *Varāhas* occurred during the time Kṛṣṇamūrti was officiating for him. Ayyā Śāstri's salary may have been raised to four *Varāhas* after Raṅgāçārlu's return.

[217] A *Varāha* was the equivalent of ten *Hanas.* See footnote 115. Ayyā Śāstri would have been twenty-two at this time. He was honoured with the title *Kavitilaka* in 1912 C.E.

[218] See page 299 for a biography of Ayyā Śāstri.

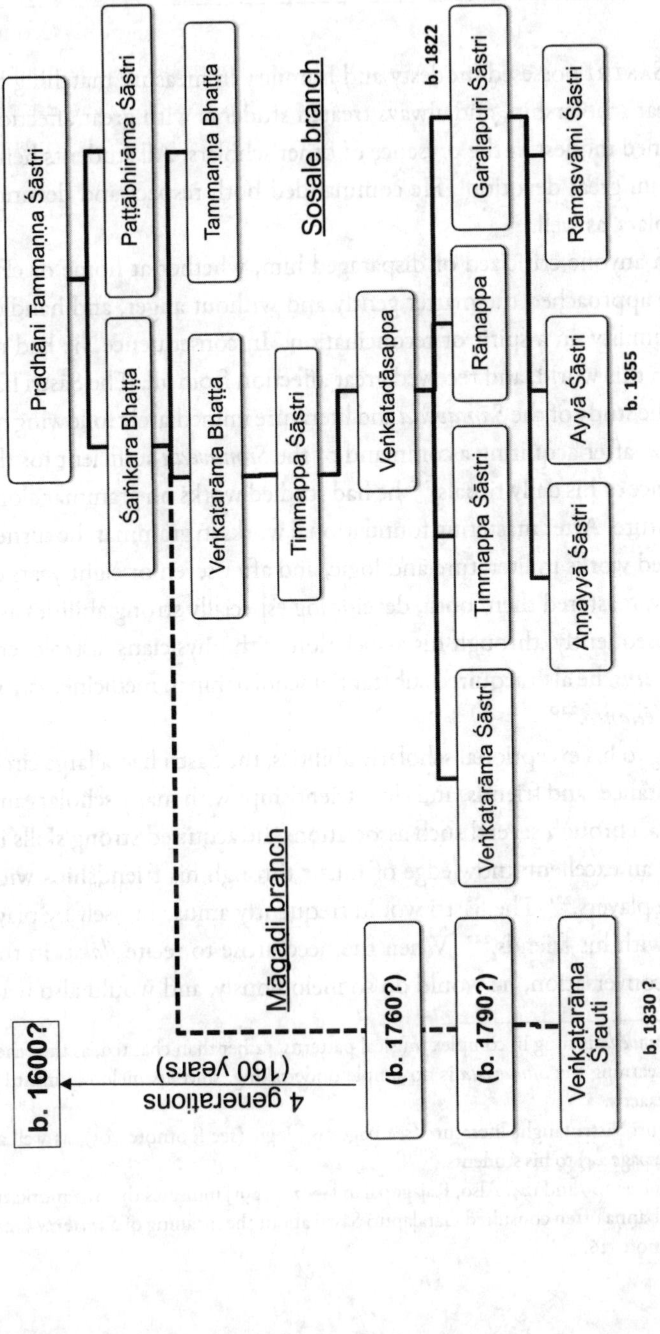

Plate 9: The family tree as depicted by Ayyā Śāstri (see page 312). The Māgadi branch and the estimates for years of birth are interpolations by the translator, and are not present in Ayyā Śāstri's original manuscript.

Chapter Ten: The Many Great Virtues of Garaḷapurī Śāstri

The Śāstri possessed modesty and humility in measure matching his great scholarship, and always treated students with great affection. He remained modest in the presence of other scholars. All students hence showed him great devotion. He commanded both respect and devotion from scholars, as well.

When anyone criticized or disparaged him, whether at home or elsewhere, he approached the matter gently and without anger, and handled it with humility, in a spirit of reconciliation. In consequence, he had no enemies in this world, and received great affection from all. The Śāstri had pursued the study of the *Sāmavēda* and literature immediately following his *upanayana;* after acquiring a command of the *Sāmavēda* sufficient for the performance of his daily rituals,[219] he had studied works on grammar along with literature. After mastering foundational works in grammar, he turned to advanced works in literature and logic, and after seven or eight years of deep study, mastered them both, developing especially strong abilities as a poet. Subsequently, through his association with physicians, astrologers, and *Vēdāntins,* he also acquired substantial scholarship in medicine, astrology, and *Vēdānta.*[220]

Owing to his exceptional scholarly abilities, the Śāstri had a large circle of acquaintances and friends, and close friendships with many scholars and aristocrats. Through several such associations, he acquired strong skills in chess, and an excellent knowledge of music through his friendships with many *vīṇa* players.[221] The Śāstri would frequently amuse himself by playing chess with his friends.[222] When the need arose to recite *ślōkas* in the course of conversation, he would do so melodiously, and would also read

[219]The *Sāmavēda* is sung in complex musical patterns, rather than chanted, as the other *Vēdas* are. Learning the *Sāmavēda* is no simple undertaking, since its melodies must be reproduced exactly.

[220]Garaḷapurī Śāstri taught literature (see page 26), logic (see footnote 705), as well as medicine (see page 24) to his students.

[221]See footnotes 109 and 124. Also, Rajagopalan [1992, p. 291] indicates that the musician Mūgūru Subbaṇṇa often consulted Garaḷapurī Śāstri about the meaning of *Saṁskṛta kṛtis*.

[222]See footnote 126.

aloud the *Rāmāyaṇa* daily, its verses set to many melodious rāgas.[223] Many were the listeners who derived pleasure from this. That such a profound scholar should also be so musically accomplished was akin to gold exuding fragrance.

The Śāstri was born with an exceptional memory. As a result, he had retained in memory everything he had learnt from his gurus. Any book he taught his students even once also became committed to memory, so that he could, with complete ease, teach the same work again without ever needing to refer to the book.[224] In addition, he carried in his memory all the books he had written, the thousands of verses of his own composition, innumerable compositions of ancient poets, and a number of *cūrṇikās*;[225] they have all been lost with him. Printing was not prevalent at his time, nor was it the practice to commit to writing most material, with some exceptions, such as works studied with a guru, new works written by oneself, and certain works required in the conduct of daily life. The practices of education had not reached their current levels of sophistication, nor were there printing presses, newspapers, or schools. One can only imagine the impact such a scholar would have had were he to have lived in our modern world.

When there were errors in the books he was teaching, the Śāstri's deep insights into the poet's style and design allowed him to confidently interpolate corrections exactly matching the poet's intent. On one occasion, when he had just moved to Maisūru from Sōsale, he happened to be teaching the ninth canto of the *Raghuvaṁśa* to a group of four students. One of the four had a palm-leaf manuscript, from which the other three were making their own copies. This manuscript included a commentary, but nine of the original *ślōkas* happened to be missing from the manuscript, leaving only the commentary intact. Considering that waiting to obtain a complete copy would amount to undue delay, he proceeded to reconstruct all

[223] Sarōjā Veṅkaṭarām, the great-granddaughter of Garaḷapurī Śāstri, recalls a palm-leaf manuscript of the Rāmāyaṇa in the possession of Mr S.G. Śāstri, the eldest son of Ayyā Śāstri. This may well have been the same manuscript that Garaḷapurī Śāstri had used for his *pārāyana*.

[224] Garaḷapurī Śāstri's namesake grandson S.G. Śāstri, speaking on the occasion of the centenary celebration of Basappa Śāstri, recalled Garaḷapurī Śāstri's advice to his son Ayyā Śāstri not to attempt poetical composition before first committing at least ten thousand verses to memory, offering Basappa Śāstri as an example [Venkaṭasubbayya and Gītāçārya 2000, p. 15]. Basappa Śāstri was, of course, Garaḷapurī Śāstri's student and Ayyā Śāstri's teacher.

[225] A *cūrṇikā* is a composition in rhythmic prose.

nine verses using the available commentary, and taught the students accordingly. When a new copy of the work was finally obtained, the nine verses in it were completely identical to the reconstructed verses. Similarly, when he happened to be teaching the following verse from the sixth canto of the *Naiṣadha* to some students,[226]

çandr'ābham'ābhran'tilakan'dadhānā
çandr'ānavasthām'iva yatra kāntā |
sasarja kāçandra samē sakhī·mukhē
tadvan'nijāsy'ēndu kṛt'ānubimbam ‖

he noticed that the third quarter of this verse improperly followed the 12-syllable *Vaṁśastha* metre, instead of the 11-syllable *Vajrā* metre. After some reflection, he proceeded, correcting the third quarter to read *"sakhīmukhē çandra samēsasarja"*. This turned out to be the correct form when an old copy of the work was consulted.

Even from his very first days in Maisūru, Garaḷapurī Śāstri never sought anyone's patronage, unless that person himself approached him. He refused such patronage even when offered by persons of note, unless it was also accompanied with due and proper respect. He would treat as a close friend any benefactor who treated him with genuine regard. He was always content with what support he received, and never, on his own accord,

[226] The *Naiṣadhaçarita* or *Naiṣidhīya* is a complex poem of about 3000 verses by Śrīharṣa, a poet and *Advaita* philospher of the 12th century C.E. It is based on the story of Nala and Damayantī from the *Mahābhārata.* It is seen as a poetical masterpiece, but also as complex and difficult reading, especially since its treatment reflects Śriharṣa's philosophical disposition. The saying *"naiṣadham vidvadauṣadham"*, meaning "the *Naiṣadha* is as tonic for the intellect", is often used to allude to its technically abstruse nature. Similarly, the verse *"tāvad bhā bhāraver bhāti yāvan māghasya nodayaḥ | udite naiṣadhe kāvye kva māgha kvaça bhāravi ‖"*, meaning "Bhāravi's lustre shines bright till Māgha has risen. But of what account, truly, are Māgha and Bhāravi once the Naiṣadha has risen?" is frequently quoted to indicate the high poetic regard this work is held in. Also see footnote 121. The verse referenced here is the 62nd verse in the 6th canto. Given the age of the work, we should expect to see variations across editions. For instance, Śrīharṣa [1912] gives: *"çandrābhamabhrantitilakandadhāna tadvannijāsyēndu kṛtānubimbam | sakhīmukhēçandra samēsasarja çandrānavasthāmiva kāpi yatra ‖"*, which exchanges the second and fourth quarters, compared to the version Garaḷapurī Śāstri was using, but the third quarter still matches Garaḷapurī Śāstri's correction. The metre is *Upēndravajrā.* It is technically permissible to mix this metre with *Vaṁśastha* (the mixed metre would be in the *Upajāti* class). However, the mixed metre would clearly be inconsistent with the rest of the canto.

solicited assistance from anyone. If ever the need arose for him to make a request of some person, he would, at some proper time, make his meaning known through a clever *ślōka* of his own composition. Thereby delighted, the person would fulfil the Śāstri's wishes unstintingly. Many people of lesser character would impose themselves on affluent patrons, and gain material benefit by inducing a sense of obligation upon them. Garaḷapurī Śāstri could have gained enormous wealth, had this been his way. He commanded great respect from everyone, since he disdained all wealth thus acquired, and always remained uncovetous.

Having been born into a family of high standing, he was high-minded, and always conducted himself honorably, regardless of material incentive to do otherwise. He was fully content with any generosity his patrons may have bestowed upon him, of their own accord. Indeed, he had also inherited land in sufficient measure to allow him to live contentedly, imparting learning without expectation of remuneration, and rendering material support to others in need.

He ensured that all special occasions and events in his household were celebrated with grandeur, matching the dignity and esteem that he and his family commanded. Despite such prosperity, the Śāstri lived modestly and without undue pride, conducting himself as a simple and pious *vaidika* brāhmaṇa, ever hard-working and virtuous, and earning great respect and acclaim from all quarters.

Śrī Kṛṣṇārpaṇamastu

Kādambarī Saṅgraha Granthamāla, No. 36

BIOGRAPHY OF
ÇĀMARĀJANAGARA ŚRĪKAṆṬHA ŚĀSTRI

By

Çāmarājanagara Veṅkaṭaramaṇa Śāstri

Printed in our own Bhuvanēśvarī Press

1917

Price 8 *Āṇe*] [Postage extra

Plate 10: *Dharmadhikāri* Ċāmarājanagara Śrīkaṇṭha Śāstri (1833–1917). Photograph by Varadāċārya, 1917 C.E. Frontispiece from original biography.

1. Birth and Childhood

jātasya hi dhruvō mṛtyur'dhruvaṁ janma mṛtasya ca |
tasmād'aparihāryē–'rthē na tvaṁ śōcitum'arhasi [227] ‖

We witness daily in this world, as it is manifest to us, that birth and death are the experience of all creatures. Many are the luminaries who have lived here, and then passed on. Truly have the wise observed in the saying *"naraḥ patitakāyōpi yaśaḥkāyēna jīvati"* that man lives on in the body of his fame, even when his earthly body has ceased to be.[228] When a man, whose human form has obtained from good deeds over many incarnations, departs this world having chosen to merely indulge himself in selfish and sensual pleasures, engaging in no works yielding merit in this world or the next, we would be right to consider him no better than a beast. But we would be right to think the scholar exalted who, having grasped the purpose of this human life, engages himself in reflections on matters of Truth and spirituality, and devotes himself to the service of others. The *darśana* of such a luminary, honoring him, conversing with him, contemplating his life, and chronicling his life, are all acts that surely bring one merit.

Our intent in undertaking this effort is to acquaint our readers with our protagonist as having been among this very group of illustrious individuals. This is not a full biography of Śrīkaṇṭha Śāstri. It is, rather, a broad account of his life, but which includes many specifics. It should suffice to acquaint the reader with the life of our protagonist, and fulfil this writer's purpose.

This venerable individual was born on the tenth *śuddha tithi (Vijayadaśami)* of the month of Āśvayuja in the Vijaya *saṁvatsara* of Śālīvāhana *Śaka* 1756 (October 15, 1833 C.E.),[229] in the Katvāḍipura Agrahāra of Nañjanagūḍu *tālūk,* which lies halfway between Maisūru and Nañjanagūḍu. At

[227] *Bhagavadgīta* (2:27), Kṛṣṇa to Arjuna: *"Certain indeed is the death of one who is born, and the rebirth of one who dies. Therefore, it is unbefitting of you to lament the inevitable."*

[228] This is the second hemistich from Ballāladeva's *Bhojaprabandha:* 53 (16th century): *"dēhē pātini kā rakṣā yaśō rakṣyamapātavat | naraḥ patitakāyōpi yaśaḥ kāyēna jīvati ‖"*, meaning "to no purpose is care for this fleeting body; esteem endures, it alone is worth our care, for Man lives on in the body of his fame even when his mortal body has ceased to be".

[229] The *tithi* given corresponds to Wednesday, October 23, 1833 C.E., not October 15. For the record, Śrīkaṇṭha Śāstri was of the Bhāradvāja *gōtra,* and the *Āśvalāyana* school of the *Ṛgvēda* [Śāstri 1925b, p. 9].

the time, Kṛṣṇarāja Voḍeyar III, the grandfather of our present king, had established an *agrahāra* in Katvāḍipura, and bestowed the homes therein upon many excellent scholarly and *śrōtriya* brāhmaṇas along with *vṛttis* for their sustenance.[230] Among those to have received homes in this manner was Rāmaśēṣa Śāstri,[231] who gifted away both his home and his *vṛtti*
1831 to a selfless and noble individual called Veṅkaṭaramaṇa Śāstri, who had moved to Maisūru from Sindhughaṭṭa.[232] As a mark of special regard, the king had also arranged for a monthly stipend of twelve *Haṇas* for him. This same Veṅkaṭaramaṇa Śāstri was Śrīkaṇṭha Śāstri's father.[233]

---

[230]Kṛṣṇarāja Voḍeyar IV (1894–1940 C.E.) was the king of Maisūru in 1917 C.E., when this biography was written. His grandfather Kṛṣṇarāja Voḍeyar III bestowed the name Çāmarājanagara upon the village of Arikuṭhāra in 1818 C.E., upon learning that it was the birthplace of Çāmarāja Voḍeyar, his own father [Rice 1877a, p. 227]. According to Row [1922, p. 153], Kṛṣṇarāja Voḍeyar III established an *agrahāra* with 74 homes and *vṛttis* at a village called Kattavāḍipura on the banks of the river Kapilā in Nañjanagūḍu district on Sunday, August 1, 1819 C.E., and named it the Kṛṣṇarājēndrapura Agrahāra. Rice [1897a, p. 316] indicates that this *agrahāra* was near the Arkēśvara temple, and that subsequently, in response to complaints from residents of this *agrahāra* about thieves, the king gave them homes in a new *agrahāra* he constructed to the southwest of the palace in Maisūru; Row [1922, p. 155] indicates that he established the Dēvīrāmbā Agrahāra to the south of the palace on June 26, 1845 C.E., with homes for 24 brāhmaṇas and for the palace *ṛtvik* Veṅkaṭaramaṇa Śāstri (see page 97). Such appear to be the origins of the Katvāḍipura Agrahāra in Maisūru.

[231]Lakshminarasimhaiya *et al.,* [1970] identify him with Kāśī Śēṣa Śāstri. See footnote 465. Śēṣa Śāstri moved to Maisūru in June 1818 C.E. and grew very close to Kṛṣṇarāja Voḍeyar III.

[232]According to Śāstri [1925b, p. 34], Veṅkaṭaramaṇa Śāstri's move to Maisūru occurred in 1831 C.E. Veṅkaṭaramaṇa Śāstri had studied at Śṛṅgēri, and had been a fellow-student of *Śrī Vṛddha* Nṛsiṁha Bhāratī (1798–1879 C.E.), the pontiff of the Śṛṅgēri Maṭha [Śāstri 1925b]. He was an accomplished scholar in the *Vēdas,* literature, logic, astrology, and ritual, and came to Maisūru in 1831 C.E. with his younger brother Lakṣmīpati Śāstri. Veṅkaṭaramaṇa Śāstri lodged with Rāmaśēṣa Śāstri (see page 174), and Lakṣmīpati Śāstri found patronage under the *Daḷavāi* of Maisūru, who, at this time, seems to have been a Dēvarājayya [Arasu 1993, p. 151]. Recognizing Veṅkaṭaramaṇa Śāstri's profound scholarship, Rāmaśeṣa Śāstri presented him at the court of Kṛṣṇarāja Voḍeyar III, who granted him a monthly salary of twelve *Haṇas.* Rāmaśeṣa Śāstri also gifted away to Veṅkaṭaramaṇa Śāstri his own house in the Katvāḍipura Agrahāra, as well as the associated *vṛtti.* We note in passing that the British rescinded Kṛṣṇarāja Voḍeyar III's executive authority as of October 19, 1831 C.E., after intervening militarily to quell an insurrection (September 1830–June 1831 C.E.) in the Nagara province near present-day Śivamogga. This would have been a difficult time for the ruler.

[233]Veṅkaṭaramaṇa Śāstri's great-grandfather Gaṅgādhara *Vāraṇāsi* was originally from Bādāmi, acquiring his sobriquet after having made several trips to Vāraṇasi. Around 1730 C.E., rising political unrest in the region of Bādāmi caused him to move to Honnavaḷḷi (13.34°N 76.39°E), a village close to Tipṭūru in Tumakūru district [Śāstri 1925b]. Bādāmi, historically a Çālukya stronghold, had passed into the control of Bijāpur even during the

Śrīkaṇṭha Śāstri's mother was a lady by the name of Bhāgīrathamma. Such being his origins, our protagonist had remained at Katvāḍipura during his early years.

When His Highness sent for Veṅkaṭaramaṇa Śāstri, intending to appoint him a scholar at court, he replied: "Your Majesty, city life is unsuitable for a *vaidika* like myself. If it pleases you to arrange for me to reside in some village akin to a hermitage, conducive to an ascetic life and the performance of rituals such as *Aupāsana* and *Vaiśvadēva*, I would be content to spend my days praying for your prosperity, sustained by the patronage of others."[234]

Bhāgavata Subbarāya, who was *Mukhtasar* of the *Zenāna Bāgilu*, conveyed this message to His Highness.[235] Bhāgavata Subbarāya had the very highest regard and reverence for Veṅkaṭaramaṇa Śāstri. Not taking even the slightest offense at this response, His Highness once again bade Bhāgavata

---

time of Vijayanagara, and subsequently into Mughal hands after 1687 C.E. The loosening of Mughal control in the 1690s C.E. resulted in a great deal of unrest in the region, as the Marāṭhas under Pēśva Bāji Rao I, as well as various local chiefs began to assert themselves. Gaṅgādhara *Vāraṇāsi's* stay at Honnavaḷḷi, however, turned out to be short [Śāstri 1925b]. Suffering much due to the depredations of the local Muslim chief (perhaps Dilāvar Khān, then *Navāb* of Sīra), he moved within two years to Sindhughaṭṭa in the Aṣṭagrāma region and remained there, the local *pāleyagāra*, a Vīraṇṇa Nāyaka, having welcomed him and supported him with a *vṛtti*. Gaṅgādhara *Vāraṇāsi* had two sons, Kṛṣṇabhaṭṭa being the elder, and Narasiṁhabhaṭṭa being the younger [Śāstri 1925b]. After his sons came of age, Gaṅgādhara *Vāraṇāsi* retired to Kāśī, where he passed away a *saṁnyāsi*. Kṛṣṇabhaṭṭa had a son who had been named Gaṅgādhara after his grandfather, and Narasiṁhabhaṭṭa had a son named Kṛṣṇa. A genealogy appears on page 151. Narasiṁhabhaṭṭa's descendants remained in Sindhughaṭṭa, which is at 12.695°N, 76.550°E.

[234] The *Aupāsana* is a twice-daily ritual sacrifice of curds and rice performed by a householder using the *Aupāsana* fire established at the time of his marriage. This fire is maintained throughout marriage, and used in all domestic rituals, and even to light the funeral pyre upon death. The *Vaiśvadēva* consists of the *pañça mahāyajñas* or five great sacrifices [Pande 1994], namely the *dēva yajña, bhūta yajña, pitṛ yajña, manuṣya yajña,* and *brahma yajña*, representing sacrifices to the gods, all animals, the ancestors, people, and the *Vēdas*, respectively. These rituals are mandatory for all brāhmaṇas, and represent the obligations of a brāhmaṇa to each of the above.

[235] See Plate 21. Bhāgavata Subbarāya was a distinguished public servant and close confidant of the king, but but surprisingly little seems to be known known about his life. A biography appears in Sāstri [2002]. *Zenāna* literally means "women's quarters", but at the time, it was one of the two sections (*Khās* and *Zenāna*) of the *Sammukhada Ūlige* department, responsible for the palace indoor employees. The *Zenāna Sammukha* had three departments, called *Ambā Vilāsa*, the *Zenāna Bāgilu,* and the *Oḷa Bāgilu.* Bhāgavata Subbarāya appears to have retired in 1868 C.E., after Kṛṣṇarāja Voḍeyar III died, with the honorary title of *Second Bakhśi* of the Treasury [Elliot 1878]. See pages 87 and 196.

Subbarāya determine Veṅkaṭaramaṇa Śāstri's wishes, so that he might be accommodated whereever he desired.

Upon receiving this message through Bhāgavata Subbarāya, Veṅkaṭaramaṇa Śāstri responded: "Good Sir, His Highness has recently made great improvements to the village of Arikuṭhāra, renamed it Çāmarājanagara in honour of his father, built a divine temple and established in it an Īśvara *liṅga* donated by the Śṛṅgēri pontiff, giving it the name Çāmarājeśvara.[236]

His Highness has provided support for many brāhmaṇas through
1834 employment at that temple.[237] Were I to obtain some appointment there, I would devote myself to my daily observances and to teaching my students." Bhāgavata Subbarāya submitted this response to His Highness. Inquiries revealed a vacancy at the temple for someone to fulfil the function of *dharmādhyayana*,[238] the incumbent Çandraśēkhara Śāstri of Diḍḍepura having passed away, and none of his children being competent to serve as instructors. His Highness selected Veṅkaṭaramaṇa Śāstri, who had deep scholarship in literature, the *Vēdas*, ritual, and astrology, for the post, and sent him a letter of appointment. The Śāstri moved to Çāmarājanagara with his wife and son.[239]

---

[236] Kṛṣṇarāja Voḍeyar III's father *Khāsa* Çāmarāja Voḍeyar was born in Arikuṭhāra. The *liṅga* bears his name, so that he is implicitly deified. See footnote 264. According to Row [1922, p. 136], this temple was completed on the third day of the waxing fortnight of Jyēṣṭha of the Vyaya *saṁvatsara* corresponding to the *Śaka* year 1749. This corresponds to June 8, 1826 C.E. Inscription CH 86, located at the entrance to the Çāmarājeśvara temple gives the date as Monday, the second *tithi* of the waxing fortnight of the *nija* Āṣāḍha of the Sarvadhārin *saṁvatsara* corresponding to the *Śaka* year 1750, which would be July 14, 1828 C.E. [Rice 1898]. However, Rice [1877a] incorrectly dates this event to 1825 C.E.

[237] Kṛṣṇarāja Voḍeyar III was noted for his munificience to scholars, temples, and charitable institutions. Royal grants nearly doubled from about 7% of total revenue in 1799 C.E. to 13.5% in 1823 C.E. (Pūrṇayya was *Divān* 1799–1811 C.E.) The British saw this increase as an example of Kṛṣṇarāja Voḍeyar III's maladministration, and used such arguments to justify their administrative takeover in 1831 C.E. [Stein 1989, p. 269]. There may be merit in that position, but a strong argument is presented by Ikegame [2007] that the king was merely discharging his traditional duty under the Indian doctrine of *rājadharma* as protector of his subjects, the concepts underlying which would have been alien to the British.

[238] Study of matters relating to the *dharmasūtras* and *dharmaśāstras*, all part of the *smṛti* corpus. This huge corpus includes the *Āpastamba, Gautama, Baudhāyana*, and *Vāsiṣṭha sūtras*, as well as the *Manu, Yājñavalkya, Nārada, and Viṣṇu smṛtis* and related commentaries. There remains a massive amount of material still in manuscript form.

[239] We can date this move as being after the birth of his first son Śrīkaṇṭha Śāstri in October 1833 C.E., but before the end of 1834 C.E., when Veṅkaṭaramaṇa Śāstri began work on his

At this time, Gaṅgādhararāya, a worthy *laukika* brāhmaṇa, made available a portion of his house for the Śāstri's residence.[240] Some time later, Jīvaṇḍarāya, an acquaintance of Gaṅgādhararāya, gifted away a home of his to the Śāstri.[241,242] As the Śāstri pursued this dignified life at Nagara,[243] three sons, Narasiṁha, Kṛṣṇa, and Rāma, and two daughters, Nañjamma and Śaṅkaramma, were born to him following Śrīkaṇṭha Śāstri.

Veṅkaṭaramaṇa Śāstri was especially attached to Śrīkaṇṭha Śāstri, both because he was his eldest son and because he had an exceptionally sharp intellect. This child was capable of clear and articulate speech by the age of three.[244] The Śāstri would seat the child near himself each morning and

---

Nañjarājaçampū (see footnote 288). We know for certain that he had already moved to Çāmarājanagara by then [Śāstri 1925b].

[240] See footnote 67 for an explanation of *laukika*. The honorific "Rāya", a corruption of *rājan* in *Saṁskṛta*, becomes "Rāv" in Marāṭhi. This Gaṅgādhararāya was surely Gaṅgādhara Rāv (see page 198), son of the highly respected public servant *Baççe* Rāv, whose real name was Bhujaṅga Rāv, the sobriquet *Baççe* obtaining from Ṭippu's fatherly affection for him. *Baççe* Rāv had been *Huzūr Gumāstah* under Pūrṇayya during Ṭippu's time, and *Head Śeristedār* of Kaḍappa after Ṭippu's defeat of 1799, at the extraordinary salary of *Rs.* 700 per month [Gribble 1875, p. 132]. Upon retirement in 1837, he was granted two villages free of tax, with annual revenues of *Rs.* 5,600. His son and grandson were also entitled to these revenues, but required to pay half as tax. *Baççe* Rāv's son Gaṅgādhara Rāv was himself a significant figure, participating prominently in the politics of the time, holding the title of *Musāhib* of the *Tośakhāna*, and held in good regard by Kṛṣṇarāja Voḍeyar III, but held in very low esteem by the British, as were many of the king's other advisers [Gopal 1993, p. 394]. Gaṅgādhara Rāv's son appears to have also been called Bhujaṅga Rāv, and modestly employed in 1874 as 3rd Clerk in the office of the Sub-Collector in the district of Kadappa [Revenue Board 1875, p. 25]. He would of course, have had access to his inherited revenues.

[241] This name was most likely Jīvan Rāya, transformed into Jīvaṇḍarāya when articulated. We observe a "Jivan Rao Tank" to the northwest in the map of Maisūru (Plate 12), suggesting that Jīvan Rāv was an important figure at the time. A memorandum dated 30th May 1826 from Sir Thomas Munro [in Arbuthnot 1881, p. 336], takes the Collector of Tinnevelly to task for improperly suspending *Head Śeristedār* "Jivan Rāv" on flimsy evidence, and ordering that the extraordinary fine of *Rs.* 4000 levied on him be returned with interest. Munro also notes that while it would be desirable to restore this Jivan Rāv to his former office, it would be unlikely that the Collector and he could work together cordially. There is a strong possibility that this same person was subsequently transferred to Maisūru, which was also within Madras Presidency at the time.

[242] Such remarkable kindness from the king and important officials such as Gaṅgādhara Rāv and Jīvan Rāv, as well as such distinguished scholars as Rāmaśeṣa Śāstri suggests that Veṅkaṭaramaṇa Śāstri was held in extraordinary esteem indeed.

[243] "Nagara" means "city", but is used here as a contraction of Çāmarājanagara.

[244] This is a subtle point. Clear and accurate pronunciation is highly esteemed by learned

evening, and teach him *stōtras* such as the *Navaratnamālikā Stōtra* and the *Pañçāyudha Stotra*.[245] The child was capable of concentrating on its lessons for as long as two hours, showing no signs of boredom. This child
1841 underwent the sacrament of tonsure at the age of three, and that of *upanayana* at the age of eight.[246] By this time, he had learned all three *kāṇḍas* of the *Amara Kōśa*, the grammatical formulæ of the *Aṣṭādhyāyī*, the list of *Saṁskṛta* verbal roots and *samāsa* forms, numerous prayer *stotras*, the *Raghuvaṁśa*, the work of Māgha, and the *Naiṣadha*, all by heart, and with an understanding of their meaning.[247]

The Śāstri decided to teach his son his own *Vēdic śākha* in its entirety, and began teaching him the *Rgveda*. Awakening him at four each morning, he would teach him a new chapter to be committed to memory, and would make him recite it repeatedly between seven and ten or eleven that evening.[248] Śrīkaṇṭha Śāstri's task in the afternoons was to study poetry, and to review his previous lessons.

---

brāhmaṇas, fastidious practitioners of the ancient tradition of orally transmitting the vast *Vēdic* corpus. Their insistence on fidelity of pronunciation has allowed the preservation of the subtleties of the *Vēdic* language and intonation over the millenia. That Śrīkaṇṭha Śāstri was capable of such clarity of articulation so early is to be taken as a mark of distinction.

[245] There are several compositions under the name *Navaratnamālikā Stōtra*. The one referred to here is most likely one attributed to *Ādi* Śaṅkarāçārya that begins *hāra nūpura kirīṭa kuṇḍala…* The *Pañçāyudha Stotram* praises the five weapons of Viṣṇu, namely the *sudarśana* discus, the *pāñçajanya* conch, the *kaumōdakī* mace, the *nandaka* sword, and the *śārṅga* bow.

[246] The sixteen traditional *samskāras* (sacraments) are *garbhādhāna* (conception), *puṁsavana* (male quickening), *sīmantonnayana* (parting of mother's hair), *jātakarma* (birth), *nāmakaraṇa* (naming), *niṣkramaṇa* (first outing), *annaprāśana* (weaning), *çūḍākaraṇa* (tonsure), *karṇavedha* (ear piercing), *upanayana* (initiation), *vedārambha* (start of *Vēdic* instruction), *keśānta* (shaving), *snāna* (bath marking end of study), *vivāha* (marriage), and the *antyeṣṭi* (funeral).

[247] It is impressive that an eight-year-old would have learned this corpus. The *Amara Kōśa* is a *Saṁskṛta* thesaurus, traditionally learned by heart. Pāṇini's *Aṣṭādhyāyī* is a monumental work on *Saṁskṛta* grammar, noted especially for its terse formulæ that comprehensively represent *Saṁskṛta* syntax and semantics in several thousand context-sensitive production rules. The *Raghuvaṁśa* is an epic poem about Rāma from Kālidāsa's mature period. Māgha is a highly respected poet (see footnote 121). The *Naiṣadhaçarita* is an epic by Śrīharṣa that deals with the story of Nala from the *Mahābhārata.* Also see footnote 226.

[248] The *Vēdas* were always fully committed to memory, preserving the tonal accents of the original *Vēdic* language. Errors were not tolerated. To guard against inadvertent changes, each verse had to be recited in seven different permutations of its words, with the proper changes in tonal accents for each. See footnote 446 for some details of such recitation.

By the age of fifteen, Śrīkaṇṭha Śāstri had learned all eight *aṣṭakas* of the *Ṛgveda,* and was accomplished in literature and drama. Impressed by the brilliance of this promising youth, Subbādīkṣita, a *Ṛgvedi* resident in Çāmarājanagara, made a proposal of marriage for his nine-year-old daughter Subbamma. Veṅkaṭaramaṇa Śāstri accepted it. The marriage was conducted in conformance with all formally prescribed rituals (1843 C.E.).[249] Within six months of his marriage, he began studying the ancillary *Vēdic* disciplines, such as the *Āśvalāyana Pūrvaprayōga* (*Nṛsiṁha Pārijāta*),[250] *Saṁskṛta* phonetics, grammar, prosody, etymology, astrology, and formal practice of ritual.

As he made systematic progress in these studies, he developed a strong interest in undertaking a formal study of the Pāṇinian *Siddhānta Kaumudi*, and expressed this interest to his father.[251] His father advised him: "Dear child! I have already taught you everything I know. You may proceed with a study of grammar, in accordance with your wishes. There is no one here capable of instructing you systematically in grammar. The city of Mahisūru is filled with scholars deeply learned in various disciplines. Go there to study grammar, as is your wish. Remember that you will be an alien there, and treat everyone with courtesy. Avoid bad company. Sustain yourself either as a teacher in a household, or by *vārānna*.[252] Review again and again what you have learned. Never be apathetic in your study. You have my permission to proceed on this journey."

---

[249] This is a typographical error in the original. Śrīkaṇṭha Śāstri would have turned fifteen only in 1848 C.E.

[250] A treatise on ritual practices pertaining to the living, for brāhmaṇas maintaining the *Ṛgvēdic* tradition. Āśvalāyana is an ancient *ṛsi* (c. 400 B.C.?), to whom are attributed the eponymous *gṛhya* and *kalpa sūtras,* covering household and formal rituals, respectively. The *Pārijāta* is a work by Nṛsiṁha (1360–1435 C.E.), which is based on these works. It remains a standard.

[251] This refers to the *Vaiyākaraṇa Siddhānta Kaumudi*, a work not by Pāṇini, but by the 17th-century grammarian Bhaṭṭoji Dīkṣita, who had studied *Vedānta* under the astonishingly prolific Appayya Dīkṣita (see footnote 203). This landmark work simplifies the arcane and highly formal *Aṣthādhyāyī* grammar of Pāṇini, making it more generally accessible, and restoring the Pāṇinian tradition to its former preeminence over competing grammatical traditions.

[252] Literally "weekly board". It was common for charitable households to sponsor students by giving them free board once a week. The students would sustain themselves by rotation among several such households.

2. Formal Study

The Śāstri arrived in Maisūru at the age of sixteen to study grammar, and began his studies in grammar and logic under Kāśī Śēṣa Śāstri and Kavi Varadāçārya,[253] who had distinguished themselves in grammar. Among his fellow-students were Çakravartyayyaṅgār and Śrī Kṛṣna Brahmatantra, the previous pontiff of the Parakāla Maṭha.[254] They were all most methodical in pursuing their studies, but of the three, Śrīkaṇṭha Śāstri's were the most impressive study habits and intellect. His gurus and fellow-students were most astonished by how he would commit the formulæ and the commentaries to memory, and study them day and night. Within just three years, he had completed a study of grammar and logic in their entirety. We will now describe his method of study.

Awaking at three o'clock, in the latter half of the night, he would review his previous lesson until it was fully committed to memory. He would next review all his prior lessons. It would be around seven in the morning by this time. He would then complete his bath and morning rituals, and
1849 proceed to receive instruction from his gurus. These lessons would last till about eleven in the morning. His fellow-students would find it a little tiresome to remain focussed for this length of time. After his lunch, the Śāstri would once again review all his lessons, till the evening. He would sometimes feel drowsy. At such times, he would splash cold water on his eyes and walk around for a bit. If anyone came by for a chat, he would send them on their way quickly, remove himself to some more isolated place, such as the Trinayanēśvara temple, and continue his study.[255] Such unrelenting application to his study allowed the Śāstri to achieve complete mastery of grammar within three years. It took his fellow-students several more

[253] See the list of scholars on page 23 and Kuṇigala Rāmaśāstri's students on page 201.

[254] Çakravarti Ayyaṅgār was a distinguished citizen, who held the honorary title of *Dharmādhikāri.* He ran the Vidyātaraṅgiṇī press out of his home in the Kempunañjāmbā Agrahāra of Maisūru. Srī Kṛṣna Brahmatantra Svatantra Parakāla Mahadeśikan was pontiff of the Parakāla Maṭha 1885–1915 C.E. He was born in 1839 C.E. in Amidala, some 40 km west of Anantapur in present-day Āndhra Pradēsh, and was known as Kṛṣṇamāçārya prior to his becoming a *saṁnyāsi.* As the author of a large number of *çampū* and poetical works, he acquired the sobriquet *kavisārvabhauma.*

[255] The Trinayanēśvara temple is a landmark within the Maisūru fort.

years to attain his level of accomplishment.[256] At this point, the Śāstri had to return to Nagara, having received a letter saying that his wife was expecting.

The Śāstri became a family man after his return to Nagara. In his
twentieth year, he celebrated the birth of his son, whom he named 1852
Narasiṁha. After this son were born, in order, two sons named Veṅkaṭakṛṣṇa and Subrahmaṇya, respectively, and a daughter named Lakṣmīdēvī.[257]

There were excessive demands at the time on the Śāstri's household in Çāmarājanagara, which consisted of Veṅkaṭaramaṇa Śāstri, his wife, five sons, daughter-in-law, as well as grandchildren. His eldest daughter Nañjamma was also now married, and he himself had become her husband's teacher.[258] Because this young man did not pursue his studies seriously and would often take himself away, and because the children in the household had to be looked after despite its limited income, the household experienced frequent discord, and Veṅkaṭaramaṇa Śāstri began to feel an aversion to the ways of this world. Bearing all this with fortitude, he stayed true to his path as a householder. Witnessing this situation, Śrīkaṇṭha Śāstri began to think to himself: "My household makes substantial demands despite its small income. I should be careful not to cause our *yajamāna* distress.[259] It would be best to move my household elsewhere."

---

[256] It will soon become clear that Śrīkaṇṭha Śāstri was in fact an extraordinarily strong all-round scholar. We can, however, begin to understand the intensity of his dedication to the study of *Saṁskṛta* grammar in the context of his view that a human lifetime barely sufficed for mastering more than a single subject. In the preface to the *Dhāturūpaprakāśikā*, his *magnum opus*, he is quite explicit: *"purā khalu dharmādi puruṣārthādhigamahētuṣu ṣaḍdarśanyāditantrēṣvēkaikamapyambudhirbāhubhyāmiva sudustaramitimatvā prāñçaḥ paṇḍitāēkasmin janmanyaikaikam śāstram paṭhitavyamiti dhṛḍhīkṛtaniṣçayāḥ pṛthakbṛthagvibhajyājanmanaḥ āçāvadhērēkaikam śāstramēva parigṛhya tatrātirāgēṇa śrāmyanta uttējināsīniva nijaśāstrāṇi bhibharāmbabhūva"*. We may paraphrase this as: *"Ancient scholars, seeing that dharma and puruṣārtha could be attained through means such as the six darśanas, each of which was a vast ocean that human strength did not suffice to cross, determined to commit themselves in each life to a single subject, divided learning amongst themselves, and studied their branch with the deepest devotion and effort."*

[257] Narasiṁha was born in 1852 C.E. (see page 97). Veṅkaṭakṛṣṇa, being forty-eight in late 1900, was likely born in 1853 C.E. (see page 112). Lakṣmīdēvī appears to have been a year older than Subrahmaṇya, being eight when he was seven, *c.* 1868 (see page 100). They were likely born in 1860 and 1861 C.E., respectively.

[258] The reference here is to Veṅkaṭaramaṇa Śāstri, not to his son Śrīkaṇṭha Śāstri.

[259] Literally, *yajamāna* means "performer of *yajñās*", but is commonly a respectful way of referring to the head of the household, who conducts all rituals on behalf of the family.

The Mahārāja once visited Çāmarājanagara with his retinue.[260] Śrīkaṇṭha Śāstri was then temporarily officiating in the role responsible for delivering the *rājāśīrvāda*.[261] The king happened to visit the temple for *darśana* one evening at the time of *dīpārādhane*.[262] The ambience during worship that evening was suggestive of Śiva himself holding court, both because a large number of people were present at the ceremony, and because the gloriously resplendent Çāmarājeśvara was pleased to accept their devotions. After services had been rendered to the deity based on the four *Vēdas*, the *Itihāsas*, the *Purāṇas*, the *Sthaḷa Mahima*, and various devotions to Śiva,[263] the person in charge of announcing the *avadhāraya* proclaimed: *"śrī kempunañjāmbikāsamēta śrī çāmarājēśvarasvāmin! rājāśīrvādamavadhāraya!"*[264] At this point, our

November 1858

[260] This visit is difficult to date precisely, but the circumstances match the report by Row [1922, p. 138] that Kṛṣṇarāja Voḍeyar III visited Çāmarājanagara during the month of Kārtika of the Kāḷayukti *saṁvatsara* of *Śaka* year 1781, which corresponds to November 1858 C.E., bringing gifts of gold and jewellery for the deities at the temple.

[261] Literally "conferring blessings on the king". See footnotes 264 and 266

[262] Literally "worship with light", an important activity towards the end of the worship ritual. A plate or a candelabra with burning camphor (or oil lamps) is waved in circles before the deity, and *mantras* chanted. The effect is spectacular, especially in subdued light. Also see footnote 528.

[263] A traditional worship ritual renders to the deity the respectful attentions due to a distinguished person or guest, to the accompaniment of the appropriate mantras from the *Vēdas*, and passages from the *Itihāsas* and *Purāṇas* ("histories" containing traditional accounts of cosmology, lives and genealogies of heroes, and geography). The *Sthala Mahima* or *Sthala Purāna* is an account of the traditions and the history of the specific temple or locale.

[264] "O *śrīmān* Çāmarājēśvara, accompanied by *śrīmatī* Kempunañjāmbikā, now hear the *rājāśīrvāda*". See footnote 266. The *āśīrvāda* is a blessing or benediction bestowed upon the *yajamāna* (the nominal or actual performer of the ritual) by the brāhmaṇas in attendance. This suggests that the worshipper here is *Khāsa* Çāmarāja Voḍeyar (accompanied by his wife Kempunañjāmbikā, as required by the *śāstras*), in whose memory the temple was built by his son Kṛṣṇarāja Voḍeyar III. The tradition of conducting all temple rituals in the name of the king has precedent, and is followed to this day in the Jagannātha temple in Pūri, Orissa [Tripathi 2004]. The long-standing tradition at Pūri is that the true ruler of the kingdom is the deity, the king merely being his *sevaka* or servant who discharges his obligation through worship. *Rājōpaçāras* (acts of deference due to a king) are offered to the deity, consolidating its status as king. The *rājāśīrvāda* is offered to the incumbent ruler, in whose name the ritual was conducted. Also see Appadurai and Breckenridge [1976]. Applying this logic here gives rise to a paradox, however, since Śiva is worshipped in this particular temple in the form of the Çāmarājēśvara *liṅga*, with statues of Kempunañjāmbikā and Çāmuṇḍēśvarī on either side. That is, Śiva and Pārvatī are being worshipped in the form of Kṛṣṇarāja Voḍeyar III's

protagonist, the *Śabda-Brahman* incarnate,[265] composing numerous verses spontaneously, delivered an articulate and majestic *āśīrvāda* that held the audience spellbound for a full half-hour.[266] This performance both enthralled the king, as well as filled him with joy. Similar proceedings took place at the Svāmi Temple, the Çāmuṇḍēśvarī Temple, and the Ammanavara Temple. After the *dīpārādhane*, everyone returned to their homes, and the king's retinue too, returned to the palace. As he was about to retire after dinner, the king asked Bhāgavata Subbarāya: "Who was that boy who delivered the *rājāśīrvāda* in the temple?" Subbarāya intimated that the boy was Veṅkaṭaramaṇa Śāstri's son, and that he was very proficient in the *Vēdas,* literature, ritual, and grammar. The king commanded: "Excellent! Please have the boy see me tomorrow."

The following morning, the king's messenger arrived at Veṅkaṭaramaṇa Śāstri's home and announced: "Sir, His Highness has commanded me to conduct your son to his presence." The Śāstri, a strict *vaidika* brāhmaṇa,

---

parents "Khāsa" Çāmarāja Voḍeyar and Kempunañjāmbikā, his first wife. They appear to be at once both the worshippers and the worshipped. We find an interesting explanation for this actual deification of this king and his consort in Row [1922, p. 135], where it is suggested that owing to the king's deep devotion to Śiva, the term *śivaikya*, meaning "oneness with Śiva", generally used to connote the demise of a member of the *Liṅgāyata* community, which the king belonged to, be taken to have literally occurred in this case, so that the king is indistinguishable from Śiva. A similar case is made for his wife. A fundamental problem remains, however, since Çāmarāja Voḍeyar and Kempunañjāmbikā appear both as worshippers and the worshipped. (The *āśīrvāda* is for the benefit of the king as worshipper. The deity is in no need of blessing.)

[265] Literally "word-*Brahman*", often taken to mean the *Oṁkāra* sound, but more broadly to comprehend the *Brahman,* or Universal Reality. Here, the term is intended to convey that Śrīkaṇṭha Śāstri was Speech (that is, Knowledge) incarnate. In the *Advaitic* tradition, *Śabda-Brahman* connotes the *saguṇa Brahman*, or the *Brahman* with attributes, representing the "lower" knowledge, rather than the *nirguṇa Brahman*, or the pure *Brahman* representing the "higher" knowledge. In the philosophical traditions of the Indian grammarians, *Śabda-Brahman* represents the "higher" knowledge.

[266] The *āśīrvāda* or benediction occurs at the end of the ritual, and serves several purposes. First, it formally reassures the *yajamāna* of the success of the ritual, and of the fulfilment of its intended purpose. Since the domain of the ritual is largely inaccessible to the attendees, the *āśīrvāda* also communicates the significance of the ritual to all present. The *āśīrvāda* is an elaborate performance, incorporating verses from the *śrutis* and *smṛtis*, and links the domain of formal ritual to the everyday world. See Prasad [2007] for an exploration of *āśīrvāda* with reference to its practice in the local traditions at the town of Śṛṅgēri, home to the influential Śaṅkara Maṭha. A royal *āśīrvāda,* such as this one, would be especially demanding. *Vēdic* rituals culminate not with an *aśīrvāda,* but in the *āśis,* which is part benediction and part an expression of the the ritual's desired outcome [Gonda 1989].

was alarmed, and wondering why the king had sent for his son, asked him what transgression might have led to such a circumstance. When his son replied that the king had visited the temple the previous evening, and that he was unaware of any lapse on his part, the Śāstri, obliged to obey a royal command, sent his son along.

Upon seeing Śrīkaṇṭha Śāstri, the king exclaimed: "So you are the son of our Śāstri, young man! Indeed, what else could the offspring of a lion be but a lion? I am pleased at your brilliance! Be that as it may, you delivered a magnificent *āśīrvāda* last night, in stately language. Who did you learn this from?" Śrīkaṇṭha Śāstri responded with humility: "Your Highness, this is simply the result of your munificence. My achievements owe entirely to your benevolence. Compared to those of the many great scholars at Your Highness's court, my accomplishments are trifling." Pleased with this response, His Highness said: "Śrīkaṇṭha Śāstri! You appear well qualified to be a scholar at our court. Come see us in Maisūru eight days hence. We will arrange for your employment at the palace."

Śrīkaṇṭha Śāstri conveyed this command of His Highness to his *yajamāna.* Pleased, he sent Śrīkaṇṭha Śāstri to Maisūru.

3. The King's Regard

Dear reader, these are events from sixty years ago. No amenities existed then for travel between towns, such as exist today. Bullock-drawn carts were the only transport available. Our protagonist always travelled between Maisūru and C̣āmarājanagara on foot. On such occasions, he would arise at dawn, bathe and finish his daily rituals, and walk all the way while reciting the *Vēdas* and grammatical formulæ, his books and clothing in a cloth bag upon his shoulder. He would arrive in Maisūru by noon. He would not feel fatigued in the least, having walked while engaged in such recitation. Maisūru and C̣āmarājanagara are thirty six miles apart. For him, walking this distance was much as an evening walk is for our citizens of today. He travelled between Maisūru and C̣āmarājanagara frequently. Indeed, he was quite used to it.

The Śāstri lodged as a guest in Bhāgavata Subbarāya's home after arriving in Maisūru. Bhāgavata Subbarāya was then a person of eminence and renown. He had enormous regard for *Vēdic* learning, as well as for *vaidikas* who had achieved erudition in these fields. He himself lived the life
of a *śrōtrīya* brāhmaṇa, observant of the practices that the *Vēdas* en- 1859
join. Hundreds of brāhmaṇas were honored guests each day at the home of this prosperous individual. A constant stream of guests arrived between ten in the morning and five in the evening each day. His home truly functioned as a *c̣hatra* at the time.[267] A large number of students from elsewhere lived there. Scholars and travellers from elsewhere frequently lodged there as well.

Upon arriving at Subbarāya's home, the Śāstri acquainted him with the purpose of his trip. Subbarāya promised to bring the matter up with the king at an opportune moment, and asked him to remain his guest at home until such time. Accordingly, the Śāstri waited there for some days, busying himself with his studies. After returning to Maisūru, the king had forgotten the conversation he'd had with Śrīkaṇṭha Śāstri in C̣āmarājanagara, it being only natural that a ruler would be occupied with many matters. When

[267] *C̣hatra* is the Kannaḍa form of *sattra*, which in *Saṁskṛta* means a facility providing free board and lodging to the public. This is not to be confused with *c̣hattra*, an umbrella or parasol.

Subbarāya brought up the matter, the king merely responded: "Ah, yes! I remember. You mean the matter about Śrīkaṇṭha Śāstri? Very well!"

Śrīkaṇṭha Śāstri remained as he was for many days, unable to secure an audience with the king. Bhāgavata Subbarāya himself being an important official, the Śāstri was hesitant to speak with him. Instead, he occupied himself in enhancing his own knowledge, engaging scholars at the palace in discussions of scholarly matters, as time permitted. Despite his deep scholarship, the Śāstri was child-like in his simplicity and innocence. There was not a trace of pride in him. Other scholars took great delight in his erudition and simplicity.

One Śāmaṇṇa, who was the father of the present pontiff of the Śivagaṅge *maṭha* before he accepted *saṁnyāsa,*[268] expressed his desire to study poetry with the Śāstri. Veṅkaṭanārayaṇa Śāstri, the brother of Śāmaṇṇa's mother, was among the foremost scholars at the court. He arranged for his nephew's studies with the Śāstri.

Having high regard for the Śāstri, Veṅkaṭanārāyaṇa Śāstri asked Subbarāya to appoint the Śāstri to the position of raconteur of stories to the king at night.[269] Arrangements were made accordingly. But who, indeed, can divine the king's thoughts! After a few days had passed in this fashion, the king happened to ask Śrīkaṇṭha Śāstri one day: "Ah, there you are, Śāstri! Anything new?" When the Śāstri responded: "Your Highness, all is the result of your munificence. Our household in Çāmarājanagara is large. Our income is insufficient. Yet, my present situation will not permit me to bring my family here. Your command in Nagara of a position for me in the palace remains unfulfilled. I face many difficulties," the king recalled his words in Nagara and the Śāstri's uncommon eloquence, called Subbarāya right away, and appointed the Śāstri as a scholar at the palace at a salary of three *Varāhas* (nine *Rūpīs*).

---

[268] This appears to have been Śri Subrahmaṇya Śivābhinava Saççidānanda Bhāratī *Svāmi.* A *saṁnyāsi,* having renounced the world, retains no attachments, and has no family. He is ritually dead to the world. Hence, any reference to the *Svāmi's* father must be in the context of his life prior to having accepted *saṁnyāsa.*

[269] Given Śrīkaṇṭha Śāstri's background, these would have been stories from the *Purāṇas, Itihāsas,* or literary or poetic sources.

The Śāstri moved his family to Maisūru very shortly after this appointment. At this time, a wealthy individual by the name of Liṅgōpant accommodated the Śāstri and his family in his own home, where he had made arrangements for him to present discourses on works such as the *Purāṇas.*[270] By this time, his eldest son Narasiṁha had undergone his *upanayana.*[271] In him was reflected his father's nature. He pursued his studies with the same vigour that his father had, and had become a dear son to his father.

[270] We can speculate that Liṅgōpant may have been a descendant of Biṣṭopant, the *Bakṣi* of the *Savāri Ilāqa,* who commanded the Maisūru forces fighting in support of the British in their war against the Marathās in 1802–1804 C.E. Biṣṭopant's grandfather Rāmarāv appears to have been a commander with *Navāb* Aṅkuś Ḳhān, a Bijāpur army general who fought alongside Randullah Ḳhān in the Bijapur campaigns in Maisūru in 1648 C.E. Ramarāv's son Liṅgōpant was in service with Nānā Faḍnavīs, a leading statesman and minister with the Pēśvas of Mahārāṣtra. Biṣṭopant was the second son of this Liṅgōpant. The Liṅgōpant who hosted Śrīkaṇṭha Śāstri was no doubt a descendant and namesake. Despite their martial traditions, the family were *Smārta* brāhmaṇas, explaining the willingness of the strictly observant Śrīkaṇṭha Śāstri to live with them.

[271] A ritual marking the formal transition from the stage of childhood to that of a student. See footnote 246 for a list of *saṁskāras.*

4. This Anguished World

No one could possibly remain unmoved by the tragedies that now transpired at Çāmarājanagara.

We have seen that Śrīkaṇṭha Śāstri was followed by three siblings, whose names were Narasiṁha, Kṛṣṇa, and Rāma.[272] Narasiṁha, too, had studied poetics and drama with passionate intensity. His *upanayana* had been completed by the age of eight. He was two years younger than Śrī-
1845 kaṇṭha Śāstri. His intellectual abilities truly surpassed those of his elder brother. This child, which had shown so much promise, passed away within two years of having completed his *upanayana*. The loss of his son shook the spirit of Veṅkaṭaramaṇa Śāstri, whose life so far had been entirely free of misfortune.

Kṛṣṇa was two years younger than Narasiṁha. His intellect was in no way inferior to that of his elder brothers. He too had undergone sacraments such as tonsure and *upanayana* in timely fashion. At fourteen, he
1854 was married to Veṅkaṭalakṣamma, the elder sister of Mūgūru Kubērayya. Due either to *daivayōga* or to the Śāstri's own *prārabdha*,[273] however, this Kṛṣṇa succumbed to an untimely death within three years of marriage.

Owing to such sorrows, the Śāstri did not pressure Rāma on matters of education. Rāma's intellect was sharper than that of his brothers. However, he was not diligent in pursuing his studies. Getting him to learn *Vēdic* recitation was a special challenge. As are many other students, he was diligent only in studying the *Amara Kōṣa,* declensions, nominal compounds, poetry, and *ċampu.* He truly liked to enjoy himself. Studying the *Vēdas,* however, would give him a headache. He was married in his fifteenth year to Nañjamma, the daughter of Kuççamma and Rāmappayya from Ālūru in Çamarājanagara district. He was especially skilled in literature and poetics.

[272] Rāma was born on Wednesday, Āṣāḍha *bahula aṣṭami* of the Sōbhakṛtu *saṁvatsara* corresponding to Śālīvāhana *Śaka* 1765 [Śāstri 1925b]. His birth particulars are given as Rēvati *nakṣatra,* Mīna *lagna,* Mīna *navāṁśa.* This corresponds to July 19, 1843 C.E.

[273] *Daivayōga* is a coincidence of providentially determined circumstances. *Prārabdha* is the operation of prior *karma* in this life.

His failure to learn the *Vēdas,* however, remained a source of concern for the Śāstri.[274]

The Śāstri's eldest daughter was Nañjamma. She was two years older than Rāma.[275] She was married to a Raṅgaṇṇa, the son of Kāḷanañjuṇḍayya of Nañjanagūḍu. Raṅgaṇṇa's mind was fickle. As we have already seen, he was under the tutelage of his own father-in-law. The extent of his learning did not approach even that of his own wife. As she had listened to her brothers study,[276] Nañjamma too had mastered the *Amara Kōśa,* declensions, nominal compounds, verbs and conjugations, poems such as the *Raghuvaṁśa,* and in the end, even *Vēdic* recitation. She would correct her husband if he made an error during his study. This caused great embarrassment to Raṅgaṇṇa. Due to his fickle nature, he was often found to have absconded entirely. In the end, that is exactly how his fate turned out. He failed even to remain long a householder. He had a daughter, but that child died. In his very youth, he forsook his family, and moved away somewhere.

Veṅkaṭaramaṇa Śāstri had enormous affection for his eldest daughter. He was deeply anguished that she should have suffered such troubles so early in her youth. He continued to shelter and protect her in his own house. Her word was never challenged at home.

Śaṅkaramma was some two or three years younger than Rāma.[277] She was married to Kṛṣṇaśāstri, the son of Bhāskarayya of Çāmarājanagara. This young man had mastered literature as a student of his own father-in-law. As a result of the marriage having occurred between families in the same town, indescribable distress ensued in household affairs. In the end, this Kṛṣṇaśāstri moved away to Rāmanāthapura with his family.[278]

The loss of his children and domestic strife now convinced the Śāstri's mind of the trifling nature of this world. Even though a householder, this deeply learned and insightful man began to meditate upon Truth, remaining radiant as a water droplet upon a lotus leaf.[279] Be this as it may!

---

[274] This Rāma became *Mahāvidvān* Cāmarājanagara Rāmaśāstri, a renowned scholar and poet. See pages 53ff. for some of his poetical interactions with Garaḷapurī Śāstri.

[275] That would make 1841 C.E. the year of her birth.

[276] Traditionally, learning was acquired not by reading, but orally, through repetiton.

[277] Śaṅkaramma would have been born around 1845 C.E.

[278] Rāmanāthapura is at 12°37′N, 76°5′E, and some 120 km from Çāmarājanagara.

[279] This is a purposeful simile, being an allusion to the fourth verse of the *Bhajagovindam,* a popular composition of *Ādi* Śaṅkarāçārya, which urges one to recognize the world

Let us now recall that Śrīkaṇṭha Śāstri and his family were resident in Liṅgōpant's home in Maisūru. On the eleventh *tithi* of the waxing fortnight of the month of Çaitra of the Kāḷayukti *saṁvatsara* of Śālīvāhana *Śaka* 1783 (1860 C.E.),[280] his wife *Sau*|| Subbamma passed away. The Śāstri was stunned. Veṅkaṭaramaṇa Śāstri's brother Lakṣmīpati Śāstri was then
1861 in Maisūru under the *Daḷavāyi's* patronage. Upon learning of the demise of his elder brother's daughter-in-law, he immediately stepped in and provided a great deal of assistance. When this news reached Veṅkaṭaramaṇa Śāstri in Çāmarājanagara, he exclaimed, "Ah, Fate! How strange are your workings! What perversity! *Kṣate kṣārāvaseçanam* (akin to rubbing salt in one's wounds)", and remained engrossed in his thoughts for a long time. But what indeed, is in the power of man to call to a halt? He himself carried out the final rites for his daughter-in-law, on behalf of his grandchildren.

How could Śrīkaṇṭha Śāstri have now cared for his orphaned children? Deeply anguished by his wife's demise, he sent his children back to Nagara, and feeling that living with Liṅgōpant would only increase his distress by evoking memories of his wife, he took up boarding and lodging in the home of *Vīṇe* Sāmbayya,[281] and became his son's teacher. The Śāstri was now twenty-eight years of age.[282] His scholarship, like the waxing moon, grew ever brighter each day.

---

as transitory, and seek refuge in devotion to Govinda. Its fourth verse says:

"naḷinī-daḷa-gata-jalam'ati-taralaṁ tadvaj'jīvitam'atiśaya-çapalam |
viddhi vyādhy'abhimāna-grastaṁ lōkaṁ śōka-hataṁ ça samastam ‖"

This translates to: "Even as a droplet of water on the lotus petal has a fleeting existence, so is life transitory. Know indeed that all the world is tormented by disease, conceit, and sorrow."

[280] The given *Śaka* year and *saṁvatsara* name are inconsistent. *Śaka* 1783 matches the Durmati *saṁvatsara* if reckoned as elapsed and Dundubhi if taken as current. The Kāḷayukti *saṁvatsara* matches *Śaka* 1780, or 1858 C.E. The *tithi* given matches Thursday, March 25, 1858 C.E. in the Kāḷayukti *saṁvatsara*, Sunday, April 21, 1861 C.E. in the Durmati *saṁvatsara*, and Thursday, April 10, 1862 C.E. in the Dundubhi *saṁvatsara*. Given the traditional practice of referring to dates by *saṁvatsara* names, we would have favored the year 1858 C.E. However, that would be inconsistent with the information in the following paragraph.

[281] See Plate 18c. He was a senior and influential *vīṇā vidvān* in the court of Kṛṣṇarāja Voḍeyar III, and was descended from *vaiṇikas* from Tañjāvūr [Vedavalli 1992, p. 56]. See Vasudevaçarya [1994, p. 129], for an amusing story involving him and *Vīṇe* Padmanābhayya.

[282] That allows us to date this to 1861 C.E.

5. Śaṅkarānanda Sarasvatī

Veṅkaṭaramaṇa Śāstri's mind, which had abided sorrow and happiness equally, now attained full detachment from this world. He was being transformed profoundly. The distress within his household continued to grow unabated. He had endured it all with great patience. His days as a householder were nearing an end! Knowledge of the divine began to take root in his mind. The ability to discriminate between Self and non-Self blossomed in him.[283] The cloak of Illusion slipped away from within his heart.[284] What now remained? When the *ariṣaḍvarga* have all fled from the Self in fear,[285] when attachment to the world has removed itself and vanished, when certainty has dawned that the Self alone is the Truth, what then remains? Dear reader! Have you an answer to this question? If renouncing the world and embracing supreme asceticism appear right for you, then surely that is the right course for you to adopt.[286]

It is now the Siddhārthi *saṁvatsara* corresponding to the Śālīvāhana *Śaka* year 1784.[287] The month of Śrāvaṇa, the first part of the season of *Varṣa,* is lending splendour to all nature. Today is the seventh *tithi* of the *śuddha* fortnight of that Śrāvaṇa. As the Śāstri was seated at dawn that day, a divine radiance stood before him said: "No longer remain in this world of impermanence. Follow me this very afternoon. Distance yourself from your life as a householder," and disappeared.[288] *1861*

[283] The original uses the expression *ātmānātma vivēka,* also the title of a famous work by *Ādi* Śaṅkarāçārya expounding the principles of his philosophy of *Advaita,* non-dualism. The expression means "discrimination between Self and non-Self".

[284] This is an allusion to Śaṅkarāçārya's concept of *Māya,* the cloak of ignorance that prevents one from perceiving the identity of the Self and the Brahman. Veṅkaṭaramaṇa Śāstri was a follower of the *Advaitic* tradition.

[285] The *ariṣḍvarga* or "six internal foes" are *kāma* (lust), *krōdha* (anger), *mada* (pride), *lōbha* (avarice), *mōha* (attachment), and *mātsarya* (jealousy).

[286] The expression used is *paramahaṁsa parivrājaka,* a term applied to the most accomplished of ascetics, whose characteristics are described in the *Paramahaṁsa Parivrājaka Upaniṣad.*

[287] Unfortunately, we have an inconsistency again. Siddhārthin *saṁvatsara* actually corresponds to *Śaka* 1781 (expired). However, if we read the text as referring to *Śaka* 1784 (current), we get the Durmati *saṁvatsara,* corresponding to 1861 C.E. This matches the year quoted in [Śāstri 1925b, p. 55]. The date referred to is August 12, 1861 C.E.

[288] Another vision, dating to an earlier time, is described [Śāstri 1925b]: Lord Veṅkaṭēśvara

The Śāstri arose immediately, completed his morning observances, his bath, and rituals such as the *Aupāsana* and *Vaiśvadēva*, and regarding himself henceforth freed of his debts to the *dēvas*, *ṛṣis*, and *pitṛs*,[289] left home without declaring his resolve, and determining to proceed to a deserted site, this omniscient luminary arrived at the Bṛhadrājavīdhītaṭāka (Doḍḍarāyapēṭe lake) some three miles distant from Çāmarājanagara,[290] bathed there, and leaving all his clothes at the spot, ritually discarded his sacred thread and top-knot, donned a loincloth, thrice recited the mantra *"saṁnyastōhaṁ, saṁnyastōhaṁ, saṁnyastōhaṁ"* (I am a *saṁnyāsi* who has forsaken all his worldly attachments),[291] meditated on the *Oṁkāra*, which brings salvation, incorporating within itself the *a-*, *u-*, and *m-* syllables as well as the World, Life, and the Self, proceeded towards the village of Ālūru, and accepting alms from a householder there, remained contented and blissful.[292]

Over here, as the family sat anxiously, all its meals delayed in anticipation of the long-absent Śāstri's return, news arrived that the Śāstri had accepted *saṁnyāsa*, and quickly spread all over town. His wife and children,

visited Veṅkaṭaramaṇa Śāstri in a dream, declared him to have been born of the sage Vyāsa, and charged him with continuing Vyāsa's account of him in the *Skānda Purāṇa*. He also foretold the birth of a great poet within his family, presumably his youngest son, Rāma. In fulfilment of this charge, Veṅkaṭaramaṇa Śāstri wrote the *Nañjarājaçampū* between 1834–1838 C.E. This date is earlier than the one given in footnote 287.

[289] Tradition has it that Man is born with three *ṛṇa*s or debts: to the *devas*, *ṛṣis*, and the *pitṛs*. These debts are discharged, respectively, by performing *yajñas* and *yāgas*, observance of *brahmaçarya*, and the begetting of children. A person may not enter *saṁnyāsa* until these obligations have been met. The *Manusmṛti* (6.35) is explicit: *"ṛṇāni trīṇapakṛtya mano mokṣe niveśayet"*.

[290] This lake is directly north of Çāmarājanagara, and just northwest of the town of Doḍḍarāyapēṭe.

[291] The *Nāradaparivrājakōpaniṣad* specifies the mantra *"Auṁ bhūḥ saṁnyastaṁ mayā | Auṁ bhuvaḥ saṁnyastaṁ mayā | Auṁ svaḥ saṁnyastaṁ mayā |"*

[292] In principle, *saṁnyāsa* is only permissible after one's *ṛṇas* have all been discharged (footnote 289) and one's wife has granted permission. In his *vārtika* on the dialogue between Yājñavalkya and Maitreyī in the *Bṛhadāraṇyakōpaniṣad*, for example, Surēśvara says: *"bhāryādanujñyāpūrvo hi saṁnyāso vihitaḥ śrutau | ato'nujñārthamēvā'ha maitrēyīmṛṣirātmanaḥ ‖"*, which translates as [Hino 1991]: "Indeed, in the Śruti, renunciation is prescribed only when it is allowed by a wife, etc., therefore, the sage addressed (his wife) Maitreyī for (securing) her consent." An accompanying footnote indicates that in Yājñavalkya's case, the *śruti* refers to *kramasaṁnyāsa* (footnote 298). In practice, however, this mandated permission is not always sought. Ālūru is some 7 km northeast of Çāmarājanagara.

who remained in the clutches of this world, lamented greatly. It is impossible to describe here the sorrow of Bhāgīrathamma, who was a model wife, and of serene temperament.

Puṭṭayya, who was then *Amaldār,*[293] wrote to the king with the news of the Śāstri's having accepted *saṁnyāsa.* Kṛṣṇarāja Voḍeyar III had the ultimate regard for Çāmarājanagara and the brāhmaṇas who lived there. The *Subedār* had strict orders to communicate any unusual news in writing. The news of the Śāstri's having accepted *saṁnyāsa* reached the king even before it reached Śrīkaṇṭha Śāstri. When the king, grieving greatly for the difficulties that had confronted Śrīkaṇṭha Śāstri, condoled with him when he came to the palace, saying: "Dear Śrīkaṇṭha Śāstri! Your father appears to have accepted *saṁnyāsa,* and departed. Do not grieve on this account!", the Śāstri, suffering even greater grief than he did upon his wife's death, burst into tears, and begged of the king: "Your Majesty! We are now orphans![294] As protector of those bereft of help, you now stand in place of our parents. You must protect us, in fulfillment of the saying *rājāpratyakṣadēvatā.*"[295] The king consoled the Śāstri, and sent him home. He also appointed him to the role of reciting the *Mantrapuṣpa* at the Nañjarājēśvara temple in Çāmarājanagara.[296] Rāma continued in Nagara, fulfilling both this duty as well as that of *dharmādhyaya.*[297] The Śāstri continued living in Maisūru.

Six years went by in this manner. The *Svāmi* (Śrīkaṇṭha Śāstri's father) had lived on the banks of the Kāvērī at Yeḍatore during this time. At this place also lived a person by the name of "Ātmānanda", who *1867* had accepted *krama saṁnyāsa,*[298] being formerly known as Subrahmaṇya Śāstri of Homma. Our *Svāmi* too was initiated into *krama saṁnyāsa*

[293] Chief administrative officer for a *tālūk* or district. This officer is known variously as *Amaldār, Tehsīldār, Māmlatdār,* or *Subedār.* We should note in passing that the person referred to here is a Puṭṭayya, not to be confused with M.S. Puṭṭaṇṇa, the author of the biography of Kuṇigala Rāmaśāstri, the third of the biographies in this volume. He too had served as *Amaldār* of Çāmarājanagara, but this date is too early for him. He finished his B.A. in 1885 C.E., and served in various locales as *Amaldār* between 1897–1908 C.E.

[294] A nosisim use of "we", connoting either the first person singular, or the larger family.

[295] This means "the king is a divinity our eyes are able to behold".

[296] The *Mantrapuṣpa* is an extract from the *Aruṇapraśna* of the *Taittirīya Āraṇyaka* of the *Kṛṣṇa Yajurveda.* It is traditionally recited as a benediction at the conclusion of the *pūja* ceremony.

[297] Veṅkaṭaramaṇa Śāstri had earlier fulfilled this role in the Çāmarājeśvara temple. See footnote 238.

[298] *Kramasaṁnyāsa* is the acceptance of *saṁnyāsa* in the normal course, at the fourth

by him. Soon after our *Svāmi* had accepted *saṁnyāsa,* our benevolent king had invited him to Maisūru, arranged for an honorarium through the palace, and hosted him where the Uttarāji Maṭha is located.[299] After remaining here for some time, the *Svāmi* returned to Yeḍatore, considering the city life unsuitable. The *Svāmi* lived there happily in the company of *Svāmi* Ātmānanda. Our *Svāmi* was known as "Śaṅkarānanda Sarasvatī".

āśrama or stage of life. The *Nāradaparivrājakōpaniṣad* describes the *vidvat, jñāna, vividiṣā,* and *karma* categories of *saṁnyāsa. Karma saṁnyāsa* is divided into the *nimitta* (causal) and *animitta* (non-causal) kinds. *Ātura saṁnyāsa,* taken on account of impending death, is of the *nimitta* type. *Krama saṁnyāsa* (the regular kind) is of the *animitta* category.

[299]This should read Uttarādi Maṭha, which is a *maṭha* belonging to the *Mādhva* sect. The Uttarādi Maṭha in Maisūru is now located adjacent to the Śaṅkara Maṭha, whose location marks the precise spot where Kunigala Rāmaśāstri's house once stood.

6. A Mingling of Happiness and Sorrow

The Akṣaya *saṁvatsara* was under way. Veṅkaṭaramaṇa Śāstri, *ṛtvik* at the palace, proposed marriage between the seven-year-old Veṅkaṭalakṣamma, who was the daughter of his son Rāmāśāstri, and Narasiṁha, the eldest son of Śrīkaṇṭha Śāstri. This news becoming known to the king, he personally arranged for this marriage, feeling that this would be an excellent match. Though Narasiṁha was then only fourteen, it would have been wrong to reject the match on account of his youth. The bride was from an excellent family! Besides, there was the matter of the king's command! Śrīkaṇṭha Śāstri therefore agreed to the marriage.

Narasiṁha took Veṅkaṭalakṣmī's hand on the third *śuddha tithi* of the month of Jyēṣṭha of the Akṣaya *saṁvatsara.*[300] The king supervised the ceremony personally. But who can stand to challenge divine will? Who indeed can fight Death! This world is subject to Īśvara. Man is unenlightened. On the fourth day of his marriage (*Haribhauma*),[301] the 1866 bridegroom Narasiṁha was racked by violent vomiting and purging, and died the same night. This pen of ours is incapable of writing of the anguish of Śrīkaṇṭha Śāstri, his in-laws, and of the king. To the same corpse were dedicated auspicious sacraments such as the *Nāgavalli* as well as the funerary sacraments such as cremation.[302] We have set our heart to stone, being forced to write of such anguish. We could not continue our account otherwise. We will simply write of what occurred.

When Śrīkaṇṭha Śāstri went to the king's presence a month after the above events transpired, and mentioned his troubles, the king, mentally anguished, said: "Dear Śāstri! Can anyone oppose divine will? I can not bring your dead son back to life. But you are still young. I will find you a bride from a good family. I will increase Śaṅkarānanda *Svāmi's* stipend, and send him to Yedatore. Your family has sufficient income in Nagara to support

[300] Unfortunately, an *adhika* Jyēṣṭha month occurs in this Kṣaya *saṁvatsara.* This date corresponds to either Thursday, May 17, 1866 C.E., or Friday, June 15, 1866, according to whether the Jyēṣṭha is taken to be *adhika* or *nija.*

[301] The couple's first meal together. Marriages were complex social affairs, and lasted up to a week.

[302] The concluding marriage rituals.

itself. Do not let what transpired in the past bother you." After consoling Śrīkaṇṭha Śāstri in this fashion, he directed: "Send for Veṅkaṭanārayaṇa Śāstri,[303] and let us have a bride found for Śrīkaṇṭha Śāstri". Inquiries now being made among *Hoysaḷa Karṇāṭaka* families all over, it was learned that Gōpāla Bhaṭṭa from Mēlukōṭe in Hirōḍe *tāllūk* had a marriageable daughter, that the match was excellent in all respects, and that the girl was also becoming and graceful. The king arranged this match for Śrīkaṇ-
1867 ṭha Śāstri, and in the Prabhava *saṁvatsara*, had the marriage conducted with grandeur, had the bride and bridegroom carried in an *howdah* atop an elephant, had them brought from Mēlukōṭe to Maisūru, lodging them en route in the Dariyā Daulat at Śrīraṅgapaṭṭaṇa, holding a grand *santarpaṇa* for brāhmaṇas, and arranging for ceremonies such as *ārati-akṣate* for the couple.[304]

After he came to Maisūru, the king appointed Śrīkaṇṭha Śāstri's father-in-law Gōpālabhaṭṭa to a position in the palace at a salary of thirty *Haṇas.*

The workings of this world are strange indeed! Does anything ever endure in this impermanent world? All is momentary! In the Vibhava *saṁvatsara*, Death had *Śrīmanmahārāja* Kṛṣṇarāja Voḍeyar III con-
1868 ducted to its presence with great grandeur. When the king left this world, the world itself became consumed by the flames of anguish. When this king, who always extended patronage to scholars, showed great empathy towards the sufferings of others, and treated the poor, the destitute, and the helpless with such respect, passed away, the world lost its radiance. Scholars, in their great anguish, recited the following *ślōka*:[305]

ratna·garbhā nirādhārā nirālambā sarasvatī |
paṇḍitāḥ khaṇḍitās'sarvē kṛṣṇa·rājē divaṅgatē ‖

---

[303] See page 88.

[304] This is a celebration on a grand scale, made possible only by the direct orders of the king. Carriage atop an elephant is a singular honor, typically reserved for royalty. The Dariyā Daulat was Ṭippu Sultān's summer palace, and later became the king's personal resort in Śrīraṅgapaṭṭaṇa. A sojourn here would be a very special favor from the king. The *ārati* ceremony is a common ritual intended to remove evil influences, and consists of filling a plate with a reddish-brown combination of water, turmeric, and lime, and moving it in circles before the couple. The *akṣate* is a benediction ritual, where rice grains stained with turmeric (the *mantrākṣate*) are thrown on the couple.

[305] See Ballāladeva's *Bhojaprabandha* 294: *"adya dhārā nirādhārā nirālambā sarasvatī* | *paṇḍitāḥ khaṇḍitāḥ sarve bhojarāje divaṅgate* ‖*"* Dhāra was King Bhoja's capital city.

Meaning: With Kṛṣṇarāja Voḍeyar III having ascended to heaven, this land of Karnāṭaka has lost its benefactor. Sarasvatī, the godess of learning, is now bereft of support. Scholars are all now destitute.[306]

Our protagonist was plunged into an ocean of grief at the demise of this crest-jewel of scholarly patronage. The honorarium that Śaṅkarānanda *Svāmi* had received also ceased with the passing of the king into the other world. This *Svāmi,* who had renounced all attachments, paid not the slightest heed, sustaining himself on the alms of householders. Although he received word both of the indescribable distress in the household of his prior *āśrama* and of the demise of the king, he maintained the dignity of his present *āśrama*, and remained engrossed in seeking the Self.

Çāmarāja Voḍeyar was now king. Raṅgāçārya was *Dīvān*.[307] Upon hearing a full account of the *svāmi's* merits from other scholars, Raṅgāçārya applied to the king, and restored the *svāmi's* honorarium (four *Varāhas*), thus becoming the object of our protagonist's gratitude.[308] At this time, our protagonist was engaged in having the Royal genealogy and the history of Maisūru compiled.[309] Our protagonist was now thirty-five years of age. When he turned thirty-six, he moved to Nagara with his second wife, to ensure the welfare and education of his children, who

1869

[306]Major C. Elliot, with the assistance of Raṅgāçārulu, who became Palace Controller after the king's demise, reduced the number of scholars in the palace's employ from 464 to 125, of whom 22 were acknowledged as leading men in different branches of learning. The rest were terminated, with some level of gratuity. The total number of palace employees dropped from 9,687 to 3,196 [Stanhope 1878, p. 57].

[307]This is inaccurate. In 1868 C.E., the year Kṛṣṇarāja Voḍeyar III died, Çāmarāja Voḍeyar was just over 5 years old. Raṅgāçārlu was still Palace Controller, and did not become *Dīvān* until the Rendition of 1881 C.E., which formally restored the rule of the Voḍeyars.

[308]No intercession would have been required of the five-year old king for the restoration of the honorarium. Also see Vāsudevāçārya [1962] for an account of how he was left without support when his father Kānkānhaḷḷi Subrahmaṇyāçārya (see page 25) died, and his pension was terminated during Raṅgāçārlu's restructuring of the palace affairs. The pension was restored following the persistent appeals of Vāsudēvāçārya's grandfather to Raṅgāçārlu.

[309]Footnote in the original: "This same book has now been published by the controller of the palace." The work being referred to is the so-called *Annals of the Mysore Royal Family*, that is, the *Śrīmanmahārajaravara Vaṁśāvaḷi,* edited by B. Rāmakṛṣṇa Row, the Palace Controller. Volume 1 of this work was published in 1916 C.E., the year before this biography was published.

were growing up without their mother, as well as to take charge of the leaderless household. He would travel to and from Maisūru occasionally. Living in Çāmarājanagara at the time were his household, that of his younger brother Rāmaśastri, his two sisters, and his mother. A school was started in the temple there, and Śrīkaṇṭha Śāstri appointed as instructor. The Śāstri lived there, teaching his students and continuing his own studies.

The Śāstri's daughter Lakṣmīdēvamma was now eight years of age and running her ninth year.[310] The *śāstras* decree that a girl be married at eight.[311] In accordance with this injunction, the Śāstri married his daughter to Ayyā Śāstri,[312] the son of the Royal scholar and distinguished poet Garaḷapurī Śāstri. He had achieved distinction in poetry and drama. The Śāstri rejoiced, thinking: "How fortunate to have such a learned son-in-law!" By this time, he had completed the *upanayana* ceremony for his second son Veṅkaṭakṛṣṇa. He also took great care in the education of his youngest son Subrahmaṇya, who was only seven.

When the Śāstri was forty, he had a daughter by his second wife.[313] The Śāstri was especially attached to her both because she was the daughter of his junior wife and because this child possessed great intellectual acuity as well as charm. This girl learned the *Amara,* grammar, and poetry with her brothers. Her name was Bhāgīrathī. Joy and sorrow must yet exist together in this world! Before one could say that the Śāstri's life had reached a certain equilibrium, that is, in the Śāstri's forty-sixth year, died in succession his youngest son Subrahmaṇya, yet unwed, his dearest daughter Bhāgīrathī a year later, and two years thence, his second wife, who had stood as his greatest worldly treasure.

1879–1883

In the interim, that is, a year or two after Lakṣmīdēvamma was married, *Svāmi* Śaṅkarānanda left Yeḍatore and travelled to Kāśī.[314] At this same time, an ascetic *brahmaçāri* from Rāmanāthapura was initiated into *krama*

[310] See footnote 178. This marriage must have taken place in 1868 or 1869 C.E., making 1860 the year of Lakṣmīdēvamma's birth.

[311] For example, *Yājñavalkyasmṛti* (*āçārādhyāyaḥ*:64) declares that the father of an unmarried maiden incurs the sin of fœticide at every menstrual period. There was urgency to ensure marriage before puberty, but there was more leeway regarding how soon brides had to join their new households after puberty. The high infant and maternal mortality rates of the time likely had much to do with such early-marriage practices.

[312] Footnote in original: "He is the Royal Scholar 'Kavitilaka' Ayyāśastri."

[313] This child was born in 1873 C.E.

[314] Śaṅkarānanda Sarasvatī's move to Kāśī can thus be dated to 1869–1871 C.E.

saṁnyāsa by our *Svāmi.* This younger *svāmi* accompanied our *Svāmi* on his trip to Kāśī. This *mahātma,* a treasure-house of Truth, lived in a small cottage on the banks of the Gaṅgā, engaged in contemplating the Self. His honorarium from the king of Maisūru was collected each month and sent to Kāśī by Sōsale Garaḷapurī Śāstri.

It was during these times that Rāmaśāstri had also suffered the loss of his first wife.[315]

[315] Rāmaśāstri had been married at sixteen, that is, in 1858 C.E.. to Nañjamma (see page 90). He had taught at the *Saṁskṛta* Pāṭhaśāla at Yeḍatore between 1873–1876 C.E., since his income had been insufficient [Śāstri 1925b]. He had lost his first wife Nañjamma during this time, and as the text to follow indicates, married Lakṣmīdevamma, affectionately called *Ammaṇṇa.* By her, he had a son (C.R. Narasiṁha Śāstri, Professor of *Saṁskṛta,* University of Maisūru), and a daughter, Bhāgīrathī.

7. Flowering of Scholarship and Authorship of Book

Dear reader! I leave it to you to consider what emotional composure any human who had undertaken to engage himself in matters of this world might be left with after suffering a series of calamities such as described above! *Paramātma* alone of transcendental awareness might fathom the depths of grief in Śrīkaṇṭha Śāstri's heart; the likes of us could not even venture to guess at it. Even confronted with such sorrow, the Śāstri faced it all with courage, and became ever more virtuous. What, indeed, are happiness and sorrow to those possessed of knowledge? Isn't this the sign of the true *mahātma*?

The Śāstri now no longer wished to remain in Çāmarājanagara. In keeping with custom, he had arranged for the timely marriage of his younger brother Rāma with Lakṣmīdēvamma,[316] daughter of Nāgappa from Sāgare in Heggaḍadēvanakōṭe *tāllūk*. He had also arranged for the marriage of his only surviving son Veṅkaṭakṛṣṇa with Kṛṣṇamma, the second daughter of Śaṅkarabhaṭṭa of Çandakavāḍi (Diṇḍēpura) in Çāmarājanagara *tāllūk*. When the Śāstri suffered his series of misfortunes, his son and brother had both lived in Çāmarājanagara. Veṅkaṭakṛṣṇa had a daughter, as well.

Deciding that he did not want the responsibilites of a household any longer, and considering it best for everyone to take charge of their own households, he returned to Maisūru when he was fifty-one years old (1884), leaving their respective household responsibilities to each. It is fair to say that his scholarship had thus far remained hidden, like the moon

1884

obscured by clouds, or embers cloaked in ash. Now there was opportunity for the brilliance of his scholarship to show itself. His brother too, following his example, moved to Maisūru, and set up his own household. Śrīkaṇṭha Śāstri's son Veṅkaṭakṛṣṇa had no equal in the practice of ritual, *Vēdic* recitation, and literature. His æsthetic sensibilities were simply unmatched. His discourses on the *Purāṇas* were marked by extraordinary fluency. He continued in the role of *dharmādhyayana* at the

[316] Footnote in original: "This is the well-known Royal Scholar Çāmarājanagara Rāmaśāstri. We plan to publish his biography in the future." This biography appeared in Śāstri [1925b], but is loosely structured, containing a great deal of ancillary material, including extracts from the *Nañjarājaçampū* by Veṅkaṭaramaṇa Śāstri, the father of Śrīkaṇṭha Śāstri.

Çāmarājēśvara temple, and lived in Çāmarājanagara, maintaining his dignity, never transgressing his father's word.

After returtning to Maisūru, Śrīkaṇṭha Śāstri sought patronage from *Darbār Bakśi Ma*‖ Ambil Narasiṁha Ayyaṅgār and *Ma*‖ M. Veṅkaṭakṛṣṇayya, acquainting them with his story, from beginning to end.[317] Impressed with his scholarship, *Ma*‖ Ambil Narasiṁha Ayyaṅgār appointed him instructor for *Saṁskṛta* in Mahārāṇī's College.[318]

The monthly magazine *Hitabōdhinī* began publication in Maisūru in 1883.[319] There were no monthly publications in Kannaḍa before this time. *Hitabōdhinī* was followed by other publications such as *Ānandamandira, Nibandhamālike,* and *Sudarśana,* all of which rendered great service to the cause of the language. The magazine *Sudarśana* began in Uḍupi in 1886, and published articles in the Maṅgaḷūru dialect of Kannaḍa.

Hitabōdhini was started by *Ma*‖ M.S. Puṭṭaṇṇa, B.A., *Ma*‖ M.B. Śrīnivāsayyaṅgār, and *Ma*‖ M. Veṅkaṭakṛṣṇayya. Among the scholars who contributed many excellent articles on a variety of subjects were *Ma*‖ K. Śyāmayyaṅgār, K. Veṅkaṭasāmayyar, B.A., *Ma*‖ Çuṁ. Raṅgāçār, M.A.,

---

[317] Ambil Narasiṁha Ayyaṅgār (1845–?) was a highly respected public official, on whom was conferred the title of *Rai Bahādūr* on February 16, 1887. He is especially remembered for his work on education, and with M. Veṅkaṭakṛṣṇayya on the emancipation of women. Narasiṁha Ayyaṅgār founded the Mahārāni's High-Caste School on January 21, 1881, with a class of 28 girls. This school enrolled several hundred girls in a short time. An excellent account of the school appears in Knowles [1889]. M. Veṅkaṭakṛṣṇayya (1844-1933 C.E.), a journalist of distinction, was equally committed to the cause of education, and served as the principal of the Marimallappa School from its very inception. He writes [in Śāstri 1934, p. 23] that he had known Śrīkaṇṭha Śāstri since the time they had both lodged at Bhāgavata Subbarāya's house, as new arrivals in Maisūru. *Ma*‖ is an abbreviation for *mahārājaśrī*, a respectful form of address.

[318] Mahārāṇī's College grew out of Mahārāṇī's High-Caste School (see footnote 317), which had been founded three years earlier. It seems certain that this was still called a "school", rather than a "college" in 1884 C.E. However, since it acquired the status of a college in 1902 C.E., well before this biography was written, the author's reference to a "college" is understandable.

[319] Although some sources, such as Narasimhacharya [1934, p. 155], indicate that the *Hitabodhinī* started publishing in 1881 C.E., 1883 C.E. is the correct date. This date was confirmed by M. Veṅkaṭakṛṣṇayya in the October 1887 issue of *Hitabōdhinī* as reported in the October 1939 issue of the publication of *Kannaḍanuḍi.* M. S. Puṭṭaṇṇa began the magazine in collaboration with M. B. Śrīnivāsayyaṅgār, and ran it for six months, having to move to Madras in 1884 to take his examination for the B.A. degree, at which time M. Veṅkaṭakṛṣṇayya took charge of the magazine. It was later in the charge of A.C. Subbarāv, who remained in charge until it ceased publication about ten years later.

Ma‖ M. Śāmrāv, M.A., *Ma*‖ B. Rāmasvāmi, B.A., *Ma*‖ H.V. Nañjuṇḍayya, M.A., B.L., *Ma*‖ M. Gaṇēśasiṅg, *Ma*‖ A.C. Subbarāv, B.A., *Ma*‖ H. Kṛṣṇarāv, M. Kṛṣṇayyaṅgār, and the Ānandāḷvār Svāmi.[320]

Ma‖ Veṅkaṭakṛṣṇayya was especially committed to the *Hitabōdhinī's* publication, and devoted himself to its development. Knowing Śrīkaṇṭha Śāstri's abilities well, he arranged for him to be employed in the offices of the *Hitabōdhinī.* His work consisted of editing the writings of the
1884 aforementioned scholars, correcting the press proofs, and selecting the best articles for publication. During this time, *Ma*‖ M. Veṅkaṭakṛṣṇayya and *Ma*‖ M. Śāmarāv, who is now the Inspector General of the Maisūru Department of Education, were both engaged in advanced studies in *Saṁskṛta* with the Śāstri.[321] The high regard both these illustrious gentlemen had for the Śāstri will become apparent in what follows.

At this same time, the Śāstri quit his post at the Mahārāṇī's College, and worked as a teacher in the Sarasvatīprāsāda Pāṭhaśāla (*Saṁskṛta* College) for some time. His brother Rāmāśāstri and Sajjaya Tātāçārya also taught literature, logic, and science at the Pāṭhaśāla during this period.

As is well known, the Bhāṣōjjīvinī Pāṭhaśāla was founded in the city of Maisūru in 1887. Śrīkaṇṭha Śāstri was then appointed *Saṁskṛta* instructor at a monthly salary of twenty *Rūpīs.* In 1894, this same Pāṭhaśāla became

---

[320] The Ānandāḷvār Svāmi was known by the name of Āsūri Anantāçārya before he became a *saṁnyāsi.* The following information appears in Venkatasubbayya [1991]:

> Vidwan Asoori Ananthacharya (also known as Anadalvar) was a direct descendant, in the male line, of Sri Ramanujacharya, the famous Sri Vaishnava saint... Sri Anandalvar was born on 24-2-1859. He studied Veda, Vedanta, Sastras, and and Sahitya at the feet of Natampalli Alasingacharya, the then famous Mathadhipati of Yathiraja Matha and later under the guidance of Panditharatnam Kuppannayyangar Swami of Mandaya Agrahara... It is learnt that he was a *sahadhyāyi* of Sosale Ayyasastri (1854–1934), the son of the famous Samskrita scholar Sri Sosale Garalapuri Sastri. Ananthacharya stayed for some time at Badarinath, and on his way back, visited Tehri-Garhwal, Bikaner, Reva, Baroda, Thiruvananthapuram and Thanjavur, where he received high honours from the rulers. After his return to Mysore, he joined the Sadvidya Pathashala, and worked as a Samskrita Pandita... On 11-2-1921, he entered Samnyasashrama and became the head of Melkote Yathiraja Matha, founded by Sri Ramanujacharya, as the 36th Acharya of the Parampara... (His scholarly works are listed...) The Acharya left this world on 17-5-1943.

[321] M. Veṅkaṭakṛṣṇayya confirms [in Śāstri 1934, p. 23] that he studied *Saṁskṛta* for thirty years with Śrīkaṇṭha Śāstri.

known as the Normal School.[322] At this time, the Śāstri taught the *Saṁskṛta* portion for the *"Paṇḍita"* examination. Bhābhā *sāhēb,* who was Inspector General at the time, was well acquainted with the Śāstri's abilities.[323] He appointed him to the Textbook Committee, as well as Examiner for various Local Examinations, such as *"Paṇḍita"*, *"Upādhyāya"*, and for students who chose *Saṁskṛta* as a First Language.[324]

The Śāstri's renown as a scholar grew by the day. Since he had extraordinary mastery over grammar, persons with ordinary ability in grammar and those learned in fields such as logic and literature were ever hesitant to challenge him. Though he was as a lion in his scholarship, his nature was as meek as that of a cow. He never declared himself a scholar even when his self-interest was involved. He never applied to the government for a promotion, unlike the scholars of today. Pleased with his gentle nature, Bhābhā *sāhēb* himself raised his salary from thirty to forty-five *Rūpīs,* and encouraged him in many other ways, besides. Since he was an observant brāhmaṇa,

---

[322]Rice [1868] observes: "From this institution are derived the masters of the Government schools. It contains two classes in one of which the instruction is Anglo Vernacular and in the other purely Canarese. The course of study embraces besides the ordinary school subjects daily lessons on school management. Each student receives while under training an allowance of Rs. 9, 7, or 5 a month according to his standing and progress. Before appointment to a mastership he is required to pass an examination for a certificate of qualification. This test was adopted for the first time during the past year and has had a beneficial effect." Śrīkaṇṭha Śāstri taught in the Normal School for around 18–20 years [Śāstri 1934, p. 13]. This institution later became the "Training College".

[323]Hormusjī Jehangīr Bhābhā had been Head Master of the Mahārājā's College, and was appointed Education Secretary for Mysore on April 25, 1890, and Inspector General of Education in July 1895. He was the grandfather of the well-known physicist Homi Jehangīr Bhābhā.

[324]Śāstri [1925b, p. 24] documents that whenever the strictly observant Śrīkaṇṭha Śāstri went to Beṅgaḷūru for Textbook Committee work, he would refrain from eating in anyone's home, and would take along some pounded rice to sustain himself. Rice [1897b, p. 793] notes regarding this Committee: "...A Text book Committee has charge since 1892 of the selection and preparation of suitable school books...In 1887 the Mysore Local Examination for pupils and teachers in vernacular schools was instituted under the management of a Committee. This gave a definite aim to vernacular studies similar in effect to what was provided for English by the University and Middle School examinations and proved a great stimulus to the Taluq and Hobli schools. It was modified in 1891 by substituting a Lower Secondary examination in English, Sanskrit and the vernaculars with a Vernacular Upper Secondary and a Teachers Certificate examination. A Sanskrit Pandits examination is held every year before the Dasara at the Maharaja's Sanskrit College Mysore and an examination for Kannada Pandits was established in 1893."

a special exception was made for him, allowing him to report to work after one o'clock in the afternoon, after completing his bath, *Sandhyā,* and other daily rituals.[325]

We have seen that *Dharmādhikāri* Çakravartyayyaṅgār and the *Śrī* Śrīkṛṣṇa Brahmatantra Parakālasvāmi were his fellow-students. They knew the Śāstri's abilities well. They urged the Śāstri: "Dear Śāstri! Your knowledge of grammar is extraordinary. One is even led to believe that elements of the great Pāṇini himself are discernible in you. *Saṁskṛta* is among the hardest of languages to master. *Saṁskṛta* grammar is harder still. Verbal conjugations are truly the hardest. You have mastered grammar in its entirety, including the various commentaries. Write a book that details all known verbal conjugations in a form that would be accessible to the ordinary scholar." Encouraged thus, he toiled for seven or eight years and produced the *Dhāturūpaprakāśikā,* a massive and comprehensive compendium of all verbal conjugations. Since this work exceeded a thousand pages in length, he had despaired of ever having it published. Çakravartyayyaṅgār then stepped in, and had it published in his own publishing house, the Vidyātaraṅgiṇī Press.[326]

1891–1898

[325]This accommodation caused unhappiness among his fellow-workers, which Bhābhā dealt with cleverly [Śāstri 1934, p. 13]. He acknowledged the complaints, and agreed to replace Śrīkaṇṭha Śāstri if the complainants could find a scholar of equal calibre to replace him. Other accommodations that H.J. Bhābhā made for Śrīkaṇṭha Śāstri included bringing him on as a government employee when he was well past the mandatory retirement age of 55 (the rules required government service to start before age 25). Śrīkaṇṭha Śāstri remained a government employee till the age of 70, an unheard-of accommodation. Śāstri [1934, p. 38] reports that Bhābhā also purchased some number of copies of the *Dhāturūpaprakāśikā,* Śrīkaṇṭha Śāstri's magnum opus, published in 1898 C.E., and arranged for him to obtain nearly 1000 *Rūpīs* in return. Perhaps not coincidentally, Śrīkaṇṭha Śāstri moved that same year to a new house which he bought for 600 *Rūpīs* in the Rāmaçandra Agrahāra opposite the *Ānekarohaṭṭi* [Śāstri 1927, p. 1]. Till that time, Śrīkaṇṭha Śāstri had lived within the Maisūru fort, in a street called Kandukada Bīdi, near the Diḍḍī Bāgilu. This date differs from the date inferred from information on page 110.

[326]Amazingly, the *Dhāturūpaprakāśikā* was Śrīkaṇṭha Śāstri's second work on grammar. The educator and journalist M. Veṅkaṭakṛṣṇayya, reports [in Śāstri 1934, p. 23] that Śrīkaṇṭha Śāstri's first work, the *Tiṅantarūpāvali,* was misappropriated by a trusted friend, who published it as his own. The translator has been unable to locate this work. The *Dhāturūpaprakāśikā,* however, begins with verses rebuking this unnamed person: *"kārye duṣkaranirvāhe yatitvā yō–ticāpalāt | prōtsāhya māṁ śramaṁ nītvā pralōbhya phalagauravāt ‖4‖ madhyē–nyathā samāśvāsya kṛtārthassvayamanyathā | atyākṣīdudyamaṁ tatra svahānim nāpyajīgaṇat ‖5‖ matphalasyāyatiṁ bhavyāṁ vilambāddarśayanbahuṁ | chadmanāntē*

There is absolutely no way to comprehend the calibre of this work, or the effort that it entailed, without inspecting the book itself. This book has been thoroughly scrutinized and greatly lauded by numerous scholars of great repute, including *Vē*‖ *Gau*‖ A. Mahadēvaśāstri, who is curator of the Oriental Library, the Śrīkṛṣṇa Brahmatantra Parakālasvāmi, *Paṇḍitaratnaṁ* Kastūriraṅgāçār, *Paṇḍitaratnaṁ* Sītārāma Śāstri, Sajjaya Tātāçārya, S. Veṅkaṭarāmāśāstri of Mahārāja's College.[327] We do not provide details here due to lack of space.[328] Interested readers may examine the book and judge its merits.[329]

We are all familiar with the work well-known as the *Arabian Nights*, or as the *Yavanayāminī Vinōda Kathegaḷu* in English and Kannaḍa.[330] Upon being urged to convert this work into *Saṁskṛta*, the Śāstri proceeded to complete three-quarters of it. However, this work was not published owing to lack of subsequent interest on the part of those who were originally so encouraging.[331]

At this time, Çañçala Rāv, who was Councillor in the State of Maisūru, was accomplished in *Saṁskṛta*, but was not particularly strong in verbal conjugations. He had indicated to *Dīvān* Sir K. Śēṣādri Ayyar his interest in having a compendium of verbal conjugations published, if a person

---

nijāvāsaṁ vyajahāddeśamēva yaḥ ‖*6*‖ *guṇāṁstasya bahiṣkartuṁ kurvāṇasyēmamudyamaṁ* | *samīhitaṁ mē bhagavāntsandadhātu nṛkēsarī* ‖*7*‖*"* The *Dhāturūpaprakāśikā* was published in 1898 C.E., and is in Telugu script, not unusual for the time. Śrīkaṇṭha Śāstri would have been sixty-five years old, which would then have been reckoned a ripe old age. This monumental work has recently been published in *Devanāgari* script by Avadhūta Prakāśanaṁ of Sōmapuraṁ in Çikkamagaḷūru district in Karṇāṭaka, under the editorship of *Vidvān* So. Ti. Nāgarāja Śarma.

[327] Footnote in original (*re* Veṅkaṭarāmāśāstri): "He is the author of well known works such as the *Kathāśataka* and *Akṣaraśikṣā*. He possessed extraordinary scholarship in English as well as *Saṁskṛta*."

[328] Many of the persons mentioned above have expressed their admiration for this monumental work in their eulogies of Śrīkaṇṭha Śāstri [in Śāstri 1934].

[329] Footnote in original: "This book is priced at three *Rūpīs*. Interested persons may contact the editor of the Kādambarisaṁgraha in Maisūru. The book runs to a thousand pages of demi 8 size." The page size referred to is 8″ × 5.5″.

[330] The *Yavanayāminī Vinōda Kathegalu* is a version of the *Arabian Nights* in Kannaḍa by P. Veda-mitra, published at Mysore in 1905.

[331] M. Veṅkaṭakṛṣṇayya writes [in Śāstri 1934, p. 24] that he encouraged Śrīkaṇṭha Śāstri to write the *Saṁskṛta* version of the *Arabian Nights*, and that he had also planned to have him translate many *Saṁskṛta* works into Kannaḍa.

thoroughly knowledgeable in the subject were available.[332] Accordingly, the *Dīvān* discussed the matter with a group of *paṇḍitas,* but no one brought up the Śāstri's name. Many years later, when Śēṣādri Ayyar came across the *Dhāturūpaprakāśikā* after its publication, he sent for the Śāstri, recalled his conversation with Çaṅçala Rāv, and expressed much regret. After all, has it not been common for scholars, all through the ages, to look upon each other with envy? This point will be obvious to anyone who reads the story of Rāja Bhōja.[333]

By this time, the Śāstri's father, of his earlier *āśrama,* had attained salvation in Kāśī.[334] After a few years, the Śāstri's mother too, attained the Eternal State.

---

[332]Çaṅçala Rāv, known within the Mysore administration as the Honorable P. Chentsal Rao, C.I.E, held many significant administrative posts in the Madras Presidency, and was appointed member of the Council of His Highness the Maharaja of Mysore in April 1889. In 1890–91, the Council consisted of Chentsal Rao, Mr Thamboo Chetty, and *Dīvān* Śēṣādri Ayyar. See Sundaram [2012, p. 123] for a biography of Chentsal Rao.

[333]Bhōja is the king of Malwa referred to in footnote 147. According to legend, Bhōja lost his father Sindhula when still very young, and his uncle Muñja took the throne. Bhōja soon became a great scholar, and began to attract great acclaim. His uncle began to see him as a threat, and asked Vatsarāja, one of his tributary princes, to take the young Bhōja into the forest and kill him. Vatsarāja, who could not bring himself to murder the boy, hid him in his own house. When Muñja inquired as to what Bhōja said before his death, Vatsarāja showed him a palm leaf with the verse *"māndhatā sa mahīpatiḥ kṛta-yugālaṅkāra-bhūto gataḥ | seturyena mahodadhau virachitaḥ kvāsau dashāsyaāntakaḥ ‖ anyechāpi yudhiṣṭhira prabhṛtayo yātā divaṁ bhūpate | naikenāpi samaṁ gatā vasumatī manye tvayā yāsyati ‖".* This rebuke in this verse brought Muñja back to his senses. He was greatly relieved to learn that Bhōja was still alive, and in due course, abdicated in his favour.

[334]Śāstri [1925b, p. 55] gives the date of Śaṅkarānanda Svāmi's passing as "... *bahuḷa dvitīya* of the month of Vaiśākha of the Dhātu *saṁvatsara* (1874 C.E.)." We see an inconsistency. The *tithi* given corresponds to Wednesday, May 10, 1876 C.E., not to a date in 1874 C.E. Reference is made to the "previous *āśrama*", as a *saṁnyāsi* has no father, having renounced all worldly attachments. A *saṁnyāsi* is, in fact, ritually dead.

(a) Portrait of Kṛṣṇarāja Voḍeyar III seated.

(b) Equestrian portrait of Kṛṣṇarāja Voḍeyar III.

Plate 11: Portraits of Kṛṣṇarāja Voḍeyar III. Images from the San Diego Museum of Art.

Plate 12: Map of Maisūru north, 1876 C.E., from Rice [1877a].

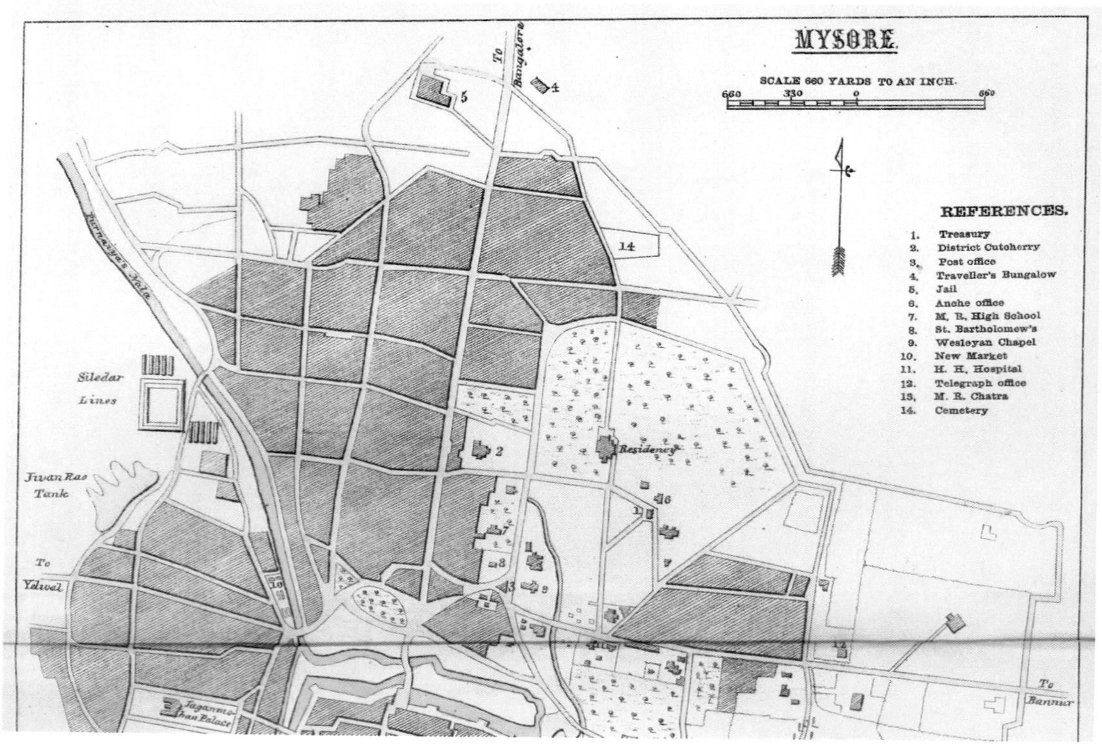

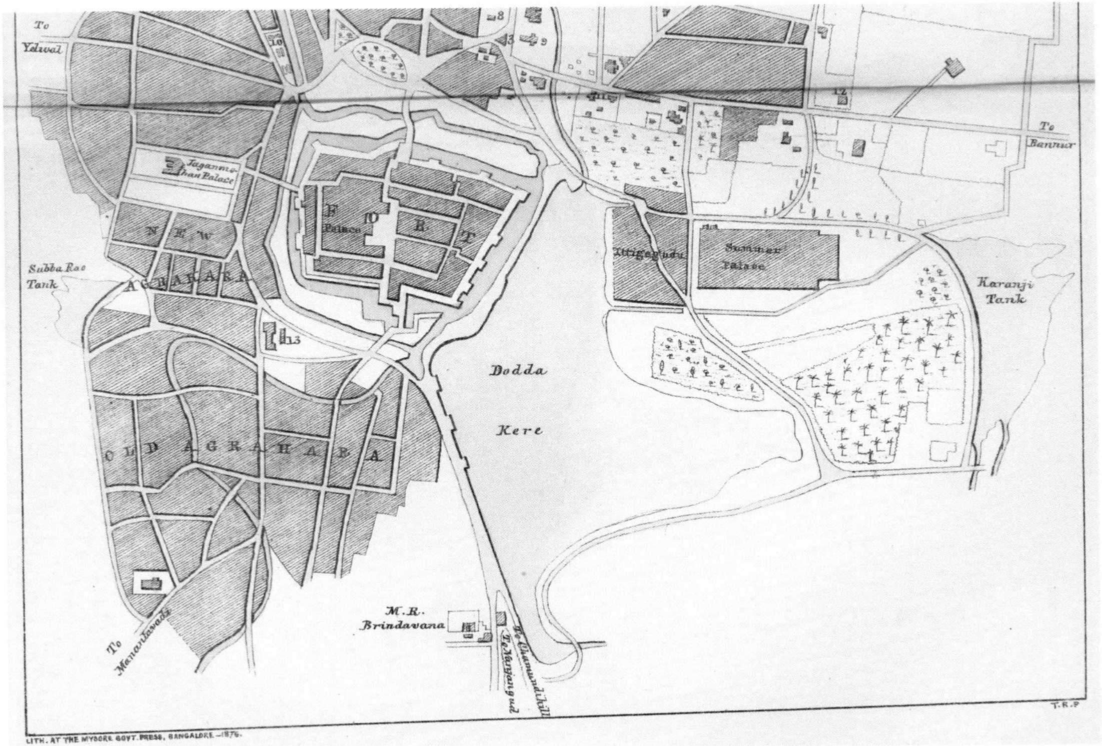

Plate 13: Map of Maisūru south, 1876 C.E., from Rice [1877a].

Plate 14: The interior of the Sōsale Vyāsarāja Maṭha, 2010. In earlier times, the floor would likely have been made of limestone plaster, rather than tile.

Plate 15: The Parakāla Maṭha in Maisūru. (Adapted by the translator, under a Creative Commons license, from an image of current façade by C.J. Fynn.)

Plate 16: Traditional house in Maisūru's Katvāḍipura Agrahara, where Garaḷapurī Śāstri built his house. This house belongs to Mr Gōpayya, who stands in the foreground, 2008.

(a) *Vyākaraṇa* Narasiṁha Śāstri

(b) Karūra Śrīnivāsāçārya, *Viśiṣṭādvaita* scholar.

(c) Kempu Śāstri

Plate 17: Some luminaries at the court of Kṛṣṇarāja Voḍeyar III. (Images by courtesy of Professor T.V. Venkatachala Sastri.)

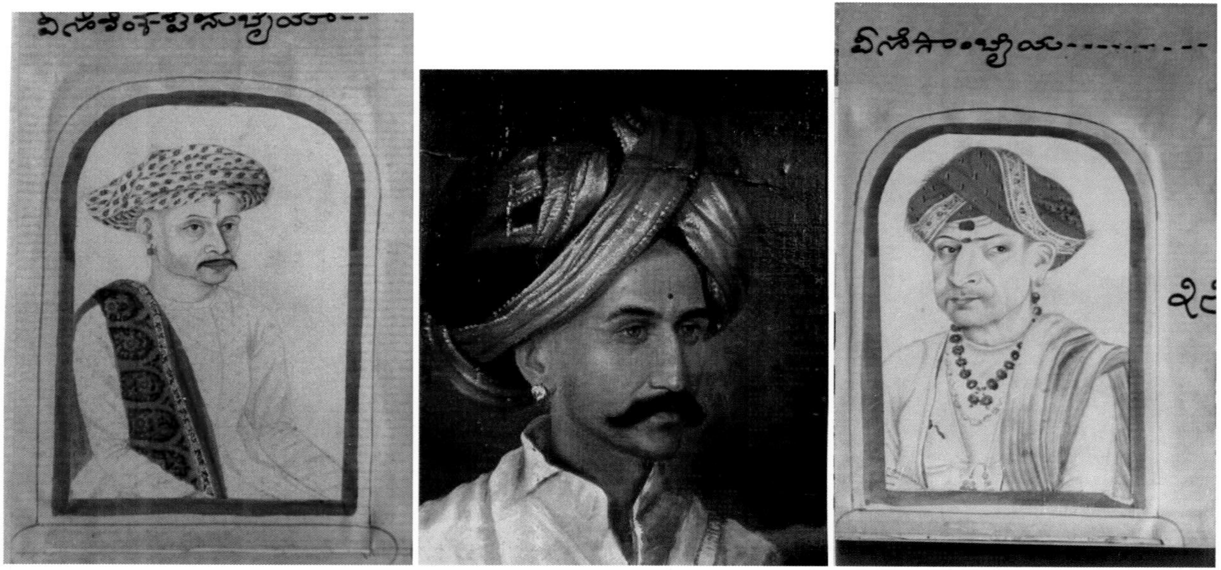

(a) *Vīṇe* Veṅkaṭasubbayya. *Vīṇā* expert and close confidant of the king.

(b) *"Çikka" Vīṇe* Śēṣaṇṇa.

(c) *Vīṇe* Sāmbayya. *Vīṇā* expert.

Plate 18: Some musicians at the Maisūru court. Images of Veṅkaṭasubbayya and Sāmbayya by courtesy of Mr Niranjana Rājē Arasu. Image of Śēṣaṇṇa by courtesy of Mr Soolamangalam Rammohan.

Plate 19: *Ubhaya Bhāṣā Vidvān* Perīsvāmi Tirumalaçārya, student of Sōsale Garaḷapurī Śāstri. Portrait at entrance to the Sadvidyāśāla.

Plate 20: *Aḷiya* Liṅgarājē Arasu. Original painting is in the possession of his grandson Mr Nirañjana Rājē Arasu of Maisūru.

Plate 21: Portrait of Bhāgavata Subba Rāv standing behing Kṛṣṇarāja Voḍeyar III. Note the striking similarities between this depiction of Kṛṣṇarāja Voḍeyar III and that in Plate 11(a), a representation of Kṛṣṇarāja Voḍeyar III which appears in many variants. It is unrealistic to expect that such portraits were painted from actual sittings with the monarch. This image is by courtesy of Mr Sunil Subbakrishna.

Plate 22: Portrait of *Dīvān* Pūrṇayya (1746–1812) by Thomas Hickey, c. 1800. Pūrṇayya had been *Dīvān* under Ṭippu Sultān, and following Ṭippu's defeat and death at the hands of the British in 1799, served as *Dīvān* to Kṛṣṇarāja Voḍeyar III till 1811. He was highly respected in the administrations of both Ṭippu and Kṛṣṇarāja Voḍeyar III for his administrative and financial acumen. He had kept the numerous restless local *pāḷeyagāras* in check, and at the time of his retirement in 1811, left the Maisūru treasury flush with cash to the extent of two crores of *Rūpīs* [Rice 1897b].

Plate 23: *Portrait of Three Princesses from Mysore*, by Thomas Hickey, *c.* 1805. Long believed to have been a painting of three courtesans in the Maisūru court, the painting's current title derives from strong arguments made by Chancellor [2001] that the subjects are in fact, royals. The lady on the left is believed to be *Paṭṭamahiṣī* Dēvājammaṇṇi, the seniormost queen of Kr̥ṣṇarāja Voḍeyar III, whom he married in 1801. The lady in white on the right, believed to be *Lakṣmīvilāsa Sannidhāna* Dēvājammaṇṇi, the second queen of Kr̥ṣṇarāja Voḍeyar III, draws attention to the region of her left arm where a vaccination against smallpox would have been administered. It is certain that she had been vaccinated, and that she became a symbol of the safety and value of the practice of vaccination [Row 1916]. The identity of the lady in the middle remains uncertain. See footnotes 596 and 599.

Plate 24: The Çāmarājeśvara temple at Çāmarājanagara. Image courtesy of www.goroadtrip.com.

(a) Kuṇigala Rāmaśāstri. Image courtesy of Professor T.V. Venkatachala Sastri.

(b) Tryambaka Śāstri. Image courtesy of Professor T.V. Venkatachala Sastri.

(c) Kāśī Śēṣa Śāstri. Frontispiece in Lakshminarasimhaiya *et al.*, [1970].

Plate 25: Kuṇigala Rāmaśāstri, Tryambaka Śāstri, and Kāśī Śeśa Śāstri (Rāmaśēṣa Śāstri).

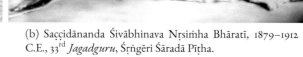

(a) Lakṣmīnarasiṁha Śāstri. Painting in the possession of Mr Kuṇigala Rāmaśāstri, Maisūru.

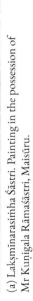

(b) Saççidānanda Śivābhinava Nṛsiṁha Bhāratī, 1879–1912 C.E., 33rd *Jagadguru*, Śṛṅgēri Śāradā Pīṭha.

Plate 26: Elder son and younger son of Kuṇigala Rāmaśāstri.

Plate 27: The Abhinava Śaṅkarālaya, a branch of the Śṛṅgēri Maṭha in Maisūru. The structure marks the birthplace of *Jagadguru* Saççidānanda Śivābhinava Nṛsiṁha Bhāratī, the spot where Kuṇigala Rāmaśāstri's house once stood.

8. Sorrows Without End

Let us recall that Veṅkaṭakṛṣṇaśāstri's household was resident in Cāmarājanagara. Śrīkaṇṭha Śāstri regularly visited Nagara, as occasioned by the need to perform obsequial rites for ancestors or worship rituals for divinities. On such occasions, he would also share words of advice and counsel with his son. Veṅkaṭakṛṣṇaśāstri has a daughter named Veṅkaṭalakṣmī and two sons named Narasiṁha and Veṅkaṭaramaṇa.[335] Veṅkaṭalakṣmī had now completed her tenth year, and was running her eleventh year. At this time, he had her married to Narasiṁhaśāstri,[336] the eldest son of a *śrōtrīya* brahmaṇa called Narasiṁhabhaṭṭa from Mattigūḍu, near Rāmanāthapura. This individual had achieved great proficiency in *Vēdic* recitation, ritual practice, literature, astrology, and *dharmaśāstra.*

Narasiṁha was his second-born. The Śāstri had taken him along to Maisūru when only four, and had been caring for him there, while also instructing him in the traditional manner. Having been born into a scholarly family, this boy had an excellent intellect. There is no more need to describe his manner of study! The third child was Veṅkaṭaramaṇa.[337] His father had tutored him since childhood. He was particularly adept at the *Amara,* declensions, and poetry. Veṅkaṭaramaṇa and Narasiṁha were two years apart. A daughter followed three years after Veṅkaṭaramaṇa. This child was named "Veṅkaṭasubbi", but everyone calls her "Subbatāyi" out of affection.[338] Thus, when this child was born, her elder sister was already in her husband's house, managing her own household. Veṅkaṭakṛṣṇaśāstri was in Nagara with his wife and family.

---

[335] This Veṅkaṭaramaṇa is of course, the author of this biography and of that of Garaḷapurī Śāstri.

[336] Footnote in original: "*Vē*‖ Narasiṁhaśāstri is now *jōḍidār* in Mattigūḍu in Hāsana district. He is a member of the Representative Assembly."

[337] This Veṅkaṭaramaṇa, of course, is the author of this biography and that of Garaḷapurī Śāstri.

[338] "Veṅkaṭasubbi" is a diminutive of "Veṅkaṭasubbamma". *Subba* in Kannaḍa is the *tadbhava* or vernacular adaptation of the *Saṁskṛta* word *Śubhra,* meaning "white" or "pure". "Subba" is a common male name in Karṇāṭaka, and refers to Ādiśeṣa, the lord of the realm of serpents, especially in the form "Subbarāya". "Subbamma" could be taken either as the feminine version of this reference, or instead, as meaning "the pure one". "Veṅkaṭa" is a common prefix, and is often elided in diminutive forms of names. *Tāyi* and *amma* both mean "mother", and are used in constructing affectionate or respectful forms of address.

All will recall that some twenty years ago, in the Viḷambi and Vikāri *saṁvatsaras* (1899–1900), the demoness Plague arrived in Maisūru, and began to sate her hunger, engorging herself on entire families. Many husbands lost their wives and children, and many ladies lost their husbands, and all suffered great sorrow at this time. The disease spread to all regions of Maisūru, and flames of anguish seared the entire country. Who would not be heartbroken at the death and desolation in Maisūru and Beṅgaḷūru? The sounds of lamentations everywhere! The scramble of funerary activities everywhere! Graveyards choked with people! Such cries of anguish! Such tales of suffering on everyone's lips! More often than not, it was the children who died right before the eyes of their elders. Surely, no household was spared suffering at the time, and if there were one or two, they have surely escaped our attention. This demoness first entered Ċāmarājanagara in the Vikāri *saṁvatsara*. Frightened, the people left town, becoming forest-dwellers. Undeterred, the demoness devoured lives enough to sate her hunger.[339]

Veṅkaṭakṛṣṇaśāstri's household, too, sheltered in a little hut at the time. Somehow, Providence saved them from danger that year. The *saṁvatsara* Śārvari arrived all too quickly. In those times, plague would drop into every town each year. Plague began as early as the month of Mārgaśira. As usual, everyone began leaving town. Only a handful of brave souls remained, having sent their families away to live with friends and relations elsewhere.

When Veṅkaṭakṛṣṇaśāstri wrote to his father, thinking it better to send his wife and children to Maisūru than force everyone to endure suffering in a little hut, our protagonist agreed to this course. It had been four
1900 years since Śrīkaṇṭha Śāstri had moved from his house in the fort to the Rāmacandra Agrahāra.[340] The administration demolished his house, which had been near the *Diḍḍī Bāgilu* on the eastern side of the

[339] The chances of surviving the disease were very low. According to testimony in March 1899 by Mr P.R. Cadeil before the Plague Commission [1900, p. 275], there occurred 4,000 plague cases and 3,298 deaths in Bangalore between 15th September 1888 and 28th February 1899, for a mortality rate of over 82%. In Maisūru, there were 1,930 plague cases and 1,519 deaths between 1st October 1898 and 28th February 1899, for a mortality rate of 78.7%. Plague was responsible for around half of all deaths during this period. The annual number of deaths in the state of Maisūru were 6,382 (in 1898), 6,629 (in 1899), 13,268 (in 1900), 11,936 (in 1901), 28,316 (in 1902), and 22,088 (in 1903), respectively [Sim̀pson 1905, p. 72].

[340] See footnote 325.

fort, and similarly razed to the ground other squalid areas that were focal points for the development of disease. The Government of Maisūru expended large sums of money, with the aim of somehow eradicating plague. After that time, this disease began to diminish gradually each year.[341]

The Śāstri had his daughter-in-law and grandchildren come to Maisūru in the *bahuḷa* half of Mārgaśira.[342] Veṅkaṭakṛṣṇaśāstri alone remained in Nagara. The need for final rites commonly arose unexpectedly, and he won the gratitude of the many people on whose behalf he performed them. No one in the region could match his skill in performing rites for the living or the dead. It was now the month of Puṣya. A telegram arrived from Nagara for the Śāstri at four in the afternoon, on the third.[343] It read: "Your son is ill with plague. Please leave immediately."

The grief of the Śāstri and his daughter-in-law upon receiving this news is beyond description. Wasting no time, the Śāstri left with everyone by

---

[341] See Parsons [1930, p. 135]:

> Less than 20 years ago the interior of the fort was a mass of houses and narrow streets. They were picturesque in the extreme. The streets of the brass-sellers (from which the vendors would always obligingly produce any kind of antique brass or copper utensil desired—given a fortnight to 'find' it), and the street of the flower-sellers were eminently so; masses of gorgeous colours against a background of dark and elaborately carved doors and windows. They were streets which, during Dasara and Birthday weeks, were thronged with Government House guests—royally mounted on elephants, or riding in barouches which almost filled the width of the narrow streets—bargaining with shopkeepers who naturally demanded extortionate prices from people so great.
>
> But the packed dwellings, however picturesque, were anything but healthy; plague broke out in 1898, and in that and the years that followed, again and again took a heavy toll of human lives. So a scheme for removing all inhabitants to higher, healthier sites, where each house should have air and light on at least two sides, where streets should be wide and tree-bordered, and where pure water and electric light should be supplied to even the poorest homes, was put in hand.
>
> Most of the uprooted Sirdars—whose houses in the fort resembled small fortresses—built spacious dwellings on the windswept uplands to the south-east of the city. For the poorer people land and facilities for building were given in the south-west extensions.

Similarly, Vāsudevāçārya [1962, p. 40] indicates that the houses in the fort were massively built, and that some wooden columns were so heavy as to have required two elephants to move. Residents of homes within the fort were allowed to purchase land outside the fort at the rate of 2 *Āṇe* per square foot [Śāstri 1927, p. 1].

[342] His daughter-in-law was Kṛṣṇamma (see page 102).

[343] That is, on the third *śukla tithi* of Puṣya of the Śarvari *saṁvatsara* (Monday, December 24, 1900).

the 5 o'clock train for Nañjanagūḍu. Three-fourths of the households in Çāmarājanagara lived in huts at this time; the town was very sparsely populated. People would come to town only at the time of the temple rituals, and then leave promptly. When the Śāstri arrived in Nagara the morning of the fourth, he found his helpless forty-eight-year-old son bedridden. Everyone was completely overcome by grief at this sight. But what does grief accomplish? They arranged for medical treatment. He begged Providence humbly to spare his only son. But what can mere Man do to thwart the Boatman of Time?

On the eighth day was the anniversary of the Śāstri's mother's death.[344] Here lay his son, incapable even of speech. Somehow or the other, and as quickly as he could, he completed the *śrāddha* rites for his mother. The sun slowly set. The moon rose in the heavens and spread its immortal rays across the world. Veṅkaṭakṛṣṇa gradually prepared to face death. The grandchildren were young! It was the dead of night! Concerned that they might be frightened, the Śāstri sent the three children to the home of Bank Agent *Ma*‖ Rāmaṇṇa, who lived across the street. Midnight too, came and passed. As dawn was breaking, Veṅkaṭakṛṣṇa's life departed this mortal world and vanished.[345] At his head was his father, and at his side was his wife, both enduring their grief and thinking of Nārāyana. Here lay the Śāstri's only son dead in his prime… Is further account needed of the father's grief and of that of the wife?

This pen deserves to be reduced to ashes! We are unable to write of what follows! Dear reader! This pen refuses to move! This tightness in this throat is unbearable! Tears of sorrow flow freely from these eyes! These events of seventeen years ago stand clearly before these eyes. A wretch is this writer! Here he sits, writing of his own father's death: his anguish is beyond control. Forgive him, it was not his intention to bring these matters up with you. It is his duty, however, to be honest in writing this biography. Do bear him out with patience.

After his son's death, the Śāstri returned to Maisūru with his widowed daughter-in-law, the fourteen-year-old Narasiṁha, the twelve-year-old Veṅkaṭaramaṇa and the eight-year-old Subbatāyi. Things must go on, as ever.

---

[344] Puṣya *śukla aṣṭamī* of Śarvari would be Saturday, December 29, 1900 C.E.

[345] This would have been Puṣya *śukla navamī*, or December 30, 1900 C.E.

After Śrīkaṇṭha Śāstri suffered the inconsolable loss of his son, his brother Rāmāśāstri came to to see him in Maisūru. No sooner had their eyes met, than grief descended on them, surging as a torrent of tears from the eyes of both these learned brothers.

9. Grandchildren's Progress. A Time of Change

Śrīkaṇṭha Śāstri was a man of courage. Consoling himself that such were the ways of the world, he devoted himself to the education of his grandchildren. Narasiṁha, his eldest grandson, had passed the Maisūru Lower-Secondary Examination in the First Class.[346] He now wanted to study English. The Śāstri, determined to educate him in the traditional areas of scholarship, stopped sending him to school. He also stopped sending his younger grandson to school, wanting him to study with his elder brother, and began to teach them both poetry and *Vēdic* recitation.

In the meanwhile, the Government decided to impose retirement on the Śāstri when he turned seventy in 1903, although he remained fully capable of teaching.[347] The Śāstri petitioned for a continuance of his term of service on the grounds that he would remain competent to teach for many more years. This petition was not granted. The Śāstri then applied for his grandson Narasiṁha to be appointed as a teacher in the A.V. School in Çāmarājanagara, considering that he had passed his *Prathama* examination in Kannaḍa.[348] This request was approved. However, Narasiṁha did not agree to this course. Not wanting to start working at such a young age at such a low salary, he now expressed a preference for working towards his Upper Secondary Examination,[349] were he to be granted the same amount as a scholarship. That request was approved. Given the acuity of his intellect, he passed the examination for a Teaching Certification within two years, finishing at the top of his class. By this time, the Śāstri had taught both his grandchildren the cantos of Māgha as well as the *Naiṣadha*.[350]

---

[346] This corresponds to the eighth grade or standard, which was the last grade before High School. At the time, it was possible to finish school with a "Lower-Secondary" certificate (commonly referred to as "LS").

[347] See footnote 325.

[348] The *Prathama* examination typically certifes the first level of competence in a field, usually a language. Subsequent levels may progress from *Dvitīya* to *Viśārada*. The A.V. School would be the Anglo-Vernacular School in Çāmarājanagara.

[349] The usual "High School" course of study.

[350] This refers to the twenty cantos of the *Śiśupāla Vadha* by Māgha and the *Naiśadhaçarita* by the 12th-century poet Śrīharṣa. Also see footnote 226.

A surprising turn of events occurred in Maisūru at this time. We may recall that Śrīkaṇṭha Śāstri had joined the ranks of the palace scholars when he was twenty-eight. One day, our present king Kṛṣṇarāja Voḍeyar IV personally reviewed a list of palace scholars, their accomplishments, and details of how long they had served in their capacity.[351] The king used to be taught Kannaḍa and *Saṁskṛta* by Sōsale Ayyā Śāstri, who was Śrīkaṇṭha Śāstri's son-in-law. On some occasion, when Ayyā Śāstri was away on leave, he had asked his father-in-law to substitute for him. Our king, having studied with our protagonist, came to know his abilities well. Çāmarāja Voḍeyar X, the father of our king, had also entrusted the education of our king and the *Yuvarāja* to our protagonist.[352] The Śāstri would instruct these these two children, aged six and eight, in various elementary subjects, including material that they were to commit to memory. Remembering this well, and being generous and a great patron of scholarship, our king ordered that he be appointed to the rank of *Mahāvidvān.* He obtained a salary commensurate with this status.

Deciding to return to Çāmarājanagara after he became a pensioner, he went there with his younger grandson Veṅkaṭaramaṇaśāstri. There, he instructed him in subjects such as the *Ṛgveda Saṁhita*, the *Aṣṭādhyāyī*, and *śikṣā*.[353] He would also ensure that he constantly reviewed the poetry he had learned in Maisūru. During this time, this boy studied Kannaḍa on his own, on the strength of his knowledge of *Saṁskṛta.* He also subscribed to various Kannaḍa magazines, and began to write in Kannaḍa. The Śāstri did not approve of this course. However, he remained silent, not wanting to become an obstacle in his path.

His grandchildren were both married by this time, so their wives were at home, as well. Following his Upper Secondary, Narasiṁhaśāstri had also completed various certifications, such as in Training and Drawing. Śrīkaṇṭha Śāstri applied to the Government to find him a position in Çāmarājanagara on this basis, and they happily obliged.

---

[351] Kṛṣṇarāja Voḍeyar IV (1884–1940 C.E.) ascended to the throne in 1894 C.E.

[352] These children were Kṛṣṇarāja Voḍeyar IV and *Yuvarāja* Kaṇṭhīrava Narasiṁharāja Voḍeyar, his younger brother and heir to the throne. These princes were both sons of Çāmarāja Voḍeyar X by Mahārāṇī Kempa Nañjammaṇṇi, Vāṇī Vilāsa *Sannidhāna.*

[353] The *Ṛgveda Saṁhita* is the metrical portion of the *Ṛgveda.* The *Aṣṭādhyāyī* is Pāṇini's work on *Saṁskṛta* grammar. *Śikṣā* is the science of proper pronunciation and articulation of the *Vēdas.*

Śrīkaṇṭha Śāstri's entire family lived in Çāmarājanagara in 1908. Narasiṁha Śāstri and Veṅkaṭaramaṇa Śāstri were employed as teachers in the A.V. School and in the *Saṁskṛta* Pāṭhaśālā, respectively. The Śāstri was teaching them both grammar at this time.

Kṛṣṇamma, the Śāstri's daughter-in-law, was now in charge of household matters. Everything functioned as she directed. The Śāstri was devoted entirely to his own studies, teaching his grandchildren, his daily rituals and worship, and to spiritual matters. He had distanced himself from worldly discord.

"Kālasya kuṭilā gatiḥ."[354] We seem to be returning often to the topic of Time! Time operates in strange ways, indeed. No one could stand firm to oppose its course. Time has no compassion. It cares little for who is rich, who is learned, or who is good. It should be clear to our readers that Time has been especially cruel to our protagonist. Going forward, Time showed particular intransigence with regard to the Śāstri.

In 1909, on the seventh *śuddha tithi* of the month of Vaiśākha in the Saumya *saṁvatsara*, Veṅkaṭaramaṇaśāstri's wife passed away in Mattigūḍu, near Rāmanāthapura, after giving birth to a daughter.[355] It is impossible to describe the Śāstri's grief. Bearing this with fortitude, he had had Veṅkaṭaramaṇaśāstri married to the daughter of Gaṇapatiśāstri of Çāmarājanagara on the tenth *śuddha tithi* of the month of Śrāvaṇa of the very same year.[356] Strange indeed were Veṅkaṭaramaṇaśāstri's fortunes. Whether this was designed to increase the Śāstri's grief, or due to Veṅkaṭaramaṇaśāstri's ill fortune, or for some other reason, we cannot say. But this girl, too, died of the plague within two months of her marriage. Now ensued a battle between *Kālapuruṣa* and the omniscient Śāstri.[357] The one was all-knowing, the other a master of deception. But could the master of subterfuge stand firm before the omniscient? Subduing *Kāla*, the Śāstri arranged for Veṅkaṭaramaṇaśāstri to wed a girl from Śrīraṅgapaṭṭaṇa in the month of Māgha that same year.[358]

---

[354] "Time flows in devious ways." The original is *"apsu plavante pāṣāṇā mānuṣā ghnanti rākṣasān | kapayaḥ karma kurvanti kālasya kuṭilā gatiḥ ‖"*

[355] The given *tithi* corresponds to April 26, 1909 C.E. In keeping with South Indian custom, the wife would have been in her father's house for the child's birth.

[356] See Plate 28. The *tithi* given corresponds to July 27, 1909 C.E.

[357] *Kāla-puruṣa* ("death-person") may be taken to mean either Death personified, or as Death's messenger.

[358] The individuals in Plate 28, as identified by Sarōjā Veṅkaṭarām, granddaughter of

Plate 28: Veṅkataramaṇa Śāstri's second wedding, 1909 C.E. The bride sits at extreme right next to the turbaned bridegroom. See footnote 358 for the names of the individuals in this photograph. Image courtesy Smt. Pārvatī Upavarṣa, granddaughter of Veṅkataramaṇa Śāstri.

Kālapuruṣa became ever more resentful of the Śāstri. To sate his grudge, he opposed himself to the Śāstri by assuming the name *Virōdhikṛt*, and on the fourteenth *śukla tithi* of Vaiśākha, seized as sacrifice the mortal body of the Śāstri's younger brother *Āsthāna Mahāvidvān* Çāmarājanagara Rāmāśāstri.[359] The Śāstri now burned with regret at having challenged someone as base as *Kāla*. Recalling the saying *"alparasaṅga abhimānabhaṅga"*,[360] he refused to engage this base individual, and thinking only of the deep regard he had for his brother, composed several *çaramaślōkas* on him. We give only one of these here.[361]

aham'apy'anuyāsyāmi bhavantam'açirād'iva |
vatsa rāma mayi prītiṁ nijān'draḍhaya mānasē ||

Meaning: Dear child! Rāma! Ever keep in mind my love for you! My only wish is to follow you!

What love the Śāstri had for his brother! What compassion! How unbearable his sorrow! What a paragon of brotherly affection! Bravo! An exalted Self! Bravo! An ample example of brotherly love!

Ayyā Śāstri: *Standing, L–R:* Subbamma (wife of Narasiṁhaśāstri, who is seated to her left), Veṅkaṭalakṣamma (daughter of Ayyā Śāstri), Veṅkaṭasubbamma ("Subbatāyi", sister of Narasiṁhaśāstri, daughter-in-law of Ayyā Śāstri), Lakṣmīdevamma (wife of Ayyā Śāstri, daughter of Śrīkaṇṭha Śāstri), *Seated on chairs, L–R:* Narasiṁhaśāstri (grandson of Śrīkaṇṭha Śāstri), Veṅkaṭalakṣmī (with baby, elder sister of Narasiṁhaśāstri and wife of Mattigūḍu Narasiṁhaśāstri), Mattigūḍu Narasiṁhaśāstri, Çāmarājanagara Veṅkaṭaramaṇaśāstri (bridegroom), Veṅkaṭaramaṇaśāstri's bride (second wife). *Seated on ground, L–R:* unknown girl in the background (daughter of Narasiṁhaśāstri?), Māṇikyā (eldest daughter of Veṅkaṭalakṣamma, granddaughter of Ayyā Śāstri), Subbamma (Ayyā Śāstri's daughter-in-law, wife of Kṛṣṇasvāmiśāstri), Śēśagiri (Veṅkaṭalakṣamma's third son), Veṅkaṭaramaṇayya (Śeśagiri's elder brother, also called "Subbaṇṇa"), Śāmaṇṇa (Veṅkaṭalakṣamma's second son), Lalitā (Veṅkaṭalakṣamma's youngest daughter)

[359] *Virōdhikṛt* means "The Opposer". Virōdhikṛt is also the name of a *saṁvatsara* in the South Indian calendar. The given *tithi* corresponds to May 12, 1911 C.E.

[360] "Keeping company with the dishonorable leads to naught but dishonour."

[361] These *ślōkas* appear in Śāstri [1925b, p. 83]: *"vidvadvṛndair aśeṣairvinutasukavitāsīmapāṇḍityagehai | śrīkṛṣṇabrahmatantrāṅkitavara parakālākhya karmandivaryaiḥ || bhūyobhūyassaharṣaṁ praçalita śirasā śyāghyamānātyudāra | śeṣotprekṣāpratīpaprabhṛti bahuvidhālaṁkṛti prauḍhamedhaḥ ||1|| śrīmatçāmedra kṛṣṇakṣitipa nṛpasabha prollasaççhoṇaratnaṁ | vidvaddhṛdyānavadyābhinavakaviçaḥ prauḍhapadyādhvanīnaḥ || jātorāmassumedhāssurasadasi mahāvaiduṣīślāghanīyaḥ | lokāślokān yatheṣṭaṁ raçayatakavayaḥ prākṛtaślāghanīyān ||2|| yathābaroḍāprabhuṇihayo bhavatkavitvam ākarṇa jaharṣanirbharaṁ | tadvatsarāmādya sa çāmarāṭṭathā niśamyahṛṣyatyahi vidviṣādivi ||3|| ahamapi anuyāsyāmi bhavantamaçirādiva | vatsarāma mayiprītiṁ nijāndhraḍayamānase ||4||"*

10. The King's Favour

We recall that Narasiṁha Śāstri is now working as Assistant Teacher at the school in Çāmarājanagara. At this time, he was invited by the Government to obtain his *Paṇḍita* certification from the Normal School in Maisūru.[362] Narasiṁha Śāstri went alone to Maisūru to complete his course of study. Veṅkaṭaramaṇa Śāstri lived with his grandfather in Nagara, and continued his *Vēdic* studies while working as instructor at the *Saṁskṛta* School there. He started the monthly magazine *Kādambarīsaṅgraha* in 1912. Narasiṁhaśāstri obtained his *Paṇdita* certification in a timely manner, and returned to Nagara. The Śāstri's income being modest, and there being many hindrances to the smooth publication of his monthly, Veṅkaṭaramaṇa Śāstri came to Maisūru with his grandfather's permission.

On November 1st, 1913, the Kannada teacher in the Marimallappa High School happened to be on leave. At this time, *Ma*‖ M. Veṅkaṭakṛṣṇayya, a great admirer of learning, having heard accounts of Veṅkaṭaramaṇa Śāstri's learning through others, sent for him and asked him to begin work as a Kannaḍa *paṇḍita.* He knew the all-round scholarship of Śrīkaṇṭha Śāstri very well. Even to this day, he continues to foster Veṅkaṭaramaṇa Śāstri, engaging with him on discussions of the Śāstri's scholarship, and sharing with him many valuable suggestions related to teaching. The writer wishes to salute and acknowledge his gratitude to the Headmaster.[363]

At this time, Kuṭṭanarasiṁhaśāstri, who held the title of *Dharmādhikāri* at the palace, passed away.[364] Our king, personally considering the question of who was deserving of the title of *Dharmādhikāri,* selected our protagonist, as a great scholar and fully qualified for the honour.

Narasiṁha Śāstri, of course, was still in Nagara. His income was insufficient to sustain his household. Śrīkaṇṭha Śāstri had remained in Maisūru, having to visit the palace frequently after his appointment as *Dharmādhikāri.* The Śāstri was concerned that his family continued to face financial

[362] This school trained teachers. See footnote 322.

[363] M. Veṅkaṭakrsṇayya served as Headmaster for thirty-five of the forty-three years he worked at the Marimallappa School. He became a revered figure in Maisūru, and was affectionately known as *Maisūru Tātayya*, or "Maisūru Grandfather". See page 104.

[364] Kuṭṭi Narasiṁha Śāstri was the son of Kuṭṭi Śāstri, who also had been *Dharmādhikāri.* See footnotes 573 and 589.

hardships, and that his grandchildren's earnings were not commensurate with their learning. He wrote about his grandchildren's situation to *Ma*‖ M. Śāmrāv, then Inspector General of the Maisūru Department of Education, and who had earlier studied *Saṁskṛta* with him. We give the letter here for the information of our readers.

ślō ‖
śyāmarāyaś'çirāyus'syāt saha·putra·prapautrakaḥ |
mahāmātra·padē sthitvā jagad'rakṣaṇa·dakṣiṇaḥ ‖1‖

vēdē śāstrē pravīṇān avitari viduṣi sthūla·lakṣyē kudaivā
j'jātē svarg'āvataṁsē yadu·kula·tilakē kṛṣṇa·rājē tṛtīyē |
tatpautrē rakṣati kṣmāṁ sadasi saçivatām'ētya rakṣan budhēndrān
jīyāç'çhri śyāmarāyas'saha·suta·sasutaḥ pūrṇa·kāmaś'çirāyuḥ ‖2‖

yaṁ kañçit samayaṁ prapāṭhya mahatīṁ prāptaḥ pratiṣṭhāṁ jaga·
ty'ēṣō–dya sthavirōbhavan budhamaṇiḥ śrīkaṇṭha·śarmā budhaḥ |
lōkādṛtya·kalā·pravīṇa·sasut'ānālamba·pautra·dvayaḥ
sīdan' prārthayatē bhavantam'adhunā vidyāvatāṁ jīvitam ‖3‖

alpīyasī sthāvira·jīvikā mē nālaṁ tath'ālpaṁ nija·vētanaṁ'ça |
ēvaṁ viniśçitya jagat·pratīta·kalā·vidagdhatvam' avāpatus'tau ‖4‖

gurau purāṇē mayi pakṣapātā·t'svatantra·suślāghya·padē niviṣṭaḥ |
vatsāv'ih'ēmāv'açirān'madīyaṁ padam bhavān prāpayat'iti manyē ‖5‖

triṁśad'anyūna·rūpyāṇi bhṛtir'yatra na tatpadam |
na kāṁkṣati pravīṇatvāt' pautrō jyāyān kalāsu mē ‖6‖

rājājñ'ōddiṣṭa·vidyāsu niṣṇātas'suçiraṁ mama |
pautraḥ kutsayatē matka·bhavad'ēkānta·saṁgatam ‖ 7‖

yath'aitat'kutsanaṁ mēdya na syāt kṛtvā tathā bhavān |
mahāmātr'ādhikār'ārhō bhavatv'ity'arthayē–niśam ‖8‖

pañçōnapañçāśad'rūpyāṇy'āsan mē vētanaṁ purā |
tat·padaṁ nēṣyas'īmaṁ drāg' iti manyē dṛḍhaṁ vibhō ‖9‖

mahīsūra·purī	*iti bhavataḥ śrēy'ābhilāśī*
ānanda·saṁvatsara	*çā* ‖ *śrīkaṇṭha·śāstri.*

A paraphrase of this in Kannaḍa is as follows.

May Śāmrāv, who is devoted to the service of the people, live long, together with his children and grandchildren. ‖1‖

May Śāmrāv, who protects scholars and graces his ministerial position in the reign of the grandson who rules after the ascension to heaven of Kṛṣṇarāja Voḍeyar III, ornament to the Yadu race and great patron of learning, live a long and exalted life, his wishes fulfilled, and in the company of his children and grandchildren. ‖2‖

A scholar named Śrīkaṇṭha Śāstri, having spent his time on teaching his students and attaining some distinction, is now aged, but has two grandchildren who have families but insufficient income. Both his grandchildren are learned in fields that are valued in this world. Therefore, this old man makes this request of you, who provide livelihood to the learned. ‖3‖

These two grandchildren, considering that their aged grandfather's income is meager, have attained scholarship in the currently valued fields of Kannaḍa and *Saṁskṛta.* ‖4‖

Being in a distinguished position of independent authority, and out of regard for me as your former teacher, I am hopeful that you will be able to appoint my grandchildren to the position I once occupied. ‖5‖

My elder grandson being well-learned in Kannaḍa and *Saṁskṛta,* believes it would be unbefitting to accept a salary of less than thirty *Rūpīs.* ‖6‖

Having passed all his examinations in accordance with the Government's directives, he now urges me to request the benevolent Śāmrāv to find him an appointment. ‖7‖

I trust that you, who are in a position of authority, will be able to oblige me in accordance with his wishes. ‖8‖

My salary in the Normal School was forty-five *Rūpīs.* I am hopeful that you will definitely appoint him to that position. ‖9‖

Maisūru — wishing for your greater acclaim
Āṣāḍha *māsa,* Ānanda *saṁvatsara* — Çā ‖ Śrīkaṇṭhaśāstri.

This letter reached *Ma*‖ *Rā*‖ Śāmrāv in a timely manner. He read it, and on account of his great regard for the Śāstri, appointed Narasiṁha at a salary of twenty-five *Rūpīs,* although deserving of more, and transferred him to the Normal School in Maisūru. In a short while, in accordance with new Government rules fixing the salary for all Kannaḍa teachers at thirty *Rūpīs,* Narasiṁha Śāstri began to receive a salary of thirty *Rūpīs.* In due course, he is certain to qualify for the position that Śrīkaṇṭha Śāstri held, and we have every expectation that his salary will soon match the amount the Śāstri received.

Let us now recall that our king, after deep reflection and consideration, had appointed Śrīkaṇṭha Śāstri to the position of *Dharmādhikāri.* As the Śāstri, immersed in an ocean of joy at the unbidden benevolence of the king, fervently wished for his greater glory, reflecting again and again upon his generosity, compassion, and commitment to scholarly patronage, the gratitude in his heart expressed itself in the form of several *ślōkas.* He had Veṅkaṭaramaṇa Śāstri write down these *ślōkas,* which issued forth spontaneously. He now wanted to recite these *ślōkas* himself, in the king's presence. Veṅkaṭaramaṇ Śāstri had these verses and their meaning published, as the Śāstri's directed, as a book with the title *Mahārājābhyudayapraśaṁsā.*

It is, of course, impossible for the common man to have an audience with the king. Śrīkaṇṭha Śāstri had the book published, but how was he now to fulfill his wish to read it before the king and express his gratitude? Upon discussing this matter with several officials at the palace, they recommended that he apply to the king's Private Secretary. After the Śāstri accordingly submitted his request, an envelope arrived from the Office of the Private Secretary at ten in the morning of the ninth *śuddha tithi* of Āṣāḍha of the Ānanda *saṁvatsara.*[365] Upon being opened, it read as follows:

> The Palace
> Maisūru
>
> To *Dharmādhikāri* Śrīkaṇṭha Śāstri.
>
> Your application was received. Upon being presented with it, His Majesty was pleased to grant you an audience between 1 O'clock and 2 O'clock in the afternoon of *Prathamēkādaśi,* and to hear a reading of the verses you have composed.[366] You are requested to favour us with your presence accordingly.

The Śāstri, elated upon learning the contents of the letter, called out: "Veṅkaṭaramaṇa! Come here!", and as his grandson too was delighting in the letter, said to him: "The king's command is that he wishes to hear my *ślōkas.* Rather than go to the palace alone, it appears better for me to take you with me, have you read the *ślōkas,* and explain their meaning myself.

[365] This date corresponds to July 2, 1914 C.E.

[366] *Prathama ekādaśi* is the name given to the eleventh *śukla tithi* in the month of Āṣāḍha.

(a) H.H. Kṛṣṇarāja Voḍeyar IV.

(b) Yuvarāja Kaṇṭhīrava Narasiṁharāja Voḍeyar

(c) Mirza Ismail

Plate 29: Kṛṣṇarāja Voḍeyar IV, his brother Kaṇṭhīrava Narasiṁharāja Voḍeyar, and Personal Secretary Mirza Ismail.

(a) Procession at the marriage of H.H. Yuvarāja Kanṭhīrava Narasiṁharāja Voḍeyar to H.H. Kempu Çeluvammaṇṇiyavaru, June 17, 1910. Construction of this new palace began after the fire of 1897, and was completed in 1912.

(b) Karikallu Toṭṭi reception area in the new palace.

Plate 30: Palace facade and the Karikallu Toṭṭi around the time of Śrīkaṇṭha Śāstri's visit in 1914 C.E. The current facade of the palace differs from that seen above. By permission of the British Library.

You have never had the opportunity to visit the palace. Our family has been well known to the Palace since the reign of Kṛṣṇarāja Voḍeyar III. The two of you (grandchildren) will need the Palace's patronage in the future. The king is well acquainted with the scholarly tradition within our family. You must maintain this reputation going forward. Be ready by noon on the day after tomorrow. Let us go to the palace together," and proceeded for his bath.

The day of *Prathamēkādaśi* arrived. The Śāstri and his grandson Veṅkaṭaramaṇa completed their baths, daily rituals, and *pūjas* by ten that morning, and readied themselves to go to the palace. They both wrapped on their turbans, and wearing shawls and crisp dhotīs, arrived at the *Karīkallu Toṭṭi* with *phalamantrākṣate* in their hands at half past noon.[367] The officer in attendance seated them, and informed Private Secretary Mirzā *sāhēb* of their arrival.[368] Mirzā *sāhēb* arrived immediately, and respectfully inquiring after the Śāstri's well-being and that of Veṅkaṭaramaṇa Śāstri, conveyed news of their arrival to the king's presence. The king, observing that it was nearly one o'clock, and thinking to himself: "The Śāstri is fasting today, since it is *Ekādaśi*. He is advanced in years. He must be very tired, having been asked to come here today," directed Mirzā *sāhēb* to request the Śāstri to come up if he weren't too tired. Accordingly, Mirzā *sāhēb* asked the Śāstri to proceed upstairs, and began ascending the stairs himself.

[367] This is the traditional formal dress in Karnāṭaka. See the picture of Śrīkaṇṭha Śāstri in the frontispiece. The *Karīkallu Toṭṭi* ("black stone courtyard") is one of the entrances to the palace. See Plate 30b. (British Library notes accompanying this photograph: "The room is at the extreme end of the Palace on the west. Its construction is in the Hindu style, with carved wooden pillars, spaced 10 feet every way, connected at top with arched carved panels, and roofed with ceiling planks. It is furnished in the European style, and is the room chiefly used by the late Maharaja for receiving visitors and the chief officers of state.") *Phalamantrākṣate* is a gift of coconut and fruits, accompanied by a benediction in the form of *mantrākṣate*, which are whole grains of rice (*"akṣata"* meaning "unbroken"), dyed with turmeric and consecreated with *mantras*. These are cast on a person while delivering a benediction. Also see footnote 152 for a different meaning of *akṣate*.

[368] This "Mirzā *sāhēb*" is none other than Mirzā Ismail, a distinguished public servant who became Private Secretary to Kṛṣṇarāja Voḍeyar IV after R.H. Campbell retired from service in 1912 C.E. He went on to serve as *Dīvān* of Mysore 1926–1941 C.E., *Dīvān* of Jaipur 1942–1946 C.E., and *Dīvān* of Haiderābād 1946–1947 C.E. Mirza Ismail's family came to India from Iran in the 1800s, and sold horses to the British and regional armies. The family had always been close to the Voḍeyars, and Mirza Ismail and Kṛṣṇarāja Voḍeyar IV were even classmates at the Royal School [Gundappa 1970, v. 4, p. 149].

When Veṅkaṭaramaṇa Śāstri began to follow them, the *Sāhēb* asked him to remain behind. When Śrīkaṇṭha Śāstri politely requested the *Sāhēb:* "It is important that he remain with me. May it please you to allow that," he was pleased to conduct them both to the king's chamber, and leaving them outside, went into the room, informed the king, returned, and indicating that the Śāstri should proceed into the room, and that Veṅkaṭaramaṇa Śāstri could enter if the king so directed, sent the Śāstri into the room, and returned downstairs. Veṅkaṭaramaṇa Śāstri seated himself next to a curtain near the door.

Since our readers may be interested in seeing the Maisūru palace, it would not be out of place to say a few things in that regard. Certainly, all visitors to Maisūru will have seen the marvellous palace within the fort. The present structure was only recently built. The old palace was not as robust as the present building. After it burned down, the present beautiful stone structure was built at an expense of crores.[369] Some parts of the old palace remain. That point is what we must now elaborate.

The palace facade, as it now appears, is called the *sejje*. The royal darbār is held on the second floor during the Navarātri festivities. That is familiar to all. If one enters the palace, turns left, and walks a few steps, one beholds the magnificent *maṇṭapa* of Bhuvanēśvarī. The *darbar* is also held here, on occasion. Upon ascending the staircase to Bhuvanēśvarī's left, one arrives at the royal *maṇṭapa* called the Ambā Vilāsa. This is a unique sight. Nowhere else does such an attractive structure exist. Across from the Ambā Vilāsa is the Çāmuṇḍī Toṭṭi.[370] Here are performed daily *ahōrātra abhiśēkas, pūjās*, various sacraments, *japās, tapas*, and *Vēdic* recitations, for Çāmuṇḍēśvarī, our king's family deity. To the Çāmuṇḍī Toṭṭi belong many officials and great scholars.[371] The palace also has many other sections, including the

[369]The old palace was erected in 1799 C.E., when the Vodeyar dynasty was restored after the death of Ṭippu Sultān in the Fourth Mysore war. This palace was constructed primarily of wood, and partially burned in February 1897 C.E., during the wedding of Princess Jayalakṣammaṇṇī and M. Kaṇṭharāj Arasu, who went on to become *Dīvān* of Mysore. The current palace is a stone structure designed by Henry Irwin, and was completed in 1912 C.E., at a cost of approximately 4.1 million *Rūpīs*.

[370]The term *toṭṭi* is best translated as "courtyard", and can have various meanings. It may, for instance, refer to the apartments within the palace of the various queens. In other contexts, it refers to administrative units of the palace.

[371]The Çāmuṇḍī Toṭṭi had a significant religious function. In 1868 C.E., when the palace

Sammukhada Toṭṭi, Madanavilāsada Toṭṭi, Kannaḍi Toṭṭi, and the Karikallu Toṭṭi.

To the west of Bhuvanēśvarī is the Kannaḍi Toṭṭi. Here are performed during Navarātri many *japas, pārāyaṇas,* and worship rituals for Çāmuṇḍī. During this time, the king presents himself both morning and evening, at the time of *dīpārādhane* for the deity.

To the west of the Kannaḍi Toṭṭi is the Karīkallu Toṭṭi.[372] Across from the Lakṣmīramaṇasvāmi temple in the fort is the large door that leads to the Karīkallu Toṭṭi. On special occasions, such as the king's birthday, ceremonies such as *ārati* and *akṣate* are performed here. The offices of the king's Private Secretary are in the Karīkallu Toṭṭi. A fortress wall runs next to it, and a charming garden faces this *toṭṭi.* If one enters through the door opposite the Jaganmōhana Palace and turns right, one sees the garden mentioned above on the right and the Karīkallu Toṭṭi on the left. This *toṭṭi* is so called because it is built entirely of black stone. On the upper floor of this *toṭṭi,* facing the garden, are visible many large windows. These windows are covered with thin curtains of silk. Inside the Karīkallu Toṭṭi is a staircase. If we ascend this staircase and turn left, we espy a small apartment. This small apartment is the king's residence.

Śrīkaṇṭha Śāstri entered here, and was seated on a cane couch before the king. The king, whose compassion is boundless, reminisced with the Śāstri about many matters, starting with his early years of education down to the present. When the Śāstri, amazed that the king had remembered such details, profusely praised the king's virtues and his generosity, declared his eternal gratitude for having been favoured with the status of *Dharmādhikāri,* and said that he had composed some *ślōkas* in his praise, and that he had brought along his grandson to read them, the king said: "*Oho!* Where is he, then? Why did he not come in?" to which the Śāstri responded that he was awaiting the king's command. Ever playful, the king himself arose immediately, went and turned the knob of the apartment's spring door, peeked at Veṅkaṭaramaṇa Śāstri seated outside, and called him in. While Veṅkaṭaramaṇa Śāstri sat astonished at having been called by the king himself, the king returned and stood within the

July 3, 1914

---

was reorganized by Raṅgāçārlu and Elliot after the death of Kṛṣṇarāja Voḍeyar III, this *toṭṭi* had 96 religious employees and 100 *paṇḍitas* attached to it [Elliot 1878].

[372] See Plate 30b.

apartment. As Veṅkaṭaramaṇa Śāstri stood struggling and distressed by the door, not knowing how to open it, the king came outside, smiling and saying: "Is there a problem? Do open the door and come in!" and showed him how to open the door. They both entered the room. "Where are the *ślōkās*? Do read them," the king commanded.

Veṅkaṭaramaṇa Śāstri now read the *ślōkas* slowly, and with clear articulation.[373] The Śāstri translated the verses as they were read. It took about three-quarters of an hour to read them all. Delighted at having heard the verses, the king again asked after the well-being of the Śāstri and the grandson, taking great satisfaction in hearing about the grandson, graciously accepted the books, and bid farewell to the Śāstri. After returning home, the Śāstri remained afloat in an ocean of happiness, repeatedly praising the king's excellent disposition, his high character, and the clarity of the memories of his childhood.

[373]Footnote in original: "These *ślōkas* have been published with their translations. The book is priced at one *Āṇe.* They describe the virtues of the king, and of the Vāṇīvilāsa and Lakṣmīvilāsa matriarchs, the glories of the Navarātri celebrations, the wonders of plumbing and electricity, and prayers for the king's welfare. Interested readers may obtain this work by writing to the offices of the Kādambarī Saṅgraha." There were sixteen *Āṇe* to the *Rūpī* at the time. The lady Vāṇīvilāsa was the king's mother H.H. Kempanañjammaṇṇī, and the lady Lakṣmīvilāsa was H.H. Mahārāṇī Srī Pratāpa Kumārī Ammaṇṇī, the king's consort. Also see footnote 718.

11. PERSEVERANCE

RIGHTLY HAS IT been said: *kālaḥkrīḍati gaçchatyāyuḥ.*[374] Two years slipped away into the ocean of time. The *Varsha* season of the Naḷa *saṁvatsara* was under way. Festivals such as *Gaurīhabba, Vināyakana Çauti,* and *Anantapadmanābha Vṛta,* followed by the *Apara Pakṣa* and then *Śarannavarātri* turned with the wheel of time and vanished. The festival called *Narakaçaturdaśī* arrived in the waning fortnight of the month of Āśvayuja.[375] It is the tradition on this day for everyone to arise at four o'clock in the morning and bathe. According to the *śāstras,* the practice of bathing after annointing oneself with oil on this day protects against the possibility of perdition. Everyone, widows included, is hence enjoined to apply some oil to one's head, even in token deference to the *śāstras,* and then bathe.[376]

---

[374] This is from the *Bhajagōvindam* by *Ādi* Śaṅkarāçārya, and translates to "time sports and life ebbs away". The full verse is *"dinayāminyau sāyaṁ prātaḥ śiśiravasantau punarāyātaḥ | kalaḥ krīḍati gaçchatyayuḥ tadapi na muñçatyāśāvāyuḥ ‖"* This translates to: "Day and night, evening and morning, winter and spring, arrive one upon the other. Time sports and life ebbs away, and yet we remain ensnared in the tempests of desire."

[375] *Narakaçaturdaśī* fell on October 25, 1916 C.E. this year. The festivals mentioned are as follows. *Svarṇagaurīvrata,* or *Gaurīhabba,* as it is popularly known, falls on Bhādrapada *śukla tritīyā,* and *Gaṇēśa Çaturthī* falls on the following day. The *Anantapadmanābha Vṛta* falls on Bhādrapada *śukla çaturdaśī.* The *apara pakṣa* is the following *bahula* fortnight. *Śarannavaratrī* is the name given to the first nine days of the *śukla* fortnight of the month of Āśvayuja, with the tenth day being *Vijayadaśamī,* more popularly known as Dasara, the state festival of Maisūru. *Narakaçaturdaśī* is the fourteenth *tithi* in the *bahula* fortnight of Āśvayuja, marking the killing of the demon Narakāsura by Kṛṣṇa.

[376] *Abhyaṅga* (or *abhyañjana*) *snāna* (bathing after inunction) is regarded as a propitious act, and is traditionally mandated on all auspicious occassions, including on one's birthday, wedding day, and on important festive occassions. *Abhyaṅga* is also used as an *Āyurvedic* prescription. It is an ancient practice. See, for example, Kālidāsa's *Kumārasambhava* (2:7): *"sā gaurasiddhārthanivēśavadbhirdūrvāpravālaiḥ pratibhinnaśobham | nirnābhikauśeyamupāttabāṇamabhyaṅganepathyamalaṁçakāra ‖"* The last *pāda* of the verse describes how Pārvatī's beauty, as she is about to be ritually bathed following anointment with oils just before her marriage to Śiva, embellishes the charm of her clothing (rather than the other way around). The extraordinary value attached to *abhyañjana* is illustrated by the tradition in the region of Śṛṅgēri in Karnāṭaka of showing hospitality to guests by inviting them home for the specific purpose of *abhyañjana* [Prasad 2007, p. 55]. Traditionally, oil is liberally massaged into one's skin and head, and permitted to soak in. This is followed by a bath in water as hot as can be tolerated, and the oil removed using the flour of chickpeas (*Cicer arietinum*) on one's body and powdered soap nuts (*Sapindus*) or *sīgekāyi* (*Acacia concinna*) in one's hair.

The ladies and children in the Śāstri's household arose at four that morning and completed their ritual oil baths. Everyone was done by a half past seven. The Śāstri alone was yet to start annointing himself with oil. He had planned to start doing so after finishing his morning chores and washing up, and now entered the backyard. Adventitious Fate caused the Śāstri to trip next to the drain and fall.[377] The injury from the fall caused him to sprain his back. The Śāstri somehow managed to wash up, came indoors, and said that he would forego his ritual bath that day, since his back was hurting. He obtained some relief when his back was immediately massaged with oil, and in about three days, he felt better. He had his oil-bath after these three days. After this, the month of Kārtīka ended after festivals such as *Dīpāvali* and *Utthānadvādaśī.*[378]

Oct. 25, 1916

The Śāstri who had thus far been very robust bodily, now began to show signs of weakness. We all know the month of Mārgaśira as the season of harvest. Disregarding his infirmity, the Śāstri travelled to Çāmarājanagara with his daughter-in-law Kṛṣṇamma in the *bahuḷa* fortnight of Mārgaśira, since the rice paddy fields needed harvesting. It being the time of Christmas vacations, Veṅkaṭaramaṇa Śāstri also travelled to Nagara to assist the Śāstri. The Śāstri never depended on anyone else. He always relied on his own exertions in accomplishing all tasks. He would supervise the threshing of the paddy himself. He would also wash all his own clothes himself. If his daughter-in-law or his children said to him: "Do not exert yourself! Let things be! We will do this work for you!", he would simply remain silent. He never said to anyone: "Do this for me. This is too much for me to do." Things remained as they were, until others perceived what was on his mind, and did what was required.

At this time, the Śāstri was studying the one hundred and eight *Upaniṣads* and various *Vēdic* commentaries. As had been his practice since his

[377] The original uses the term *aniççhāprārabdha. Prārabdha* (see footnote 273), fructification of prior *karma* in this birth, is classified into three kinds: *iççhā, parēççha, and aniççhā.* The first is driven by one's own intention, the second by that of someone else, and the third operates independently, not subject to anyone's intention. See, for example, Vidyāraṇya's *Pañçadaśī*, chapter 7, verse 152: *"naiṣa doṣo yatonekavidhaṁ prārabdhamīkṣyate | iççāniççhā pareççhāça trividham smṛtaṁ ‖"*

[378] *Narakaçaturdaśī* begins the three-day period celebrated as *Dīpāvali. Utthānadvādaśī* is the twelfth *śukla tithi* in the month of Kārtīka, celebrated as the day when Viṣṇu awakens, having gone to sleep on Āṣāḍha *śukla ekādaśī.*

younger years, he would arise at three in the morning and review the formulæ of the *Aṣṭādhyāyī* and recite the Vedas. If he tired of sitting at home, he would walk two miles in the afternoon to the paddy fields, supporting himself with his stick. His body continued to diminish every day. He conducted himself in accordance with the injunction[379]

ajarāmaravat' prājñō vidyāmarthaṁ ça sādhayēt |
gṛhīta iva kēśēṣu mṛtyunā dharmam'āçarēt ‖

People who observed him on his walks feared for his well-being, concerned that he was weak, that he might fall, or that he might suffer confusions, even as they marvelled at his devotion to work and duty. The Śāstri paid no heed to what anyone said, performing all his work with care and thoughtfulness.

The Śāstri returned home at eleven in the morning on the third day of the *śukla* fortnight of the month of Puṣya, after supervising work in the fields.[380] Veṅkaṭasubbayya of Nagara then approached him, saying that a *śrāddha* ritual was to be conducted at his home, that a priest was unavailable, and asking him to greatly oblige him by conducting the ritual. It was the middle of the afternoon! The possibility loomed of losing his brahminhood![381] Despite facing this dilemma, the kind-hearted Śāstri considerate of Veṅkaṭasubbayya's abject state, agreed to go to his house. The afternoon past, Veṅkaṭasubbayya's work was done, by the Śāstri's goodwill. It was now about six in the evening.

[379] This *slōka* is from the *Hitopadeśa*. It translates to: "Let the wise man pursue knowledge and wealth as if he were ever youthful and immortal. Let him pursue dharma as if Death had in its grasp the very hair on his head."

[380] This would be December 16, 1916 C.E.

[381] The sentence is ambiguous, and the reasoning is unclear. The obvious reading is that the afternoon is an unsuitable time for the *śrāddha*. However, according to Manu (III, 278), and the *Āpastamba Sūtra* (II, 7, 16), the afternoon is better than the forenoon for the ritual. Veṅkaṭasubbayya is a brāhmaṇa name, so the chances of Śrīkaṇṭha Śāstri coming into contact with impure materials at his home is unlikely. (See footnote 324.) The most likely possibility is that the *śrāddha* being a mandatory ritual, severe demerit accrues to one who fails to perform it. The demerit would clearly attach to Veṅkaṭasubbayya, but could also attach to Śrīkaṇṭha Śāstri if his unwillingness to perform the ritual were to prevent Veṅkaṭasubbayya from performing it.

At this time, Veṅkaṭasubbayya lived in a hut near the Kaṭṭe Haḷḷa bridge on the road to Nañjanagūḍu.[382] This hut is half a mile distant from the Śāstri's farm. When the Śāstri indicated that he wished to look over the farm and then proceed home, and Kāśī Pāṇḍuraṅga Bhaṭṭa and Kempina Veṅkaṭarāmāvadhāni, who were both there, said: "Dear Śāstri! It is almost dark, and you are of advanced age. Please come with us, and we will take you home. Will it not be a problem if it gets dark by the time you reach your farm?", the Śāstri responded: "There really is no problem. I will be sure to hurry. Please do not trouble yourself. Please go on," and having sent them away, he proceeded alone along the path to the farm at dusk. It gradually became dark.

When the Śāstri, thinking that he would look over the farm and proceed home with one of the workers, called out, he found no one. The farm hands had all left for home before dusk. There was little moonlight, and there was a fence all round. Considering it best to proceed home, the Śāstri finished his *Sandhyāvandane* in the Kaṭṭe Haḷḷa, crossed the fence, and began walking between the hedgerows. Getting home from the Śāstri's farm required crossing several farms, fields, hedgerows, and fences. This distance is about three-fourths of a mile. Since the fields had just been ploughed, there lay about many large and heavy clumps of dirt, each of which a man could barely lift. Since it was dark and he was unable to discern the proper path, the Śāstri strayed from the proper hedgerows and paths, and turned the wrong way, his clothes becoming ripped by thorns as he crossed several thorny fences, his feet hurting as they were pricked by thorns, reached a freshly ploughed field, and having lost his bearings, wandered in that field for quite a while. He was utterly unable to find his way. Deciding it best to spend the night in the field, and walk to town in the morning, he spread a cloth on the ground, and using a clod of earth for a pillow, declared: *"Svāmin! Nṛsiṁha! Māmuddhara!"*,[383] and lay himself down. The exhausted Śāstri soon fell asleep.

Dec. 16, 1916

[382] Kaṭṭe Haḷḷa appears to have been a spring fed by an aquifer that has now run dry due to groundwater depletion. Electricity is provided free of cost for agricultural use, so indiscriminate pumping of groundwater is widespread. As a consequence, many long-standing groves of trees in the region, such as coconut palms, are now dead.

[383] "Lord! Narasiṁha! Protect me!" Clearly, this is a prayer to his family deity Yadugiri Lakṣmīnarasiṁhasvāmi of Mēlukōṭe [Śāstri 1934, p. 40]. According to Śāstri [1925b, p. 8], Śrīkaṇṭha Śāstri's great-great-grandfather Gaṅgādhara Vāraṇāsi had remained childless after he moved to Sindhughaṭṭa, even until the age of forty (see footnote 233). His meditations

The Śāstri not having returned for so long even after dark, his daughter-in-law Kṛṣṇamma and Veṅkaṭaramaṇa Śāstri awaited his return till ten that night, their minds filled with anxiety, trying to reassure themselves that he would soon return.[384] The Śāstri having failed to return even at that late hour, they became truly fearful. Carrying a lighted lantern, they went up to Puṭṭammaṇṇi's farm, but learned nothing from inquiries they made of a couple of people and a cart driver they encountered. They finally returned home and went to bed, deriving some reassurance from the possibility that he had slept at the farm, it having become very late. But it was impossible to sleep. Unpleasant thoughts kept disturbing the mind.

Veṅkaṭaramaṇa Śāstri, who had anxiously awaited the morning, left for the farm at six o'clock, as soon as it was light. Going slowly, and looking carefully this way and that, he walked some distance along the route to Narasīpura, and turned left near Pāpaṇṇa's farm en route to the farm. On his right was Pāpaṇṇa's farm. A freshly ploughed field was to his left, next to a thorny fence. As Veṅkaṭaramaṇa Śāstri walked down the hedgerow in between, he met Siddha, the *guttige* holder on Pāpaṇṇa's farm,[385] who asked: "How is this, master? Up and about at this early hour?"

As Veṅkaṭaramaṇa Śāstri replied: "*Yelā,* Siddha! Our grandfather did not return home last night. I understand he came to the farm. I have come by to see if he slept in the field last night...," the Śāstri, hearing these words, shouted from a few yards past the adjacent fence: "*Yelā,* Veṅkaṭaramaṇa! I am over here, come this way!" When Veṅkaṭaramaṇa Śāstri, hearing his grandfather's voice, looked over the fence, he saw the Śāstri covered in a shawl, reclining against a large clod of earth. Veṅkaṭaramaṇa Śāstri, greatly distraught at this sight, crossed the fence, and stood sobbing out loud by the Śāstri: "*Aṇṇayya!* I cannot bear to see you suffering in this manner! How could we have let this happen to you! Arise, and let us go home!" Siddha, seeing the state that the Śāstri was in, burst into tears and wept: "Master! My lord! How could I have missed your presence in the farm, being right

upon the deity Lakṣmīnarasiṁhasvāmi of Mēlukōṭe bore fruit, and he was blessed with two sons. This deity has remained the family deity since. The name Narasiṁha remains common to this day in this household.

[384] Kṛṣṇamma was Veṅkaṭakṛṣṇa's widow, and Veṅkaṭaramaṇa Śāstri's mother.

[385] *Guttige* is a type of land tenancy in which the tenant bears the cost of cultivation, but gives the owner a fixed rent in cash or kind.

here! Is there a greater sinner than me? If I had known, I would have made sure that you slept in warmth and comfort in my hut! Śiva, Śiva!"

At this, the Śāstri's eyes, too, filled with tears. He said to his grandson: "Dear Veṅkaṭaramaṇa! I tried mightily to return home last night. But the stars were aligned otherwise. I became lost, and had to endure this trouble. I would surely have returned home had I known either that Pāpaṇṇa's farm or that the road was nearby. But let us put this aside! Compared to all else I have endured, this is but a trifle," and returned home. Although overjoyed at the Śāstri's safe return, the eyes of his daughter-in-law Kṛṣṇamma flowed with tears when she heard what had transpired the previous night.

Obsequial rites and worship of deities, respectively, were observed in the Śāstri's household on the eighth, ninth, and fourteenth *śukla tithis,* and on the day of the full moon in Puṣya.[386] Narasiṁha Śāstri was to arrive from Maisūru during this period. When Kṛṣṇamma suggested asking her younger daughter Subbatāyi to come from Maisūru, feeling that it would be very helpful to have some young ladies present at such a time, the Śāstri agreed with her, and had a letter written accordingly to Narasiṁha Śāstri. Subbatāyi is married to Garaḷapurī Śāstri,[387] the eldest son of her

[386]The anniversaries of the Śāstri's mother's death and that of his son were on the eighth and ninth *śukla tithi* of Puṣya, respectively (see footnotes 344 and 345). The anniversary of Śrīkaṇṭha Śāstri's father's passing was observed as an *ārādhana* on the third and fourth *bahuḷa tithi* of the month of Vaiśākha (see page 142). The *vratas* called *Śākaṁbarī* and *Banaśaṅkarī* occur on the fourteenth *tithi* and on *pūrṇima,* respectively. The family had observed these rites of worship for the deity *Banaśaṅkarī* (also called *Śākambarī*) even in their ancestral home of Bādāmi, from where Gaṅgādhara *Vāraṇāsi* originally came (see footnote 233). According to Śāstri [1925b], certain rules are to be strictly followed in these observances. For instance, only members of the *Hoysaḷa Karṇāṭaka* community could be invited for meals on these days.

[387]Footnote in original: "Having passed the B.A. examination from Madras in the First Class, he is presently in London on a scholarship from the Government of Mysore, and has completed advanced degrees there, such as the M.Sc. He is to return to his native land shortly. He is the first son of Mahāvidvān *Kavitilaka* Ayyā Śāstri." Ayyā Śāstri's first son Garaḷapurī Śāstri (1888–1955 C.E.) was named after his grandfather, and graduated in 1911 from the Presidency College, Madras, with a degree in Chemistry. Following two years as a research student at the Tata Institute in Bangalore with Professor J.J. Sudborough on a scholarship from the Mysore Government, he proceeded to London on a Dāmodar Scholarship in 1913, where he completed his M.Sc., and conducted research at the University College and the Imperial Institute of Science and Technology, publishing several scientific papers. After returning to India in 1918, he joined the Mysore Soap Factory, which he ultimately managed. His accomplishments there included creating Mysore Sandal Soap, which is still

own paternal aunt Lakṣmīdēvamma.[388] She has a lovely daughter called Rukmiṇī. Narasiṁhaśāstri, Subbatāyī, and Rukmiṇī arrived in Çāmarājanagara on the evening of the seventh *śukla tithi* of Puṣya. After the rites on the eighth and ninth were complete, the Śāstri travelled to Maisūru, and returned to Nagara after eight days. The *Śākambarī* and *Banaśankarī* rituals were performed in Maisūru by Narasiṁhaśāstri, and in Nagara by Veṅkaṭaramaṇaśāstri.

---

being manufactured. Subsequently, he became Director of the Department of Industries and Commerce in Mysore. His work took him to Japan and the United States of America, in addition to England. He retired in 1943. He also made significant literary contributions, starting as early as 1913. His literary output included original plays and short stories, as well as translations of many English works into Kannaḍa. He was a leading citizen of the time, and socially well connected. He was one of the founders of Century Club in Beṅgaḷūru.

[388] *Gōtra* being a patrilineal attribute, cross-cousin marriages (where the bride and bridegoom have different male lineages) automatically respect *gōtra* exogamy, provided it was also respected in the marriage of the parents. In this case, the *gōtras* would have been Bhāradvāja for Subbatāyi (footnote 229) and Kāśyapa for Garaḷapurī Śāstri (page 8). Exogamy practices vary considerably between northern and southern India. In the north, a very rigid system of patrilineal descent and virilocal residence often leads to strict exogamy forms, such as village exogamy. In such cases, there may be few pre-exisiting social or familial ties between the families, visitations by the bride's family may be uncommon, and visitations by the husband's family to that of the bride may be even rarer, to preclude the possibility of obligations being incurred. It is even common for the bride's family to consider her a *parāyī* (alien, outsider) after marriage. Brides can experience considerable alienation under such conditions. This is in marked contrast to southern India, where kinship ties play an important role in determining marriages, marriage within the extended family is welcomed, and *gōtra* exogamy seen more important than any other form. Matrilocal or uxorilocal residence is widely accepted, as was apparently the case with Veṅkaṭaramaṇa Śāstri's son-in-law (see page 91). South Indian brides may therefore feel less alienation than their northern sisters, and can typically count on family support in adversity or abandonment (again, see page 91). Cross-cousin marriages have always been common in southern India, and were in fact viewed very favourably. This fact may be reflected in the Kannaḍa terms for maternal uncle and paternal aunt, *sōdara (sahōdara) māva* and *sōdara (sahōdara) atte*, literally "co-uterine father-in-law" and "co-uterine mother-in-law". It is striking how the "co-uterine" relationship at the parent level is secondary, and appears merely as a qualifier for the more important "in-law" relationship at the child level. In contrast, the terms for younger/elder maternal aunt and paternal uncle happen to be *çikka/doḍḍa amma* and *çikka/doḍḍa appa*, or "junior/senior mother" and "junior/senior father", suggesting marriage there to be incestuous. Cross-cousin marriages are by no means unique to southern India, and are still seen all across the world.

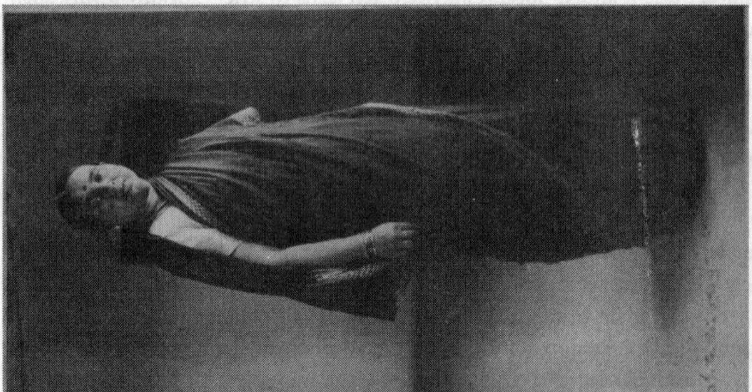

(a) Veṅkaṭasubbamma, granddaughter of Cāmarājanagara Śrīkaṇṭha Śāstri

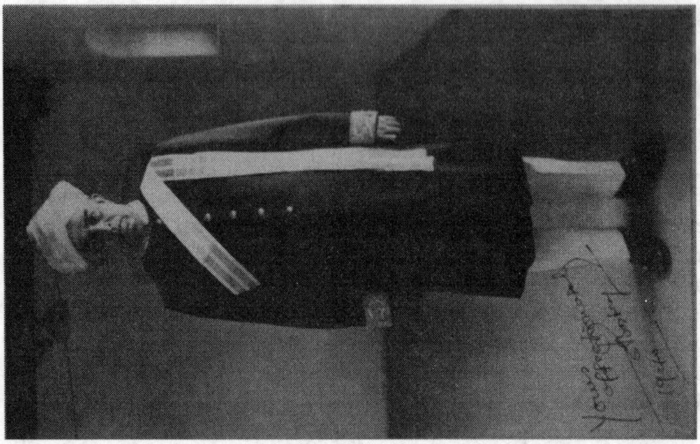

(b) Sōsale Garaḷapurī Śāstri, son of Ayyā Śāstri

Plate 31: Portraits of Sōsale Garaḷapurī Śāstri and his wife Veṅkaṭasubbamma

12. The Final Days

Though the Śāstri had no surviving sons, Lakṣmīdēvamma had helped diminish the anguish in his heart by being both daughter and son to him. Lakṣmīdēvamma was a virtuous and talented lady. Her skills in managing the household were exemplary. Her house is filled with children and grandchildren. Her sons are all well-educated. Her daughters are all virtuous wives, and accomplished ladies of discrimination. In them has truly been realized the meaning of the saying *"asārēkhalusaṁsārē sārabhūtānitambinī"*.[389] The noble housewife who manages the household in a principled manner, brings joy to her beloved, nurtures her children, and promotes their progress, is indeed worthy of the highest praise. It is known to all that households, nations, and even this world achieve greatness only due to the efforts of such gems of womanhood. It is proper to regard such noble ladies as being mothers to all Humanity. Lakṣmīdēvamma, a lady of high character and principled upbringing, had devoted herself to the care of her husband and children, never letting them experience the slightest sorrow, and being a source of joy to them through her many virtues. It is no small accomplishment to have managed a household with judgment and sagacity, maintaining propriety and decorum in dealings with all relatives, and becoming the object of universal praise. Lakṣmīdēvamma held fast the reins of the household, indeed as Īśvara holds the world in his grasp.[390] This is why her children and grandchildren are upright, widely-respected, honorable,

[389] This quote is intended to convey the sense that while this world may be without worth, a virtuous woman is a noble exception. It is based on two verses from the *Vikramaçarita* that appear in the story told by the sixth statue, where king Vikramāditya indulges a dishonest ascetic. These verses read [Edgerton 1926]: *"asārabhūte saṁsāre sāraṁ sāraṅgalōçanā | tadarthaṁ dhanamiçchanti tattyāge dhanena kiṁ ‖ asārabhūte saṁsāre sārabhūtā nitambinī | iti sañçintya vai śambhurardhāṅge kāminīṁ dadhau ‖"*, and translate as follows: "In this unprofitable round of existence the best thing of all a gazelle-eyed woman. For her sake men seek after wealth, and without her, what is the use of wealth? 'In this unprofitable round of existence the best thing of all is a fair-hipt woman;' it was with this thought in mind, I ween, that Śambhu took his beloved on his lap." It may seem surprising that the *bahuvrīhi* compound *nitambinī*, meaning "heavy-hipped one", is used instead of "woman", but it is common in *Saṁskṛta* poetry to refer to such physical characteristics. Nitambinī is used as a first name even today.

[390] Although *Īśvara* denotes Śiva in common usage, *īśa* literally means "master" or "controller". Accordingly, *Īśvara*, the possessor of the attribute of *īśa*, is the one who controls.

well-educated, and virtuous individuals. Rare indeed are such households in this world, or housewives such as Lakṣmīdēvamma. Lakṣmīdēvamma was not educated. Yet, much would it behoove the so-called educated ladies of these times to apprentice themselves to her, that they might learn what it means to be a homemaker. Her word was never transgressed within the household. It is on account of her many admirable virtues and excellent counsel that her daughters Mīnākṣī and Viśālākṣī, though widowed in childhood, are distanced from worldly atrractions, and remain immersed in spirituality and devotion to Īśvara. In all, it would be right to say that Lakṣmīdēvamma's household was a model of good conduct, ethics, and virtue.

But *Kālapuruṣa* is indeed hard of heart.[391] He is devoid of even the smallest iota of mercy. Making the soul of Lakṣmīdēvamma, the model consort, the target of much anguish starting the morning of the eighth *bahuḷa tithi* of the month of Puṣya of the Naḷa *saṁvatsara*, he wrested it away into the other world within eight days, that is, on the first *śuddha tithi* of the month of Māgha.[392]

If a relative inquired after her health, she would simply respond: "This body is subject to illness! This world is subject to Īśvara! Even the gods are subject to *karma*! Man is not at liberty! One must not covet this body!", and if her husband or children urged her to take some medicine, she would smilingly take some, and lie down composedly. She would inquire unhurriedly after the well-being of all visitors, giving them her good counsel. If her husband or children said to her: "Conversation is exhausting; you should rest quietly", she would refrain from expressing her suffering overtly, so as not to alarm them. For their satisfaction, she would take her medicine, and observe the salutary dietary norms prescribed for her.

Ayyā Śāstri, wishing to save his wife somehow, had excellent medicines prescribed by the greatest and most accomplished physicians. *"Apidhanvantarirvaidyaḥ kimkarōti gatayuṣi?"*,[393] that is, even Dhanvantari, the physician of the gods, cannot save one whose time has come. Lakṣmīdēvamma's breathing became laboured at four o'clock in the morning on the first *tithi*

[391] See footnote 357.

[392] The first date alluded to is January 16, 1917 C.E.

[393] This hemistich is from the *Hitopadeśa (vigrahaḥ,* 146*)*: *"prakṛtiḥ svāminā tyaktā samṛddhā'pi na jīvati | api dhanvantarirvaidyaḥ kiṁ karoti gatāyuṣi ‖"*.

of Māgha.[394] She was immediately given Gaṅgā water to drink.[395] As her breathing weakened, Lakṣmīdēvamma began to lose her powers of speech. Even so, she gestured for her husband to come near, and touching his feet, she pressed her hands to her eyes, and speaking indistinctly, said that she was about to depart, and sought his permission. She then looked long and well at her sons and daughters seated nearby. As she meditated on Nārāyaṇa, her soul left this mortal body, even as they all looked on.

Jan. 24, 1917

The loss of a thing so precious plunged everyone into sorrow, not just the family, but even those who knew her as acquaintances, or even merely by reputation. Many lamented that such a treasury of virtue would never again be seen. Narasiṁha Śāstri and Veṅkaṭaramaṇa Śāstri, the nephews of the deceased, arrived at seven in the morning, and seeing the corpse and the strong resemblance of its facial features to those of their father, lamented: "When our father died, his face appeared to bear a smile, exactly as this face does! *Ayyo!* Kiṭṭaṇṇayya! *Ayyo!* Maisūrakka![396] have you now both departed this world? Where shall we ever again see such a brother and sister?" Be everyone else's sorrow as it might, the deep anguish of Ayyā Śāstri and that of his children who had just lost their mother, especially that of Mīnākṣamma and Viśālākṣamma, was beyond description. But one must accept what transpires. Lakṣmīdēvamma's virtues and high character underwent cremation with her body, and accompanied her soul, giving it much comfort en route to the other world.[397]

[394] This would be the early morning of January 24, 1917 C.E.

[395] A common service to a dying person, the Gaṅgā being the holiest of the Indian rivers.

[396] *Kiṭṭaṇṇayya* is a compound of *Kiṭṭa* and *Aṇṇayya. Kiṭṭa* is a diminutive of Kṛṣṇa, itself a contraction of Veṅkaṭakṛṣṇa, the name of the writer's father. When the noun Veṅkaṭa appears as the first component of a compound name, it is often treated as a qualifier and elided in contractions, leaving the second component, which may further suffer diminution. Thus, Veṅkaṭa-Kṛṣṇa becomes *Kiṭṭa,* and Veṅkaṭa-Subrahmaṇya becomes *Subbu* (but also see footnote 338). *Aṇṇa* and *Akka* are the Kannaḍa terms for elder brother and elder sister, respectively, with *Aṇṇayya* being a honorific form for *Aṇṇa.* It may seem odd that the speakers of these words refer to the two deceased individuals as *Aṇṇa* and *Akka,* despite being the sons of the first and nephews of the second. However, it is common in South-Indian joint families for children to adopt the form of address for adults prevalent in the household. It is not uncommon for children to grow up referring to their fathers as *Aṇṇa,* or even *Bhāva* (brother-in-law).

[397] Agni, the only *Vēdic* deity present on this earth, is seen as the conduit through which things pass from this world to that of the gods. Cremation is not mere destruction of the material body, but rather, the means of conveyance to the other world through Agni's agency.

Let us recall that Śrīkaṇṭha Śāstri, Kṛṣṇamma, and Lakṣmīdēvamma's daughter-in-law Subbatāyī were now still in Nagara. The news of Lakṣmīdēvamma's illness reached them. The Śāstri left Nagara on the night of her demise, and upon reaching Maisūru on Thursday morning, he inquired: "Where is Lakṣmīdēvi? Is she well?" When the Śāstri, still ignorant of his daughter's death, learned of her demise, he sat stunned and speechless for a long time, thinking, "What? Is it all over? Is Lakṣmīdēvī gone?" We have not the skill to describe his anguish. This elderly, august, and venerable personage, reflecting over and over on his daughter's demise, finally arose and walked away, as his anguish surpassed the bounds of his endurance.

Grief, like woodworm, began to eat away at him. First, his own sons had died. His younger brother had died next. What now remained for the Śāstri, who had yet consoled himself that his daughter remained, and saw her as his source of contentment? His anguish continued to grow. An aversion to worldly matters began to build. Passions such as anger and attachment began to diminish in him, and his spirit exalted itself through contemplation of spiritual matters. His bodily strength began to wane. Feeling that he would have no respite from worldly sorrows as long he remained in Maisūru, he returned to Nagara in the month of Chaitra. Kṛṣṇamma remained at hand to serve him. In the month of Phālguṇa, the Śāstri had already developed dysentery.[398] This turned especially severe after his return to Nagara.

Paying no regard to his bodily infirmities, the Śāstri continued his physical activities, his daily ritual observances, his spiritual meditations, and his well-being, while accepting treatment from skilled physicians. His physical vigour and his ambulatory capacity, however, continued to diminish each day. Nonetheless, his mental and sensory abilities remained acute. His teeth remained strong. After his meals, it was his practice to eat *hurigāḷu, çakkuli,*

[398]The month of Chaitra (Piṅgaḷa *saṁvatsara*) commenced on March 24, 1917 C.E. The prior month of Phālguṇa (Naḷa *saṁvatsara*) had commenced on February 22, 1917 C.E.

Plate 32: Ayyā Śāstri (1855–1934) and Lakṣmīdevamma (1860–1917). On his right wrist, Ayyā Śāstri wears the bejewelled bracelet inscribed *Kavitilaka*, bestowed upon him in 1912 C.E. The photograph thus dates to between 1912 and 1917, the year of Lakṣmīdēvamma's passing.

followed by *tāmbūla*.[399] He always consumed the areca nut sliced in halves, never when cut into pieces.

The *ārādhana* of Śaṅkarānanda *Svāmi*, who had attained unity with the Absolute, was to take place on the third and fourth *bahuḷa tithis* of the month of Vaiśākha of the Paiṅgaḷa *saṁvatsara*.[400] The Śāstri, who had always performed this ritual himself, and with great devotion, was feeling especially weak, and just this once, had the ceremonies completed on both days by his eldest grandson Narasiṁhaśāstri. Both grandsons were in Nagara at this time, all schools being closed on account of summer vacations. They both returned to Maisūru after the *ārādhana*.

The eleventh *śuddha tithi* of Jyēṣṭha being the birthday of the Mahāraja,[401] the Śāstri determined to be in Maisūru on that day, and had Narasiṁhaśāstri come to Nagara four days prior, leaving for Maisūru in his company. While still in Nagara, the Śāstri suddenly being troubled by the loss of his hearing and eyesight, he had a *paṇḍita* brought from Rāmasamudra, from whom he obtained treatment.[402] This treatment succeeded in restoring his previous health and his sensory capacities. At ten o'clock on the morning of Sunday, the sixth *śuddha tithi* of Jyēṣṭha,[403] the Śāstri, Kṛṣṇamma, and Veṅkaṭaramaṇaśāstri had finished their meal, and were ready for the trip. Before departing, the Śāstri had a look all around the house, approached the vehicle, prayed to the family deity Nṛsiṁhasvāmi, looked long and well at the Çāmarāja temple, prayed to that deity, and ascended into the

---

[399] *Hurigāḷu* is a savoury and pungent preparation of dried legumes with chillies, salt, and spices. *Çakkuli* (*śaṣkuli* in *Saṁskṛta*) is spiced rice flour paste extruded in circular rings and fried in oil. *Tāmbūla* is a combination of betel leaf (*Piper betle*), areca nut (*Areca catechu*), and slaked lime, consumed after meals as a carminative. In its natural spherical form, the areca nut is called *gōṭ-aḍike*, but is usually cut into halves (*baṭṭal-aḍike*), slices, or into fine pieces. Strong teeth and gums are essential if the areca nut is to be eaten in the first two forms.

[400] These dates correspond to May 9 and 10, 1917 C.E. *Śrāddha* rites are not performed for the soul of a *saṁnyāsin*, since it has attained unity with the Absolute, and thus has no need of propitiatory *kārmic saṁskāras* performed on its behalf by earthly descendants. Instead, an *ārādhana*, or worship ritual is performed in its memory. The act of accepting *saṁnyāsa* is ritually equivalent to death; the associated rites include *ātmaśrāddha*, which is a *śrāddha* rite performed for oneself. For some interesting conundrums involving renunciation, see Freiberger [2005].

[401] This would be Friday, June 1, 1917 C.E. Kṛṣṇarāja Voḍeyar IV was born on June 4, 1884, but his birthday would have been observed on the *tithi* corresponding to that date.

[402] Rāmasamudra is about 3 km due east of Çāmarājanagara.

[403] This would be May 27, 1917 C.E.

vehicle. This was to be the last time the Śāstri would be in Çāmarājanagara. "The heart knows, even if the eye does not," so goes an old saying. Accordingly, it appears that the Śāstri's heart had indeed come to recognize that his end was near.

On that sixth *tithi,* they arrived at the railway station at Nañjanagūḍu in the evening,[404] bought their tickets, and reached Maisūru at nine o'clock that night. Since they were unable to find any conveyances that night, the Śāstri, his grandson, and his daughter-in-law lodged with his son-in-law Ayyā Śāstri, whose house was near the Çāmarājapuram railway station.[405] After his *Sandhyāvandane* and dinner, he stayed there the night, and travelled by foot to his house in the Rāmaçandra Agrahāra the next morning.

On the day of the birthday, the Śāstri made his trip to the palace without anyone's help. When a number of palace officials urged the king to prevent the Śāstri, who was awaiting death, from coming to the palace, the Mahārāja, a most pious person, is said to have replied that his well-being and that of the kingdom both being contingent on his receiving blessings in the form of *mantrākṣate* from this elderly and venerable person, his coming to the palace was most essential! We leave it to the reader to judge the sincere and upright character of our king.

June 1, 1917

After the day of the birthday, the Śāstri visited the Çāmuṇḍi Toṭṭi on two occasions, once to collect his honorarium, and once to participate in a *dhārmic* discussion. Around this time, our Mahārāja, for some reason, ordered the well known photographer Varadāçārya to photograph the Śāstri and send the picture to the palace. Unwilling to contravene the kings orders, the Śāstri consented, and was photographed. The image has been handsomely framed and kept in the Maisūru palace. We have included that photograph in this volume, so that our readers may view that image.

[404] This town is 40 km northwest of Çāmarājanagara, en route to Maisūru. The Maisūru–Nañjanagūḍu railway line, a metre-guage track 15.8 miles in length, was opened to the public on December 1, 1891 C.E. It had been built as an extension of the track from Bangalore to Maisūru. Nañjanagūḍu served as the southern terminus of the Mysore State Railway. This route's reputation as being agonizingly slow remained intact even decades after the events mentioned. The 25 km trip took around three hours, so the Śāstri is likely to have boarded the train at around 6pm. The Maisūru-Nañjanagūḍu track was not extended to Çāmarājanagara until August 27, 1926.

[405] *Kavitāvilāsa*, Ayyā Śāstri's house, was a couple of hundred yards from the railway station. He had received this house as a gift from the palace, most likely in 1894, when Çāmarāja Voḍeyar X died.

After this, the Śāstri's movement outside the home diminished even more. He remained at home, performing his bathing and daily rituals and his spiritual devotions. It is of course normal for high officials to visit the capital during the king's birthday celebrations. During this time, *Prāktana Vimarṣā Viçakṣaṇa Rāvbahādūr* R. Narasiṁhāçār, M.A., M.R.A.S.,[406] visited the Śāstri, inquired after his health, and becoming much distressed at his condition, left lamenting that Learning itself would be lost if the Śāstri, a treasury of knowledge, were to be lost. The extent of the Śāstri's scholarship was certainly well known to Narasiṁhāçār.[407]

July 20, 1917

As the Śāstri's ability to move about diminished, so did the strength of his limbs. His activities were limited to arising and bathing with the help of others, and then performing his rituals and eating by himself, then rising with help and washing his hands, and then lying down.[408] He remained in bed except when he bathed or ate. He would sit up for a bit if he tired of lying down. After completing his evening *Sandhyāvandane,* he would

[406] As this list of titles and honours suggests, Narasiṁhāçār was a distinguished literary scholar, as well as epigraphist and historian. The title *Prāktana Vimarṣā Viçakṣaṇa* ("one distinguished in historical research") was conferred upon him by the king in 1913. The title *Rāv Bahadūr*, reserved in British times for individuals who had rendered exceptional national service, was conferred on him by the Government of India in 1916. He also held the titles *Karṇāṭaka Prāçyavidyā Vaibhava,* conferred on him by the All-India Literary Association, Calcutta, and *Mahāmahopādhyāya,* conferred on him by the Government of India. He served as Director of Archeological Research in Mysore. Among his many accomplishments are his editorship of the *Mysore Gazetteer* after B.L. Rice, and his *Karnāṭaka Kaviçarite*, a monumental work on Kannaḍa poets. He died December 6, 1936, aged 77.

[407] Narasiṁhāçār recalls [in Śāstri 1934, p. 38]:

> ... When I was in positions of authority, the Śāstri would often stop by to see me. I would spend much time in discussions with him, and end up shaking my head in wonder and appreciation for the depth and extent of his scholarship... When the Śāstri was close to his impending death, I had visited him a week prior to his demise. Despite his extreme weakness, he gestured for help, and getting up with great difficulty, said tearfully: 'A visit by a luminary such as yourself is surely a sign of my *puṇya*'. I too, responded with words appropriate for the occasion. We are truly unlikely to ever again see such a scholar as him... His younger brother Rāmaśāstri was also a well-known scholar. He was without peer in literary scholarship. His elder brother was without peer in grammatical scholarship. Scholars of such great ability are born to this blessed soil but only rarely...

[408] Śrīkaṇṭha Śāstri would have eaten his meals with his hands sitting cross-legged on the floor, and would have needed help in getting up and washing up.

drink some milk and go to bed, to arise only to bathe the following morning. During these times, Kṛṣṇamma would wash his clothes every day, prepare his bed, and remove the dirtied linen. Indeed, she built herself a stairway to Heaven through her unselfish devotion to her father-in-law. Both grandsons were also deeply engaged in serving their grandfather. The Śāstri had his grand-daughter Subbatayī come stay with him.[409] This young girl too, served her grandfather tirelessly, spending time with him and speaking pleasantly to him.

In this manner, on account of the regard his daughter-in-law and his grandchildren had for him, and their service, the Śāstri remained contented and free from worry. He continued his medicines and salutary dietary prescriptions both owing to the possibility that his dysentery would relent, as well as in conformance with social protocols. He never expressed his suffering overtly. He appeared perfectly healthy. Yet, his feeble body continued to decline. It was impossible to tell that he was ill, from just looking at him. Nor did one feel any sense of anxiety.

On the eighth *śuddha tithi* of the month of Śrāvaṇa, he began to suffer extreme bodily anguish.[410] However, he endured it without telling any of the children. That was a Friday. His grandsons Narasiṁha Śāstri and Veṅkaṭaramaṇa Śāstri had left for school, which had been moved to the morning, that day being the *vrata* of Varamahālakṣmī. At eight that morning, his suffering increased greatly. He immediately called out to his daughter-in-law Kṛṣṇamma, and asked what time it was. Upon being told that it was eight-thirty, he replied that there was no stopping things now, since this body would no longer endure, and that since he had not the strength to turn over, she should place him on a bed of *darbha* grass on his left side; lying with his right ear upwards, he then asked where Narasiṁha was.[411]

Upon being summoned, Narasiṁha Śāstri came immediately, and seeing his grandfather on his deathbed, cried our tearfully: *"Aṇṇayya!"* The Śāstri, seeing that his grandson had arrived, said, "Have you arrived? Come near," and simply looked at his grandson once. His ability to speak having left him by this time, he began to meditate upon Īśvara. When Narasiṁhaśāstri, quite alarmed, called a physician to examine him, that inexperienced

[409] Subbatāyi's husband S.G. Śāstri was still in England at this time, working on his Master's degree in Chemistry. See footnote 387.

[410] This would be Friday, July 27, 1917 C.E.

[411] See footnote 211.

physician said: "There is no imminent danger. This will hold till evening," and departed. It was about ten o'clock now. By this time, Narasiṁhaśāstri had dispatched his seven-year-old son Vidyāmūrti to fetch his brother, bathed, completed his daily rituals and worship, asked all his relatives to have their meals and arrive quickly, and began reading the *Viṣṇusahasranāma* aloud, sitting by his grandfather. When Veṅkaṭaramaṇaśāstri arrived, and seeing what had come to pass, tearfully cried *"Aṇṇayya!"* gazing at his grandfather's face, the Śāstri looked at him once and remained silent.

Narasiṁhaśāstri admonished his brother, saying: "Weeping at such a time? Keep your courage, go bathe, and finish your meals," and continued reading the *Viṣṇusahasranāma.* The Śāstri continued listening, his mind fully engrossed. His breathing had begun to diminish. By about eleven-fifteen, Kṛṣṇamma and Veṅkaṭaramaṇaśāstri, having finished their baths and rituals, sat by the Śāstri's head. Narasiṁha continued reading the *Viṣṇusahasranāma.* Kṛṣṇamma fed him Gaṅgā water. Veṅkaṭaramaṇaśāstri ritually bathed his grandfather through *mantrasnāna*,[412] applied *vibhūti* to his forehead,[413] and began reciting the name of Nārāyaṇa into his right ear. The Śāstri's soul, finding this to be a propitious time, now left this material body and blissfully departed. Just then, the noon hour was announced by the sound of a cannon.[414]

July 27, 1917

Relatives, from spiritual ignorance, were distressed at the sight of the Śāstri's lifeless body.[415] Narasiṁhaśāstri, the son of the Śāstri's brother,[416] upon beholding the death of his uncle said:

---

[412] *Mantrasnāna* is a ritual bath performed by the sprinking of water accompanied by the recitation of a *mārjana mantra.* A commonly used *mantra* is *"apavitraḥpavitrovā sarvāvasthāṅgatopiva | yassmaret puṇḍarīkākṣaṁ sa bāhyābhyanntaraḥ śuciḥ ‖"* Another, of greater antiquity, is *"āpohiṣṭhā mayobhuvastā na ūrje dadhātana | mahe raṇāya çakṣase ‖ yovaḥ śivatamo rasastasya bhājayate ihanaḥ uṣatīriva mātaraḥ ‖ tasmā araṁ gamāmavo | yasya kṣayāya jinvatha | āpo janayathāçanaḥ ‖"*

[413] Three stripes of ash worn across the forehead by brāhmaṇas of the *Smārta* tradition.

[414] During the period, the hours of 5 a.m., noon, and 9 p.m. were marked by the sound of cannon fired within Maisūru fort, as Vāsudevāçārya [1962, p. 41] documents. Daily life in the city would largely have been bracketed by these markers. Also see page 167 for additional significance of a cannon shot at this instant.

[415] See footnote 227.

[416] Footnote in original: "This is none other than the well-known C.R. Narasiṁhaśāstri, B.A. He is the son of Çamarājanagara Rāmāśāstri. He is now lecturer at the Mahārāja's College in Maisūru, having completed his B.A. degree. His scholarship in English and *Saṁskṛta*, and his poetic abilities are both exceptional." Narasiṁhaśāstri went on to become Professor of Sanskrit at the Mahārāja's College.

tāta·pāda·viyōgō'ttha·ś'śōkō vismāritas'tvayā |
tridivaṁ prastithēn'ādya pitṛvya dviguṇīkṛtaḥ ||

Meaning: "Uncle! Your presence had diminished the sorrow of our father's death. Your demise has now doubled the intensity of this grief." He then began to weep, as common people do.

It took only a little while for the news of the Śāstri's demise to spread across the city. A large number of people soon assembled. The corpse was taken to the cremation grounds by a half past three in the afternoon. Acceding to requests from Narasiṁhaśāstri and Veṅkaṭaramaṇaśāstri, *Asthāna-mahāvidvāṅ Dvivēdi* Subrahmaṇya *Ghanapāṭhi* arrived, oversaw the rituals, ensuring that the officiating priest performed the funerary rites without the slightest lapse, and himself recited *Vēdic mantras* sonorously and with great dignity. The sound of *Vēdic* recitation continued to resound in all ten directions till the evening.[417] Many relatives, including the Śāstri's son-in-law Ayyā Śāstri, were present. At six in the evening, the Śāstri's mortal remains were placed on the pyre, and made an oblation to the fire-god.

Grammatical scholarship has now come undone. The Śāstri's grandchildren both performed the post-funerary rituals with respect, devotion, and in the prescribed manner.[418] Although the din of the grandchildren and great-grandchildren filled the Śāstri's house at this time, yet bereft of the Śāstri, the house was like the night sky bereft of the moon. Things continue as always; the days dawn and the evenings come, people are born and die, but one may never again behold the Śāstri. Though his physical body has turned to ashes, he lives on in the body of his fame.[419]

The talented poet Mattigūḍu Vāsudēvaśāstri, who is the son-in-law of Ayyā Śāstri,[420] describes his scholarship and abilities in this manner:

ÇARAMA·ŚLŌK'ĀVAḶI

nūnam prāk'saṁbhavē–sau vibudha·gaṇa·maṇiḥ pāṇinēs'sūtrajālaṁ
vyāçakhyāv'adya janmany'api kṛtim'akarōd'dhātu·rūpa·prakāśam |
itthaṁ śabd'āgam'ābdhiṁ vibudha·jana·tatēr jānu·daghnaṁ vidhāya
śrīkaṇṭhā'khyaḥ phaṇīndrō vitata·nija·yaśā dhāma naijaṁ jagāma ||1||

[417] The four cardinal and the four intercardinal directions, as well as the zenith and nadir.
[418] Only the male descendants are entitled to perfom these rituals.
[419] See footnote 228.
[420] He was married to Jānakīamma, Ayyā Śāstri's second daughter.

bhō bhō nāgās'tvaradhvaṁ vyajanam'ayi sakhē vasukē tvaṁ gṛhāṇa
ç'çhatraṁ kārkōṭaka tvaṁ maṇi·gaṇa·rucirāṁ takṣaka tvaṁ patākām |
yasmād'asmākam' adya prabhur'avatarati kṣmā·talād'ity'abhīkṣnaṁ
nūnam śēṣ'āvatārē tvayi jahati bhuvaṁ saṁbhramō–nyatra jātaḥ ‖2‖

gurō tvaṁ yāhy'agrē tad'anuja·kaviṁ rāma·vibudhaṁ
kavē tvaṁ kṛtv'āgrē vraja bhaja gaja·dvāra·savidham |
asau śrīkaṇṭh'ākhyō budha·maṇir'ih'āyāti sucirāt
saparyāṁ tasy'ārhāṁ kuru suragurō tvaṁ vyavahitaḥ ‖3‖

surais'sārdhaṁ tasy'āgatim'iha sudharmām'adhigataḥ
pratīkṣē raṁbhā'dyā apasarata yuyaṁ bahir'itaḥ |
śaçī·nāthēn'ētthaṁ viraçita·saparyaṁ budha·varaṁ
dhruvaṁ svargō vismārayati bhuvam'ēnām'atitarām ‖4‖

tvayi budha·maṇau śābdaṁ tantraṁ gurōḥ purataḥ kramā·
d'apagata·bhayaṁ vyākurvāṇē kavēr'dhuri tē–nujē |
sarasa·kavitā'lāpān kurvaty'ahō maghavā yuvāṁ
amara·sadasō bhūṣā·yugmaṁ çirād'iva manyatē ‖5‖

nijāgra·nakha·kuṭmal'āhati·vipāṭit'ēbhaç'çhaṭā
visṛtvara·yaśā gatō divam'asau mṛg'ādhiśitā |
ahō bata bilād bahis'sarata nirbhayaṁ phēravaḥ
rutam kuruta sāṁprataṁ śruti·vidāraṇaṁ dāruṇam ‖6‖

yātē'staṁ sva·kara·tirōhit'ānya·rūpē
mārtāṇḍē divam'abhitō yath'aiva tārāḥ |
lakṣyantē vibudha·śikhāmaṇau ça tad vat
śrīkaṇṭhē jahati bhuvaṁ budhā vayaṁ ca ‖7‖

svarga·pratīhāra·gataṁ bhavantaṁ
putrō–nujas'tē duhitā ça pūrvam |
gatās'samēty'ābhimukhaṁ praharṣā
d'aṇṇayya tē svāgatam'īrayanti ‖8‖

Meaning:

In an earlier birth, this Śrīkaṇṭha Śāstri composed a commentary on the *sūtras* of the *Aṣṭādhyāyī*.[421] He wrote the *Dhāturūpa Prakāśikā* in this birth. Thus did this Śāstri, an incarnation of Patañjali (Ādiśeṣa) himself, change grammar from the vast ocean it is into what is only knee-deep,

[421] The translation of the *Saṁskṛta* verses given in the Kannaḍa source also incorrectly says here that Śrīkaṇṭha Śāstri was Pāṇini reborn. As is clear in the rest of the verse, the suggestion is that he was Patāñjali reborn. Patāñjali is a revered grammarian, and is the author of the *Mahābhāṣya*, the most respected commentary on Pāṇini's *Aṣṭādhyāyī*.

making it easy for the community of scholars to wade through it with ease, achieved great acclaim, and then returned to his own home.[422]

O serpents! Rejoice that your lord is returning to your world from ours.[423] O Vāsuki, take up that fan! O Karkōṭaka, hold you that umbrella! O Takṣaka, hold aloft that bejeweled flag! When the Śāstri, an incarnation of Ādiśeṣa left this world, much elation there was in *Pātala*.[424]

O Bṛhaspati! Walk ahead of this distinguished scholar called Śrīkaṇṭha Śāstri, who is leaving this world! O Śukrāçārya! Approach the gateway of heaven, with Rāmakavi, the Śāstri's brother! O Guru! Venerate the Śāstri, as indeed his great accomplishments warrant![425]

Is it any wonder that the Śāstri should forget about this world when Indra himself, seated in his court Sudharma, bade Rambhā and the other *apsaras* leave upon learning of the Śāstri's arrival, and then began to venerate him?

O jewel of learning! As you sit in Indra's court discoursing upon grammar, and your brother composes delicate verses, the two of you are indeed ornaments to this divine assembly!

The fearless lion has departed for heaven. Now let the foxes exit their burrows and shriek their cacophony!

When the sun has set, only then are the stars visible. Only when Śrīkaṇṭha, the crest-jewel of learning, has left this earth, do scholars like us begin to appear.

Aṇṇayya! Your son, your brother, and daughter are eagerly waiting to welcome you, who are now approaching the gates of heaven.

---

[422] This "own home" is heaven. Patañjali is traditionally regarded as an earthly incarnation of Ādiśeṣa, who is the king of all serpents, a primal being of creation, and a manifestation of Nārāyaṇa.

[423] A reference to Ādiśeṣa.

[424] The fan, the umbrella, and the flag are all insignia of royalty, to which Ādiśeṣa would be entitled. The serpent Vāsuki was used as a rope around Mount Meru by the *dēvas* and *asuras* as they used Meru to churn the primordial ocean of milk. In the *Nalopākhyānam* of the *Mahābhārata*, the serpent Karkōṭaka transforms the handsome Nala into an ugly being by biting him. Takṣaka is also a serpent mentioned in the *Mahābhārata*. In Indian cosmology, *Pātala* refers to the nether regions, the lowest of which is inhabited by the Nāgas, the serpent-people.

[425] Bṛhaspati is the *purohita* of the gods, and also the deity of wisdom and eloquence. Śukrāçārya is the preceptor of the *daityas*. Guru (here, *suraguru*) is the preceptor of the gods, also identified with Bṛhaspati.

Dear readers! All who knew the Śāstri's abilities agree that this poet's words are literally true. Such a luminary it was who left this world in his eighty-fourth year.[426]

mahāvidvān dharmādhikṛd'api mahāraja·bhavanē
çirād'apy'āsīd yas'taraḷa iva mālāsu sudhiyām |
çatasraś'ç'āśītiṁ śarada iha bhuktvā sura·purī·
m'avāptuṁ śrīkaṇṭhō nijam'iha jaḍam dēham'ajahāt ‖

[426]The following verse is by Mattigūḍu Narasiṁhaśāstri, the brother of Mattigūḍu Vāsudēvaśāstri, who wrote the verses that appear immdiately above [Śāstri 1934, p. 5]. Narasiṁhaśāstri was the husband of Veṅkaṭalakṣmī, who was the daughter of Veṅkaṭakṛṣṇa, and granddaughter of Śrīkaṇṭha Śāstri. See footnote 336.

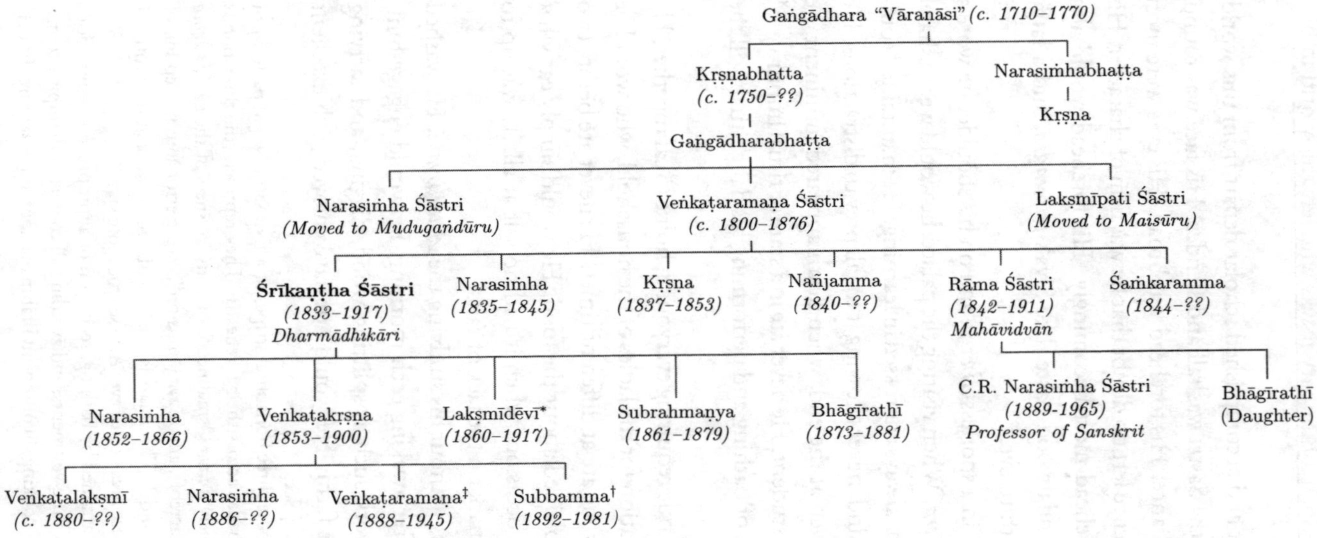

*Lakṣmīdēvī married Sōsale Ayyā Śāstri (1855–1934), son of Sōsale Garaḷapuri Śāstri (1822–1877).

†Subbamma married Sōsale Garaḷapuri Śāstri (1888–1955), son of Sōsale Ayyā Śāstri.

‡Veṅkaṭaramaṇa Śāstri is the author of the biographies of Sōsale Garaḷapuri Śāstri and Çāmarājanagara Śrīkaṇṭha Śāstri.

Plate 33: Genealogy of *Dharmādhikāri* Çāmarājanagara Śrīkaṇṭha Śāstri, compiled by the translator from the information in this biography and in [Śāstri 1925b].

13. His Many Virtues

Thus did this great and accomplished scholar depart from this world. In aspect, Śrīkaṇṭha Śāstri was tall and slender. His face was round, and full of a divine radiance. His forehead was broad. His eyes were most handsome. His appearence left no doubt that he was firm of character. His *vibhūti* covered his forehead most becomingly. His forehead would also bear three stripes of sandalwood paste, like Śiva's *tripuṇḍra*, and a large *akṣate* mark, like Śiva's third eye.[427]

He dressed himself in a spotless *dhōtra*, and on his shoulder he wore a shawl folded with a *dhōtra*. When visiting the palace, he would wear a shawl as turban. The Śāstri was always engrossed in learning. He maintained complete control over his mind, never allowing it to fall prey to distractions. He was always teaching. Even at the end, when death appeared imminent, he took the time to teach a student. He never ate in a state of ritual impurity.[428] He kept up his practice of bathing and performing his daily rituals, till the very end.

He had instituted a rule requiring everyone at home to eat together. He did this out of consideration for the ladies of the household, who would be inconvenienced if everyone ate at different times. He never ate before two o'clock. He never complained about the food. He would simply eat what he was served, even on occasions when it had no salt at all. It was up to others to notice and remark on the lack of salt.

Never did a day pass without his studying the *Aṣṭādhyāyī*. He washed his clothes himself. After awaking each morning, he would engage himself in back-breaking work such as splitting wood, digging, and carrying in heavy loads from the farm. He would not have enjoyed such excellent

[427] The *tripuṇḍra* refers to the three horizontal stripes of ash or sandalwood paste worn by Śaivaite or *Smārta* brāhmaṇas across their foreheads. They represent the three bonds which ensnare the soul, namely *aṇava* ("smallness", or consciousness of the ego), *karma* ("action", that is, the fruits thereof), and *maya* ("illusion", or the erroneous perception of the world mediated by our minds). The *akṣate* is a red circular mark work at the centre of the *tripuṇḍra*, said to symbolize Śiva's third eye. Also see footnote 134.

[428] Ritual purity (*maḍi*) is attained by bathing, recitation of appropriate *mantras*, donning a minimal set of ritually pure vestments, and avoiding all contact with impure items. Even household tasks (such as cooking) in observant brāhmaṇa households require the performer to be ritually pure.

health had he not performed such hard work. He was never known to take to bed due to illness. He would go to bed at ten, awake at three, and begin to study. He would say nothing if he saw a grandchild of his whiling away the time without studying, but would himself begin to study what the child was to study. The child, ashamed of seeing his grandfather study in his stead, would start studying.

It is clear from many indications that he was always engaged in introspection. During his final illness, he would remain in bed, covered in a sheet from head to toe. If a grandchild came by and called out *"Aṇṇayya!"* to him, he would uncover his face, and after speaking, cover himself again. Someone looking at him as he lay silently and still, might indeed wonder if he were still alive. He was a great devotee of Narasiṁhasvāmi of Mēlukōṭe.[429] He worshipped him constantly. At night he would sometimes loudly exclaim: "*He!* Lakṣmīnarasiṁha!"

While no one could face him when was angry, he was always calm and collected. There was little opportunity for conversation with him on matters other than scholarly and technical. As hard as it was for beginners to study with him, in equal measure did advanced students derive pleasure and satisfaction from their studies with him. Many are those who have undertaken advanced studies with him and achieved great distinction as scholars. Starting with *Ve*‖ Kānkānhaḷḷi Varadāçārya, who teaches Kannaḍa and *Saṁskṛta* at Mahārāja's College in Maisūru, and *Ve*‖ Timmappayya Śāstri, a distinguished scholar at the Normal School in Maisūru, it is universally accepted that practically all the Kannaḍa and *Saṁskṛta* scholars in the colleges and high schools of the state of Maisūru were among his students.

The Śāstri always spoke the truth. He would have no patience with those who spoke falsehoods. A person called Mādana who tended his fields had cheated and lied to him, not giving him his proper share of the grain the fields yielded. The Śāstri discovered his dishonesty after some considerable time, and discharged him. Although the Śāstri, out of consideration, caused him no unpleasantness, Mādana's own deceit caused him to lose both his eyes, even in this birth. Our eyes have been witness to many others who have, in this same fashion, cheated, lied, and otherwise troubled this gentle soul, and are now suffering greatly, experiencing the results of their misdeeds. It has been said in this connection:

---

[429] See footnote 383.

dāru·ċarma·viniśvāsaṁ dahatē lōha·pañċakam |
sādhu·sajjana·santāpaṁ kim'āṣċaryaṁ kula·kṣayam ||

Meaning: Even the breath that the bellows blows burns all metals. It it any wonder that the suffering of the good and gentle should ruin an entire clan?

satāṁ santāpam'utpādya śāpaṁ dēh'īti nō vadēt |
satāṁ santōṣam'utpādya hy'āśiṣaṁ naiva yāċayēt ||

meaning that those who bring suffering to the good and gentle need invite no one to curse them. Those who bring them happiness have no need of blessing. Indeed, stealing the property of a brāhmaṇa, causing suffering to the meek and gentle, causing the ruin of someone without just cause, not helping the righteous when one is able to render such help, and killing a brāhmaṇa, are all considered as being the worst among evils. The *śāstras* assure us that perpetrator of such evils is certain to suffer the consequences of his misdeeds.

tribhir'varṣais'tribhir'māsais'tribhiḥ pakṣais'tribhir'dinai |
aty'utkaṭaiḥ puṇya·pāpair ihaiva phalam'aśnutē ||

meaning that the perpetrator of these worst of evils is certain, even in this very birth, to suffer their consequences, whether in three years, three months, three fortnights, or in just three days.[430] Because good deeds, in like manner, have good consequences, it is simply this writer's purpose that everyone reflect upon good and evil in their pursuit of piety.

It would upset the Śāstri exceedingly to hear anyone disparaging the *Vēdic śāstras.* Indeed, he would stop speaking with such persons altogether. His radiant appearance would cause people to remark that in him were present elements of Īśvara's divinity. This feeling was expressed not just by Hindus, but also by many Muslims. When he was teaching at the Normal School, the resident *Maulavi* would respectfully render him *"salāms"*, remarking that he was indeed godly, not merely human. On one occasion, the Śāstri was returning home from his fields. It was about ten in the morning. The Śāstri had worn his *vibhūti* broadly across his forehead, and was dressed in a substantial *dhōtra* and a gold-embroidered shawl, and held a

[430] This verse is from the *Hitopadeśa (mitralābha: 82).*

stick in his hand. A Muslim from south of the valley,[431] who had come to trade at the Tuesday fair at Marahaḷḷi, looking at the Śāstri from head to toe, prostrated himself before him, saying: "*Svāmi,* to my eyes you appear divine. Your shawl surpasses the sort that ordinary people wear. Your radiance is extraordinary. I am truly blessed to have seen you this day." The inner qualities that the heart of a pious person has accumulated from good deeds over many births are often outwardly manifested in this manner.

Abdul Khāliq *sāhēb,* who is now *Amaldār* of Nagara used to be *Śirastedār* of Çāmarājanagara. Whenever the Śāstri visited his offices to collect his pension, the *sāhēb,* moved by the Śāstri's radiance, would have him sit on the chair next to him, and proceed to discuss Hindu *śāstras* and *Purāṇas.* Devotion to god and good nature always go together. These qualities are generally to be found in the hearts of the pious.

The Śāstri always wrote in verse to those whose stature matched his own. His poetry was most dignified. We are in possession of many of his verses, but have not published them due to lack of space. He would never abandon any task he undertook, until it had yielded results. While employed in the Çāmarājanagara temple, the Śāstri was much troubled by regulations changing with administrations. The Śāstri endured such vexations.

In the middle of *prākāra* on the western side of the Çāmarājēśvarasvāmi temple that Kṛṣṇarāja Voḍeyar III built in his father's name, he also established a *śivaliṅga* called "Khāsa Prasanna Nañjarājēśvara", his father's given name, and ensuring that it would unfailingly receive *abhiṣēka* and other devotions by placing his beloved Śrīkaṇṭha Śāstri in charge of its *mantrapuṣpa* ritual and making various other arrangements, he also established inscriptions, in which he has had the following *ślōka* carved:

mad'vaṁśajāḥ para·mahīpati·vaṁśajā vā
yē bhūmipās'satatam'ujvala·dharma·çittāḥ |
mad'dharmam'ēva satataṁ paripālayanti |
tat'pāda·padma·yugaḷaṁ śirasā namāmi ||

---

[431] From the Coimbatore region, that is. The valley referenced is the Gajjala Haṭṭi valley in the Nīlagiri mountains. The epithet "from south of the valley" is also applied to brāhmaṇas, as elaborated by Lakshminarasimhaiya *et al.,* [1970, p. 4]: "Another group of Vadadesha Vadamas moved south to Karur, Coimbatore and Bhavani along the upper Kaveri, and quietly entered Mysore rajya from Satyamangalam and became known as Kanive-Kelaginavaru (the settlers from Coimbatore district through Gajjala Hatti Valley in the Nilgiri mountains)."

Meaning: I offer my salutations at the feet of the one who, in devotion to *dharma,* preserves my *dharmic* works, be he from my own family or from that of another king.[432]

Dear reader! We shall not ever see another such king born. What an upright and pious king! What a symbol of righteousness! Could such a generous heart really have existed? We are not competent to take the measure of the generosity of such a king, born from sparks of divinity, or of his deep devotion to god and brahmaṇas! Ah, did Death, in his heartless way, take away from us a person of such greatness?

[432] The noble sentiment expressed here is is in fact quite old, and found in earlier inscriptions. For example, Baḷḷāla Dēva's Gaddak inscription no. 2 of 1192 C.E. ends in a very similar fashion [Fleet 1873, p. 301]: *"madvaṁśajāḥ paramahīpativaṁśajā vā pāpādapētamanasōbhuvibhavibhūpaḥ | yē pālayanti mama dharmamimaṁ samagraṁ tēṣāṁ mayā viraçitoṁjalirēśa mūrdhni ‖"*

|| ŚRĪ ||

BIOGRAPHY OF KUṆIGALA RĀMAŚĀSTRI

Maisūru Sūryanārayaṇabhaṭṭa Puṭṭaṇṇa

ŚUBHAMASTU

Plate 34: *Dharmādhikāri* Kuṇigala Rāmaśāstri (1807–1860). Frontispiece from original biography.

Preface

I begin by doing reverence to Gaṇapati and Sarasvatī. I next prostrate myself at the lotus feet of the *Jagadguru* of the Śṛṅgēri *maṭha*.[433]

Many great personages, possessed of special endowments, have lived in the past. They have accomplished many great works. The fruits of their deeds are now ours to enjoy. By learning of those from whom these fruits have obtained, and how they lived their lives, we might learn to live our lives as they did. Their biographies therefore hold special value for us. Such biographies, however, are rare in the languages of our nation.

Kuṇigala Rāmaśāstri was a scholar of extraordinary calibre. No one like him has been born since. New ways are now pervading the customs of our people, as old ways continue to disappear. Rāmaśāstri lived at a time when the old ways were drawing to an end. This biography allows us to draw comparisons between his times and our own.

We have not the means, however, to describe his exceptional accomplishments in all areas. Being a *vaidika*, he maintained no diaries or journals to document his daily routine. I was therefore led to collect a great deal of information on him from his many students, using one account to confirm another. I took detailed notes. It has been 16 years since I began this effort.

Kuṇigala Rāmaśāstri having been among the foremost of the scholars at Kṛṣṇarāja Voḍeyar III's court, we have taken the opportunity to describe such matters, whenever they directly or indirectly relate to this biography, as the state of the royal court and its practices, the accomplishments and virtues of the *vaidikas* and *laukikas* at court, the manner of study at the time, the accomplishments of his scholarly peers, and the many virtues of the king himself, the pillar who sustained this enterprise. Our account would lack felicity were we to disregard the character of this royal *ṛṣi*, whose dedication to scholars might eclipse that of Vikrama, Bhōja, and the Peśvas. We have hence been led to provide accounts of court itself, even if briefly. These matters are by no means irrelevant.

---

[433] This would be *Jagadguru* Saççidānanda Śivābhinava Nṛsiṁha Bhāratī, who was in fact, the son of Kuṇigala Rāmaśāstri. See Plate 26b.

Rāmaśāstri was a strict *Advaitin*; on many occasions, he refuted the tenets of *Dvaita* and *Viśiṣṭādvaita* in debates with their proponents. No disrespect to *Vaiṣṇavas* or the followers of Rāmānuja should be inferred from my accounts of such episodes. I beg forgiveness for any lapses in my writing.

Many scholars of *Saṁskṛta* look down upon books in our vernacular languages, as they contain few materials relevant to their interests. English scholars are already indifferent to these works. There are hence few readers for works in our regional languages. To understand the brilliance of the Śāstri, who authored many works on *Nyāya* and *Vēdānta*, it is also essential to discuss such works of his. However, a discussion of such works would make the biography very difficult reading, and lose most readers. Omitting these matters would not reveal the depth of the Śāstri's abilities. Difficulties such as these arose repeatedly during my efforts. I have nevertheless persevered sufficiently to finished what I started. Discerning readers must look upon my shortcomings with forgiveness, bearing in mind instead my enthusiasm for placing before them the biography of a great personage.

I am deeply grateful to many of the Śāstri's students, including Vāsudēvaśāstri of Doḍḍabaḷḷāpura, Nārāyaṇaśāstri of Sāggere, Subrahmaṇyaśāstri, Gaṅgādharaśāstri of Soṇḍekoppa, Śrīnivāsāçārya of Dhāravāḍa, and *Dharmādhikāri* Kāśī Rāmaśāstri, who provided me with so much of the information I have needed. I cannot forget the assistance I received from Nārayaṇaśāstri of Doḍḍabele, who provided me with much essential information from *Saṁskṛta* books. Always foremost in my mind is the special help I received from Śrīkaṇṭha Śāstri, the *Sarvādhikāri* of the Śṛṅgeri *maṭha* and from *Dharmādhikāri* Rāmaśāstri, as well as the help throughout this endeavor from B.C. Kṛṣṇaśāstri. Yet, if all these persons were weighed together and their worth multiplied by ten, ten times greater still would be the merit of the lotus feet of the *Paramahaṁsa Parivrājakāçārya*, the *Jagadguru* of the Śṛṅgeri *maṭha,* which feet I salute at each of the three *sandhyās* each day.

Mai. Sū. Pu.

Beṅgaḷūru
Saumya *saṁvatsara* ‖ *uttarāyaṇa*
puṇyakāla Puṣya *śukla* ‖ 3 Śukravāra
Śaka 1832[434]

[434] This date would be Friday, January 2, 1910 C.E.

śrī
śubhamastu
śrī lakṣmīnarasiṁha prasīda

CHAPTER I: PREAMBLE

THERE ARE stars in the sky. They shine brightly. They appear to all. They shine, more or less, in all parts of the sky. Fewer stars are visible in cold regions, such as Europe, than in warm regions, such as India. Westerners, the people of Europe, have used means such as telescopes to research stars both visible and invisible to them, to determine their nature, their distances from the Earth, the materials they comprise and their properties, the causes of their luminosity, and the thousands of years that it takes their light to reach our Earth. Despite the many stars visible only in our India, few among our people are acquainted with their nature. Were one to inquire "What are stars?", it appears too much to expect even the response "The lights that twinkle in the night sky!"

Thus also it is that if we make our populace our sky, we may witness the genius of the Westerners and the dullness of our own people. Whether they take a person endowed with the genius of Bṛhaspati and the learning of Sarasvatī, or an ordinary person who might add three and four to get seven, one may count on Westerners to present splendid analyses of the abilities of such people, how they developed these abilities, and what benefits accrued to mankind from their works. Yet, among our people, who consider it improper to display portraits or to praise oneself or others, and lean strongly towards asceticism, holding the sole purpose of life to be the search for salvation, few realize the benefit to their intellectual progress of learning about the contributions of our own geniuses, such as Pāṇini, Āryabhaṭa, Śaṅkarāçārya, Kāḷidāsa, and Vidyāraṇya, or that of viewing themselves in the context of the lives of such people. Owing to such indifference among our people, many of the great personages of India might as well have never existed, at least as far as outsiders and the uninformed are concerned. Foreign writers have gained prestige even as we have continued stroking our beards in expression of amazement at their scholarship. To those familiar with both the traditional and modern approaches to learning, it will surely seem proper that we should document the lives of the luminaries about whom information may still be gathered, although we must inevitably set aside the many whose biographies it is no longer feasible to write.

Ten *haridāris* west of Maisūru is a place called Yeḍatore.[435] The Kāvērī flows prodigiously near this town. A section of that stream is called *Arkapuṣkariṇi.* Nearby is the temple of Arkēśvara. According to local tradition, the rays of the sun fall upon the crown of the Arkēśvara idol in the sanctum sanctorum on the morning of the *Rathasaptami* festival.[436] Due to the Kāvērī's influence, the land is green as far as meets the eye. Not only is bathing in the *Arkapuṣkariṇi* and worship of Arkēśvara conducive to fulfilment in the next world, the richness of the soil and the abundance of water are conducive to fulfilment in this world as well. This site being most fitting as a habitation for brāhmaṇas, long has there existed a large settlement of brāhmaṇas in this place. These brāhmaṇas were largely teachers, scholars, and *agnihōtris,* deeply devoted to their daily observances, and unwearied by worldly matters.

A narrative exists, relating to the accomplishments of these very brāhmaṇas. A king once arrived at Yeḍatore. He set up camp there, and having found a suitable house among those available, lodged therein with the members of his family. After a day or two, while walking about in the courtyard in the morning, he noticed a small chamber with the sign *'Agnihōtra Chamber'* above the door.[437] Upon inquiry, he learned from local officials

---

[435] A *haridāri* is about three miles. Yeḍatore is about 45 km northwest of Maisūru. This town had a population of 2,413 in 1876 C.E. [Rice 1897a, p. 316]. Also see page 95.

[436] The Archeological Department of Maisūru [1936] gives the following information: "An undated inscription, No. 64 of Yedatore taluk, Mysore District Supplement, which is in Tamil and Grantha characters and belongs probably to the time of Kulōttunga Chōla I, mentions that a certain Ankakkāran, son of Ponnāndān, errected a temple named Ankakkārēśvara for the god Nāyarukilavar, lord of Aiyamapolil alias Uyyakkonda-Śolapattanam in Turaināḍu and granted lands to it. There is no doubt that Ankakkālēśvara is the same as Arkēśvara or the sun god (Nāyarukkilavar) for whom the temple is built in Yedatore." Much of the current temple dates to the time of the Hoysaḷa kings. *Rathasaptami* is the seventh day of the *śukla* fortnight of the month of Māgha, the start of the northerly movement of the sun. Metaphorically, the sun turns his chariot (*ratha*) northwards. Local tradition has it that the rays of the sun fall upon the head of the Arkēśvara idol on this day.

[437] The *Agnihōtra* ritual, an ancient rite likely dating back to pre-*Vēdic* times, is performed

that the house belonged to a *sōmayāji* devoted to the practice of *yajñas.*[438] When the king called the *sōmayāji* to his presence, and asked: "Why sir, is there a sign saying *'Agnihōtra Chamber'* above the door of this small chamber?" the brāhmaṇa replied: "Your Highness, I have placed this sign to prevent this chamber from being used for any base purpose." The king decided to honor this brāhmaṇa by giving him the gift that it was his practice to give daily. The *sōmayāji* extended his left hand to receive this gift. The king was greatly angered by this insulting gesture.[439] He said angrily: "What impertinence to proffer your left hand to receive my gift!" The *sōmayāji* responded:

---

at sunset and sunrise, and may be seen as establishing a ritual connection between Agni, the fire here on the earth, and Sūrya, the sun, the fire in the heavens. The epithet *agnihotri* can refer either to an observant brāhmaṇa who performs this ritual, or to one who maintains three sacred domestic fires, namely the *Gārhapatya, Āhavanīya,* and *Dakṣiṇāgni.* An *agnihotri* (also, *āhitāgni*) who maintains these fires all his life has acquired such special merit that his past sins are destroyed with his body when he is cremated upon his death. The chamber dedicated to maintaining these fires is called the *agnyāgāra* or *agniśāla,* ("fire-chamber"), or *agniśaraṇam* ("fire-refuge"). See Kālidāsa's *Abhijñānaśākuntalam,* Act 4 (Priyamvada): *"agniśaraṇaṁ praviṣṭasya śarīraṁ vinā ḉhandomayya vācayā |"* The term *Agnihotra* is also used as a synecdoche to refer to the seven *haviryajñās,* namely *Agnyādheya, Agnihotra, Darśapūrṇamāsau, Ḉaturmasyāni, Paśubandha, Sautrāmaṇī,* and *Pākayajña.* Thus, when the *Maitrāyaṇī Upaniṣad* (6:36) says *"agnihotraṁ juhuyāt svargakm̄aḥ"*, meaning *"let him, who seeks salvation perform the Agnihotra"*, it is using the term *Agnihotra* in this sense.

[438] A *sōmayājin* is a person who conducts the *sōmayāga* sacrifice or partakes of the *soma* libation during this sacrifice. *Yajñas* are elaborate ancient *Vēdic* rituals that are by far the most complicated religious rituals found anywhere, the details of whose performance are specified in excruciating detail. *Somayāgas* are especially complex. The *Agniḉayana* ritual, for instance, lasts twelve days, and as Converse [1974] explains:

> The immediate practical purpose of the Agnicayana rite is to build up for the sacrificer an immortal body that is permanently beyond the reach of the transitoriness, suffering, and death that, according to this rite, characterize man's mortal existence. The purpose is to be achieved by ritual analogy in the rebuilding of the 'unstrung' body of the god Prajapati. The rite includes a year's preparation and then the placing of a minimum of 10,800 kiln-fired bricks (a sizable brick-making operation) in minutely prescribed sequence and position, in five layers, with the sacrificial fire placed on top. At every point, with every brick, special mantras are to be recited, special actions carried out, and the religious meanings of each part of the rite carefully explained."

Vēdic yajñas are also the most ancient religious rituals known. See Converse [1974] for strong evidence of the indigineous, pre-*Vēdic* origins of the *Agniḉayana.* Amazingly, an unbroken tradition of performance of this ritual exists in India, especially in Āndhra Pradeśa (see Knipe [2015]) and among the Nambūthiri brāhmaṇas of Kerala [Staal 2001a].

[439] The left hand being inauspicious, as in most cultures, one never gives or receives with this hand.

"Do not be angry Your Highness. The *śāstras* declare that Agni resides in the brāhmaṇa's right hand.[440] I merely extended my left hand from fear that my right hand might scorch your gift." When the king asked: "Indeed, does Yajñēśvara reside in your hand even now?" the *sōmayāji,* saying that he was ready to be tested, had some dried cowdung sprinkled on his hand.[441] The powder began to smoulder and smoke. The king was astonished at such powers. He arose, prostrated himself before the brāhmaṇa, and after doing him great honors and arranging for a monthly stipend, departed from the place.[442] Such a tradition exists regarding Yeḍatore. Even if we choose to see this as hyperbole, there is little doubt that the residents of this place were sufficiently pious to have inspired such a tale.

In this hallowed place lived contentedly a brāhmaṇa family belonging to the Telugu *Mulukunāḍu* community, the Kāśyapa *gōtra* and the *Āpastamba Sūtra,* and second to none in their scholarship, rigor of observance, or conduct. In this family there was a Yajñanārāyaṇa Śāstri, especially observant of ritual, maintaining the tradition of *agnihotra,* performing *yajñas* such as the *Agniṣṭōma* and the *Atirātra,* and who, in his sixtieth year, left this province for a village called Sēramahādēvi near Tirunelvēli south of the valley, and giving up all attachments to his wife and family, lived ten years a *saṁnyāsi,* attaining *siddhi* in his seventieth year. Eight years after his death, a brāhmaṇa arriving in Yeḍatore from that region conveyed this information to Yajñanārāyaṇa Śāstri's son Pāpaśāstri. All funerary rites were thereupon completed. Yajñanārāyaṇa Śāstri's resolve and the asceticism it engendered were praiseworthy indeed.

---

[440] See *Manusmṛti,* Chapter 3, v.212: *"agnyabhāve tu viprasya pāṇavevopapādayet | yo hyagniḥ sa dvijo viprairmantradarśabhiruççyate ‖"* meaning "But if no (sacred) fire (is available), he shall place (the offerings) into the hand of a Brahmana; for Brahmanas who know the sacred texts declare, 'What fire is, even such is a Brahmana.' "

[441] Dried cowdung is widely used in India as kindling and fuel.

[442] This anecdote also appears in Vāsudevāçārya [1962, p. 79]. In this version, Kṛṣṇarāja Voḍeyar III, being once beset by the evil influences of an inauspicious planetary configuration, was advised to counter them through the gift of a golden cow to a virtuous brāhmaṇa. Nobody at court having the courage to come forward as deserving of such a gift, the king was informed that a certain pious *sōmayāji* living in Yeḍatore was surely sufficiently deserving. When called to the palace and asked to accept the gift, the *sōmayāji* proffered his left hand, but upon being admonished, accepted the gift with his right hand. He then demonstrated the reason for his apparent impertinence, as described. The king, himself well versed in astrology, saw immediately that his gift would now not have the intended exculpatory effect. The *sōmayāji,* too, begged the king's forgiveness. Owing to this transgression, the king lost his kingdom to the British in due course (in 1831 C.E.).

His son Pāpaśāstri, or Nārāyaṇaśāstri, was learned in the *Vēdas,* knowledgeable in the *śrauta* rituals, and also very devout. Not once did he forego his ritual morning bath, his recitation of a thousand *Gāyatrīs*, or other such observances. Even when his son died before his very eyes and his corpse lay before him did he show no undue emotion, having the corpse removed only after completing his daily ritual of bathing in the river *1822*
at early dawn.[443] It is no ordinary person who can still his mind under such adverse circumstances and show such unwavering commitment to his observances. He lived for ninety-three years before he passed away. His son Narasiṁhaśāstri was learned in the *Vēdas* and was a literary scholar.[444] He was reputed as an outstanding teacher of logic and *Vēdānta.* He was employed by the Maisūru palace at a salary of five *Varāhas*. He died in his fiftieth year, right before the eyes of his father Pāpaśāstri.

Narasiṁhaśāstri's wife was from Śivagaṅge. Her family too, was learned to a fair degree; it appears that this family was originally from Kuṇigal.[445] Narasiṁhaśāstri's two eldest children were sons. The first was named Narasiṁhaśāstri. He was an excellent *ghanapāṭhi*.[446] We have learned that he

[443] A brāhmaṇa's ritual duties fall into three categories: *nitya* (obligatory), *naimittika* (mandated for specific occasions) and *kāmya* (to achieve certain goals). With some variations, the *dharmaśāstras* mandate that *nitya* duties, such as *Sandhyāvandana*, be performed under all circumstances, including the death of a close relative [Kane 1953a]. This absolute insistence on performing one's ritual duties was an important traditional value in India, with ancient roots in the *Vēdic* notions of *ṛta*, the principle of natural order in the universe. Everything and everyone has a role in this natural order. Performance of this role ensured harmony, and violations of it had adverse consequences. In subsequent periods, this notion gave rise to the concept of *dharma*, etymologically derived from the root *dhṛ*, "to uphold" (these roles). *Dharma* is upheld through an individual's performance of *karma*, or actions. Rituals, especially of the *nitya* category, were an important part of the *karma* enjoined upon brāhmaṇas. Uncompromising performance of these *karmas* ensured harmony, and brought merit not merely upon the individual, but also upon the society that promoted these practices. This was a major reason for the support such rituals had from society and from kings and other notables despite the enormous cost associated with them. *Vēdic* rituals are easily the most elaborate and complex in the world. Also see footnotes 437 and 438.

[444] His name appears as Lakṣmīnarasiṁhaśāstri in what follows. It will become clear shortly that he died in 1822 C.E., at the age of fifty, so he must have been born in 1772 C.E.

[445] Śivagaṅge is about 50 km northwest of Bengaḷūru, en route to Tumakūru. Kuṇigal is about 25 km southwest of Śivagaṅge.

[446] The oral tradition of *Vēdic* recitation has preserved the *Vēdas* with such fidelity that variant readings are extremely rare, despite the intervening millennia. Such fidelity is attained by learning the text not simply as it is, but also in numerous variant forms, each

left for Kāśī in the Saumya *saṁvatsara*, and attained *siddhi* in the Sādhāraṇa *saṁvatsara*.[447]

The second son was the great scholar Rāmaśāstri. Somehow, Kuṇigal, his maternal grandfather's place of origin, became a sobriquet or surname, and he became known as Kuṇigala Rāmaśāstri. He was well known in the Maisūru region as Kuṇigala Rāmaśāstri, in the Beṅgaḷūru region as Yeḍatore Rāmaśāstri, and in the regions south of the valley as Maisūra Rāmaśāstri.[448]

---

following the original rules of *Vēdic* intonation and euphony. These patterns of recitation are called the *saṁhitā, pada, krama, jaṭa, mālā, śikhā, rekhā, dhvaja, ratha*, and the *ghana pāṭhas*, respectively. The simplest is the *saṁhitā pāṭha*, the original text recited directly, preserving the intonation and *saṁdhi* structure. The next is *pada pāṭha*, where the words are separated, and recited in sequence, as $w_1, w_2, w_3, \ldots, w_N$. In *jaṭā pāṭha* recitation, we see the first variant, with words permuted pairwise, as w_1w_2, w_2w_1, w_1w_2, w_2w_3, w_3w_2, $w_2w_3, \ldots$ In *dhvaja pāṭha* the words are recited pairwise from each end, proceeding towards the middle, as w_1w_2, $w_{N-1}w_N$, w_2w_3, $w_{N-3}w_{N-2}, \ldots, w_{N-1}w_N, w_1w_2$. Mentally most demanding is the *ghana pāṭha* mode, which requires recitation in the word order w_1w_2, w_2w_1, $w_1w_2w_3$, $w_3w_2w_1$, $w_1w_2w_3$, w_2w_3, w_3w_2, $w_2w_3w_4$, $w_4w_3w_2$, $w_2w_3w_4$, and so on. All recitation is purely from memory. Expert *ghanapāṭhis* are highly respected, and for good reason.

[447] These years correspond to 1849–1850 C.E., and 1850–1851 C.E., respectively.

[448] See footnote 431.

Chapter 2: Birth and Childhood

This Rāmaśāstri was born in in Śivagaṅge in his maternal grandfather's house, under the *nakṣatra* Svāti, on the third *bahuḷa* day of the Çaitra month of the Prabhava *saṁvatsara*, the eighth year after the loss of Śrīraṅgapaṭṭaṇa.[449]

Śivagaṅge is about 34 miles distant from Beṅgaḷūru. His mother used to say that the sound of a cannon fired in Beṅgaḷūru on account of some royal occasion was heard at the instant of this infant's birth. The belief is common to all nations and cultures that such auspicious omens accompany the births of great and virtuous benefactors of Humanity. It is not easy for us to analyse such events, and reject the possibility of there being a causal connection between them. It appears to be beyond our present abilities to determine if such omens, whether at the births or deaths of such great persons, signify deep connections between the universe of intellect their minds naturally incline to and the external universe born of the five elements, or are mere coincidences. Whatever these links may be, such omens occur invariably in conjunction with great events.

April 25, 1807

Even from childhood, Rāmaśāstri was healthy and robust. He was full of mischief as a child, and especially interested in play. Many are displeased when children are mischievous. A strong intellect does not, however, remain still; it occupies itself with all manner of work, engaging with big things if one is mature, and if still young and lacking in experience, it engages with smaller works, providing the right experience and learning from each activity. But children are only capable of learning from their activities; because they are not yet capable of leaving things as adults may have left them, it is often the practice to blindly regard this as idle mischief and punish them. Because the value gained from mischief does not accrue from inactivity, one must consider that the child has gained ten times more from engaging in mischief, even if it means a certain inconvenience. Play in children improves both their intellect as well as their physical well-being. It is

[449] This *tithi* matches Saturday, April 25, 1807 C.E. However, the corresponding *nakṣatra* appears to have been Jyeṣṭhā, rather than Svātī.

important, therefore, to leave children to their play without undue interference, except to watch for excessive dangers.

Such playfulness and mischief were present in great measure in Rāmaśāstri. He would excel in any game he played, outdoing all his playmates. If a conflict arose with any of his playmates, he would give them a thrashing. One *Dīvān* Sūrappa, who was *Amīl* in the Beṅgaḷūru *tālluk,* and held the office of *Śirastedār,* had been soundly thrashed in childhood by this Rāma.[450] After Rāmaśāstri attained renown, this official would tease him, saying: "Śāstri! The marks of your handiwork are still visible on my head!" and displaying the scar, would add: "In those days, you defeated all by pummelling them with your hands, you now defeat the world by pummelling it with your scholarship!" This pursuit of victory, then a mere germ, grew in strength over time. Rāma would repeatedly swim from one bank of the Kāvērī in Yeḍatore to the other. He was an enthusiastic swimmer. A woman once fell into the Kāvērī by accident, and was being swept away. Rāmaśāstri jumped into the river, seized the woman by her hair, and brought her to shore. He and the others around him rubbed her body with ash to expel the water she had swallowed. Ramā had thus saved her life. That he played in this manner in his childhood greatly benefited his robustness in later life.

His father Lakṣmīnarasiṁhaśāstri was not unaware of his son's precocity. His *upanayana* and other ceremonies proceeded in the prescribed manner. His grandfather Pāpaśāstri began to teach him the *Vēdas.*
1822 This was followed by the tradition of teaching him the *Raghuvaṁśa* and other poetic works, to develop his knowledge of *Saṁskṛta.* As soon as he had learned the language began his training in logic.[451] At this

[450] A *Śirastedār* is the head of a revenue or judicial office. Sūrappa was appointed *Huzūr Head Śirastedār* in 1838. See footnote 509 for details. There is a street even today in the Çikkapēṭe section of Beṅgaḷūru called Dewan Surappa Street. Also see Appendix III of Lakshminarasimhaiya *et al.,* [1970] for a memorial dated October 27, 1840 C.E. by one 'Anneayah Sastree' to the Governor General of India, complaining of corruption in the administration of Colonel Cubbon, and specifically naming a 'Dewan Soorappa' as a conduit of bribes to Cubbon. This document indicates that this Soorappa had been so ill some two years prior as to have been unlikely to recover. *Śirastedār* Sūrappa died in 1840 (see footnote 509).

[451] Presumably under the guidance of his father, whom we know to have been well versed in logic. The discussion to ensue refers to the *Navya Nyāya* development of Indian logic. Indian logic has a long and rich history, its origins being independent of, but contemporaneous with that of logic in Greece. The Indian syllogism differs structurally from that of the

time, his father Lakṣmīnarasiṁhaśāstri passed away in Yeḍatore. Rāmaśāstri was fifteen years old.

There were now obstacles to Rāmaśāstri's continued education. This concern also arose in Rāmaśāstri's mother's mind. Although the modern practice of female education was not then current, it is clear that she was discriminating enough to grasp the acuity of her son's intelligence, and realize that it would not flower without education and training. Yeḍatore was not suitable for the education of such a talented child. Although home to numerous devout individuals, this place was not able to support scholars. Scholarship, as is well known, cannot be sustained without the support of a generous king or a person of affluence. Such support being substantially forthcoming in Kṛṣṇarāja Voḍeyar III's court, many scholars from the towns around Maisūru were at his court. It was hence difficult, except in Maisūru, to find a teacher with the competence to instruct a student with Rāma's abilities and eagerness. Rāma therefore left Yeḍatore and came to Maisūru.

An occasion arose that illuminated the extent of this young man's abilities at the time he arrived in Maisūru. Although he was young and had only studied a limited number of works, he never had the slightest hesitation in taking issue with even the greatest of scholars. When Rāma was still a student in Maisūru, the *Svāmi* of the Śṛṅgēri *maṭha* once came to Maisūru with his retinue of scholars.[452] In keeping with tradition, scholarly debates had been organized in the Śrī Maṭha. Students, too, were demonstrating their learning and skills by participating in debates. The *1822*
discussions centered around the concept of cause in *Nyāyaśāstra.* It is usual for logicians to first illustrate cause-effect relationships using simple instances involving ordinary entities, before proceeding to more complex

Greeks, having five components, rather than the three of the Aristotelian syllogism. Many independent schools of Indian logic existed as far back as 200 B.C.E., including multivalued logic systems, such as the *Syādvāda* system of the Jainas. The *Navya Nyāya* school is the most recent, and technically the most difficult. Bhattacharyya [1990] correctly calls it a logic of cognition, in contrast to the formal logic that has developed in the western world. *Navya Nyāya* has a rich technical vocabulary, and insists on extreme technical precision in describing cognitions and concepts. The *Navya Nyāya* vocabulary has been used widely in other fields, including literature. See, for instance, footnote 77.

[452] This was *Svāmi* Nṛsiṁha Bhāratī (1817–1879). It is recorded [in Narasimhachar 1913] that the *Svāmi* was invited to Maisūru in 1822 C.E. by Kṛṣṇarāja Voḍeyar III, matching the information in this biography. Rāmaśāstri would have been fifteen at the time.

examples. The example of a pot is often used. Such things as clay, the potter, his wheel, the stick used to turn the wheel, and so on, are the causal agents involved in the making of a pot. Although certain unusual entities may first appear to be involved in the making of a pot, these are in fact irrelevant. For example, the clay used to make the pot may have been carried on a donkey. It does not follow that the donkey is among the causes of the pot. Such irrelevant entities are called *anyathāsiddhas* in logic.[453] There are some additional details to be presented in this context.

There is a concise summary called the *Tarkasaṅgraha*. This work has given rise to a commentary called the *Dīpikā*.[454] There exists a commentary called the *Muktāvaḷi* on the *Dīpikā*.[455] The *Dīpikā* states that the *anyathāsiddhas* number only three.[456] The *Muktāvali* gives the number of

---

[453]We are beginning an expedition into a technically difficult series of ideas. Following Sastri [1951], we begin by noting that *anyathā* means "otherwise", and *siddha* means "made out". In this context, "otherwise" is to be taken as "otherwise than indispensable." Hence, *anyathāsiddha* means "made out to be otherwise than indispensable", or "made out to be such as one can do without".

[454]The *Tarkasaṅgraha* is a landmark work by Annambhaṭṭa, dating to the second half of the 17th century. It is essential reading for all students of *Navya Nyāya* logic. The *Dīpikā* commentary that usually accompanies editions of the *Tarkasaṅgraha* is also by Annambhaṭṭa. Technical works in *Saṁskṛta* can be unintelligible without a commentary, since they are often written in the *sūtra* style, which prizes extreme terseness, making *sūtras* analogous to mathematical formulæ. The characteristics of a *sūtra* are summarized in the *Viṣṇudharmottara Purāṇa* as follows: *"alpākṣaramasandigdham sāravadviṣvatomukham | astobham anavadyañça sūtram sūtravidoḥ viduḥ ‖"* meaning: "In the view of experts, a *sūtra* is terse yet unambiguous, concentrated in meaning yet comprehensive, unfragmented and leaving no cause for reproach". The satisfaction obtained from a well-crafted and concise *sūtra* is very similar to that resulting from a well-crafted mathematical theorem or formula. Nāgeśa Bhaṭṭa's *Paribhāṣendu Śekhara* ends with the following memorable quote: *"ardhamātrālāghavena putrotsavaṁ manyante vaiyākaraṇāḥ ‖133‖"*, meaning: "for grammarians, the saving of even half a mora in a *sūtra* is cause for as much celebration as the birth of a son." Such brevity and precision makes *sūtras* invaluable as mnemonic aids, but they can be impenetrably opaque by themselves. Opacity can even be a matter of pride, as in *Bhaṭṭikāvyam*, 22:34: *"vyākhyāgamyamidaṁ kāvyamutsavaḥ sudhiyāmalaṁ | hatā durmedhasçāsmin viduṣāṁ prītaye maya ‖"*, meaning: "With a commentary may this poem be understood, and for the proficient it is a feast; the dull-witted are crushed by it, but I care only for the learned."

[455]This *Muktāvali* is the *Siddhāntamuktāvali*, which is a commentary not on the *Dīpikā*, but on the *Bhāṣāpariççheda*. The *Pariççheda* and the accompanying commentary *Muktāvali* are both by Viṣvanātha *Nyayapañçānana* Bhaṭṭāçārya of the 17the century C.E.

[456]Footnote in original: "In the *Dīpikā*–(1) *daṇḍatva*, (2) *ākāśa*, (3) *rūpaprāgabhāva* relating to *gandha*."

anyathāsiddhas as five.[457] Logicians have defined the technical term *avaśya*, however, to refer specifically to the fifth *anyathāsiddha*, that is, to such things as the donkey, horse, or cart used to transport the clay. This terminology arises since the fifth *anyathāsiddha* is seen as *avaśya kl̥ptaniyatapūrvavr̥tti*, that is, although these entities are not viewed as being the causes of the pot, their existence must be granted as essential precedents of the pot.[458]

Now, as a scholar by name Hosahaḷḷi Rāmaśāstri from the Śrī Maṭha was discoursing on these very *anyathāsiddhas*, Rāma, who was seated with a group of students, spontaneously asked: "Is the *rāsabha*, or donkey, an

[457] Footnote in original: "In the *Muktāvali*–(1) *daṇḍatva,* (2) *daṇḍarūpa,* (3) *ākāśa,* (4) *kulāla's* father, (5) such things as the donkey."

[458] This paragraph, and footnotes 456 and 457 may appear rather obscure, the *anyathāsiddhas* listed may appear odd, and the reference to the word *avaśya* unclear. The technical difficulties of *Navya Nyāya* are considerable, but we will attempt to clarify matters a little, albeit through recourse to much simplification. First, it must be understood that *Nyāya* advocates a very robust realism, and generally treats universals as real. Thus, in the case of a potter creating a pot on a wheel, which he spins by means of a stick (*daṇḍa*), *Nyāya* would regard this stick, *daṇḍatva* ("stick-ness", the universal characterizing sticks), and *daṇḍarūpa* (color, shape, and other properties of the stick), as all real, and as potential causes of the pot.

Now, a cause is defined as an invariable antecedent to the effect that is not also an *anyathāsiddha* (*anyathāsiddhiśūnyasya niyata pūrvavartitā kāraṇatvaṁ bhavēt*). The stick itself clearly meets this criterion. As in Sastri [1951] and Röer [1850], we note that an entity being considered as a cause is made out to be an invariable antecedent only as determined by a delimiting adjunct (*avaçchedaka*), which in the case of a stick is stick-ness (*daṇḍatva*). However, *daṇḍatva* does not participate in the creative process, and represents the first class of *anyathāsiddhas*. The second class of *anyathāsiddhas* comprises such things as cannot be considered as causes for an effect, except via the intermediacy of some other real cause. Examples include the shape or colour of the stick (*daṇḍarūpa*). We cannot say, for instance, that the pot is a given, once the colour of the stick is given, nor that the pot is not a given if this color is not given. The third class comprises things which arise as causes of an effect if they have already been applied to another effect. This class is represented by the ether (*ākāśa*), which can only be seen as an invariable antecedent of the pot when perceived under the delimiting adjunct of ether-ness (*ākāśatva*), which defines it to be the intimate cause of sound. This delimiting adjunct now makes the ether primarily the cause of sound, and only secondarily the cause of the pot. The fourth category of *anyathāsiddha* is represented by the potter's father, who is the cause of the cause (the potter), and not directly the cause of the pot. The fifth category is represented by the donkey used to carry the clay. It may be that a certain donkey is an invariable antecedent for a particular pot. However, this pot, as all others, can also be produced without this donkey, as long as the other essential antecedents are present.

Annambhaṭṭa, following Gaṅgēśōpādhyāya, combines the first two categories into one, and the last two into one, obtaining three categories. Viśvanātha lists all five in the *Bhāṣāpariçchēda*.

avaśyaka anyathāsiddha?"[459] Hosahaḷḷi Rāmaśāstri, interpreting the word *avaśya* in its ordinary, non-technical sense, replied: "Essential to you, perhaps, but surely not to us!" Rāmaśāstri immediately countered: "We find the donkey essential, indeed! For though the donkey is not a causal agent for the pot, and yet the good *śāstri* attached the meaning to the term that he did, we need the donkey so we can arrange for him to ride it!" Everyone was astonished at his skill and wit.

This event occurred six months after Rāma's father's death. The extent of Rāma's accomplishments is clear from this episode. He had mastered *Saṁskṛta* and achieved such a mastery of logic, even by the age of fifteen. He also had the judgment and discrimination to hold his own in public debates with adults on the topics he had studied. His ability to completely grasp what he had read, to internalize the ideas and make them his own, his situational understanding, and his ability to bring his knowledge to bear as the occasion required, were all clear evidence of his growing intellect and acumen. His supreme confidence in his own understanding, and his willingness to take issue with opponents, regardless of their reputation, also showed his exceptional courage.

[459] Continuing the discussion in footnote 458, the *Bhāṣāpariççhēda* reduces all five *anyathāsiddhas* into the one represented by the donkey, declaring it to be the only *avaśyaka* (essential) *anyathāsiddha*: *"ētē pañçānyathāsiddhāḥ daṇḍatvādikamādimaṁ | ghaṭādau daṇḍarūpādi dvitīyamapi darśitaṁ ‖21‖ tṛtīyaṁ tu bhavēdvyōma kulālajanakō–paraḥ | pañçamō rāsabhādiḥ ētēṣvāvaśyakatvasau ‖22‖"* The expression *"ētēṣu avaśyaka tu asau"* means "of these (superfluities), only this (the fifth) is essential", i.e., it serves the purpose of the rest. Rāmaśāstri has used the word *avaśyaka* in this sense.

Chapter 3: Study in Rāmadurga

Many great scholars had found patronage from Peśva Bājirāv, ruling from Puṇe, and adorned his court. Their number included such luminaries as Bhaṭṭoji Dīkṣita, Nāgoji Dīkṣita, Puruṣottama Śāstri, Tryambaka Śāstri, and Trivikrama Śāstri.[460] The Peśvas were brāhmaṇas by birth, and were themselves learned. They sponsored a scholarly conference called *Śrāvaṇapāṭhi* every year, during the month of Śrāvaṇa. Scholars from all over participated in this event, displayed their scholarship in the learned debates that took place, and returned with accolades and prizes.[461] Many of these scholars remained in Puṇe, having found support from the Peśva.

A jewel among such scholars was Tryambaka Śāstri. Among his many works is a book on *Advaita* called the *Bhāṣyabhānuprabhā*, which stands out as a service to mankind.[462] His fame had spread far and wide. He was originally from Kalyāṇadurga in Baḷḷāri district, where he had substantial lands and property.[463] His scholarship was unmatched. A large number of

---

[460]There appear to be significant errors here. The dates of Peśva Bāji Rāv I are 1700–1740 C.E., and those of Bāji Rāv II are 1775–1851 C.E. Bhaṭṭoji Dīkṣita, however, was a famous grammarian who flourished in Vārāṇāsi towards the end of the 16th century, and Nāgōji Dīkṣita (Nāgeśa Bhaṭṭa) was Bhaṭṭoji Dīkṣita's great-grandson, and active between 1670–1750 C.E. He was patronized by Rāmavarman of Śṛṅgaverapura near Allahābād [Coward *et al.*, 1990]. Clearly, neither could have been at Bāji Rāv's court. Tryambaka Śāstri was active during Bāji Rāv's time, but it is not immediately clear who Puruṣottama Śāstri and Trivikrama Śāstri are.

[461]See Deshpande [2001, p. 121] (based on Ranade [1992, p. 373]): "Each year, in the month of Śrāvaṇa, the Peshwas distributed Dakṣiṇā to a large number of Brahmins who gathered in Pune… The tradition of annually distributing Dakṣiṇā to Vaidikas and Shastris was initiated by the Maratha king Shahu's commander Dābhāḍe… With the expansion of the power of the Peshwa, this amount increased by 1758 to Rupees 1,800,000. We are told that in the year 1770, the Peshwa distributed Dakṣiṇā in Pune to 39,912 Brahmins who had come from all parts of India, north and south…"

[462]This work is a commentary on the *Śārirakabhāṣya*, often called the *Śāṅkarabhāṣya*, by *Ādi* Śaṅkarāçārya itself a commentary on the *Brahmasūtra* of Bādarāyaṇa [Roodermum 2002, p. 28]. Tryambaka Śāstri's works include *Dṛgdṛśya Praṇibandhanoupapatti Prakāśa, Prakṛtyādhikaraṇa Vicāra, Pramāṇa Tatva, Basavabādha, Bhāṣyabhānuprabha, Śāstrārambhasamarthanam, Śrutimatprakāśa, Śrutimatānumānopapatti, Śrutimatodyota, Advaitasiddhāntavaijayanti*, and the *Avidyālakṣaṇaupapatti* [Saraswathi 1957, p. 24]. The *Siddhāntavaijayantī* is a critique of the *Dvaita* work *Vanamālamiśrīya* by Vanamālamiśra.

[463]A property dispute involving this property is documented in Lakshminarasimhaiya *et al.*, [1970, p. 123]. Lakṣmī Baī, daughter-in-law of Tryambaka Śāstri, submits a petition

students studied with him. He would sit supporting himself with a pillow, paying no heed to whether it was day or night, engrossed in his books, and writing occasionally; if overcome by drowsiness, he would doze off for a bit, then awake and return to his reading and writing. When he came for the first time to the court of Kṛṣṇarāja Voḍeyar III, it was decided that a debate should take place between him and the scholars then at court. Rāmaśēṣa Śāstri, who was a leading scholar at court, came forward to debate Tryambaka Śāstri.[464]

This Rāmaśēṣa Śāstri was apparently of boundless scholarship. He was a *Smārta* brāhmaṇa of the *Drāviḍa* tradition, from south of the valley.[465] This scholar had migrated to Maisūru, and had been awarded much in the form of rewards and land.[466] Kṛṣṇarāja Voḍeyar III had a great deal of regard for him. It appears that he was a worshipper of Uc̣chiṣṭa Gaṇapati,

dated May 20, 1840 to the Governor General of India for the restoration of her property and personal freedom. The petition states that a certain Veṅkaṭaramaṇa, who had been purchased as a slave by her father-in-law Tryambaka Śāstri after the death of her husband, had improperly established himself as heir to all her property through a decree of Maisūru Commissioner Colonel Cubbon passed on October 17, 1838, and that she was no longer being paid the sum of 40 *Rūpīs* per month that the decree granted her, and further, that she was being kept under house arrest. Clearly, Tryambaka Śāstri and his son had both passed away by 1838 C.E.

[464]The date of this debate remains unclear. Lakshminarasimhaiya *et al.,* [1970] give the year as around 1815 C.E. on page 9, but as 1819 C.E. on page 24. On page 25, they claim that Kuṇigala Rāmaśāstri was a judge at this debate, but that cannot be correct. He would have only been 12 years old in 1819. Besides, we know he moved to Maisūru only in 1822.

[465]For an explanation of the expression "south of the valley", see footnote 431. Lakshminarasimhaiya *et al.,* [1970] have argued that the Rāmaśēṣa Śāstri alluded to here is the same as Kāśī Śēṣaśāstri. The case is defensible, but weakened by several factors. First, while the name Rāmaśēṣa Śāstri is used consistently in the pages immediately following, the name Kāśī Śēṣaśāstri also explicitly appears in the present work on pages 224 and 267, suggesting that these were different persons. Also, Rāmaśēṣa Śāstri and Kāśī Śēṣaśāstri both appear in the list of scholars in Kṛṣṇarāja Voḍeyar III's court given by Arasu [1993, pp. 116–118], which is apparently based on a catalog in the Jaganmohana Palace in Maisūru. The translator has not been able to consult the catalog to verify this information. One must recognize the possibility that these were different individuals, but that some of the stories pertaining to the one may have inadvertently been attributed to the other in the present work. Confusion on the part of Puṭṭaṇṇa's sources for these stories, or on the part of the sources used by Lakshminarasimhaiya *et al.,* [1970] is understandable, given the shared "śēṣa" in the two names. See footnotes 100, 102, and 589 for other inconsistencies in Lakshminarasimhaiya *et al.,* [1970].

[466]This was the same Rāmaśēṣa Śāstri who gifted away his house and *vṛtti* in the Katvāḍipura Agrahāra to Veṅkaṭaramaṇa Śāstri, the father of Ċāmarājanagara Śrīkaṇṭha Śāstri. See page 76.

and of exceptional intellect.[467] It appears that extreme intelligence is associated with unusual behaviours. There are accounts of him standing from 9 a.m. till 4 p.m. in Maisūru's Kalyāṇī grounds, on his head a load of grass for his cow, in his hand ten seers of *togari bēḷe* tied in a bundle, deeply engaged in a *śāstric* discussion with Ānavaṭṭi Śrīnivāsāçār.[468] The king, who happened to be on the fifth floor of the palace, looking through a pair of binoculars, observed these proceedings. He finally sent word through a palace guard, inquiring whether standing for so long wasn't causing the legs to be fatigued. Once, on the occasion of the king's birthday, he went to the palace carrying flowers and *phalamantrākṣate*.[469] He was late; the *darbār* had ended, and the Royal Retinue had departed for Ambāvilāsa. The Śāstri went to the Ambāvilāsa entrance. The gate was closed, and the guard denied him admission. The Śāstri simply placed the garland he had around the neck of one of the soldiers, handed him the *phalamantrākṣate,* and departed. The king learned of this episode. The next day, when the Śāstri arrived at the palace, the king said to him, smiling: "I believe you came to the palace yesterday, but I was not available. I understand that you therefore garlanded the palace guard and gave him the *phalamantrākṣate*. To this, the Śāstri replied: "Your Highness, this is surely not objectionable! The guard bore your insignia and wore your uniform, so doing him respect, as your representative, is the same as doing you respect!" The king was silent. Those seeking to slander the Śāstri were shamed.

On another occasion, as the Śāstri was leaving Ambāvilāsa, a guard with drawn sword asked him: "Good sir, would you please tell me my future?" The Śāstri replied: "Why do you ask me about such trifling things? I don't know. Ask some astrologer, if one happens to come by." The guard retorted: "What, sir! You are a great scholar! Can't you even tell me this much?" The Śāstri left without responding. A few days later, as the same soldier stood guard with sword drawn, the Śāstri showed up with a towel

[467] Uççhiṣṭa Gaṇapati is a *tāntric* form of Gaṇapati, whose worshippers follow the "left-hand" path of worship, forbidden to worshippers of other Gaṇapati forms. *Tāntric* practices are associated with special powers.

[468] Ānavaṭṭi Śrīnivāsāçār is the author of the *Kṛṣṇaprabhāvodaya*. *Togari beḷe* is *Cajanus cajan*, or the pigeon pea, widely used in Karṇāṭaka. Foodgrains were sold by volume at the time. A *pakkā seer*, used for measuring dry goods such as grains, was 74.8125 cubic inches [Rice 1897b, p. 810], so that ten seers would amount to about 12.26 litres, and likely weighed about 7–8 kg.

[469] See footnote 367 for an explanation of *phalamantrākṣate*.

wrapped around his head, his sacred thread around his ear, and carrying a flask of hot water. He went up to the guard and said: "You! Come here, and give me a shave!" The guard reacted: "Sir, you are a person of eminence. It is wrong to insult me in this fashion. Am I a barber?"[470] The Śāstri responded: "When you desired me to tell your future the other day, and I directed you to an astrologer, you asked why I, though such a scholar, could not deal with such a simple matter. Now here you are, carrying such a big sword, yet unable to even give me a shave!" Reports of this incident reached the king. He arrived with his Retinue. Seeing what was going on, and amused by it, the king counseled the guard, and admonished him not to take issue with persons of substance.

For some time, Kṛṣṇarāja Voḍeyar III had performed the *Aupāsana* ritual regularly.[471] During this time, one of his queens began her monthly period. The question arose whether it was proper to continue to perform the ritual. The king ordered that Rāmaśēṣa Śāstri be consulted. The Śāstri was at home, having leaves stitched together to make dinner plates, and sunning himself.[472] The king's messenger arrived and informed the Śāstri of the royal order. The Śāstri made no response. Another messenger arrived, saluted the Śāstri, and stood before him. The Śāstri remained silent. Then arrived a palace guard, and then another. The Śāstri made no response to any of them. Finally, they said together: "It is already past the king's mealtime. What is your response, your bidding?" The Śāstri shouted in anger: "Tell the king that permission to perform the *Aupāsana* when the queen has her period is granted in the same place that grants him permission to perform it when she does not have her period! It is all the same whether he performs it or not!" The king's guards and messengers returned with this information. The king listened to their account, and expressing no anger, he accepted the Śāstri's pronouncement as a blessing, and stopped observing the *Aupāsana*.

Another incident occurred that showed Rāmaśēṣa Śāstri's exceptional abilities. He had once travelled to Tiruçirapalli. It was his practice every day to bathe and perform his daily rituals in an isolated location. One day, he

[470] Barbers are from the lowest caste.

[471] See footnote 234.

[472] Leaves of the *muttaga* tree *(Butea fronderosa, Butea monosperma)* are stitched together with little sticks and dried to make flat, rimless circular "plates" in Karṇāṭaka. These are used after they are dried, in contrast to leaves of the banana plant, which are used when still green.

sat on the bank of a channel of the Kāvērī, engrossed in his *japa*. A small detachment of soldiers of the the East India Company had been stationed at Tiruçirapaḷḷi. Two of these soldiers came to this channel, removed their clothes, jumped in the water, and as they swam, began an altercation. They shouted, pummelled, and soon bloodied each other. They lodged complaints against each other with their commanding officer, a colonel. When he asked for witnesses, they indicated that a brāhmaṇa covered in ash had been sitting some distance away, referring to Rāmaśēṣa Śāstri. The officer had him identified, and called and questioned him. The Śāstri replied: "I really know nothing. These two soldiers were shouting at each other in anger. I do not speak their language, but I can repeat their words," and then proceeded to repeat their words from beginning to end. The soldiers agreed to his account of their conversation. The officer was astonished at the Śāstri's performance. He was unconvinced of the Śāstri's professed ignorance of English. A small group gathered to test him. The Śāstri agreed to repeat everthing that he heard once. The District Collector retrieved two old books from a chest at home, one in English, and the other in Latin. As soon as a a page from either book was read, Rāmaśēṣa Śāstri would repeat the entire page without error. Everyone was truly astounded.[473] There being no account of his extraordinary abilities anywhere, I have chosen to document them here.[474]

The anecdotes relating to His Highness Kṛṣṇarāja, too, illustrate his virtues well. He was not in the least arrogant, although he was very well

[473]The translator had seen this episode described in a contemporary British account, and recognized it immediately when reading this work. Unfortunately, he had not recorded the reference, and has been unable to trace it since.

[474]Continuing in the spirit of the author, we mention some other episodes concerning Rāmaśēṣa Śāstri, as recounted by Śāstri [1925b]. Once, a brother-in-law of the king's was bothering passers-by, by riding his horse near the fort entrance. When he disregarded the Śāstri's pleas to ride elsewhere, the Śāstri recited the following verse in rebuke: "*çaturaṁ turagaṁ pathi nartayataḥ pathikāṅ bahuśaḥ parimardayataḥ | nahitē bhujavirya bhavo vibhavo bhagini tava bhāgya bhavo vibhavaḥ ‖*" meaning "Oh, rider, your equestrian antics make it clear that the might which you are here displaying derives not from your arms, but from your sister's marriage to the king." On another occasion, as the Śāstri was hurrying to the palace on the occasion of some ritual, he slipped into some mud, and stained his clothes. When the king remarked on his stained clothing, the Śāstri replied: "*kṣuttṛḍāśā kuṭumbinyaḥ mayitiṣṭhanti nānyagāḥ | tāsāmantyā çasubhagātasyāḥ śṛṅgāra çēṣṭitaṁ ‖*" meaning: "Oh king, I have three wives named hunger, thirst, and greed, who never leave me. Of these, the third I hold dearest. She is the loveliest. The stains on my clothing are the marks of her loveplay."

informed from all that came to his notice. He would converse with everyone as the occasion required, without the slightest conceit. He had a special regard for scholars, and took great pains to support them, providing all they needed. O virtuous king! Why did Death have to make you his target!

It appears that this Rāmaśāstri, while debating Tryambaka Śāstri in the royal court, challenged him with a great many propositions concerning the very word "Tryambaka".[475] It also appears to be the case that Kṛṣṇarāja Voḍeyar III recognized the peerless scholarship of Tryambaka Śāstri with many awards.

Enthralled by accounts of the brilliance of Tryambaka Śāstri's scholarship, and deciding that he could do no better than to study with him, Rāma left Maisūru for Kalyāṇadurga, gained an audience with Tryambaka Śāstri, and became one of his students.

The means of learning in times past were very unlike those of today. Institutions such as schools, colleges, and universities did not exist for the dissemination of knowledge. Titles such as Master or Professor were unheard of. The government did not include a Department of Education. There were no regular government expenditures towards education. Instead, there were *maṭhas* established in villages, towns, and in the homes of the wealthy, where children would be taught, starting with the *Ōnāma*,[476] to the extent of being able to read papers given to them, writing down what they were told, and performing simple and compound addition, as well as subtraction. Instead of books, there were teachers; if a teacher could read Kannaḍa poetry and teach multiplication and division, he would be considered especially accomplished. Such was the manner of elementary education. The languages used in the *maṭhas* was the local vernacular.[477] These

---

[475]This echoes the account of Kāśī Śēśa Śāstri's great-grandson Kāśī Subrahmaṇya Śāstri [Lakshminarasimhaiya *et al.*, 1970, p. 145]. According to this account, Kāśī Śeśa Śāstri declared after Tryambaka Śāstri was formally introduced at the debate: "It is of no consequence whether his name is *Tryambaka* (Śiva), *Ambaka* (effeminate), or just *Baka* (a crane). This is an occasion for *śāstric* debate." Surprisingly, the debate is said to have raged for three days on the issue of whether the word *Nārāyaṇa* means Viṣṇu or Śiva. Tryambaka Śāstri and Kāśī Śeśa Śāstri, both being *Smārtas,* might have been expected to quickly agree that the word means Śiva. Also, see page 250.

[476]It was traditional to begin instruction with the auspicious words *Om Namaḥ Śivāya*, meaning "salutations to Śiva". This sentence is colloquially referred to as the *Ōnāma*.

[477]Needless to say, these languages garnered far less respect than did *Saṁskṛta* or English. Nonetheless, many of these languages, such as Kannaḍa and Tamiḷ, have rich traditions of

teachers were awarded annual or monthly allowances by the parents of their students. During the month of Āśvayuja, it was customary for the teachers to provide entertainment by having these students visit the homes of the local leaders, well dressed and holding colourful sticks, and reciting Kannaḍa songs called *ċaupadas*. The students would be fed, and the teachers would receive monetary awards.

Students of *Saṁskṛta* seeking instruction in subjects such as literature, grammar, logic, and *Vēdānta* would approach the many great scholars who lived in those times. It was the practice to concentrate on, and achieve scholarly depth in one single field. Such scholars would receive support from the many kings at the time who held traditional learning in high regard. There were no examinations, other than the debates that took place in the royal courts. Not only did these kings support such scholars generously with monthly stipends and grants of lands and property, thereby safeguarding them from the gloom of penury, but also bestowed on them special honors and rewards as and when special aspects of their scholarship came to light.

Contented thereby, these scholars taught many students in their homes. They expected nothing in return from their students. On the contrary, because they hosted these students in their homes, feeding them and treating them as their own children, students had a special reverence for their teachers, and served them with great devotion. Neither did the teachers accept compensation for their teaching from their royal patrons or from their students. They regarded it as sins equally heinous to accept money for learning, food, or for a damsel.[478] Such was the mode of education until the govern-

---

literature going back thousands of years. Interestingly, it has been argued that the language spoken by an Indian character in the Charition Mime, from the Oxyrhynchus Papyri 443, is an archaic form of Kannaḍa (see, for example, Hultzsch [1904] and Sastri [1927]). Others, such as Rai [1985] and Salomon [1993], have made the case that the language spoken is Tuḷu, a language from the coastal region of Karṇāṭaka. The latter possibility is even more interesting, since Tuḷu is not a dominant language at the present time.

[478] *Kanyāvikraya*, the selling of a damsel, is treated in the *śāstras* as a serious offense. See *Manusmṛti*, 3:51: *"na kanyāyāḥ pitā vidvān gṛhṇīyāċċhulkamaṇvapi | gṛhṇanhi śulkaṁ lobhena syānnaropatyavikrayī ‖"* ("The well-informed father must never accept even the smallest sum as dowry for his daughter; for if driven by greed, he accepts a dowry, he becomes a seller of his own offspring.") This proscription arises not because a low value is attached to this gift, but precisely because the great value attached to it makes it a meritorious gift, when given freely. This consideration also extends to food and learning. See Mahimabhaṭṭa's *Vyaktiviveka*, 1: *"ayāċitāni dēyāni sarvadravyāṇi bhārata | annaṁ vidyā kanyā anarthithab-*

ment established schools and colleges. Every scholar's home was a college for advanced learning.

I used the expression "in the past" above. This should not be taken to mean in ages past. This was the state of affairs even fifty years ago.[479] This system of education had come down to us through tradition. This tradition has now been upset by the current arrangements for education in various languages. We now see such deplorable developments as students paying for their learning, teachers accepting payment for imparting knowledge, a different teacher holding forth each hour on a topic familiar to him and then departing, teachers lacking the concern, patience, and time to address the questions and confusions of their students, students therefore losing their regard for teachers, teachers losing confidence in their students, ultimately causing students to lose all respect for their teachers, and commit the sin of speaking of their teachers with contempt. There is now the artifice of the government charging students for their education, but this practice has not raised the salary of a single scholar.[480] Neither has the government seen a reduction in its expenses. What has diminished is the respect that students have for their teachers. The traditions of seeing education as a gift to be given freely have also diminished. Shortcomings such as these are inherent in the Western method of education.

These new ways are not right for us. The great scholars of the past, in keeping with traditional ways, had made their homes sanctuaries where

hyo na dīyate ‖" ("Oh Bhārata! It is proper to give away all things without being asked, but never food, learning, or a damsel, unless asked.")

[479] That is, even in 1860 C.E. This work was published in 1910 C.E. See footnote 480.

[480] We use the word "scholar" here to denote a teacher or learned person, not a student. The following excerpt from a memorandum in 1854 C.E. by G.N. Taylor, Sub-Collector in charge of Rajahmundry, makes for very interesting reading here [Bourdillon 1859, p. 29]:

> It will be observed that the scheme I am now proposing, contemplates the improvement of the existing village schools... The schoolmaster in this case, being a resident in the village, and, as it were, one of themselves, needs but a small salary, but this salary which is now dependent on chance or charity, will be secured to him by the plan of fixing an annual addition to the demand of the village... The sum of five rupees monthly, or 60 rupees a year, is perhaps the minimum upon which persons of this class could make a respectable appearance..., but I would give him an additional stimulus to exertion, by allowing him to receive a fixed fee from every class of person who did not contribute to the fund assessed upon the land... and it would show the people that the instruction was the more valuable because it must be paid for. Two annas a month would probably be a high enough fee...

food and learning were given away. It was on this account that a great many students studied in Tryambaka Śāstri's home.

Rāmaśāstri arrived in Rāyadurga, paid his respects to Tryambaka Śāstri, and appraised him of his purpose. Since he was still studying the basics of logic, Tryambaka Śāstri sent him to his son Bāpuśāstri for instruction. Bāpuśāstri was himself a great scholar. He taught advanced works to many students who had come to his father for instruction, and helped them with their learning. Rāmaśāstri became a member of this group of students.

According to traditional observances, no instruction was imparted on three days of each half of the lunar month.[481] On the thirteenth day of each half, the day of *Pradōṣa*, students would demonstrate their knowledge of the material they had learned by recitations, discussions, and debates. If any doubts or controversies arose, Bāpuśāstri would resolve them. Rāmaśāstri was still studying the elements of logic. Bāpuśāstri had an attitude of great indifference towards him. One *Pradōṣa*, however, provided an opportunity for Rāmaśāstri's natural brilliance to become manifest.

There are many expository works on logic, such as the *Muktāvaḷi* and the *Dinakarī*. There is also a new work called the *Çintāmaṇi*. This work has been authored by Gaṅgeśvaramiśropādhyāya.[482] It is traditional to speak of him with the greatest of respect, always using the plural form of address. Raghunātha Bhaṭṭāçārya has written a commentary called the *Dīdhiti*, or *Śirōmaṇi*,[483] on the *Çintāmaṇi*. The *Çintāmaṇi* is composed on the topics

[481] This corresponds to the *Pradōsa Vrata*, an observance starting on the evening of the twelfth and continuing through the thirteenth day of each half of the lunar month. Śiva is worshipped.

[482] This work is the *Tattvaçintāmaṇi* by Gaṅgēśa (Gaṅgēśvara Miśra Upādhyāya), dating to 1310 C.E. [Potter and Bhattacharya 2008]. It is a classic work, marking the beginning of *Navya Nyāya* logic. It is a "new work" only in the sense that it is the point of departure for *Navya Nyāya*, or the New *Nyāya*. In matter of fact, the *Tattvaçintāmaṇi* predates the other two works mentioned. The *Siddhāntamuktāvalī* is a commentary by Viśvanātha *Nyāyapañçānana* Bhaṭṭāçārya on his own work, the *Bhāṣāpariççheda* (also called the *Kārikāvali*), written around 1634 C.E. The *Dinakarī* is a commentary on the *Muktāvalī* by Mahādeva Bhaṭṭa, also known as Dinakara. The full title of the work is *Nyāyasiddhāntamuktāvalīprakāśa*, although it is better known as the *Dinakarī*.

[483] *Dīdhiti* means illumination, an apt title for a commentary. *Śiromaṇi* or "crest-jewel" was an appellation of Raghunātha, the author. He is by far the most original and brilliant of the modern Indian logicians. *Śiromaṇi* is used here as a metonym for the *Dīdhiti*.

pratyakṣa, anumāna, upamāna, śabda.[484] The *Dīdhiti* is a commentary on this work. In this work are given fourteen definitions.[485]

Before proceeding further with this account, it is necessary to explain a few matters that may appear strange to today's students. In those times, it was not the practice to carve letters on blocks, arrange them as desired, and print books thereby. We did not even have machines capable of this function. As a result, books were not common. To a large extent, scholars committed everything to memory, and when needed, reproduced the material verbally. They had committed to memory the entire corpus of the *Vēdas,* the *śastras,* the various commentaries on them, and so on. Native scholars could reproduce verbally, and without hesitation, the equivalent of the contents of many chestfuls of books. Every one of these scholars was a veritable library. Some English scholars poke fun at them, accusing them of merely parroting this material without understanding it, and contending that such recitation is pointless. On closer analysis, however, the ignorance of such detractors becomes clear.

Today, many seem to believe that an ability to respond to a given word with a synonym, or with several words strung together, demonstrates their understanding. They boast of their abilities as if they were limitless, just because they are able to respond with *tok* as the meaning of *tik.*[486] This is wrong. The native scholar is able to expound on a word, starting with how the vowels and consonants in it come about, and continuing all the way through its proper application, utility, and all other relevant aspects.

Setting this aside, let us consider how many ancillary branches of learning have been developed just for the purpose of *Vēdic* interpretation. There

[484]These are the four *pramāṇas* or the means to right knowledge recognized in Indian logic. *Pratyakṣa* is perception, the knowledge that arises through the senses. *Anumāna* is inferential knowledge. *Upamāna* is comparison (or identification). *Śabda* is knowledge through testimony.

[485]These are fourteen definitions of *vyāpti,* which translates into English as *pervasion.* The equivalent concept in modern logic is *implication.* Thus, if *s* is true whenever *h* is true, we would say *h* implies *s*, or, in Indian logic, that *h pervades s*. An enormous amount of effort is devoted in Indian logic to obtaining an accurate definition of pervasion. In this case, Raghunātha is commenting in his *Dīdhiti* on Book 2 of the *Tattvaçintāmaṇi,* which is concerned with topic of inference. These definitions occur in Section 5 thereof.

[486]*Tik* and *tok* are nonsense syllables, used pejoratively here to denote shallow learning.

is also the entire field of *Mīmāṁsa* devoted just to the analysis of this meaning.[487] Given that native scholars have developed such an elaborate apparatus to ensure deep understanding of just one aspect of their heritage, it is hardly proper to accuse them of rote memorization without understanding. Memorization is an essential tool to facilitate deeper understanding. It would be better for those who are ignorant of the sciences devoted to understanding, and do disservice to these sciences by making much of simple glosses written for monetary gain, to speak after due consideration.

While our scholars committed these texts to memory, many of them did also commit them to writing. Students approaching them for instruction would have possessed no books. All books would have been with the teacher. After each day's lesson, the students would have borrowed the book from the teacher, copied out the parts required for the following lesson, and studied that material. This was the only way available to them for study and reflection. Printed books, as we now have, were not available.

Let us, however, continue with our story. Tryambaka Śāstri's students happened to be engaged in debate on the occasion of a certain *Pradōṣa.* The discussion centred around the fourteen definitions. The current focus was the twelfth definition. Rāmaśāstri, who had been listening intently, said by way of refutation, that the twelfth definition could be established in the manner of the thirteenth. He had not yet studied the thirteenth defintion. Nevertheless, he defended his proposition with greater facility than did others who had studied and mastered the thirteenth.[488] The other students

[487] The six *vēdāṅgas* are *śikṣā* (phonetics, phonology, and morphophonology), *vyākaraṇa* (grammar), *kalpa* (ritual), *nirukta* (etymology), *ḉhandas* (poetic metre), and *jyotiṣa* (astronomy). The *upāṅgas* are the six systems of philosophical thought, namely *Nyāya, Vaiśeṣika, Saṅkhya, Yoga, Pūrva Mīmāṁsa, and Uttara Mīmāṁsa. Mīmāṁsa* is *Vēdic* hermeneutics. *Pūrva Mīmāṁsa* deals with the *karmakāṇḍa*, the ritual or sacrificial aspects of the *Vēdic* corpus, and the *Uttara Mīmāṁsa* deals with the *jñānakāṇḍa* or *Vēdānta*, the aspects dealing with the knowledge of the *Braḥman*, the ultimate truth.

[488] Some sense of the technical difficulty of these debates is conveyed by the brief summaries of these definitions in Potter and Bhattacharya [2008, p. 555]. Below, *s* refers to the *sādhya*, or what is to be proved (the "major term"), *h* to the *hetu*, or cause (the "middle term") and *p* to the *pakṣa*, or the locus where *h* resides (the "minor term"). The twelfth definition of *vyāpti* is summarized as follows:

> *Pervasion is* h*'s being characterized by the absence of every existent which is an absence of* s. This definition has to be understood as requiring that each existent in question must be absent in the relation by which the *h* is related to the *p*.

The thirteenth definition is summarized as follows:

were unable to refute Rāmaśāstri's thesis, which appeared novel to them. These students, who lacked a deep understanding of the material, were also indignant at Rāmaśāstri, who was junior to them both in age and in formal instruction. Such is the difference between natural talent and learning acquired through mere practice.

An interesting tradition had been in practice among the students. Any student unable to effectively contest the arguments of another student was required to copy out the next lesson from the teacher's book, or perhaps even more, for the student who had prevailed. This was a punishment of sorts for the one who showed himself less capable. Since none of the students was able to deal with Rāma's arguments, they all suffered embarassment. They were forced to copy out the lesson for this student from Maisūru. This became cause for them to compete ever more fiercely with Rāma.

> *Pervasion is* h*'s being characterized by the absence of every existent locus of all absences of* s. Here the entire locus of the absence of *s* is what is to be taken as the counterpositive of the absence characterizing *h*. Again, the counterpositive must be limited by the relation in which the *h* is related to *p*. And it should be understood that *s* must pervade the counterpositive of the *absence of* s, and that the limitor of the counterpositve must pervade the *s*. Thus, there is no overextension to the invalid inference "it possesses earthness, because it had a universal property.

The definitions above have the form they do because *Navya Nyāya* does not use quantifiers, but uses negation instead to serve the same purpose. This aspect of *Navya Nyāya,* and its extreme insistence on precision is illustrated in Srinivas [1986] by the *Navya Nyāya* formulation of the statement *"All that possesses smoke possesses fire"*, which would be written in modern Western formal notation as $\forall x$, Smoky$(x) \rightarrow$ Fiery(x):

> Smokeness is not a limitor of occurrentness limited by relation of contact and described by locus of absence of fire which absence describes a counterpositiveness limited by fireness and contact.

A rather more spectacular illustration of the technical complexity of the language of *Navya Nyāya* appears in the translation in Ingalls [1951, p. 117] of Mathurānātha's *Vyāptipañcaka-rahasya* (64.1–4):

> [Answer. The above objections should not be made] because what is meant is: a generic absence of occurrentness to a substratum of that unlimited locusness the [limiting] relation of which is the aforementioned one and which is described by [an entity] qualified by absence-ness of *sādhya,* absence of *sādhya* being as before mentioned; [to this absence of occurrentness the counterpositiveness] being limited by a particular qualification relation where the adjunct is a superstratumness limited by the limiting relation of *hetutā* and described by locusness to *hetu,* which locusness is limited by the limiting properties of *hetutā*.

The other students joined forces, and calling Rāma's arguments arrogant, complained to the junior *śāstri* Bāpuśāstri. When Rāma succeeded in defending his thesis with him as well, Bāpuśāstri took the matter to Tryambaka Śāstri, the senior *śāstri,* intending to break his perceived arrogance.

After listening to the controversy that had arisen, Tryambaka Śāstri desired to know how far Rāma's own study had progressed. He learned that Rāma had not yet studied the thirteenth definition, which had been the subject of the controversy. He asked whether Rāma had been given the pages with the thirteenth definition to copy. Bāpuśāstri and the other students conceded that he had not been given those pages. Tryambaka Śāstri then snubbed them, saying: "It is extraordinary that this student from Maisūru should have developed such an understanding of the thirteenth definition by himself, without studying or even having read the relevant topics. Indeed, the thesis he has established has also been articulated by none other than Raghunātha Bhaṭṭācārya himself. That he should have outperformed students who have studied this topic, without even being exposed to it demonstrates his brilliance. He has shown himself equal to the writer of the *Dīdhiti*. Despite having studied advanced works such as the *Gadādhari*, none of you has seen this subtle point. This boy is surely more capable than you are." From that day onward, Tryambaka Śāstri himself began to instruct Rāmaśāstri.

Tryambaka Śāstri had a very demanding method of teaching. Students were not permitted to ask questions. If a student did ask a question, it had to be relevant. Tryambaka Śāstri would be furious if it turned out to have been even slightly irrelevant. He would declare such a student unfit to study with him, and send him away. This caused Rāmaśāstri much apprehension. During one lesson, however, a certain doubt arose in Rāmaśāstri's mind. He did not raise the question, fearful of being sent away if his guru were to become furious. He simply waited for a suitable opportunity to have his doubt clarified.

Let us recall that the students all lived with the guru in his home. The students were extremely devoted to the guru. As service to their guru, they performed all the household chores, such as drawing water from the well, washing clothes, cleaning up after meals, and applying *gōmaya*.[489] Students were not yet accustomed to putting on airs and demeaning their gurus.

[489] *Gōmaya* is cowdung, which is mixed with water and smeared on the floors of dwellings

Now, an opportunity arose for Rāmaśāstri's doubt to be clarified. One day, the Śāstri came to wash his hands after his meal. Rāma filled a pot with water and handed it to him. As he was washing his hands, Rāma summoned up his courage, and asked his question. The Śāstri said nothing at the time. The next day, however, he called out to Rāma at the time of his daily worship, and answered his question.

The conditions at Rāyadurga were not conducive to Rāma's study. He had no proper place to sit and study. There was not enough light to study by. Yet, Rāma saw no obstacles to his study. He would gather twigs and branches during the day, set them alight in a field at night, and study by that light. Tryambaka Śāstri called him one day, and said: "Dear boy, you are still very young, and not strong enough to sustain yourself so far from home while you study. Return to your own town and find a suitable guru there to continue your study."[490] Rāmaśāstri replied: "Good sir, my goal
1823 was to further my learning in your presence. This ambition appears to have been shattered." Tryambaka Śāstri said to him: "Dear boy, a Tirupati Śrīnivāsāçārya lives in Maisūru. He studied with Viṭhalōpādhyāya of Paṇḍharapura. I studied with Hanumantāçārya of Nāgapura.[491] I know Śrīnivāsāçārya to be a great scholar. Approach him without any hesitation."

---

as a ritual act of purification. The ground where meals are eaten is ritually impure or *uççhiṣta*, having come into contact with the plate, which is rendered impure when touched by the hand, which is impure, having touched the saliva in one's mouth. This ground must be cleansed before it is fit to be used for other activities. Also see footnote 641.

[490] We might speculate that symptoms of the seizure disorder alluded to in footnote 617 were responsible for Tryambaka Śāstri's advice that Rāmaśāstri return to Maisūru.

[491] The following information is available regarding the two great scholars being referenced here. The first, Viṭṭhalēśa Upādhyāya, is the author of a commentary known as the *Viṭṭhalēśōpādhyāyī* on the *Gauḍabrahmānandī* by Brahmānanda. Viṭṭhalēśa Upādhyāya was a leading scholar of logic and *Vēdanta*. The *Advaitasiddhi* and several commentaries, including the *Viṭṭhalēśōpādhyāyī*, appear in Śāstri [1937]. The *Saṁskṛta* introduction in Śāstri [1937] yields the following information. He was the ninth or tenth child of Govindabhaṭṭa, who was of Gurjara (of modern-day Gujarāt) origins, but hailed from a village called Kaśaḷī near Rājāpur in the Ratnāgiri region of modern-day Mahārāśtra. Govindabhaṭṭa had the title of Paṭavardhan, and held a position of great honour and distinction as a scholar in the service of the prince of Panhāḷagaḍh in the Ratnāgiri region. Viṭṭhalēśa began his studies locally, and then proceeded to Kāśī for further study. His descendants were still in Kāśī in 1937 C.E. He subsequently came to Paṇḍharapura in the Śolāpura district of modern-day Mahārāśtra, where he taught. (Tirupati Śrīnivāṣāçārya would have been among his students here.) Viṭṭhalēśa studied *Nyāya* with Kṛṣṇabhaṭṭa Paṇḍita, who wrote the *Kṛṣṇabhaṭṭi* commentary on the *Gādādharī* and the *Jāgadīśī*, and grammar under a *Mādhva* of Paṇḍharapura called Kṛṣṇāçārya Śarma. Footnote 662 gives further details on Kṛṣṇabhaṭṭa, who

Following Tryambaka Śāstri's bidding, Rāmaśāstri came to Maisūru, and studied all the works on logic and *Vēdānta* under Tirupati Śrīnivāsāçārya; he then completed his *bhāṣyaśānti* under Aṇṇāśāstri of Gargeśvarī.[492]

Another episode occurred during the time that Rāmaśāstri was studying with Tirupati Śrīnivāsāçārya. At this time, Tryambaka Śāstri visited the Maisūru court for the second time. Kṛṣṇarāja Voḍeyar III welcomed him with special honors. The Śāstri visited the palace. All the palace scholars were in attendance. However, nobody had the courage to challenge Tryambaka Śāstri, who was seated as if here were Dakṣiṇāmūrti himself.[493] Finally, the palace *paṇḍita* Kuṭṭiśāstri rose to the occasion, but had to ultimately hold his silence, being unable to prevail in the debate.[494] Many scholars from the Southern kingdoms had travelled to Maisūru, having learned that Tryambaka Śāstri would be visiting. A *Śrīvaiṣṇava* scholar called Kāñçīpura Śrīnivāsāçārya had also come to Maisūru, and was at the assembly. He too began a debate with Tryambaka Śāstri, and fell silent, unable to hold his own. Rāmaśāstri, who was still a student, was also present at the gathering. Let us keep this in mind as our story progresses.

Tirupati Śrīnivāsāçārya and Tryambaka Śāstri met each other on this occasion. Tryambaka Śāstri brought up Rāmaśāstri's name, and praising

---

appears to have been in Kāśī circa 1800 C.E. It is conjectured in Śāstri [1937] that Viṭṭhalēśa died at the end of the eighteenth century.

Regarding Hanumantāçārya, the second scholar referenced here, we see in Ballantyne [1851]: "...(refering to Annambhaṭṭa's *Tarkadīpikā*)...This commentary has been elucidated by...The *Hanumadīya*, by Hanumadāçārya, a follower of the Vaisnava school of Madhwa Āçārya. The writer was a native of Karnāṭa, but spent the greater part of his life in the service of the Rāja of Nāgpur, at his capital. He is said to have died about a hundred years ago. The *Hanumadīya* consists of nearly 6000 ślokas." The *Hanumadīya* is also recorded as item 1145 in the *Nyāya* section of works by Rice [1884, p. 122], listing Nāgapuri Hanumantāçārya as author. A "Hanumad Āchārya" is mentioned by Hall [1859, p. 38] as the author of the *Vākyārtha Dīpikā*, a commentary on the second section of Gaṅgēśa'a *Tattvaçintāmaṇi*. He is stated to be the student of a Vīrarāghava, and son of Vyāsavarya of the Kāśyapa *gotra*. The likelihood of there being two different Hanumadāçāryas, both with expertise in logic, seems low.

[492]The *bhāśyaśānti* is a propitiatory rite, including a *santarpaṇa*, performed after a student has completed the study of the *bhāṣyas* of *Ādi* Śaṅkarāçārya under the guidance of a guru. Saṅkara's *bhāṣyas* comprise his commentaries on the *Brahmasūtras*, the *Bhagavadgītā*, and ten *Upaniṣads*.

[493]Dakṣiṇāmūrti is Śiva, in his aspect as teacher. He has supreme awareness, as the god of wisdom.

[494]See footnote 573 for information on this scholar.

his intellect greatly, said: "You will be assured of acclaim if you teach him well and turn him into a great scholar."

Rāmaśāstri was about sixteen years of age when he returned to Maisūru from Kalyāṇadurga.[495] Although his travel to Kalyāṇadurga did not advance his education to any great extent, it brought his exceptional abilities to light. If one acquires a sound grasp of the principles underlying the opponent's position, uses it to predict the arguments the opponent might make, determines the elements prejudicial to his position, unravels all their complexities, and thinking with a perfectly a clear mind, constructs a counter-argument that denies the opponent all recourse, it is possible to master even a subject that one is seeing for the first time. One also needs the intellectual calibre and maturity to bring these abilities to bear as the occasion demands. It is such an intellect that is called brilliant. It is the way of the world, however, that people who find themselves lacking the capacity to match such abilities give in to jealousy. This evil demon possessed even a scholar such as Bāpuśāstri. There is little doubt that Rāmaśāstri's desire to study with such a great scholar as Tryambaka Śāstri went unfulfilled mainly due to the low-mindedness of Bāpuśāstri and others like him.

Regardless, Rāmaśāstri continued to see Tryambaka Śāstri as his guru, holding him in the highest regard. Tryambaka Śāstri entered *saṁnyāsa* in his later years, and attained *siddhi.* His *samādhi* is in a place called Raṅgasamudra near Kalyāṇadurga.[496] Let us recall that Rāmaśāstri completed his *bhāṣyaśānti* with Aṇṇāśāstri of Gargēśvarī. Subsequently, Rāmaśāstri went to Raṅgasamudra, and seating himself near the *samādhi,* recited the entire *sūtrabhāṣya* from beginning to end, paid his respects at the *samādhi,* and returned. Today's students may consider this a baseless tale. This is, however, a true story.

[495] Clearly, he spent only a few months as Tryambaka Śāstri's student.

[496] Lakṣmībāī, the daughter-in-law of Tryambaka Śāstri alludes to Raṅgasamudra as her *jāhgīr* village in the petition referenced in footnote 463. Clearly, Raṅgasamudra would have been Tryambaka Śāstri's *jāhgīr* village when he was alive.

Chapter 4: Residence in Maisūru: The State of the Darbār

Rāmaśāstri, as we saw, mastered many works under Tirupati Śrīnivāsāçārya. The guru had special regard for his student. He was beyond observing the distinctions between *Smārta* and *Vaiṣṇava.*[497] Unlike the current day, where we see this distinction in excessive form, this distinction was significant in those days only in matters relating to debate and scholarship.[498] These differences are stronger among those who are not conversant with the *śāstras.* The pride that Śrīnivāsāçārya had in Rāmaśāstri exceeded even that which Drōṇāçārya had in Arjuna.[499] This will become clear presently. Out of affection, he always called him "our Rāmuḍu", or "Rāmuḍuśāstri".[500] The brilliance of Rāmaśāstri's scholarship grew by the day. His father, who had been a scholar in the palace *Sammukhada Ūḷige* department, had received a salary of five *Varāhas.* This salary had stopped upon his death. Upon learning of Rāmaśāstri's abilities, Kṛṣṇarāja Voḍeyar III arranged for Rāmaśāstri to receive the same salary. Some say that his father's salary was three *Varāhas*, and that Rāmaśāstri received that amount. After some time, Rāmaśāstri was married.[501]

At this time, Śrī Śrīnivāsa Brahmatantra Ghaṇṭāvatāra *Svāmi* was the pontiff of the Parakāla Maṭha.[502] He was himself a great scholar. He had

---

[497] *Smārtas* tend to be more identified with the *Śaiva* tradition. There are long-standing differences between the *Śaiva* (Śiva-worship) and *Vaiṣṇava* (Viṣṇu-worship) traditions. Technically, *Smārtas* are simply followers of the *smṛtis*, the corpus of religious literature seen as being of human origin, in contrast with the *śruti* corpus, believed to be divinely inspired. The *smṛtis* include the *dharmaśāstras*, the *itihāsas*, and the *purāṇas. Smārtas* worship both Śiva and Viṣṇu. In contrast, the *Vaiṣṇava* tradition tends to focus solely on Viṣṇu.

[498] There is some merit to this assertion. In addition to what is said here, the *Advaitin* Tryambaka Śāstri studied with Hanumadāçārya, a *Vaiṣṇava,* and Tirupati Śrīnivāsāçārya, a *Vaiṣṇava,* was a student of Viṭṭhalōpādhyāta, an *Advaitin.* Among Rāmaśāstri's own students were *Smārtas, Vaiṣṇavas,* and *Śrīvaiṣṇavas.* Nonetheless, the followers of the various *maṭhas* were not above petty squabbling. See Sastri [1932, pp. 66–67], for some instances of serious, sometimes violent, differences between the various *maṭhas.*

[499] In the *Mahābhārata,* Drōṇāçārya was the teacher who taught the Pāṇḍavas and Kauravas archery. Arjuna was by far the most accomplished, and was Drōṇa's favourite.

[500] Rāmuḍu would be an affectionate diminutive in the Telugu language.

[501] His wife's name was Lakṣamma. See page 260.

[502] Śrīnivāsa Brahmatantra Ghaṇṭāvatāra *Svāmi* became pontiff of the Parakāla Maṭha

debated such scholars as Tryambaka Śāstri, and won honours in the court of Pēśva Bājirāv. This *Svāmi,* greatly impressed by Rāmaśāstri's abilities, appointed him a scholar at the *maṭha* at a monthly salary of fifteen *Rūpīs.* Rāmaśāstri also received annual honoraria of twenty-five *Rūpīs* each from the Sumatēndra Maṭha at Nañjanagūḍu, and from the Vyāsarāya *maṭha* at Sōsale.[503]

These *svāmis* were followers of the *Vaiṣṇava* tradition, and Rāmaśāstri was a *Smārta.* I have not the words to describe the sheer caliber of the Śāstri's scholarship, to have deserved this recognition from these *maṭhas* that were such great centres of the *Dvaita* and *Viśiṣṭādvaita* traditions. I am not fit to praise the greatness of spirit of these most excellent ascetics, the *svāmis* of these *maṭhas,* who thereby demonstrated their esteem for scholarship alone, casting aside all sectarian considerations. On what pair of scales, indeed, might this caliber of scholarship and such greatness of spirit be measured? And where is the merchant competent enough to hold this pair of scales?

Behind Doḍḍakere in the southern part of Maisūru city is a place called the Old Agrahāra. In that section is an old *satra* called Pūrṇayya's Ċhatra. The street it is on is called Ċhatra Street. Rāmaśāstri bought a house on that street, and lived there.[504]

This house had belonged to the *Nāyaka* of Tañjāvūru. The Marāṭha king then ruling Tañjāvūru had no male heir. The British, who were acting as emperors of India even at that time, had usurped many of India's kingdoms, and were intent on preventing the king of Tañjāvūru from adopting an heir, and insistent that his kingdom should come under their control after the king's demise.[505] In keeping with tradition, the aforesaid *Nāyaka*

on June 28, 1836. He was born in 1790 C.E. In his *pūrvāśrama,* he had been known as Kṛṣṇamāċārya.

[503] The Sumatīndra *maṭha* is a *Mādhva maṭha,* also called the Rāghavendra Svāmi *maṭha.* It is common for the individual *maṭhas* of a sect to acquire the name of the founding guru, Sumatīndra Tīrtha (1692–1725 C.E.) in this case. See footnote 75 for information about the Sōsale *maṭha.*

[504] Most regrettably, Pūrṇayya's Ċhatra has now been demolished. Despite protests from a large segment of the residents of Maisūru, the administration shows little regard for the preservation of the rich heritage of the city. Commercial interests prevail in such situations, and are able to attain their objectives through all such means as required.

[505] Although the British ruled their possessions by proxy, through the East India Company, India was not formally part of the British empire till 1857 C.E., following the First War

had come to Maisūru as ambassador. Having heard of Rāmaśāstri's brilliance, he sold him the house for about four hundred *Rūpīs.* This house is next to the Uttarādi Maṭha.[506] It appears that the son of the daughter of the Śāstri's elder brother had lived there recently. Subsequently, the house has been repaired and kept in good condition. *Dharmādhikāri* Rāmaśāstri, the grandson of Rāmaśāstri, is apparently desirous of using the house for some charitable purpose.[507]

There appears to have been another reason for the Tañjāvūru *Nāyaka's* sale of this house. The East India Company took over the reins of power in Maisūru in the Khara *saṁvatsara* (1830–1831 C.E.). Kṛṣṇarāja Voḍeyar III was given an allowance of around thirty-five thousand *Rūpīs* a month for his expenses.[508] This sum was insufficient to maintain this monarch's dignity and generosity, which were known the world over. Veṅkaṭē Arasu had been *Dīvān* at the time the king still retained control.[509] Timmapparājē Arasu, the eldest of his younger brothers, was the *Faujdār* of Nandīdurga.

---

of Independence, otherwise known as the Sepoy Mutiny. Lord Dalhousie, the Governor General of India 1848–1856 C.E. was the architect of the Doctrine of Lapse, under which a kingdom passed into British hands if either its ruler were deemed manifestly incompetent by the British, or died without a direct heir. The region around Tañjāvūru was ceded to the British in 1799 C.E., with the royal family retaining control only over the capital and a small region around it. The nominal rulers during the period were Serfōji II (1798–1822), and Śivāji II (1823–1855). Serfōji II had been educated by missionaries, was fluent in English, and was a great patron of the arts. Tañjāvūru reached the height of its artistic glory during this period. Artists in the Tañjāvūru court included the "Tanjore Quartet" who gave *Bharatanāṭyam* its modern form: the composer and singer Ponnayya, the composer and violinist Vaḍivēlu, the choreographer Çinnayya, and the percussionist Śivānandam [Weidman 2006]. Śivāji II continued this patronage of the arts, but died without an heir, and the kingdom "lapsed" into British hands. The British ended the expenditure on the arts as wasteful, causing many of the artists to emigrate to Maisūru and Travancore. The Tañjāvūru prince at the time being referenced was Śivāji II.

[506] This house has now been converted into the local branch of the Śṛṅgēri Śaṅkara Maṭha (see footnote 507). The Uttarādi Maṭha and the Śaṅkara Maṭha are adjacent to each other.

[507] Kuṇigala Rāmaśāstri's son Śivasvāmi later became Saççidānanda Śivābhinava Nṛsiṁha Bhāratī, the *Jagadguru* of the Śṛṅgēri Maṭha (see footnote 630). In 1924 C.E., during a visit to Maisūru by his successor *Jagadguru* Çandraśēkhara Bhāratī III, this house was acquired by the Śṛṅgēri Maṭha, and a temple and *maṭha* consecrated there, under the name *Abhinava Śaṅkarālaya* (Plate 27). Footnote 653 gives further details on Kuṇigala Rāmaśāstri's family.

[508] Kṛṣṇarāja Voḍeyar III actually received the sum of 13 lakh *Rūpīs* a year, or just over 100,000 *Rūpīs* a month. This included an allowance of one lakh *Star Pagodas* and a fifth of the net revenues of the state [Ikegame 2013, p. 18]. These terms were guaranteed by the Subsidiary Treaty of 1799. See footnote 603.

[509] The *Dīvāns* of the kingdom are listed by Row [1916, pp. 100–114] as follows: Pūrṇayya

Dāsappāji, the next of his brothers, was *Sarmokhtasar* at the palace. All the palace deparments came under his purview. Since the expenses of the *Mujarāyi* department had become excessive, Dāsappāji took measures to reduce them. References are still made to *Dāsappāji's lavājame* in the *Mujarāyi* department.[510] Himself a scholar of *Saṁskṛta* and Kannaḍa, he was patron to a large number of scholars. He had a reputation as an excellent administrator. Veṅkaṭē Arasu's third brother Nārayaṇarājē Arasu occupied himself with attaching himself to the king, complaining constantly about his brothers to the king, informing his brothers about developments that they might disapprove of, and meddling in affairs both inside and outside the royal court.

These four brothers were becoming a great nuisance for the entire kingdom. Despite their royal heritage and their nationalism, they had very limited vision. Companions to these princes in their mischief were a number of *dēśastha* brāhmaṇas from the Marāṭha regions who had established themselves in positions of power, with no intention other than to plunder the kingdom and return home with booty.[511]

(*Sarmokhtasar* from July 1, 1799–November, 1810, *Dīvān* from 1810–March 1811), *Bārgīr Bakṣi* Bāḷāji Rāya (April 1811–January 1812), *Savār Bakṣi* Rāma Rāya (February 1812–October 1812), Bābu Rāya (November 1817–April 1818), Siddharājē Arasu (May 1818–February 1820), Bābu Rāya (March 1820–August 1821), Liṅgarājē Arasu (September 1821–November 1822), Bābu Rāya (December 1822–November 1825), Veṅkaṭē Arasu (May 1827–October 1831), Veṅkaṭaramaṇayya (October 1831–May 1832, Bābu Rāya (May 1832–1834). Subsequently, the role of *Dīvan* was moved into the offices of the Commissioner and renamed as the office of the *Huzūr Head Śirastedār*. A Veṅkaṭaramaṇayya was appointed to this office, but was not allowed to continue because he did not accomplish a sound accounting of *inām* and revenue lands. Bābu Rāya was reappointed to this office in May 1832, but died in 1834. Kollam Veṅkaṭa Rāya was appointed to this office at a salary of *Rs.* 800 per month. When he left to become *Dīvān* of Travancore in 1838, Sūrappa replaced him. Veṅkaṭa Rāya returned to this office when Sūrappa died in 1840. Sūrappa had been a childhood associate of Kuṇigala Rāmaśāstri. See page 168.

[510] The terms used here have the following meanings [Rice 1897a]. *Faujdār:* military commander. *Divân:* Minister. *Mokhtesar:* head of a department. (The *Sarmokhtasar* oversaw all departments.) *Muzarâi:* A department for the control of temple funds and other religious property. *Lavajame:* Establishment of a department drawing pay.

[511] We see in Rice [1897b]: "In 1830 symptoms of disaffection began to show themselves in the Nagar country. A Brahman named Rama Rao, from the Mahratta territory, who had served with credit under Haidar and Tipu as a commander of cavalry, had been appointed Faujdar of Nagar in 1799, and held that office till 1805. He afterwards became Bakshi of the Sowar Cutcherry, and was one of the Raja's most intimate counsellors, and virtually

The depredations of these officials caused a number of faithless *pāle-yagāras* in the kingdom to rise up in revolt. The farmers rose up as well. It appears that a number of officials actively fomented this rebellion, calculating that if Maisūru were to come under the control of the East India Company, outsiders from places such as Āndhra, Coimbatore, and Mahārāṣtra would be assured of high positions. Such were the reasons for the administration to pass into the hands of the Company.[512]

The four Arasus mentioned above had come to be seen as the incarnations of Karaṭaka and Damanaka of the *Pañçatantra.*[513] Regardless, they

the Dewan for a few years after Purnaiya's retirement. By his influence almost every public situation of importance in Nagar down to 1828 was, with a slight interruption, filled up by his dependents or relatives. Though charged with flagrant frauds and embezzlements, their conduct was shielded from scrutiny; while some of them even enriched themselves by giving encouragement to robbers—for whose operations the wild nature of the country offers many facilities—and partaking of the plunder. The outstanding balances of revenue having accumulated to upwards of thirteen lakhs of rupees, the Bakshi contrived that he himself should be deputed to inquire into and settle the claims. He made large remissions to the extent of seven-and-a-half lakhs, and returned to the Darbar in 1828. The Raja being led to question the propriety of these proceedings, resolved to appoint a relative of his own, named Vira Raj Arasu, as Faujdar. The latter discovered that much fraud had been practised in the remissions, and re-imposed the claims, which naturally excited dissatisfaction in those affected. The Bakshi's party, also, fearful of the consequences to themselves if the inquiries which Vira Raj Arasu was pursuing should expose the corruption and malversation they had practised during so many years, connived at the seditious proceedings of a pretender to the throne of Nagar…

"…But during the greater part of this time the principal authority had been left too much in the hands of one family. Every office was gradually filled with Deshasta Brahmans, who made themselves obnoxious to the Lingáyits. A system of secret plunder was connived at, of which they and their patrons reaped the benefit. At the same time the mode of farming the revenue laid the people under burdens from which there was no redress. Matters grew to such a pitch that in 1830 the gauḍas and ryots assembled in kúṭas or indignation meetings at Basavapatna and Honnali. The discontent was fomented by a pretender to the Bednur throne, named Budi Basavappa, who formed insurgent bands; and these again were shortly joined by Rangappa Náyak, the head of the Tarikere family, and by numbers of Thugs, professional stranglers. The Raja's troops failed to put down the now open revolt, and he was obliged to seek the aid of British force…"

[512] A strong argument is made by Stein [1985] that the Nagar insurgency was triggered in large part by the extension of central control into previously semi-autonomous regions in Mysore, in response to British demands for revenue. Mysore was required to pay "subsidy" revenues of 24.5 lakhs per annum (57% of the projected revenues of the region), for the maintenance of a subsidiary force of the British. For perspective, this sum was a staggering 50% of the total tribute collected by the British from the 198 princely states of India.

[513] In the story from the *Pañçatantra,* Karaṭaka and Damanaka are two jackals who are

were experts in the art of real-world politics. They continued to plot against Kṛṣṇarāja Voḍeyar III even after the loss of his kingdom. The righteousness of the king, however, caused all their schemes to go up in flames. A certain Veṅkaṭappāji, who was under the patronage of these brothers and was well informed of their activities, entered the king's inner circle. He is believed to have known some English, and was therefore known as *Iṅgrēji* Veṅkaṭappāji. At this time, the king was in correspondence with the British, making the case that the allowance of twelve thousand *Varāhas* was insufficient to meet expenses, and that he should be granted a fifth of the revenue of the kingdom. For the benefit of the king and his countrymen, *Iṅgrēji* Veṅkaṭappāji played a leading role in this matter.

Few restrictions had been placed by the Company on Kṛṣṇarāja Voḍeyar III while he was in power. It is true that there was a Resident, who ensured that the king took no measures prejudicial to the interests of the Company. This official, however, operated more as if he were the ambassador of a foreign nation. The rulers of various kingdoms interacted and corresponded with each other freely, maintained mutual relations, and sent ambassadors to each other.[514] The Tañjāvūru *Nāyakā* had come to Maisūru as a lawyer, and in accordance with protocol, interacted with the king through Veṅkaṭappāji.

General Cubbon was then in charge of administration, as the Mysore Commissioner. During this period, there was constant warfare between the

---

retainers to the lion king Piṅgalaka, and connive to break up the friendship between him and a bull named Sañjīvaka. They are held out as the archetypical faithless retainers.

[514] This statement may be correct in the sense that the king remained the nominal head of state, and performed the attendant functions in some *pro forma* manner. However, the king had no power to communicate with other potentates on matters of State. The Subsidiary Treaty of 1799, which formally installed Kṛṣṇarāja Voḍeyar III as the nominal ruler of Maisūru is explicit in this respect, as the following excerpt amply demonstrates:

Article VI.

> His Highness Maha Rajah Kistna Rajah Oodiyaver Behauder engages, that he will be guided by a sincere and cordial attention to the relations of peace and amity, now established between the English Company Behauder and their allies, and that he will carefully abstain from any interference in the affairs of any state in alliance with the said English Company Behauder, or of any state whatever. And for securing the object of this stipulation, it is further stipulated and agreed, that no communication or correspondence, with any foreign state whatever, shall be holden by his said Highness, without the previous knowledge and sanction of the said English Company Behauder.

British and the Afghāns, Marāṭhās, and Sīkhs.[515] At such times, the Company was especially mindful of their subject states. It was in this context that the Company, suspecting Veṅkaṭappāji and the Tañjāvūru *Nāyaka*, among others, of being part of a plot against them, suddenly moved them to Beṅgalūru and placed them under house arrest.[516] The Tañjāvūru *Nāyaka* having hurriedly sold his house around this time, Rāmaśāstri was able to purchase it from him.

One might wonder what connection might exist between Rāmaśāstri's scholarship and the political goings-on in Maisūru. The kingdom's condition will have a bearing on the progress of our story. We have been brief in our summary of the reasons for the decline in the king's income. Indeed, had there not been this shortfall in resources, the king, who had bestowed so much wealth and property on scholars such as Rāmaśēṣa Śāstri, Kuṭṭiśāstri, Ānavaṭṭi Śrīnivāsācārya, *Julapi* Kṛṣṇāçārya, and Rājēśvaraśāstri, would certainly have shown similar favour to Rāmaśāstri, who in a way, was an even greater scholar. Indeed, after he lost ruling powers, the king was prevented by the Company from granting *jāhgīrs*. On this account, the Śāstri did not receive rewards to the extent he deserved. It was for this reason that we felt it necessary to describe the political situation at the time.

Rāmaśāstri remained content with what he received, and lived happily, without ever craving for more.

---

[515]General Mark Cubbon was appointed Commissioner of Mysore State in 1834 C.E. However, the British had largely overcome Marāṭha oppositon by 1818 C.E., when Pēśva Bāji Rāv II was exiled to Biṭhūr near present-day Kānpur, and granted a pension of 800,000 *Rūpīs*. (See footnote 553.) When Bāji Rāv died in 1851, his adopted son Dhōṇḍo Pant (Nānā Sāhib) was denied this pension, and became a leader of the 1857 uprising. Conflict with the Sīkhs continued till 1848, when Pañjāb was annexed. Conflict with the Afghāns lasted much longer, with the First Afghan War fought 1839–1842, the Second Afghan War fought 1878–1880, and the Third Afghan War in 1919.

[516]This note from Sastri [1932, p. 125] may be relevant here: "The maharaja, in his turn, was most cordial to the commission... But one important note should be added here. While he held Cubbon in high esteem as a man, he was jealous of him as a commissioner, and would not see eye to eye with him in public measures. Something of this attitude was due to the counsels of Stokes the resident, Arapoor Basappaji Urs, Seebiah, Venkatappaji Urs, and Vanderlowen (an English writer). *Cubbon succeeded in separating the Maharaja from them.*" The italics are by the translator.

Chapter 5: Residence in Maisūru: A Wealth of Students

Rāmaśāstri was now resident in his house in Maisūru. His tutelage under his guru was complete. Many students now came to him for instruction, on account of the excellence of his scholarship, his speech, and his capabilites as a teacher. As the Śāstri's fame spread, students began to arrive from places far away. Though himself a *Smārta*, he was a student of the *Vaiṣṇavite* Tirupati Śrīnivāsāçārya, and a recipient of a monthly salary from the Parakālasvāmi, the crest-jewel of the *Śrivaiṣṇavite* sect. Thus, Rāmaśāstri, respected by all faiths, was not partial to any sect. Adherents of all three faiths studied with him. Many students from far away having no means of sustenance, the Śāstri arranged for them to board twice daily in his own house, and gifted them a *pañçe* set annually.[517]

In addition to scholars who themselves both boarded and taught students, many officials supported the advancement of learning by feeding hundreds of students in their homes twice a day. A great many students studied in Māgaḍi with the great scholar Mahādēva Śāstri. Their number grew year after year. These students all boarded twice a day in the home of Karaṇīka Kṛṣṇappa of Māgaḍi, who performed this meritorious service out of righteous devotion. If a student arrived late for the evening meal, Kṛṣṇappa himself would come bearing a torch, inquire after the student's welfare, and ensure that he was fed.

A distinguished citizen of Maisūru called Bhāgavata Subbarāv was also such a person of virtue.[518] He had made available a large house of his own to serve as a school. Teachers lived in this house and taught the *Vēdas* to students. These students studied many other subjects from other scholars in Maisūru. Bhāgavata Subbarāv boarded around a couple of hundred such students in his home, and also gifted them a *pañçe* set each year. This Bhāgavata Subbarāv was most pious. He had built many *çhatras,* temples,

[517] A *pañçe* set includes a *pañçe* worn around the waist, and an *aṅgavastra* worn on the upper body.

[518] See footnote 235 and page 87.

lakes, watering places for cattle, and *maṇṭapas.*[519] He had also sponsored many *yāgas*. He was himself very observant of religious ritual. He would arise at the crack of dawn, complete his daily rituals and his *pārthivapūjā* in a timely manner, attend to his duties at the palace, return around noon, and complete his afternoon rituals. He would eat with the students, seating himself among them. He never had a special place reserved for him, as might befit a head of household. He would eat the same food that everyone ate. He followed this practice to prevent *paṅktibhēda*.[520] On one occasion, his young son, seated nearby, ate some food that was too pungent for his tender palate, causing his mouth and nose to start watering copiously. Subbarāv called out to him to drink water, rather than favour him specially by asking for ghee to be brought to him to sooth his palaṭe. Subbarāv never gave in to self-aggrandizement, always treating everyone as equals.

Bhāgavata Subbarāv belonged to the *Bobbūru Kamme* community.[521] He was a palace official of the *Khāsa Bokkasa* department.[522] The king had enormous regard for him. He supervised all the activities of the *Zenāna* department. He was exempt from *goṣā* in the queen's quarters.[523] The king was very pleased with the acts of charity and goodwill that Subbarāv engaged in. The palace discharged Subbarāv's debts, whenever they happened

[519] For instance, Desikāchārya [1949, p. lxxvi] records that Bhāgavata Subbarāv built an *agrahāra* called Subrahmaṇyapura as well as a temple to Śrī Narasiṁha near Kannambāḍi, and had the two inaugurated by His Holiness Ghaṇṭāvatāra Parakālasvāmi on April 22, 1839 C.E.

[520] *Paṅktibhēda*, meaning "separate rows", indicates different seating for different classes of people, reflecting differences of status. This is seen as a serious offense, as the following *śloka* from the *Vyāsa Smṛti* indicates: *paṅktibhedī pṛthakpākī nityabrāhmaṇanindakaḥ* | *ādeśī vedavikrīta pañçaite brahmaghātakāḥ* ‖, meaning that anyone who engages in *paṅktibheda*, has food cooked for himself separately, speaks ill of brāhmaṇas, asserts himself unduly, or teaches the *Vēdas* for money, is no different from a killer of brāhmaṇas.

[521] This is a community of Kannaḍa-speaking *Smārta* brāhmaṇas. The Kannaḍa-speaking brāhmaṇa communities include *Aravattuvokkalu, Baḍaganāḍu, Havyaka, Hosalanāḍu, Hoysaḷa, Hoisaṇige, Kamme (Bobbūru, Karna, Ulaça), Kandāvara, Kōṭa, Māraka, Sīrnāḍu*, and *Śivaḷḷi*. See Rice [1877b, pp. 321–325] for more details on brāhmaṇa communities.

[522] See footnote 235.

[523] The word *gōṣa* or *gōśa* (sometimes *ghōṣa*, etc.) is generally used as a synonym for *pardah* (*pardeh* in Persian), meaning "veil", and refers to the practice of requiring Muslim or upper-class Hindu women to wear veils in the presence of males who were not close relations. *Gośa* is just an alternate pronunciation of the Persian word *gūśeh*, meaning "corner", an allusion to the confinement of women to a small room or apartment, appropriately called the "corner". Thus, *gōṣa* is closer in meaning to the Persian word *zanāneh*, meaning "women's quarters", rather than to the word *pardeh*.

to mount. Subbarāv, too, was extremely devoted to his king. Being like-minded, servant and master were close to each other. Other major officials, including *Musāhib* Gaṅgādhararāv, also participated in providing food for students as well as to those who were destitute.[524] There being many other ways for the wealthy to spend their money today, the charitable practies of old have now come to an end.

This would be an appropriate place to make another point. The ever-munificent Kr̥ṣṇarāja Voḍeyar III had provided for brāhmaṇa boys of the three sects to have their own spaces,[525] the better for them to study both the books specific to their sects, as well as the various universally used *mantras*. *Smārtas* were taught in the temple of Triṇēśvara, *Vaiṣṇavas* in the temple of Kr̥ṣṇasvāmi, and *Śrīvaiṣṇavas* in the temple of Varāhāsvāmi.[526] Many students, according to their abilities, were given stipends of one *Muppāga* (3 *Āṇe*, 6 *Pai*), one *Haṇa* (4 *Āṇe*, 8 *Pai*), or one *Haṇa Vaḍḍa* (7 *Āṇe*).[527] These stipends were disbursed from the palace each month in the form of loose change. Thus, there was encouragement in Maisūru for the continuance of the traditional ways of acquiring learning. The current prevalence of English education has caused both the minds of our people, as well as their wealth, to be committed to other matters. The ways of our people have indeed changed.

Be this as it might. Rāmaśāstri looked upon all his students fondly, no matter how dull, treating them all as his own children. It is unusual for a guru to have as much pride in his other students as he might have in his brightest. As a result, the bright students thrive on his encouragement and

[524] See footnote 240 for further details on this Gaṅgādhararāv.

[525] Boys from the *Smārta*, *Vaiṣṇava*, and *Śrīvaiṣṇava* sects, that is.

[526] These are three of the twelve temples within the Maisūru fort.

[527] The *Rūpī* was divided into 16 *Āṇe*, and each *Āṇe* was divided into 12 *Pai*. The currency and coinage in use at the time was complicated. The larger denominations were the *Rūpī*, *Varāha*, and *Pagōḍa*, each coming in several variants, depending on the issuer. The smallest denomination was the *Kāsu* (whence we have the English *cash*), also referred to as the *Pai*. Then there was the *Haṇa* or *Paṇa*, also referred to as the *Fanam*. A *Fanam* was worth 4 *Āṇe*, 8 *Kāsus*, or at somewhat more than half a *Rūpī*. A *Pāga* (the derived or *tadbhava* form of the *Saṁskr̥ta* word *pāda*, or quarter) was a fourth of a *Paṇa*, or 1 *Āṇe*, 2 *Kāsus*. A *Muppāga* was three *Pāgas* (three-quarters of a *Paṇa*), or 3 *Āṇe*, 6 *Kāsus*. A *Duḍḍu* was a copper coin worth a third of an *Āṇe*, or 4 *Kāsus*. An *Aḍḍa* was 7 *Duḍḍus*, or 2 *Āṇe*, 4 *Kāsus*. The *Haṇa Vaḍḍa* alluded to in the text, is of course, a *Haṇa Aḍḍa*; the source text is clearly using the terms *Duḍḍu* and *Āṇe* equivalently. Also see footnote 543.

excel, while students receiving less recognition from the guru lose confidence, thereby magnifying their dullness, and are dismissed as dim-witted. Because Rāmaśāstri treated all his students equally, however, and taught them himself, the talented among them became outstanding scholars, but even the dull were recognized as scholars.

We might also call attention to another reason for his students to be devoted to their guru. Many teachers do not follow the practice of teaching novice students themselves. It is usual to assign an advanced student to teach beginners. As a result, novice students gain no benefit from having become students of the senior *śāstri.* They must be content with receiving instruction in the homes of advanced students. This practice often creates indifference in the minds of these students. Rāmaśāstri had himself faced this difficulty in Kalyāṇadurga. The indifference he had experienced in Kalyāṇadurga was half the reason why he came to Maisūru to study with Tirupati Śrīnivāsāçārya. Tryambaka Śāstri's scholarship drew him to Kalyāṇadurga, but his experience there only served to remind him of the proverbial unfortunate who jumps into what looks like an ocean, only to find himself knee-deep in mud.

Determined to be on guard against such a failing, the Śāstri, after completing his morning rituals, would instruct one group of his advanced students from 9 a.m. to noon, another group from 4 p.m. to 6 p.m., and novice students in the evening. His advanced students Sāggere Nārāyaṇaśāstri and Kavi Varadāçārya would help students review their lessons. A great many students were attracted by his insistence on teaching all his students himself. During *Pradōṣa* times, he would review old lessons and organize debates, instead of teaching new material. As a result, the Śāstri was left with very little time. His renown spread far and wide because of this manner of structuring his teaching. The number of his students grew enormously. If any of his students were taken ill, the Śāstri showed concern as if the illness were his own, and administered medication and other treatment by his own hand. His students were deeply devoted to the Śāstri, because he was a treasure house of such virtue, besides being such a great scholar.

Çhatra Street, where Rāmaśāstri's house was located, was in excellent order. Many eminent officials and public servants had built homes on this street. Rāmaśāstri's students would rehearse their lessons, seated on the porches of each of these houses. Their voices could be heard for quite a distance, according to senior people who were witnesses. Each year, on the fourth *śukla tithi* of Bhādrapada, the Śāstri would celebrate the festival of Gaṇēśa. Starting that day, there would be no lessons for twenty-one days. During this time, there would be debates on the subject of *Vēdānta* and logic every evening before the time of *maṅgaḷārati*. Students studying the same topic would be organized into two opposing groups, another student would serve as the debate moderator, and the Śāstri would be on hand to clarify doubts and confusions. Many *vaidikas* and officials would be invited for the *maṅgaḷārati*.[528] Many would attend, because it was a distinction to be invited to the Śāstri's home. The Śāstri himself would take part in these debates, if another distinguished scholar happened to be among the guests. On such occasions, when the Śāstri himself participated, the *maṅgaḷārati* would occur as late as 2, 3, or even 4 a.m.

Tirupati Śrīnivāsāçārya, the Śāstri's guru, often came to these Gaṇeśa *maṅgalārati* gatherings. He would always delight in his dearest student's scholarship and his eloquence. On one such occasion, after watching the students debate each other, his own scholarly instincts got the better of him. He felt impelled to take part in the debate himself. Nobody was capable of debating him but Rāmaśāstri himself. Teacher and student began their debate. Arguments and counter-arguments came in a cascade, one on top of the other. All the blustering from the ordinary students quickly died away. It was a battle as might have been between Drōṇa and Arjuna, or indeed a debate between Sarasvatī and Dakṣiṇāmūrti. Learning of these proceedings, all the notables in Maisūru took themselves over to the Śāstri's house. It was almost dawn. Rāmaśāstri challenged his guru with yet another argument. At that point, in full view of everyone, Śrīnivāsāçārya declared: "Our Rāmuḍu Śāstri! Dakṣiṇāmūrti incarnate! Who indeed can counter your arguments!", and with tears of joy in his eyes, embraced his student. Jubilant shouts of "*jaya! jaya!*" resounded among those gathered.

Even Drōṇāçārya asked Ekalavya, who had the utmost regard for his guru, to cut off his thumb; infuriated by the blows of his long-cherished student Arjuna, he unleashed a fierce flood of arrows, giving him no pause

---

[528] In this essential part of the worship ritual, a lamp or platter containing a light is waved (moved in circles) before the deity. The word is a compound of *maṅgala* (auspicious) and *ārati*. The latter word is obtained from the *Saṁskṛta* word *ārātrika* by way of its *Prākṛta* form *ārattiya*, and could refer to either the plate holding the light, or the ceremony itself. Also see footnote 262.

to recover.[529] The arrows of the intellect inflict greater torment than do ordinary arrows. To bear them, and embrace his student, shedding tears of affection, surely places the nobility of Śrīnivāsāçārya's character a smidgen higher than even that of Drōṇāçārya's. That the student of such a teacher should possess boundless ability goes without saying. Who but the two themselves could even judge the abilities of such a teacher and such a student?

It appears necessary to give the names of some students of the Śāstri, who went on to become great scholars. Among them were:

1. Rīma Raṅgāçāraya, who was recently *svāmi* of the Parakāla Maṭha,[530]
2. Ānandāḷvār,[531]
3. Siṅgaḷāçārya,
4. Raṅgaśrīnivāsāçārya of the Sōsale Maṭha,
5. Rāmagiri Śāmāçār,
6. Bānamballi Veṅkaṭaramaṇaçārya,
7. Śēṣaśāstri of Gaddavāla,
8. Anantāçārya,
9. Kavi Varadāçārya,
10. Kuraçci Raṅgāçārya of Kumbhakōṇe,
11. Vijayarāghavāçār of Śōbhattūr in Kāñçipura district,
12. Raṅgappāçārya of Kocci[532]
13. *Vidyānidhi* Vāsudēvā Śāstri of Doḍḍaballāpura,

[529] The battle between Drōṇa and Arjuna occurs in Canto 103 of the *Bhīṣma Parva* of the *Mahābhārata,* on the eighth day of the eighteen-day war. Ekalavya is the paradigm of devotion to the guru. He seeks to learn archery from Drōṇa, who rejects him because he is from a low caste. Undeterred, he creates a clay image of Drōṇa, practices before it, and soon attains unmatched skill. When Drōṇa discovers this, he demands Ekalavya's right thumb as his *gurudakṣiṇa*. Ekalavya unhesitatingly gives it to him.

[530] This appears to be Śrī Raṅganātha Brahmatantra Parakāla Svāmi, who was born in 1812 C.E., and was the head of the Parakāla maṭha from 1873–1885 C.E. [Desikāchārya 1949].

[531] See footnote 320.

[532] Koççi Raṅgappāçārya (1820–1891 C.E.) is listed in [Sharma 1981] as a leading scholar of the age, and as a student of Śatakōṭi Rāmaśāstri of Maisūru, that is, of Kuṇigala Rāmaśāstri.

14. Paṇḍita Bhāṣyāçārya,
15. Kupanaiyyaṅgār of Kumbhakōṇe,
16. Nārāyaṇaśāstri of Sāggere,
17. Lakṣmīnarasiṁhaśāstri, the eldest son of Rāmaśāstri,
18. *Vēdānta* Rāmappa,
19. Kuppaśāstri,
20. Kuṭṭi Narasiṁhaśāstri,
21. Jōyisa Siṅgaḷāçārya,
22. Tōgire Śrīkaṇṭhaśāstri,
23. Koyimattūr Bhīmāçārya,
24. Niḍagallu Kṛṣṇaśāstri,
25. Tiramakuḍi Appaṇṇāçārya,
26. Muttūru Rāmaśāstri,
27. Subrahmaṇyaśāstri,
28. Śrīnivāsāçārya of Dhāravāḍa,
29. Kaṇagāla Śāmaśāstri,
30. Gaṅgādharaśāstri of Soṇḍekoppa.

All his students always accompanied Rāmaśāstri whenever he went for a scholarly debate, or on an excursion. Rāmaśāstri never ate his meals in anyone's house, in the places he visited.[533] Either Vāsudēvāśāstri of Doḍḍaballāpura or Nārāyaṇaśāstri of Sāggere always prepared the Śāstri's meals.

[533] This was to maintain his ritual purity. He would have had no way of knowing whether the food in anyone else's house met his strict standards of ritual purity. In South Indian brāhmaṇa households, the kitchen is an area of the highest ritual purity, and eating itself entails certain formal protocols and rituals. Also see footnote 324.

Chapter 6: Residence in Maisūru: The Śriyappāçārya Episode

Rāmaśāstri maintained the practice of visiting the palace every day. He would arrive in the morning at the time of the king's *Śivapūja*, spend some time in the Ātmavilāsa or Nāmatīrtha courtyards, and return after conferring his blessings on the king once the *Śivapūja* was complete. Many scholars followed this practice. On days when the gatherings of scholars appeared interesting, the king would join them in the Ambāvilāsa, and enjoy some time in their company.

Those unfamiliar with the Maisūru palace may wonder at the name Ambāvilāsa. This was a courtyard in the old palace. Kṛṣṇarāja Voḍeyar III would spend his time here, managing the affairs of the palace. Manōvilāsa, Ātmavilāsa, and Rājēndravilāsa were some of the other courtyards. For the queens and their retinues, there were other courtyards with interesting names, such as the Lakṣmīvilāsa, Ramāvilāsa, Sītāvilāsa, Kṛṣṇavilāsa, Çandravilāsa, Madanavilāsa, Kamāna Toṭṭi, Jantada Toṭṭi, Baṇṇada Toṭṭi, Sammukhada Toṭṭi, Karīkallu Toṭṭi, Kudurē Toṭṭi, and the Nāmatīrtha Toṭṭi. These *toṭṭis* have all been consumed in the recent conflagration in the palace.[534]

Some people, while nominally scholars in the *Sammukha* department, do little more than display the trappings of the position, nurturing with care the habit of going to the palace once a month just to collect their salary. They do visit the palace on special occasions, when there is the possibility of some special reward. Is there much chance indeed, of their foregoing attendance on such occasions? But I will refrain from singing their full praises here. There are only a few of this number who will content themselves with a dignified exit. I lack the space here to write at length of the others, who are given to such antics as marking their foreheads with marks designating their sect, dressing themsleves in fancy shawls, and declaiming loudly while standing in the middle of the street: "And oh, if anyone comes looking for me, be sure to let them know I have gone to the palace!" and if they meet some ordinary soul on their way, assaulting everyone's ears by inserting ghastly mispronunciations of English words into their speech, and

[534] See footnote 369.

if they happen upon an acquaintance, saying, while detaining them in conversation on some frivolous topic: "A palace messenger and a guard both arrived yesterday; a *kuhayōga śānti* is being observed today;[535] we are sure to be called to the palace if we are absent," and making their way slowly to the palace while constantly adjusting their garment to ensure that everyone gets a good look at its grand border.

Rāmaśāstri had a very different attitude. He knew well that any wealth he received from the king was ultimately debasing. Yet, without royal patronage, scholarship would neither be recognized nor find fulfilment. Accepting the king's wage was hence a necessity. The Śāstri believed, however, that the chief responsibility of a *vaidika* like him being to advance scholarship and to bestow blessings on the king, the wage he received from the palace would be justifed if he saw the king in person every day and prayed for his well-being.

We are already familiar with the depth of Tryambaka Śāstri's scholarship. He had authored many works promoting *Advaita*. Scholars of many other persuasions tried to refute Tryambaka Śāstri's arguments. A fellow-student of Tirupati Śrīnivāsāçārya called Hulagi Śriyappāçārya arrived in Maisūru from elsewhere, and claiming that he would refute Tryambaka Śāstri's works, met with Kṛṣṇarāja Vodeyar III.[536]

---

[535] *Kuhayōga* refers to a malevolent conjunction of planets, signifying doom for the king. The *śānti* is a rite intended to avert this fate.

[536] This scholar appears to be none other than the Hulugi Śriyaḥpatyāçārya mentioned in Sharma [1981]. Because this scholar figures so prominently in this biography, we excerpt the information in Sharma [1981] in its entirety:

> "He is another celebrated writer of the early XIX century. His most important work is the *Dvaita Dyumaṇi*, which is supposed to be a refutation of the *Brahmānandīya*, but is in reality a very recondite commentary on the *Tattvodyota* and its *tīkā* by Jayatīrtha. He is also credited with a commentary on the *Bhedojjīvana*, and another in defense of the *Tarkatāṇḍava* against certain contemporary criticisms. The *Sattattvapeṭikā* is mentioned as another of his works. He was a contemporary of the well-known Advaitic scholar Tryambaka Śāstri whom he is supposed to have encountered in several debates and whose *Śrutimatodyota* and other tracts (containing adverse comments on certain of Madhva's works) have been refuted by him in the course of his commentary on *Tattvodyota*. The commentary on the *Pramāṇapaddhati* called *Ādarśa* (published at Dharwar) is by one of his disciples. Śriyaḥpatyāçārya belonged to the village of Hulugi near Koppal on the Hubli-Guntakal section."

Having come to Maisūru for the purpose of debate, it was necessary for Śriyappāçārya to learn something about the local scholars. The scholarship and daring of Rāmaśāstri was sufficient to be alarming to visiting scholars. Having learnt something of these matters, Śriyappāçārya said to his former fellow-student Tirupati Śrīnivāsāçārya: "Dear *Āçārya*, perhaps it would be best for you to speak with Rāmaśāstri, so his recklessness in debate does not cause harm to my dignity." To this, Tirupati Śrīnivāsāçārya replied: "It is indeed true that Rāmaśāstri is my disciple, but he has a very independent mind, and is not likely to listen to what I might say in this regard. I would prefer to leave this matter alone."

Later, Śrīnivāsāçārya saw Rāmaśāstri and said to him: "Rāmuḍu, I had a conversation with Śriyappāçārya. He desired me to ask you not to overwhelm him with your arguments and humiliate him in the debate set for tomorrow. This did not seem right to me. One should build a reputation on one's competence and ability. Respect gained by pleading for mercy will never endure. Don't spare him. Show him what you are capable of!" However, Śriyappāçārya declined to debate Rāmaśāstri, proffering as excuse the fact that Rāmaśāstri was the equivalent of his own disciple, being a disciple of his fellow-student Tirupati Śrīnivāsāçārya.

This occurred in the Śhubhakṛtu *saṁvatsara*. At the time, Rāmaśāstri was thirty-six years of age. The exuberance and intensity of his scholarship was not about to aquiesce to Śriyappāçārya's appeals. He stood ready to debate him. A debate in writing was finally set to take place between Rāmaśāstri and Śriyappāçārya, with Śrīnivāsa Brahmatantra Parakālasvāmi as moderator. However, the Parakālasvāmi had to leave for Mēlukōṭe at that time.[537]

Śriyappāçārya then sent the Parakālasvāmi several papers he had written, attempting to refute the propositions that Tryambaka Śāstri had established. This most excellent ascetic who adorned the *Hayagrīva Pīṭha*, and who was himself a great scholar, sent these papers to Rāmaśāstri, having great faith in his abilities to prevail. A disciple from the *maṭha* brought these to Rāmaśāstri's home. Rāmaśāstri was in bed, with the covers drawn over his face. He had the messenger

Early 1843

[537]The Parakālasvāmi made frequent trips to Mēlukōṭe. Records indicate that he was been in Mēlukōṭe on January 14, 1843 [Desikāchārya 1949, p. lxxxii].

who brought the papers read them to him just once, and asked him to return immediately with the papers. Śriyappāçārya, upon learning that the *Svāmi* had left for Mēlukōṭe, also departed Maisūru.

When Rāmaśāstri went after him to Mēlukōṭe, he found this scholar there. Rāmaśāstri declared that he would not rest until he had substantiated all of Tryambaka Śāstri's theories that had been attacked, and the very next day, forwarded to the *Svāmi's* presence a document refuting every word in the documents Śriyappāçārya had sent the *Svāmi*. It is incredible that Rāmaśāstri, after hearing it read just once, recalled everything in such detail, and even built such strong counter-arguments.

In reply, the *Āçārya* said: "I did not write anything in refutation of Tryambaka Śāstri's disquisitions. I merely wrote some notes and commentary from the *Dvaita* perspective." The *Svāmi,* unable to directly call this a prevarication, fell silent.[538]

Śriyappāçārya then made an appointment to meet Rāmaśāstri the next day, but quietly left for Beṅgaḷūru that night, and lodged in the home of a person by the name of Kōlāra Śāmrāv. This news reached Kṛṣṇarāja Voḍeyar III. As Rāmaśāstri was about to follow Śriyappāçārya to Beṅgaḷūru, the king said to Rāmaśāstri: "Dear Śāstri! Why kill a person who is already dead?"

Rāmaśāstri replied: "Indeed, I harbour no resentment against Śriyappāçārya, but Tryambakaśāstri, that treasure house of learning, was my guru. When a person travels to many countries, bragging that he has refuted the theses established by such a great scholar, and even comes here, but will not stay for a debate, escapes, and then boasts that nobody in Maisūru could stand up to him in debate, that is merely demeaning the scholarship of someone who is no more. Even worse, if it comes to be believed elsewhere that this court, which is home to all manner of scholarship, is great in name only, we who are so greatly obliged to it would be no better than walking dead, Your Highness. After your bidding, however, I will pursue him no more."

---

[538] See the excerpt from Sharma [1981] in footnote 536, however. It is suggested there that Śriyaḥpatyāçārya's refutation of Tryambaka Śāstri's work appears in his *Dvaita Dyumaṇi*, a work that is supposedly a refutation on the *Brahmānandīya*, but being in reality more of a commentary on the *Dvaita* principles appearing in Madhvāçārya's *Tatvodyota*.

Nevertheless, he wrote a paper and two *ślōkas* refuting Śriyappāçārya's theses, and sent them to Baṅgalī Çauḍappa in Beṅgaḷūru. These *ślōkas* are printed below in Rāmaśāstri's own handwriting.[539]

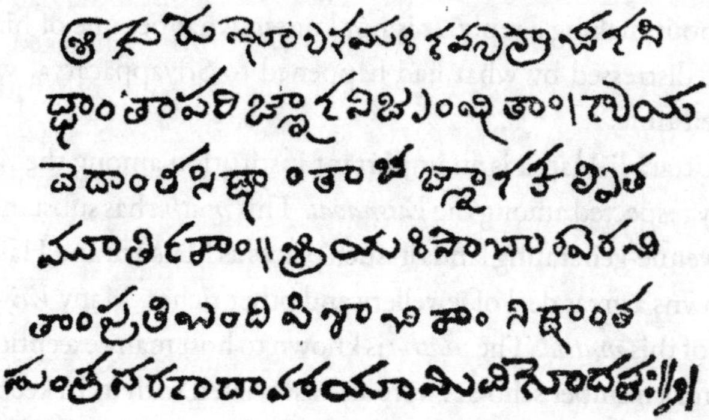

Meaning: By reciting the *mantra* called *siddhānta* will I playfully exorcise the demon *pratibandi*,[540] whose ostentation arises from ignorance of *siddhāntas* old and new, and who was conceived by Śriyaḥpāçārya, in his abject ignorance of *Nyāya* and *Vēdānta.*

Baṅgalī Çauḍappa was head *Śirastedār* in the office of the British Resident. He had acquired the nickname *baṅgali* since he was employed in the Resident's bungalow.[541] Although he held what was considered a very important position, he had not abandoned traditional practices or adopted unprincipled behaviours. He remained committed to traditional customs,

[539] These *slokas* read as follows. *"śrī gurubhyo namaḥ | navya prāçina siddhāntā parijñāna vijrambitāṁ | nyāya vēdānta siddhāntāçajñāna kalpita mūrtikāṁ ‖ śriyaḥpāçāryaraçitāṁ pratibandi piṣāçikāṁ | siddhānta mantra paṭhanādāvarayāmi vinōditāḥ ‖"*

[540] *Pratibandi* refers to a logical or dialectical fallacy in which the refutation of an argument as flawed suffers from the same flaw.

[541] Here is what Rao [1936a, p. 403] says: "Chowdiah the Residency Sheristedar was originally a shanbogue or village accountant of Hirisave in the taluk of Kickery. Then he became a clerk in the taluk of Gudibande on a salary of three pagodas a month. Next he became a clerk to the Residency surgeon at Mysore. At the same time he paid court to Ramaswamy Mudaliar and through the latter's influence with Casamaijor he was appointed Sheristedar in the Resident's office… Chowdiah by virtue of his appointment made himself an indispensable factotum of Casamaijor who succeeded Cole and he also became generally the medium of communication between the Resident and the Raja. Casamaijor under the semblance of non-interference is stated to have suffered his agent to meddle and dictate in everything, much to the latter's advantage…"

and maintained a deep respect for scholars, as well as to his countrymen. As soon as the above document and *ślōkas* reached Beṅgaḷūru, Çauḍappa followed his instructions to ensure that it reached Śriyappāçārya in Kōlāra Śāmrāv's home; the document arrived at mealtime. Śriyappāçārya left Beṅgaḷūru without making a reply. It is not known what became of him. Some *Mādhvas,* distressed by what had happened to Śriyappāçārya, were now biding their time.

The Uttarādi Maṭha is an important institution among the *Mādhvas.* It is deeply respected among the *Vaiṣṇavas.* This *maṭha* has substantial amounts of revenue-generating lands in such places as Maisūru and Haiderābād, and also owns a great deal of jewellery and other riches. Many *Vaiṣṇavas* are followers of this *maṭha.* The *maṭha* is known to host many exceptional individuals, and a number scholars were also associated with it. In keeping with long-standing tradition, an accomplished scholar named *Gūḷi* Bāḷāçārya was appointed pontiff of this *maṭha.* We have already seen that there were debates in the Maisūru palace on the occasion of Tryambaka Śāstri's visit to Maisūru. On that occasion, when Bāḷāçārya had carried on the debate with extraordinary eloquence, Tryambaka Śāstri had remarked: "This Bāḷāçārya attacks one as a bull does!" From that point forward, Kṛṣṇarāja Voḍeyar III nicknamed him "Gūḷi" Bāḷāçārya.[542] Kṛṣṇarāja Voḍeyar III, indulging in a bit of playfulness, often gave people unusual nicknames, such as *Julapi* Kṛṣṇāçārya, *Onṭe* Rāmaçārya, *Pāyasa* Kṛṣṇa, *Prēta* Narasiṁhaśāstri, *Hāgū-beḷe* Rāmarāv, and *Muççagaṇṇu* Śrīnivāsāçayra.[543]

---

[542] *Gūḷi* means bull in Kannaḍa. Gūḷi Bāḷāçārya took on the name Śrī Satyasantuṣṭa Tīrtha when he became 30th pontifical head of the *maṭha.* The Uttarādi Maṭha's account of how he acquired the nickname "Gūḷi" is similar to the one here, except that it alludes to a debate with a visiting scholar called Çandramouḷi Avadhāni, instead of with Tryambaka Śāstri. According to the *maṭha's* account, Śrī Satyasantuṣṭa Tīrtha served only 8 months and 14 days as the pontiff (Āṣāḍha *śuddha pūrṇima* to Phālguṇa *bahuḷa amāvasya* of the Plava *saṁvatsara,* or July 3, 1841 to March 12, 1842), the shortest tenure in the *maṭha's* history.

[543] These nicknames have the following meanings: *Julapi:* a small decorative tuft of hair left on the head of a child who has undergone tonsure, *Onṭe:* camel, *Pāyasa:* sweet pudding or porridge made from milk, *Prēta:* spirit of a dead person, *Muççagaṇṇu:* eye(s) with drooping or closed eyelids. Vāsudevāçārya [1962, p. 40], associates the nickname *Hāga-bēḷe* with a Bhīmarāv, rather than with a Rāmrāv, as it is here, and gives the values of *hāga* and *bēḷe* respectively, as one and two *Āṇe,* a sixteenth and eighth of a *Rūpī.* By his account, this Bhīmarāv acquired his nickname upon discovering a discprepancy of merely three *Āṇe* in some complicated account. Common names for fractions include *pāga (hāga), pāvu, pala, kālu* (one quarter), *bēḷe* (an eighth), *vīsa, gira:* (a sixteenth), and *kāṇi* (a sixty-fourth). In

There was an outstanding scholar called Timmaṇṇāçārya in the Uttaradi Maṭha.[544] Several *Vaiṣṇavite* scholars were determined to avenge the loss of face that Śriyappāçārya had suffered. Arrangements were made for a debate between Timmaṇṇāçārya and Rāmaśāstri when the *Svāmi* of the Uttarādi Maṭha came to Maisūru. This *Svāmi* was known as *Gūḷi* Bāḷāçārya in his prior *āśrama*.[545] The scholars were all gathered. The debate began, and made some progress. The Śāstri's arguments then began to overwhelm Timmaṇṇāçārya. It became impossible for Timmaṇṇāçārya to respond effectively. Finally, Rāmaśāstri said to the gathering: "The scholar from the Maṭha has been silenced. I see no reason to hold back. I am happy to continue this debate with any number of those present here, one after the other." At this point, the diplomatic and far-sighted king called an end to the debate, and caused the scholars to be honored at the palace. Just as the *darbār* was coming to an end, Timmaṇṇāçārya rose and paid a tribute: "Your Highness, I have engaged in many debates in my time, but never have I seen such a great scholar as Rāmaśāstri!"

c. 1841

---

this context, the values given for *hāga* and *bēḷe* in Vāsudevāçārya [1962] appear to have been reversed. Also see footnote 527.

[544] Given the information on page 275, we may discount the possibility of this person having been Kāśī Timmaṇṇāçārya. This is most likely Varkheḍ Timmaṇṇāçārya. He was a student of Satyavijaya Tīrtha, the pontiff of the Uttarādi Maṭha 1726–1737 C.E. We learn in Sharma [1981] that he was "...a powerful glossator and controversialist. His commentary on the *Viṣṇutatvanirṇaya, Gajapañçānana,* and *Sudhānārambhaṇīyakhaṇḍanam* are to be found in the Tanjore Palace Library." Timmaṇṇāçārya is a name from Karṇāṭaka, though Varkheḍ is in Ahmadnagar district. It appears that he ultimately migrated to Tañjāvūru.

[545] This information allows us to date this debate as having occurred sometime between July, 1841 and March 12, 1842 C.E. Rāmaśāstri would have been around thirty-five years old.

Chapter 7: Travels in the South (The First Time)

The first four of Rāmaśāstri's children were all sons. They all died immediately after birth. Deeply distressed, Rāmaśāstri decided to travel to Rāmēśvaram.[546] Thinking it proper that a great scholar from his court should carry symbols appropriate to his standing, Kṛṣṇarāja Voḍeyar III granted him insignia such as the *çhatra* and *çāmara*.[547] The Śāstri, accompanied by his family and a small retinue of students, accepted these insignia,

[546]Rāmēśvaram is one of the holiest pilgrimage sites in the Hindu tradition. The great litterateur D.V. Guṇḍappa relates the following story connected with this trip, which he credits to V.S. Śrīnivāsa Śāstri [Gundappa 1970, v. 5, p. 140]. As Rāmaśāstri was en route to Rāmēśvaram in his palanquin, a substantial retinue accompanied him, including cooks, carriers of luggage, his students, as well as curious locals. As he passed Māyāvaram, the elderly Mannārguḍi Rājuśāstri, a highly-respected *Vēdantic* scholar, joined this group with his students, but without divulging his identity, and without requesting any support from Rāmaśāstri. His students were upset, because the much younger Rāmaśāstri travelled by palanquin, showing no apparent regard for the far older Rājuśāstri, who walked beside him. Rājuśāstri urged patience, reassuring them that Rāmaśāstri was a great scholar, that he hoped to learn *Navya Nyāya* from him, and that Rāmaśāstri's true worth would soon reveal itself. A few days later, Rāmaśāstri asked Rājuśāstri who he was. As soon as he learned the truth, Rāmaśāstri alighted from his palanquin, prostrated himself before Rājuśāstri, recited his *pravara*, touched his feet, pronounced his supplication to the great Rājuśāstri, and then insisted that they travel together in the palanquin.

This fascinating story, sadly, cannot be accurate. We will see shortly that Mannārguḍi Rājuśāstri did study with Rāmaśāstri during this trip. Rājuśāstri, however, was born only in 1815 C.E., making him eight years Rāmaśāstri's junior. He would have been a vigorous 25-year-old at the time of this trip, rather than an old man. We might acknowledge some other possibilities, however. First, perhaps the kernel of the story is accurate, but the elderly individual mentioned is misidentified. Second (see footnote 653), Rāmaśāstri's grandson was also named Kuṇigala Rāmaśāstri, and was a *Dharmādhikāri* in the palace. Perhaps the reference to Mannārguḍi Rājuśāstri is accurate, but the Rāmaśāstri was the grandson. Their relative ages would match the story. This is a far-fetched possibility, however. Mannārguḍi Rājuśāstri was a revered scholar by this time, and the grandson Rāmaśāstri did not have nearly the stature that his grandfather had. A record of the grandson Rāmaśāstri travelling to Rāmēśvaram in a palanquin might lend support to this possibility.

[547]The *çhatra* (parasol) and the *çāmara* (fan or fly-whisk) are among the most important of the insignia of royalty, and may be used by others only by royal sanction. (See Plate 11b.) The heads of various *maṭhas* are allowed to use these insignia, a practice that is said to date to the time when Vidyāraṇya temporarily officiated as the king of Vijayanagara, at a time when an inauspicious time was predicted for the ruler.

and departed. Upon his return, he also performed the *Nāgapratiṣṭhe* ceremony.[548]

A male child was born on the day of *Narasiṁha Jayanti* during the *śuddha* fortnight of the month of Vaiśākha of the Śārvari *saṁvatsara*.[549] This boy was given the name Lakṣmīnarasiṁha. He is now the well-known scholar Lakṣmīnarasiṁha Śāstri.[550]

May 15, 1840

The father had a special affection for his son. He took him everywhere he went. He would bathe his son himself, massage him, wipe and shake his hair dry, and tie his hair in a knot. He began to teach him, even in early childhood. The child was extremely intelligent. We have heard accounts of people who absorb everything at the first or second telling. This quality was manifest in this child. The Śāstri started teaching him *Nyāya* at the age of nine.

The Śāstri would teach him as one of a group of fellow-students. The son would raise a challenge to some point the father made during the lesson, and run off to play at marbles or *ciṇṇikōlu* while the father came up with a response to his question.[551] The Śāstri would consult his books, think deeply about the matter, come up with a response, call out to his son, answer his question, and proceed with the lesson. The son would immediately raise a new objection to what the father said, and run off again to play. We say this here not merely to indicate that this child, even as a nine-year-old, had the intellectual capacity to challenge his father, but also that teachers might learn from the the Śāstri, who worked patiently to answer the questions of a child, instead of simply dismissing them as frivolous.

Let us, however, continue with our narrative. In the Krōdhi *saṁvatsara*, the Śāstri departed with his students for travels through the southern

---

548 This is the consecration of the image of a snake in a shrine, a ceremony often recommended to childless couples. It may be performed to counter the effects of *kālasarpa dōṣa*, an inauspicious planetary configuration.

549 *Narasiṁha Jayanti* is observed on the fourteenth *tithi* of the *śukla* fortnight of Vaiśākha. The date given corresponds to May 15, 1840 C.E.

550 See Plate 26a.

551 *Ciṇṇikōlu* is an Indian game where a small stick with both ends sharpened (the *ciṇṇi*) is placed on the ground, and struck on one sharpened end with a longer stick (the *kōlu*). As the *ciṇṇi* rises into the air, it is immediately struck again, sending it flying some considerable distance.

countries. He was then 37 years of age. He travelled steadily, breaking journey at various places of note. There were large numbers of students here, and a great many of them became his students. Munnārguḍi Gōpālaśāstri and Rājuśāstri were considered great scholars in the region.[552]
1844–1845 They both studied several advanced works with the Śāstri, as he travelled through the region. They all came together, and took him to Pudukōṭe. This was a place of long-standing renown. The Śāstri intended to demonstrate his scholarship by debating the scholars there, and by succeeding in these debates, to win acclaim. He realized both these objectives.

Word spread in Pudukōṭe of the presence of a great scholar from the kingdom of Maisūru. The court of Kṛṣṇarāja Voḍeyar III in Maisūru was second in glory only to the court of the Pēśva Bājīrāv, and was home to many scholars. Battles had raged between the British and the Marāṭhas in the Dhātu and Īśvara *saṁvatsaras*, and Bājīrāv lost his kingdom. He was imprisoned by the British in *Brahmāvarta* near Kāśī.[553] The Marāṭha kingdom came apart. The large number of scholars under the patronage of the nobles and affluent notables became widely dispersed. In the kingdom of Maisūru alone, which was second only to Puṇe, did scholars survive, continuing to obtain sanctuary from the munificient king. It being well known in the south that Maisūru was the one place where great scholarship survived, Rāmaśāstri, as a scholar from that kingdom, was highly esteemed in Pudukōṭe. The Śāstri was received by the king.[554]

A scholar called Brahmāçāri was well known in that kingdom. Arrangements were made for him to debate Rāmaśāstri. At the debate, however, the

[552] See footnote 546.

[553] Pēśva Bājīrāv II was imprisoned by the British in Biṭhūr, near the city of Kānpur. The region around Biṭhūr has been known as *Brahmāvarta* since classical times. For instance, Kālidāsa's *Meghadūtam* (*Pūrvamegha:* 50) places it to the north of *Çarmaṇvatī* (the Chambal river) and *Daśapura* (Mandasaur in Madhya Pradeśa). Also see *Manusṛti* 2.17: "*sarasvatīdṛṣadvatyordevanadyoryadantaram | tam devanirmitam deśam brahmāvartam praçakṣyate* ‖" meaning "Brahmāvarta is the land that lies between the divine rivers Sarasvatī and Dṛṣadvatī". Contrary to what the present author says, however, this place is not near Vārāṇasi (Kāśī), bur rather, some 330 km northwest of it.

[554] This king would have been Rāja Srī Bṛhadāmba Dāsa Rāja Rāmaçandra Tondaimān Bahādūr, ruler of the princely state of Pudukōṭe from July 13, 1839 to April 15, 1886. He was born in 1829, so the kingdom was administered by the British resident in his early years. He formally assumed ruling powers in 1844. He would have been about sixteen at the time of his meeting with Rāmaśāstri.

opponent disgracefully refused to open the debate. At that point, Rāmaśāstri himself opened the debate, and shortly silenced that scholar. Brahmāçāri then heaped praise on Rāmaśāstri, declaring him a great scholar. The Pudukōṭe ruler recognized the Śāstri with a most excellent reward. The Śāstri, having achieved this victory, now proceeded to Kāñçipura with his students.[555]

There were many *Śrīvaiṣṇavite* scholars in Kāñçipura. After Rāmaśāstri's arrival, a date was determined for him to debate these scholars. The *Śrīvaiṣṇavite* scholars began elaborate preparations for this debate, devoting themselves day and night to studying many books. Rāmaśāstri, on the other hand, continued as usual, devoting himself to merely performing his daily rituals and teaching his students. The *Smārtas* of Kāñçīpura gathered in anxiety, greatly concerned at the possibility of humiliation for the sect of *Advaita,* since the Śāstri's opponents were making such great efforts, in contrast to the Śāstri's unconcern. Rāmaśāstri was a scholar visiting from Maisūru, making it difficult to suggest to him that he should study in preparation for the debate. Nevertheless, the leaders among this group, deciding that it would be best to acquaint the Śāstri with the situation, arrived at the Śāstri's camp, and hesitated a long time before summoning up their courage. The Śāstri received them with respect, and upon his inquiring for the reason for their visit, the locals said: "It is nothing, really. We just wanted to inform you that your opponents have been studying a great number of books in preparation for the debate."

Grasping their meaning immediately, the Śāstri replied: "Self-praise is contrary to the *śāstras.* Neither is it a sign of virtue. Merit, if present in a person, is sure to express itself when the opportunity arises. Immodesty is indeed a sign of conceit. However, immodesty is not objectionable if necessary to allay the concerns of so many others, especially before merit has had an opportunity to show itself, or when such an opportunity may not be forthcoming. Let me therefore be clear. Even Paramēśvara, were he to descend from Kailāsa to oppose me in debate, would only match me; even in this situation, you may set aside any thoughts of my suffering a loss." Although the Śāstri disliked boasting about his own abilities, the circumstances and the pride he had in his own scholarship conspired to make him

[555] An inscription attests to Rāmaśāstri's presence at Kāñçīpuram on January 22, 1840 (see footnote 573).

utter these words. The visitors departed, pleased and reassured. This incident illustrates how much confidence the Śāstri had in his own scholarship.

We have already noted that a scholar named Kāñçīpura Śrīnivāsāçārya had debated Tryambaka Śāstri in Maisūru, and failed to prevail in the encounter.[556] This same Kāñçīpura Śrīnivāsāçārya, after returning to Kāñçī, had written a tract claiming that he had debated Tryambaka Śāstri at the Maisūru palace, that there had been eleven points of disputation, that the eleventh point had been his, to which Tryambaka Śāstri had been able to make no reply, and having concocted eleven such points, had proceeded to distribute the tract in his circle. This came to Rāmaśāstri's notice in Kāñçi. Rāmaśāstri then wrote a book laying out his eyewitness account of what had actually transpired in the Maisūru court, and refuting the eleven points that Śrīnivāsāçārya had laid out. We give two *ślōkas* from that book below.

dvaitavādi matadhvānta vidhvaṁsana viçakṣaṇaṁ |
vande tryambaka mārtaṇḍaṁ sarvaśāstrābja bōdhakaṁ ‖

Meaning: I salute the sun Tryambaka, who is capable of dispelling the darkness called *Dvaita,* and unveiling the lotus-flower representing all the *śastras.*

bhaṭṭatryambaka śiṣyeṇa rāmēṇa tadanugrahāt |
śrīnivāsakṛtassvēyōtprēkṣā mūlā nirākṛtā ‖

Meaning: The work of Śrīnivāsāçārya, whose basis is self-exaltation, is soundly rejected by Rāma, the disciple of Tryambaka Bhaṭṭa.

These actions by Rāmaśāstri humiliated Śrīnivāsāçārya, and became another reason for the *Śrīvaiṣṇavas* to prepare for the debate with vigour. This anecdote well illustrates the deep regard the Śāstri had for Tryambaka Śāstri.

Another incident is noteworthy, in this context. A *Śrīvaiṣṇava* scholar called Vigrahadēśikāçārya, finding Rāmaśāstri's attitude insufferable, spoke contemptuously of Rāmaśāstri, saying: "Why does he have a *çhatra* and *çāmara*? Who gave them to him? What did he see in him to give him such

---

[556] See page 187.

things?"[557] The Śāstri learned of this, but remained silent, waiting for his opportunity.

As previously arranged, the debate began in the Kāñçi temple. A large number of *Śrīvaiṣṇavas* came to the debate as opponents. The Śāstri too, went to the assembly with his students, and sat down. Some ten thousand people, both brāhmaṇas and others, came to witness this spectacle. Even though they understood none of the technicalities of the debate, they were fascinated by the eloquence of the scholars and thrilled by the spectacle. The Śāstri prevailed in argument after argu- *1846–1847* ment, and finally, established the doctrine of *jaganmithyatva* in the manner that a scholar called Madhusūdana Sarasvatī had done in the book *Advaitasiddhi.*[558] No argument or device succeeded in refuting what the Śāstri had established. At this time, the Śāstri, mindful of Vigrahadēśikāçārya's contemptuous comment, thumped his chest with his right hand and declared to the assembly: "I understand that Vigrahadēśikāçārya asked 'What did he see in him that he granted him a *çhatra* and *çāmara*?' This is what he saw, truly, this is what he saw!" Everyone was left speechless. They were all extremely pleased with the Śāstri's scholarship. This occurred in the Parābhava *saṁvatsara.* The Śāstri travelled with his students in the south for over three years, and then returned to Maisūru with his students. It was at this time that the Śāstri established a *Saṁskṛta* school in Kāñçi, in accordance with the wishes of the locals, and appointed his dear student Vijayarāghavāçārya as its principal.

[557] This Vigraham Dēśikāçārya appears to be the author of *Brahmasūtra Bhāṣya Ṭippaṇī*, a short gloss on the *Śrībhāṣya* [Varadachari 1972], and of the *Aṇṇayāryamahādēśikamaṅgala*, a eulogy of his guru Aṇṇayārya Śrīśaila [Raja 1968]. The *Srībhāṣyapariṣkāraḥ* is a work by Sarasvatīvigraham Deśikāçārya [Deśikāçārya 1989]. The work is undated, and it is possible that "Sarasvatīvigraham" has been transformed into "Vigraham" by elision.

[558] Madhusūdana Sarasvatī is a towering figure within the tradition of *Advaita,* or non-dualism. He was a master not simply of *Advaita,* but also of *yoga, Navya Nyāya, alaṅkāra* (æsthetics), and *vyākaraṇa* (grammar). Two traditional verses illustrate the high regard he is held in: *"madhusūdana sarasvatyāḥ pāraṁ vetti sarasvatī | pāraṁ vetti sarasvatyāḥ madhusūdana sarasvatī ‖"* meaning that only Sarasvatī, the goddess of learning, knows the limits of Madhusūdana Sarasvatī's knowledge, and only Madhusūdana Sarasvatī knows the limits of Sarasvatī's knowledge, and *"navadvīpe samāyāte madhusūdana sarasvatī | çakampe tarkavāgīśaḥ kātaro-bhūdgadādharaḥ ‖"* meaning that when came Madhusūdana Sarasvatī to Navadvīpa, then became fearful Mathuranātha Tarkavāgīśa and Gadādhara.

The Śāstri subsequently wrote a book on logic called *Śatakōṭi.*[559] He has now become well-known as *"Śatakōṭi"* Rāmaśāstri.

It was also during his travels in the south that a son named Yajñanārāyaṇa was born to him in Kāñci, in the month of Vaiśākha, in the Parābhava *saṁvatsara*. This Yajñanārāyaṇa was very bright and enthusiastic. He became especially learned in the *Vēdas,* literature, and *Nyāya.*

[559] This work is the *Gadadharīya Śatpratipakṣa Kroḍapatram*, and offers a hundred refutations of the definitions of the fallacy of *satpratipakṣa* offered by Gadādhara. Anantaçāriyar (Anantāḷvār) and Kṛṣṇatātāçāri have written refutations of this called *Śatakōṭikhanḍana*, which has in turn been refuted in *Śatakōṭikhanḍanamanḍana* by Rāmaśāstri's student Sokattur Vijayarāghavāçārya.

Chapter 8: The Minister Timmaṇṇaśāstri. Rāmaśāstri's Scholarship

We have already seen that Kṛṣṇarāja Voḍeyar III had lost administrative control over the kingdom, that the East India Company had appointed a Commissioner to oversee the administration, and that he was given an allowance of about 25,000 *Rūpīs* a month.[560] We have also seen that *Iṅgrēji* Veṅkaṭappāji had been imprisoned on some pretext. Now, a certain *Smārta vaidika* brāhmaṇa from Mulaknāṭu, Timmaṇṇaśāstri by name, had been close to Veṅkaṭappāji, and had established himself in the king's inner circle. The king had taken on debt, since his expenses were too large.[561] Timmaṇṇaśāstri, with the help of some British officials, became deeply engaged in politics, especially in the king's ongoing correspondence with the government in Kalakatta. Kṛṣṇarāja Voḍeyar III, justifiably, yearned to reclaim control over his kingdom, which he had lost due to imprudence. This concern gnawed away at him, like a worm.

Though the Company controlled a great many regions of India at the time, their supremacy had not yet been established. There was a growing concern over open hostilities breaking out between the British and the Marāṭhas under Sindhya.[562] Raṇajītsiṅgh having died, power in the Pañjāb had passed into new hands. The strength of the Sīkh army had grown unbounded under this new leadership. The Company remained ever vigilant, not knowing when this valiant army might fall upon a kingdom it controlled, or what trouble might ensue, at what time. The armies of Sindhya and Raṇajītsiṅgh having both been trained by French generals, victory

[560] This is not entirely accurate. See footnote 508.

[561] These debts were massive. As noted by Sastri [1932, p. 134], the Company directors wrote in July 1847 that "…on the 30th June, 1845, the debt still remaining due from the Mysore state to the British Government, amounted (inclusive of interest at 5 per cent) to no less than Rs. 23,59,619, although Rs. 31,70,864 had been liquidated since our assumption of the administration." In 1855, it was similarly noted that "the whole amount, principal and interest, which has thus been paid on account of arrears due by the former government, has been Rs. 56,91,660-12-1/2, or Rs. 57 lakhs."

[562] Sindhya is the Anglicised form of Śinde, and is commonly spelled Scindia. Daulat Rāv Sindhya was defeated in the Third Anglo-Maraṭha war of 1818 C.E., and was forced to accept local autonomy. He died in 1827 C.E., and was succeeded by Jaṅkōji Rāv II, and then by Jayāji Rāv in 1843, these reigns being interspersed with the regencies of Daulat Rāv's widow Baiza Bāī and Jaṅkōji Rāv's widow Tārābāī Rāje.

against these adversaries, who stood up to Company troops as equals, depended entirely on which way Jayalakṣmī glanced at the last moment; this was sufficient to cause apprehension among humans.[563]

Under these circumstances, it was essential for the Company to maintain the southern provinces, which remained peaceful, in a state that was quiet and conducive to their goals. Was it thus not natural for the Kalakatta government to seek to maintain the goodwill of the large and well-respected kingdom of Maisūru, and establish themselves as benefactors of the virtuous Kṛṣṇarāja Voḍeyar III, for whom there was sympathy in all kingdoms? The ongoing correspondence he had pursued provided just the opportunity. The government decided to grant Kṛṣṇarāja Voḍeyar III a fifth of the revenues of the kingdom, just as he had desired.[564]

It now became well known that Timmaṇṇaśāstri's efforts had managed to bring in funds sufficient to match expenses, although they fell short of regaining control of the kingdom. Efforts to restore control over the kingdom continued, despite this success. Determining that the expenses of the Maisūru palace were too high, Timmaṇṇaśāstri reduced the salaries of employees, according to their abilities. Arrangements were also made to repay the monies the king had borrowed from many farmers, wealthy Gujarātis, and others. The king therefore developed a great regard for Timmaṇṇaśāstri, who had worked so hard to his advantage. It is hardly natural, however, for wild creatures to display the superior nature of domestic animals, for domestic animals to display the superior nature of humans, nor for humans to display the superior nature of the gods. This power went to Timmaṇṇaśāstri's head, impairing his vision and judgment of the internal and external worlds, rendering him half-blind, as it were. With such numbers of important officials seeking to ingratiate themselves with him, might such a person as him be expected to care for a *vaidika*? Never.

The worldly benefits that Timmaṇṇaśāstri's efforts had accrued, however, could hardly be compared with the achievements of Rāmaśāstri, whose *vaidika* ways and scholarship were instrumental in spreading far and wide the glory of Kṛṣṇarāja Voḍeyar III, the person who sustained it all. The

[563]The Sikh army was trained by the Italians Jean-Baptiste Ventura and Paolo Avitabile, and the Frenchmen Jean-Françoise Allard and Claude August Court. Sindhya's army was led by French generals, such as Perron and Bouquin, in its battles with the British.

[564]This information is inaccurate. See footnote 508.

benefits from the first kind service were transient, those from the second, enduring. That stalwart of scholarship, Rāmaśāstri, understood this, and never followed Timmaṇṇaśāstri around, as others did. Timmaṇṇaśāstri, ever mindful of this, was biding his time.

Rāmaśāstri and Timmaṇṇaśāstri were both Āndhra brāhmaṇas from the Mulaknātu community.[565] It is only natural for people from the same community to socialize, and visit and dine with each other. Such practices are seen as being especially appropriate among people who are observant of ritual. People from Maisūru, Beṅgaḷūru, and elsewhere saw it as a special privilege to be invited to Rāmaśāstri's house for a meal. There can be no doubt that one's body and mind are both purified by dining in the home of one who is pure and virtuous, and earns his living by righteous means. Nevertheless, it appears that Timmaṇṇaśāstri was reluctant to dine in Rāmaśāstri's home, seeking instead to flaunt the prerogatives of power and position. Rāmaśāstri himself never ate in the home of anyone who was not also extremely observant of tradition and rituals such as the *Aupāsana* and *Vaiśvadēva*.[566] Not having a great deal of faith in Timmaṇṇaśāstri when it came to such matters, Rāmaśāstri never dined in his house. It was natural for everyone to see this as evidence of mutual antipathy between the two. Such feelings are never enhancing of stature. Both parties were conscious of this shortcoming in their relationship.

Now, an inauspicious planetary configuration having arisen at some point that cast an evil influence on the king's horoscope, scholars determined that its effects could be averted by performing a *lakṣa tila hōma*. Accordingly, preparations were undertaken in the palace for the *hōma*. Astrologers determined the most propitious time for the ritual. The main procedure underlying this ritual is the offering of oblations of sesamum seeds a hundred thousand times into a fire. It was important for the ritual to begin shortly after dawn on the appointed day, and proceed without interruption till it was complete. It was also required that the king, as chief performer of the ritual, was to maintain a fast until the ceremony was complete. To this day, it remains the practice that all *vaidikas* associated with the

---

[565] This is a community of expatriate Telugu-speaking *Smārta* brāhmaṇas, spread out across present-day Karṇāṭaka and Tamiḻnāḍu. This community has produced a number of outstanding individuals across a broad range of disciplines, well out of proportion to its small size. Śāstri [2000] is an excellent resource on the community.

[566] See footnote 533.

palace complete their baths and rituals early on such occasions, come to the palace, and oversee all the observances. Accordingly, Rāmaśāstri completed his bath and morning rituals, and arrived at the palace within 3–4 *gaḷiges* of sunrise.[567] The *havana* had started by the time he arrived.

Ten brāhmaṇas were seated around the fire altar, offering oblations into the fire in synchrony. As each of them, in turn, proclaimed the *saṅkalpa*, and the others offered the oblations, they were making the serious lapse of using the singular person in the *saṅkalpa*.[568] As soon as the Śāstri arrived, he heard the ill-formed *mantras* being chanted, asked that the ritual be paused, and made his objections known to the priest who was in the role of the *brahma*.[569] No proper answer was forthcoming. A discussion ensued. Nobody was able to hold their own against this lion. Thus far, ten priests had each offered three thousand oblations each into the fire. Together, they had completed about thirty thousand oblations. That number

[567] A *galige* is 24 minutes, so 3–4 *galiges* are between an hour and an hour-and-a-half.

[568] The *saṅkalpa* is a formal declaration of intent or resolution to undertake the ritual. The *saṅkalpa* is critical; absent a proper *saṅkalpa*, the actions of the ritual are a mere charade, are devoid of all ritual significance, and bear no fruit. The *saṅkalpa's* structure is also critical. It begins with an elaborate declaration of the time and location of performance, and announces the proposed ritual action, after stating its intent (*artha*) and the desired outcome (*kāma*). The sentence must be structured using finite verbs conjugated in the *ātmanēpada* (middle) voice and future tense. A *saṅkalpa* for the morning *Sandhyā* ritual might include the sentence "*... mama upātta samasta durita kṣaya dvāra śrīparamēśvara prītyarthaṁ prātassandhyāmupāsye,*" declaring the ritual to be *prātaḥ sandhyā*, with the intent (*artham*) of winning the favour of *paramēśvara* by effacing one's accumulated misdeeds (*upātta duritakṣaya*). When the ritual action is being performed by an individual, the singular form, such as *kariṣye* ("I will perform"), is appropriate. In this case, however, although the *yajamāna* is the king, an individual, the ritual actions are being performed by ten priests at once. (It is acceptable for the actions to be performed on behalf of the *yajamāna* by priests.) Each priest, in turn, is pronouncing the *saṅkalpa* before all ten priests offer the oblation. Rāmaśāstri's argument appears to be that when the priest who pronounces the *saṅkalpa* uses the singular form *kariṣye*, he is referencing his oblation only. The nine other oblations are not covered since this *saṅkalpa* is in the singular form, and become external to the ritual performance. The *saṅkalpa* should be using an action verb in plural conjugation, such as *kariṣyāmahe* ("we will perform").

[569] The *brahma* is the officiating priest responsible for coordinating a *Vēdic* ritual. He issues directions, and bears responsibility for its conduct in strict conformance with the elaborate ritual prescriptions. *Vēdic* rituals are elaborate affairs, and can require as many as sixteen priests for *soma* rituals. The following four are the main priests: *hotṛ, udgātṛ, adhvaryu*, and *brahma*, corresponding to the *Rik, Sāma, Yajur*, and *Atharva Vēdas*. See footnote 585.

was about a third of what was required for the entire ritual. Rāmaśāstri insisted, however, that these efforts came to naught because of the lapse in the *mantra* chanted.

News of this controversy reached the presence of the king. Though in a state of ritual purity, he arrived at the fire altar without ceremony, and inquired what the issue was. Timmaṇṇaśāstri said: "Although 30,000 oblations have been completed, Kuṇigala Rāmaśāstri insists that only 3000 oblations have effectively been offered because of a lapse in the *mantra.* Could 30,000 oblations be negated because of some minor error in language? This can hardly be a real issue. A third of the ritual is already done. We can complete the rest by 11 o'clock today. If, however, we listen to every person who loiters by, take the issue of the lapse in *mantra* seriously, and restart the entire *havana,* as Rāmaśāstri insists, the king's repast will be unduly delayed."

This angered Rāmaśāstri. His face reddened. He roared: "Your Majesty, the purpose of this ritual of propitiation is to ensure your well-being. It must be performed in accordance with *śāstric* prescriptions, and all *mantras* recited in the prescribed manner. *Karma* does not accrue without *mantra.* When the *mantra* is deficient, so is the *karma.* This can only work to the detriment of both king and kingdom. The only proper course now is to atone for the lapse in the *mantra,* and begin afresh the *hōma,* for the sake of ensuring your prosperity. This is not idle blather, but the *Vēdic* prescription; I do not know how to speak like a blockhead, idly asking what of this and what of that, with no understanding whatsoever of result or consequence."

This king, the very embodiment of respect for scripture, said: "We have undertaken this *hōma* to secure our prosperity and that of our people. This *hōma* will be fruitless if performed without the proper *mantra.* All becomes deficient when the *mantra* is deficient. The only proper course is for us to atone for the lapse and start afresh, as Rāmaśāstri bids us do. We began with the *saṅkalpa 'śrī paramēśvara prītyarthaṁ'.* Shall I bare myself to the fury of *Paraśiva*, knowing as I do that the *Vēdas* and *mantras* are merely forms in which he is manifest? It matters little if I remain awake and hungry; I will happily remain so for three days, if need be. Let us ensure that everything proceeds as it should," indicating satisfaction with Rāmaśāstri's words, and disapproval with those of Timmaṇṇaśāstri. Indeed! Which other kingdom might have for king such a virtuous person as this? Following the king's bidding, Rāmaśāstri himself took charge, and supervised the *hōma* from beginning to end. The king was very pleased. Timmaṇṇaśāstri's anger at Rāmaśāstri was now greater than ever, his statements having been called the babblings of a blockhead, in open assembly.

This incident clearly illustrates that Rāmaśāstri completed every task he undertook, with no tolerance for even the slightest flaw, and never giving cause for reproach or objection. The truly great never see any task as unimportant. Even the least important tasks have their consequences. To demean the task as trifling, is to demean its consequence. Those who lack the ability to discern the consequences of a task are the ones who disdain it as unimportant. It would not be wrong to see a person's worth as diminished in the same measure as his disdain for such tasks. An analogy may also be drawn with people. Everyone has unequalled ability in some respect. It is fair to see a person as worthy if he can perceive the merits of each individual. Others strut around egotistically, dismissing everything and everyone else as unimportant. A person's true worth is betrayed by his egotism.

Chapter 9: Anugama Vāda. Sarvatōmukha Yāga

Many of Rāmaśāstri's students, such as Kavi Varadāçārya, Vijayarāghavāçārya, Kuraççi Raṅgāçārya, and Rāmagiri Śāmāçārya were stalwart scholars. Kavi Varadāçārya remained in Maisūru. Kuraççi Raṅgāçārya returned to his home province. Vijayarāghavāçārya went to Kañçi. Rāmagiri Śāmāçārya remained in Maisūru.

There was also a scholar at the time called Viṣṇupādāçārya. He was the son of the scholar *"Julapi"* Kṛṣṇāçārya. Viṣṇupādāçārya studied for some time with his own father, then with Rāmaśāstri, and attained unmatched excellence in logic and *Vēdānta.* He developed a special intellectual affinity for *Advaita.* He was not a person who thought one way, yet acted another. People were often startled by his insistence on saying what he believed, and doing what he said. Indeed, when Viṣṇupādāçārya debated, he would argue against the tenets of *Dvaita* and in favour of the tenets of *Advaita.* This led to ill-feeling between him and his fellow *Mādhvas.* The *Vaiṣṇavas,* declaring they were ostracizing him, cut him off socially. Undeterred, Viṣṇupādāçārya declared that he was ostracizing the *Vaiṣṇavas,* began inviting *Smārta* rather than *Vaiṣṇava* priests to officiate at religious and obsequial ceremonies, and started speaking of *Vaiṣṇavas* with disdain. Internecine conflicts can take a toll. Even the head of the Maṭha was cautious, out of his great respect for Viṣṇupādāçārya's learning. On one occasion, when the *Svāmi* of the Uttarādi Maṭha visited Maisūru, Kṛṣṇarāja Voḍeyar III arranged for a reconciliation between him and Viṣṇupādāçārya.[570] The scholar even began receiving a salary from the Maṭha. The *Svāmi* spoke to the small-minded members of his community, asking them not to bring disgrace upon themselves by provoking this lion of scholarship and learning.

This Viṣṇupādāçārya had great scholarship not just in logic and *Vedānta,* but also in astrology. Unlike other astrologers, however, he was not one to while away his time talking about propitious times of the day, the influences of stars, or in computing and casting horoscopes. His house was on the street that ran along the northern wall of the fort in Maisūru. That was

---

[570] This *Svāmi* was likely Śrī Satyapārāyaṇa Tīrtha, who was head of the Uttarādi Maṭha between March 12, 1842 and October 19, 1863.

a large house, and was two stories high. The *Āçārya* had installed a small planetarium in a room in the house which represented the nine planets and various stars using spheres and lamps, and demonstrated their movements through a clockwork mechanism. Many elderly people in Maisūru have recollections of this device. Such abilities are indeed rare and unusual. He reminds one of brilliant minds such as Bhāskarāçārya and Āryabhaṭa.[571]

There was also a *Smārta* scholar at the time called Kāśī Śēṣaśāstri, of the *Drāviḍa* tradition.[572] He was a great scholar of grammar, and had a large number of students. A scholar called Kuṭṭiśāstri belonging to the *Hoysaḷa Karṇāṭaka* community had settled in Maisūru, having come from south of the pass.[573] He was an expert in all the *Śāstras.* He was especially knowledgeable in the *śrauta* rituals. These scholars, among others, were Rāmaśāstri's

---

[571]Bhāskara II was a celebrated mathematician of the 12th century C.E., who made deep contributions to Algebra, Diophantine equations (including a general approach to Pell's Equation), trigonometry, and had even developed several ideas relating to differential calculus. Āryabhaṭa was a mathematician of the fifth century C.E. His astronomical work the *Ārya Siddhānta* is lost, but the *Āryabhāṭīya*, his work on mathematics, survives. This work covers a wide array of topics, including arithmetic, algebra, trigonometry, continued fractions, and quadratic equations.

[572]Explicit references such as this and on page 267 to Kāśī Śēṣaśāstri considerably weaken the argument by Lakshminarasimhaiya *et al.,* [1970] that he is the same as the Rāmaśēṣa Śāstri referred to earlier. See footnote 465.

[573]Kuṭṭiśāstri's name was actually Vāñçhēśvara Yajvan (Sūri). He was named after his great-grandfather Vāñçhēśvara Kavi, who was given the sobriquet *Kuṭṭi Kavi* ("little poet" in Tamiḷ) as a child by the king Śāhji I of Tañjāvūru in recognition of his remarkable poetic talents [Śāstri 1946]. The sobriquet "Kuṭṭi" continued to be used by succeeding generations of the family as a family name. Kuṭṭi Kavi's *Mahiṣaśatakam* is a masterful double entendre, rich in *ślēṣa alaṅkāra* on the theme of misrule by king Pratāpasiṁha of Tañjāvūru. Kuṭṭi Kavi was a descendant of the venerated Govinda Dīkṣita, who belonged to the *Hoysaḷa Karṇāṭaka* community, but served as minister to the Tañjāvūru kings Açyutappa Nāyaka and Raghunātha Nāyaka. Govinda Dīkṣita was renowned as a scholar, statesman, and musicologist. His descendants continued in the Tañjāvūru region.

Kuṭṭiśāstri (the great-grandson of Kuṭṭi Kavi) grew up in Tiruvisanallūr near Kumbhakōṇam. He studied first with his father, then with Īśvaraśāstri in his own village, then with Śrīnivāsārya from Maṇalūr nearby, and finally with Ahōbalaśāstri in Vārāṇasi. Around 1800 C.E., Sarbhōji II established a *Saṁskṛta* school in Orattanāḍu nearby, and appointed Kuṭṭiśāstri as an instructor. Finding the king's attitude overbearing, he soon left for the Maisūru court, where he was welcomed by Ṭippu. Feeling pressured by Ṭippu to convert to Islām, however, he moved to the court of the Pēśva in Puṇe, where he remained for a while. Subsequently, he travelled to Kāśī, studied with Ahōbalaśāstri, and taught there for some time. He composed the *Ślēṣārthaçandrikā*, his commentary on his namesake ancestor's *Mahiṣaśataka* while in Kāśī in 1813 [Sarma and Sarma 1939]. He returned to the Pēśva's court, and then moved to Maisūru in 1818 C.E., as Marāṭha power began its

contemporaries. Kṛṣṇarāja Voḍeyar III's court, with scholars such as these, was home to the nine treasures.[574] This virtuous patron of scholarship, always granting scholars whatever they needed, and supporting the advancement of scholarship is so many ways, acquired fame not just in India, but also in England and other countries.

Two scholars came to Maisūru in the Saumya *saṁvatsara*, attracted by the king's renown. Rāmaśāstri's fame grew even greater on account of these

---

decline. Kṛṣṇarāja Voḍeyar III welcomed him, and appointed him *Dharmādhikāri*. He performed the *Jyōtiṣṭōma* sacrifice in Maisūru (see footnote 584). When he travelled to Śṛṅgēri to visit the Śaṅkara Maṭha, he discovered that the pontiff Nṛsiṁha Bhāratī had been his student in Kāśī. He travelled to Rāmēśvaram, and then returned to his own village, where he is believed to have died at around the age of eighty. His works include *Hiraṇyakēśīśrautasūtravyākhyā, Satsāmānyasūtravyākhyā, Dattaçintāmaṇi, Śrāddhaçintāmaṇi, Brahmasūtrārthaçintāmaṇi, Kākatālīyavādārtha, Dhūrgānaçandrikā, Tarkasaṅgrahavyākhya, Śrīmahaliṅgaśatakam,* and the *Bhāṭṭaçintāmaṇi.*

An inscription commemorating the consecration of the Kāmākṣī temple at Kāñçi on January 22, 1840 C.E. records the presence of the scholars Vāñçhēśvara Yajvan and Kuṇigala Rāmaśāstri.

We reproduce a genealogy from the introduction to Kuṭṭiśāstri's *Bhāṭṭaçintāmaṇi* (see Gode [1939]).

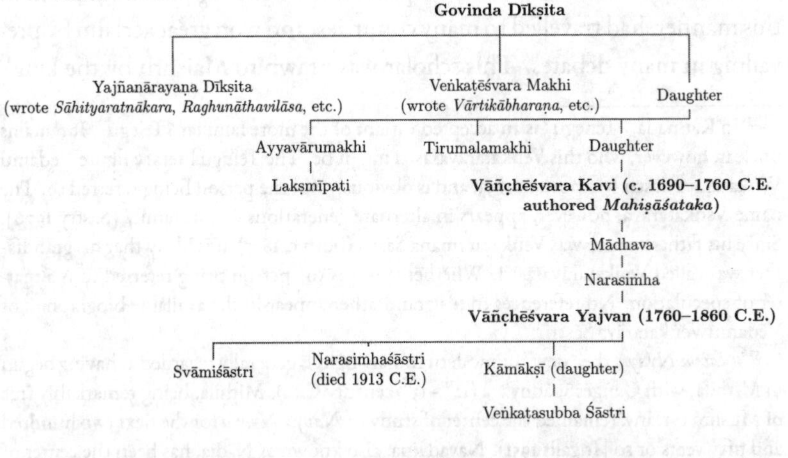

[574] It is common to refer to an exceptionally distinguished group of luminaries as *navaratnas* (the nine jewels) if they number nine, or as the *aṣṭa diggajas* (the eight mythical elephants supporting the earth in the eight cardinal and intercardinal directions) if they number eight. The nine great treasures of Kubēra, the (demi) god of wealth: *padma, mahāpadma, śankha, makara, kaçchapa, mukunda, nanda, nīla,* and *kharva.* The *Amarakōśa (digvarga:6)* lists the *aṣṭadiggajas* as: *"airāvataḥ puṇḍarīko vāmanaḥ kumudō-ñjana | puṣpadantaḥ sārvabhaumaḥ supratīkaşça diggajāḥ ‖"*

scholars. The first of these scholars was *Anugamabhaṭṭācari* Veṅkaṭarāya-śāstri; he was from the Tenugu kingdom.[575] Not content with the learning he acquired studying *Nyāya* and *Vēdānta* in his own country, he travelled to Navadvīpa in Beṅgāl for futher study, and became famous as *Anugamabhaṭṭāçārya.* Navadvīpa in Beṅgāl has, since time immemorial, been the source site of advanced learning in the *vēdaśāstras.*[576] The great reputation of that academy remains unblemished to this day. All the great scholars from the northern countries have acquired their learning either in Kāśī or in Navadvīpa. Just as the inhabitants of Beṅgāl and the north have, through their exceptional erudition in English, defended the reputation of the descendants of the Āryan lineages as matchless, so did they secure India's reputation in times past through their learning in *Saṁskṛta.* Just as they are now the pacesetters in India, they were even then, pioneers in all respects. It has long been the practice for the council of scholars in Navadvīpa to award titles and agnomena to students who have demonstrated accomplishment. Great names such as Brahmānanda and Gadādharabhaṭṭāçārya are from Navadvīpa.[577]

1849–1850

Veṅkaṭarāyaśāstri, who had acquired the title *Anugamabhaṭṭāçārya* in this manner, had travelled to many countries, and won great acclaim by prevailing in many debates. This scholar was drawn to Maisūru by the king's

[575] In Kannaḍa, "Tenegu" is an accepted variant of the more familiar "Telegu". It remains unclear, however, who this Veṅkaṭarāyaśāstri might be. The Telugu literary figure Vēdamu Veṅkaṭarāya Śāstri was born in 1853, and is obviously not the person being referred to. The name Veṅkaṭarāya, however, appears in alternate generations of this family [Sastry 1976]. Since his father's name was Veṅkaṭaramaṇa Śāstri (born c. 1817), it is likely that his grandfather was called Veṅkaṭarāyaśāstri. Whether this was the person being referred to is a matter of speculation. No references to his grandfather appear in the available biographies of Vēdamu Veṅkaṭarāya Śāstri.

[576] *Navya Nyāya*, the "new" or modern Indian logic, is generally regarded as having begun in Mithila, with Gaṅgēśōpādhyāya (12th–13th century C.E.). Mithila, being remarkably free of Muslim tyrrany, remained the center of study of *Navya Nyāya* for the next two hundred and fifty years or so [Ingalls 1951]. Navadvīpa, also known as Nādia, has been the center of *Navya Nyāya* since the time of Vāsudeva *Sārvabhauma,* who flourished around 1480 C.E. [Potter and Bhattacharya 2008].

[577] The Brahmānanda being referred to is Gauḍa Brahmānanda Sarasvatī, author of the *Guruçandrikā* and *Laghuçandrikā*, also known as the *Gauḍabrahmānandī.* Brahmānanda flourished around 1680 C.E. [Phillips 1997], and was a student of Nārāyaṇatīrtha, who was a student of the great Madhusūdana Sarasvatī (1540–1640 C.E.), author of the *Advaitasiddhi.* Gadādhara Bhaṭṭāçārya is another great logician of the Navadvīpa school, and dates to around 1650 C.E. He wrote numerous glosses, collectively known as the *Gādādharī.*

reputation for generosity and the renown of Rāmaśāstri who graced his court, pulled both by the desire for reward as well as his scholarly arrogance. He made an ostentatious entrance into Maisūru, and obtained an audience with the king. His great ambition was to humble Rāmaśāstri in debate.

A debate lasting six or seven days took place between Veṅkaṭarāyaśāstri and Rāmaśāstri in the Parakāla Maṭha. Veṅkaṭarāyaśāstri began presenting his various arguments in accordance with the *anugamavidhi* as propounded by Śaṅkara Bhaṭṭāçārya.[578] The great scholars of Maisūru were all present. Kāśī Timmaṇṇāçārya, the debate moderator, declared that he was unable to follow Veṅkaṭarāyaśāstri's logical development.[579] Nobody else was able to follow it, either. Everyone remained still and silent, inert like images in a painting. The *prakāravidhi* that Tryambaka Śāstri had developed was prevalent in Southern India.

When Timmaṇṇāçārya indicated his inability to follow the argument being presented, Rāmaśāstri said: "No cause for concern. Let Veṅkaṭarāya-śāstri finish what he has to say." After this, the debate continued for eight days at the palace. Not only did Rāmaśāstri completely comprehend the arguments Veṅkaṭarāyaśāstri made using the technique of *anugamavidhi*,[580]

---

[578] This Śaṅkara Bhaṭṭāçārya is most likely the person listed in [Potter 1995] as "Kālī Śaṅkara (Siddhāntavāgīśa) (Bhaṭṭāçārya) (1810) (*New Catalogus Catalogorum* IV, 80)". He is credited with *kroḍapatras* on Jagadīśa's *Jāgadīśī* and *Śabdaśaktiprakāśikā*, Mathuranātha's *Māthurī*, Gadādhara's *Muktivāda, Śaktivāda,* and *Vyutpattivāda,* Udayana's *Nyāyakusumāñjali, ṭīkā* on *Tarkagrantha*, and *Vyākhyā* on the *Upamāna* section of Gaṅgēśa's *Tattvaçintāmaṇi.*

[579] Sharma [1981] gives the following information: "KĀŚI TIMMAṆṆĀÇĀRYA (C. 1800–50): He was a native of the Mysore state and is reputed to have studied Śastras in Banares and established his reputation as the foremost scholar of his day, in Navya-Nyāya. He was a contemporary of Tryambaka Śāstri and Satyadharma Tīrtha. He wrote half a dozen works, mostly glosses, on the *TS, Td, Bhedojjīvana, Krsnāmrtamahārṇava, PP,* and the *NS* (for the i adhikaraṇa alone). The *Dvaitabhūṣaṇam* is evidently a work of the same author refuting the *Çandrikākhaṇḍanam* of Raghunātha Śāstri. His descendants are still living."

[580] Footnote in original: "1. *anugamavidhi*–The technique of presenting the initial premise in an argument in a concise manner, without a detailed discussion of the properties and characteristics relating to the topic. 2. *prakāravidhi*–The technique of presenting the initial premise in an argument by detailing all the properties and characteristics." We see in Bhattacharyya [1990, p. 106]: "The technique of stating a very simple property as simply qualifying an object, and then stating explicitly in what sense the 'qualification' is to be taken so that the property is shown to be common to all and only the objects to be defined*, in called *anugama* of the defining* mark; i.e., showing how the defining* mark is related to all and only the objects to be defined*." Also see Chapter IX, "The Technique of Anugama", in Guha [1979] for a detailed discussion of this technique.

he both refuted his arguments as well as presented entirely new counter-arguments, using the very same technique. Only Veṅkaṭarāyaśāstri was able to follow his arguments; everyone else sat there completely bewildered.

Finally, the new techniques that Rāmaśāstri used turned out to be too much for even Veṅkaṭarāyaśāstri to comprehend. Everyone was stunned. *Anugamabhaṭṭāçārya* had been silenced. The roar of this lion of logic from Maisūru filled the palace. At this point, Bhaṭṭāçārya embraced Rāmaśāstri, and declared to the assembly in the presence of the king: "I have been to many kingdoms and debated many scholars; this Rāmaśāstri is Gautama himself; he is a source authority on *Nyāyaśāstra;* this is not mere scholarship, this is exceptional brilliance." The king, who had been very concerned that the kingdom of Maisūru would suffer loss of face, was very pleased. The king awarded 4000 *Rūpīs* to Rāmaśāstri and 3000 *Rūpīs* to Veṅkaṭarāyaśāstri, as well as *khillats.*[581] *Anugamabhaṭṭāçārya* remained in Maisūru for some time and then returned to his country.

After this, Rāmaśāstri began instructing his students in the techniques of *anugamavidhi* as well. They all learned to debate both in the traditional mode of *prakāravidhi* as well as in the new mode of *anugamavidhi*. Subsequently, whenever debates occurred in places such as Kāśī, Gaya, Prayāga, Navadvīpa, Brahmāvarta, Vardhamāna, Darbhaṅga, or Kalakatta, it became the practice to accept Rāmaśāstri as an authority, and to use his techniques in debates.

Another scholar's arrival in Maisūru became an occasion for Rāmaśāstri's fame to grow even more. He was Gaṅgādhara Somayāji of Pāvagaḍh.[582] Having determined to perform a *yāga* called *Sarvatomukha,* he came to Maisūru in the belief that he was likely to get the resources he needed for

[581] The word *khillat* originally referred to robes of honor, but later was used for any gift given to show royal esteem, especially one marked in a way that made clear its significance.

[582] A *sōmayāji* is a person who has performed a *sōmayāga,* the most elaborate of *Vēdic* rituals. It was long believed that the practice of *Vēdic yāgas* was nearly extinct, and that the *Agniçayana* performance documented by Staal in 1975 [Staal 2001a,b] was perhaps the last performance of the extraordinarily elaborate ritual. However, as Knipe [2015] documents, there survives to this day a significant *Vēdic* tradition, including that of the performance of *Vēdic yāgas,* in coastal Āndhra. Pāvagaḍh is a small town near Tumakūru in present-day Karṇāṭaka. Pāvagaḍh is also a site of considerable antiquity in the state of Gujarāt, which now has UNESCO world heritage site status. It has several temples, the most important of which is the Kāli temple situated on top of a hill. The reference is surely to the local Pāvagaḍh.

the *yāga,* and having met with important officials, gained an audience with the king. Being the very fount of support for tradition, the king was very pleased, and said to the Somayāji: "Peace and prosperity is sure to accrue to us and our kingdom from a worthy person as yourself performing such a meritorious act. You may rest assured that your expenses will be covered by the palace."[583] Unfortunately, Kuṭṭi Śāstri, who was seen as without equal in the performance of *śrauta* ritual, failed to give the Somayāji the proper directions for performing this ritual.[584] The Somayāji then approached Rāmaśāstri, and pleaded for his help. The Śāstri, having first taken him by the hand and reassured him, had all the *śrautis* from the province of Maisūru and elsewhere invited to Maisūru. Among them was Kṛṣṇasomayāji of Beṅgaḷūru. The Śāstri was able to construe the procedure for the *yāga* using the various books that the *śrautis* had brought with them.

Four sacrificial halls were constructed for the *yāga.*[585] A hundred priests were appointed for the ritual.[586] The Śāstri himself assumed the roles of

---

[583] The resources required for this *yāga* were very substantial. In [Versaikar 2013], it is reported that several brāhmaṇas in Puṇe and Nāgpur had received letters in 1857 C.E. (roughly contemporaneously with our story) inviting them to participate in a *Sarvatōmukha yāga* being planned by the dowager queen Baiza Bāi, widow of the late Daulat Rāv Śinde, ruler of Gvāliar, who had set aside seven or eight hundred thousand *Rūpīs* for that purpose. Even allowing for some hyperbole, the sum must have been substantial.

[584] In his *Saṁskṛta* introduction to the *Mahiṣaśatakam*, Śāstri [1946] indicates that Kuṭṭi Śāstri once performed the *Jyōtiṣṭōma* sacrifice, with his students and relatives serving as the priests. Desikāchārya [1949, p. lxxxii] records that on May 13, 1842 C.E., the Parakāla *Svāmi* visited the *yajñaśāla* of Kuṭṭi Śāstri, who had performed the *Agniṣṭōma* sacrifice. However, Śāstri [1946] goes on to say that Kuṭṭi Śāstri later declined to perform the *Vājapēyam* sacrifice for Kṛṣṇarāja Voḍeyar III because it involved the sacrifice of too many animals.

[585] The *Sarvatōmukha* is so called because four *Jyōtiṣṭōma* sacrifices of different *saṁsthās* (or varieties) are performed at the same time in four different enclosures located in the directions north, south, east, and west [Utgikar 1928, p. 132]. *Jyōtiṣṭōma* has the following *saṁsthas: Agniṣṭōma, Atyagniṣṭōma, Ukthya, Ṣoḷaśin, Vājapeya, Atirātra,* and *Aptoryāma.* Three animal sacrifices are required for the *Agniṣṭōma*—the *agnīsomīyāpaśu* on the fourth day, the *savanīyapaśu* on the fifth day, and finally, the *aunbandhyapaśu.*

[586] Knipe [1997, 2015] reports that an *āhitagni* called Mitranārayaṇa in Āndhra performed the *Sarvatōmukha yāga* in 1980 C.E., with 72 priests. Since the *Sarvatōmukha* is effectively four simultaneous *Jyōtiṣṭōmas,* the large number of priests is hardly surprising. The sixteen priests are in four classes, with the *mahartvija* for each of the four *Vēdas* being the chief priest, and his assistants the *ardhi, tritīyi,* and the *pādi* receiving only a half, a third, and a fourth, respectively, of the *dakṣiṇa* payment given the *mahartvija.* Some *yāgas* require the *sadasya,* a seventeenth priest. The priests required are shown in the following table:

sadasya and *somapravāka* in the *yāga.*[587] Many people and scholars had come from other countries to witness this *yāga.* The Śāstri himself supervised this *kratu* from beginning to end. Kuṭṭi Śāstri and his son Vāñçhēśvara Śāstri, who witnessed this flawless performance, were pleased and were full of praise in the royal court.[588] Kuṭṭi Śāstri was indeed no ordinary person. He was an accomplished expert in ritual, and very pious; he was also reputed as an outstanding all-round scholar. Kṛṣṇarāja Voḍeyar III had a very special regard for him. He would travel to the palace in a palanquin. By order of the king, this venerable person was exempt from the *goṣa* custom in the palace. It is clearly no small matter that a person such as him heaped so much praise on Rāmaśāstri.[589] At this time, Kṛṣṇarāja Voḍeyar III bestowed honours on Rāmaśāstri, and also designated for him a salary of 10 *Varāhas.*[590] He also

MAHARTVIJA	*ARDHI*	*TRITĪYI*	*PĀDI*	*VĒDA*
adhvaryu	*pratiprasthatṛ*	*neṣṭr*	*unnetṛ*	*Yajurveda*
hotṛ	*maitrāvaruṇa*	*açcāhvāka*	*grāvastut*	*Ṛgveda*
udgātṛ	*prastotṛ*	*pratihartṛ*	*subrahmaṇya*	*Sāmaveda*
brahma	*brāhmaṇāççhamsin*	*āgnīdhra*	*potṛ*	*Atharvaveda*

[587] The *sadasya* is the seventeenth priest required for some *yāgas* (see footnotes 585 and 586). The *somapravāka* is the messenger sent by the *yajamāna,* or sacrificer, who informs the *agnihotris* from whom the officiating priests are chosen that a *yāga* is being planned, the name of the *yajamāna,* and the fee proposed for the priests. The *yajamāna* chooses the officiating priests from those who find the terms agreeable.

[588] Vāñçhēśvara was, in fact, Kuṭṭi Śāstri's own name, not that of his son (footnote 573).

[589] Given what we know about Kuṭṭi Śāstri (see footnote 573) the following quote from Lakshminarasimhaiya *et al.,* [1970] seems not just inaccurate but downright amusing:

> Among the four such eminent scholars who were appointed as *dharmadhikaris,* Sesha was, as stated already, the first in the order of precedence. How the portfolios should be divided, Sesha was requested to advise. Sesha reserved *Rajadharma* for himself; Kunigal Rama Sastri was to advise on purely religious matters; Vyakarana Narasimha Sastri had to supervise and regulate the patronage of literature and learning; and Kutty Sastri was to look after odds and ends and being quite a 'boy' treated as a probationer. This arrangement did not continue for long, because Sesha died within less than twelve months.

Kāśī Śeṣa Śāstri died in April 1860 C.E., so the appointments alluded to were in 1859 C.E., at which time Kuṭṭiśāstri would have been seventy-nine years old, hardly a 'boy', and in fact, significantly older than the others mentioned. It is also inconceivable that a person of this stature would have been asked to, or agree to "look after odds and ends!" Also see footnotes 100 and 102.

[590] A *Varāha* (or *Kaṇṭhīrava Pagōḍa*) was valued in 1868 C.E. at 2 *Rūpīs,* 14 *Āṇe* and 6

appointed the Śāstri to the role of *Dharmādhikāri*. While all this surely enhanced the Śāstri's prestige, it also raised the intensity of Timmaṇṇaśāstri's jealousy.

Moved by anger, and determined to ensure Rāmaśāstri's humiliation at the hands of other scholars, Timmaṇṇaśāstri maintained a steady correspondence with the aim of accumulating information on the names and whereabouts of other scholars. Even now, there are principalities in such places as Gaddavāla and Vanaparti, under the dominion of Haiderābād. Their rulers have maintained their deep respect for our traditions and practices. They organize a scholarly conference each year, in which they honor scholars and award them annual stipends. Such royal patronage has attracted a number of scholars to these small domains. A well-known scholar called Muddukṛṣṇācārya lived in this region.[591]

Timmaṇṇaśāstri determined to assuage his torment by inviting Muddukṛṣṇācārya to Maisūru to let him loose on Rāmaśāstri and humiliate him. But alas, wretched Timmaṇṇaśāstri! He had not the competence to judge the accomplishments of these two. He was not learned in any *vaidika* way, nor proficient in any *laukika* way. It was a great strain for this person, who survived by proclaiming himself a *laukika* Bṛhaspati when among *vaidikas,* and a *vaidika* Sarasvatī when among *laukikas,* to come to terms with very much.[592] When asked whether he was an *Āśvalāyana* or an *Āpastamba,*[593] a certain pitiful brāhmaṇa who had never heard these words in his entire

---

Pai, or about 3 *Rūpīs*. Ten *Varāhas* are about thirty *Rūpīs*. Even after Kṛṣṇarāja Voḍeyar III's demise in 1868 C.E., there were only four *paṇḍitas* in the palace with salaries of thirty *Rūpīs* or more (see letter from Major C. Elliot to L.B. Bowring in Stanhope [1878, p. 68]).

[591] It is really unclear who this Muddukṛṣṇācārya might be. The most likely candidate may be Kṛṣṇāvadhūta Paṇḍita [Sharma 1981, p. 513], who was also known as Muddu Kṛṣṇa. However, his dates appear as either 1835–1909 or 1864–1909 C.E. in the literature, making him no older than 17 or 18 at the time of this episode, perhaps explaining why he began by debating not Rāmaśāstri, but his students. He was born in the region of Baḷḷāri, and became the *Āsthāna Paṇḍita* at the principality of Saṇḍūru, nearby. Saṇḍūru is not especially close to Gaddavāla and Vanaparti, the regions mentioned in the text, but these all happen to be locations in the northern part of Karṇāṭaka, bordering what was then Haiderābād. He is held in extremely high regard for his broad scholarship, and his religious devotion. The text calls him a "well-known scholar" from the region, so this is a possibility. There are problems with the dates, however.

[592] Bṛhaspati is teacher to the gods and their chief priest, and thus personifies the *kārmic* aspect of existence. Sarasvatī is the goddess of learning, and personifies scholarship.

[593] In effect, the question asks what *Vēda* the individual is a follower of. *Āśvalāyana* is one of the *śākhas* or branches of the *Ṛgveda*. The reference here is to the *Āśvalāyana Kalpasūtra*,

life, responded that he was not aware of being much more than perhaps a little of either *Āśvalāyana* or *Āpastamba*, but that he was quite sure of being a relative of *Pradhāna* Veṅkappayya.[594] Thinking of Timmaṇṇaśāstri brings to mind just such a worm of a brāhmaṇa. Perhaps Timmaṇṇaśāstri drew inspiration from the manner in which wrestlers are paired in matches during Navarātri, in the arena opposite the palace. At any rate, he secretly invited Muddukṛṣṇācārya to Maisūru to do battle with Rāmaśāstri, apparently seeing scholarly debate as little more than a boxing or grappling match between wrestlers.

Muddukṛṣṇācārya arrived with much fanfare, and met with the king. A scholarly assembly gathered A debate was arranged between him and Rāmaśāstri in the palace. The Śāstri quietly sat down. A debate began between his student Rāmagiri Śāmācārya and Muddukṛṣṇācārya. The debate

---

which includes the manual of *Vēdic* rituals (*śrautasūtra*), domestic rituals (*gṛhyasūtra*), and of law and conduct (*dharmasūtra*). The *Āpastamba Sūtras* are the corresponding manuals for the *Kṛṣṇa Yajurveda*. The ritual identity of a brāhmaṇa is defined by reference to his ancestral *ṛsis*, his *gōtra*, his *sūtra*, and the *Vēda* that he follows. Ignorance of one's *sūtra* is a mark of disgrace.

[594] *Pradhāni* Veṅkappayya, also known by various other names, such as Veṅkappa, Veṅkāmātya, Veṅkaṭapati, and Veṅkaṭabhūpati, was a remarkable scholar, statesman, general, and strategist, who deserves to be far better known than he appears to be. Born around 1727 C.E., he rose from modest origins to serve as *Pradhāna* (Chief Minister) between 1763–1779 C.E. to *Navāb* Haidar 'Ali, who had usurped the Maisūru throne. He was a skilled statesman, and served Haidar 'Ali as the administrator for various provinces, military strategist and general, as well as chief negotiator and emissary to a number of contemporary powers, including the Marāṭhas and the Portuguese. Veṅkappa was deeply involved in military operations when the Marāṭhas surrounded Mēlukōṭe in April of 1771 C.E., and put Haidar's son Ṭippu in grave danger of being taken prisoner. Ṭippu was saved mainly by Veṅkappa's ingenuity and intervention. In addition to his military, political, and administrative accomplishments, Veṅkappa was also an extraordinary scholar, with deep scholarship in both *Saṁskṛta* and Kannaḍa. His literary and scholarly output easily matches or exceeds the accomplishments of a great many better-known scholars. His *Karṇāṭa Rāmāyaṇa*, for example, is the largest Kannaḍa *Rāmāyaṇa* in the *Vārdhaka Ṣaṭpadi* metre [Veṅkāmātya 1954]. He also has an extraordinary volume and breadth of work in *Saṁskṛta*, ranging over *alaṅkāra, kāvya*, and *nāṭaka*. He has the distinction of having written each of the ten types of plays enumerated by Bharata in the *Nāṭyaśāstra*. Despite Veṅkappa's exemplary record of service, Haidar 'Ali, who was both illiterate and untrusting of people around him, accused him in 1779 C.E. of improper remittances of taxes, publicly humiliated him, fined him 60,000 *Varāhas*, stripped him of his property, and imprisoned him. Intervention by Appāji Rām succeeded in securing his release from prison, and retirement at a monthly pension of 1000 *Rūpīs*, and permission to keep his title of *Pradhāna*. Veṅkappa died of complications from diabetes in November 1782 C.E., at the age of 55. For more information about Veṅkappa, see Rao [1954] and Svāmi and Bhāratī [2007].

made some progress. Another dear student of the Śāstri's, Vijayarāghavāçārya, entered into debate. Muddukṛṣṇāçārya was unable to comprehend his arguments. The visiting scholar then said: "I have not come here to debate you and your fellow-students. Your guru Rāmaśāstri must enter the debate." Hearing these words, a scholar who was present in the audience retorted: "Good sir, we would consider it ample for you to respond just to Vijayarāghavāçārya. It seems hardly necessary for Dakṣiṇāmūrti himself to come forth to debate you!" Yet, because he foolishly insisted on ignoring the advice of so many in the audience that he should not take on Rāmaśāstri, the Śāstri himself entered the debate, and made short work of him. Muddukṛṣṇāçārya's cute countenance shrivelled up.[595] So did Timmaṇṇaśāstri's bravado. This occurred in the Paridhāvi *saṁvatsara*.

1852–1853

[595] "*Muddu*" means cute in Kannaḍa.

Chapter 10: The Situation in the Royal Court

Kṛṣṇarāja Voḍeyar III had three queens consort. The seniormost, the lady of Lakṣmīvilāsa, was a daughter of the household of Bāgaḷi Dēśē Arasu.[596] This lady would be the paternal aunt of Dēśē Arasu, the father by adoption of Colonel Dēśarājē Arasu, of our own time.[597] His second wife was the lady of Ramāvilāsa. She was a daughter of the household of Katti Gōpālarājē Arasu; she would be paternal aunt to Kṛṣṇē Arasu, who was the biological father of the now deceased Çāmarājendra Voḍeyar.[598] Both these ladies were the formally consecrated queens of Kṛṣṇarāja Voḍeyar III. Both were from real Arasu households. General Harris and Colonel Wellesley (the Duke of Wellington) gained fame by capturing Śrīraṅgapaṭṭaṇa, destroying Ṭippu, and crowning Kṛṣṇarāja Voḍeyar III king of the region that is now Maisūru. *Dīvān* Pūrṇayya had arranged for the marriage of Kṛṣṇarāja Voḍeyar III with these princesses, with the consent of these officers. More recently, Kṛṣṇarāja Voḍeyar III has also married the lady of Sītāvilāsa, who is a daughter of the household of Taruvēkere.[599] The seniormost of these queens, the lady of Lakṣmīvilāsa, was learned, intelligent, and conducted herself with decorum. She had apparently been expecting at one time, but it came to naught. A youthful Kṛṣṇarāja Voḍeyar III had been led astray by faithless retainers who had managed to gain his confidence, and

---

[596] See Plate 23. Kṛṣṇarāja Voḍeyar III's first marriage had been in April 1801 C.E., to Dēvājammaṇṇi, daughter of Sardār Gōpālarājē Arasu [Row 1916, p. 247], but she appears to have died young. This queen's name appears as Dyāvājāmbādēvī in some sources [Arasu 1993, Archeological Department 1936]. The lady of Lakṣmīvilāsa, being referred to here, was his second wife, and was also named Dēvājammaṇṇi [Row 1916]. She too appears in Plate 23, and would have become the *paṭṭamahiṣī*, or the senior queen consort upon the death of her more senior namesake queen.

[597] Lieutenant Colonel Deśarāj Arasu was appointed Chief Commandant, Mysore State Troops in 1897 C.E.

[598] Çāmarājendra Voḍeyar X was the adopted son of Kṛṣṇarāja Voḍeyar III. As a young prince, he had been instructed by Garaḷapurī Śāstri. See page 43.

[599] Kṛṣṇarāja Voḍeyar III had twenty legitimate wives [Archeological Department 1936, p. 174]. By tradition, queens are formally addressed by stating the name of the royal quarters of the respective queen, followed by *Sannidhāna* (presence). The names of his first several wives were as follows: Dēvājammaṇṇi (Dyāvājāmbādēvī), Dēvājammaṇṇi (Dēvāmbādēvī, Lakṣmīvilāsa *Sannidhāna*), Çaluvājammaṇṇi (Çaluvāmbādēvī, Ramāvilāsa *Sannidhāna*), Liṅgājammaṇṇi (Liṅgājamāmbādēvī, Kṛṣṇavilāsa *Sannidhāna*), Dēvāmbādēvī (Sītāvilāsa *Sannidhāna*).

the people of the state were suffering deeply on account of maladministration. A great many people attempted to petition the king, but were ignored. The king had become deaf when it came to hearing the people's complaints, their sentiments, or the advice of far-sighted individuals. His eyes, even in his youth, had become in need of eyeglasses when it came to perceiving the truth around him. Dishonorable natives of the state were being joined by avaricious non-natives in converting him to the ways of ruin. Counsels of madness from his evil companions were to him as sonorous music, good advice like hideous braying.[600] The kingdom was in shreds, like so much tattered clothing. Beholding all of this, the lady of Lakṣmīvilāsa began to give good counsel to the king. The king was vexed by this, however, and his annoyance soon grew into hatred. He stopped speaking with her entirely.

Dāsappāji, the younger brother of *Dīvān* Veṅkaṭē Arasu, a person we have already encountered, had an attitude of arrogance and disregard for the king. The king also began to draw closer to his morganatic wives than to the queens consort. It appears he required the Arasus to treat the son born to the lady of Madanavilāsa with all the deference due to an heir apparent, requiring them, in fact, to eat their meals in his immediate company.[601]

Many Arasus had therefore turned against the king. Dāsappāji was one of this group. His hatred of the king deepened. It appears that he conspired to write to the Government in Kalakatta in the name of the lady of

[600] There appears to be much truth to this statement. As early as 1817, just six years after the retirement of Pūrṇayya, Sir Thomas Munro writes to Marquess Francis Rawdon-Hastings, then Governor General, as follows [Arbuthnot 1889, p. 131]:

> ... Wherever the subsidiary system is introduced, unless the reigning prince be a man of great abilities, the country will soon bear the marks of it in decaying villages and decreasing populations. This has long been observed in the dominions of the Peshwa and the Nizam, and is now beginning to be seen in Mysore. The talents of Purnayya, while he acted as Diwan, saved that country from the usual effects of the system, but the Raja is likely to let them have their full operation. He is indolent and prodigal, and has, besides the current revenue, dissipated about sixty lakhs of pagodas of the treasure laid up by the late Diwan. He is mean, artful, revengeful, and cruel. He does not take away life, but he inflicts the most disgraceful and inhuman punishments on men of every rank, at a distance from his capital, where he thinks it will remain unknown to Europeans, and, though young, he is already detested by his subjects...

[601] The lady of Madanavilāsa was Kṛṣṇarāja Voḍeyar III's ninth wife, born Muddaliṅgamāmbādēvī. Her son was Ċāmarājabahādūr. Because the lady of Madanavilāsa was a morganatic wife, and not queen consort, her son was excluded from the line of succession.

Lakṣmīvilāsa, complaining that the king had lost his senses, and that the lady of Lakṣmīvilāsa should become regent.[602] It is not possible to say if the lady of Lakṣmīvilāsa was even aware of these goings-on. Dāsappāji had also apparently suggested surrendering Maisūru as a tributary state to the British for 44,00,000 *Varāhas*.[603] His great ambition was to ruin the king's reputation in a great many ways, before his selfish machinations might be discovered. There is sufficient reason to believe that Dāsappāji, seeing that the name of the lady of Lakṣmīvilāsa carried great weight, used it in his correspondence.[604]

By this time, the Company had taken over the reins of administration from the king. The communication with Kalakatta in the name of the lady of Lakṣmīvilāsa came to the king's attention. In the belief that this letter was responsible for his debacle, he developed an even more malevolent contempt for her. He had the door leading from within the palace to

[602] Kalakatta (Calcutta) was then the seat of government for the British in India.

[603] The tone of this statement suggests perfidy, but it is possible that these negotiations involving 44,00,000 *Varāhas* were intended to secure a higher status (perhaps as a tributary state) for the state of Maisūru than it enjoyed at the time under the rule of the East India Company. The terms of the Subsidiary Treaty of 1799 were quite onerous. At the time, Indian states were either *subsidiary* or *tributary* states. The primary distinction was that while military duty in a subsidiary state was performed by the troops of the East India Company, this was not necessarily the case in a tributary state [Commons 1840, para. 451]. Maisūru was a subsidiary state (but see below). A subsidy was extracted from the state, ostensibly for the maintenance of the British military force. Under Article II of the Subsidiary Treaty of 1799, this subsidy from Maisūru was set at 7,00,000 *Star Pagodas*, or the equivalent of 57% of the estimated revenues of the state at the time. Maisūru's contribution was to be even higher at times of war involving the Company, as happened in the Marāṭha wars of 1802–1805 and 1817–1818. In 1804 alone, Maisūru incurred expenses of over 4,10,000 *Star Pagodas* in support of the Marāṭha campaign [Rao 1936a, p. 357]. The treaty of 1807 required Maisūru to maintain a standing cavalry of 4000 horse to support the British, which accounted for 70% of the annual military expenditures of 9,50,000–11,10,000 *Rūpīs* [Rao 1936a, p. 491]. The treaty of 1799 granted the king an annual allowance of 100,000 *Star Pagodas*, as well as a fifth of the *net* revenue of the state. This treaty also allowed the British to assume the government at any time, so Maisūru was seen practically as a British possession, not simply as a subsidiary state [Commons 1840, para. 459]. No other Indian state, excepting Travancore, was in this situation. In 1831 C.E., following the Nagar insurrection, the British invoked the terms of the treaty, and assumed full control of the administration of Maisūru.

[604] Such intrigue was apparently not unknown in the Maisūru Palace. See, for example, Rao [1936a, p. 405]: "Chowdiah and Veene Venkatasubbiah were in league and often did not scruple, it is said, to fabricate communications between the Maharaja and the Resident to serve their own ends. They also prevented proper information from reaching the ears of the Maharaja or Casamaijor." This Chowdiah is the same Residency *Śeristedār* alluded to in footnote 541.

Lakṣmīvilāsa walled up, thus isolating these quarters from the rest of the palace. It is a classic quip that a king angry with a queen banishes her to the farthest palace quarters, and forces her to subsist on coarse millet and stale legumes. This turned to reality in the case of the lady of Lakṣmīvilāsa.

She often lamented to the ladies closest to her: "*Śiva, Śiva!* The life of a woman is indeed one of woe! I thought the husband who took my hand my god, and forsook my parents, my siblings, and all the comforts of my home. Isn't a child a part of a parent's very own being? Should ever a child torn away from a parent's bosom and given to another who promises to care and protect, be reduced to such a state? No good fortune or prosperity could ever make up for a husband's indifference to his wife. Securing the lineage is the chief object of a marriage. There now remains no prospect for preserving the kingdom.[605] When the wife wed with *Agni* as witness is forsaken,[606] what does it matter when the others beget children? How shall I describe the misfortunes of the king of Maisūru! The righteous do suffer thus when the malicious prevail. It is far better for husband and wife to suffer the pangs of abject poverty but live in harmony, than for them to enjoy great opulence but live estranged. The ordinary person may be shown the right path through good counsel, but when the king's mind is corrupted, that is indeed an incurable disease. I am now suffering the consequences of my misdeeds in my lives past. I am a woman, and thus helpless. But blaming others gains one nothing. The more suffering one causes a woman, the closer one gets to the great crime of gynæcide. But can one avert fate?" The greater her disappointments, the more high-minded she became. Dressing herself in a simple white *sīre* costing three *Haṇas,* she divested herself of her golden and bejewelled ornaments, wore the ashes of *vibhūti* on her forehead and a necklace of *rudrākṣi* beads around her neck, and since she was not a widow, some *kuṁkuma* on her forehead, and spent her time studying books on *Vēdānta,* acquiring insight into *jñāna yōga* and *rāja yōga,* living the life of a *yōginī.* Her life was so exemplary in every respect, that not a tongue could wag, even with lips closed. She waned in body because she subjected herself to such rigours as eating a single meal a day, subsisting on fruits and milk, and fasting. Her delicate figure wasted away. Many years

[605] See footnote 505.

[606] That is, the formally wed wife, with the status of Queen Consort, rather than a morganatic wife.

passed in this manner. Born into a noble family and being a lady of resolve, however, her mind remained steadfast.

But who can divine the future? One never knows what might happen, or when. Indeed, a reason arose for the king's heart to soften in regard to this queen. This is a story I have heard first-hand from my maternal grandmother's sister, that is, my birth mother's maternal aunt, who heard it from the princess herself.[607] By publishing this story here, we hope to bring to light the great virtues of the royal couple.

Also, this narrative is essential to provide context for the king's displeasure with the queen, its abatement and its transformation into regard, the king's indignation at the Śāstri because of his aversion to the king's attitude, and the Śāstri's consequent determination to leave the kingdom.

A daughter had been born to a lady with whom the king had a concubinal relation. This daughter was beautiful, and bore a strong resemblance to the king.[608] In due course, she was married, and became pregnant. The king would meet the daughter as many as four times a day. The king had unlimited regard for his daughter. She was in the fifth month of her pregnancy. In accordance with tradition, preparations were made for the bangle-wearing ceremony.[609] The father said to the daughter one day:

---

[607] The sentence in the original is ambiguous: *"namma mātāmahiya taṅgi endare ċikka hettammanu doreya baṅgārada kumāriyinda kēḷi nōḍida saṅgati endu hēḷida mātannu nānu kiviyāra kēḷidēne."* The sentence refers to the same person as *mātāmahiya taṅgi*, or grandmother's younger sister, and also as *ċikka hettamma,* the obvious reading of which would mean his biological mother's younger sister. Since these relationships cannot both apply to the same person, it seems reasonable to read the latter relationship as *hettammana ċikkamma*, or mother's maternal aunt (grandmother's sister). M.S. Puṭṭaṇṇa's given name was Lakṣmīnarasiṁhaśāstri, but he was called Puṭṭaṇṇa ("the little one") for affection; the appellation stuck. His father was Sūryanārāyaṇabhaṭṭa of Ċannapaṭṭaṇa, whose father Lakṣmīkānta Bhaṭṭa was learned in the *Vēdas* and in *jyotiṣa*, or astrology. In appreciation of his abilities, the king had granted Lakṣmīkanta Bhaṭṭa 20 acres of land in Ċannapaṭṭaṇa. Puṭṭaṇṇa's mother died a few days after he was born. There is no record of her identity, or of her mother's. Puṭṭaṇṇa grew up in the house of his birth mother's older brother Aṇṇayyaśāstri of Aṇṇapēṭe. He was cared for by his grandmother and a widowed paternal aunt named Ammaṇatte, whom he would have seen as his foster mother. The family had connections in the palace, so it would be no surprise for one of the ladies to have known something of the internal goings-on in the palace.

[608] In praising Puṭṭaṇṇa's sensitive treatment of this episode, Sujātā [2001] gives the name of this young lady as "Ratnājī". The source of this specific information is unclear.

[609] In this South Indian ritual, a number of married ladies place green (and red) glass bangles on the expectant mother's wrists. In wealthy households, bracelets of gold may also

KING: Lady, your pregnancy is a divine blessing. Is there anything you wish for? Tell me without hesitation. I will have it brought for you.

DAUGHTER: *Appāji,* will you really have brought to me what I want?

KING: I assure you, I will. I will not go back on my word.

DAUGHTER: *Appāji,* I really wish for a bracelet embedded with the nine precious gems.[610]

KING: You are well-acquainted with our treasury. You may choose any bracelet you wish.

DAUGHTER: The Royal Treasury contains none I would want.

KING: Then I will have one made for you.

DAUGHTER: I do not want one that is new. I want one that has been worn by a *muttaide*.[611]

KING: Who might have one such? Tell me, and I will have it brought to you.

DAUGHTER: *Appāji,* I fear you will be angry.

KING: No, just tell me.

DAUGHTER: Hold me by the hand, and promise me that you will not be angry, *Appāji.*

KING: Lady, one does not swear on a pregnant woman.

DAUGHTER: If I tell you, you won't restrain your anger, and neither will you have it brought to me. Oh, why did I ever wish for this bracelet!

KING: Do not be upset. That pains me. I will have it brought, no matter where it may be. Tell me.

DAUGHTER: It is with the lady of Lakṣmīvilāsa. Do have it brought to me.[612]

---

be given. The ceremony is a ritual of blessing, and is connected with the *sīmantonnayana* ritual, which is one of the sixteen *saṁskāras* (see footnote 246).

[610] The list of *navaratnas* can vary a bit, but generally, these are pearl, ruby, topaz, diamond, emerald, lapis lazuli, coral, sapphire, and zircon.

[611] A *muttaide* is a respectable lady whose husband is still alive. The presence of such ladies at auspicious occasions is a good omen, and brings blessings and good fortune. Wearing items of jewellery that have been worn by *muttaides* is seen as auspicious.

[612] This would be the queen Dēvājammaṇṇi (Dēvāmbādēvi). See footnote 599. Much more is at work here than fatherly affection; the wishes of a pregnant woman must always be

As soon as he heard this, the king left the matter where it was, and on some pretext, went outside, away from the presence of his daughter. However, his daughter's words remained lodged in his mind. It bothered him that there was no way to fulfil her wish. His previous resentments had all came gushing forth at the mere mention of Lakṣmīvilāsa; how was a message to be sent to that residence? How was that bracelet to be brought away from there? This did not seem possible. Yet, the wishes of his dear daughter had to be fulfilled. This was not a matter that could simply be forgotten. Nor could he bring himself to speak the needed words. His mind could not just continue bearing this burden. Thus was his state. His daughter was depressed that her wish had gone unfulfilled. The glow upon her countenance had dimmed. Her body too, appeared to be wasting. Seeing her decline, the king finally spoke:

KING: Lady, I am anguished that your wish has gone unfulfilled. Do go to where the bracelet is, and ask for it yourself.

DAUGHTER: This is not such a simple matter, *Appāji.* The senior lady will not give me the bracelet just for the asking. Neither is the ornament an ordinary one.

KING: What sort of a bracelet is it? Is it not one that we had made? Is it not of our palace? Could I not have one made that is even better?

DAUGHTER: That bracelet was not made in this palace. It was gifted to the senior lady by *Dīvān* Pūrṇayya when she was seated on the ritual platform for some special ceremony. Whether good comes of it or not, it must be mine, even if only for a couple of days. Your Retinue must arrive and request it.[613]

KING: (Deeply anguished) It appears that I must do what you ask to restore your happiness. I am having to break my vow for you. I will walk behind you to the that apartment, and stand at the door. You can go in and ask for the bracelet.

---

accommodated, both by tradition and scriptural mandate. For example, see *Yājñavalkyasmṛti* 3.79: *"dohadasyāpradānena garbho doṣamavāpnuyāt | vairūpyam nidhanam vā-pi tasmātkāryam priyam striyaḥ ‖"* meaning "If the wishes of a pregnant woman are denied, detriment accrues to the fœtus. It suffers deformity or demise. One should hence do as the lady desires." The king bears a particular burden in this respect, as the supremely munificient patron of everyone and everything in his realm.

[613] The word "Retinue" is used in what follows as a metonym, and is an allusion to the king himself.

DAUGHTER: Sir, that will not work. You must hold me by the hand and take me inside. When the king's feet enter the apartment, I will follow.

KING: Those with children have left no dignity. As you wish, lady.

At this, a person from the queens' apartments, who stood nearby, lay prostrate before the king, and said: "Great Sire, it is not befitting that such thoughts should enter one's mind. Indeed, it is those with children who are due the highest respect. Affection for one's children soothes the mind and softens one's heart. When one sees others suffering, one's children come to mind, and one's heart feels for others. Those who can, then work to alleviate the suffering of others. Those who cannot, still feel the anguish. Sire, don't such blessed people, who work to help others, receive respect? They receive respect even from the gods themselves."

The king's mind now turned mellow. The great many virtues of the lady of Lakṣmīvilāsa came to mind, one after the other. The conspiracies hatched recently by such rogues as as Dāsappāji also came to mind. It became clear in his mind that blame for what had transpired belonged to such scoundrels, not to the lady of Lakṣmīvilāsa, who always remained in her apartments, committed to asceticism. The order went out that the wall that closed off the internal door to Lakṣmīvilāsa was to come down. The lady of Lakṣmīvilāsa commanded great respect everywhere, not just in her quarters, but also among the workers, the servants, and indeed among all the kingdom's subjects. Overjoyed that the king's anger had subsided, they pulled down the wall in an instant. The lock that had closed the door for so many years was forced open.

The servants rushed to convey the news of the door's opening to the lady of Lakṣmīvilāsa, who was seated on a deerskin in the shrine in her apartment, immersed in reading the *Gītā,* after having completed her daily worship. She remained silent and distant. At this moment ran in another maid, saying: "Your Majesty! The Royal Retinue approaches this apartment, accompanied by the junior lady!" The naturally calm mind of the lady became disquieted. She worried herself: "I wonder what punishment now awaits me. But then, there would be no reason to bring along the expectant daughter; I wonder why the Retinue approaches!" Just then, the king stood outside the threshold of the door that led from inside the palace to the apartment. The princess stood inside the threshold. The king said: "I will remain here. Go in and ask for the bracelet." The princess replied: "That will not do. The Retinue must enter." The king then grasped his daughter's hand, and entered the apartment. Hearing of this, the lady put down her book, and entered the large hall of the apartment. The king looked at his daughter and said: "Ask for the bracelet that you want." The daughter replied: "You ask for it, *Appāji!*"

Nobody knows what can transpire at what time, and for what reason. What had not happened for so many years now came to pass. Husband and wife looked at each other. The king at once saw her pure, borderless white *sīre,* the ash that she wore on her body and forehead, the small mark of *kuṁkuma* on her forehead, her well-grayed and tousled hair tied in a knot, the many layers of *rudrākṣi* beads at her neck, among which was her circular *tāḷi* hanging from a turmeric-dyed thread, her bracelets of *rudrākṣi* beads, her palm-leaf earrings, her emaciated figure, her once-beautiful face now wrinkled and plain, and her sunken eyes.[614]

The king said to his royal consort: "Your daughter is expecting. She wants the bejewelled bracelet that *Yajamān* Pūrṇayya gifted to you when you were seated on the ritual platform; please have it given to her." The lady's eyes flooded with tears. The king's mind had been distressed at the state in which he found his wife. The tears in the eyes of his royal consort brought tears to the eyes of the kindhearted king. The lady paid her respects to her husband's feet, washed them, wiped them clean with the edge of the *sīre* she wore, and pressed it to her eyes. With a tremulous voice, she said: "My lord, today, my sins are all atoned for. My life has attained its meaning." Thinking back over everything that had transpired, at his wife's virtues, and deeply remorseful at the difficulties he had caused her, the king held his wife's hand and sat transfixed and silent for a while. A tingling in his nose caused his eyes to swell with tears. Tears streamed from the lady's

[614] This is the paradigmatic image of spousal and spiritual devotion. The borderless white *sīre* signifies purity and asceticism. The *vibhūti* ash and *rudrākṣi* beads are also symbols of asceticism. The *kuṁkuma* on her forehead and the *tāḷi* pendant are marks of her status as a *sumaṅgalī,* an unwidowed woman. Her tousled hair, her earrings of palm-leaf rolls, and the turmeric-dyed thread necklace for her *tāḷi* are signs of her rejection of worldly pleasures and her focus on the spiritual. The latter two ornaments are seen only among the poorest of the poor. A queen consort would of course, have otherwise worn substantial and bejewelled gold ornaments.

eyes; hiccups caused by excessive weeping were clearly audible. The daughter paid her respects to her mother, and stood before her. Tears appeared like pearls on her cheeks at the plight of her parents.

The lady of Lakṣmīvilāsa now saluted her husband once again, embraced her daughter, and had brought to her the bracelet she sought, as well as many other ornaments, and gifted them to her along with auspicious materials like turmeric and *kuṁkuma.* The palace was overjoyed. The Arasu relatives were all jubilant. From that day forward, the king placed not just great faith in the lady of Lakṣmīvilāsa, but also the greatest regard. Her asceticism roused feelings of devotion. All the recognition and reverence that she once enjoyed were again granted her, in increased measure. Whenever an occasion presented itself, the king would remark: "The lady of Lakṣmīvilāsa is most virtuous. Our splendour and prestige are all on her account." He also often remarked that everything she had warned him about had come true, and that her intelligence and far-sightedness were unequalled.

Thus lay matters, when the time the lady of Lakṣmīvilāsa had on this earth came to an end, and she passed away. The obsequial ceremonies were completed with special reverence. The order was given for all the palace employees and *vaidikas* to come to the cremation grounds. It was a little late, however, by the time Rāmaśāstri finished his morning rituals and arrived at the place. Timmaṇṇaśāstri, who had been waiting for just such an opportunity to sate the fires in his belly, went up to the king at this time of sorrow, and said: "Your Majesty, everyone is here except for Rāmaśāstri." The malevolent smoke from that fire caused the great regard the king had for the Śāstri to become obscured, even to the extent of making him say in reproach: "Why has Rāmaśāstri not come? He really ought to have come!" This episode illustrates the extreme regard in the king's mind for the lady of Lakṣmīvilāsa. In proportion to his regard grew the king's great sorrow, and in the same proportion, his umbrage at the Śāstri. This became known to Rāmaśāstri, who had just arrived.[615]

Now, Rāmaśāstri never left home before completing his morning bath and other rituals. He awoke each morning just as dawn was breaking, and went to the side of Çāmuṇḍī hill to attend to personal matters appropriate

---

[615] This insistence on performing one's mandatory rituals before all else is to be respected as a sign of great merit, rather than disdained as a sign of self-indulgence. See footnote 443.

for the outdoors. He would be accompanied by Sāggere Nārāyaṇaśāstri, Subrahmaṇyaśāstri, or some other student. They would discuss interesting topics as they proceeded. He would clarify any doubts or questions they might have had relating to their studies. It was the practice for the student to carry a large pot of water. When they got to the hill, the student would remain behind, and the Śāstri would proceed, taking the pot of water. After he returned home, he would bathe, complete his morning rituals, such as *Sandhyāvandane,* his recitation of scriptures, worship rituals, and *Aupāsana.* This would take about a *jāva* or so.[616] He would then instruct some students, go to the palace, returning home only after the king had left for his meals after completing his Śiva worship. He would then bathe again, and complete his afternoon rituals, such as *Sandhyāvandane, Brahmayajña, Vaiśvadēva,* and *Baliharaṇa.* It would now be around two or three in the afternoon. At this time, he would seat himself with his students, and have his meal. He would eat well, and without haste. Later, he would complete his evening rituals, such as *Sandhyāvandane,* and retire to bed after dinner, at around 9–10 p.m. He would instruct his students during the times in-between. He would also constantly engage himself in studying his books.

A new fact came to light on one occasion. The Śāstri had left for the side of Çāmuṇḍī hill in the morning, accompanied by Sāggere Nārāyaṇaśāstri. When they neared the hill, the student remained behind, as was the practice, and the Śāstri went ahead with the pot of water. It was still misty. It was difficult to see even those who passed right before one's eyes. The student completed his morning activities, and sat, waiting for his guru. The sun came up after a while, and it became quite warm; it was now around eight o'clock. The Śāstri had still not returned. Narāyaṇaśāstri began to tire of his waiting. He went in search of the Śāstri. At around nine o'clock, something white was visible in the distance, at the the foot of the Çāmuṇḍī mountain. When the student went up to it, he saw a shallow hollow in the rock, full of clean, clear water. There was a cave nearby. The Śāstri was standing next to it. He had his outer garment around him. A *pañçe* was wrapped around his head. His head, spine, and feet were all stiffly stretched out in a straight line. His eyes were closed. His eyeballs were slightly visible, and turned upwards.

[616] A *jāva (jhāva)* is the *tadbhava* or derived form of *yāma* in *Saṁskṛta.* This would be an eighth part of a day, that is, about three hours.

There appeared to be no movement in his body. Nārāyaṇaśāstri just stood there, not knowing what to do. After a bit, a sound was heard. The Śāstri opened his eyes. Seeing his student standing there, he said: "Why did you come here? I would have returned on my own," and charged him not to speak to anyone about what he had witnessed. The guru and student walked back home.[617]

After completing his morning rituals, the Śāstri would meditate, regulating his breath. In light of all this, there remains little doubt that the Śāstri was not merely knowledgeable in Yoga, but was really very accomplished in Yogic practices. He would do nothing until he had completed his bath and his morning rituals. This was common practice among *vaidikas* in times past. Indeed, he could be possessed of no other temperament; he was the grandson of Pāpaśāstri, who proceeded to complete his morning bath even when his son lay dead before him, and before he had his corpse removed for cremation. Given his rigorous Yogic practice, it was impossible to know how much time might pass when he meditated upon his breathing and entered a state of deep concentration. Neither is it proper in this case for one to consult clocks, and speak in terms of hours and minutes. Truly, such exalted beings are not captives to the flow of time; rather, time itself is subject to their control. These Yogic and ritual practices on the Śāstri's part were the real reason for the delay in his arrival at the cremation grounds, when the lady of Lakṣmīvilāsa passed away.

Timmaṇṇaśāstri took great care to sustain the king's unhappiness with the Śāstri, by continuing to speak vicious untruths about him. On some other occasion, the king sent for Rāmaśāstri, wishing to speak with him on some matter. Timmaṇṇaśāstri's machinations had brought about this circumstance. Guards and servants came a couple of times to call him to the palace. However, the Śāstri had not yet completed his daily rituals, and there were some additional ceremonies due for performance on that day. The Śāstri said to the messenger that he would leave in a little while. By the time this word reached the king, it had been completely transformed, and grown into a being with hands, feet, ears, and a nose, as it were. The king was very displeased that the Śāstri had not arrived instantly.

---

[617] These symptoms are obviously consistent with conditions such as seizure disorders. Puṭṭaṇṇa, the author, is aware of, and alludes to this possibility. See page 263.

Even a small black dot stands out starkly against a white and spotless cloth. That same black dot on a dirty and grimy cloth merges with the dirt, and is not even visible. A single fingerprint on a clean mirror appears like a major blemish, and seems to disfigure the countenance of anyone looking into the mirror. But no matter how much dirt settles on a tarnished mirror that has lost its brightness, it remains unseen. Neither does a face reflected in it appear disfigured. In this same way, Kṛṣṇarāja Voḍeyar III's mind, which was pure and principled, saw even a small flaw as substantial, even when placed there by devious minds.

The Śāstri learned of the king's displeasure. He said: "A brāhmaṇa lives but on the patronage of others. The world is, after all, a large place. There are many countries besides this one. If this king is unhappy, we
1854–1855 shall not remain in this kingdom, in which malicious individuals have such say," and departed in short order for Kāñçi, accompanied by his family, his chief disciple Vijayarāghavāçārya, and twenty students. The Śāstri did not visit the king when he departed. The king learned of all this. He said nothing, and remained silent.

Chapter 11: Southward Travels (The Second Time). Nārāyaṇa Shown to Mean Śiva. The King's Regard

People saw the world very differently fifty or sixty years ago than they do today. Their views have changed over time. English education has now become prevalent. But English education is foreign education. Those who teach it are Christians. Most important, such education was brought to this country by Christian missionaries, who are Christian priests. It is understandable for them to preach their religion. However, the teachers in English schools established by the government were also Christians. Even when it was forbidden to preach Christianity in government schools, and even when teachers desisted from preaching their religion, it was indeed the rare teacher who did not deride or ridicule our Āryan traditions.

The scorn aimed at our religion and tradition naturally targeted brāhmaṇas, as the intellectuals who sustained it all. Because such disdain and ridicule comes from teachers, the very individuals our students maintain the greatest regard for, innocent children come to believe that our religion is no religion at all, and that our ancients and elders must have lacked intelligence and discernment. When such children are grown, and work for the government in positions of responsibility, the deplorable views they were exposed to as children remain ingrained in their minds, and they carry out with exemplary ability such tasks as abandoning our traditional practices, and like foreigners, speaking of our own people with censure. Others, out of fear of authority, hesitate to correct their flawed opinions. When such officials or dignitaries happen to be brāhmaṇas, their words of censure may be somewhat restrained; if they are non-brāhmaṇas, their intensity is magnified tenfold.

Means to express contempt for brāhmaṇas arise naturally, in this fashion. It would be going a step farther, and cause for even greater pride, if a brāhmaṇa were especially well versed in many branches of learning, and one expressed contempt for him and his learning. If, however, some foreign scholar were to suggest that there might be commendable elements in our traditions and learning, then that is believed, there awakens a spark of pride, and one hears non-brāhmaṇas saying out loud: "These accursed brāhmaṇas hide everything from us! They tell us nothing!"

Even when it comes to goverment employment, non-brāhmaṇas are heard complaining that brāhmaṇas keep such jobs securely locked away in coffers, which they open as they see fit, but only to hand out jobs to their own. These are the views of those who do not know the truth. With the decline in royal patronage, brāhmaṇas naturally gravitated towards government jobs, knowing no way of earning livelihoods other than by relying on their education. When one considers who holds the power to fill government jobs, however, one sees only non-brāhmaṇas. Why, then, do they appoint brāhmaṇas? The reason becomes clear upon some reflection. Persons in positions of ultimate responsibility in the government, regardless of the community they are from, give due consideration to the weight of their responsibilities. Such officials are ever mindful of such factors as intelligence and ability. When the focus is on ability, rather than on caste, there is no room for partisanship. The point of a needle is able to pierce a piece of cloth without tearing it, and join the two edges of this cloth as if they were one. A crowbar may be made of the same substance, but could it pierce cloth? But a crowbar may be sharpened, to make it like a needle. Then it does become possible. Matters do become clear upon reflection.

Thus have arisen ways for discord to grow among our own people. This is a big reason for the lack of consensus in our nation. People assume incorrectly that this problem is rooted in English education.

This, at any rate, is how the situation stands at present.[618] I have no legal brief to argue the case for brāhmaṇas. I have written what appears clear to me after analysis. It is possible that I am being unconsciously dogged by a bias in favour of my own community. I have no desire, however, to harbour such a bias.

This degree of conflict between brāhmaṇas and non-brāhmaṇas did not exist in times past. Brāhmaṇas did see themselves as more accomplished in matters relating to religion and the associated areas of scholarship, but had appropriate regard for non-brāhmaṇas in all other matters, in proportion to their abilities. Non-brāhmaṇas were well aware of this, and in fact, learned a great many things from the brāhmaṇas.

---

[618] It is fair to say that the situation is not better, and indeed much worse, a hundred years after these words were written.

Thus, there were a great many scholars among non-brāhmaṇas. Among these was an individual called Vāsaraḍḍi Veṅkaṭācala *Nāyaka* from a *pāḷeyapaṭ* that is now under the jurisdiction of the Madras Corps.[619] He was always engaged in studying scholarly works, and was patron to a great many scholars. He referred to the scholars in his court as the *Aṣṭadiggajas*.[620] He was very protective of them, always showing them great generosity.

---

[619]This is Vāsireḍḍi Veṅkaṭādri Nāyaḍu (1783–1816 C.E.), a powerful and wealthy local ruler, renowned as dynamic and extravagant, and as a great patron of learning and the arts. An excellent summary of his life and legacy appears in Lakṣmīnārāyaṇa [1963]. He was the last king of a line of *pāḷeyagāras* dating back to the Vijayanagara empire, and was originally based in Çintāpalli. He later moved to Amarāvati in Guntūr district, which he built up and made his base. He is said to have left an estate that included 50 *lakh Rūpīs* and half a million pounds sterling, in addition to vast lands. All this wealth was quickly dissipated after he died. This family's history after Veṅkaṭādri's death is fascinating.

Veṅkaṭādri adopted two sons: Jagannātha Bābu in 1798 and Rāmanātha Bābu in 1807, both children of cousins. Upon Veṅkaṭādri's death, a court battle ensued between his sons for control of his estate, with Sabnavis Antanna Pantulu, one of Veṅkaṭādri's two ministers, backing Jagannatha Bābu, and Pottūri Kāḷidāsa, the other minister, backing Rāmanātha Bābu. This battle dragged on for a quarter of a century. Even by 1818, two years after Veṅkaṭādri's death, the wealth he had amassed had largely been dissipated, partly due to the litigation, but also because of embezzlement and mismanagement. The collectors of Maçilipaṭṭaṇam and Guntṭūru attached most of the estate to cover arrears. In June 1824, the Provincial Court decided against Rāmanātha Bābu, who appealed to the Sadr Court at Madras. The elder brother Jagannātha Bābu died on February 28, 1825. Rāmanātha Bābu now claimed to be his heir, but the Provincial Court decided in favour of Aççamma, his senior widow. In 1826, the junior widow Raṅgamma filed suit against Rāmanātha Bābu, Aççamma, and Pottūri Kāḷidāsa, claiming that she and her late husband had adopted a boy named Lakṣmīpati in 1819 (her mother's sister's son), who was thus the heir to the whole estate of Rāja Veṅkaṭādri. This suit was dismissed with costs in 1827, but Raṅgamma appealed. On March 14, 1832, the Sadr Court at Madras found that Lakṣmīpati had not been properly adopted by Jagannātha Bābu, and that whatever remained of Veṅkaṭādri's estate belonged to Rāmanātha Bābu. However, in 1848, the Privy Council turned this judgment on its head, finding Lakṣmīpati's adoption by Jagannātha Bābu to be valid, and Rāmanātha Bābu's adoption by Veṅkaṭādri to be invalid, and denying him the right to inherit any of the property, except that given him explicitly by Veṅkaṭādri. In 1852, the Privy Council directed the Collectors of Maçilipaṭṭaṇam and Guntūru to restore to Lakṣmīpati Nāyaḍu the property they had attached. Rāmanātha Bābu died in 1859. The Madras Government maintained that all that remained for Lakṣmīpati to inherit was the monthly allowance of *Rs.* 1,000 that Rāmanātha Bābu had received. See Mackenzie [1883] and Lakṣmīnārāyaṇa [1963] for more details.

[620]Terms such as *diggaja* or *digdanti* are frequently used metaphors denoting stalwarts in any field. See footnote 574 for further details. *Aṣṭadiggaja* is used in Lakṣmīnārāyaṇa [1963] for the scholars in Veṅkaṭādri Nāyaḍu's court.

The chief point here is that our scholars would not have prospered as they have without the support of non-brāhmaṇas, nor would there have been as many scholarly works in *Saṁskṛta*. After Veṅkaṭāçala *Nāyaka*, his son Lakṣmīpati *Nāyaka* continued as a great patron of *Saṁskṛta* scholarship.[621] Father and son were both learned in *Saṁskṛta*, and showed great regard for scholars and brāhmaṇas.

Lakṣmīpati Nāyaka would sponsor a scholarly meeting each year. Debates and such activities took place at this meeting. At a conference some long time past, a discussion took place on whether the word *nārāyaṇa* could in fact, be interpreted to mean Śiva. It is said that a long time ago, Appayya Dīkṣita determined that while the word *nārāyana* could be shown to mean Śiva, it was difficult to construe *nārāyaṇa* as Śiva, that the syllable *ṇa* was grammatically troublesome, but that if the *ṇa* sound in *nārāyaṇa* were to be *na* instead, one could construe the resulting *nārāyaṇa* as Śiva.[622]

We have seen that Rāmaśāstri departed for Kāñçi around the Ānanda *saṁvatsara* or so. At this time, Lakṣmīpati Nāyaḍu, who was now resident in Kāñçi, cordially invited Rāmaśāstri to participate in the symposium the following year. With Rāmaśāstri, renowned all over as a great scholar, resident in the same town, would a scholarly symposium without his presence not be akin to the sky absent the moon? The Śāstri attended the symposium. There he recited the *śloka*:

1854–1855

kēçana mūrkhānatvaṁ bādhata iti dīkṣitavaraira bhāṇīti |
pralapanti tanmusyaiva sphurati śivādityadīpikādi dṛśām ||

Meaning: Some fools babble on that the great Appayya Dīksita said that he was discomfited by the syllable *na*. It is clear that this is false when one examines works such as the *Śivādityadīpikā*.[623]

Then he entered into the debate, and established using arguments by a certain *Smārta* grammarian that the meaning of the word *nārāyana* was indeed *Śiva*. The *Śrīvaiṣṇava* scholars present objected strongly that this was contrary to the *Vaiṣṇava* tenets. The Śāstri responded that those who felt this was incorrect were welcome to point out the errors in his argument,

---

[621] Lakṣmīpati Nāyaḍu was not Veṅkaṭādri's son, but his grandson. See footnote 619.
[622] See footnote 203.
[623] Appayya Dīkṣita was a proponent of a branch of *Advaita* called *Śivādvaita*. Also see footnote 203.

and silence him. After some quibbling, the *Śrīvaiṣṇava* scholars agreed that it was difficult to counter the Śāstri's arguments.

At this time, the Śāstri composed a work called *Navakōṭi*. Finally, the matter not having been resolved, some 600–700 *Vaiṣṇavas,* deciding that matters must be taken into their own hands when all else fails, arrived, bent upon a physical confrontation. The Śāstri replied to them thus: "Gentlemen, this fact has been established more recently than Appayya Dīkṣita, by a great grammarian called Śaṅkara Bhaṭṭāçārya.[624] This is not a new determination. Besides, this is not a dispute involving sectarian tenets, but a scholarly debate. The arguments we have presented are based purely on statements from the *Śāstras;* there is no disparagement of religion."

Everyone was then full of praise for the Śāstri. Lakṣmīpati *Nāyaka* gave him the gift of a palanquin, and honoured him greatly. This news reached Kṛṣṇarāja Voḍeyar III, the king of Maisūru. The king anguished, saying: "What sorrow it is that this great scholar, born and brought up in our own country, and who was such an ornament to our court, should have left our kingdom! When will he step on our soil again, and sanctify it?"

Rāmaśāstri then travelled to Madarās with his family. A gathering took place, in which were present such luminaries as *Pāḷeyagāra* Lakṣmīpati *Nāyaka,* Kollā Kannayyaśeṭṭi, Madarās Sadar Adālat Court scholar Gōpālaśāstri, Appaṇṇaśāstri, Çaṅgalpaṭ Collector's Office Head *Śirastedār* Śrīnivāsarāv, *Nāyab Śirastedār* Varadāçāri, who were themselves scholars and important local leaders. The topic of debate was once again whether the word *nārāyaṇa* could be construed to mean *Śiva.* The Śāstri took one side of the issue. Opposing him was a foursome: Kunapākaṁ Appāsāmayyaṅgār, Tirupakuḍi Appanaiyyaṅgār, Muñjālagaḍḍe Veṅkaṭāçāri, and Vāsudēvāçāri, a *Mādhva* of Kāñçipura.[625] This topic had been debated first in the *maṭha* of Upaniṣat Brahma in Kāñçi and later in the temple of Pārthasārathi in Tiruvaḷakkēṇi in Madarās. Rāmaśāstri succeeded in establishing his thesis. Everyone praised Rāmaśāstri's scholarship greatly. They conferred excellent awards on him. Kollā Rāghavaśeṭṭi gave him the gift of a palanquin.

[624] See footnote 578.

[625] In the original, the last name appears as Vāsuveēvāçāri, clearly a typographical error.

The Śāstri then established the doctrine of *jaganmithya* through his student Vāsudēvaśāstri of Doḍḍaballāpura.[626]

This news, too, reached Kṛṣṇarāja Voḍeyar III. His anguish regarding Rāmaśāstri's departure from his kingdom grew. The king continued his efforts to secure the Śāstri's return, regretting that he had listened to evil-doers and gone too far, and concerned about whether such a luminary would ever return to his province, and whether he would ever see him again.

Around this time, a reason arose unexpectedly for the Śāstri to visit Śrīraṅgapaṭṭaṇa. The Śāstri's fame having spread everywhere, he was also well-known in the city of Beṅgaḷūru. The Śāstri arrived in Beṅgaḷūru en route. He had to remain there a few days, at the urging of some officials. Whether it be affection or aversion, its intensity diminishes at distance, but grows in proximity. Some *Vaiṣṇavas* saw the thesis the Śāstri had established in the region south of the pass, namely, that the word *nārāyaṇa* actually means *Śiva,* as a denigration of their beliefs. It appears that a group of people who held these views had decided to debate Rāmaśāstri on this topic, and if unsuccessful in debate, to mete out punishment befitting the devilish arguments of the *Smārtas.*

The Śāstri received news of the planned debate. The venue too, was decided. Yet, the fisticuffs planned if the debate outcome were unfavourable were still kept secret. A person acquainted with the plot, however, sent an anonymous petition to General Cubbon, who was then Commissioner. When this petition came up for hearing, it came to the hand of Beḷḷāvi Sōmayya, who was *Ghaṭaka Munśi* in the Commissioner's Office. As per the officer's orders, he opened it and read it aloud. It became clear that there was the strong likelihood of brawls and fisticuffs, and possibly risk to life and limb, on the day scheduled for the debate between Rāmaśāstri and the residents of Beṅgaḷūru. As soon as Cubbon heard this, he forbade such a debate, and issued orders directing the *Amīl* of Beṅgaḷūru to stop its occurrence. For this reason, nothing ontoward occurred in Beṅgaḷūru. The plans of the Śāstri's opponents came to naught.

[626] *Jaganmithyā* is the *Advaitic* position that the world is illusion. See Śaṅkara's *Vivekaçūdāmani,* 20: *"brahma satyam jaganmithyetyevaṁrūpo viniṣcyaḥ | so-yam nityānityavastuvivekaḥ samudāhṛtaḥ ‖"* Gundappa [1970] states that Vāsudēvaśāstri of Doḍḍaballāpura put forth the *Advaitic* doctrine *"brahma satyaṁ jaganmithyā"* and established it in a debate before the *Jagadguru* of the Śṛṅgēri *maṭha.* Pleased with his scholarship and eloquence, the *Jagadguru* awarded him the agnomen *Jaganmithyā Vāsudēvaśāstri.* He also received the title *Vidyānidhi* from the king of Maisūru. See page 283.

Plate 35: The royal bathing *ghāṭ* at Paścimavāhinī. Department of Image Collections, National Gallery of Art Library, Washington, DC.

Sometime later, the Śāstri came to Śrīraṅgapaṭṭaṇa for some personal reasons. On one occasion, he came to bathe in the Paṣçimavāhinī.[627] This came to the attention of the king. He came to Paṣçimavāhinī on some pretext, and visited the place where the Śāstri was staying. The Śāstri offered *phalamantrākṣate* to the king, and blessed him. Kṛṣṇarāja Voḍeyar III inquired after his health, and seizing the opportunity, invited the Śāstri graciously, saying: "Dear Śāstri, I am very gratified to learn of your triumphs in places such as Madarās and Kāñçi. I am unfortunate not to have been able to witness these events. My misfortune is the result of my having listened to wicked individuals. You are all-knowing, and should not take such umbrage at me. Please do definitely come to Maisūru."

In accordance with the king's wishes, the Śāstri travelled to Maisūru with full regalia and retinue. He and his family received such magnificient gifts as carriages drawn by a pair of horses. He entered Maisūru in a manner befitting a great ruler. The king bestowed much recognition on him.

---

[627] The Kāvērī bifurcates around Śrīraṅgapaṭṭaṇa, and a small offshoot of the river forks off from the Western branch. This offshoot flows briefly westwards at one spot, where it is regarded as very holy, especially for the purpose of immersing the ashes of the cremated. A royal bathing ghat exists at this spot. See Parsons [1931] for the following delightful passage:

> Paschimavahini means "flowing to the west" and the westerly direction gives the river here an added sanctity. For the Kaveri, holy from source to mouth, is doubly so where it is joined by a tributary; trebly so when, as here, it flows opposite to its general direction.
>
> Whatever non-Hindus may feel about her sanctity no one whatever his creed or country can refuse a tribute to the extraordinary beauty of these two or three acres of river side. There can be few places on earth, which in such small compass, offer more loveliness: few as quiet, except when an eclipse or some saint's day draws multitudes to bathe and worship; and chattering monkeys clamber over the temple roofs and on the bridge, making sudden raids on any eatables in sight, exacting willing or unsanctioned toll of plantain, bread and nuts.

Indeed, it is within living memory for troops of monkeys to be resident in groves, and for all manner of wildlife to be observed in backyards, even in major cities such as Beṅgaḷūru. But no more, alas, may we witness such loveliness as the passage describes, but gaze in horror at the insults and ravages visited upon it by what passes for modernity across the land.

Chapter 12: Birth of Third Son. His Passing

A significant event occurred in the month of Puṣya of the Paiṅgaḷa *saṁvatsara.* Whenever an important official or scholar travelled from Maisūru to some place nearby, it was customary for them to receive transportation from the palace stables, such as a carriage drawn by a pair, a carriage drawn by a single horse, or an ox-drawn carriage, in accordance with status. At such times, it was the practice for Rāmaśāstri to receive a carriage drawn by a pair of horses. He never cared for such ostentation, however. He would simply walk to wherever he was going.

Thus, on one occasion, he needed to go to Nañjanagūḍu. He began walking to Nañjanagūḍu carrying his belongings in a bag on his shoulder, and accompanied by his student Subrahmaṇyaśāstri. This student was especially close to his guru. The Śāstri, conversing casually to pass the time en route, said: "Subrahmaṇya, the lady of our house is expecting. A son is to be born. You are from south of the pass, and your people find excellent names for children. Suggest a name connoting Śiva."

December 1857

Subrahmaṇya: *Amma* is still expecting. The child is yet in the womb. Has it already been determined that it is a boy? And what does it mean to name a child that is yet unborn? What manner of wonder is this?[628]

[628] Given the background of Rāmaśāstri and his student, we take note of the expression *"ajātaputra nāmōtkīrtana nyāya"* (the adage of shouting out the name of the unborn), a proverbial expression employed to illustrate the foolishness of naming the unborn. There is variability in naming practices, but the *sūtras* proscribe the naming of a child for at least ten days after birth. In some practices, the child may not be named for a year after birth. Among other functions, the delay accommodates the duration of ritual impurity resulting from childbirth. A child may be given several types of names, including a name based on the *nakṣatra*, an *abhivādanīya* name to be used in salutations, a secret name known only to the child and the parents, a common name, a name based on the *gotra,* and so on [Kane 1953b]. According to some authorities, the secret name is based on the *nakṣatra* of birth. Similarly, some state that the *abhivādanīya* name is given by the guru at the time of his *upanayana.* See, for instance, the famous story of Satyakāma, (*Chāndōgya Upaniṣad* 4:4:1,2), who is asked for the name of his *gotra* when he approaches the sage Gautama for instruction.

RĀMAŚĀSTRI: *Chi!* You know nothing! I have performed the *puṁsavana* ceremony.[629] A boy is certain to be born. There can be no doubt about this. Stop uttering nonsense. Shall we name him Śiva?

SUBRAHMAṆYA: Well, in that case, we could certainly name him Śiva.

RĀMAŚĀSTRI: If we name him Śiva, uncultured people from our Telugu community will shorten it to Śivu, and destroy its meaning. We could name him Śivasvāmi, which would be a handsome name. Give me such a name.

SUBRAHMAṆYA: In that case, we could name him Śivasvāmi.

RĀMAŚĀSTRI: Let us name him Śivasvāmi, then.

(Up ahead, after walking quietly for a little while.)

RĀMAŚĀSTRI: Subrahmaṇya, we have named this child Śivasvāmi. Perhaps being called *"svāmi"* will cause him to become a *saṁnyāsi!* That seems likely. Yes, he will accept the *saṁnyāsa āśrama* and become an ascetic, that is certain.

SUBRAHMAṆYA: A son has just been born, he has already acquired a name, and he has already become an ascetic! Is this some sort of delusion? Is there anything more?

RĀMAŚĀSTRI: This is how you always speak, but what do you know of these secrets? What I have said will surely come true. You will see.

(Guru and disciple walked to Nañjanagūḍu, conversing in this manner.)

A few months after this episode, a son was born in Maisūru on Thursday, the eleventh *bahula tithi* of the month of Phālguṇa of the Paiṅgaḷa *saṁvatsara*. As decided in the conversation with Subrahmaṇyaśāstri during the walk to Nañjanagūḍu, the child was named Śivasvāmi. Rāmaśāstri immediately went to the palace, with his students carrying articles such as different kinds of fruit, sugar, and betel leaves, and gifted them to the king. The king examined the child's horoscope, and said: "Dear Śāstri, this is the horoscope of one who will be *svāmi* to both you and me. You have even now aptly named him Śivasvāmi. Is there anything you do not see?"

March 11, 1858

[629] This pre-natal *saṁskāra* is performed to ensure the birth of a male child. See footnote 246.

Thus, the Śāstri knew even before the child was born that his destiny was to enter *saṁnyāsa āśrama,* and the king knew this after the child was born. It appears from this that Kṛṣṇarāja Voḍeyar III was especially skilled in reading horoscopes. The king, who remembered both this episode and the horoscope, subsequently arranged for this Śivasvāmi to enter *saṁnyāsa āśrama.*[630] This *Svāmi* now adorns the seat of the pontiff of the Śṛṅgēri Maṭha. Thus did the words of the Śāstri come true. We cannot say what unusual power or ability this represents. Those with Yogic accomplishments can see the unseen, and hear the unheard. This enigma falls only within their understanding.

Subsequently, the Śāstri travelled south once again in the Kāḷayukti *saṁvatsara.* This was his last trip. He returned in about a year's time. It is not known where he went, or what he did. The king remained concerned that the Śāstri might still harbour some residual anger towards him, and whenever the Śāstri travelled, he remained anxious to ensure his return. An opportunity arose to satisfy this wish of his. *1858–1859* A debate was arranged between Kavi Varadāçārya's student Beṅgaḷūra Sītārāmaśāstri and Kāśī Timmaṇṇāçārya's son.[631] The king arranged for Lakṣmīnarasiṁhaśāstri to serve as debate moderator.[632] Two nights prior, the king had experienced a dream in which someone had said *çaṇḍamuṇḍaniṣūdini* to him, by way of a riddle.[633] The thesis Lakṣmīnarasiṁhaśāstri established appeared to the king to be a solution to this riddle. The king was very pleased. Saying: "Lakṣmīnarasiṁhaśāstri is indeed a cub

[630] It is the prerogative of the *maṭha* to choose its *svāmi;* the king has no say in the matter. Kuṇigala Rāmaśāstri had died, however, when Nṛsiṁha Bhāratī, then pontiff of the Sṛṅgēri *maṭha,* selected Śivasvāmi as his successor, in 1866. Śivasvāmi, who was only 8 years old, was under the care of his eldest brother Lakṣmīnarasiṁhaśāstri, who was himself only 26 years of age. He was reluctant to give up his younger brother to *saṁnyāsa.* It took the king's intervention to convince the elder brother to let the child enter *saṁnyāsa.* Śivasvāmi took the vows of asceticism on Friday, August 2, 1866, and assumed the name Saççidānanda Śivābhinava Nṛsiṁha Bhāratī. The name Śivābhinava acknowledges the name his father gave him, and Nṛsiṁha Bhāratī acknowledges his guru, the 32nd pontiff. Saççidānanda Bhāratī had been the name of the 31st pontiff.

[631] It is unclear who the son of this illustrious scholar might have been.

[632] He would have been around fifteen or sixteen years old.

[633] This is a common epithet for Durgā, and means "slayer of Çaṇḍa and Muṇḍa", both of whom were demons. *Çāmuṇḍī,* another name for Durgā, is derived from the initial syllables of these demons. See *Mārkaṇḍeya Purāṇa,* 87.25: *"yasmāççaṇḍañça muṇḍañça gṛhītvā tvamupāgatā | çāmuṇḍeti tato loke khyātā devi bhaviṣyasi ‖"*

befitting that tiger," he honoured him by gifting him items such as a pearl necklace, a bracelet with the head of a lion, and a pair of shawls with gold borders. This information reached Rāmaśāstri, who was still in a different country. He returned to Maisūru immediately. The king had achieved his goal. The Śāstri wrote scholia on several advanced works on *Nyāya* and *Vēdānta.*

On the fourth *bahuḷa* day of Puṣya in the Siddhārthi *saṁvatsara*, the Śāstri developed a fever. He lay ill for fifteen days, and passed away on the fourth *śuddha* day of Māgha the same year. Shortly before he died, he called his wife and children, and speaking words of advice to them, said: "Give up all attachment to me. Please take yourself far from me." He then drew his blankets over his head, began meditating upon his breathing, and gave up this life.[634] This news reached the king immediately. The following morning, before the corpse was removed, the Royal Retinue arrived at the Śāstri's house. The king beheld the Śāstri's face, and moved to tears, said: "The world of scholarship is now in ruins. Never again shall we see the likes of what we have seen," and consoled his children and his students; to his wife, he said: "Dear lady, please look upon me as the eldest of your children. We cannot bring back such a precious thing as we have lost, but you need have no

January 27, 1860

[634]The suggestion here is that Rāmaśāstri's death was an act of volition on his part. Accomplished *yōgis* are seen as capable of such feats as causing their *cittas* (minds) to leave their bodies and enter the bodies of others, and knowing the times of their own deaths (see Patāñjali's *Yōga Sūtras* 3.38 and 3.22). There are even accounts attesting to such abilities on the part of contemporary *yōgis* [Swami Rama 2002, p. 150]. Accomplished *yōgis* are able to attain the *yōgic* state of *samādhi*, a unique mental state characterized by full awareness, but also simultaneously of detachment from the world. A number of varieties of *samādhi* are recognized, of which *kaivalyam* represents ultimate freedom, and unity with the Absolute. The *samādhi* state is characterized both by unresponsiveness to worldly stimuli and by a slowdown of physiological processes to the extent of their cessation. A *yōgi's* death is hence generally not distinguished from a state of *samādhi,* since it may be impossible in practice to tell the two apart. A *yōgi* is hence buried, instead of being cremated. A *yōgic* death has long been considered the ideal, and a fitting end to a life lived in harmony with traditional values and principles. It is common for exalted individuals to be credited with the ability to achieve a *yōgic* death. See, for instance, Kālidāsa's description in Canto 1 of the *Raghuvaṁśa* of the attainments of the kings of the *Raghu* lineage: *"śaiśavē-bhyastavidyānāṁ yauvanēviṣayīṣiṇāṁ | vārdhakē munivṛttīnāṁ yogēnānte tanutyajāṁ* ||8||" meaning: "(Of the kings of the Raghu lineage I speak...) of those who acquired great learning in childhood, who in youth engaged with worldly issues and pleasures, who in advanced years attained the temperaments of *munis,* and who, in the end, gave up their bodies in the *yōgic* manner."

worries about other matters," and ensured that the funerary rites all proceeded without impediment, with the costs being borne by the palace.[635] The Royal Retinue returned to the palace after having appointed Lakṣmīnarasiṁhaśāstri to a position with the salary befitting a scholar. The obsequial ceremonies were duly finished, with no aspect neglected. All required supplies and expenditures came from the palace.

[635] Kṛṣṇarāja Voḍeyar III was fully 66 years of age in 1860 C.E. Rāmaśāstri was 53 years old, so his wife would likely have been in her forties. Given the deep respect for age in Indian culture, the king's urging of Rāmaśāstri's wife to consider him her son is a mark of the deep regard he had for Rāmaśāstri. His scholarship and learning would have made him a father-figure even to the king, who is honoring Rāmaśāstri's wife, a far younger lady, by treating her as a mother-figure.

Chapter 13: His Many Virtues (1)

Thus did this brilliant scholar depart this world. Rāmaśāstri was tall in aspect, slender in form, and of reddish complexion; his face was elegant, neither long nor round. His head was large, and somewhat round. His forehead was large and broad, and protruded slightly. His eyes were handsome and unusual, and gave the impression of his being engrossed in thought over some deep issue. His nose was a little too big for his face, and slightly hooked at the tip. His ears were large and long. His mouth and teeth were small. His lips were thin, and conveyed intellectual determination. He had long limbs. There was hair on his cheeks, chest, and back. There was also hair on his ears.

He always exuded a certain radiance. He wore no ornaments, but dressed himself in a *dhōtra* with a big border, also covering his upper body with one. He would also wear a shawl. When going to the palace, he would wear a turban. Elegant *vibhūti* lines would grace his forehead. *Rudrākṣi* beads would adorn his neck. In his hand would be prayer beads of rock crystal. He never sought to embellish his appearance.

The Śāstri was always engaged in introspection. He always maintained full control over his intellect, never surrendering himself to the inconstancies of the mind. Śrīnivāsāçārya, his guru, was well aware of his introspective nature. The *Āçārya* was over eighty years of age. He would visit the Śāstri's home on occasion. Upon his arrival, the Śāstri would arise, and would touch his feet. All the students of the Śāstri would then do the same. The *Āçārya* would delight in listening to the Śāstri teach his students. He would tell the Śāstri: "Rāmuḍu, I won't be returning home; I will stay, and eat my meal here." He would then tell the Śāstri's wife: "Lakṣamma, I am an old man, and like to indulge my palate; please cook me a good meal. I will eat first; it will not do for me to wait for your husband. If he sits down holding his nose, it may be three days before he stirs again."[636] Lakṣamma would immediately come and touch his feet, ask: "What feast shall I prepare?" and cook the meal according to his wishes. The *Āçārya* would rest after his

[636] The jocular reference to Rāmaśāstri's holding his nose is an allusion to his practice of *prāṇayāma*, or breath control. The comment about sitting still for three days is a hyperbolic allusion to his immersion in a meditative state. Reference has already been made to both.

meal, and return home at about four or five in the evening, supporting himself with his stick. Śrīnivāsāçārya, though a *Vaiṣṇava,* had never the slightest hesitation nor any airs, about eating in the home of a *Smārta.*

The issue of Śrīnivāsāçārya's meal is one illustration of the Śāstri's immersion into deep meditation. There are other instances where the Śāstri had lost himself in this state. When teaching his students, the Śāstri would sometimes suddenly become silent and sit still. His eyes would turn upwards. His students would also sit silently. After his mind turned outward again, the Śāstri would continue the lesson from where it had been left off. It would appear to the observer that he had just fallen asleep while seated.

On another occasion, the Śāstri was walking to Yeḍatore with his students Subrahmaṇyaśāstri and Gaṅgādharaśāstri of Soṇḍekoppa. Beyond Ilavāla, en route to Lakṣmaṇatīrtha, a small path branched off the main road, and headed towards a village nearby.[637] As the Śāstri was walking along this path, these students happened to be about forty or fifty steps ahead of the Śāstri. Some women from a village off to the side were going to fetch water, and said to the two students: "What, sirs! The brāhmaṇa who walks behind you is in a swoon. Poor man! You have abandoned him! What manner of people are you?" When Subrahmaṇya Śāstri and Gaṅgādhara Śāstri looked back in alarm, Rāmaśāstri was standing silently in the middle of the path. His eyes were turned upwards. The students stood by and waited. The Śāstri's consciousness turned outwards. The Śāstri and his students then continued their journey. It is clear that the Śāstri possessed exceptional ability to engage in concentrated introspection, no matter how he was occupied.

The discipline of stilling one's mind, and the joy that this engenders enraptures the mind and induces tranquillity. This is how self-knowledge is attained. Çidānanda has said in his book *Jñānasindhu:*[638]

---

[637] Ilavāla is about 10 km northwest of Maisūru. Lakṣmaṇatīrtha is a river originating in the Brahmagiri region, which is the southern border of the Koḍagu region of Karṇāṭaka. It joins the Kāvērī near the village of Sāgarakaṭṭe near the Kṛṣṇarājasāgara reservoir. One must cross this river en route to Yeḍatore from Maisūru.

[638] Çidānanda *Avadhūta* was a Kannaḍa *Vīraśaiva* poet, whose best-known work is *Jñānasindhu.* The appellation *avadhūta* indicates that he had shaken off all worldly attachments. This verse translates as: "never censuring, accepting all censure | giving all away, urging all to take | forgiving those who speak no words of kindness ‖ lost in self-contemplation | with eyes open or shut slowly | know these to be the marks of the saintly ones ‖"

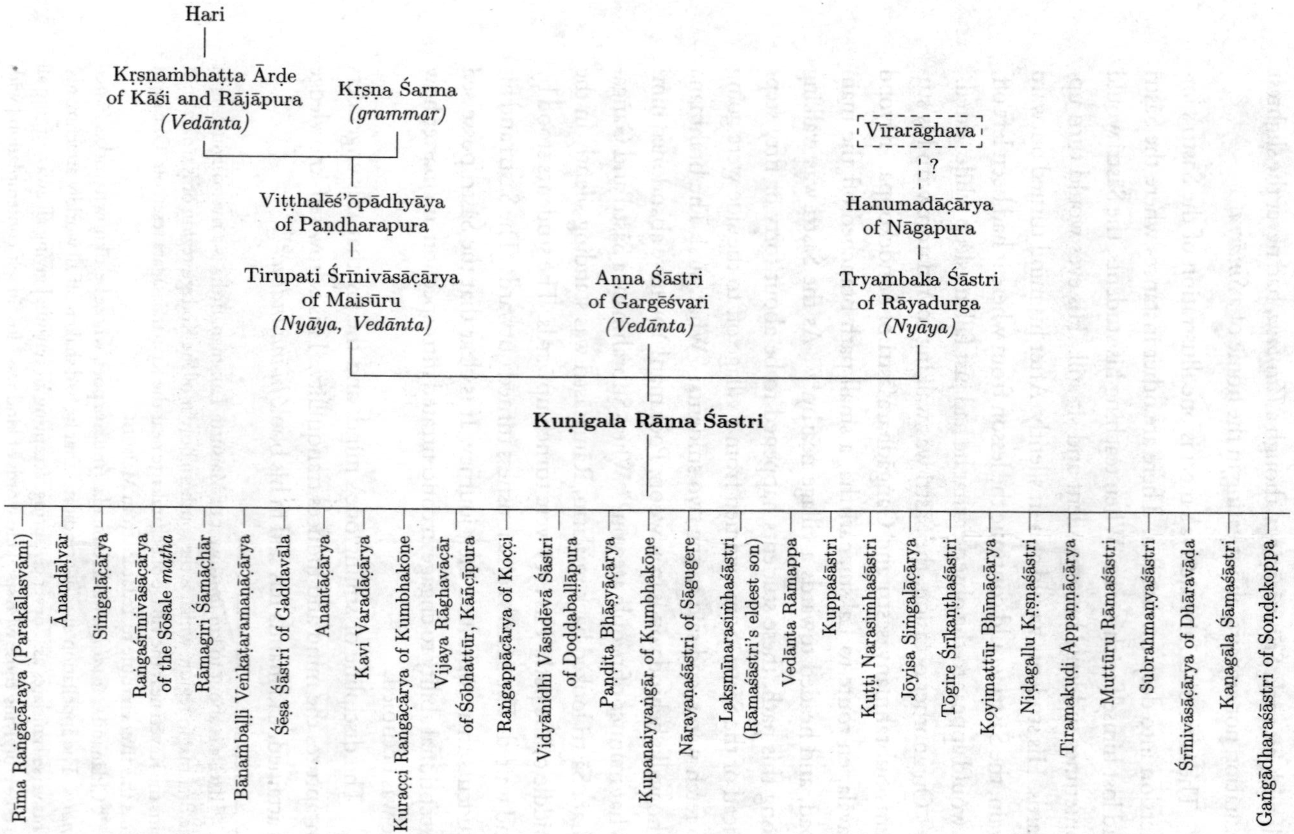

Plate 36: Translator's reconstruction of the academic genealogy of Kuṇigala Rāmaśāstri. See footnotes 491, 491, 662, and page 201.

bayyarāranu bayyakēḷvaru | ayyakoḷirendenutalīvaru | priyavaçanava nuḍivarārādoḍeyu mannisuta ‖ mayyamarevaru ātmaçinteya | loyyane kaṇderedu muççuta | ayyanenapiru jagake idu sādhugaḷa guṇavenda‖

Such is the description of this phenomenon by an omniscient being. If this indeed be sleep, then it is *yōgic* sleep; if this be sickness, then it is *yōgic* sickness. Some people even call this a sort of madness, or *śivalīle*.[639] Experience shows that this phenomenon occurs naturally in the case of many exceptional individuals. People everywhere who are accomplished in *yōgic* practices understand that this is merely regulation of the inner self. Those who do not understand *yōgic* practices think of this as *śivalīle*.

Rāmaśāstri never coveted anyone else's wealth. He hesitated even to dine in the homes of others. He would dine in someone's home only when invited, and only if they were strictly observant of tradition, rites, and rituals. Even many *laukikas* would observe rituals such as *Aupāsana*, since it would be an honour for them to have the Śāstri accept an invitation to eat in their home. The Śāstri would hesitate to even speak with someone whom he discovered to be unethical or immoral. Many people were especially fearful of him.

The Śāstri always spoke softly and carefully. His words and speech, however, flowed freely in a cascade, without the slightest impediment. He was always calm and peaceful, rarely losing his temper. It will shortly become clear that his wife Lakṣamma was of the same temperament.

We have seen that many of his students lived and boarded in the Śāstri's home. Subrahmaṇyaśāstri, who was from south of the pass, lived in the Śāstri's home in this manner. This Subrahmaṇyaśāstri once contracted a fever, having been afflicted with an excess of biliousness. Rāmaśāstri gave him his medicine. Subrahmaṇyaśāstri would not take it. Realizing that hunger was making his discomfort worse, the Śāstri and his wife mixed some rice with a little soup, and brought it to him on a leaf.[640] He took a little into his mouth, and retched. The Śāstri's wife then mashed the mixture, put it into a cup, and gave it to him to drink. At this point, Subrahmaṇyaśāstri, who was tormented by fever, spat the food in his mouth over the couple, threw

[639] *Śivalīle* literally means Śiva's sport, implying that the actions of the person afflicted are a manifestation of this divine sport.

[640] This soup was almost certainly *sāru*, a light broth of lentils and spices. It is traditional to eat meals on a banana leaf, or on plates of leaves stitched together. See footnote 472.

the leaf holding the remnants of his meal on them, shouted at them, and fell back asleep.[641] Rāmaśāstri laughed and stood up, saying: "Subrahmaṇya, you always were given to such foolishness! Why you fall ill is more than I can know! Never mind. Go back to sleep." His wife too, laughing, removed the impure and unclean mess, and applied *gomaya*. The couple both bathed. They were bothered only that all this should have befallen Subrahmaṇya, and carried not the least resentment in their minds at his having committed this base deed. Ordinary people would never display such forbearance. It is difficult for people to put up with this even from the children they have borne themselves.

The Śāstri, however, would be furious at anyone who disparaged *Vēdic* literature. On one occasion, in the Ātmavilāsa section of the palace, the *Mukhāmi* of the Ahōbala Maṭha called *Nyāya* an atheistical science.[642] He said this right in the very presence of Rāmaśāstri. The Śāstri was furious; he went right away to Ambāvilāsa. The king had just completed his Śiva worship, and was walking unclothed, still in a state of ritual purity. The Śāstri saw the king, and said: "Sir, this has now turned into a kingdom of imbeciles!" The king, seeing that the Śāstri was unusually upset, tried to calm him down.

A similar incident occurred on another occasion. Many people were envious of the Śāstri's renown not just in the local region, but also in other countries. An individual called Pantōji Subbarāya had been the recipient of the king's favour, for some reason.[643] Some of his people would gather in the palace, and were always on hand for idle chatter. The king had occasion to call the Śāstri to the palace one day. Before the Śāstri arrived at the palace, however, a loudmouth from among Pantōji Subbarāya's people said: "Rāmaśāstri come now? Hardly likely! He is seated, busily teaching

[641] Across all Indian cultures (except, of course, among Muslims, who eat communal meals) contact with saliva is regarded as causing extreme ritual impurity. Traditional brāhmaṇas will not even bite into a fruit, preferring to, say, eat a banana by breaking off pieces with their fingers. They will tilt their heads upwards and pour hot coffee into their mouths, rather than allow the cup to touch their lips. There are few greater insults in Indian culture than spitting on someone, even among Muslims. This is an almost inconceivable insult to a guru and his wife. See footnote 489.

[642] The Ahōbila Maṭha is a major *Śrīvaiṣṇava* institution, founded by Ādivaṇa Śaṭhagōpa Yatīndra Mahādēśikan, born in 1378 C.E., near Mēlukōṭe in present-day Karṇāṭaka. The *Vaḍagalai* (northern) sect of *Śrīvaiṣṇavas* are followers of this *maṭha*.

[643] Pantōji Subbarāo (Subbarāya) appears to have been an important palace official.

his students the atheistic doctrines of *Nyāya*!" Rāmaśāstri arrived just then. Upon hearing of this remark, Rāmaśāstri said angrily to the king: "Good sir, could it be permissible for this brāhmaṇa to speak thus? There are such things as the *Āstikaṣaṭka* and *Nāstikaṣaṭka*.[644] The *Āstikaṣaṭka* comprises *Tarka, Vēdānta, Jyōtiṣa, Vyākaraṇa, Mīmāṁsa,* and *Ayurvēda*.[645] Let this *Śrīvaiṣṇava* brāhmaṇa prove that logic is a *nāstika* science. I will then give up my status as a brāhmaṇa. If he fails, let him give up his status as a brāhmaṇa. I will not tolerate such words from base individuals!" The king summoned this *Śrīvaiṣṇava* brāhmaṇa, severely admonished him, terminated his salary, and had him removed from the palace. Finally, this brāhmaṇa came to Rāmaśāstri's home, waited for him, and then followed him around everywhere, apologizing for his remarks. Finally, Rāmaśāstri interceded with the king, and had his salary restored. Such were the incidents that angered the Śāstri.

The Śāstri's disposition was always cheerful. He would speak with his students with familiarity and humour, treating them like friends. He would play games with them, such as taking them to the woods, and plucking a particularly prickly fruit, and throwing it a distance for his students to run and catch; the one who caught it, he would call skilful. The students would run after it, struggling against each other, anxious to catch it. Catching it in a hurry, however, would cause the prickles to hurt their hand. This spectacle would be a great source of merriment to them all. This would be a good source of fun and exercise for students, and also alleviate any of their anxieties.

He would look for stammerers among students, and get them to participate in debates. He would do this for fun during the Gaṇēśa *maṅgaḷārati* celebrations in the month of Bhādrapada. The spectacle of the contestants

---

644 These terms mean 'theistic sextet' and 'atheistic sextet', respectively. They could also mean 'orthodox sextet', and 'heterodox sextet'.

645 This is not the standard listing of the *Āstikaṣaṭka*. In the *Sarvasiddhāntasaṅgraha* (1:23), attributed to *Ādi* Śaṅkara, the *Āstikaṣaṭka* is enumerated in terms of the progenitors of the respective *darśanas* as Akṣapāda *(Nyāya)*, Kaṇāda *(Vaiśeṣika)*, Kapila *(Saṅkhya)*, Jaimini *(Mīmāṁsa)*, Vyāsa *(Vēdānta)*, and Patañjali *(Yoga)*: *"akṣapāda kaṇādaṣca kapilo jaiministathā | vyāsa patañjaliṣcete vaidikā sūtrakārakā ‖"* At the end of Chapter 4, the *Nāstikaṣaṭka* is listed as *Lokāyatā*, *Arhata*, *Mādhyamika*, *Yogāçāra*, *Sautrāntika*, *Vaibhāsika*. The first two correspond to the *Çārvākas* and *Jainas*, and the last four correspond to the *Bauddha* schools.

debating each other while uttering a word every other minute would be amusing to the audience.

The Śāstri also played pranks to amuse others. A certain brāhmaṇa from Kōlāra, who called himself *Mahāpuruṣa,* visited the Śāstri occasionally. He was somewhat delusional; he had declared himself omniscient, and claimed that he could bring about the end of all creation. There was another brāhmaṇa called Gōdāvarī Veṅkaṭaśāstri, who was an expert in grammar. He had a stated desire to conduct a *santarpaṇa* for ten million brāhmaṇas, and kept asking Rāmaśāstri how he might accomplish this goal.[646] Rāmaśāstri suggested to him that if he were to carry a large pot on his head and call it an *akṣayapātra,* someone would be sure to put a handful of rice in it, and that he should then be able to feed ten million brāhmaṇas.[647] This Veṅkaṭaśāstri began to act accordingly. Whenever Rāmaśāstri met Veṅkaṭaśāstri, he would inquire: "How is the collection coming along? How many million now remain?" Such folk were always targets of ridicule. For people of exceptional brilliance, who spend all their time engrossed in issues of substance, such amusements are essential for maintaining their mental balance and to prevent their minds from becoming delusional due to excessive engagement with a single matter.

He had set a number of goals for himself. He wanted to train a number of his students in logic and *Vēdānta,* and send them to various countries. This goal was certainly attained. Even today, in Maisūru and the southern countries, the best-known scholars of logic and *Vēdānta* tend to be first-, second-, or third-generation students of Rāmaśāstri. In the great centres of *Saṁskṛta* scholarship in the northern regions of our country, such as Navadvīpa, Kāśī, and Darbhaṅga, students undertake a study of his works, such as *Śatakōṭi, Vyutpattivāda,* the *Pañçavādas, Uttaṛavāda,* and his numerous scholia, in their pursuit of great scholarship.

His other great wish was to complete all the *kratus* in the formally prescribed manner.[648] This was not an unrealistic desire on the part of Rāmaśāstri, who was looked upon with such favour by Kṛṣṇarāja Vōḍeyar III.

[646] See page 22.

[647] An *akṣayapātra* is a pot that serves as an inexhaustible source of food.

[648] A *kratu* is technically a *yajña* that includes an animal sacrifice, but the term is being used here in a generic sense to signify a *Vēdic* ritual. There are seven *saṁsthas* (varieties) each of the *pākayajña, haviryajña,* and *sōmayajña* classes. These are *nitya,* or mandated *yajñas,* as is clear from *Vēdic* injunctions such as *"yāvajjīvam agnihotram juhoti," "yāvajjīvam darśapūrṇamāsābhyām yajeta,"* and *"vasante vasante jyotiṣā yajeta."* Consequently,

Fate just happened to intervene. Because of his sudden, untimely demise, this goal, and his wish to accept *saṁnyāsa* in the sixtieth year and go to Kāśī both remained unfulfilled.

It appears that the Śāstri had land in Yeḍatore. Regardless, the yield from that land, the salary he received from places such as the Parakāla Maṭha and the palace, the various rewards that he received, as well as the considerations he received in symposia in other countries, were together insufficient to meet his expenses. He had to borrow money on occasion. As soon as his debts reached a thousand *Rūpīs*, he would embark on travels. Kāśīpati Śāstri and Kāśī Śēṣa Śāstri were his primary lenders. These two, Tōgire Sāmbamūrti Śāstri, and Tōgire Subbaśāstri of Çhatrada Bīdi were the Śāstri's chief friends. When the Śāstri died, he owed Kāśīpati Śāstri 3000 *Rūpīs.*[649]

Many of the Śāstri's scholarly contemporaries were ever quick to praise him. On one occasion, a debate took place between the Śāstri and the *Teṅgalai Śrīvaiṣṇava* scholar Govardhana Raṅgāçārya.[650] A *Vaiṣṇava* scholar called Mānamāḍi Madhvāçārya also joined the debate on the side opposing Rāmaśāstri. While presenting arguments in favour of the doctrines of Ānandatīrtha, Mānamāḍi Madhvāçārya said: "You don't understand the principles underlying *Mādhva* doctrines. This is not a logical argument," instead of responding to the points Rāmaśāstri had raised. Unable to countenance those words, Kāśī Śēṣa Śāstri, who was present in the audience said: "*Açārya,* you would do well to consider *Mādhva* doctrine sanctified by Rāmaśāstri's mere utterance of its name. Such bluster as you are attempting will not work against this Dakṣiṇāmūrti!"

Even when money came into Rāmaśāstri's hands, he would not keep it. He would hand his money over to others to keep for him. As he spent the money he had, he would request more, but would never ask for an accounting of the original sum. He was very trusting of others, and did not believe anyone would cheat him. A composed and steadfast mind is essential for

---

no merit accrues from their performance, but demerit does accrue from ignoring them. This may be one reason for Rāmaśāstri's interest in performing them all.

[649] Kāśī Śēṣa Śāstri appears prominently in the early part of this biography. Insufficient information is available regarding the others.

[650] Govardhana Raṅgāçārya (1810–1874 C.E.), a highly regarded *Śrīvaiṣṇavite* scholar, was originally from Kāñçi, but settled in Bṛndāvana near Mathura. Among his works are the *Sahasragītī*, a translation of Śaṭhakopa Nammāḻvār's *Tiruvāyamoli* from Tamiḻ verse into *Saṁskṛta* verse. He has also translated Nambillai's *Iḍumuppatārāyirappaḍi* into *Saṁskṛta.*

study and serious effort. If one keeps and manages money, one feels anxiety when it is spent and pleasure when it accumulates. Such emotions suffice to dissipate one's time, and disturb mental composure. The mind will not remain steadfast, but behave as a lamp might in a whirlwind.

Rāmaśāstri had three sons, named Lakṣmīnarasiṁhaśāstri, Yajñanārāyaṇaśāstri, and Śivasvāmi. He also had a daughter called Śrīlakṣmī. This daughter was born in the Paridhāvi *saṁvatsara* in Nañjanagūḍu.[651] She was married into the household of Kōṇūru Śāmaśāstri. This Śrīlakṣmī and the second son Yajñanārāyaṇa both died the same day in the Raktākṣi *saṁvatsara.*[652] We have already seen what became of the other two sons. Lakṣmīnarasiṁhaśāstri's son Rāmaśāstri is still a *Dharmādhikāri* in the palace.[653]

[651] She was born in the year 1852–1853 C.E.

[652] This would be the year 1864–1865 C.E., barely four or five years after Rāmaśāstri's demise.

[653] Kuṇigala Rāmaśāstri's descendants are still resident in Maisūru. According to the current head of the household of descendants (also named Kuṇigala Rāmaśāstri), Lakṣmīnarasiṁhaśāstri's son Rāmaśāstri was adopted. He was born to Narasiṁhaśāstri and Subbamma, and his name was originally Kṛṣṇaśāstri. However, he acquired the name Kuṇigala Rāmaśāstri after adoption. Since he too was known as *Dharmādhikāri* Kuṇigala Rāmaśāstri, it is easy to confuse him with his grandfather.

Chapter 14: His Many Virtues (2)

Rāmaśāstri possessed another great quality. He never spoke any untruths. He always spoke the truth in any circumstance. He firmly believed that one should not speak untruths even to forestall mischief by children, to the insane, or even in jest. Speaking falsehoods gives occasion to many evils. One must consider that good unto others underlies truth, and evil underlies falsehoods. Here, the word "others" does not merely signify one or two individuals. One must take it to mean everyone. People with even larger hearts would include all living beings in this creation.

Some people have come to accept falsehoods as justifiable if they are well intentioned. Thus, the police mislead criminals through falsehoods, gain their confidence, and then lead them to punishment. While it is proper to punish wrong-doers, jurists and ethicists do not see such falsehoods as acceptable, since people can be led to collude with police to escape mistreatment, and cause innocent people to be falsely implicated. Even when this leads to punishment for lawbreakers, the benefits that accrue thereby are less than the injuries resulting from the intervening falsehoods, so that the overall outcome is negative, on balance.[654] Similarly, in the domain of politics, some officials believe that any means they employ are justified, as long as it is done under the pretext of public service. Such ways result only in one measure of benefit for every nine of injury.

---

[654] The author M.S. Puṭṭaṇṇa is speaking from painful personal experience here. The following account comes from Puṭṭaṇṇa's granddaughter Sarōjā Veṅkaṭarām. A few years before this work was originally published, his two eldest sons M.P. Sōmaśēkhara Rāv and M.P. Sāmbamūrti Rāv arrived by train to Maisūru with a young student named Nañjuṇḍa, who was boarding and lodging in Puṭṭaṇṇa's home, although he was no relation. Their intention had been to study in Maisūru, while living with the well-known educator and journalist M. Veṅkaṭakṛṣṇayya (*Tātayya*), a good friend of Puṭṭaṇṇa's. A Tamilian lady who had travelled with them falsely accused them of having stolen her luggage. Nañjuṇḍa had gone to look for Veṅkaṭakṛṣṇayya's house, leaving the two young boys at the train station. The police arrested the three after he returned, and subjected them to painful tortures, including such outrages as inserting needles under their fingernails. After the boys fainted, a telegram was sent to Puṭṭaṇṇa, who rushed to Maisūru, abandoning the naming ceremony of his newborn son Kṛṣṇa. Puṭṭaṇṇa, a well-respected figure, secured the release of his sons from custody, and had the responsible police officials discharged from service.

False praise is said to be acceptable, since it allows the attainment of one's goals, yet causes no injury. There are many naïve individuals, however, who come to believe such false praise, and begin to see themselves as veritable mountains of virtue. The roots of any harm caused by such conceited individuals will truly lie in such false praise.

Some may regard the old saying *"a thousand falsehoods to make a marriage, a thousand falsehoods to save a life"*, as a moral guide. Such people concede at the outset that a falsehood, even under the said circumstances, is a transgression. The one who hides the truth and speaks untruth shares responsibility for the fruits of this transgression, as and when they become apparent. If, on the other hand, the beneficiary of an untruth cannot be blamed for the untruth, it is permissible to speak an untruth to bring them reward? This is a subtle ethical and moral question.

Falsehoods spoken as hyperbole, in jest, or in fear, are unpremeditated. Neither are they calamitous in effect. These have hence not come to be seen as infractions. If a calamity does result, however, the infraction will then have manifested its natural outcome.

People in the West sometimes distinguish white lies from black lies. They view a black lie as one that results in harm to someone and a white lie as one that does not, and see it as unacceptable to tell a black lie, but acceptable to tell a white lie if the occasion so demands. Even a white lie, as described above, does bring some harm into this world, and hence cannot be condoned. In certain narrow circumstances, perhaps, no harm results from a white lie; yet, if it becomes known that a person spoke an untruth, his reputation is sure to be damaged. This is certainly harm of one kind.

Even if no damage ultimately results, it was Rāmaśāstri's view that one should forswear untruths in all circumstances. Someone with this wicked habit may otherwise cause us harm, whether deliberately, or unknowingly. The outcomes of such untruths are forced upon us. Hence, in order that people may act rightly, even the *Vēdas* contain the injunction *"satyaṁ vada, dharmaṁ çara"*, meaning, speak the truth, and act righteously.[655]

---

[655] This is from the *Taittirīyōpaniṣad* (*Śīkṣāvallī* 19): *"vēdaṁanūççayāçāryō–ntevāsinamanuśāsti | satyam vada | dharmam çara | svādhyāyānmā pramadaḥ | āçāryāya priyam dhanamahṛtya prajātantum mā vyavatççhētsīḥ | satyānna pramaditavyam | dharmānna pramaditavyam | kuśalānna pramaditavyam | bhūtyai na pramaditavyam | svādhyāyaprvaçanābhyām na pramaditavyam ‖"* Meaning: "Having instructed the student in the

There is another approach to considering the effects of a falsehood on the mind of one who hears it.[656]

satyaṁbrūyāt priyaṁbrūyānnabrūyāt satyamapriyaṁ |
priyañçanānṛtaṁbrūyāt sūkṣmādharmagatiḥparā ‖

This means: "One must speak the truth. One must speak what is pleasant. One must not speak the truth if unpleasant. One must not speak untruth even if it is a pleasant one. This is the subtlest moral path." The truth is surely pleasant. The truth, however, may be unpleasant for some. When we are constrained to answer a question, we must speak the truth whether or not it is pleasant to all. However, when there are no such constraints, we are not compelled to speak the truth for everyone to hear. There are many disagreeable aspects about the human body. There are many delicate aspects. It would be speaking the truth to discuss these at length. But who is ignorant of these facts? Even if someone were thus ignorant, it would offend respectable people were a woman to speak truthfully about these matters to a man. There is no requirement that such truths be spoken. Neither would there be detriment to anyone if these were left unspoken. Such truths need not be spoken in these circumstances.

However, if it were necessary to discuss such a matter at length in a court of law, where it is being determined whether an accused is to be punished or set free, it is irrelevant whether or not the truth is pleasant. This consideration does not apply to other, and more ordinary situations.

When Drōṇāçārya's blows gained in strength, the Pāṇḍavas feared impending defeat. To cause Drōṇa to cease battle, Kṛṣṇa said to Dharmarāya: "Shout out loudly that Drōṇa's son Aśvatthāma has died." Dharmarāya replied that this would be a falsehood, since Aśvatthāma had the boon of eternal life. He agreed to Kṛṣṇa's suggestion, however, that he shout out

Vēdas, the teacher exhorts him | speak the truth | act according to dharma | do not neglect the study of the *Vēdas* | having gathered the wealth for your teacher that he desires, do not sever the line of procreation | do not stray from the truth | do not neglect dharma | do not stray from what is beneficial | do not stray from prosperity | do not stray from *Vēdic* learning and teaching ‖"

[656] This is verse 4:138 of the *Manusmṛti.*

that an elephant named Aśvatthāma had died.[657] Upon consideration, it is clear, however, that Dharmarāya well knew that Drōna would suffer hurt, no matter in what manner he declared Aśvatthāma dead. Thus, an elephant by that name did die, and announcing that fact was not an untruth. Yet, there is no doubt that this constitutes an unpleasant truth.

A gang of thieves once broke into the house of a brāhmaṇa who always spoke the truth. The people next door to him were rich. When the brāhmaṇa said to these thieves: "I am truthful, but poor. My neighbours are rich," the thieves entered the neighbour's home and looted it.[658] It is certainly true that these neighbours were rich. Yet, this brāhmaṇa's speaking this truth when the thieves did not ask him to, indeed makes it an unpleasant truth. No demerit accrues from not speaking such a truth. Demerit does accrue, however, from speaking such a truth. In such circumstances, it is important to consider the ethical and moral consequences of one's actions.

False praise and hyperbole are rather related to the category of pleasant untruths. While it is wrong to speak untruths, it is heinous indeed to speak unpleasant untruths. Even if this is pleasant to one person, it is unpleasant to another, and causes detriment. Some people speak pleasant untruths to children. We can be certain, however, that such people lack foresight. Even if children believe us in the interim, there is the risk of their losing all faith in us, if they come to see the untruth in our words. In fact, if these children make a habit of speaking untruths, there are no limits to the criminality engendered thereby. We can estimate in advance the end results of speaking untruths to the insane.

Most importantly, the truth is what comes naturally. Untruths are unnatural. The first is indispensable for those of upright character, the second to those whose character is warped. Even if one disregards the principle that one should speak the truth regardless of consequences, and looks at it from

---

[657] This is a famous episode from the *Mahābhārata* (*Drōṇaparva*). Drōṇa proved impossible to vanquish in battle, so Kṛṣṇa contrived the following deceit. He had Yudhiṣṭhira shout out that an elephant called Aśvatthāma had been killed, and arranged to have loud noises made to coincide with the word "elephant". (In some recensions, Yudhiṣṭhira utters the word "elephant" under his breath.) Given Yudhiṣṭhira's reputation for honesty and integrity, Drōṇa was thereby led to believe that his son Aśvatthāma had been killed, and lay down his arms. Droṇa was then killed by Dhṛṣṭadyumna.

[658] A version of this story appears in the *Nīticintāmaṇi* by M.S. Puṭṭaṇṇa, a collection of stories for children illustrating moral principles. The immediately preceding *Saṁskṛta* verse appears as epigraph in this story.

the perspective of outcome, it will still be apparent that the truth leads to benefits, while untruth leads to detriment. This is why the Śāstri had established the principle of speaking the truth under all circumstances.

Not only did Rāmaśāstri himself never speak untruths, he would not tolerate untruths from anyone else, either. On one occasion, it came to the Śāstri's attention that one of his students had spoken an untruth in some context. He immediately called the student, and said: "From now on, you are forbidden from entering this house, or coming to me for instruction. Take yourself away immediately," had him removed from the house, and forbade his other students from speaking with him. The student was deeply remorseful from that moment on. The Śāstri would not change his mind even though the student lay down fasting for two whole days in front of the Śāstri's doorstep. He changed his mind only after the Śāstri's wife pleaded with him in a great many ways to show the student mercy.

Chapter 15: His Many Virtues (3)

A unique radiance was manifest on the face of this virtuous Śāstri. His greatness was widely known. No official who visited Maisūru would leave without visiting him. Once, a person called Kṛṣṇamanāyaka, who was head *Śirastedār* at the Commissioner's office in Beṅgaḷūru, and was respectfully addressed as *Dīvān,* came to Maisūru; after meeting Kṛṣṇarāja Voḍeyar III, he visited the Śāstri's house.[659] It was about 8–8:30 in the morning. The Śāstri's students saw him, and seated him with due respect. The Śāstri, who was inside, came out after finishing his bath, and having donned his *vibhūti* and *rudrākṣi*. He spoke with the *Nāyaka* most graciously, and saw him off with respect. The Śāstri inspired great respect in the *Nāyaka.* As he was returning, he said to his companions that he had never seen such radiance on anyone, and that seeing him was like experiencing divinity. The Śāstri's brilliance and his mental composure were clearly evident upon his countenance.

Rāmaśāstri was never partial to anyone. Neither did he tolerate such behaviour on the part of others. On some occasion, the palace distributed gifts to all *vaidikas.* Many of Rāmaśāstri's students received a pair of shawls. Somehow, a person called Dhāravāḍada Śrīnivāsāçārya happened to be overlooked. The issue was not raised at the time. The next day, as the students were speaking with each other, it became clear that only the *Āçārya* from Dhāravāḍa had not received a gift. When some students asked him why he had not received a gift, Dhāravāḍada Śrīnivāsāçārya replied: "I too would have received a pair of shawls, had I but worn *vibhūti.*"[660]

The next morning, as the students were studying, someone informed the Śāstri of what had transpired. When the Śāstri heard this, he immediately anguished that he had not learned of this on the day the oversight occurred, and went inside, brought out a shawl, and draped it on the student. Dhāravāḍada Śrīnivāsāçārya struggled with a dilemma—if he accepted the shawl, that would cause the Śāstri a loss, but if he did not, the Śāstri would

---

[659] This is surely Kollam Krisnama Naidu, who was *Huzūr Head Śirastēdār* during 1844–1858 [Rao 1936a, p. 487; Row 1916, p. 114]. He had apparently served as the head of the English Department at the palace and next as a *Munsif* under the British Commission.

[660] *Vibhūti* is only worn by *Smārtas. Vaiṣṇavas* and *Śrīvaiṣṇavas* wear vertical marks on their forehead called *nāmas* in Kannaḍa. See footnote 134.

be displeased—but finally, considering the shawl a blessing from the guru, accepted it.

Rāmaśāstri would not bear causing hurt to others. He would anguish even if it were an animal that was suffering. Compassion for all creatures was present in ample measure in this great man. One day, the Śāstri was returning home at around noon. It was summer, and the heat intense. Water had to be fetched from some distance. He saw his student Dhāravāḍada Śrīnivāsāçārya, who was weak in body, struggling to carry a pot of water, and rueing the student's situation, helped carry the pot home.

Other scholars who were his contemporaries had enormous respect for the Śāstri. Kāśī Timmaṇṇāçārya was a leading scholar of logic in Maisūru.[661] Gadādhara Bhaṭṭāçārya is the author of an eponymous masterwork called the *Gadādharīya.* A commentary on this work has been written by Kṛṣṇa Bhaṭṭāçārya.[662] This Kṛṣṇa Bhaṭṭāçārya had two students called Ramaṇāçārya and Viṭṭhalōpādhyāya. We have seen that Rāmaśāstri's guru Tirupati Śrīnivāsāçārya was a student of Viṭṭhalōpādhyāya. Ramaṇāçārya happened to be Kāśī Timmaṇṇāçārya's elder brother. Rāmaśāstri had special faith and regard for Timmaṇṇāçārya because of this connection in their academic lineage. As soon as the news arrived one morning that Timmaṇṇāçārya had passed away, the Śāstri, who was seated, teaching his students, stopped his teaching, sent his students away, and before the corpse was removed, went

---

[661] See footnote 579.

[662] This Kṛṣṇa Bhaṭṭāçārya is likely none other than Kṛṣṇaṁbhaṭṭa Ārḍe, the son of Raṅganātha and Kamala, and brother of Nārāyaṇa, dated to 1750–1825 C.E. in [Gode 1956]. On page 19, this reference also alludes to an Ārḍe family still resident in Rājapur Tāluka of Ratnāgiri, as late as 1856 C.E., corroborating the information in footnote 491. We quote from [Gode 1956]: "Aufrecht records about 74 works of this author. In CG II, 23 and CG III, 26 Aufrecht calls him son of Raṅganātha. In CC III, 114 he informs us that one Raṅganātha Ārad, son of Mahādeva, wrote *Daśakumāraçaritapūrvapīṭhikāsāra* (Stem 81). Hall in his edition of the Vāsavadatta (Bib. Ind. 1859) states that a rumour had reached him regarding a commentary on the Vāsavadatta by Kṛṣṇabhaṭṭa Ārḍe but Aufrecht makes no mention of this commentary. Hall farther informs us in footnote 1 on p 47 of his Preface to Vāsavadatta as follows—Krsnabhatta was 'a Maratha of Benares, son of Raṅganātha and pupil of one Hari. Among his works are huge commentaries on the *Nirṇayasindhu, Gadādharī,* and *Jagadīśī.* The second is called *Kāśikā* or *Gadādharīvivṛtti,* and the third *Mañjūṣā* or *Jagadīṣatōṣiṇī....*' M M Professor P.V. Kane makes the following remarks... The foregoing remarks of several scholars like Hall, Aufrecht, Kane, reveal that Kṛṣṇabhaṭṭa Ārḍe was not only a great logician but also a learned commentator on works pertaining to Dharmasastra and Kāvya..."

to Timmaṇṇācārya's home, spoke words of courage to his children, and returned after having accompanied the body to the cremation grounds.

A nearly forgotten piece of information is that the Śāstri had a weakness for sweet foods. He liked hot foods rather less. He always ate in the company of his students. He never ate without them, regardless of how late the hour was. As they ate, he would engage his students with humour. He would recount amusing anecdotes and tales, making everyone laugh. No one would feel any tedium, no matter how long the meal took. The Śāstri went to bed after 10–11 o'clock. It is not clear whether he slept for even three hours. According to the students who were close to him, the Śāstri could be seen sitting on his bed no matter how late the hour; it appears that he would be in a state of *samādhi*, having meditated upon his breathing.

The Śāstri's students all had enormous love and respect for him. Every student who spoke of the Śāstri did so with great enthusiasm, and recounting stories of his life, would say: "We will never again see a thing such as this", and shed tears. I have beheld this with my own eyes.

The biography of this great man has all been about his scholarship. It is impossible to take its measure, or tell its beginning, or its end. On another occasion, a scholar from Navadvīpa who held the title *Tarkabrahma* came to Maisūru from the North. This *Tarkabrahma* met the king, and proceeded to visit the Sarasvatī Bhaṇḍāra in the palace.[663] When he perused the works on *Nyāya*, he found but a few of them. He spoke disparagingly, saying: "When the palace library, with such a name as Sarasvatī Bhaṇḍāra has so few advanced works on logic, what could a famed scholar of logic, such as Rāmaśāstri have studied?" He went to the Śāstri's home, but did not find many books there, either. This foreign scholar's pride in his own scholarship swelled. A debate lasting several days took place between *Tarkabrahma* and Rāmaśāstri. As *Tarkabrahma* began presenting propositions from books that existed only in the North but not in the South, Rāmaśāstri continued responding to him and making refutations. This scholar then praised Rāmaśāstri before the king, saying that even when challenged with arguments in books he had never read, Rāmaśāstri had responded perfectly, and that such scholarship must be counted as exceptional brilliance.

[663]This is the Royal Library. Sadly, according to Rao [1936b, p. 178], the fire of 1897 C.E. destroyed a fifth of the entire palace "...including the *Sejje* and the three stories above it to the gold pinnacles, the Sanskrit Library, the armoury, the music-room and the Balakhana."

The Śāstri was especially devoted to God. He would occasionally walk to Nañjanagūḍu with his family.[664] Some of his students would carry the luggage, others would carry his children, and still others would carry the *Aupāsanāgni*.[665] En route, near Mallanamūle, if the Kabinī was full and flowing, the Śāstri would jump off the bridge into the water, and swim to the opposite shore.[666]

He would stand before the deity at the Nañjanagūḍu temple and start reciting *stōtras* with great devotion, his eyes full of tears.[667] It is natural for such tears to flow from the eyes of those in whose hearts are combined devotion and compassion. A *paramahaṁsa* has said that certain emotions expressed in divine presence are especially strong in the case of those who have left no remaining births, and are fulfilling their final birth. Rare indeed it is for such blessed individuals to be born in this world. Some believe the Śāstri to have been a devotee of Narasiṁha.

Rāmaśāstri had high regard for ritual. We have already seen that he had wished to perform all *kratus*. He kept up efforts towards this goal. Preliminary to performing *kratus*, the *śāstras* require the performance of a ritual called *Ādhāna* to establish the *Śrautāgni*. The Śāstri made efforts to perform this ritual. Four *ṛtviks* are needed for this ritual. They are to receive such *dakṣiṇa* as horses and chariots. He made preparations for such gifts.

An *araṇi* was required for the ceremony. The performer of the ritual had to seek out an *araḷī* tree that had grown entwined with a *banni* tree, find a branch growing in a specific direction, cut this branch down on a certain prescribed day after having bathed and completed his daily rituals, while reciting certain prescribed *mantras*.[668] An *araṇi* may be constructed from this branch if it were to fall to the ground in a particular direction when cut. The *araṇi* resembles a wooden basin. If one places bits of dried cowdung in it, and churns it with another piece of wood in the manner of a drill, heat is produced, causing the pieces of cowdung to ignite. The *yajña* is to be performed with that fire.

[664]Nañjanagūḍu is about 25 km from Maisūru.

[665]The *Aupāsanāgni* is the domestic fire in which the *Aupāsana* sacrifice is offered. See footnote 234.

[666]This is likely the bridge built by *Daḷavāi* Dēvarājayya in 1753 C.E., which was later converted into a railway bridge. It is now in disuse, but enjoys the status of a heritage monument, being the oldest railway bridge in India.

[667]This deity is Śrīkaṇṭhēśvara, that is, Śiva.

[668]The *araḷī* tree is *Ficus religiosa*. *Banni* is *Prosopis cinerāria*.

He had the region searched for a suitable *araḷī* tree. A suitable tree was found in a village in the district of Hoḷēnarasīpura.[669] He cut down the branch himself, in the prescribed manner. It fell in the direction prescribed in the *śrautas*. The Śāstri was very pleased. He had two *araṇis* constructed from that branch. He had other implements for the *yajña* made from other woods.[670] The most auspicious date and time for the *yajña* was determined. Everything was in order.

When the Śāstri returned home after bathing in the lake on the appointed day, however, he learned that his wife had started her monthly period.[671] The Śāstri felt deep sorrow at what had come to pass, despite his planning for the ritual having taken into account such impediments. As he approached his home, and heard this news, he stopped there awhile. He

---

[669] Hoḷēnarasīpura is 80 km from Maisūru. The search for the right tree clearly had been extensive.

[670] The construction of these implements is specified in great detail in the *sūtras*. The *araṇi*, for example, is to be constructed of *aśvattha* (*araḷī* in Kannaḍa) wood, and measure 16×12×4 inches. There are some 36 other implements of various shapes and sizes, and used for various purposes in the performance of the *yajña.* For instance, the *Taittirīya Saṁhita* specifies the following implements: *sphai, kapālāni, agnihōtrahavaṇī, śūrpa, kṛṣṇājina, śamyā, ūlūkhala, musala, dṛṣat, upala, juhū, upabhṛt, sruva, dhruvā, prāśitraharaṇa, iḍāpātra, mēkṣaṇa, piṣṭōdvapanī, praṇītāpraṇayana, ājyasthālī, vēda, dārupātrī, yōktra, vēdaparivāsana, dhṛṣṭi, idhmapravraṣçana, anvāhāryasthālī, madantī, antardhānakaṭa, phalīkaraṇa, asida, aśvaparśu, upavēṣa, dōhana, sānnāyatapanī,* and the *śākhāpavitra,* made from a variety of different woods. In addition, there are implements such as the *nirvāpapātrī, sadaṁṣa, śikya, śakaṭa, pariśrayaṇa,* various pots, and so on.

[671] The menstrual period is a period of ritual impurity for a woman, who would have been confined during this time. All Indian rituals require the presence of the *yajamāna* and his wife, so the *yajña* he was contemplating could not have been completed at the appointed auspicious time. The most propitious time for the ritual would have been determined by astrological calculations, and would have passed by the time his wife's ritual purity had been regained. See *Manusmṛti, 5.66: "rātribhirmāsatulyābhirgarbhasrāve viśudhyati | rajasyuparate sādhvī snānena strī rajasvalā ‖"* The concern over various forms of ritual pollution (see *maḍi*, footnote 208) is extreme, and in observant brāhmaṇa households, entry to certain sections of the house, such as the household shrine and the kitchen, is reserved for those who are ritually pure. The timing here appears to have been most unfortunate. The *yajña* would have commenced with a *dīkṣa* ritual for Rāmaśāstri and his wife, which is a ritual equivalent of birth and death [Knipe 2015, p. 50]. After *dīkṣa*, the couple would have been immune to ritual pollutions, including those due to death in the family, or menstruation. If the wife menstruates after *dīkṣa* (a certainty for non-menopausal women, since some *yajñas* last weeks or months), she does not pollute the ritual; she may remain in the *yajña bhūmi* or sacrificial ground, and would continue her duties while confined to the *patniśāla.* She would, however, be untouchable for the menstrual period.

thought to himself: "Alas! With such preparations, and the care with which I would have conducted this ritual, Yajñēśvara himself would have come to accept the sacrifice.[672] Because this impediment has arisen in this circumstance, it appears to be divine will that I should not conduct this ritual. One cannot go against this," and without entering his home, he left for Paṣcimavāhinī without even eating his meal. He returned only after three days, after his friends and his students urged him to overcome his deep sadness.

It appears that after Yajñanārāyaṇa, the Śāstri had three daughters including Śrīlakṣmī, and that excepting for Śrīlakṣmī, the others all died without having left the birth-chamber. The Śāstri performed the *puṁsavana,* or the *sīmanta,* ceremony to ensure the birth of a son. The *sīmanta* is one of the sixteen *karmas.*[673] He believed firmly that performing this rite would result in the birth of a son. This was the substance of the conversation he had with his student Subrahmaṇyaśāstri.

A son was indeed born, in conformance with his beliefs in these rituals. Neither was this any ordinary son. Born to him was one to whom even the greatest monarchs must bow down, one with the rank of emperor among ascetics. Every emperor has his subordinate kings. He also has enemies who will not salute him. But this son has only followers, and no enemies. An emperor may hold temporal sway, but has no assurance of any standing in the other world. This son holds sway in both worlds equally, is truly without enemies, and reigns over the kingdom of deliverance.

Saṁpūrṇa

---

[672] Yajñēśvara, the lord of the sacrifice, is Viṣṇu.

[673] See footnote 246.

APPENDIX A: EXCERPTS FROM D.V. GUṆḌAPPA'S *JÑĀPAKA ÇITRAŚĀLE*

Some Students of Kuṇigala Rāmaśāstri. Other Reminiscences

The following selection from Gundappa [1970, v. 5] provides some additional information about Vāsudēvaśastri, one of Kuṇigala Rāmaśāstri's foremost students, and other contemporary scholars. It also provides additional insight into a period of transition for traditional Indian scholarship.

The Students of Vāsudēvaśastri

It is my understanding that Vāsudēvaśastri was from Doḍḍaballāpura.[674] His Highness had conferred upon him the title *Vidyānidhi*. He was surely the foremost of the scholars in Maisūru who might rank as *Vidyānidhis*.[675] He had also acquired renown as *"Jaganmithyā"* Vāsudēvaśastri. In a debate in a scholarly assembly held in the presence of the *Jagadguru* of Śṛṅgēri,[676] he established the *Advaitic* doctrine *"brahma satyam jaganmithyā"* using the *Vēdas* as well as ingenious arguments. It appears that the *Svāmi,* impressed by his scholarship and eloquence, praised him by referring to him as *"Jaganmithyā"* Vāsudēvaśastri.[677]

His Students

Vāsudēvaśastri had no peer in logic, grammar, and hermeneutics. A great many of the renowned scholars in Beṅgaḷūru were his students. I have been privileged to have had the opportunity to speak to several of them on occasion. Chief among them were Sāggere Nārāyaṇaśāstri, Dēvanagondi Nārāyaṇaśāstri, Doḍḍabele Nārāyaṇaśāstri, and Veṅkaṭēśaśastri of Soṇḍekoppa. I have forgotten the names of many others. Vāsudēvaśastri had a great many students.

---

[674] Vāsudēvaśastri was a senior student of Kuṇigala Rāmaśāstri, and appears repeatedly in the biography of Rāmaśāstri. Not surprisingly, many of his students also appear as students of Kuṇigala Rāmaśāstri.

[675] Others had received the same title, such as Virūpākṣa Śāstri [Gundappa 1970, v. 5, p. 154].

[676] This would have been *Jagadguru* Śrī Saccidānanda Śivābhinava Nṛsiṁha Bhāratī, the son of Kuṇigala Rāmaśāstri, who was Vāsudēvaśāstri's teacher.

[677] Vāsudēvaśastri had already done this earlier, in the company of Kuṇigala Rāmaśāstri, in Madrās. See page 252.

Doḍḍabele Nārāyaṇaśāstri

Doḍḍabele Nārāyaṇaśāstri has performed immense service to the cause of Kannaḍa literature. He has composed verbatim notes and commentaries on works such as the *Jaimini Bhārata*. He has also published notes and commentaries on works such as the *Bhagavadgīta, Viveka Çūḍāmaṇi,* and the *Raghuvaṁśa.* In Kannaḍa, he has written a book called *Devaraseve*, a book of bhajans called *Hanūmannāmāmṛta*, and many other smaller works. Bhajans such as *"Śuddha brahma paratpara rāma"* were popular in those times. Doḍḍabele Śāstri has composed several works of the same sort on bhajans in praise of Śiva, Hanumān, and other deities. Doḍḍabele Śāstri was eloquent, and a courageous debator. With the support of the Śivagaṅgā *saṁsthāna,* he ran the monthly *Śāradā*, and sometime later, the monthly *Vidyānanda*. It was in these monthlies that the *Viveka Çūḍāmaṇi* and the poetical works mentioned above appeared. In addition to works such as these, he also published works relating to the *śāstras* and literature. His style was simple, and motivated the average reader.

Dēvanagondi Nārāyaṇaśāstri

I studied logic for a bit with Dēvanagondi Nārāyaṇaśāstri. I became aware that his income had become seriously deficient. I wrote to B. Rāmakṛṣṇarāya, the Palace Controller, bringing this to his notice. Four or five months went by. I received no reply. One afternoon, I happened to be seated in the offices of the magazine *Karnāṭaka* on Guṇḍōpant street, occupied with something. Dēvanagondi Nārāyaṇaśāstri arrived, and stood before me with an envelope in his hand. I spoke up:

Me: Do have a seat.

Śāstri: (In Telugu) You are younger than I am. But I feel obliged to do you obeisance.

Humility was written on his face. Tears seemed about to flow from his eyes. I blocked his attempt to do me reverence, and asked: "What is going on?"

He handed me the envelope, and asked me to read it. It contained a letter from the palace. "Dēvanagondi Nārāyaṇaśāstri has been appointed a scholar at the palace." I thanked Rāmakṛṣṇarāya in my mind, and asked the Śāstri:

Me: How is this of value to you?

Śāstri: This will mean five (or six) *Rūpīs* a month.

Me: Is that all? Why all this fuss, then?

Here is the gist of what he said:

"Good sir, you are still young. It is important that people such as you know how difficult our circumstances are. I was a student of Sāggere Nārāyaṇaśāstri. I visited him at home one afternoon. I saw him sitting immersed in worry, with his elbow on his knee and his head in his hand. He did not raise his head to look at me. Whenever he had seen me, he had always greeted me, saying 'Come dear boy.' That afternoon, he had not even noticed that I had arrived. His mind was completely absent. I waited a couple of minutes as asked: 'Dear Śāstri, are you bothered by a headache?' He then raised his head, looked at me, smiled a little, and said: 'Yes, dear boy. I do have a headache now. But it awaits you tomorrow.' 'What does this mean?' I asked. He said: 'I studied logic with Vāsudēvaśāstri for twelve years. This headache is its fruition. Tomorrow is the anniversary of my sire's passing. I was worrying about how to arrange for the necessities. The storekeepers who would lend me money have lent me all they can lend. I cannot ask them to lend me more. I am concerned about where to turn now. I would not have had such a headache had I become a clerk or a schoolmaster instead of studying logic. It is still not too late for you to learn this. This is all that logic is good for. The child is dead. What remains is the fragrance of the clothes in its crib. My study of logic is done. What has remained is this headache.'

"Such is my plight, as well. Now that you have arranged for me to receive this salary from the palace, I can at least look forward to rice gruel once a day. I thank God a thousand times for this favour."

Dēvanagondi Nārāyaṇaśāstri was a person of great dignity. He was also most observant of precept and ritual. He was not the sort to speak up loudly. I was given to some light-hearted teasing: "Logicians are garrulous, long-winded. Despite this reputation, how is it that you are polite and decorous?"

***

Vidyānidhi Vāsudēvaśāstri's house was large. It extended from Guṇḍōpant street to Haḷeteregupēṭe.[678] He hosted, fed, and taught a number of students in his house.

He generally taught *Tarka, Vyākaraṇa, Pūrva Mīmāṁsa, Uttara Mīmāṁsa,* and *Jyōtiṣa.* All his students became well-known scholars.

Vāsudēvaśāstri belonged to the Velanāḍu community. Chief among his relatives was V.B. Subbayya, the owner of well-known publishing houses and presses. (An institution called V.B. Subbayya and Sons flourishes even to this day.)

Subrahmaṇya Śāstri

Siddhānti Subrahmaṇya Śāstri was the husband of Vāsudēvaśāstri's sister. He was a renowned astrologer. He has written commentaries on numerous Kannaḍa works such as the *Siddharāmapurāṇa.* He used to publish an almanac under the aegis of the Śṛṅgēri *maṭha.*

Subrahmaṇya Śāstri has written a translation of the *Upaniṣads* called the *Upaniṣatsāra.* He has discussed the essence of the *Upaniṣads* and the *Brahmasūtras* in this work. Garaṇi *vaiyākaraṇi* Kṛṣṇāçārya[679] was a very close friend of his.

Siddhānti Subrahmaṇya Śāstri's son was *Mahāmhōpādhyāya* Śivaśaṅkara Śāstri. Like his father, he too was learned in many fields, and had scholarship in both Kannaḍa and *Saṁskṛta.*

---

[678] The distance between Guṇḍōpant street and Haḷeteregupēṭe street, marking the extent of Vāsudēvaśāstri's property, appears to be about 400 feet.

The following fascinating details appear in Gundappa [1970, v. 5, p. 88]. Guṇḍōpant was an administrative official during the times when the administration Mysore was entrusted to various Commissioners. His home was in the middle of the northern side of the street that bears his name. A printing press called the "Irish Press", and the offices of the Kannaḍa magazine *Karṇāṭaka* (in a hall on the upper floor) were both in this structure. Subsequently, it was home to the offices of the magazine *Economic Review* run by Hayavadana Rāv, and later, it became a wholesale market. A few houses to the east of the home of Guṇḍōpant was the *çhatra* of Pūrṇayya. Vāsudēvaśāstri's house was situated between this *çhatra* and the home of Guṇḍōpant. This area was called *Siddhī Kaṭṭe.*

As an aside, the translator speculates *Siddhī Kaṭṭe* to be a derivative of "City Market". The change from "City" to *Siddhī* (a common girl's name in Kannaḍa) is obvious. Further, the English word "market", to Kannaḍa ears, sounds very close to *Māru Kaṭṭe,* which literally means "sales platform". The net result is *Siddhī Maru Kaṭṭe*, or simply *Siddhī Kaṭṭe.*

[679] Footnote in original: "*Jñāpaka Çitraśāle,* 1, pp. 104–110."

Śivaśaṅkara Śāstri

Śivaśaṅkara Śāstri was the president of the Kannaḍa Literary Conference in Bijāpura. I recall that he delivered his presidential address in poetry. He was capable of effortlessly composing poetry of any form in any desired metre, starting with any syllable. His compostions were grammatically pure and conformed to all relevant rules and principles. They were a bit difficult, however, for those who were less knowledgeable.

> *çinmaya rūpanīśanabhavam sale rājase çittadoḷ*
> *sanmati sadvidhēya śivaśaṅkara śarmaninādudu buddhibhā*
> *svanmahasīyarellaridanōdi...*

Śivaśaṅkara Śāstri had undertaken another task—that of showing in verse, the meaning of every name in each of the five *sahasranāmas*—the *Veṅkaṭēśa Sahasranāma,* the *Śiva Sahasranāma,* the *Lalitā Sahasranāma,* and the *Gaṇēśa Sahasranāma.* Five thousand verses in all. He had the first five or eight hundred verses published on glossy paper in the Bangalore Press. Included with the verses were images of various deities. I had seen it when the work was in progress. I had marvelled at it. What scholarship, what fluency, what courage, and what determination! I had never seen the like before. When the Śāstri lectured, it was the same. An astonishing level of eloquence.

The Śāstri was knowledgeable in matters of the divine—he understood the deeper significance of *mantras, tantras,* and the *śāstras,* and was a devotee of Subrahmaṇya. Beḷḷāvi Veṅkaṭanāraṇappa had spent several months in Madarās studying for his M.A. degree.[680] Veṅkaṭanāraṇappa's dedication was profound. He had curtailed his eating and sleeping during his preparations. He became ill as a result of his reading, writing, and working on mathematics all day and night. His intensity would apparently often result in his losing consciousness. At the time, Veṅkaṭanāraṇappa's house was in Beṅgaḷūru's Alasūrupēṭe, near B.V. Subbayya's house. Alarmed, the members of Veṅkaṭanāraṇappa's household brought this situation to Śivaśaṅkara Śāstri's attention, who was able to effect a cure with *vibhūti, kuṁkuma,* and *bilvākṣate.*

Towards the end of his days, Śivaśaṅkara Śāstri took over the management of the Kumārasvāmi temple on the Mount Joy hill in Beṅgaḷūru from

[680] A detailed biography of Veṅkaṭanāraṇappa appears in [Gundappa 1970, v. 5].

the government,[681] and did a great service to devotees by arranging for regular worship and other ceremonies. He had a new icon of *Aṣṭabhuja Gaṇapati* installed. I too, had attended that ceremony. His work brought grace upon that hill.

> *pratyakṣādbhuta ṣaṇmukha mṛtyuñjaya kumāra giri śṛṅgam |*
> *bhaktāpraṇamata... śivaliṅgam ||*

Those troubled by inauspicious planetary configurations, the machinations of evil spirits, or by illnesses such as fevers, seizures, or leprosy would visit this Kumārasvāmi temple, seeking relief through the Śāstri's *māntric* or *tāntric* interventions.

* * *

The following appears in Gundappa [1970, v. 5, p. 114].

Viśvēśvara Śāstri's Occupation

Viśvēśvara Śāstri's family name was Çhappalli. It appears that there were three or four branches of the family. I have not inquired whether it is the name of a village, and if so, where it might be. I do not know when the Śāstri came to Beṅgaḷūru, and under what circumstances. I do not know the name of his teacher. He must have moved to Beṅgaḷūru before 1890. The Çāmarājēndra *Saṁskṛta* Pāṭhaśāla was not yet in existence. Viśvēśvara Śāstri began by teaching in the homes of several people. Chief among them were V.N. Narasiṅgarāya and B. Veṅkaṭappayyaṅgār. He was also a teacher in the private school that started in the Tulasi garden through the efforts of Bhāṣyam Tirumalāçārya and others. It appears that the government took over this private school. Such were the origins of the Çāmarājēndra *Saṁskṛta* Pāṭhaśāla. After this change, Viśvēśvara Śāstri became a government employee. The day that he received the appointment letter, the Śāstri visited V.N. Narasiṁhayyaṅgār to give him the good news. The Ayyaṅgār was very pleased, and congratulated him with:

> *śāstri bhāvamapākṛtya mēstri bhāvamupākṛtaḥ ||*

---

[681] Mount Joy used to be called *Naraharirāyana Guḍḍa* (Narahari Rāya's Hill) after Narahari Rao, a judge at the Maisūru high court. See Gundappa [1970, vol. 2].

"You were a *śāstri* all this while, but now you are a *mēstri.*" This is a pun. It may mean a schoolmaster, but it may also mean an overseer of manual labour.[682] V.N. Narasiṁhayyaṅgār was well known for such playfulness. He was a free spirit.

Viśvēśvara Śāstri moved from the *Saṁskṛta* Pāṭhaśāla to Central College as a *Saṁskṛta paṇḍita.* It is probably around this time, when Ārkāt Śrīnivāsāçārlu, the chief of the *Mujrāyi* Department, was trying to regularize the administration of the various temples, that Viśvēśvara Śāstri, at his urging, edited a book called *Śaivāgamasāra* and readied it for publication.

Rāmaśēṣa Śāstri was *paṇḍita* at Central College before him. There is a story about him that bears retelling.

Rāmaśēṣa Śāstri

I know nothing about Rāmaśēṣa Śāstri myself. I will recount a story I heard from one of his students.

Rāmaśēṣa Śāstri was a great scholar in both *Saṁskṛta* and Kannaḍa. It appears that his lectures on poetry were exceptional. He would recite and explain Kannaḍa verses and poems in captivating style. When he lectured, students from other classes, and even professors, would gather at the windows to hear him. Even J.G. Tait, who was Professor of English, had apparently partaken of this pleasure.[683] Tait had learned some Kannaḍa. He was also learning a little *Saṁskṛta.*

One morning, Rāmaśēṣa Śāstri arrived as usual at the college. He did not have any classes at that time. Being free, he and two other instructors were engaged in conversation in the hallway. Mr. Tait arrived there around the same time, and joined the conversation. After some five minutes or so, Mr. Tait excused himself. He then shook hands with some four or five people who were present. He extended his hand towards Rāmaśēṣa Śāstri.

R: Please forgive me. I cannot grasp your hand.

T: (in Kannaḍa) Why not?

---

[682]The word *mēstri,* that is.

[683]John Guthrie Tait (1861–1945) was Professor of English Literature and Principal of Central College, Bangalore. He was appointed Professor of Languages after his predecessor R.H. Piggot died on October 31, 1889. He retired from Central College as Principal in 1917, and returned to Edinburgh, where he worked on Sir Walter Scott.

R: Your hands have touched the cigar that you have had in your mouth. That was tainted with your saliva.[684]

Mr Tait discarded the cigar in his hand, went inside, washed his hands, returned, and extended his hand again.

T: Now we should be able to do it.

R: It is still not possible. Today happens to be *amāvāsya*. When I return home, I must bathe and perform certain holy rituals. I cannot touch you.

T: When might I shake your hand, then? That would give me great pleasure.

R: I would be pleased to accommodate you if that would make you happy. I will myself come to you one morning. You can then shake my hand.

Mr Tait was very impressed by this. He praised Rāmaśēṣa Śāstri's devotion to his observances, and commented on this to his students.

The Scholarly Assembly of Çāmarājapēṭe

A great number of scholars were visitors at Viśvēśvara Śāstri's home. Chief among them were such scholars as Hosakōṭe Veṅkaṭarāma Śāstri, Narasiṁhaśāstri, Mōṭagānahaḷḷi Śaṅkaraśāstri, Mōṭagānahaḷḷi Rāmaśēṣaśāstri, Tirumalāçārya, Garaṇi Kṛṣṇāçārya, Muttūru Narahariśāstri, and Çennarāyapaṭṭaṇa Veṅkaṭaramaṇayya. Among them all, Viśvēśvara Śāstri was especially close to Mōṭagānahaḷḷi Śaṅkaraśāstri. Viśvēśvara Śāstri would sit in his verandah in the evenings. The other scholars would arrive. Some discussion would then ensue on some aspect of grammar, poetics, or some commentary. Śaṅkaraśāstri would recite some verses he had composed. Everyone would engage in the conversation enthusiastically.

---

[684]See footnote 641. Saliva is particularly impure. Of course, contact with Tait would also be problematic for the Śāstri, since Tait was outside the caste system. Contact with him would have been ritually polluting for a *vaidika*, especially on an auspicious *tithi*.

The Assembly at Tiruvāḍi

Around 1911, a scholarly assembly took place in a place called Tiruvāḍi in the Southern Country.[685] The assembly had convened to determine how to bring about essential reforms in Hindu traditions and practices. Viśvēśvara Śāstri attended the conference. As soon as he returned and alighted from his carriage, I did him reverence, as I always did. He was in good spirits. I inquired after his well-being, and then asked him about the conference. He replied as follows:

V.: Many great scholars were at the conference. In attendance were Professor Maḷūru Raṅgāçārya, Professor Kuppusvāmi Śāstri, Professor Sundararāma Ayyar, two judges of the High Court, as well as lawyers.[686] What was remarkable was that these *laukika* scholars know as much *Saṁskṛta* as we do. They are as familiar with the *śāstras* as we are. Thus, not only do they know the *śāstras,* they are also knowledgeable about worldly matters to which we *vaidikas* have no access. What you call the census—the numbers of people, the numbers of people of each faith—what do we know of such matters? A number of miracles of science are now under way. They do have an understanding of such matters. Thus, they are not inferior to us in *sāstric* matters. They may even be superior in some ways. Now, with respect to *dhārmic* matters, could it be right to claim that we are superior and they inferior? Who can possibly claim that Raṅgāçārya or Sundararāma Ayyar come up short in devotion to *dharma* or in their devotion to worldly service?"

I: In that case, did the *vaidikas* accept their conclusions?

---

[685] The conference at Tiruvāḍi, some six miles north of Tañjāvūru, took place in December 1912. An earlier conference had been held in April 1912 in the town of Kāñçīpuram. Their purpose was for *paṇḍitas* to confer on how to bring traditional practices and beliefs, including those having to do with age of consent and loss of caste due to foreign travel, in line with modernity.

[686] Rao Bahadur Mālūru Raṅgāçārya, M.A., was formerly Professor of Sanskrit and Comparative Philology at Presidency College, and Curator of the Government Oriental Manuscript Library at Madras. *Mahāmhōpādhyāya* Kuppusvāmi Śāstri had held the same positions, as well as several others, including that of Principal of Madras Sanskrit College in Mylapore. Professor Sundararāma Ayyar was professor at Kumbhakōṇam.

V.: All the conclusions of the conference were entirely proper from the perspectives of both *sāstras* and policy.

I: Do you accept them, then?

V.: Some matters are not right for me to follow personally. Is my age proper for me to marry a widow, or even contemplate a second marriage? Some such matters cannot touch me personally. By and large, however, we have all accepted the disposition and sentiments of the conference. Surely, everyone is bound to find that acceptable!

Such was the humility and the liberality of the Śāstri's spirit.

***

The following appears in [Gundappa 1970, v. 5, p. 173].

An Incident

On one occasion, The Right Honourable Śrīnivāsa Śāstri had been invited to dinner at a wedding when he had visited Beṅgaḷūru.[687] D. Veṅkaṭarāmayya, Deputy Director of the Department of Education, was the host. Veṅkaṭarāmayya and Śrīnivāsa Śāstri were close friends. They had been fellow-students in Madrās while studying for the L.D. examination.[688] Many scholars were also present as invitees on this occasion. A conversation was in progress during the customary partaking of *tāmbūla* after dinner.

A few weeks earlier, the Śāstri had delivered a lecture at an annual conference of *paṇḍitas*, in which he had urged *paṇḍitas* to rise above their traditionalism, and become free thinkers. His intention had been to bring about positive social change.

Presumably with this in mind, a notable in the group, however, spoke diparagingly of *purōhitas*. This notable had come to a senior administrative role, having passed the Mysore Civil Service Examination. He held the position of Secretary in the government. The Śāstri's response to his comments about *vaidikas* was as follows.

---

[687] The Rt. Hon. Valaṅgaimān Śaṅkaranārāyaṇa Śrīnivāsa Śāstri (1869–1946) was one of India's leading statesmen, and its most eloquent orator, as the Encyclopædia Britannica recognized. He was born to an orthodox brāhmaṇa family, and was intimately familiar with Indian tradition and Sanskrit. At the same time, his command of English was exceptional.

[688] This is a typographical error. It should read LL.D. (Doctor of Laws), rather than L.D.

"Good sir, when you visit the barber—how much do you pay him?"

"Four *Āṇe* for a haircut."

"What do you pay the *purōhita* who comes to your home to perform *pūja*?"

"Four *Āṇe*."[689]

"What sir, do you not see the contradiction in your statements? You find it reasonable that the barber should take four *Āṇe* from you, though he may be ignorant. You find it agreeable though he may not be clean. If, however, the person who accepts the same four *Āṇe* is a brāhmaṇa, you complain about what he knows or does not know, and how he is or how he is not. How might this be seen as proper?

"Have you even considered how it might be possible for a *vaidika* brāhmaṇa to have income enough, food enough to eat, and clothes enough to wear? How dare you, before you even consider this matter, insist that he be fully proficient in the *śāstras,* understand all the deeper meanings of the *mantras,* and the significance of all ritual?

"But let us set that aside. Have you understood these matters yourself? Things are all in your favour now, by the grace of God. You hold an office of importance. You have acquired knowledge in English and in Science. You earn a generous income. Given all this, how much time do you devote to learning about your religion or traditions? Do you even devote as much time to them as you devote to a haircut? Let us grant that *vaidikas* are ignorant of deeper meanings. You, however, do have the opportunity now to learn these deeper meanings. How are you using this opportunity?"

Such indeed, was the flow of the Śāstri's eloquence. The company was utterly dumbfounded. The gathering was at an end.

* * *

[689] If we compute earnings on an hourly basis, the barber's earnings would far exceed those of the *vaidika* brāhmaṇa.

The following appears in Gundappa [1970, v. 7].

Rāmasvāmi Śetti

Rāmasvāmi Śetti lived in a village called Kappalamaḍuga some five or six miles distant from Muḷubāgilu. He was a very wealthy man. He had arranged for the grand image of Veṅkaṭaramaṇasvāmi, which stood with arms reaching down to its knees in the courtyard of the Śrīmadāñjanēya temple in Muḷubāgilu, to be caparisoned in a corset, and having resolved that an image of Śrī Padmāvātīdēvī was to stand alongside, had arranged for this image to be sculpted and installed...[690]

Three or four years thence, Rāmasvāmi Śetti passed away in his own house in Kappalamaḍuga. A group of brāhmaṇas had travelled to Kappalamaḍuga from Muḷubāgilu to partake in the feast associated with the *vaikuṇṭha* ceremony, and to receive the *dakṣiṇa* benefaction.[691] I was among that group. I remember well that I had managed to snag the amount of one *Doḍḍāṇe* (a silver coin worth two *Āṇe*). I also remember well that I had subsequently received a sound thrashing at home. The reason for the thrashing was that we were not *vaidikas*. A *laukika* may never reach for anything that should rightly go to a *vaidika*. I was, of course, a *laukika*.

---

[690] Long arms, often represented as extending to below the knees, are a sign of distinction, associated with great or divine beings. Rāma is often referred to as *mahābāhu* (great- or long-armed) or as *ājānubāhu* (one with arms long enough to reach the knees). Indian tradition recognizes thirty-two physical characteristics that distinguish great or divine beings, including exceptionally long arms, the *śrīvatsa* mark on the chest, large earlobes, and a broad chest. Buddhist iconography also depicts the Buddha with these thirty-two *mahāpuruṣa lakṣaṇas*.

[691] The *vaikuṇṭha samārādhane* is a celebration held on the twelfth or thirteenth day after death, depending upon practice. After death, the spirit of the deceased does not automatically join the ranks of the *pitṛs*, or ancestors. Instead, it remains in limbo in the form of a *prēta*, and must be formally incorporated into *pitṛ* status through sixteen ritual stages, mirroring the sixteen *saṁskāras* for the living. The first ten days of post-mortem ritual are *ekoddiṣṭa*, or "directed at the one", namely the *prēta*, and are designed to construct a new body for the *prēta*. The final stage is the *sapiṇḍīkaraṇa* ritual, which formally confers *pitṛ* status. The *pitṛs* also progress through four stages; those in the first three stages are recipients of ritual services. The fourth stage being more transcendental, ancestors at this stage do not require the same attention. The names of the ancestors of the last three generations are recited at the annual *śrāddha* ceremonies, for instance, but the names of ancestors in earlier generations are not. The *sapiṇḍīkaraṇa* ritual promotes the list of ancestors upwards, so that the name of the earliest ancestor need no longer be recited. See Knipe [1977] for details. In some accounts, the *vaikuṇṭha samārādhane* marks the entry of the departed soul into *Vaikuṇṭha*, the abode of Viṣṇu. A special feast (a *santarpaṇa*) is held for family members and brāhmaṇas on this day, with all participants receiving a *dakṣiṇa* gift, usually in cash.

* * *

The following appears in Gundappa [1970, v. 7].

Gōdāvarī Brāhmaṇas

Some sixty years ago, the region of Gōdāvarī was not well-served by canals or other means of irrigation; much of it was dry grassland.[692] Groups of brāhmaṇas from the region would frequently travel south with the purpose of visiting holy sites such as Rāmēśvaram or Tirupati. These were extremely observant brāhmaṇas.[693] A *sattra* built by a merchant named Tavva existed, adjacent to the front of the Śrīmadāñjanēyasvāmi temple in Muḷubāgilu. The Gōdāvarī brāhmaṇas who passed through the town would usually sojourn in this *sattra*.

The Gōdāvarī brāhmaṇas normally travelled by foot. Vinōbā Bhāve's travels are renowned in our own time.[694] Sixty years ago, however, walking was the universal mode of travel. It was no hardship at all for the Gōdāvarī brāhmaṇas to walk fiteen or twenty miles each day. Among them were devotees of Çauḍēśvarī and Bhadrakāḷī, as well as those well versed in *Śrīvidya*.[695]

Our homes were visited mainly by individuals who were devoted to the study of the *Vēdas*. They had unabashed faith in the power and greatness of the *Vēdas*. They were physically robust. As a result, their voices resounded grandly in the upper register.

These brāhmaṇas would not hesitate to come home and ask: "This is surely a brāhmaṇa home. Would it be convenient for us to dine here?" The *yajamāna* of the house, regarding the inquiry as a supreme blessing, would

[692]This work was published in 1970, so the allusion "sixty years ago" is to around 1910.

[693]Observant brāhmaṇas were likely found everywhere at the time, but brāhmaṇas of the Gōdāvarī region appear to stand out even today. As detailed in Knipe [2015], among the brāhmaṇa communities of the Gōdāvarī delta are some of the last known *āhitāgnis* in India. It has recently come to light that in these communities are also found the last known routine performers of the ancient *śrauta* rituals, including the *sōmayāgas*, especially the elaborate *Sarvatōmukha*. See footnote 586. Sadly, these traditions are quickly becoming extinct.

[694]Vinōba Bhāve (1895–1982) was a respected figure, and very much in the Gandhian tradition. He travelled the country on foot, promoting his *bhūdāna* movement, asking people to donate land to indigent farmers. Needless to say, the movement had limited success.

[695]The suggestion here is that these brāhmaṇas engaged in practices with *tāntric* overtones. Çauḍēśvarī and Bhadrakāḷī are both manifestations of Durgā, who is associated with *tāntric* ritual. *Śrīvidya* is a system of ritual that does have *tāntric* overtones, although it is practiced mainly by *Smārta* brāhmaṇas.

immediately respond: "Please do us this great favour!"[696] The brāhmaṇas would never begin their meal until they had recited the *Vēdas* for at least half an hour.

Neither was preparing their meal particularly difficult. All they wanted was rice, *tovve*, very spicy *huḷi* (*pappu dappaḷam*), *gojju* or *caṭni*, plenty of *ghī*, and some buttermilk.[697] Even approaching them with our *sāru* in hand would elicit the reaction "No illness here!"[698] Light *sāru* was only for the ill! Such was their view. They would not refuse vegetables or delicacies. What they wanted chiefly, however, was rice, *pappu dappaḷam*, and *ghī*.

They would eat no dinner in the evenings.

Carefree Natures

They would normally travel between five and eight or nine in the mornings. They would travel again between four and seven in the evenings. In this manner, some six or seven hours would be devoted each day to travel. They always remained carefree.

One of them would always carry a *śivaliṅga*. That *bāṇaliṅga* was about a foot tall.[699] He would place it in a platter and perform the *Rudrābhiṣēka* ritual.[700] The two individuals chanted the *namakas* and *camakas* in perfect unison; their voices sounded as one. They made no demands of us. They even made sure to obtain the flowers required for the worship ritual on their way. It would suffice to give them some milk or jaggery for the *naivēdya* offering.

---

[696] Hospitality to guests is *mānuṣa yajña*, a *nitya* ritual. See footnote 53.

[697] *Tovve* is typically cooked *togari bēḷe* (pigeon peas) seasoned with salt, asafœtida, cumin seeds, and mustard seeds. *Huḷi* is a spicy vegetable stew from Karṇāṭaka with *togari bēḷe* as base. *Pappu dappaḷam* is the equivalent term in Telugu. *Gojju* and *caṭni* are both types of spicy vegetable sauce or relish.

[698] *Sāru* is a light and spicy soup, with a small amount of lentils (typically *togari bēḷe*). Because it is light, *sāru* is usually served when someone is ill. See footnote 640.

[699] A *bāṇaliṅga* is an elongated ellipsoid polished stone obtained from the bed of the Narmadā river, and is a symbol of Śiva.

[700] In the *Rudrābhiṣēka* worship ritual, the chief act is to bathe the *śivaliṅga* with substances such as milk, sugar, and *ghī*, to the accompaniment of *Vēdic mantras*, especially the *Rudranamakas* and *Rudracamakas*.

APPENDIX B: FAMILY HISTORY OF SŌSALE GARAḶAPURĪ ŚĀSTRI

BIOGRAPHY OF SŌSALE AYYA ŚĀSTRI

Sōsale Kṛṣṇasvāmi Śāstri[701]

[701] Sōsale Kṛṣṇasvāmi Śāstri was the second son of Sōsale Ayya Śāstri. This biography appeared in the *Kannaḍa Sāhitya Pariṣad Patrike*, 19-3, 1934, p. 281, and was reprinted in Venkaṭasubbayya and Gītāçārya [2000].

Plate 37: *Āsthānamahāvidvān Kavitilaka* Sōsale Ayya Śāstri (1855–1934). The photograph is unattributed, but the similarity of the backgrounds in this plate and Plate 10 very clearly suggests that it was taken in the studio of Varadāçārya.

THE LATE *ĀSTHĀNAMAHĀVIDVĀN* *"KAVITILAKA"* SŌSALE AYYA ŚĀSTRI

VĒDABRAHMA *"Kavitilaka"* Sōsale Ayya Śāstri was born in the village of Sōsale in Tirumakūḍalu Narasīpura *tāllūk* on Thursday, the first *bahuḷa tithi* of Phālguṇa in the Ānanda *saṁvatsara* corresponding to 1776 of the *Śaka* era (March 20, 1854 C.E.).[702] His parents were *Vē*‖ Garaḷapurī Śāstri and *Śrīmatī* Subbamma. He was from the *Hoysaḷa Karṇāṭaka* community of *Smārtas,* and was a descendant of Tammaṇṇabhaṭṭa, who had been a minister in the realm of Ānegondi. He belonged to the Kāśyapa *gōtra* and the *Drāhyāyaṇa sūtra* of the *Sāmavēda;* his father was a renowned poet and *mahāvidvāṁsa* in the court of Kṛṣṇarāja Voḍeyar III, and had authored such subtle and exquisite works as the *Çampūrāmayaṇa Yuddhakāṇḍa,* the *Kṛṣṇabhūpālīyam,* and the *Harihara Stōtra. Vē*‖ Ayyaśāstri's father-in-law was Çāmarājanagara Śrīkaṇṭha Śāstri. A *śrōtri* and a deep *Vēdic* scholar, he was also an expert on *Vēdic* rites and rituals, and the author of the grammatical treatise *Dhātur̄upa Prakāśikā. Vē*‖ Ayyaśāstri was the second among his brothers.[703] He also had two sisters, named Nañjamma and Sītamma. Although the Śāstri had been named Veṅkaṭasubbaśarma, the name "Ayya", which his father called him by, became the popular way to address him.

The Śāstri remained in Sōsale in childhood for about six or seven years, and then moved to Maisūru with his father. After he learned how to read and write, his elementary education proceeded for two or three years under the tutelage of his own father. Following his *upanayana,* he studied the *Sāmavēda* under *Vē*‖ Magu Śrauti, who was accomplished in *śrautic* matters, and had authored the *Huṁkāraçandrike,* a work on the *Sāmavēda.*[704]

---

[702] This appears to be an error. March 20 corresponds to the first *śukla tithi* of Phālguṇa of the Ānanda *saṁvatsara.* The first *bahuḷa tithi* actually corresponds to Sunday, March 4, 1855 C.E. When such conflicts arise, it is wise to take the *tithi* as correct, so the date should be Sunday, March 4. The year should be 1855 C.E., rather than 1854 C.E., in either case. This is a widely reproduced error.

[703] The three brothers were, in birth order, Aṇṇayya Śāstri, Ayya Śāstri, and Rāmasvāmi Śāstri.

[704] One was, of course, required to study one's own *Vēdic śākha. Huṁkāra* is the first of seven *bhaktis* or segments of a *sāman* recitation. The others are *prastāva, udgīta, pratihāra, upadrava, nidhana,* and *praṇava.* Syllables such as *huṁ, hā,* and *ū* are extensively interpolated into the text in *Sāmavēdic* recitation as textual and musical fillers.

At the time, *Vē‖* Garaḷapurī Śāstri's home was indeed a small school devoted to the study of literature. More than twenty or thirty students, both local and from elsewhere, studied such subjects as literature, medicine, and logic with the senior (Garaḷapuri) Śāstri.[705] In addition, spirited poetical contests, such as *antarlāpa, bahirlāpa,* and *pratidattākṣara*, took place regularly.[706] A luminary by the name of Periyasvāmi Tirumalāçārya had gained the elder Śāstri's regard and affection owing to his exceptional brilliance, his consummate scholarship, and his poetical abilities. The elder Śāstri sent his son to Periyasvāmi Tirumalāçārya for study, requiring him to return occasionally, so that he might evaluate his progress.

Respectfully following his father's bidding, *Vē‖* Ayyaśāstri pursued his studies under the *Āçārya,* covering all aspects of literature, including poetry and *alaṅkāra*, as well as works on grammar and logic, and as directed, presented himself regularly to be tested, both by his father, as well as in *Pradoṣapūja* assemblies.

Vē‖ Ayyaśāstri also pursued advanced studies for some time with Kumbhakōṇa Śēṣāçārya. Just as both his father and Periyasvāmi Tirumalāçārya had done, he applied himself to poetical composition even from childhood, soliciting the suggestions of his guru and his father. In his spare time, he learned music and the graphic arts.[707] *Vē‖* Ānandāḷvār (the current head of the Yatirāja Gurupīṭha, known as Āsūri Anantāçārya in his prior *āśrama*) was his fellow-student.[708]

---

[705] See page 26 and footnote 77. This is the first explicit reference anywhere indicating that Garaḷapurī Śāstri taught logic, in addition to literature and medicine.

[706] An *antarlāpikā* is a riddle whose answer is hidden within itself, while a *bahirlāpikā's* answer lies outside it. A *pratidattākṣara* changes meaning when one syllable is substituted for another in the composition.

[707] This is the first documented indication that Ayya Śāstri had expertise in these areas, although his name does come up in the context of art and music of the period [Pranesh 2003]. Much of his poetry has been set to music, and his granddaughter Smt. Sarōja Veṅkatarām, now in her eighties, is still able to sing many of his compositions from memory. Consistent with the regrettable history of indifference of brāhmaṇa families to their own heritage, however, no verifiable examples of his art appear to have survived. An unsigned painting of his wife Lakṣmīdevamma, clearly copied from her likeness in Plate 32, is in the possession of *Smt.* Anasūyā Śāstri, widow of Ayyā Śāstri's grandson Veṅkaṭakṛṣṇa Śāstri (nicknamed *Puṭṭasvāmi*). Whether the artist was Ayyā Śāstri is a matter of speculation.

[708] Ayya Śāstri also knew Saççidānanda Śivābhinava Nṛsimha Bhāratī, the 33rd pontiff of the Śṛṅgēri Maṭha, known as Śivasvāmi in his prior *āśrama* (see page 256). In fact, Ayya Śāstri's grandson S.R. Śivasvāmi indicates that his own name had originally been Śivaśaṅkara, but that Ayya Śāstri began to call him Śivasvāmi after the pontiff, and the name stuck.

Çāmarājanagara Śrīkaṇṭha Śāstri arranged for the marriage of his daughter *Sau*‖ Lakṣmīdevamma with Ayya Śāstri in the Akṣaya *saṁvatsara* corresponding to 1866 C.E., when the Śāstri was fourteen years old.[709] Subsequently, the Śāstri advanced his poetic skills greatly through his association with Çāmarājanagara Rāmaśāstri, his father-in-law's younger brother.

At the time, *Aḷiya* Liṅgarāje Arasu, the wealthy royal kinsman, was resident in the street within the Maisūru fort known as Hūvina Bīdi. He would engage himself in melodious recitation of the *Kannaḍabhārata Jaimini*, study of *Saṁskṛta* poetry, and being poetically talented, in the composition of small *yakṣagānas*. Impressed by Garaḷapurī Śāstri's poetical skills and scholarship in literature, he began studying plays and poetics with him. Basappa Śāstri, who since childhood had been a fellow-student of the Arasu, was also present during these lessons. He became an even greater scholar than the Arasu.

The elder Śāstri often took his son *Vē*‖ Ayya Śāstri with him on visits to the Arasu's residence. Through his association with the Arasu and Basappa Śāstri, Ayya Śāstri developed a deep interest in Kannaḍa poetry. *Yakṣagāna* performances were held weekly at the Arasu's residence. The Arasu and Basappa Śāstri encouraged the younger Śāstri by having him compose poetry in Kannaḍa. The enthusiastic Śāstri directed his scholarly abilities towards the study of numerous literary and grammatical works in Kannaḍa, and thereby greatly enhanced his poetical skills in both Kannaḍa and *Saṁskṛta*.

His first major accomplishment was a *çampū* work based on the coronation ceremony of Śrī Çāmarājēndra Voḍeyar in 1884. Everyone, including the elder Śāstri, was delighted with the work.[710] Around this time, *Vē*‖ Periyasvāmi Tirumalāçārya, who had been a student of Garaḷapurī Śāstri, established the Sadvidyāśāla in the capital city, with the assistance of scholars and other notables.[711] Ayya Śāstri taught here for a number of years.

[709]This cannot be correct. Ayya Śāstri would have turned fourteen only in 1869 C.E.

[710]There are a couple of significant errors here. First, the "elder Śāstri" here referenced cannot be Garaḷapurī Śāstri, who died in 1877 C.E., well before the events referenced. Second, the coronation of Çāmarājēndra Voḍeyar was in 1881 C.E., as part of the "rendition" proceedings restoring the Arasu family's rule over Maisūru. The work being alluded to is the *Çāmarājēndra Paṭṭābhiṣēka*, a *çampū* composition in *Saṁskrta*.

[711]The Sadvidyāśāla was founded in 1870 C.E., well before the coronation. A detailed account of its founding appears in the undated anonymous manuscript that the translator discovered in 2008 among Ayya Śāstri's papers. (See footnote 175.) This manuscript now appears in [Śāstri 2012, p. 83].

Among his students here were M.N. Kr̥ṣṇarāv, who graced the position of *Dīvān,* his brother Prof. (retd.) M. Hiriyaṇṇa, *Amaldār* Veṅkataramaṇa Śrauti, *Br‖* Maisūru Sītārāma Śāstri, and *Br‖* Narahari Joyisa. He also established a *Saṁskr̥ta* association during his well-regarded tenure at this institution.

Vē‖ Garaḷapurī Śāstri passed away on the eleventh *bahuḷa* day of the month of *Çaitra* of the Īśvara *saṁvatsara.*[712] Deeply saddened at his demise, Śrī Çāmarāja Voḍeyar appointed Ayya Śāstri to a position as a palace scholar, with the charge of editing Kannaḍa works at the Jaganmōhana Printing Press.[713]

Around this time, that is, in 1887–1888, a Kannaḍa school called Bhāṣōjjīvinī was founded in Maisūru. Many well-known scholars worked at this institution. *Ma‖ Rā‖* Mallappa invited Ayya Śāstri to teach Kannaḍa at this institution. The Śāstri furthered his scholarship in the company of Kannaḍa scholars here.

H.H. Çāmarāja Voḍeyar appointed the Śāstri, who was well known for his character, his virtues, his appearance, his scholarship, and his poetic abilities, as tutor to the princesses, and directed him to pursue poetic composition in the time that remained. In accordance with the king's wishes, the Śāstri engaged himself in composing many new literary, musical, and dramatic works, as well as in translations of such works, and gained the respect and regard of the king, his associates, and scholars. Around this time, a learned lady by the name of Jñānasundarī arrived at the court from the region of Pūnā, recited her *Saṁskr̥ta* poetry, impressed the king and the assembly of scholars at the palace, and gained their regard.[714] The king honoured her,

---

[712] See page 63 for further details.

[713] Çāmarāja Voḍeyar X was only fourteen years old at the time. The appointment was made by Palace Controller Raṅgāçārlu. See page 65.

[714] The identity of this lady has long remained a mystery, and indeed, her association with Pūnā (the modern Puṇe) implied here turns out to be misleading. The translator has discovered the following information [in Krishnamachariar and Srinivasachariar 1974]:

> Jnanasundarī was a dancing girl of Kumbakonam. She lived there and passed away about 1910. She was the pupil of Kuppuswami Sastri of Śrīvatsagotra and was, as she says, the author of several works; of these however only one *Hālāsyacampū* in 6 *stabakas* has been traced. There are old gentlemen living in the southern districts who remember her discourses, dancing and recitals, well and with delight and R. Fisher, Bar-at-law, of Madura was her particular patron. She visited the Mysore court and there received the title *Kaviratna.* Her narration of the wedding of Mīnākṣī

while thinking to himself: "Is there nobody at our court capable of defeating her?" The assembly of scholars nominated Ayya Śāstri. Within a week, the Śāstri composed and submitted to the assembly numerous *ślōkas* of extraordinary merit. The assembly was impressed. The king was pleased. The Śāstri was then honored. The learned lady, her natural shyness amplified, prostrated herself before the Śāstri in the assembly.

A drama company visited Maisūru from the Sāṅgali region during the reign of Çāmarāja Voḍeyar.[715] This company performed several plays in Marāṭhi. Many were impressed, including the king, who resolved to have plays composed and performed in the Kannaḍa language. The king's Retinue visited Bombay around that time. The Śāstri was directed to accompany the king.

During its sojourn there, the Royal Retinue visited several Pārsi playhouses. The Śāstri had been directed to accompany the Retinue on these occasions, and witnessed the performances with the king. The Śāstri immediately saw what the king had in mind.

After the Royal Retinue returned to Maisūru, the king had the play *Śākuntala* written by the poet Basappa Śāstri, the play *Vikramōrvaśīya* written by *Vē‖* Ayya Śāstri, and the play *Mṛçchakaṭika* written by Nañjanagūḍu Subbāśāstri, all in Kannaḍa, and arranged for them to be performed by a drama company he established. Many plays, including *Othello*, *Çaṇḍakauśika, Pratāpasiṁha Çaritre,* and *The Merchant of Venice* were translated into Kannaḍa by poets at his court.[716] Ayya Śāstri oversaw the operations

---

and Sundareśa makes a pleasant reading. In verse she is fond of alliteration: *"madhurīkṛtagaralatvāt madhurābhikhyā tadādi sā nagarī | nijasīmasthaphaṇitvāt vibhāti hālāsyanāmataśçeha ‖ tasyā lalāṭalīnasvāhāpatireva śāntasantāpaḥ | reje kuṁkumatilakavyājānnūnaṁ budhā hi kālavidaḥ ‖"*

[715] Saṅgali is in southern Mahārāṣtra.

[716] The drama company referred to is the *Çāmarājēndra Karnāṭaka Nāṭaka Sabha*, established in 1880 C.E. The *Abhijñāna Śākuntalaṁ* and *Vikramōrvaśīya* are among the best-known plays of Kālidāsa. The *Mṛçchakaṭika* is a play by Śūdraka. These three plays belong to the *Saṁskṛta* classical period. *Othello* was translated by Basappa Śāstri as the *Śūrasēna Çaritre* (1895), and *The Merchant of Venice* was the *Pāñçālī Pariṇaya* by Ānandarāv [Trivedi and Bartholomeusz 2005]. This reference also lists Śrīkaṇṭhēsa Gauḍa's *Pratāpa Rudradēva* (Macbeth, 1895) and *Pramiḷārjunīya* (A Midsummer Night's Dream, no date), *Hemaçandrarāja Vilāsa* (King Lear, 1889) by M.S. Puṭṭaṇṇa, and *Çaṇḍī Mardana* (The Taming of the Shrew, 1910) by Lakṣmaṇa Rāv. The *Çaṇḍakauśika* is a 10th century play by Kṣemīśvara, and tells the well-known story of the righteous king Harīṣçandra. The origi-

of this drama company for some time, and ensured its development and growth.

He accompanied His Highness on trips to places such as Madrās, Bombay, Calcutta, Kāśi, and Delhi, where he came into contact with scholars, officials, and other notables. Consequently, and due to his scholarship, his poetic abilities, and the encouragement of H.H. Çāmarāja, his works attained considerable renown. He completed such works as the *Śēṣarāmāyaṇa,* the *Damayantī Çaritre*, the *Naḷa Çaritre* (play), and the *Pratāpasiṁha Çaritre* (play) even during the lifetime of His Highness, and brought them to his notice.

His Highness Çāmarāja Voḍeyar passed away in 1894 C.E. The Śāstri was deeply anguished by this loss. The Regent Queen of the Vāṇī Vilāsa Sannidhāna appointed the Śāstri instructor to her children, who are now the king and the Yuvarāja.[717] At this time, the Śāstri composed many *ślokas* in Kannaḍa and *Saṁskṛta* suitable for the purpose, and taught them to his royal disciples and their fellow-students.

The Śāstri remained instructor in Kannaḍa and *Saṁskṛta* to His Highness and the Yuvarāja till 1901 C.E. Subsequently, he was appointed instructor in the Lakṣmīvilāsa Sannidhāna.[718] At this time he also worked at the Royal School for the grandchildren of *Śrī* Vāṇī Vilāsa Sannidhāna. The queen *Mahāmātṛśrī* Vāṇī Vilāsa Sannidhāna had deep regard for the Śāstri, and would frequently have him recount stories from the *Purāṇas,* which she listened to respectfully.

---

nal of the *Pratāpasiṁha Çaritre* has apparently long remained a mystery (see, for example Venkaṭasubbayya and Gītāçārya [2000, p. 37]); in his introduction, Ayya Śāstri merely states it to be a translation of a play originally in the "Hindustāni" language. The translator has found several plays with matching titles, but none with matching content.

[717] These children would be His Highness Kṛṣṇarāja Voḍeyar IV and Yuvarāja Kaṇṭhīrava Narasiṁharāja Voḍeyar. Also see page 115.

[718] H.H. Lakṣmīvilāsa Sannidhāna was the princess Sri Pratāpa Kumārī Ammaṇṇi Avaru (b. 1889), who married H.H. Kṛṣṇarāja Voḍeyar IV in 1900 C.E. This appears to have been a surprising alliance. She was the youngest daughter of Raṇa Srī Bane Sinhji Sāhib, Rāṇa Sāhib of Vana in the Kaṭhiavār region of present-day Gujarāt state. While Maisūru was one of the largest and most significant kingdoms of the time, Vana was a minor *tālūk* of Jhālwār *prānt,* in the Kāṭhiavār Agency, comprising a mere three villages, with a total population of 2,600 in 1901 C.E., and a total revenue of just 26,000 *Rūpīs* [Gazetteer 1908, p. 164]. In his prime, Kṛṣṇarāja Voḍeyar IV is said to have been the world's wealthiest man, with a personal fortune of $56 billion at current values.

The Śāstri helped Mr B.L. Rice edit the *Karṇāṭaka Śabdānuśāsana.*[719] He was also a member of the textbook committee from the time of Mr Bhābha until 1920 C.E.[720] He also performed editorial work on the *Karṇāṭaka Kāvyakalānidhi* series.

He solicited criticism of his poetical compositions from his relative *Ā*‖ *Ma*‖ *Vi*‖ *Brahmaśrī* Çāmarājanagara Rāmaśāstri, and his friends, such as *Brahmaśrī* Lakṣmīnarasiṁha Śāstri, *Ma*‖ *Rā*‖ B. Mallappa, *Vē*‖ *Br*‖ Timmappayya Śāstri, and *Karṇāṭa Bhāṣāratnaṁ Ma*‖ *Rā*‖ P. R. Karibasava Śāstri.

The king endowed him with the titles *Mahāvidvān* in 1905 and *Kavitilaka* in 1912. To celebrate the grant of these titles and to express their appreciation to the king, his friends felicitated him in a celebration held in the Raṅgāçārlu Memorial Hall in the capital city. Starting 1913, he served as a member of the Maharāja's *Saṁskṛta* College Committee for three years, and contributed greatly to its growth and advancement. Subsequently, he served for three years on the committee to advance *Saṁskṛta* education, and assisted greatly in improving the quality of *Saṁskṛta* education. Dr. Brajēndranāth Śīla invited him to deliver three lectures on Kannaḍa literature at the University of Maisūru.[721] He became a member of the Karṇāṭaka Sāhitya Pariṣad in 1914.

He contributed greatly to the establishment of the Bālabōdhinī school within the Maisūru fort in 1894–1895. This school was founded due to the joint efforts of such persons as *Ma*‖ *Rā*‖ Veṅkaṭakṛṣnayya, *Ma*‖ *Rā*‖ Ambaḷe Aṇṇayya Paṇḍita, *Ma*‖ *Rā*‖ Biḍadi Muddurāja Arasu, and *Ma*‖ *Rā*‖ Nañjuṇḍa Rāja Arasu. Following the suggestion of Rāv Bahādūr Ambil Narasiṁhayyaṅgār, a great promoter of women's education in Maisūru, he composed many poems and songs suitable for a girl's school. Many of these compositions appear in the *Bālikā Gīta Muktākalāpa*, but without specific attribution to him.

---

[719] The *Karṇāṭaka Śabdānuśāsana* is a classical work on Kannaḍa grammar by Bhaṭṭakalaṅka Dēva. The edition by B.L. Rice appeared in 1890 C.E.

[720] See footnote 324.

[721] Brajēndranāth Śīla was a well-known philosopher, humanist and thinker, and a close associate of many leading Beṅgāli figures of the time, including Rabīndranāth Tagore and Svāmi Vivekānanda. He became Vice-Chancellor of the University of Mysore in 1921.

His Works:

In Kannaḍa: (1) *Śēṣa Rāmayaṇa* (*śaṭpadī mahākāvya*), (2) *Maisūru Mahārāja Çaritaṁ* (*çampū mahākāvya* in old Kannaḍa), (3) *Vikramōrvaśīya* (play translated from *Saṁskṛta*), (4) *Rāmāyaṇa* (play), (5) *Naḷa Çaritre* (play), (6) *Pratāpasiṁha Çaritre* (play), (7) *Damayantī Çaritre* (poem in *śaṭpadī* metre), (8) *Yakṣapraṣne* (poem in *śaṭpadī* metre), (9) *Rājabhakti Laharī* (poem in *śaṭpadī* metre).

In *Saṁskṛta*: (1) *Çāmarājēndra Paṭṭābhiṣeka* (*çampū*), (2) *Kṛṣṇāmbā Pariṇaya* (*çampū*).

Edited Works: (1) *Karṇāṭaka Śabdānuśāsana* (2) *Karṇāṭaka Kādambarī*, (3) *Nāgarasana Karṇāṭaka Bhagavadgīte*, (4) *Karṇāṭaka Vaçana Bhārata*

In additon, he composed many smaller works such as the *Daśastōtra*, the *Āśīrvaçana Pañçaka*, the *Bhagavatpādāçārya Praśaṁse*, as the time and occasion demanded.[722] He also served as a judge for the poetry competition that His Highness organized in 1925. The Government Department of Education and palace officials would often send him books for review.

Over the last couple of years, his body greatly weakened, he had organized all his personal affairs, and devoting himself to his daily observances and rituals, and distancing himself from worldly matters and discontinuing his regular visits to the palace entirely, he had immersed himself in *japa* and meditation, and remaining a strong *saṁnyāsi* within though seeming externally as if a weakened child, he continued full of dignity and effulgence, and at last, unbowed and resolute, he departed this physical body and reached the lotus-feet of *Bhagavanta* on the fourth *śuddha tithi* of the month of Vaiśākha in the Bhāva *saṁvatsara* (April 17, 1934).

His was a large family. Including his four sons, five daughters, grandchildren, and great-grandchildren, more than sixty persons continue their lives with the blessings of the Śāstri.[723]

---

[722] The *Daśastōtra* is the well-known composition beginning *"Svāmi dēvane lōka pālane te namōstu namostu te"*, which was used as a school prayer for decades in Karṇāṭaka. It was also used as a song in the Kannaḍa movie *School Master* (1958).

[723] Ayya Śāstri's children were: Veṅkaṭalakṣamma ("Akkayya", *w/o* Veṅkaṭaramaṇayya of Dēvarāyanadurga), Jānakīamma (married Mattigūḍu Vāsudēva Śāstri), Veṅkaṭasubbamma

Reconstructed Timeline of Garaḷapurī Śāstri's Life

Tammaṇṇa Śāstri's *Hoysala* ancestors arrived in Ānēgondi from Dōrasamudra *c.* 1300–1400 C.E. Tammaṇṇa Śāstri appears to have been minister to *Aliya* Rāma Rāya's descendants, who had continued at Ānēgondi after Tāḷikōṭe. After a devastating attack by Gōlkōṇḍa in 1638 C.E., Tammaṇṇa Śāstri left Ānēgondi for Anantaśayana. He appears to have arrived at Ānēkallu just as Tammēgauḍa of the Sugaṭuru lineage was fortifying Ānēkallu, having been forced to move there after losing Hosakōṭe to the Bijāpur army under Śivāji's father Śāhji. The following table gives a detailed timeline for the events of interest.

Date (C.E.)	Event	Pages
1300s–1400s	Tammaṇṇa Śāstri's ancestors come to Ānēgondi from Dōrasamudra.	7, 358
1400s–1600s	Tammaṇṇa Śāstri and ancestors in ministerial roles at Ānēgondi.	7
~1600	Tammaṇṇa Śāstri is born.	67
~1638–1639	Haiderābādi army devastates Ānēgondi. Tammaṇṇa Śāstri departs southwards.	8, 348–354
1638–1639	Tammēgauda loses Hosakōṭe to Bijāpur army under Śāhji. Moves to Ānēkallu and begins fort's construction.	315–330
~1639	Tammaṇṇa Śāstri arrives at Ānēkallu.	10, 319–331, 348–354
1822	Garaḷapurī Śāstri is born.	12
1830	Garaḷapurī Śāstri starts formal studies under Rāmāśāstri of Tirumakūḍalu.	12

("Ajjubu", *w/o* Veṅkaṭanarasiṁhayya), Mīnākṣīamma, Garaḷapurī Śāstri ([1888–1955], *h/o* Veṅkaṭasubbamma, *d/o* of Çāmarājanagara Śrīkaṇṭha Śāstri), Kṛṣṇasvāmi Śāstri (*h/o* Subbamma, and author of this biography), Rāmasvāmi Śāstri ([July 17, 1892–September 9, 1973], *h/o* Sītamma [September 21, 1904–December 17, 1991], *d/o* of M.S. Puṭṭaṇṇa), Viśālākṣamma ("Śālamma", tragically widowed in childhood), and Gōpālasvāmi Śāstri.

Date (C.E.)	Event	Pages
1838	Garaḷapurī Śāstri marries Subbamma.	15
1838	Garaḷapurī Śāstri composes *"vāmāṅkegirija..."* in response to Veṅkaṭasubbayya's challenge.	18
~1840	Garaḷapurī Śāstri begins study of logic with Tammayyāçārya in Sōsale.	17
1842	Garaḷapurī Śāstri composes *"anāghrāta..."*, lamenting the work of inferior poets.	20
~1845?	Aṇṇayya Śāstri's passing.	21
Mar. 4, 1855	Ayyā Śāstri is born.	301
~1858	Garaḷapurī Śāstri moves to Maisūru.	24
~1859	Garaḷapurī Śāstri composes *kṛṣṇabhūpālīyam*.	29
~1859	Garaḷapurī Śāstri appointed as scholar at the Maisūru court.	29
~1860	Garaḷapurī Śāstri called upon to judge the merit of Varadāçārya's *ślōka*.	30
1861	Garaḷapurī Śāstri appointed instructor at the *Saṁskṛta* Pāṭhaśāla.	36
~1862–1865	The Āśukavi comes to Maisūru.	36
1865	Çāmarāja Voḍeyar X adopted. Garaḷapurī Śāstri appointed as his tutor.	39
1866	Garaḷapurī Śāstri and Gōpālakṛṣṇāçārya begin editing *Aṣṭāṅgahṛdaya*.	40
1868	Episode of pun on *kari* with Ayyā Śāstri.	43
Mar. 27, 1868	Demise of Kṛṣṇarāja Voḍeyar III.	43
Aug. 12, 1868	*Aṣṭāṅgahṛdaya* published by the Palace Press.	40
Dec. 24, 1868	Garaḷapurī Śāstri composes response to *Bhāgavatsaptāha* invitation.	47
~1868–1869	Garaḷapurī Śāstri composes *Hariharāṣṭōttara*.	43

Date (C.E.)	Event	Pages
~1869	Ayyā Śāstri marries Lakṣmīdēvamma.	53, 100
~ 1870	Garaḷapurī Śāstri completes his *Campūrāmāyaṇa Yuddhakāṇḍa*.	41
~1873	Garaḷapurī Śāstri composes *tvamasirasika*… Liṅgarāje Arasu gifts new house.	34
Dec. 5, 1874	Demise of *Aḷiya* Liṅgarājē Arasu.	52
1877	Garaḷapurī Śāstri begins his commentary on the *Nīlakaṇṭhavijaya*.	62
Mar. 26, 1877	Demise of Sōsale Garaḷapurī Śāstri.	63
1877	Ayyā Śāstri is appointed as scholar at Maisūru court.	65
1891	Ayyā Śāstri publishes the *Yuddhakāṇḍa*.	41
1931	Ayyā Śāstri publishes *Kṛṣṇabhūpālīyam*.	29
Apr. 17, 1934	Demise of Ayyā Śāstri.	308

Genealogical Account in Ayyā Śāstri's Hand

The translator has located two undated pages, both in the possession of S.R. Śivasvāmi, Ayyā Śāstri's grandson, containing historical and genealogical information in Ayyā Śāstri's own hand. The first is an account of the family's move from Ānēgondi to Sōsale, and carries the page number 2. The other sheet, bearing no page number, is a family tree (see Plate 9, page 67). It is likely these were prepared together as a two-page manuscript. The second page reads as follows.

> *ānēgondiyallidda pradhāni tammaṇṇa śāstrigaḷu haiderābādina turukara hāvaḷiyinda ā saṁsthānadalli sarvasvavannū kaḷedukoṇḍu enṭu kōṇagaḷa mēle ōle pustakagaḷannu hērikoṇḍu anataśayana prāntyakke hōgabēkendu baruttiruvāga ānekallina baḷige bandu alli kōṭe kaṭṭisutidda pāḷyagāraninda maryādeyannu hondi ātana prārthaneyinda ānekallinallē nintaru. ā pāḷyagāranu hattu vṛuttigaḷannu koṭṭu doḍḍadāgi mane kaṭṭisi koṭṭanu. alli kelavu kāla ivaru sukhavāgiddu allē kālādhīnarāda kelavu varṣagaḷa mēle avara makkaḷu śaṅkarabhaṭṭaru māgaḍige hōgi alliyē nintaru. ī śaṅkarabhaṭṭara munde 5-nē taleyavaru veṅkaṭarāmaśrautigaḷembavaru ī 7–8 varṣagala keḷage bahaḷa vṛddharāgi māgaḍiyalliddaru. hinde vidyāraṇyara kāladindalū tammaṇṇa śāstrigaḷavarige aydu taleya tanaka ī vaṁśadavarige ānegondi saṁsthānadalli pradhāni kelasavu nadedu bandiruvudu.*
>
> *śaṅkarabhaṭṭara makkaḷu veṅkaṭaramābhaṭṭaru ṭī. narasīpurada tāllōku sōsale grāmakke bandu ā grāmashtharanēkara avalambavannu paḍedu allē nintaru. ī venkaṭaramābhaṭṭara makkaḷē sōsale timmappaśāstrigaḷu– ī timmappaśāstrigaḷa makkaḷu veṅkaṭadāsappanavarembavarē sōsale aṇṇayya śāstrigaḷendu prasiddharāgiddaru.*

The translation of this passage is as follows.

> *As Tammaṇṇa Śāstri, having lost his all to the depredations of Haiderābādi Muslims, was en route from Ānēgondi to the region of Anantaśayana, carrying his palm-leaf manuscripts on eight buffaloes, he came to Ānēkallu and remained there at the request of the local pāḷyagāra, who received him with great respect, and who was then engaged in building a fort. This pāḷyagāra gifted him ten vṛttis and built him a large house. A few years after he passed on,*[724] *having lived there contentedly for some*

[724] Tammaṇṇa Śāstri, that is. This is clear in the original, which refers to him respectfully in the plural, and to the *pāḷyagāra* in the singular.

time, his son Śaṅkarabhaṭṭa moved to Māgaḍi and settled down there. A very aged descendant in the fifth generation after Śaṅkarabhaṭṭa, called Veṅkaṭarāma Śrauti, lived in Māgaḍi as recently as 7–8 years ago. In the past, for the five generations from the time of Vidyāraṇya to the time of Tammaṇṇa Śāstri, members of this same family had served in the role of minister in the state of Ānēgondi.

Veṅkaṭrāmabhaṭṭa, the son of Śaṅkarabhaṭṭa, came to Sōsale and remained there, finding support from many of its residents. The son of this Veṅkaṭrāmābhaṭṭa was none other than Sōsale Timmappaśāstri – the son of this Timmappaśāstri, Veṅkaṭadāsappa, was renowned by the name of Aṇṇayya Śāstri.

Establishing a Basis for Analyzing the Genealogy

This account by Ayyā Śāstri closely matches the account starting on page 8, and may well have been used by the author of this biography. This invaluable document is, however, not specific on several crucial points, particularly on the date of Tammaṇṇa Śāstri's departure from Ānēgondi, as well as the reason for his curious choice of Anantaśayana as destination. Anantaśayana (modern-day Tiruvanantapuram [Sircar 1971]) is at a distance of 750 km from Ānēgondi as the crow flies, but the actual distance must have been much greater over the roads of the period. Tammaṇṇa Śāstri's journey took place at a very restive time in the region, and would have been a gruelling and hazardous undertaking for a family travelling with all its possessions. In addition to the eight buffaloes mentioned, the train would have included carts for the ladies and other people of the entourage, as well as for carrying provisions and possessions. There would also surely have been a retinue of attendants. In all, it would have been a substantial caravan, on a long and dangerous journey.

Garaḷapurī Śāstri's biography implies that the cataclysmic event precipitating Tammaṇṇa Śāstri's journey was the battle of Tāḷikōṭe.[725] It refers to the sack of the capital, and its allusion to the king's disappearence is suggestive of Tirumala's flight from Vijayanagara to Pēnukōṇḍa. In 1919, when this biography was written, scholarship on Vijayanagara was sparse, and the prevailing sense seems to have been that the battle of Tāḷikōṭe marked the end of the Vijayanagara empire. Thus, in discussing the murder of Sadāśiva, the last Tuḷuva king, Sewell [1900] remarks of the Āravīḍu dynasty: *"And thus began the third dynasty, if dynasty it can be appropriately called."* Subsequent scholarship has shown this view to be grossly incorrect, but there would have been little reason in 1919 to ascribe Tammaṇṇa Śāstri's journey to any period substantially later than Tāḷikōṭe.

We note, however, that Ayyā Śāstri's account makes no mention at all of the fateful battle of Tāḷikōṭe. It merely suggests that Tammaṇṇa Śāstri lost

[725]Technically, this is the battle of Rakkasa-Taṅgaḍi. For brevity, however, we will adopt the conventional practice of calling it Tāḷikōṭe, after the the site where the Muslim armies camped.

his all as a result of the actions of "Haiderābādi Muslims". As such, it provides no sound basis for the association with Tāḷikōṭe, though Ayyā Śāstri appears not to have contested this implication when he read the biography. We will see sound reasons for a different interpretation.

Ayyā Śāstri had deep ties to Sōsale, and must have heard this account from his father, and possibly his grandfather, who was only four generations removed from Tammaṇṇa Śāstri. As the only available written account of this history, by a learned descendant of Tammaṇṇa Śāstri, we must treat this document as a primary source. However, it is in the nature of oral traditions to be altered in the transmission, and to be subject to reinterpretation at each recounting. While this is an authoritative account of the tradition at Ayyā Śāstri's time, it would be risky to take it uncritically.

A Foundation for Further Inquiry

We begin by identifying the most reliable aspects of the account as those most likely to have remained unchanged in the retellings over the generations. We can consider all else in their light.

The genealogy is surely correct. Tammaṇṇa Śāstri and his descendants were all steeped in learning and culture. As proud inheritors of an illustrious family heritage going back centuries, and as descendants of scholars who were ministers at Dōrasamudra and Vijayanagara, capitals of the two most important dynasties in Karnāṭaka's history, they would have taken pains to preserve their antecedents.[726] Also, as traditional and observant brāhmaṇas, the sons would have dutifully performed the *śrāddha* rituals on each anniversary of their father's death, when they would have recited the names of their ancestors from the three preceding generations.[727] The genealogy's placement of Aṇṇayya Śāstri in the fourth generation after Tammaṇṇa Śāstri cannot be in error. We are also certain that Ayyā Śāstri was in the second generation after Aṇṇayya Śāstri.

An incidental reference in Ayyā Śāstri's account is also likely to be reliable, and indeed of crucial significance. Ayyā Śāstri states that the local *paḷeyagāra* was building a fort at Ānekallu when Tammaṇṇa Śāstri arrived.

---

[726] The family tradition holds that their remote ancestors were Hoysaḷa ministers. See page 358.

[727] See footnote 691.

Remarkably, this recollection has been preserved over six generations, down to Ayyā Śāstri's time. The construction of a fort is a major and impressive undertaking, requiring a huge investment of resources, and would have been a landmark event for the community. It seems certain that a genuine memory has been preserved; the very character of the event makes it unlikely that it is an invention arising from re-interpretations or creative retellings.

The Sugaṭūru and Ānēkallu *Pāḷeyagāras*

We will try to deduce the time of Tammaṇṇa Śāstri's arrival in Ānēkallu by identifying the fort's builder and the date of its construction. This task, however, turns out to be unexpectedly difficult.

The *pāḷeyagāras* of Ānēkallu were a branch of the Sugaṭūru lineage of *Gauḍas,* whose most distinguished ancestor appears to have been a Timmē Gauḍa of the early 15th century. The Sugaṭūru and Ānēkallu *pāḷeyagāras* tended to assume eponymous titles that were derivatives of this ancestor's name, making it hard to distinguish between them. The eponym appears in inscriptions and in the literature in numerous variant forms, including *Timme Gauda, Thamma (Tamma) Gauda, Timmappa Gauda, Tammendra,* and *Tammappagauda.* These forms appear to have been equivalent, so that the same individual is sometimes referred to by different variants in different inscriptions. The Ānēkallu *Gauḍas* were also fond of emphasizing their origins by adding the qualifier *Sugaṭūru* to their names, confounding the lineages and their members even further.

The use of qualifiers such as *Immaḍi* ("The Second") or *Mummaḍi* ("The Third"), or honorifics like *Çikka Rāya,* by members of the lineage is less helpful than we might expect. These qualifiers have been used as if they were first names, in disregard of their true meanings. Thus, the inscription HT 94, dated 1564 C.E., mentions a Çikkarāya Tamma Gauḍarayya, whose dominions included Hosakōṭe, as being the son of Tammayya Gauḍarayya and grandson of Mummaḍi Çikkarāya Tammapa Gauḍarayya. According to inscription AN 47 [Rice 1905], dated 1614 C.E., however, Mummaḍi Tammappa Gauḍa, then ruling over Hosakōṭe, was the son of Immaḍi Tammappa Gauḍa, and the grandson of Çikka Rāya Tammappa Gauḍa. AN 60 is a grant by Mummaḍi Çikka Rāya Tamme-Gaudarāya in Ānēkallu in the

Mummuḍi Çikkarāya Tammappa Gauḍa
↓
Ta(Ti)mmayya Gauḍa (1559)
↓
Çikkarāya Tammappa Gauḍa (1564)
↓
Immaḍi Tammappa
↓
Mummuḍi Çikkarāya Tammappa (1614)
↓
Çikkarāya Tamme Gauḍa
↓
Mummuḍi Çikkarāya Tamme Gauḍa (1693)

(a) FROM GOPAL [1985]

Tammappagauḍa (1422–1474)
↓
Çikkarāya Tammegauḍa 1 (1474–1542)
↓
Tammegauḍa 2 (1522–1605)
↓
Tammegauḍa 3 (1605–1642)
↓
Çikkarāya Tammegauḍa 2 (1642–1675)
↓
Çikkarāya Tammegauḍa 3 (1675–1705)
↓
Śivanēgauḍa (1705–1725)

(b) FROM RICE [2005]

Çikkarāya Tammegauḍa (1650)
↓
Mummuḍi Karaḍu Tammegauḍa (1699)
↓
Vīranañjunḍa Tammegauḍa (1757)
↓
Mummuḍi Ayyamagauḍa
↓
Çikkarāya
↓
Vīra Çikkarāya
↓
Çikkarāyalu (adopted)

(c) FROM REDDY [1995]

Plate 38: Example Sugaṭūru genealogies from the literature.

period 1639–1640 C.E. [Rice 1905]. Confusion abounds. Some 105 inscriptions relating to these two lineages are available, but great care is needed in interpreting them. These uncertainties have led to different genealogies for the Sugaṭūru lineage (see Plate 38).

An account called the *Kaifiyat of the Ānēkallu Pāḷeyagāras* has recently come to light [Reddy 1995]. It was written around 1800 C.E. to press the claims of the Ānēkallu *pāḷeyagāras* with the British after Ṭippu Sultān's death at their hands in Śrīraṅgapaṭṭaṇa in 1799 C.E. A large number of *Kaifiyats* were written at the time, mainly by village officials, such as accountants, and were informal histories, reflecting local tradition [Kalburgi 1994]. Most were sponsored by Colin Mackenzie, a surveyor and cartographer with the British army conquering South India between the late 1700s and the 1820s, C.E. These works contain both historically accurate information as well as folklore, frequently connecting local origins to *Puraṇic* and mythological events. The *Ānēkallu Kaifiyat* remains in the possession of a descendant of the Ānēkallu lineage, but is not a reliable source of its early history. We shall see, however, that it contains a piece of information of crucial value for us.

Ānēkallu's History and the *Ānēkallu Kaifiyat*

The present status of historical research on the Sugatūru and Ānēkallu *pāḷeyagāras* does not permit even an accurate reconstruction of the lineages, let alone their accurate dating. We will hence restrict ourselves to using available evidence to obtain an accurate date for the Ānēkallu fort's construction, our main object. We will also consider the identity of the *pāḷeyagāra* responsible for its construction. To allow future corrections in the light of new and more reliable information, and to relieve the more casual reader from having to consult the originals, we will include quotes from our sources. We begin with the following quote from Rice [1877a, p. 40]:

> The origin of the name—áne-kallu, hailstone—is not known. The town was founded about 1603 by Chikka Timme Gauda, a descendant of the original Sugatur chief. The general of the Bijapur State, after seizing Timme Gauda's hereditary possession of Hoskote, granted him Anekal, which formed a hobli of that pargana. He thereupon erected the fort and temple, constructed the large tank to the west, and set on foot such improvements as tended to the opulence and prosperity of the town. After a reign of 30 years he died, and was succeeded by his son Timme Gauda. The latter reigned 20 years, and left the territory to his son Dodda Timme Gauda, in whose time Anekal was conquered by the Mysore Raja. The chief, however, remained in possession, paying an annual tribute of 2,000 rupees, and died shortly after, having completed a long reign of 60 years. His son Vira Nañjana Timme Gauda then ruled for 24 years, and was in turn succeeded by his son Jama Gauda. This chief, in common with many others, was expelled by Haidar and his possessions annexed to Mysore.

The Bijāpur invasion refered to here occurred in 1638 C.E., as we will soon see. It is claimed by Sathyan [1989], however, on the basis of unspecified literary sources,[728] that the Ānēkallu fort was built in 1603 C.E. by Timmappagauda, the younger brother of Immadi Tammendra (or Tammegauda II).

[728] Perhaps one or more of the many literary works of Mummaḍi Tammēgauḍa. See page 331.

This claim conflicts with other accounts, and is hard to evaluate, since it is unclear what literary sources it is based on. Genealogical considerations, however, suggest that 1603 C.E. is too early a date for Tammaṇṇa Śāstri's arrival in Ānēkallu. If Tammaṇṇa Śāstri were even thirty when he arrived in Ānēkallu in 1603 C.E., he must have been born in 1573 C.E. or earlier. The span of two hundred and fifty or more years between his birth and that of Garalapurī Śāstri is simply too long for the five generations separating them in the genealogy (see Plate 9). We have already determined that the genealogy is likely to be fully reliable. It appears quite safe to discount the possibility that Tammaṇṇa Śāstri had arrived in Ānēkallu by 1603 C.E.

We pursue the history of the Sugaṭūr Gauḍas with the following excerpt from Rice [1877a, p. 108]:

> *Timme Gauḍa:* The history of the Bangalore District has already introduced us to the story of Baire Gauḍa and the band of refugees of the Morasu Wokkal tribe, …On their agreeing to separate, Timme Gauḍa, one of the seven, took up his abode at Sugaṭūr, near Jangamkoṭe. This was about the year 1418…
>
> Soon afterwards Timme Gauḍa repaired to the Vijayanagara court, and having ingratiated himself with the authorities, returned with the title of Nāḍ Prabhu, or Lord of the Sugaṭūr Naḍ…he had an opportunity of rendering signal service by rescuing some members of the royal family who had fallen into the hands of the Mughals. For this gallant act he was rewarded with the title of Chikka Rāyal, and soon after returned with royal permission to appropriate the treasure he had discovered and with extended authority. He accordingly repaired the fort of Kōlar, built Hoskōṭe (the new fort), and possessed himself of Muḷbagal, Punganūr and the adjacent parts, turning out the descendants of Lakhana and Madanna. To Kōlār he added the hoblis of Vemgal, Bail Sugaṭūr, Kaivara, Buradaguṇṭe, and Budikoṭe…
>
> Immaḍi (or the second) Chikka Rāyal Timme Gauḍa succeeded. On his death he divided the territory between his two sons. To Mummaḍi (or the third) Chikka Rāyal Timme Gauḍa he granted Hoskōṭe, and Kōlar to Timme Gauḍa. The latter ruled for five years under the name of Sugaṭūr Timme Gauḍa, and was succeeded by his son Timme Gauḍa, who in turn was followed by his son Chikka Rāyal Timme Gauḍa.

The precise circumstances underlying Çikka Rāya Timmegauḍa's move to Ānēkal are elaborated by Rice [1877b, p. 358] as follows.

> ...The Mughals had taken Daulatabad in 1634, and Aurangzeb was appointed viceroy of the Dekhan; but the contests with the Mughal power were shortly brought to a close for the time by the treaty which extinguished the State of Ahmadnagar and made Bijapur tributary to Delhi. The Bijapur arms were now directed to the south, under Ran-dulha Khan; with whom Shahji, father of the famous Sivaji, was sent as second in command, with a promise of a jagir in the territories to be conquered...
>
> ...The possessions of the Chikka Raya, namely, Hoskote and all the present Kolar District east of it, were then seized, in 1639, and the victorious army, passing below the Ghats, took Vellore and S'enji. Returning to the tableland, Dod Ballapur, Sira and all the south of the Chitaldroog district fell to Bijapur in 1644...
>
> The policy of the invaders was, while taking possession of the capital town, and administering the revenues of each principality, to grant the ousted chief an estate in some less productive part of his territory. This resulted in bringing under cultivation and attracting population to the more neglected tracts of the country. Thus Basavapatna and its possessions being retained, Tarikere was given to the palegar; Bangalore was taken but Magadi left to Kempe Gauda; similarly Hoskote was taken and Anekal granted; Kolar was taken and Punganur granted; Sira was taken and Ratnagiri granted.

By this account, Ānēkallu was founded in 1603 C.E. by the very *pāḷeyagāra* who had earlier founded Hosakōṭe. The inscription HT 186 carrying the date *Śaka* 1416, Ānanda *saṁvatsara,* Kārtika *śuddha* 12 (Nov. 19, 1494 C.E.), indeed refers to Tammagauda's construction of Hosakōṭe [Rice 1905]. According to Rice [1877a, p. 95], Hosakōṭe was built in 1595, its name ("new fort") distinguishing it from the old fort at Kōlār. Our analysis suggests, however, that this date is incorrect.

Mummaḍi Çikka Rāya Tammegauḍa inherited Hosakōṭe from Immaḍi Çikka Rāya Tammegauḍa, and was ousted from Hosakōṭe in 1639 C.E. by Śāhjī, who subsequently granted him Ānēkallu as a *jāhgir.* The excerpt on page 319 indicates that he built the fort in Ānēkallu only after being ousted from Hosakōṭe in 1639 C.E. We find support for this account in inscription AN 47 which mentions Mummaḍi Tammappa Gauḍa as the son of Immaḍi Tammappa Gauḍa, and the grandson of Çikka Rāya Tammappa Gauḍa, and indicates that Hosakōṭe was part of his dominions [Rice 1905]. Inscription AN 60 confirms Mummaḍi Çikka Rāya Tamme-Gaudarāya's presence in Ānēkallu at the time, being a grant by him in the period 1639–1640 C.E. [Rice 1905].

There is substantial and reliable documentation of the region's conquest in 1638–1639 C.E. by the Bijapur armies under Randullah Ḳhān and his second-in-command, the Marātha Śāhji, the father of Śivāji. Śāhji took up residence in Bangalore after driving out Immaḍi Kempēgauḍa, who was granted Māgaḍi.

Evidence from the *Ānēkallu Kaifiyat*

As we have noted, the *Ānēkallu Kaifiyat* cannot be relied on for historically accurate information for our period of interest. Many of its passages are fanciful, and many of its dates are clearly wrong. However, it accurately documents the original *pāḷeyagāra* family's own account of its history, and despite its shortcomings, deserves our attention. Its purpose at the time of its composition was to persuade the British to restore the family's hereditary rights as rulers of the region, of which they were deprived by Haider Ali in 1758 C.E., and for which the *Kaifiyat* pleads at its conclusion. It appears to have been composed around 1800 C.E., appealing Ānēkal's incorporation into the Kingdom of Maisūru after Ṭippu's death at Śriraṅgapaṭṭaṇa in 1799 C.E. in the Fourth Mysore War, putting it in the time frame of other *Kaifiyats*.

Kaifiyat writers seem to have been much more than merely literate, but not always scholarly. The *Ānēkallu Kaifiyat*, like many *Kaifiyats*, is in colloquial, and frequently ungrammatical Kannaḍa. Rather than translate the document, we will therefore paraphrase the sections most relevant to our inquiry.

> ...*(the preceding passage describes the flight of Dēvappa Gauḍa and his family from the Kanci region on Āśvayuja Bahuḷa Pratipad of the Prajāpati saṁvatsara, 1012 of the Śaka era*[729] *)*... they stopped at a convenient place in the western region, cleared the forest, and built a village, and named it Sugaṭuru after the *suraguttaḷi*. On the 14th *Bahuḷa* day of Māgha of the Śrīmukha *saṁvatsara*, 1014 of the *Śaka* era,[730] as Dēvappa Gauḍa's

[729] This corresponds to the year 1091 C.E., altogether too early for this episode.

[730] *Śaka* 1014 would be 1092 C.E., but Śrīmukha would be 1093 C.E., both too early.

son Tammēgauḍa slept under a Banyan tree,[731] a snake was seen shading him with its hood outspread...[732] they subsequently cleared the forest around, turned it into farmland, and while ploughing these fields, turned up seven pots full of treasure. They put it to good use, clearing more of the forest, and building a bastion in the form of a new fort, expanded their dominions, named the place Hosakōṭe, built the *Avimuktēśvara* temple in the fort, the large *Tammambudhi* lake, and the *Muttukūru agrahāra,* and inaugurated all three together on the 15th *śuddha* day of Māgha of the Yuvan *saṁvatsara* of the year 1016 of the *Śaka* era... they later built forts at Kōlār and Śiddlaghaṭṭa... In the Īśvara *saṁvatsara* matching *Śaka* year 1079, the Çedupaṭṭu-Çaṅgalpaṭṭu rulers attacked Narasiṅga Rāya of Pēnukōṇḍa with their forces, and the Rāya's forces having being weakened, were able to carry off the Rāya's family.[733] At this time, Tammēgauḍa of Hosakōṭe, thinking it shameful not to act when his Rāya's family was being taken away, attacked the Çedupaṭṭu-Çaṅgalpaṭṭu forces of his own accord, freed the Rāya's family, and returned them to the Rāya... Pleased, the Rāya conferred on him the following marks of recognition: (1) the title of *Çikkarāya,*[734] (2) a sword of state, (3) crown and signet, (4) thirty-two titles, (5) robes of honour, and control of the regions of Hosakōṭe, Kōlār, and Śiddlaghaṭṭa... the eldest son of this Tammēgauḍa was Ayyamagauḍa and his third son was Śivanēgauḍa... After the time of Tammēgauḍa, his sons divided his territories, Mummuḍi Ayyamagauḍa, the eldest, gaining Hosakōṭe, Immaḍi Vīranañjunḍa Tammēgauḍa, the second, getting Kōlār, and Śivanēgauḍa, the third, getting Śiddlaghaṭṭa... When Çikkarāya Tammegauḍa, the son of Vīra Nañjunḍa Tammegauḍa and grandson of Mummuḍi Ayyamagauḍa of Hosakōṭe was ruling Hosakōṭe,[735] he was asked for twenty elephants by the Rāya... Learning that elephants lived in a certain region of the forest to his south, he had twenty elephants captured near a rock formation thereabouts and sent them to his Rāya.

[731] Here we see the first occurrence of the important name Tammēgauḍa, so common in the family's genealogy.

[732] Important as an auspicious omen, inspiring the family to remain and develop the place.

[733] The word used is *kuṭumba,* which is also used in this document to mean "wife", though one would have expected the word *rāṇī* to have been used for the Rāya's consort.

[734] Literally "little king", a title reserved for royal princes or heirs presumptive. The *Kaifiyat* suggests that Tammegauḍa's actions were viewed by the Rāya as an act of filial devotion to his consort, thus justifying this title. Its conferral is surely a mark of profound gratitude.

[735] We have two Vīra Nañjunḍa Tammegauḍas here. The first, of Hosakōṭe, is the father of Çikkarāya Tammēgauḍa and the son of Mummuḍi Ayyamagauḍa. The second is "Immaḍi" Vīra Nañjunḍa Tammegauḍa of Kōlār. This genealogy differs from that in the quote above from Rice [1877a].

He then constructed a village, a lake, a grove, and a well on the spot, and appointed one Liṅgēgauḍa as their keeper... When gardeners and peasants from surrounding regions such as Patlugere, Śidi Hosakōṭe, Māsti, Mādapantla began creating trouble at Liṅgēgauḍa's village, he complained to Tammēgauḍa, who arrived with his forces, subdued these areas, and stationed some of his forces locally... In the Vyāya *saṁvatsara* of *Śaka* year 1328, representatives of the Pēśva called Ekōji and Śivōji arrived from the north, and under the command of Kāsim Ḳhān,[736] attacked and occupied Hosakōṭe; the terms of our treaty granted six months for the family to move to a rural region in the south called *Ānēmale.*[737] Tammegauḍa funded Liṅgēgauḍa to build a fort and a lake, and after himself moving to this location, added a more substantial fort, the *Tammāmbudhi* lake, the *Amṛtamallikārjuna* temple, and the *Tammasandra Agrahāra,* named the place *Ānēkallu,* and in the Sarvajitu *saṁvatsara* of the *Śaka* year 1329, dedicated all of them at the same time... Çikkarāya Tammegauḍa's son was Mummuḍi Karaḍu Tammegauḍa, whose son was Mummuḍi Çikkarāya Tammegauḍa, whose son was Vīra Nañjunḍa Tammegauḍa... In the Bahudhānya *saṁvatsara* of the *Śaka* year 1679,[738] Navāb Haidar Ali *Bahadūr* took control of the state and kept us in prison for 34 years; in the Virōdhikṛtu *saṁvatsara* of the *Śaka* year 1713, when Lord Wallis Mendis attacked Śrīraṅgapaṭṭaṇa,[739] he also occupied Beṅgaḷūru, and Mummuḍi Ayyamagauḍa, the son of Vīra Nañjunḍa Tammegauḍa and Obbayya Daṇi met him, and when after paying his respects, recited the *Kaifiyat* and reported on the state, he received a *sannad*...

Reflections on the *Kaifiyat*

The *Ānēkallu Kaifiyat's* account is in excellent agreement with those of Hunter [1908] and Rice [1877a,b]. The latter accounts in fact, give many

[736] *Śaka* 1328 (expired) is 1406–1407 C.E. The persons referred to arrived over 250 years later. The reference appears to be to the Bijāpur invasion of 1638 C.E. under the generalship of Śāhji, the father of the Ekōji and Śivāji mentioned here. There is no connection with the Pēśvas, except that they were also Marāṭhas.

[737] This means "elephant hill", substantially the same as Ānēkallu ("elephant rock").

[738] This date is accurate, as are subsequent dates.

[739] "Wallis Mendis" is obviously a reference to Lord Charles Cornwallis and General William Medows. This part refers to the Third Mysore War, and specifically to the march on Ṭippu Sultan in Śrīraṅgapaṭṭaṇa by way of Bangalore, which Cornwallis captured in March 1791. The Ānēkallu *pāḷeyagāra* contracted with the British to provision their forces during their march, thus playing an important support role. According to [Buchanan 1807, p. 426], he ravaged the countryside entirely in the process.

details not found in the *Kaifiyat*, but which we have omitted for brevity. These accounts appear indeed to have been based on reliable contemporary or historical information.

The dates in the *Kaifiyat*, however, are clearly problematic. The unfortunate practice in South India of referencing years only by their cyclic *saṁvatsara* names, paying no heed to the *Śaka* years, complicates matters. If we focus on finding a match for the *saṁvatsaras* based on historically reasonable timelines, the Prajāpati *saṁvatsara* of the fight from Kāñçi is likely to correspond to 1449 C.E., the snake episode to 1451 C.E., and Hosakōṭe's formal founding likely occurred in the Yuvan *saṁvatsara* of 1455 C.E. The *Kaifiyat* shows a lapse of 63 years between the founding of Hosakōṭe and the year Tammegauḍa is said to have received the *Çikkarāya* title. Going forward 63 years, however, places the latter event in the Īśvara *saṁvatsara* matching 1517–1518 C.E., firmly in the reign of Kṛṣṇadēva Rāya (1509–1530 C.E.), rather than during the reign of a Pēnukōṇḍa-based Vijayanagara ruler called "Narasiṅga", as the *Kaifiyat* says.

All four Vijayanagara kings called "Narasimha" ruled in succession between 1486–1509 C.E., none of them having Pēnukōṇḍa as their capital. We know of rebellions by Nāgama Nāyaka and Timma Dannāyaka during Kṛṣṇadēva Rāya's time, but none by Çaṅgalpaṭṭu. Any serious rebellion against this most powerful monarch would have been documented, especially if it involved the kidnapping of the royal family. In [Hunter 1908], however, it is suggested that this event occurred in 1577 C.E, a year that does correspond to an Īśvara *saṁvatsara*. By this time, Śrīraṅgadēva Rāya I (1572–1586 C.E.) had succeeded Tirumala, who had already moved the capital to Pēnukōṇḍa after Vijayanagara's defeat at Tāḷikōṭe. Śrīraṅgadēva was relatively weak at this time, as his vassals had begun to assert their independence. In 1577 C.E., his capital Pēnukōṇḍa was attacked by the 'Ādil Śāhi forces of Bijāpur [Sharma and Gopal 1980], and he moved his own residence to Çandragiri, causing some disarray in his personal affairs. There appear to be no other reports of a Çangalpaṭṭu revolt in this period, but the time was chaotic, and such a revolt remains a possibility. Tammegauḍa may indeed have received the *Çikkarāya* title in 1577 C.E. It is also just possible that the *Kaifiyat's* "Narasiṅga" is a corruption of "Śrīraṅga".

Çikkarāya was no trifling title, and figures prominently in subsequent events that led to a disastrous civil war. A nephew of Veṅkaṭāpati Rāya II

(1586–1614 C.E.) called Śrīraṅga seems to have initially been considered the logical heir to the throne, and addressed as *Çikkarāya*. However, a palace intrigue involving the powerful Gobbūri family, two of whose daughters were wives to Veṅkaṭāpati, managed to promote the claims of a boy said to be the Rāya's son by Bayamma of the Gobbūri family, though he was widely believed to be merely a foundling [Sharma and Gopal 1980, Subrahmanyam and Shulman 1990]. This boy appears to have been addressed as *Çikkarāya* during this period. In 1614 C.E., however, six days before he died, Veṅkaṭāpati reverted to his original choice, and handed over the reins of power to his nephew Śrīraṅgadēva Rāya II, leading to a civil war that ultimately led to Śrīraṅgadēva's murder by Gobbūri Jaggarāju. In the end, Jaggarāju was himself killed at the battle of Toppūr by the loyalist Vēlugōṭi Yaçama. At any rate, it is clear that conferral of the *Çikkarāya* title on Tammēgauḍa was an act of particular favour on the part of the sovereign.

Bijāpur and the Marāṭhās in the *Kaifiyat*

The next significant episode in the *Kaifiyat* is the one of greatest moment for us, namely, Tammegauḍa's move from Hosakōṭe to Ānēkallu. The *Kaifiyat* confirms that the Ānēkallu fort was built by Tammegauḍa after he lost Hoskōṭe and was forced to retire to Ānēkallu. Sadly, the *Kaifiyat* provides inaccurate information here in every other respect. By its account, Tammegauḍa's defeat occurred in the Vyāya *saṁvatsara* matching *Śaka* 1328, corresponding to 1405–1406 C.E. This date is too early by some 233 years.

We know from reliable historical sources [Rice 1877b, Satyanarayana 1996] that Tammegauḍa lost Hosakōṭe to Bijāpur in 1638 C.E., matching *Śaka* 1560 and the Bahudhānya *saṁvatsara*. His defeat came at the hands of the Bijāpur general Randullah Ḳhān and his Marāṭha deputy Śāhji, rather than at the hands of Śivāji, Ekōji, or Kāsim Ḳhān. There is no evidence that Randullah Ḳhān and Śāhji had any generals with those names on this campaign. In Sharma and Gopal [1980, p. 214], for example, we find names such as Aṅkuś Ḳhān, Ḳhairiyat Ḳhān, Patte Khān, Ādam Ḳhān, Abdullah Ḳhān, Mahmūd Ḳhān, Mallik Śāle Ḳhān, Galiya Ḳhān, Bilhar Ḳhān, Balavant Ḳhān, Sidde Raçein, *Siddi* Mallik Ḳhān, Śāhji, Vedōji, and Rāghava Panḍit. In Laine and Bahulkar [2001, p. 128], we see the additional names Yakut Ḳhān, 'Ambar Ḳhān, Hussein, Masūd Ḳhān, Pawār, Ghatge, Ingle,

Gaḍhe, Ghorpaḍe. Śivāji, Ekōji, and Kāsim Ḳhān are indeed names familiar to history, but nowhere do they come up among Randullah Ḳhān's or Śāhji's generals.

In this instance, the *Kaifiyat's* account appears to reflect confused lingering memories of several subsequent historical episodes. The Marāṭha influence in the region begins when Śāhji arrived as a senior commander under the Bijāpuri general Randullah Ḳhān. Śivāji and Ekōji, who both figure prominently in the later history of the region, were sons of Śāhji by his wives Jījībāi and Tukābāi, respectively. During this period, Bijāpur and Gōlkōṇḍa were busy conquering the remnants of the former Vijayanagara empire. Instead of directly attacking the Vijayanagara sovereign, who ruled by turns from Pēnukōṇḍa, Çandragiri, and Vēlūr, they went about taking it apart *pāḷeyagāra* by *pāḷeyagāra*. Bijāpur's forces came down the western coast into the region of modern-day Karnāṭaka, and Gōlkōṇḍa's armies took its eastern sections. These campaigns appear to be linked with the circumstances of Tammaṇṇa Śāstri's journey, as we will see.

Śāhji played a leading role in this Muslim conquest of the south as a Bijāpur commander under Randullah Ḳhān during the reign of Mohammad 'Ādil Śāh,[740] and had stayed on in Beṅgaḷūru to administer the newly formed Karnāṭak-Bijāpur-Bālāghaṭ province, which included Kōlār, Hosakōṭe, Beṅgaḷūru, and Sīra, and which was conferred on him as *jāhgīr* [Rice 1908]. In 1648 C.E., Śāhji had a falling out with his patron king Mohammad 'Ādil Śāh, and was arrested on July 25 [Sharma 1944], though he was pardoned and released ten months later on May 16, 1649 C.E.[741] At this time, the region of Beṅgaḷūru was restored to him as *jāhgīr*. He then took up residence at Kanakagiri near Ānēgondi, leaving his southern *jāhgīr* in the hands of his son Ekōji. The *Kaifiyat's* reference to Ekōji is surely a recollection of this period.

---

[740] Śivāji is now celebrated for having checked Muslim power. However, his grandfather Mālōji and father Śāhji had both served as distinguished generals in the service of Muslim kingdoms, Mālōji with Malik 'Ambar of Ahmadnagar, and Śāhji with Ahmadnagar, Bijāpur, and the Mughals. Śivāji himself appears to have been motivated less by a desire to check Muslim power than by a desire to dominate his adversaries, who largely just happened to be Muslim. The iconification of Śivāji may also result from a profound lack of awareness in Mahārāṣtra, even among scholars, of Vijayanagara's history and legacy. See [Guha 2009] for an analysis of this astounding phenomenon.

[741] Śāhji was arrested again in 1663 C.E., this time by 'Ali 'Ādil Śāh II, but again quickly released.

Śivāji had held Śāhji's *jāhgīr* in Puṇe since boyhood. Ekōji had taken residence at Tañjāvūru after conquering it in 1675 C.E., but had control of Śāhji's southern *jāhgīr,* headquartered at Beṅgaḷūru. Śāhji died in early 1664 C.E., and a dispute arose between Śivāji and Ekōji on how to divide their father's southern *jāhgīr.* Śivāji demanded that Ekōji hand over the *jāhgīr* in exchange for a smaller *jāhgīr* amounting to 300,000 *Haṇas,* which Ekōji refused to do. A campaign by Śivāji culminated in Ekōji's defeat in November 1677 C.E. [Sharma 1944]. Śivāji had to turn back in 1677 C.E. to defend his northern dominions against Mughal attacks, but left Ekōji in charge as a vassal. On his return journey, Śivāji took Beṅgaḷūru, Kōlār, Sīra, and several other provinces. Ānēkallu would have been among these conquests, accounting for the *Kaifiyat's* mention of Śivāji. Contrary to what the *Kaifiyat* says, however, neither Ekōji nor Śivāji had any connection with the Pēśvās, who were in control from 1749 C.E. onwards. The *Kaifiyat* is using the term Pēśvā simply as a generic allusion to a Marāṭhā power.

The *Kaifiyat* also mentions Kāsim Ḳhān, who was a Mughal general from a later date. After conquering Bijāpur and Gōlkōṇḍa in 1687 C.E. and 1688 C.E., respectively, the Mughals seized the southern districts subordinate to them, and formed a new province with Sīra as capital, composed of the *parganas* Basavapaṭṭaṇa, Būdihāḷu, Sīra, Pēnukōṇḍa, Doḍḍaballapura, Hosakōṭe, and Kōlār. Kāsim Ḳhān was appointed the *Faujdār Dīvān* of this province.

Kāsim Ḳhān, interestingly, was also responsible for Beṅgaḷūru's coming into the possession of the Maisūru kings. Ekōji had continued to rule from Tañjāvūru after Śivāji's death in 1680 C.E. Finding Beṅgaḷūru to be too far from his capital to control, he offered to sell it to Kaṇṭhīrava Voḍeyar of Maisūru for 300,000 *Rūpīs* in 1687 C.E. However, Kāsim Ḳhān first seized the city, and sold it to Voḍeyar for the same price. At any rate, the *Kaifiyat* mentions three of the four administrators of the region (Śāhji has been left out), but is quite wrong on the dates and the sequence of events.

The *Kaifiyat,* however, yields up one important nugget of information. By its account, Tammēgauḍa was given six months by Śāhji to establish himself at Ānēkallu after he lost Hosakōṭe in 1638 C.E. We know that Randullah Ḳhān attacked Śrīraṅgapaṭṭaṇa in January 1639 C.E., sometime after his conquest of Hosakōṭe [Sharma and Gopal 1980, p. 265]. Thus, Tammēgauḍa's move to Ānēkallu could not have occurred any later than the middle of

1639 C.E. The *Śaka* year the *Kaifiyat* gives for Tammēgauḍa's move (1329) is incorrect. *Śaka* years, however, are less reliable in traditional accounts than are *saṁvatsaras*. Indeed, 1639 C.E. corresponds to a Sarvajitu *saṁvatsara*, the very *saṁvatsara* the *Kaifiyat* specifies for Tammēgauḍa's move. In this respect, the *Kaifiyat's* account matches other historical information.

Tammaṇṇa Śāstri's Arrival in Ānēkallu

We now return to our primary inquiry, using the above background as context. Available evidence suggests that the Ānēkallu fort was built immediately after Tammāgauḍa lost Hosakōṭe, which, as we have seen, happened in 1638 C.E.

The *Kaifiyat* suggests that there were, in fact, two rounds of fort construction, the first by Liṅgēgauḍa at Tammēgauḍa's behest in the Vyāya *saṁvatsara*, and the second by Tammēgauḍa himself in the Sarvajitu *saṁvatsara*, after moving to Ānēkallu. Sarvajitu follows Vyāya in the southern Bṛhaspati *saṁvatsara* cycle, so we can make a fair inference that the second round of fort construction was completed within a year of Tammēgauḍa's move from Hosakōṭe.

Tammaṇṇa Śāstri must hence have arived in Ānēkallu in 1639–1640 C.E. We note in passing that this date is over seventy-five years after Tāḷikōṭe. Tammaṇṇa Śāstri was likely in the second or third generation after that event. Can we associate a timeline with the genealogy, working backwards from 1822 C.E., the confirmed year of Garaḷapurī Śāstri's birth? Reckoning 30 years per generation would place Tammaṇṇa Śāstri's birth at around 1672 C.E., and push his arrival in Ānēkallu into the 1700s C.E. By this time, however, the Mughals were firmly in control of the region, so the *pāḷeyagāra* is hardly likely to have been building a fort. Also, Ayyā Śāstri's reference to Tammaṇṇa Śāstri's travails at the hands of the "Haiderābādi" Muslims would make no sense, since the state of Haiderābād had ceased to exist after 1687 C.E., when Aurangzēb's Mughal forces had occupied its capital city Haiderābād. Even reckoning 40 years per generation yields 1622 C.E. as the likely year for Tammaṇṇa Śāstri's birth, making him barely 17 years of age in 1639 C.E. Some generations in the genealogy appear to have been even longer than 40 years.

We follow the Māgaḍi branch of the family, instead. Ayyā Śāstri belonged to the fifth generation after Tammaṇṇa Śāstri. Veṅkaṭarāmā Śrauti, of the same generation, is said to have been "very aged" seven or eight years prior 1919 C.E., the date we presume for the genealogical document by Ayyā Śāstri. Ayyā Śāstri was sixty-five years old in 1919 C.E., so Veṅkaṭarāmā Śrauti was probably in his eighties by 1910 C.E., and so was likely born in the 1830s

C.E. His father, who would have been in Garaḷapurī Śāstri's generation, was likely born in the late 1700s C.E. By this timeline, we might expect someone in Aṇṇayya Śāstri's generation, the fourth after Tammaṇṇa Śāstri, to have been born in the 1760s C.E. Reckoning back four more generations at an average of 40 years each, we arrive at 1600 C.E. as a possible year for Tammaṇṇa Śāstri's birth. This would make him just under 40 years of age at the time of his arrival in Ānēkallu, which appears quite reasonable.

It is usual to reckon 25–30 years per generation in genealogical calculations, so a figure of 40 years per generation is rather high. Unfortunately, we are constrained by a complete lack of documentary evidence, so we must construct our chronology using the most reasonable interpretation of the available facts, and on the elimination of possibilities inconsistent with such facts. Plate 9 on page 67 shows the genealogy given by Ayyā Śāstri annotated with dates.

Additional Questions About the *Pāḷeyagāra's* Identity

The *pāḷeyagāra* who built the Ānēkallu fort after being evicted from Hosakōṭe is referred to variously in the literature as Tammēgauda, Çikkarāya Tammēgauda, Mummuḍi Çikka Rāya Tammēgauda, and so on. We are unable to distinguish this individual from others of his lineage purely by name. As we have seen, names are frequently repeated in this lineage, and epigraphs and other writings use inconsistent names for the same person.

We can, however, ask a different question regarding this person's identity. One of the Ānēkallu *pāḷeyagāras,* also referred to variously as Çikkarāya Tammē Gauda, Mummuḍi Tammē Gauda, Mummuḍi Çikkarāya Tammē Gauda, and so on, was himself a considerable scholar. According to Diwakar [1968, p. 686], Mummaḍi Thamma Bhūpāla (one of the many variants we see of his name) wrote *Rājēndra Çōḷa Çarita, Kumārārjunīya* and *Sundarēśaçarita* in Telugu, *Śankara Samhita* in Kannaḍa, *Karmadivyākhyāna Rasika Manōranjana* in *Saṁskṛta,* and had the work *Śivadarpaṇa* compiled by brāhmaṇa scholars. He fostered trade and commerce, and sheltered hundreds of Hindu refugees from Muslim persecution.

That last point is significant, given Tammaṇṇa Śāstri's own story. Even though we may not be able to distinguish him by name from the others in his lineage, can we determine whether the *pāḷeyagāra* who sheltered Tammaṇṇa Śāstri in his flight from Muslim persecution was indeed the scholarly

Tammēgauḍa? According to [Krishnamurthi 2001], Mummaḍi Tammēgauḍa succeeded Immaḍi Tammēgauḍa around 1608 C.E., and went on to produce the body of scholarship listed above. This same *pāḷeyagāra* is said in [Sharma and Gopal 1980, p. 240] to have lived during the reign of Veṅkaṭa Dēva Rāya (1633–1646 C.E.), based on information from [Narasimhāçār 1929]. If this information is accurate, our answer would be in the affirmative.

Clues from the *Maḷeyarāja Çāritra*

Sadly, we must peer through murky waters once again. In the first chapter of his *Maḷeyarāja Çāritra*, the poet Sejjeya Siddhaliṅga, in acknowledging his royal patron, refers to him by the names Tamma, Mummadi Tamma, and Mummaḍi Çikkarāya Bhūpālaka, and lauds his accomplishments in having written poetry in three languages (*tribhāṣeyoḷ viraçita kavitvamuṁ*), leaving no doubt that he lived during the time of the scholarly *pāḷeyagāra* of our interest [Siddhaliṅga 1989].

The precise *Śaka* year of the work's completion is referenced in the fifty-sixth verse of the eleventh *sandhi* of the third *āśvāsa,* but is illegible in the available manuscripts. In the colophon, however, the poet declares the work to have been completed on Śukravāra (Friday), the thirteenth *śuddha tithi* of Vaiśākha of the Dundhubhi *saṁvatsara.* We see Dundhubhi *saṁvatsara*s in 1562–1563, 1622–1623, and 1682–1683 C.E. In his preface to Siddhaliṅga [1989], the editor assigns the work to 1562–1563 C.E., quoting information a colleague provided from the *Indian Ephemeris* by Svamikannu Pillai. This work matches the given *tithi* and *māsa* to Friday, April 17, 1562.

This seems too early a date for the work, however. It is earlier than our inferred date of 1577 C.E. for the *Çikkarāya* title's having come into the family, and predates even the battle of Tāḷikōṭe. If this date is correct, however, the Tammēgauḍa who moved to Ānēkallu in 1639 C.E. could not be the same person Siddhaliṅgayya refers to in 1562 C.E.

What about the subsequent Dundubhi *saṁvatsaras*? The stated *māsa* and *tithi* also correspond to Saturday, April 13, 1622 C.E., to Tuesday, May 9, 1682 C.E., and to Thursday, May 6, 1742 C.E. We can eliminate the second of these, since we are looking for a Friday. The thirteenth *śuddha tithi* of Vaiśākha began in the late evening on Friday, April 12, 1622, so this date is a possibility. Similarly, the *tithi* of interest began in the middle of the day on Friday, May 5, 1742 C.E., so this also remains a possibility.

We suggest that a clue to the correct date of this work is to be found in the first chapter of its first canto. Here, the poet praises his patron for his valour, saying that even at the age of eleven, he defeated a *Sikhīndra Pādhā* and sported with the heads of his enemies. We reproduce the verse below:

> *pannondaneya barisadeḻevareyadol śaurya*
> *dunnatikeyindā sikhīndrapādhāvanaṁ*
> *bannambaḍisi koḷuguḷadoḷātanaṁ taguḷi mannemaneyaranellaṁ*
> *pannatikeyiṁ tar̂idu talegaḷaṁ çeṇḍāḍi*
> *daṁ nirjarāṅganeyarānandisuttiral*
> *nanni mummaḍi çikkarāyabhūpālakaṅginniḷeyoḷeṇegāṇenu* ||37||

Who exactly was this *Sikhīndra Pādhā*? Almost surely, *Sikhīndra* is a corruption of Sikandar. However, no references to a ruler or other military figure by that name seem to appear around 1562 C.E. or 1622 C.E. The only possibility is that *Sikhīndra Pādhā* is a reference to Sikandar Pādśāh, the last king of Bijāpur, the boy-prince Sikandar 'Ādil Śāh (born 1668 C.E., ruled 1672–1686 C.E.).

Is it possible that Tammēgauḍa fought Sikandar 'Ādil Śāh? We recall that the Hosakōṭe-Ānēkallu region was under Ekōji, who maintained his allegiance to Bijāpur till the very end. After Ekōji's move to Tañjāvūru in 1675 C.E., he found it hard to keep these more distant provinces from becoming autonomous (whence his move to sell Beṅgaḷūru). As noted by Krishnamurthi [2001], the number of inscriptions in the name of the local chiefs shows a distinct increase at this time. Though Bijāpur was a greatly weakened kingdom by this time, it must have made attempts to subdue its vassal *paḷeyagāras,* among whom was indeed the Ānēkallu ruler. All such attempts would have been undertaken in the name of Sikandar 'Ādil Śāh, who had then come to the Bijāpur throne. The poet is likely referring to one such attempt to bring Ānēkallu to heel, in which the forces of his patron Mummaḍi Çikkarāya Bhūpāla prevailed.

A similar observation is made by Krishnamurthy [1994, p. 18], who assigns Mummaḍi Tammegauḍa to the period 1605–1642 C.E., and concludes that the *Maḷeyarāja Çāritra* has confused either Ibrāhim 'Ādil Śāh II or his son Mohammad with Sikandar 'Ādil Śāh. This conclusion is manifestly incorrect. Given its reference to Sikandar 'Ādil Śāh, a name that could hardly have been conjured up by its author, the *Maḷeyarāja Çāritra* must be later than 1668 C.E., the year Sikandar 'Ādil Śāh was born. However, the *Çāritra* refers to the scholarly Tammegauḍa in the present tense, rather than eulogistically. Clearly, this Tammegauḍa was contemporaneous with the work, and could not possibly have ruled 1605–1642 C.E.

The likelihood of a later date for the *Maḷeyarāja Çāritra* seems to be strengthened by its language. It is generally very formal, and employs both pure Kannaḍa words as well as an extensive *Saṁskṛta* vocabulary. Surprisingly, however, the work also uses Urdu words. For example (*aśvāsa-sandhi*-verse references appear in parentheses), it uses *çhappan* for fifty-six (2-2-29), *çhattīs* for thirty-six (1-1-8), *battīs* and for twenty-six (2-7-6), *jangi* and *jabar* for war and force (3-7-21), *tarkas* and *phauj* for arrow and army (2-5-11).

There was a flourishing *Dakkhani Urdu* tradition long before this time, but Urdu words had to have become common enough in Kannada by the time of this work to be acceptable in formal literary compositions. Not proof, certainly, but evidence in favour of the later date of 1742 C.E. for the *Çāritra*.

If this scholarly Tammēgauḍa were to have been born around 1670 C.E., he would have been eleven years old in around 1681 C.E. It is possible for him to have fought Sikandar 'Ādil Śāh (who ruled 1672–1686 C.E.) at the age of eleven, as *Çāritra* suggests. 1742 C.E., the possible date for the completion of the *Çāritra*, would be seventy-two years after Tammēgauḍa's birth. He could have been alive, justifying the *Çāritra's* reference to him in the present tense.

If this reasoning is correct, the *pāleyagāra* who welcomed Tammaṇṇa Śāstri to Ānēkallu was not the scholarly Mummaḍi Çikkarāya Tammēgauḍa (Bhūpāla), but an ancestor, who has been referred to by very similar names. The Sugaṭur genealogies in Plate 38 do, in fact, show a Mummuḍi Çikkarāya Tammēgauḍa in the late 1600s C.E., who may have been this scholar. It is also very likely that this scholarly Mummaḍi Çikkarāya Tammēgauḍa was educated by the company of learned brāhmaṇas, including the descendants of Tammaṇṇa Śāstri, who lived in the Tammasandra *agrahāra* that was built by this Tammēgauḍa's ancestor when he established Ānēkallu.

The Identity of the Ānēgondi *Saṁsthāna*

We know from Ayyā Śāstri's account that Tammaṇṇa Śāstri was a minister in the Ānēgondi *Saṁsthāna*. The biography's author infers that Tammaṇṇa Śāstri was a minister at the Vijayanagara court, and that his southward journey to Anantaśayana was triggered by the sack of the city in 1565 C.E. This interpretation is understandable, given the status of Vijayanagara scholarship at the time of the biography's writing. Our analysis suggests, however, that Tammaṇṇa Śāstri's journey dates to around 1639 C.E. We now ask whether we can make any inferences regarding the origin of this journey and its destination.

The term "Ānēgondi *Saṁsthāna*" being a generic allusion to an Ānēgondi-based regime, we must seek its identity in the political context of 1639 C.E. We give a brief account of the developments in the region before and after 1565 C.E.

Prelude to the Battle of Tāḷikōṭe

Contrary to popular impression, the rivalry between Vijayanagara and its Muslim neighbours (the Deccan Sultanates of Ahmadnagar, Berar, Bijāpur, Bidar, and Golkōṇḍa) appears not to have been rooted in religion. Their armies were of quite diverse composition, and included local Hindus and Muslims, as well as foreign mercenaries from Ethiopia (the *Siddis*), Turks, Persians, and Europeans.[742] Soldiers and generals frequently accepted employment with one state, later switching to another. Vijayanagara and the various Sultanates also often appealed to each other for help against one or more of the others.

Incredibly, *Aḷiya* Rāma Rāya (1484–1565 C.E.), who was effectively the Vijayanagara ruler at the time of Tāḷikōṭe, began his career as a general in the Gōlkōṇḍa army [Eaton 2005], switching his allegiance to Vijayanagara only

[742] All these different ethnicities and religions played an important rọle in the politics of the time. The word *Siddi* is applied to a group of African mercenaries of Bantu background who worked both as foot soldiers as well as commanders, Malik 'Ambar of Ethiopia being among the most famous. They were Muslims of the Śi'ā sect (the term *Siddi* is believed to be a corruption of *Sayyidi*). Large *Siddi* communities still thrive in parts of India and Pakistan.

in 1515 C.E., after being dismissed by Gōlkōṇḍa for perceived dereliction of duty. He quickly distinguished himself as a general under the great Tuḷuva emperor Kṛṣṇadēva Rāya (1509–1529 C.E.), later becoming his son-in-law (*Aḷiya* is a sobriquet meaning "son-in-law" in Kannaḍa). The practice of Hindus and Muslims serving in each other's armies continued even in later years, as the service of Mālōji and Śāhji in Muslim armies amply demonstrates (see footnote 740). *Aḷiya* Rāma Rāya also appears to have had a very warm friendship with 'Ali 'Ādil Śāh of Bijāpur, even referring to the 'Ādil Śāh as his son. The 'Ādil Śāh would ultimately become a reluctant ally against Rāma Rāya at Tāḷikōṭe.

Sadāśiva Rāya (1542–1570 C.E.), the last representative of the Tuḷuva dynasty, was nominally king at the time of Tāḷikoṭe, but his regent *Aḷiya* Rāma Rāya of the Āravīḍu clan maintained complete control of the kingdom during his own lifetime. The Āravīḍu dynasty came into being only after Rāma Rāya's brother Tirumala Rāya was crowned at Pēnukōṇḍa after Sadāśiva's death in 1570 C.E., but the Āravīḍu clan had exercised a great deal of power after the death of Kṛṣṇadēva Rāya in 1529 C.E. As Kṛṣṇadēva Rāya's son-in-law, Rāma Rāya had long enjoyed the emperor's confidence. He consolidated his power fully during the tragic prelude to Sadāśiva's coming to the throne.

Aḷiya Rāma Rāya's Ascent to Power

A bloody battle for succession followed the death in 1542 C.E. of Açyuta Rāya, Kṛṣṇadēva Rāya's successor. Açyuta had placed his son and heir Veṅkaṭa, still a child, under the charge of his brother, most likely Raṅga [Sharma and Gopal 1978, p. 180]. Raṅga, with the support of many nobles, including Rāma Rāya, imprisoned Veṅkaṭa in an attempt to seize power. *Pedda* and *Çinna* Tirumala, the late king's brothers-in-law, intervened on Veṅkaṭa's behalf, with little effect. Varadāmba, the queen mother, solicited the 'Ādil Śāh's help. Coming to their senses, the nobles now threw their support to Raṅga, averting disaster.

Subsequently, when Rāma Rāya was away on a campaign in the Malabār, the elder Tirumala seized power. When Rāma Rāya turned back towards Vijayanagara, Tirumala panicked, and invited the 'Ādil Śāh's help, reportedly even seating him on the Vijayanagara throne [Sharma and Gopal 1978, p. 181]. Rāma Rāya, biding his time, made peace with Tirumala, and

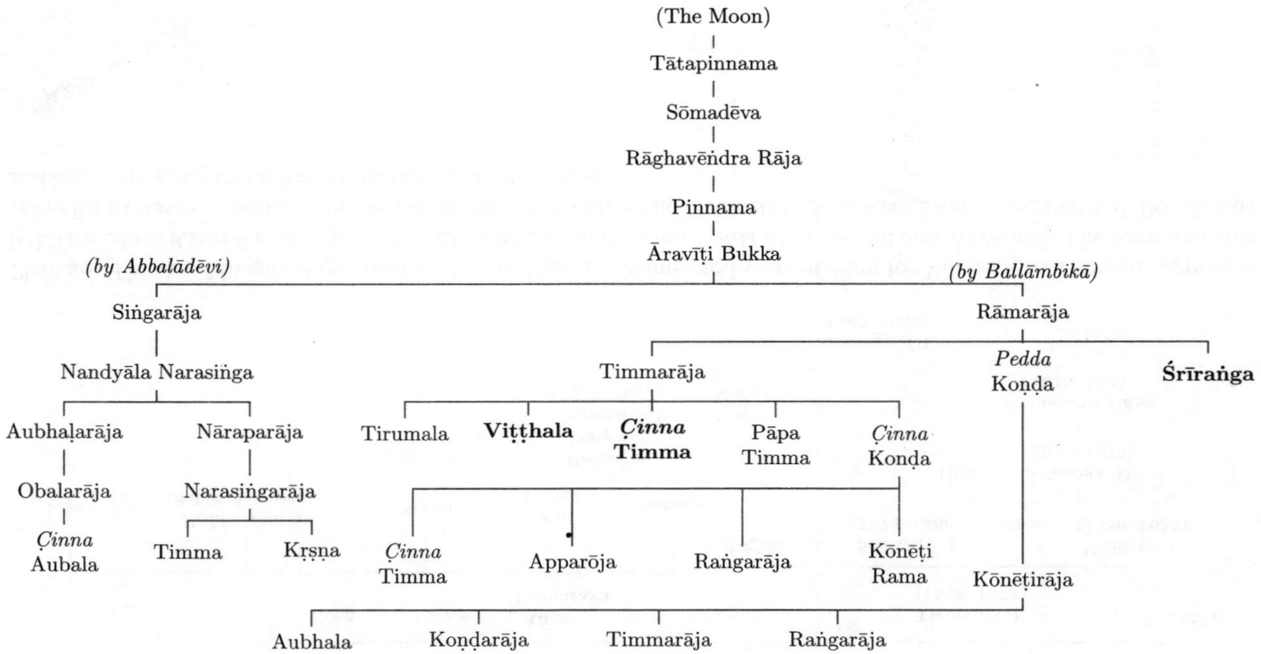

Plate 39: Narapati genealogy, as per Aiyangār [1919], the Dēvanahaḷḷi inscription, the *Bālabhāgavatam,* and the *Narapativijayamu.* Tātapinnama's great-grandfather is said to have been Vijjala, who usurped the Çāḷukyan throne. Pinnama is described in inscriptions as being the lord of Āravīṭipura. His son Āravīṭi Bukka was a general of the Vijayanagara emperor Sāḷuva Narasiṁha. The kings of the Āravīḍu dynasty of Vijayanagara were all descendants of Śrīraṅga, at right. See Plate 40.

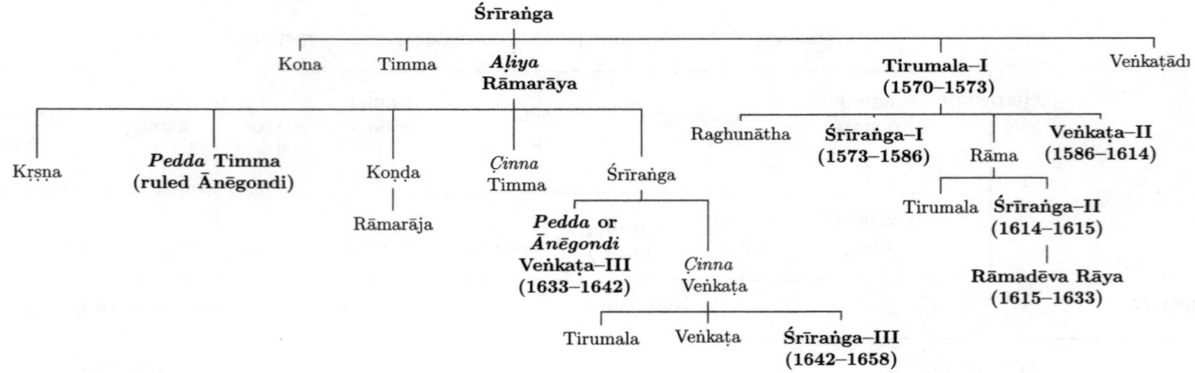

Plate 40: The Āravīḍu genealogy continued from Plate 39. Names and years of reign for Vijayanagara emperors appear in boldface. *Aḷiya* Rāma Rāya was never formally emperor, and his son *Pedda* Timma ruled only Ānēgondi. The descendants of *Aḷiya* Rāma Rāya continued to be associated with Ānēgondi, while Tirumala I's descendants were associated with Pēnukōṇḍa and other Vijayanagara capitals of the post-Tāḷikōṭe period.

convinced him of the danger of inviting the help of Muslims. The 'Ādil Śāh was persuaded to return to his dominions, albeit only in exchange for a great deal of wealth.

The elder Tirumala,[743] in a grab for power, now killed his nephew Veṅkaṭa, two of his own uncles, and one of Açyuta's nephews. He then proceeded to have a number of leading nobles blinded. Disgusted with Tirumala, the nobles rallied around Rāma Rāya, who marched on the capital. The younger Tirumala, who went out to meet Rāma's forces, lost the battle due to massive desertions, and was executed. The queens now ordered the city gates thrown open to Rāma Rāya. The elder Tirumala, recognizing that his cause was lost, destroyed much of the wealth in the treasury, and committed suicide.[744] Sadāśiva, the son of Açyuta's brother Raṅga, was still a child, but was accepted as the king by all. Sadāśiva was formally crowned, Rāma Rāya took over as regent, and kept power until his death at Tāḷikōṭe. Sadāśiva, in fact, became Rāma Rāya's prisoner after 1550 C.E, when he tried to assert power [Datta 2008, p. 96].

Sadāśiva likely enjoyed popular sympathy and support during his lifetime, given the the tragic massacre following Açyuta's death. It was clearly not expedient for Rāma Rāya to openly depose Sadāśiva and seat himself on the throne. Nonetheless, he seems to have begun preparing for a transfer of power from the Tuḷuvas to his own Narapati lineage, by promoting its association with that of the Çāḷukyas (see footnote 35), which was held in great esteem at the time.

This association is dismissed by Eaton [2005], since Kalyāṇa had been under Muslim control for hundreds of years preceding Rāma Rāya's time. This claim was ingeniously justified, however. The Devanahaḷḷi inscription and the *Narapativijayam* give genealogies showing this clan's descent from Kalaçuri Vijjala, usurper of the Çāḷukyan throne in 1157 C.E. A remote ancestor called *Çāḷukya* (92nd from the Pāṇḍava Arjuna himself), is also shown for Vijjala, a literal justification of the title "Çāḷukyan descendant" claimed by later Āraviḍus. This Çāḷukyan association was politically

[743]He is referred to as *Pedda* (or elder) Tirumala by Sharma and Gopal [1978], but as Salakarāja by Eaton [2005]. He may have been the viceroy who invaded Anantaśayana. See page 356.

[744]*Pedda* Tirumala is referred to as *Huçça* (or insane) Tirumala in many accounts. The pattern of paranoia in his actions is clear.

necessary. Rāma Rāya was an outstanding ruler and general, and was descended from a prominent warrior clan of Āravīḍu in present-day Karnūl district in Āndhrapradēśa. Even these antecedents could hardly match the acknowledged glory of the Vijayanagara lineage, however. A link to a historically prominent independent dynastic line was essential.

Vijayanagara was quite easily the dominant power of its time in peninsular India, and Rāma Rāya was an extremely confident and effective ruler. While the Muslim Bahmani kingdom, founded in the mid-14th century C.E., had functioned as a fairly effective counterweight against Vijayanagara, the Deccan Sultanates of Gōlkōṇḍa, Bijāpur, Ahmadnagar, Berār, and Bidar, which were its successors, had never been fully united against Vijayanagara. They constantly fought each other as regional rivals vying for the same territories. More importantly, the power of these Sultanates had been kept in check by the great Kṛṣṇadēva Rāya, and later by Rāma Rāya, during his rule of Vijayanagara in Sadāśiva's name.

Rāma Rāya may have lacked Kṛṣṇadēva Rāya's profile, but he proved to be supremely capable both as a general and as a politician. He kept the Sultanates under check either by force, or by forming alliances with one or more of them, as needed. However, in 1564 C.E., Gōlkōṇḍa, Bijāpur, and Ahmadnagar moved to form a league against Vijayanagara because of what they perceived a series of intolerable insults by *Aḷiya* Rāma Rāya. Some accounts suggest that Rāma Rāya had treated Muslim envoys with contempt. A detailed account of Rāma Rāya's dealings with these envoys appears in *Rāma Rāyana Bakhair* [Sastry and Venkataramanayya 1946, p. 208]. On hearing that the Sultanates were ready to move against him, Rāma Rāya expelled their envoys with disgrace from his court, thereby precipitating the confrontation [Sharma and Gopal 1978, p. 217].

The Battle of Tāḷikōṭe (Rakkasa-Taṅgaḍi)

Their famous battle was fought south of the river Kṛṣṇā, across the river from the villages of Rakkasgi and Taṅgaḍgi (Rakkasa-Taṅgaḍi). The armies of the Sultanates camped near Tāḷikoṭe (giving the battle its more common name), and initially found it impossible to cross the Kṛṣṇā, the Vijayanagara army having secured the only spot where the river might reasonably have been forded. However, the Muslim armies executed a feinting maneuver, moving along the northern bank for three days. Deceived, the Vijayanagara forces moved from their fortified positions to oppose a possible crossing elsewhere. The Muslim armies suddenly struck camp at night, and moved back to the original spot, where they effected a crossing unopposed. They then moved twelve miles to the river Hukkēri to oppose Rāma Rāya's forces.

Rāma Rāya was surprised, but remained confident of victory. Though over eighty years old at the time, he mounted his war elephant and placed himself in the thick of battle, egging on his troops and rewarding bravery instantly with treasure. His troops initially caused so much havoc among the Muslims that the Gōlkōṇḍa and Bijāpur forces on the flanks retreated. The Ahmadnagar forces, however, remained firm. The next charge by Vijayanagar forces might well have been decisive, but the Muslim artillery now began to use bags of copper coins as ammunition, causing devastating losses at close range among the charging Vijayanagara troops. According to the Italian traveler Cesar Federici, however, this sudden reversal of Vijayanagara fortunes was caused by the treachery of two Muslim generals under Rāma Rāya who abandoned their king, and went over to the enemy [Purchas 1625]. At any rate, the Muslims now gave chase to these retreating troops. Rāma Rāya himself was captured when his bearers abandoned him in the face of an enemy elephant charge. He was immediately beheaded and his head displayed at the end of a spear, causing panic among his troops, who began to flee the battlefield.

Rāma Rāya's brother Tirumala, who lost an eye in the battle, now dashed back to Vijayanagara. Instead of mounting a defense of the capital, he fled to Pēnukōṇḍa, taking with him enormous treasure, as well as the prisoner Sadāśiva. Vijayanagara was left utterly defenseless, and looted, first by marauding tribes from the neighboring regions, and then by the Muslim armies, when they arrived some six days after the battle. They are said to have remained in Vijayanagara for six months, systematically destroying the city.

The ever-present divisions between the Muslim allies quickly came to the fore after their victory, and they were unable to press their advantage and destroy Vijayanagara's residual power. Tirumala, too, sued for peace, offering to restore the lands Rāma Rāya had taken in previous wars. The conquerors were now content to withdraw, after agreeing not to invade the region again without mutual consent. Interestingly, they appear to have divided the empire among Rāma Rāya's sons and nephews before withdrawing [Sharma and Gopal 1978, p. 224]. Tirumala continued to rule in Sadaśiva's name from Pēnukōṇḍa, taking for himself the title of *Mahāmanḍalēśvara,* and finally coming to the throne when Sadāśiva died in 1570 C.E., reportedly murdered by Tirumala's son Veṅkaṭa, who himself went on to rule as Veṅkaṭa II [Heras 1927, p. 246].

The Sequel to Tāḷikōṭe

The the city of Vijayanagara appears to have been devastated following the battle. The following account of Vijayanagara was given by Cesar Federici a few years after its destruction [Purchas 1625, p. 97]:

> The city was not altogether destroyed, but houses still stand empty, and there are dwelling in them nothing but tigers and other wild beasts. The *enceinte* of the city is about four-and-twenty miles, and within the walls are several mountains. The houses stand walled with earth, and no place, saving the palaces of the three tyrants and the pagodas, other than made with earth.

After the Muslim armies withdrew, Tirumala returned to Vijayanagara the following year, with the hope of repopulating the city, reportedly spending seven months there [Purchas 1625]. Finding the task impossible, he returned to Pēnukōṇḍa by 1567 C.E. By some accounts, he was frustrated by repeated attacks by the Muslims [Heras 1927]. At any rate, the later Vijayanagara kings would never again try to re-establish their capital at this site, ruling instead from Pēnukōnda, Çandragiri, and Vēlūr.

Though its glory days ended with the battle of Tāḷikōṭe, the Vijayanagara kingdom was far from finished. It continued as a significant, albeit diminished, political and military force in the region. The rivalries between the Sultanates also continued. Hussein Nizām Śāh of Ahmadnagar died a few months after Tāḷikōṭe (in June 1565 C.E.), and his widow Khūnzā proved an incompetent ruler. 'Ali 'Ādil Śāh of Bijāpur promptly attacked Ahmadnagar, who sought the help of the other Sultanates. This pattern of warfare between the Sultanates continued, much to the advantage of Tirumala and his immediate successors, who soon managed to reclaim much of the territory lost to the Sultanates.

Nonetheless, the empire was already coming apart. Many of Tirumala's vassals refused to accept his authority after Śadāśiva's murder. Some *pāḷeyagāras* continued to pay tribute in name to the ruler in Pēnukōṇḍa, but acted freely. Bōḷa Çāmarāja Voḍeyar of Maisūru first began to assert his strength and independence during the rule of Śrīraṅga Dēva Rāya I (1572–1586 C.E.), Tirumala's son and successor.[745] It was during the rule of Veṅkaṭāpati Dēva Rāya II (1586–1614 C.E.), the brother and successor of Śrīraṅga I, however, that the empire went into a true decline. Keḷadi and Maisūru became increasingly powerful and independent after 1600 C.E. Relations between Veṅkaṭāpati II and Tirumala Rāja, his viceroy at Śrīraṅgapaṭṭaṇa (and his nephew), had completely broken down. This breach ultimately led to the effective loss of Śrīraṅgapaṭṭaṇa to the Maisūru chief Rāja Voḍeyar in 1610 C.E., who defeated Tirumala Rāja and installed himself in his viceregal position. The year 1612 C.E. saw turmoil in the region of Hosakōṭe, when Ayyama Gauḍa seized control upon the death of Immaḍi Tammēgauḍa, causing Immaḍi Kempēgauḍa of Beṅgaḷūru to intervene. Ayyama Gauḍa complained to Veṅkaṭa II, who sent his forces to subdue Kempēgauḍa, with only partial success. The bloody civil war over Veṅkaṭa II's succession (see page 325) was the first stage of the true unravelling of the empire. Veṅkaṭa II was succeeded briefly by Śrīraṅga Dēva Rāya II (1614–1615 C.E.), and then by Rāma (1615–1633 C.E.), during whose reigns the pattern of decline accelerated.

The Situation at Ānēgondi After Tāḷikōṭe

The centre of gravity of the Vijayanagara kingdom had shifted decisively southwards after Tāḷikōṭe, to Pēnukōṇḍa, Çandragiri, and Vēlūr. We note, however, that Ayyā Śāstri associates Tammaṇṇa Śāstri's ministerial role with Ānēgondi, although Ānēgondi had ceased to be the center of power a long time before Tammaṇṇa Śāstri's journey. Ayyā Śāstri specifically says *Ānēgondi Saṁsthāna,* instead of *Vijayanagara Sāmrārjya,* say.[746] Tammaṇṇa

[745]It is in the reign of Śrīraṅga Dēva Rāya I that we conjecture that the revolt by Çangalpaṭṭu occurred, during which episode Tammēgauḍa came by the *Çikkarāya* title. See page 325.

[746] *Ānēgondi Saṁsthāna* means "Ānēgondi State" or "Ānēgondi Polity". There is no allusion whatsoever to empire.

Śāstri's association with Ānēgondi was surely part of the family's oral history. We examine the political situation in Ānēgondi after Tāḷikōṭe for clues to this state's identity.

The Royal Line of Ānēgondi

According to the copperplate inscription Mb 60, *Aḷiya* Rāma Rāya had five sons, although some confusion remains regarding the specifics. Sources such as the *Rāmarājīyamu* [Aiyangār 1919, p. 184] and Heras [1927] indicate that his sons were Kṛṣnarāya and *Pedda* Timma by his first wife Tirumalāmba, Konda and Timma by his third wife Koṇdamma, and Śrīraṅga by his fourth wife Lakṣmamma. Śrīraṅga's son would go on to become the future Veṅkaṭa Dēva Rāya III. The *Rāmarājīyamu* also indicates that Timma, Koṇḍa, and Śrīraṅga were his sons by Laksmāmba [Aiyangār 1919, p. 103]. Some accounts suggest that Koṇda was the governor of Ānēgondi, although the dates of his tenure are not known. Timma is said to have governed Raicūr.

According to Farishta [Briggs 1829, p. 132, p. 181], however, one of Rāma Rāya's sons, Timma by name, but also referred to as Timma Rāja in inscriptions, remained in Ānēgondi after Tāḷikōṭe, and began pressing his claim to the throne as early as 1566 C.E., setting up a confrontation with his uncle Tirumala I, then ruling from Pēnukōṇḍa. Rāma Rāya's descendants seem to have continued living in Ānēgondi, continuing their struggle for the throne [Sharma and Gopal 1980, p. 200]. As descendants of the eldest of the Āravīḍu brothers, they had a stronger claim to the throne than the descendants of the younger siblings, a stronger claim, in fact, than Tirumala I himself had.

In 1566 C.E., Timma seems to have appealed for help to the 'Adil Śāh, who proceeded immediately to the Ānēgondi region. Tirumala I, in his turn, approached Ahmadnagar, whose queen Khūnza promptly moved to attack Bijāpur, forcing the 'Adil Śāh to withdraw. Such attempts to claim the throne by Timma and his descendants generally remained unsuccessful. It was not until 1633 C.E. that Rāma Rāya's descendants finally came to the throne.

We also have epigraphical evidence of Timma's presence in Ānēgondi after Tāḷikōṭe. For example, the following appears in Sastry [1968].

No. 685. (A.R. No. 318 of 1925.)
ON A STONE LYING BEFORE THE KARNAM'S HOUSE AT KOTTUR, KUDLIGI TALUK, BELLARY DISTRICT.

This is dated Saka 1502, Vikrama, Margasira, ba. 10, corresponding A.D. 1580 December 1, Thursday (not verifiable), in the reign of Timmarajaya-Maha-arasu, son of Ramarajayyadeva-Maha-arasu ruling from Anegondi. It records that Vadi-Nayaka, son of Machi-Nayaka of Baguli, agent of the king, exempted the shepherds of Kottura-sime from tax on their sheep. The gift was made in the presence of the god Kallinatha of Baguli, for the merit of his parents. Kottura-sime is stated to have been situated in Kogali-venthe, a sub-division of Pandya-nadu in Hastinavati-valita.

According to MB 60, Rāma Rāya's last son Śrīraṅga had two sons, called *Pedda* Veṅkaṭa and *Pina* Veṅkaṭa. *Pedda* Veṅkaṭa harbored imperial ambitions, but appears to have made little headway until around 1615 C.E., directly after the bloody struggle for succession following Veṅkaṭa II's death (see page 325). Rāma Dēva Rāya (1615–1633 C.E.) had succeeded the brief rule of Srīraṅga II, at a difficult time for the empire. Rāma Dēva Rāya had to confront two rival aspirants to the throne in *Pedda* Veṅkaṭa and his nephew Srīraṅga III, who also happened to have been adopted by Gōpāla, the grandson of Veṅkaṭādri, *Aḷiya* Rāma Rāya's youngest brother.

The *paḷeyagāras* were divided in their loyalties between Rāma Dēva Rāya, *Pedda* Veṅkaṭa, and Srīraṅga. None of these three happened to command a dedicated following in any geographical region, and the *paḷeyagāras* frequently switched loyalties. *Pedda* Veṅkaṭa seems to have moved away from Ānēgondi in pursuit of his ambitions, and his stronghold at this time appears to have been Nellore district. References to Rāma Dēva Rāya disappear around 1630 C.E., and Śrīraṅga appears to come to the fore. Shortly thereafter, in 1631 C.E., Veṅkaṭa appears to dominate, and a large number of *pāḷeyagāras,* among them Çikkarāya Tammegauḍa, declare their allegiance to him around this time.

Pedda Veṅkaṭa finally succeeded in gaining the crown in 1633 C.E., and ruled as Veṅkaṭa Dēva Rāya III. This Veṅkaṭa is also referred to as "Ānēgondi" Veṅkaṭāpati, and "Rāma Rāya" Veṅkaṭa, given his connections with Ānēgondi and his descent from *Aḷiya* Rāma Rāya. Veṅkaṭa Dēva Rāya III is reported in various inscriptions to have ruled from Pēnukōṇḍa, Çandragiri, as well as from Vēlūr, and appears to have died at Nārāyaṇavanam near Çandragiri in 1642 C.E.

The Identity of the Ānēgondi *Saṁsthāna*

It seems logical for us to identify the Ānēgondi *Saṁsthāna* referred to in Ayyā Śāstri's account with the Ānēgondi-based regime established by Rāma Rāya's descendants after Tāḷikōṭe. Contenders for the throne even from the time of Tāḷikōṭe, they must have always maintained an establishment independent of the official rulers based in Pēnukōṇḍa and Çandragiri.

Information on this *saṁsthāna* is hard to come by, since the Ānēgondi rulers do not figure much in inscriptions. Two members of this family, Veṅkaṭa Dēva Rāya III and his nephew Śrīraṅga Dēva Rāya III, do appear in inscriptions, but mainly after they became official Vijayanagara sovereigns based at places other than Ānēgondi. While the rulers at Ānēgondi may have had limited military power, their pedigree clearly made them very high-status rulers. They were descendants of *Aḷiya* Rāma Rāya, and therefore represented the senior line of succession to the Vijayanagara throne. They likely saw their status as higher than that of their cousins who ruled from Pēnukōṇḍa and Çandragiri.

In the inscription last quoted, we note that Timma is referred to by the title *Timma-rajayya-Maha-arasu* (Timma Mahārāja, effectively), identical to the title conferred upon the great Rāma Rāya in that same sentence. It would have been high treason for a mere vassal to assume such a title.

Timma's assertiveness clearly reflects weakened central authority. In 1580 C.E., the year of that inscription, the official Vijayanagara emperor Śrīraṅga Dēva Rāya I was taken to the Qutb Śāhi capital by Fazal Ḳhān, a Qutb Śāhi general, from where he returned only after concluding a treaty with the Qutb Śāh. By one account, he went as a captive having lost a battle for Pēnukōṇḍa, while in another, he went there after being persuaded by Fazal Khan [Aiyangār 1919, p. 231, 236]. Either way, the story is informative; it is hard to imagine any of the kings of Vijayanagara travelling to a rival capital during the empire's heyday. It is clear that the empire was in serious decline.

We lack any information regarding the Ānēgondi *Saṁsthāna's* rulers after Timma, until the time of *Pedda* Veṅkaṭa, the grandson of *Aḷiya* Rāma Rāya and son of Śrīraṅga. It is claimed by Sharma and Gopal [1980], on the basis of such inscriptions as Udayagiri 19 and Ck 25, that this Veṅkaṭa was assuming imperial titles by 1615 C.E. This claim is likely incorrect, since the sovereign referred to was more likely to have been Veṅkaṭa II, whose reign had just ended.

It is certain, however, that *Pedda* Veṅkaṭa had firmly established himself by 1631 C.E. For example, in 1630 C.E., we have the inscriptions Ko 164, 165 of Sugaṭūr Tammegauḍa acknowledging Rāma Dēva Rāya as his sovereign, but exactly a year later, he acknowledges Veṅkaṭa as sovereign in Ko 251. Veṅkaṭa dominates after that point. His capital is unclear, however, since he is stated as ruling from Pēnukōṇḍa as well as Çandragiri. Some inscriptions make no mention at all of his capital. It is possible that he moved around in response to situational exigencies. By 1635 C.E., however, Veṅkaṭa III was officially on the throne [Sharma and Gopal 1980, p. 201].

While it is certain that Veṅkaṭa III had left Ānēgondi to pursue his claims to the Vijayanagara throne, it is not clear which members of his family had remained at Ānēgondi. Assuming Tammaṇṇa Śāstri remained at Ānēgondi after Veṅkaṭa III left, he would have been closely associated with these individuals.

Other Clues Regarding Tammaṇṇa Śāstri's Journey

We know that Tammaṇṇa Śāstri's southward journey occurred around or just after 1639 C.E., and that *Pedda* Veṅkaṭa of Ānēgondi had become the emperor Veṅkaṭa Dēva Rāya III in 1635 C.E. We know also that Veṅkaṭa III did not rule from Ānēgondi, that he ruled from several places at different times, and that he died near Çandragiri in 1642 C.E. Was Tammaṇṇa Śāstri associated with his court? If so, where did his journey to Anantaśayana originate? Was he still at Ānēgondi, or at some other location?

We have no historical basis to approach these questions, but will give in to the temptation to speculate. We note first that Ayyā Śāstri alludes to Tammaṇṇa Śāstri's troubles specifically at the hands of "Haiderābādi Muslims", not merely "Muslims". Was his use of the qualifier "Haiderābādi" significant, or was it merely incidental and gratuitous? After all, Haiderābād had been the seat of the Āsaf Jāhi dynasty, the dominant South Indian Muslim power since 1724 C.E. This dynasty had partnered with the British in their overthrow of Ṭippu Sultān in 1799 C.E., and it is usual even today in South India to associate Muslims with Haiderābād. If so, this reference conveys little information about the circumstances or date of Tammaṇṇa Śāstri's journey.

We argue, however, that the reference to "Haiderābādi" Muslims is actually significant, and was undoubtedly a part of the family's oral history. Ayyā Śāstri himself was a man of deep erudition, and as a *Mahāvidvān* at the royal court, had a large circle of scholarly friends and colleagues. He had, in fact, been one of the circle of scholars who had assisted Benjamin Lewis Rice in his monumental works on the language, history, and epigraphy of Karnāṭaka. He had also travelled widely with His Highness Çāmarājendra Voḍeyar across the state and the country. There seems to be little doubt that Ayyā Śāstri knew the differences between the various Muslim kingdoms of the South. His use of the qualifier "Haiderābādi" could only have been deliberate.

We also note that the relevant paragraph in Garaḷapurī Śāstri's biography (see page 8) begins with a broad reference to the growing power of Muslims in India at the time. Almost immediately, however, it becomes more specific, characterizing Tammaṇṇa Śāstri's tormentors as Haiderābādi Muslims, not simply as Muslims. This sharpened focus is surely significant. It has always been well known in South India that Vijayanagara's destruction (to which page 8 alludes) resulted from an alliance among the Sultanates, and that Vijayanagara had fought different Muslim kingdoms over its history. The singling out of Haiderābādi Muslims here has to be deliberate. Ayyā Śāstri, in recounting the family history to the biographer, must have named the attackers Haiderābādis. The allusions to Haiderābād in the biography and in Ayyā Śāstri's manuscript reinforce each other, diminishing the likelihood that they are both gratuitous.

The Gōlkōṇḍa and Bijāpur Campaigns of 1638 C.E.

If Tammaṇṇa Śāstri's Muslim tormentors had indeed been based in Haiderābād, the reference is quite informative. The city of Haiderābād was founded by Mohammed Quli Qutb Śāh in 1589 C.E., who initially named it Bhāgnagar, after Bhāgmatī, a favourite concubine of his. A year later, he moved his capital from the city of Gōlkōṇḍa to Haiderābād. If Ayyā Śāstri's reference to "Haiderābādi" Muslims is a genuine part of the family history as handed down, Tammaṇṇa Śāstri's move must have occurred after the kingdom of Gōlkōṇḍa became known as the kingdom of Haiderābād. This was clearly well after 1590 C.E., strengthening the credibility of the timeline we have constructed.

Can we identify any specifics regarding the attack by Haiderābādi Muslims that precipitated Tammaṇṇa Śāstri's journey? Unfortunately, there was incessant fighting among the regional powers after 1600 C.E., as the Vijayanagara rulers began to lose their hold on the region. We will focus on the period following 1635 C.E., the time of most interest to us. In 1636 C.E., the Mughals under Aurangzeb finally annexed the Ahmadnagar Sultanate to their empire. In the process, Aurangazēb defeated Śāhji, the last significant Ahmadnagar general, who now entered the service of the Bijāpur Sultanate. He would beome one of Bijāpur's most trusted and effective generals, and serve as a chief commander in Bijāpur's southern conquests of 1638 C.E.

Bijāpur and Gōlkōṇḍa (likely identified with Haiderābād, by this time) entered into a treaty with the Mughals in 1636 C.E., agreeing to become its tributaries. This treaty secured them from Mughal attacks, and also granted them permission for southern expansion into the Vijayanagar territories.

These Sultanates now went about conquering the Vijayanagar *pāḷeyapaṭs* one at a time, Bijāpur on the west and Gōlkōṇḍa on the east. The campaigns appear to have a direct bearing on Tammaṇṇa Śāstri's story, Gōlkōṇḍa's on its beginning, and Bijāpur's on its end.

Gōlkōṇḍa began a campaign in 1638 C.E., conquering the Telugu and Tamiḷ *pāḷeyapaṭs* that were the eastern provinces of Vijayanagara. The Telugu regions were the first to be taken over, according to Sharma and Gopal [1980, p. 226], at least partly because Gōlkōṇḍa had always coveted the diamond mines in the region.[747] Ānegondi is very close to the Telugu provinces, and even today, is adjacent to the border with Āndhra Pradēsh. There is also other evidence that Vijayanagara was under the control of Gōlkōṇḍa ("Hyderābād") in 1640 C.E. Ephrem de Nevers, a Capuchin priest of French origin, is stated [in Lach and van Kley 1998, p. 257] to have travelled in 1640 C.E. from Surat to Vijayanagara, then occupied by Gōlkōṇḍa. He befriended its sultan, and proceeded in 1642 C.E. to Madras, which was also under Gōlkōṇḍa's control. The British, who had built Fort St. George the previous year, welcomed him, and de Nevers established a church there. In 1649 C.E., the Portuguese arrested him and took him to Goa, where an inquisition was in progress. They released de Nevers in 1651 C.E., under threats from the Papacy, the French and English governments, and the sultan of Gōlkōṇḍa. Tavernier [1889] confirms that de Nevers passed through Bhāgnagar, Gōlkōṇḍa's capital. By this account, Vijayanagara appears to have been under Gōlkōṇḍa's occupation in 1640 C.E. Tammaṇṇa Śāstri's move southwards was likely to have been precipitated by this attack by the forces of Gōlkōṇḍa (by then called Haiderābād).

Bijāpur's armies too, led by Randullah Ḳhān and Śāhji, swept down the west coast in 1638 C.E., overrunning the Kannaḍa regions of Keḷadi, Santebannūr, Beṅgaḷūru, Hosakōṭe, and Kōlār. It appears that only Kaṇṭhīrava Narasa Rāja of Maisūru, then ruling from Śrīraṅgapaṭṭaṇa, was able to resist this onslaught. Śāhji took Hosakōṭe in 1639 C.E., forcing Tammēgauḍa to move to Ānekallu. At the same time, he also took Beṅgaḷūru from Immaḍi

[747] The fabled diamonds of Gōlkōṇḍa, which include the Hope diamond, the *Koh-i-Noor,* the *Daryā-i-Noor,* the Orlov diamond, and the Sanc diamond, appear to have been mined in this region. The qualifier *Gōlkōnda* is still used in the trade to signify nearly perfect gems. India had been the only source of diamonds till the late 17th century, when Borneo's diamonds became known in Europe.

Kempēgauḍa, forcing him to move to Māgaḍi. We know from Ayyā Śāstri's account that Tammaṇṇa Śāstri's son Śaṅkarabhaṭṭa moved to Māgaḍi after Tammaṇṇa Śāstri passed on. Kempēgauḍa ruled for eighteen years in Māgaḍi, so Śaṅkarabhaṭṭa is quite likely to have moved to Māgaḍi during Immaḍi Kempēgauḍa's time.

Some Speculations About Tammaṇṇa Śāstri's Journey

Ayyā Śāstri's reference to the Ānēgondi *Saṁsthāna* does not imply that the starting point for Tammaṇṇa Śāstri's journey was Ānēgondi. Veṅkaṭa III, for example, had left Ānēgondi in pursuit of his imperial ambitions, and we have evidence of his presence at Pēnukōṇḍa at this time. Similarly, there is evidence that Śrīraṅga III, a nephew and rival of Veṅkaṭa III for the throne, was at Vēlūr. Tammaṇṇa Śāstri may have been in the entourage of the one or the other.

Plate 41 depicts hypothetical straight-line routes to Anantaśayana from Ānēgondi, Pēnukōṇḍa, Çandragiri, and Vēlūr, the four places where we know Vijayanagara emperors associated with the Ānēgondi *Saṁsthāna* to have been. Somewhat unexpectedly, the straight-line route that runs closest to Ānēkallu starts from Pēnukōṇḍa. Ānēkallu is within about 120 km of the straight-line routes to Anantaśayana from Ānēgondi and from Çandragiri, but within about 30 km of the route from Pēnukōṇḍa. This observation cannot be taken as sufficient evidence, however, that Tammaṇṇa Śāstri's journey started from a place other than Ānēgondi.

Roads are very rarely straight lines, and no trip follows a straight-line path, unless by air. The roads of the period surely reflected dominant local transit patterns, rather than carefully planned routes between certain points. Besides, we must keep in mind that Bijāpur was attacking down the west coast in 1638 C.E., concurrently with Gōlkōṇḍa's campaign down the east coast. Keḷadi and Santebannūr were among the first provinces to fall to Bijāpur, whose military thrust quickly overran even Basavapaṭṭaṇa and Beṅgaḷūru. The straight-line route from Ānēgondi passes through some of these very provinces. Tammaṇṇa Śāstri's party would have had no maps to guide them, and would have relied on local advice to determine waypoints on their journey. They would have adjusted their routes to go around troubled or inhospitable regions. Even if they had started from Ānēgondi, it is

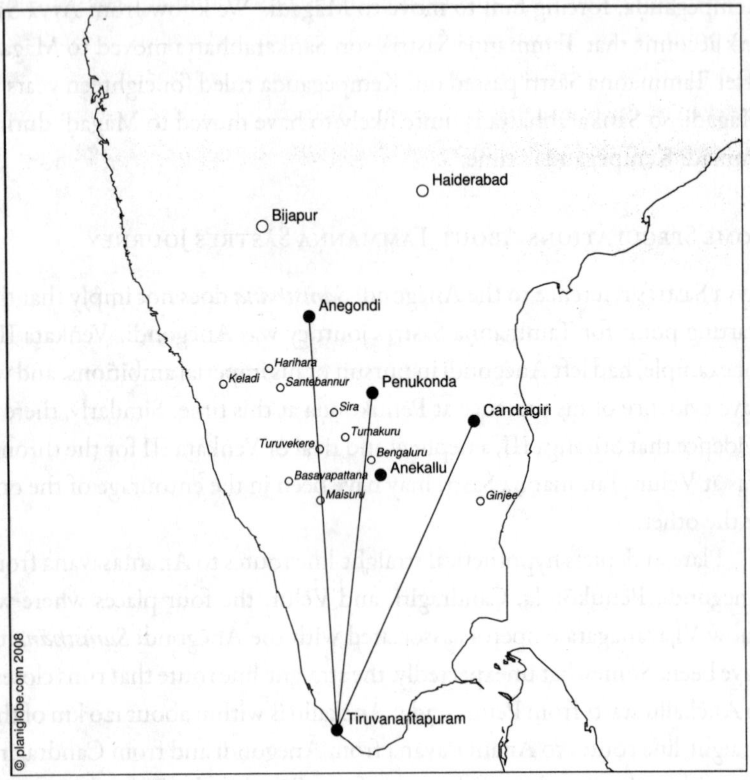

Plate 41: Hypothetical straight-line routes from possible starting points for Tammaṇṇa Śāstri's journey. The *pāḷeyapaṭs* conquered in Bijāpur's campaign of 1638 C.E. are shown in italics.

quite possible that their route followed a more circuitous course than the straight lines depicted in Plate 41.

There is also strong evidence that Veṅkaṭa III was resident at Pēnukōṇḍa at this time, and that his rival Śrīraṅga III was at Vēlūr [Sharma and Gopal 1980, p. 238]. We know that the Gōlkōṇḍa and Bijāpur campaigns of 1638 C.E. did not confront either of these symbols of Vijayanagara central power directly, to avoid rallying their vassals to their aid. Instead, they went about conquering the vassal states themselves. If Tammaṇṇa Śāstri had been in the entourage of either of these monarchs, he is unlikely to have suffered the personal devastation that the family history describes. There are no historical accounts of attacks by the Gōlkōṇḍa forces on Pēnukōṇḍa or Vēlūr during this period matching Ayyā Śāstri's account.

Ānēgondi hence remains a viable candidate as Tammaṇṇa Śāstri's starting point. Plate 41 makes clear that Ānēgondi is closer to the sphere of Bijāpur's influence than to that of Gōlkōṇḍa, and is more likely to have been attacked by Bijāpur than by Gōlkōṇḍa. Bijāpur did, in fact, wage numerous campaigns in this region, many of them under Śāhji himself. Śāhji, for example, wrote to 'Ali 'Ādil Śāh II on July 6, 1657 C.E., aggressively demanding a *jāhgīr* as reward for his earlier conquest of Kanakagiri (farther south), and of Ānēgondi just a month earlier [Patwardhan and Rawlinson 1978, p. 28].

However, these were extremely turbulent times for the region, and we have no grounds for dismissing the possibility of an attack on Ānēgondi during Gōlkōṇḍa's campaign of 1638 C.E. Such an attack is unlikely to have met much opposition. This ancient city had lost its political primacy long before this time, and despite the emotional associations it must have held for Veṅkaṭa III and Śrīraṅga III, it is unlikely to have figured prominently in their political and military calculus. Both rulers had long been gone from Ānēgondi, and neither one is likely to have wanted to invest much in its defense, even assuming he had the resources to do so. Sadly, we have no specifics on any of the battles waged in this region during the Gōlkōṇḍa campaign of 1638 C.E. We are thus left to speculate that it was most likely some attack in the locale of Ānēgondi by the Gōlkōṇḍa forces during this campaign that was responsible for Tammaṇṇa Śāstri's journey. Ānēgondi's location would have made it one of the first Vijayanagara principalities overrun by the Gōlkōṇḍa forces in their southward sweep, so such an attack would have occurred early in this campaign, that is, in 1638–1639 C.E.

The Timing and Course of the Journey

Regardless of the starting point for Tammaṇṇa Śāstri's journey, the timing of these events appears to be just right. We proceed with the working hypothesis that Tammaṇṇa Śāstri's city of residence was attacked sometime during 1638 C.E. Following this devastation, Tammaṇṇa Śāstri would most likely have taken some weeks, perhaps some months, to consider his options, choose a course of action, and make preparations for his long trip southwards to Anantaśayana. The preparations would have been substantial, since the party would have had to traverse a chaotic, war-torn region, negotiating bad roads and dense forests. They would have taken along substantial resources and provisions, a number of attendants, and would have proceeded with all deliberate caution, adapting their route to local conditions, and making their journey in legs dictated by the spacing between villages en route. They would have traveled in carts, cooked on improvised fires, and at times, perhaps even subsisted on tubers and forest produce. They would have rested in improvised campsites, guarding against marauders as well as against wild animals, including lions, tigers, and cheetahs, which would have been common in the forests at the time. We also know they were accompanied by eight buffaloes, which, apart from being tempting prey, walk at a leisurely pace. It is unlikely that this party could have traveled more than 10 km a day, on average.

At this pace, it is likely that their 320-km journey from Ānēgondi to Ānēkallu would have taken something over a month or so. A similar time frame is likely, even if they had started from a place other than Ānēgondi. This scenario makes it quite possible for Tammaṇṇa Śāstri and his family to have arrived in Ānēkallu just at the time that Tammēgauḍa had moved there. According to the *Ānēkallu Kaifiyat*, Tammēgauḍa's treaty with Śāhji granted him six months to make this move after losing Hosakōṭe in 1638 C.E. The *Kaifiyat* confirms that Tammēgauḍa was fortifying the place at the time, matching this detail from Ayyā Śāstri's account.

Tammēgauḍa acknowledges Veṅkaṭa III as his sovereign in inscription Ko 251, and would have been familiar with his Ānēgondi antecedents. He would also have been well acquainted with the Ānēgondi *Saṁsthāna,* its rulers, and perhaps even with its *pradhānis,* including Tammaṇṇa Śāstri himself. In establishing his new dominions, he would have sought people of learning and ability, and would have warmly welcomed a person of Tammaṇṇa Śāstri's accomplishments, his generous gift of ten *vṛuttis* reflecting his high esteem for Tammaṇṇa Śāstri. The large house Tammēgauḍa built for Tammaṇṇa Śāstri would have been located in *Tammasandra Agrahāra* that the *Ānēkallu Kaifiyat* mentions, and these ten *vṛuttis* would have been in its environs.

We are unable to say much more, given the lack of documentary evidence, either from within the family or from reliable historical sources. We take comfort, however, that our reconstruction of events is a plausible account, and fully consistent with available historical facts and the family's own oral history. It has a good chance of being close to what Tammaṇṇa Śāstri actually experienced and endured.

The Anantaśayana and Hoysaḷa Questions

It remains unclear why Tammaṇṇa Śāstri would have chosen Anantaśayana as his destination. Anantaśayana (literally "eternal repose") derives its name from its eponymous temple of Viṣṇu reclining on the Śēśa serpent. Its other names include Tiruvanantapuram and Travancore (a corruption of Tiruviṭaṁkūr from British times). Its rulers have been known as Tiruvadis. The kingdom of the Tiruvaḍi rulers is also referred to as Anantaśayana. Thus, Ayyā Śāstri's account refers to Tammaṇṇa Śāstri's departure for the "province of Anantaśayana".

Its rulers have enjoyed a strong reputation as patrons of scholarship and the arts,[748] and one might conjecture that Tammaṇṇa Śāstri travelled there in search of patronage. However, the high reputation of the Travancore kings as patrons dates back only to the time of Mārtanḍa Varma (1729–1758 C.E.), a much later time than that we have assigned to Tammaṇṇa Śāstri. The Travancore region does not appear to have been a particularly prominent principality at Tammaṇṇa Śāstri's time. The *Nāyakas* of Madurai and Tañjāvūru, as well as the Voḍeyars then ruling Maisūru and Śrīraṅgapaṭṭaṇa had much stronger reputations as patrons of scholarship and the arts. Tammaṇṇa Śāstri might have sought their patronage, much closer to home.

The Tiruvaḍi capital at Tammaṇṇa Śāstri's time was in fact at Padmanābhapuram, some 33 miles from Tiruvanantapuram. An edict of 1634 C.E. mentions Kalkulam, near Padmanābhapuram, as the ruler's residence [Aiya 1906, p. 302]. Padmanābhapuram remained the region's capial from ancient times until 1795 C.E., when Tiruvanantapuram became its capital. Ayyā Śāstri refers to the "province of Anantaśayana" as Tammaṇṇa Śāstri's destination, so Tammaṇṇa Śāstri may actually have been headed for Padmanābhapuram.

His choice of Anantaśayana as destination is puzzling, however. The distance between Ānēgondi and Anantaśayana is a daunting 750 km. Why would Tammaṇṇa Śāstri choose to travel in a time of crisis to a place so far removed from his home? He is very unlikely indeed to have embarked on this journey without some substantial assurance of support in Anantaśayana.

[748] Mahārāja Svāti Tirunāḷ of Travancore (1813–1846 C.E.) was a musical giant in his own right, for example.

What assurance of support drew Tammaṇṇa Śāstri to Anantaśayana? Sadly, we must deal in conjecture once again. Tammaṇṇa Śāstri's departure was almost certainly a one-sided decision, based on a strong anticipation of support at Anantaśayana. There would surely not have been time for communications to have been exchanged between Ānēgondi and Anantaśayana. Such support must have come either from some family connection in Anantaśayana, or from a person of nobility or other substantial means, who knew Tammaṇṇa Śāstri at Ānēgondi, and who invited him to Anantaśayana. Perhaps they travelled south at the same time from Ānēgondi. But what connections existed between Ānēgondi and Anantaśayana?

A Possible Ānēgondi-Anantaśayana Link

The region of Anantaśayana, or "Travancore" in recent historical accounts and analyses, had long been a vassal state on the outer edges of the Vijayanagara empire. A legend exists that the brāhmaṇas of the region had asked the emperor Kṛṣṇadēva Rāya to send them a ruler [Aiya 1906, p. 223], although no independent confirmation of this fact appears to exist. It is known, however, that the region suffered invasions by Vijayanagara.

According to the *Açyutarāyābhyudayam* by Rājanātha Ḍiṇḍima [Ḍiṇḍima 1907], a tributary chief named Çellappa (also known as Sāḷuva Nāyaka and Vīra Narasimha [Aiyangār 1919, p. 12]) and the ruler of the Çēra region (Travancore) had defeated and expelled the Pāṇḍya ruler of Madurai.[749] This account suggests that the Tiruvaḍi kingdom had a certain strength at the time. In response, Kṛṣṇadēva Rāya's successor Açyuta Rāya campaigned southwards to Çandragiri, and then further towards Śrīraṅgam. Açyuta remained at Śrīraṅgam, but sent his armies under Timma Rāja, his brother-in-law and Salakarāja's son,[750] to vanquish the Tiruvaḍi (the Çēra king). Inscriptions A.R. No. 542 of 1919 and A.R. No. 158 of 1924 confirm the broad outlines of this account [Hultzsch 1988].

According to the *Bālabhāgavatam* of Dōnēri Kōnērinātha, however, it was *Aḷiya* Rāma Rāya's cousin *Çinna* Timma who subdued the Tiruvaḍi. It appears that there were two expeditions, the first under Açyuta himself

[749] The local ruler at the time was likely one or both of Vīra Ravi Varma or Vīra Kērala Varma.

[750] See footnote 743.

in 1532–1533 C.E., and another in 1542–1544 C.E., led by *Çinna* Timma and his brother Viṭṭhala (see Plate 39). The Vijayanagara invasions may also have been prompted by the missionary activities of the Portuguese under Francis Xavier, who were busy converting the coastal Parava fishermen to Christianity. The Vijayanagara sovereign may have felt the need to respond to this *de facto* change of their alleigance from him to the king of Portugal [Aiyar 1991, p. 123].

Çinna Timma and Viṭṭhala were both sons of Timmarāja, who was brother to *Aḷiya* Rāma Rāya's father Śrīraṅga. There is solid evidence that *Çinna* Timma was at Madurai, and had been Appayya Dīkṣita's patron (see footnote 203). According to the *Bālabhāgavatam*, *Çinna* Timma restored to the Tiruvaḍi the territories that he had taken from him, thereby acquiring the title *Tiruvaḍi Rājyasthāpanāçārya*, or "establisher of the Tiruvaḍi kingdom". After this subjugation of the Tiruvaḍis, the brothers *Çinna* Timma and Viṭṭhala appear to have remained in Madurai for some ten years, establishing Madurai's supremacy in the region.

The Madurai *Nāyakas* remained the most powerful Vijayanagara vassals in the region, and their influence over the Tiruvaḍis continued to subsequent times. A grant dated 1634 C.E. exempts farmers from certain taxes, on account of Madurai's Tirumala *Nāyaka* having attacked and devastated Anantaśayana on behalf of the Vijayanagara king ("Ānegondi" Veṅkaṭāpati Rāya III, at this time), most likely because of a failure by its ruler to pay tribute.[751] Clearly, the Tiruvaḍis were far from being powerful rulers at Tammaṇṇa Śāstri's time.

Why, in the light of this last fact, did Tammaṇṇa Śāstri choose Anantaśayana as his destination? We can only speculate. We start with the observation that *Çinna* Timma and Viṭṭhala were both scions of the Āravīṭi family, the very same family that we have identified as the likely rulers of Ānegondi *Saṁsthāna* (see page 344). Perhaps it was the Āravīṭi lineage that Tammaṇṇa Śāstri's ancestors had served as trusted ministers for five generations (see page 7). If so, there would have been long and close associations between the Āravīṭi family and that of Tammaṇṇa Śāstri.

[751]This ruler was likely Unni Kēraḷavarman (1631–1661 C.E.) or Ravivarman (1625–1631 C.E.).

Might some members of Tammaṇṇa Śāstri's family have accompanied *Çinna* Timma and Viṭṭhala on their campaigns to Madurai and Anantaśayana, in their capacity as trusted ministers? We do know that *Çinna* Timma was resident at Madurai, and that he and his brother Viṭṭhala were active in the south for some ten years [Aiyar 1991, p. 91]. Their entourage and trusted advisers would have stayed there with them. Is it possible that some members of Tammaṇṇa Śāstri's family had stayed behind even after *Çinna* Timma and Viṭṭhala returned to Vijayanagara? Was this the connection that drew Tammaṇṇa Śāstri to Anantaśayana? Or was it simply the case that Tammaṇṇa Śāstri had travelled south from Ānēgondi with companions who had strong connections in Anantaśayana? We can have no answers at this point. Perhaps some new evidence will come to light in the future, allowing us to resolve some of these intriguing questions. If only some of Tammaṇṇa Śāstri's manuscripts had survived!

The Hoysaḷa Antecedents of Tammaṇṇa Śāstri

The biography suggests that Tammaṇṇa Śāstri's ancestors had been at Ānēgondi since the time of Vidyāraṇya. The family tradition holds (see footnote 41) that the remote ancestors of Tammaṇṇa Śāstri had been Hoysaḷa ministers at Dōrasamudra, the Hoysaḷa capital, and had migrated to Ānēgondi after the Hoysaḷa decline. Vidyāraṇya is himself believed to have been from the *Hoysaḷa Karnāṭaka* sect, to which we know Tammaṇṇa Śāstri belonged. Family tradition also suggests that these remote ancestors were related to Vidyāranya himself. These accounts are, of course, completely unverifiable at this point.

Nonetheless, this family tradition appears not to be in conflict with available facts. A considerable body of new evidence suggests that Vijayanagara's founders had close connections to the Hoysaḷa royals, and used them to establish legitimacy, as the inheritors of a great empire whose memories were still very much alive [Kulke and Rothermund 1998]. A prevailing theory had been that Hakka and Bukka fled Wāraṅgal in present-day Āndhra Pradēsh after its capture, settled at Kampili near Hampi, were taken prisoner by Mohammed bin Tughlaq's army in 1327 C.E., and converted to Islam. The sultan supposedly sent them back to Kampili, where they came under Vidyāraṇya's influence and founded Vijayanagara, where Hakka was crowned as Harihara I in 1336 C.E. This theory also states that Harihara I held a great celebration at Śṛṅgēri in 1346 C.E. after overcoming the weakened Hoysaḷa king Baḷḷāla IV.

However, recent epigraphical discoveries strongly indicate that Hakka and Bukka were nobles in the Hoysaḷa court already. An inscription dating to 1320 C.E. records that Baḷḷāla III founded the town of Vijayavirūpākṣa Hosapaṭṭana on the spot which became Vijayanagara. After the death of Baḷḷāla IV, the widow of Baḷḷāla III seems to have participated in the coronation of Harihara I in 1346 C.E. Even though Harihara was king in 1349 C.E., an inscription from that date actually mentions her name before that of Harihara, suggesting that he did not yet have independent legitimacy.

It is therefore not inconceivable that as *Hoysaḷa Karnāṭakas,* Tammaṇṇa Śāstri's ancestors had been in the service of the Vijayanagara kings since the earliest times. The family tradition that Tammaṇṇa Śāstri's remote ancestors migrated from Dōrasamudra at this early date does not appear to be inconsistent with available facts.

APPENDIX C: TRANSLATIONS OF SELECTED VERSES

Dr Shankar Rajaraman
Vidvān H.V. Nagaraja Rao

Various Verses

Dr Shankar Rajaraman

Verse (page 7):

prajñā·mūla·mahī vivēka·salilaiḥ siktā balopaghnikā
mantraiḥ pallavitā viśāla·viṭapā sandhy'ādibhiṣ'ṣaḍguṇaiḥ |
śaktyā korakitā yaśas'surabhitā siddhyā samudyat'phalā
samprāptā bhuvi bhāti nīti·latikā sarvottaraṁ mādhavaṁ

Translation:

Sprinkled with waters in the form of wisdom, discretion and territorial domain, supported by an army standing for a stake, having respectively for its tender shoots and vast branches the advice of ministers and the sixfold course of action starting with treaty, putting forth a multitude of buds that is regal power, fragrant with fame and fruitful at the advent of success, the tender creeper of polity, firmly rooted in earth, looks pretty in association with Mādhava (Vidyāraṇya/spring), foremost among all (men/seasons).[752]

Verse (page 18):

vāme bhūmi·sutā puras'ca hanumān paścāt sumitrā·sutaḥ
śatrughno bharataś'ca pārśva·daḷayor vāyvādi·koṇeṣu ca |
sugrīvaś'ca vibhīṣaṇaś'ca yuvarāṭ tārā·suto jāmbavān
madhye nīla·saroja·komala·ruciṁ rāmaṁ bhaje śyāmalam ||

Translation:

With Sītā on the left, Hanumān in front, Lakṣmaṇa behind, Śatrughna and Bharata on either side, Lord Rāma, dark-hued and splendidly beautiful like a blue-lotus, sits in the middle, surrounded by Sugrīva, Vibhīṣaṇa, prince Aṅgada, and Jāmabavān in the four cardinal points beginning with the northwest. Him, I take recourse to.

[752] See footnote 39 for more information.

VERSE (page 363):

vāmāṅke girijā puras'triçaraṇaḥ paśçāç'ça nandīśvarō
herambaś'ça guhaś'ça pārśva·dalayōr vāyvādi·koṇeṣu ça |
çaṇḍīśo'pi ça bhairavas'savinayo bāṇas'tathā rāvaṇaḥ
tan'madhye sphuṭa·puṇḍārīka·ruçiraṁ śrī·nīlakaṇṭhaṁ bhaje ||

TRANSLATION:
With Pārvatī seated on his left lap, the three-legged Bhṛṅgī in front, Nandī behind, Gaṇeśa and Kumāra on either side, Lord Śiva, splendid like a full-blown lily, sits in the middle, surrounded by Çaṇḍīśvara, Bhairava, the humble *rākṣasa* Bāṇa and Rāvaṇa in the four cardinal points, starting with the northwest. Him, I take recourse to.

VERSE (page 20):

anāghrāta·vyaṅgyair apariçita·śabdārtha·raçanair
abuddhā'laṅkārair'anavagata·bhāvojjvala·rasaiḥ |
yaśo·mātr'āṅkūrān'nava·nava·durāśaiḥ kukavibhiḥ
duradhvē vyākṛṣṭā bhagavati vipannāsi kavitē ||

TRANSLATION:
They catch not even the faintest smell of suggestiveness. The art of bringing sound and sense together is foreign to them. They have never figured out the various figures of speech. Words splendidly infused with aesthetic sentiments are unknown to them. And just because they have sprouted some fame, these poetasters, greedier with every passing moment, dare drag you into wrong paths. You are doomed, O divine Muse.

VERSE (page 30):

nṛsimhākhyē gaṇḍa·śailē varadākhyo mahāmaṇiḥ |
nipatya khalu tatraiva vyaśīryata sahasradhā ||

TRANSLATION:
A great gem named Varada fell on the hillock called Nṛsiṁha and split up into a thousand pieces at that very spot.

VERSE (page 34):

tvam'asi rasika·madhye maṅgaḷa·svāna·ramya·
s'samara·mṛḍiṭa·śatruḥ kiñça rambhā·ratī'ççhuḥ |
dara·dhara·hṛdayō'ham nēśvara·śrīr jitō'nyaih
mama vitara samṛddhyai mandiram kā kṣatis'tē ‖

TRANSLATION:

See page 34.

VERSE (page 37):

niḥsvatā·yuvati·çumbana·jany'onmāda·mūla·kavitā·kṛti·dakṣaṁ |
sarva·loka·parihāsa·padaṁ mām ko nirīkṣya na bhavet karunārdraḥ‖

TRANSLATION:

Poverty, my ever-youthful sweetheart, kisses me and leaves me insane enough to compose poetry. I am the subject of universal ridicule. Is there anyone at all who could look at me and yet not feel pity?

VERSE (page 52):

lakṣmī·śāradayōs'svayaṅ'gṛha·patir'dātā dayāluḥ kṣamī
jāmātā dharaṇīśa·kṛṣṇa·nṛpatēś'śrīliṅgarāja·prabhuḥ |
bhāvābdē sahasi dvipāsya·divasē vārē śanēr' viṣṇu·bhē
śrīkaṇṭh'āṅghri·sarōruha·bhramaratāṁ āpat'tapōbhir'nijaiḥ ‖

TRANSLATION:

It was on a Saturday, the day of Caturthī presided over by the asterism Śravaṇa in the month of Mārgaśīrṣa, in the year called Bhāva, that His Highness Liṅgarāja, son-in-law of king Kṛṣṇarāja Wodeyar, self-chosen groom of the Goddesses of wealth and learning alike, munificent, kind-hearted and forbearing became, by the dint of his penance, a bumblebee at the lotus-feet of Lord Śrīkaṇṭha.

VERSE (page 53):

badhnīmō vayam'añjali·
samputam'avanamritē mūrdhni |
dadhnā sikta·kalēbaram
arbhakam'ēkaṁ purāṇam'uddiśya ||

TRANSLATION:
With hands cupped on heads bent low in reverence, we offer our salutations to the primeval child whose limbs are smeared with fresh curds.

VERSE (page 55):

mukhañ'ca çandra·pratimaṁ timaṁ timam
kuçau ça pīnau kaṭhinau ṭhinau ṭhinau |
kaṭir'viśālā rabhasā bhasā bhasā
ahō viçitrā taruṇī ruṇī ruṇī ||

TRANSLATION:
Her face is moon-like-ike-ike. Her breasts are rounded and unyielding-ding-ding. Her hips are broad and sway swiftly-tly-tly. She is a wonder—this maiden-den-den! (This is nonsense verse.)

Çitrakāvya Translations

Dr Shankar Rajaraman

Verse (page 55):

smara·śriyaṁ yaṁ tarasā rasā'rasā
nirīkṣya gōpyō mumuhur' muhurmuhuḥ |
anudravad'dhēnu·paramparaṁ param
tam'ēha jihvē vada nanda·nandanaṁ ‖

Anvaya:

hē jihvē, smaraśriyaṁ yaṁ nirīkṣya tarasā rasārasāḥ (rasālasāḥ) gōpyaḥ muhurmuhuḥ mumuhuḥ, taṁ anudravaddhēnuparamparaṁ paraṁ nanda-nandanaṁ ēva vada |

Vocabulary:

jihvē: o, my tongue; *smaraśriyaṁ:* akin to the Lord of love in beauty; *yaṁ:* he that is (correlates with *taṁ*); *nirīkṣya:* glancing, beholding; *tarasā:* vehemently, quickly, instantly; *rasārasā:* languid with love (since *ra* and *la* are interchangeable, the word *rasārasāḥ* actually means *rasālasāḥ,* since *ra* and *la* are allophones; *gōpyaḥ:* cowherd women; *muhurmuhuḥ:* again and again, repeatedly; *mumuhuḥ:* lost their senses; *taṁ:* him; *anudravad + dhenu + paraṁparaṁ:* followed by a herd of cows; *paraṁ:* supreme; *nandanandanaṁ:* son of Nandagopa; *ēva:* alone; *vada:* chant (the name).

Translation:

O, my tongue! I implore you to chant the name of Nanda's son alone. Looking at Him, the Supreme Lord, who is akin to the god of love in his charm and is accompanied by a herd of cows, the cowherd-girls, instantly languid with passion, repeatedly lost their senses.

Verse (page 55):

vṛṣā'py'upēkṣā·priyayā yayā yayā·
v'adhaśca bhikṣāñ'jagṛhē gṛhē gṛhē |
dayārdray'airāvata·yātayā tayā
vayaṅ'galad'dainya·may'āmayā mayā ‖

Anvaya:

upēkṣāpriyayā yayā vṛṣā api adhaḥ yayau gṛhē gṛhē bhikṣāṁ ça jagṛhē, tayā dayārdrayā airāvatayātayā mayā (lakṣmyā) vayaṁ galaddainyamayāmayā

Vocabulary:

upēkṣāpriyayā: given to indifference, uncaring; *yayā:* by whom; *vṛṣā:* Indra; *api:* also; *adha:* below, down; *yayau:* go, reach; *gṛhē gṛhē:* at every house; *bhikṣāṁ:* alms; *jagṛhē:* accept; *tayā:* by her; *dayārdrayā:* filled with fresh compassion; *airāvatayātayā:* of a gait majestic like that of the celestial elephant Airāvata; *mayā:* by the goddess Lakṣmī; *vayaṁ:* we; *galat-dainya-maya-āmayāḥ:* freed of the disease of poverty.

Translation:

Freed are we of our disease of poverty by the goddess Lakṣmī, who is full of fresh compassion and matches the celestial elephant, Airāvata, by her measured gait. Spurned by Her, even Indra had to make a steady descent into the lower regions of the world and live on alms obtained by begging at every door.

Verse (page 56):

tav'āmba kund'ōtkara·dāradā radāḥ
kuç'ābham'ētan'na tu kantu·kantukaṁ |
dṛśōs'sakhāyō'jina·yōnayō'nayōḥ
kaçō'rçitōñcan'nalinālinā'linā ‖

Anvaya:

amba, tava radāḥ kundōtkara-dāra-dāḥ, ētat kuçābhaṁ natu (nanu?) kantukantukaṁ, anayōḥ dṛśōḥ sakhāyaḥ ajinayōnayaḥ, kaçaḥ añçannalinālinā alinā arçitaḥ |

Vocabulary:

amba: Divine Mother! *tava:* your; *radāḥ:* teeth; *kundōtkara-dāra-dāḥ:* imparting (*dāḥ*) a state of being split (*dāra*) to heaps of jasmine flowers (*kundōtkara*); *ētat:* this; *kuçābhaṁ:* appearing like your breasts; *nanu:* is verily; *kantu-kantukaṁ:* a ball for Kāma to play with; *anayōḥ:* of these two; *dṛśōḥ:* eyes; *sakhāyaḥ:* friends; *ajinayōnaḥ:* antelopes; *kaçaḥ:* tresses; *añçat + nalina + ālinā:* towards which rows (*āli*) of lotuses (*nalina*) bend in reverence (*añçat*); *alinā:* by a bumblebee; *arçita:* esteemed.

TRANSLATION:
O Divine Mother! Your teeth rip apart the pride of jasmine heaps. What appears to be your rounded breast is verily a ball for Kāma to sport with. Antelopes are your eyes' natural allies. And your curly tresses are esteemed by bumblebees that flourish amidst rows of lotuses.

VERSE (page 56):

pravāḷa·kānti·prakar'ākarā karāḥ
radaç'çhada·śrīr'taruṇ'āruṇ'āruṇā |
iti sphuṭ'ōpāsanayā'nayā nayā·
my'ahāni sarva·kratavas'tava stavaḥ ‖

ANVAYA:
(tava) karāḥ pravāla-kānti-prakara-ākarāḥ, (tava) radaçchada-śrīḥ taruna-aruṇa-aruṇā | iti anayā sphuta-upāsanayā ahani nayāmi | sarvakratavaḥ tava stavaḥ |

VOCABULARY:
(tava): (your); *karāḥ:* arms; *pravāla-kānti-prakara-ākarāḥ:* are the repositories (*ākarāḥ*) of the heaps (*prakara*) of luster (*kānti*) emanating from corals (*pravāla*), i.e., your arms are as lustrous as corals; *radaçchadda-śrīḥ:* the shine on your lips; *taruṇa-aruṇa-aruṇā:* is ruddy like that of the rising sun; *iti:* in this manner; *anayā:* by this; *sphuṭa-upāsanayā:* explicit form of worship/reverence; *ahani:* days; *nayāmi:* I will pass/lead; *sarva-kratavaḥ:* all ritualistic sacrifices; *tava:* your; *stavaḥ:* praise.

TRANSLATION:
Your arms are the repositories of coralline radiance and your crimson lips match the color of the newly risen sun. And all rituals are but your eulogies– May my days pass with such earnest adoration.

VERSE (page 56):

bhavēt'tavā'nugraha·dōha·dōhadō
dayā·plutō'pāṅga·lav'ālavālavān
manōratha·drur'mama nāma nā'manā·
k'phalaḥ katham vā'bja·padē padē·padē ‖

ANVAYA:

(hē) abjapadē, tavānugraha-dōha-dōhadaḥ, dayā-plutaḥ, apāṅga-lava-ālavāla-vān, mama manōratha-druḥ katham nāma padē padē amanāk-phalaḥ na bhavēt ‖

VOCABULARY:

abjapadē: O Goddess with feet like lotuses!; *tava:* your; *anugraha-dōha-dōhada:* with the flow of your grace for the *dōhada* ritual; *dayā-pluta:* watered by your compassion; *apāṅga-lava-ālavāla-vān:* with your casual side-glance for its basin; *mama:* my; *manōratha-druḥ:* tree of desires; *katham:* how; *nāma:* surely; *padē padē:* again and again; *amanāk-phalaḥ:* bearing plentiful fruits; *na:* not; *bhavēt:* shall become.

TRANSLATION:

O Goddess with feet pretty like lotuses! How, I ask of you, shall the tree of my desires not bear plentiful fruit? The continuous flow of your grace is the *dōhada* ritual that puts it to bloom, your compassion the water that nourishes it and your casual side-glance the basin within which it grows.[753]

VERSE (page 56):

budh'ālir'ēkā mahit'ēhitē hi tē
tav'ābhibhūtā sva·pad'āpadā padā |
nirasta·kalpa·prasav'āsavā savā·
g'rasaiḥ par'ābhukta·savā sa·vāsavā ‖

[753] *Dōhada* is a ritual that is performed by ladies before trees can put forth their flowers. The belief is that trees, like pregnant women, have certain desires that must be fulfilled. The Aśoka, for instance, craves a kick from the bejeweled feet of beautiful maidens. See, for example, Kālidāsa's *Uttaramegha,* 18: *"raktāśokaścalakisalaya kesarasçātra kānta | pratyāsannau kurabakavrtermādhavīmaṇḍapasya ‖ ekaḥ sakhyāstava saha mayā vāmapadābhilāṣī | kāṅkṣatyanyo vadanamadirām dohadaçchadmanāsyāḥ ‖"*

Anvaya:

mahita-īhite, hite, ekā sa-vāsavā budha-āliḥ svapada-āpadā, tava padā abhibhūtā (sati) nirasta-kalpa-prasava-āsavā, a-sa-vāk, para-ābhukta-savā (āsīt)

Vocabulary:

mahita-īhite: of desires that are esteemed, she that respects what others desire; *hite:* gracious, beneficial; *ekā:* one, unique; *sa-vāsavā:* accompanied by Indra; *budha-āliḥ:* assembly of gods; *svapada-āpadā:* because of the calamity (*āpata*) affecting their own (*sva*) abode (*pada*); *tava:* your; *padā:* foot; *abhibhūtā:* dishonored; *nirasta-kalpa-prasava-āsavā:* not having access (*nirasta*) to the wine (*āsava*) made from the flowers (*prasava*) of the wish-yielding trees (*kalpa*); *a-sa-vāk:* without words, mute; *rasaiḥ:* joyfully, passionately; *para-ābhukta-savā:* with the sacrificial rituals (*sava*) meant for them being enjoyed (*ābhukta*) by their enemies (*para*); *(āsīt):* (was).

Translation:

O favorable Goddess, holding high regard for the wishes of your devotees! When your feet no longer provided refuge to the assembly of demigods—their heavenly abode in grave danger—the latter, cheated of the sweet wine prepared from the flowers of the wish-yielding trees, mutely watched as their jubilant enemies partook of the sacrificial offerings.

Verse (page 57):

kamalā punātu bhava·śoka·malā·
n'avadhūya māṁ garuḍa·yāna·vadhūḥ |
sumanā natā'vana·kalāsu manā·
g'avanamra·mūrtir'agha·nāga·vanaṁ ||

Anvaya:

garuḍa-yāna-vadhūḥ, nata-avana-kalāsu sumanāḥ manāk-avanamra-mūrtiḥ, kamalā bhava-śoka-malān avadhūya agha-nāga-vanaṁ māṁ punātu

Vocabulary:

garuḍa-yāna-vadhūḥ: The beloved wife of *viṣṇu,* whose vehicle is Garuḍa; *nata-avana-kalāsu:* in the art of protecting those that bow down to Her; *sumanāḥ:* clever; *manāk-avanamra-mūrtiḥ:* with a slightly stooping form; *kamalā:* Lakṣmī; *bhava-śoka-malān:* the dirt that is the sorrow of worldly existence; *avadhūya:* removing; *agha-nāga-vanaṁ:* the forest that shelters serpents in the form of sins; *māṁ:* me; *punātu:* cleanse, purify.

TRANSLATION:
Let Lakṣmī, the beloved wife of Viṣṇu, whose vehicle is *Garuḍa,* adept in the art of protecting Her suppliants and looking graceful with a slightly stooping form, remove the dirt of distressful material existence and cleanse me, who am the forest that shelters serpents in the form of dreaded sins.
NOTE: The poet's use of the synonym *garuḍa-yāna-vadhūḥ* for the Goddess suggests her capability in destroying the serpents in the form of sins.

VERSE (page 58):

vandē śivaṁ dēśikam'apy'udañça·
d'āmōda·dāmōdara·padmayōnyōḥ |
mōhaṁ tamō hanta jighamsatāṁ svaṁ
dīpam nadī·pannaga·çandra·bhūṣam ||

ANVAYA:
hanta! udañçat-āmōda-dāmōdara-padmayōnyōḥ api dēśikaṁ, svaṁ mōhaṁ tamaḥ jighāṁsatāṁ dīpaṁ, nadī-pannaga-candra-bhūṣaṁ śivaṁ vandē

VOCABULARY:
hanta: exclamation of surprise and glee; *udañçat-āmōda-dāmōdara-padma-yōnyōḥ:* of the happy duo Viṣṇu and Brahma; *api:* also, even; *dēśikaṁ:* master teacher; *svaṁ:* personal, one's own; *mōhaṁ:* delusion, ignorance; *tamaḥ:* darkness; *jighāṁsatāṁ:* desirous to destroy; *dīpaṁ:* lamp; *nadī-pannaga-çandra-bhūṣaṁ:* adorned with the river Gaṅgā, serpents, and the moon; *śivaṁ:* Lord Śiva; *vandē:* I salute.

TRANSLATION:
Salutations to Lord Śiva—He who is Master of even Viṣṇu and Brahma, the joyous duo. Adorned with the celestial river, serpents and crescent moon, He is the lamp to those that desire to put an end to the darkness of their inner ignorance.

VERSE (page 58):

stainyēna praṇayēna vā bhuvi sakṛd yas'tē namas'stēnam'a·
py'amba tvaṁ paripāsi taṁ dalita·daurgatyā'hitā'tyāhitā |
padmē tvāṁ tu vayaṁ vaçaḥ·parimalair āmōdayamō dayā·
m'ady'āpadya na çēt prasīdasi numas'śrī·kāmataḥ kām'ataḥ ||

ANVAYA:

amba! bhuvi yaḥ stainyena (?dainyena) praṇayena vā sakṛt te namaḥ (iti vadati) taṁ stēnam api dalita-daurgatya-ahita-atyāhitā paripāsi | padmē! vayaṁ tu tvāṁ vaçaḥparimalaiḥ āmōdayāmaḥ | adya dayāṁ āpadya na prasīdasi çēt śrī-kāmataḥ ataḥ kāṁ numaḥ |

VOCABULARY:

amba: O Divine Mother!; *bhuvi:* in the world; *yaḥ:* He who (correlative of *saḥ*); *stainyāna (?dainyēna):* because of his theiving nature/improbity (?miserable state); *praṇayēna:* out of love; *vā:* or; *sakṛt:* just once; *te namaḥ:* salutations to thee; *(iti vadati):* (utters thus); *taṁ:* Him; *stēnam:* thief; *api:* also; *dalita-daurgatya-ahita-atyāhitā:* destroying (*dalita*) his poverty (*daurgatya*), enemies (*ahita*) and disagreeable state (*atyāhitā*); *paripāsi:* you protect; *padmē:* Lakṣmī, *vayaṁ:* we; *tu:* on the other hand; *tvāṁ:* you; *vaçaḥparimalaiḥ:* with our fragrant words; *āmōdayāmaḥ:* we delight (perfume) you; *adya:* today, now; *dayāṁ:* compassion; *āpadya:* having, taking; *na:* not; *prasīdasi:* become gracious; *çēt:* if; *śrī-kāmataḥ:* due to a desire for wealth and prosperity; *ataḥ:* because of this; *numaḥ:* we (shall) praise.

TRANSLATION:

O Divine Mother! O Lakṣmī! When, in this world, even a thief utters these words: "Salutations to thee", just once, whether out of desperation, love or even a desire to steal, you still protect him by putting an end to his poverty, destroying his enemies and ridding him of his despicableness. We, on the other hand, are ever ready to perfume you with our fragrant poetry. If you still choose not to be gracious by revealing to us your compassionate nature, who else should we, overcome with this intense desire for prosperity, praise? Pray tell us.

VERSE (page 58):

hṛdyas'suhṛd yas'sutarān'nidhīnāṁ
nētur'vinētur'viṣamāṁś'ca daityān |
jāyān'nijāyān'nidadhat'tanau sa
dēvō mudē vō munibhis'stutō'stu ‖

ANVAYA:

yaḥ nidhīnāṁ netuḥ sutarāṁ hṛdyaḥ suhṛt, (yaḥ) viṣamān daityān vinētuḥ ça (sutarāṁ hṛdyaḥ suhṛt), nijāyāṁ tanau jāyāṁ nidadhat, munibhiḥ stutaḥ saḥ dēvaḥ vaḥ mudē astu |

VOCABULARY:

yaḥ: He (correlative of *saḥ*); *nidhīnāṁ:* of the nine treasures; *netuḥ:* lord; *sutarāṁ:* extremely; *hṛdyaḥ:* close to the heart; *suhṛt:* friend; *(yaḥ):* He; *viṣamān:* wicked; *daityān:* demons; *vinētuḥ:* destroyer; *ça:* and; *(sutarāṁ hṛdyaḥ suhṛt):* a friend very close to the heart; *nijāyāṁ:* in one's own; *tanau:* body; *jāyāṁ:* wife; *nidadhat:* placing; *munibhiḥ:* by the sages; *stutaḥ:* praised; *saḥ:* He; *dēvaḥ:* Lord; *vaḥ:* of you; *mudē:* happiness; *astu:* may He be.

TRANSLATION:

Let Lord Śiva, who shares his body with his wife, who is a close friend of Kubēra, the guardian of treasures and of Viṣṇu, the destroyer of wicked demons and who is lauded by sages, confer happiness on you.

VERSE (page 58):

vēdyā trivēdyā'tridiva·prasūna·
dhūlī·madhūlī·masṛṇā'ṅghri·padmā |
rakṣō·bhara·kṣōbhakarī śubhāni
tanvīta tanvī taruṇēndu·mauḷēḥ ‖

ANVAYA:

trivēdyā vēdyā, tridiva-prasūna-dhūlī-madhūlī-masṛṇa-aṅgighra-padmā, rakṣō-bhara-kṣōbha-karī, taruṇēndumaulēḥ tanvī śubhāni tanvīta |

Vocabulary:

trivēdyā: by the three *Vēdas*; *vēdyā:* fit to be known, understood; *tridiva-prasūna-dhūlī-madhūlī-masṛṇa-aṅgighra-padmā:* Her lotus-feet softened by the trickle of honey from, and the pollen of heavenly blossoms; *rakṣō-bhara-kṣōbha-karī:* causing agitation in the demonic hordes; *taruṇēndu-mauleḥ:* Śiva (He who wears the tender moon on his crest); *tanvī:* slender woman; *śubhāni:* prosperity, auspiciousness; *tanvīta:* bring about.

Translation:

May the slender-limbed sweetheart of the moon-crested Śiva confer auspiciousness. With her lotus-feet softened by the trickle of honey and pollen-dust from celestial blossoms, She, fit to be known through the three *Vēdas*, terrorizes the demonic hordes.

Verse (page 58):

kāma·prakāma·prahitaṁ kaṭākṣam
lōlamba·lōlaṁ bahudhā kirantī |
bhāvaṁ svabhāvaṁ sva·vaśaṁ nayantī
pāyād'apāyād'aniśaṁ bhavānī ||

Anvaya:

kāma-prakāma-prahitaṁ, lōlamba-lōlaṁ kaṭākṣaṁ bahudhā kirantī bhāvaṁ svabhāvaṁ sva-vaśaṁ nayantī bhavānī aniśaṁ apāyāt pāyāt

Vocabulary:

kāma-prakāma-prahitaṁ: fervently (*prakāma*) dispatched (*prahitaṁ*) with love (*kāma*); *lōlamba-lōlaṁ:* as fickle as a bee; *kaṭākṣaṁ:* side-ways glance; *bahudhā:* many times over; *kirantī:* casting; *bhāvaṁ:* Śiva's, belonging to Śiva (*bhavasya idaṁ bhāvaṁ*); *svabhāvaṁ:* nature; *sva-vaśaṁ:* under one's own control; *nayantī:* bringing; *bhavānī:* Pārvatī, *aniśaṁ:* always; *apāyāt:* from difficulty; *pāyāt:* protect.

Translation:

Repeatedly casting on Śiva Her side-glance that she dispatches fervently with love, and which is as fickle as a bumblebee, She brings under Her control His very persona. May She, Bhavāni, always protect us from peril.

VERSE (page 59):

nānā'ṅganānāṁ gaṇanīya-śōbhā
dāyādadā yādava-puṅgavasya |
pāyād'apāyād'anaghā'cyutasya
jāy'ānujā yānuparōdham'indōḥ ||

ANVAYA:
nānā-aṅganānāṁ gaṇanīya-śōbhā, yādava-puṅgavasya dāyāda-dā, acyutasya anaghā jāyā, anuparōdhaṁ apāyāt pāyāt yā indōḥ anujā |

VOCABULARY:
nānā-aṅganānāṁ: Of several women; *gaṇanīya-śōbhā:* with a beauty that is worthy of consideration; *yādava-puṅgavasya:* to the foremost of Yādavas; *dāyāda-dā:* She that gifts an heir; *acyutasya:* of Kṛṣṇa; *anaghā:* faultless, sinless, pure; *jāyā:* wife; *anuparōdhaṁ:* without a break, continually; *apāyāt:* from danger; *pāyāt:* protect us; *yā:* She that (correlative of *sā*); *indōḥ:* of the moon; *anujā:* younger sister.

TRANSLATION:
May the sinless wife of Kṛṣṇa, whose beauty is esteemed by many a maiden, who is the younger sister of the moon and who gifted an heir to the foremost of the Yādavas, continually save us from calamity.

VERSE (page 59):

mātā ramā tārakit'ēva hāraiḥ
kaṇṭh'ōpakaṇṭhō'panata-pralambhaiḥ |
dīnān'nadīnāṁ na jahātu patyus'
tādṛk sutā dṛk-sudhayā'rthinō naḥ ||

ANVAYA:
kaṇṭha-upakaṇṭha-upanata-pralambaiḥ hāraiḥ tārakitēva (satī) nadīnāṁ patyuḥ tādṛk sutā dṛksudhayā arthinaḥ dīnān naḥ na jahātu |

VOCABULARY:
kaṇṭha-upakaṇṭha-upanata-pralambaiḥ: with strands (*pralamba*) dangling (*upanata*) close (*upakaṇṭha*) to the neck (*kaṇṭha*); *hāraiḥ:* pearl necklaces; *tārakitā:* starry, studded with stars; *iva* (*satī*): appearing as if she is; *nadīnāṁ:* of rivers; *patyuḥ:* lord; *tādṛk:* of such and such nature; *sutā:* daughter;

dṛk-sudhayā: with the nectar of her glances; *arthinaḥ:* supplicants; *dīnān:* poor, miserable; *naḥ:* us; *na:* not; *jahātu:* abandon.

TRANSLATION:

Let the glorious daughter of the lord of rivers never withdraw her nectarine glances from us, her poor supplicants. She appears to be studded with stars in the form of many a pearl necklace whose multiple strands dangle close to her neck.

VERSE (page 60):

śrī·vatsa·kaustabh'ālaṅkāra·sadmānō gṛhīta·padmānō |
kāmita·mati·mandārāḥ paramōdārāḥ phalantu hari·dārāḥ ||

ANVAYA:

śrīvatsa-kaustubha-alaṁkṛta-sadmānaḥ gṛhītapadmānaḥ kāmita-mati-mandārāḥ parama-udārāḥ hari-dārāḥ naḥ phalantu |

VOCABULARY:

śrīvatsa-kaustubha-alaṁkṛta-sadmānaḥ: She whose home (Viṣṇu's chest) is adorned with the auspicious mark called *śrīvatsa* and the gem *kaustubha*; *gṛhīta padmāḥ:* carrying a lotus; *kāmita-mati-mandārāḥ:* the divine tree *mandāra* that yields desires thought about; *parama-udārāḥ:* excessively glorious/generous; *hari-dārāḥ:* wife of Hari; *naḥ:* to us; *phalantu:* bear fruits.

TRANSLATION:

May the excessively generous wife of Hari, whose abode is adorned with the *śrīvatsa* mark and the gem *kaustubha,* who holds a lotus in her hand and who, like the divine tree mandāra, yields objects that are wished for, fulfil our aspirations.

VERSE (page 59):

vidyā·kairava·kaumudīṁ śruti·śiras'sīmanta·muktāmaṇiṁ
dārān padmabhuvas'trilōka·jananīṁ vandē girāṁ dēvatāṁ |
yat'pādabja·namaskriyās'sukṛtināṁ sārasvata·prakriyā
bīja·nyāsa·bhuvō bhavanti kavitā·nāty'aika·jīvātavaḥ ||

TRANSLATION:
I salute the goddess of speech. She, the beloved wife of Brahma, is the moonlight which puts to bloom night lilies in the form of the various sciences and the pearl ornament that adorns the crest of embodied *Vēdic* lore. And those that are fortunate to fall in devotion at her lotus-feet are rewarded with the gift of poesy—poesy that is a fertile ground to sow the seeds of eloquence and that alone rejuvenates the art of dramaturgy.

VERSE (page 61):

> *draupad'īna·nadīpa·drau māra·bhē śuśubhē ramā |*
> *sv'āparādha·dharā'pa·svā vēda·yānini yādavē ||*

ANVAYA:
sva-aparādha-dhara-apa-svā, ramā draupadī-ina-nadī-pa-drau, māra-bhē, vēda-yānini, yādavē śuśubhē |

VOCABULARY:
sva-aparādha-dhara-apa-svā (sveṣāṁ aparādhānāṁ dharā): She, who tolerates the mistakes of her devotees and is free of egotism (*apa-svā*); *ramā:* Lakṣmī; *draupadī-ina-nadī-pa-drau:* a wooden raft (*drau*) for the Pāṇḍavās (*draupadī-ina*) to cross the ocean (of misery) (*nadī-pa*); *māra-bhē:* similar in luster (*bhā*) to Kāma (*māra*); *vēda-yāninī:* whose vehicle (*yāna*) are the *Vēdas*; *yādavē:* in Kṛṣṇa; *śuśubhē:* shone.

TRANSLATION:
Lakṣmī, who tolerates the sins of her devotees and is free of egotism, attained great beauty by uniting with Kṛṣṇa, who is a wooden raft for the Pāṇḍavas to cross over the ocean of misery, who is similar to the Lord of love in splendor and whose vehicle are the *Vēdas* themselves.

NOTE: This is a *gata-pratyāgata* verse, each *pāda* of which is a palindrome, yielding identical readings whether read forwards or backwards.

Translations of the Invitation to *Bhāgavatasaptāha* Celebrations, and Garaḷapurī Śāstri's Response

Vidvān H.V. Nagaraja Rao

Letter from Veṅkōba Rāv and Rāmaçandra Rāv to Maisūru.
(An invitation to the *paṇḍitas* to attend the *Bhāgavatasaptāha* celebration to take place in Mahārāṣṭra. *The first 22 ślōkas of the letter of the invitation have been lost.*)

⋮

A great *yajña* in the form of reading the *Bhāgavata* is to be held shortly in the vicinity of a beautiful mansion. This will be a rare event, which will surely bring the grace of God. ||23||

This auspicious event, which will be wonderful and attractive in the extreme, should be witnessed by one and all. In it will be an assembly of brāhmaṇas reciting holy texts. ||24||

We are hence requesting you, with folded hands and bowed heads, and urge you to come here and stay with us for seven days. ||25||

Great persons will participate in this assembly of scholars, in which the story of Lord Kṛṣṇa will be presented in melodious tunes, highlighting its deep meanings. ||26||

May all of you, desirous of imbibing the nectarine sweetness of the *Bhāgavata,* kindly drop the pollen of your lotus feet on the floor of our residence. ||27||

Do please all of you arrive before the commencement of the event, and stay here till its end, relishing the ambrosia of the story of the Lord. ||28||

If, however, time does not permit, you may visit us for a day, a minute, or even half an instant, for there is surely nothing else that will bring us such prosperity. ||29||

As the *Śrīmad Bhāgavata* itself says: "To what end are many years spent without an awareness of Lord Kṛṣṇa? Even a single hour will bring all prosperity, if one knows in it God's greatness. ‖30‖

"For anyone who has entered into this cycle of birth and death, there is no path other than that of devotion. ‖31‖

"They who drink the divine nectar of Kṛṣṇa's story will purify the people whose hearts are spoiled by the taint of worldly objects of trivial pleasure. Such good persons will also reach the lotus feet of Lord Kṛṣṇa. ‖32‖

"The sun robs the lifespan of all beings when he rises and sets, except in those moments spent eulogising the stories of good persons." ‖33‖

What is the use of talking or writing too much? O, enjoyers of the study of the *Vēdas!* ‖34‖

You are all learned scholars, and your dispositions are generous. The two of us are trying to accomplish a difficult task. Do make our tree of desire bear fruit. ‖35‖

All those who covet various benefits in this world will surely obtain them from the wish-yielding tree known as the *Bhāgavata.* In this there is no doubt! ‖36‖

Please do accept our prayerful invitation, and come. We wish to be blessed by you, the connoisseurs (of the wine of the *Bhāgavata*). ‖37‖

Sirs, may you virtuous scholars kindly pardon us if we have written anything that may be erroneous or contrary to tradition, due to our haste or impetuosity. ‖38‖

GARAḶAPURĪ ŚĀSTRI'S REPLY TO THE ABOVE INVITATION

WE BOW TO KṚṢṆA, THE BELOVED OF THE COWHERDESSES.

May Lord Kṛṣṇa, who enhances love in Rukmiṇī's heart, who kindles the fire of desire in Satyabhāma, who is intoxicated from drinking the juice of Jāṁbavatī's lips, whose mind is ever in the control of Rādhā, whose eyes are riveted on Nīlā's blouse, and who is a natural servant of the cowherdesses, protect us. ‖1‖

May the world be peaceful, and may all righteous people be happy. May all works of such good persons be free of obstacles. ‖2‖

There is a city known as Maisūru, which is the capital and jewel of the state of Karṇāṭaka. Its prosperity puts even Heaven to shame. ‖3‖

There shone king Kṛṣṇarāja; he was indefatigable and most virtuous. He was as the full moon to the ocean of scholars at his court. He was as Harīṣcandra in keeping his word. ‖4‖

He was born of the powers of the Lords of Directions. He protected all his people with love as that of a father. ‖5‖

Now Çāmarāja, who is like a reflection of his predecessor, is looking after the scholars, with even greater love. ‖6‖

The scholars are engaged in realizing the Indescribable Principle by the means of listening to and memorizing the hidden meanings of the *Upaniṣads.* ‖7‖

They have gained expertise in the eighteen branches of learning, putting their rivals to shame. Even so, these scholars remained untainted even by the slightest bit of arrogance. ‖8‖

These scholars wear pearl necklaces strung with strong threads, and live in *agrahāras* donated by the king Kṛṣṇa, and which are free from diseases, possess the best qualities, and exhibit excellent characteristics.[754] ‖9‖

---

[754] This intersting verse contains a series of cleverly crafted puns. Mr Naresh Keerti offers the following: "The scholars wear and reside in that *agrahāra* [necklace/community], which is a gift from king Kṛṣṇa, *muktāmaya* [pearl-studded/healthy], *sugraha-guṇāḍhya*

These scholars take pleasure in beautiful poetry suffused with emotions, and in which refusal may signify assent, just as they relish the companionship of a wife who conveys assent through words that appear to assert refusal. ‖10‖

Just as a bee sucks nectar from a flower, leaving behind its pollen, these scholars see only good qualities in others, omitting their flaws. ‖11‖

The blessings of these scholars, following prayers and worship offered to Viṣṇu, Śiva, and other gods, and accompanied by *Vēdic* recitations are showered upon the two of you. ‖12‖

You two possess wealth in measure fit for kings, and like the mountains Mēru and Himālaya, remain steadfast, without trembling in crises. ‖13‖

You two are stamped by the footprints of Lakṣmī, which are coloured red by *lākṣā*. Your speech is sweet as cow's milk, honey, sugarcane, and grapes. ‖14‖

The rivalry between Lakṣmī and Sarasvatī has existed from the begining of creation. However, the two of you have brought about their reconciliation within yourselves. ‖15‖

The ocean of milk was covered with blue due to the shining body of Viṣṇu, who sleeps there. You two, however, have made the ocean white on account of your fame. ‖16‖

As befits your position as ministers, you are managing the affairs of your master's kingdom effortlessly, issuing commands even just by the movements of your eyebrows. ‖17‖

A couch of devotion have you spread on the swing of your mind, whose very fabric is faith. Thereupon have you placed a motherless and fatherless orphan child (i.e., Lord Nārāyaṇa). ‖18‖

May the blessings of scholars bestow great prosperity on you two, Veṅkōba and Rāmaçandra, who please all learned scholars. ‖19‖

[strung on a strong thread/accessible/well connected and prosperous] and *sadvṛttam* [well rounded/well built]."

By the grace of Rāma, the king of Kōsala, we are all well, as of this morning of the tenth day of the *bahula* half of the month of Puṣya in the year Vibhava. ‖20‖

We wish to receive a letter again from you, conveying the welfare of yourselves, your wives, children, friends, and relatives. ‖21‖

And now, we are extremely pleased to learn of your adventurous undertaking in organizing an event fit to be performed in *kṛtayuga*, even in this impious *kaliyuga*, from your letter, which was given to us by the revered sage of the Parakāla Maṭha, who is always engaged in the performance of amazing feats of *tapasya*. ‖22, 23‖

These are truly the fruits of being born, of being alive, and of possessing wealth, if a person worships Lord Hari in the company of brāhmaṇas. ‖24‖

You two are born into noble families, which great persons have adorned. The tongue is ashamed of its inability to adequately praise your extraordinary feats. ‖25‖

It would indeed be proper for us to attend the auspicious event you are organizing even in the absence of an invitation, let alone after being invited with such love and humility. ‖26‖

We are not, however, used to travelling far, and hence remain here, but truly only our bodies remain here, like wooden idols. ‖27‖

Our minds have travelled to your place with speed, along with our sentiments. When our sentiments are expressed in words, they yield the desired result, we believe. ‖28‖

When you will have completed the bath signalling the culmination of the great event you have planned, you may kindly write a letter again to bring great joy to our ears. ‖29‖

You know all, and all undesirable possibilities are ruled out in your case because you have served for long the lotus feet of revered preceptors. So, nothing remains to be wished for in your case. Nonetheless, we wish to say the following. ‖30‖

May the grace of the prime couple of all creation be showered upon you. May the king who is your helper be equal to Kubera in wealth (or, may your king become an emperor). ‖31‖

The great persons who serve the divine child Kṛṣṇa, who brought happiness to the smiling Yaśōdā, and also serve the meritorious assembly of brāhmaṇas with guileless devotion, will obtain unblemished fame. ‖32‖

Garaḷapurī Śāstri, urged by great scholars, wrote these verses due to their grace. May these words, though slight, bring delight, like the crescent moon. ‖33‖

BIBLIOGRAPHY

AAAS (2013). *The Heart of the Matter: The Humanities and Social Sciences for a Vibrant, Competitive, and Secure Nation.* American Academy of Arts and Sciences.

Aiya, V.N. (1906). *The Travancore State Manual.* Travancore Government Press.

Aiyangār, S.K., editor (1919). *Sources of Vijayanagar History.* Aryan Books International (2003 reissue).

Aiyar, R.S. (1991). *History of the Nayaks of Madura.* Asian Educational Services.

Appadurai, A. and Breckenridge, C.A. (1976). The south indian temple: authority, honour, and redistribution. *Contributions to Indian Sociology,* 10:187–211.

Arasu, A.N.N. (1993). *Mummaḍi Śrīkṛṣṇarāja Mahīpāla Vaṁśaratnākara.* A.N. Nirañjanarāja Arasu, No. 1, 10th Main Road, Sarasvatīpuram, Maisūru.

Arbuthnot, A.J. (1881). *Major-General Sir Thomas Munro, Bart, K.C.B. Governor of Madras: Selections from His Minutes and Other Official Writings.* Number v. 2. Kegan Paul & Co., 1 Paternoster Square, London.

Arbuthnot, A.J. (1889). *Major-General Sir Thomas Munro, Bart. K.C.B. Governor of Madras: A Memoir.* Kegan Paul, Trench, & Co., Paternoster Square, London.

Archeological Department (1932). *Annual Report of the Mysore Archeological Department for the Year 1932 (Mysore University).* Superintendent, Government Press, Bangalore.

Archeological Department (1936). *Annual Report of the Mysore Archeological Department for the Year 1935 (Mysore University).* Superintendent, Government Press, Bangalore.

Ayyāśāstri, S. (1916). *Karṇāta Ċampū Mahakāvyam—Mahiśūra Mahārāja Ċaritram.* G. T. A. Press, Mysore.

Ballantyne, J.R. (1851). *Tarka-sangraha of Annam Bhaṭṭa, with a Hindī paraphrase and English version.* The Tarka-sangraha, with a translation and notes in Hindí and English. Presbyterian Mission Press.

Bell, E. (1882). *A Letter to Sir James Davidson and a Letter to H.M. Durand (1882).* Chatto and Windus, Picadilly, London.

Bendall, C. (1886). *A Journey of Literacy and Archaeological Research in Nepal and Northern India During the Winter of 1884–5.* Cambridge University Press, Cambridge.

Bendall, C. (1893). *Catalogue of Sanskrit, Pali, and Prakrit Books in the British Museum Acquired During the Years 1876–92.* The British Museum.

Bhattacharyya, S. (1990). *Gadādhara's Theory of Objectivity, Part 1.* Indian Council of Philosophical Research, Motilal Banarsidass.

Bourdillon, E.D. (1859). *East India (Education).* Copy of Correspondence with the Indian Government, showing the Progress of the Measures adopted for carrying out the Education Despatch of the 19th day of July 1854. House of Commons.

Bowring, L.B. (1872). *Eastern Experiences.* Henry S. King & Co., London.

Briggs, J. (1829). *A History of The Rise of Mahommedan Power in India, till the year 1612.* Longman, Rees, Orne, Brown, and Green, London.

Buchanan, F. (1807). *A Journey from Madras through the countries of Mysore, Canara, and Malabar,* volume 1. T. Cadell and W. Davies, London.

Chancellor, N. (2001). A Picture of Health: The Dilemma of Gender and Status in the Iconography of Empire, india, c. 1805. *Modern Asian Studies,* 35:769–782.

Commons, H. (1840). Report from the Select Committee on East India Produce; together with the Minutes of Evidence, An Appendix, and Index. In *Parliamentary Papers: 1780–1849, Volume 8.* House of Commons, London, England.

Converse, H.S. (1974). The Agnicayana Rite: Indigenous Origin? *History of Religions*, 14(2):81–95.

Coward, H.G., Potter, K.H., and Raja, K.K. (1990). *The Philosophy of the Grammarians*. Number 5 in Encyclopedia of Indian Philosophies. Motilal Banarsidass, Delhi.

Cutts, E.H. (1953). The Background of Macaulay's Minute. *The American Historical Review*, 58(4):824–853.

Datta, R., editor (2008). *Rethinking a Millenium: Perspectives on Indian History from the Eighth to the Eighteenth Century*. Aakar Books, New Delhi.

Datta, S. (1989). *Migrant Brahmanas in Northern India. Their Settlement and General Impact c. A.D. 475-1030*. Motilal Banarsidass, Delhi.

Ḍinḍima, R. (1907). *Açyutarāyābhyudayam*. Śrī Vāṇī Vilās Sanskrit Series. Śrī Vāṇī Vilās Press, Srirangam. Commentary by Pandit R. V. Krishnamachariar.

Deshpande, M. (2001). Pandit and Professor: Transformations in the 19th Century Maharashtra. In Michaels, A., editor, *The Pandit: Traditional Scholarship in India*, South Asian studies. Manohar, New Delhi.

Desikāchārya, N. (1949). *Origin and Growth of Śrī Brahmatantra Parakāla Mutt*. The Bangalore Press, Bangalore.

Deśikāçārya, S. (1989). *Śrībhāṣyapariṣkāraḥ*. *Laghu Granthamāla*. Sampūrṇānanda Sanskrit University.

Diwakar, R.R., editor (1968). *Karnataka Through the Ages*. Literary & Cultural Development Department, Government of Mysore, Bangalore.

Dundas, H. (1800). *The Asiatic Annual Register*. J. Debrett, London.

Eaton, R.M. (2005). *A Social History of the Deccan, 1300–1761: Eight Indian Lives*. Cambridge University Press, Cambridge.

Edgerton, F. (1926). *Vikrama's Adventures*, volume 27 of *Harvard Oriental Series*. Harvard University Press.

Elliot, C. (1878). Letter from Major C. Elliot to L. Bowring. In *Accounts and Papers of the House of Commons*, volume LVIII. House of Commons. (Enclosure 6 in Item No. 20, letter to the Duke of Argyll, Secretary of State for India, from John Lawrence, *et al.*, December 17, 1868, Session 17 January—16 August 1878).

Fleet, J.F. (1873). Notes on Inscriptions at Gaddak, in the Ḍambaḷ Tālukā of the Dhārwāḍ district. In Burgess, J.A.S., editor, *The Indian Antiquary*, volume II. Education Society Press, Bombay.

Freiberger, O. (2005). Resurrection from the Dead? The Brāhmaṇical Rite of Renunciation and Its Irreversibility. In Gengnagel, J., Hüsken, U., and Raman, S., editors, *Words and Deeds: Hindu and Buddhist Rituals in South Asia*, Ethno Indology: Heidelberg Studies in South Asian Rituals. Harrassowitz Verlag.

Ganeri, J. (2008). Contextualism in the Study of Indian Intellectual Cultures. *Journal of Indian Philosophy*, 36(5-6):551–562.

Gazetteer (1908). *The Imperial Gazetteer of India*. His Majesty's Secretary of State for India In Council, Oxford.

George, P.T. (1970). Land System and Laws in Mysore State. *Artha Vijñāna: Journal of the Gokhale Institute of Politics and Economics*, 12:117–192.

Gode, P.K. (1939). Vāñcheśvara Alias Kuṭṭi Kavi And His Contact With the Patvardhan Sardars Of The Southern Marāṭha Country. *Annals of the Bhandarkar Oriental Research Institute*, XX.

Gode, P.K. (1956). *Studies in Indian Literary History*, volume III. Prof. P. K. Gode Collected Works Publication Committee, Poona.

Gonda, J. (1989). *Prayer and Blessing: Ancient Indian Ritual Terminology*. Orientalia Rheno-traiectina. E. J. Brill, Leiden, The Netherlands.

Gopal, B.R. (1985). *Vijayanagara Inscriptions*, volume I. Directorate of Archeology and Museums, Government of Karnataka, Mysore.

Gopal, M.H. (1993). *British Sources of the Economic, Political, and Social History of Mysore*. Popular Prakashan.

Gribble, J.D.B., editor (1875). *Manual of the District of Cuddapah in the Presidency of Madras*. Government Press, Madras.

Groves, J.P. (1887). *The Duke's Own; or, the Adventures of Peter Daly*. Griffith, Farran, Okeden, and Welsh, London.

Guha, D.C. (1979). *Navya Nyāya System of Logic (Basic Theories and Techniques)*. Motilal Banarsidass, New Delhi.

Guha, S. (2009). The Frontiers of Memory: What the Marathas Remembered of Vijayanagara. *Modern Asian Studies*, 43:268–288.

Gundappa, D.V. (1970). *Jñāpaka Çitraśāle*. Jñāpaka Çitraśāle Series. Kāvyālaya, Mysore.

Hall, F. (1859). *A Contribution Towards an Index to the Bibliography of the Indian Philosophical Systems*. Government N.W.P., Calcutta.

Heras, F.H. (1927). *The Aravidu Dynasty of Vijayanagar*, volume 1. B. G. Paul & Co., Madras.

Hino, S. (1991). *Suresvara's Vartika on Yajnavalkya-Maitreyi Dialogue*. Advaita Tradition Series. Motilal Banarsidass Publishers (Pvt. Limited), Delhi.

Hook, T.E. (1832). *The Life of General, The Right Honourable David Baird, Bart. G. C. B. K. C. &c. &c.*, volume I. Richard Bentley, New Burlington Street, London.

Hultzsch, E. (1904). Remarks on a papyrus from Oxyrhynchus. *Journal of the Royal Asiatic Society*, pages 399–406.

Hultzsch, E. (1988). *South Indian Inscriptions*, volume XVI. Archeological Survey of India.

Hunter, W.W. (1908). *Imperial Gazetteer of India*, volume 18. Clarendon Press.

Hymavathi, P. (1993). *History of Āyurvēda in Āndhradēśa (A.D. 14th c.–17th c.).* Bhargava Publishers, Warangal.

Ikegame, A. (2007). The Capital of Rājadharma: Modern Space and Religion in Colonial Mysore. *International Journal of Asian Studies*, 4(1):15–44.

Ikegame, A. (2009). Space of kinship, space of empire: Marriage strategies amongst the Mysore royal caste in the nineteenth and twentieth centuries. *The Indian Economic and Social History Review*, 46(3):343–372.

Ikegame, A. (2013). *Princely India Re-imagined: A Historical Anthropology of Mysore from 1799 to the Present.* Routledge/Edinburgh South Asian Studies Series. Taylor & Francis.

Ingalls, D.H.H. (1951). *Materials for the Study of Navya-nyāya Logic.* Number v. 40 in Harvard Oriental Series. Harvard University Press.

Kalburgi, M.M., editor (1994). *Karnaṭakada Kaifiyattugaḷu.* Kannada University, Hampi.

Kamath, S.U. (1996). *A Handbook of Karnataka.* Government of Karnataka, Karnataka Gazetteer Department.

Kane, P.V. (1953a). *History of Dharmaśāstra*, volume IV of *Goverment Oriental Series.* Bhandarkar Oriental Research Institute, Poona.

Kane, P.V. (1953b). *History of Dharmaśāstra*, volume II, Part I of *Goverment Oriental Series.* Bhandarkar Oriental Research Institute, Poona.

Knipe, D.M. (1977). *Sapiṇḍīkaraṇa*: The Hindu Rite of Entry Into Heaven. In Reynolds, F., Waugh, E.H., and of Religion, A.A., editors, *Religious Encounters With Death: Insights from the History and Anthropology of Religions*, pages 111–124. Pennsylvania State University Press.

Knipe, D.M. (1997). Becoming a Veda in the Godavari Delta. In van der Meij, D., editor, *India & Beyond: Aspects of Literature, Meaning, Ritual, and Thought*, pages 306–332. Routledge, Taylor & Francis Group.

Knipe, D.M. (2015). *Vedic Voices: Intimate Narratives of a Living Andhra Tradition.* Oxford University Press, New York.

Knowles, J., editor (1889). *The Nineteenth Century: A Monthly Review*, volume XXV. Leonard Scott (New York)/Kegan Paul, Trench & Co. (London).

Krishnamachariar, M. and Srinivasachariar, M. (1974). *History of Classical Sanskrit Literature*. Motilal Banarsidass, Delhi.

Krishnamurthi, P.V. (2001). Suguṭūru Prabhugaḷu. In Vasu, M.V., editor, *Dakshina Karnatakada Arasu Manetanagalu*, Hampi. Kannada University Prasaranga.

Krishnamurthy, P.V. (1994). *Sugutūru Vīraśaiva Arasumanetana*. Beḻḻihabba Kannaḍa Adhyāyanapīṭha, Karnāṭaka Viśvavidyālaya, Dhāravāda.

Kulke, H. and Rothermund, D. (1998). *A History of India*. Routledge, London.

Lach, D.F. and van Kley, E.J. (1998). *Asia in the Making of Europe*. University of Chicago Press.

Laine, J. and Bahulkar, S.S. (2001). *The Epic of Shivaji (Translation of Kavindra Paramananda's Sivabharata)*. Orient Longmans.

Lakṣmīnārāyaṇa, K. (1963). *Rāja Vekaṭādri Nāyaḍu*. Śrī Bhāvanārāyaṇasvāmivāri Dēvasthānamu, Ponnūru, Andhra Pradesh, India.

Lakshminarasimhaiya, M., Sastri, K.N.V., and Sreenivasan, K. (1970). *Kashi Sesha Sastri and His Descendants*. Madras Law Journal Office, Madras.

Mackenzie, G. (1883). *A Manual of the Kistna District, in the Presidency of Madras: Compiled for the Government of Madras*. W. H. Moore, printer, Madras.

Michaels, A. (2001). Traditional sanskrit learning in contemporary india. In Michaels, A., editor, *The Pandit: Traditional Scholarship in India*, South Asian Studies. Manohar, New Delhi.

Minkowski, C. (2014). Apūrvaṁ Pāṇḍityam: On Appayya Dīkṣita's Singular Life. *Journal of Indian Philosophy*, pages 1–10.

Monier-Williams, M. (1899). *A Sanskrit-English dictionary etymologically and philologically arranged with special reference to cognate Indo-European languages.* Clarendon Press, Oxford.

Murray, H. (1853). *History of British India.* T. Nelson and Sons, Paternoster Row, London.

Naidu, B.N. (1996). *Intellectual History of Colonial India, Mysore 1831–1920.* Rawat Publications, Jaipur and New Delhi.

Narasimhachar, R. (1913). *Archaeological Survey of Mysore Annual Report.* Government of Karnataka.

Narasimhacharya, R. (1934). *History of Kannada language (Readership lectures).* Government Branch Press, Mysore.

Narasimhāçār, R. (1929). *Karnāṭaka Kaviçarite.* S.L.N. Press, Bangalore.

Pande, G.C. (1994). *Foundations of Indian Culture.* Motilal Banarsidass, Delhi, India.

Pandey, R. (1998). *Hindu Samskāras.* Motilal Banarsidass, Delhi.

Parsons, C.E. (1930). *Mysore City.* Humphrey Milford, Oxford University Press, Cambridge.

Parsons, C.E. (1931). *Seringapatam.* Humphrey Milford, Oxford University Press, Cambridge.

Patwardhan, R.P. and Rawlinson, H.G. (1978). *Source Book of Maratha History.* K. K. Bagchi & Company, Calcutta. Indian Council of Historical Research.

Phillips, S.H. (1997). *Classical Indian Metaphysics: Refutations of Realism and the Emergence of 'New Logic.* Motilal Banarsidass.

Plague Commission (1900). Proceedings of the Indian Plague Commission, Volume III. In *Reports from Commissioners, Inspectors, and Others,* volume XXXII. House of Commons, London.

Pollock, S. (2001). New intellectuals in seventeenth-century India. *Indian Economic and Social History Review*, 38:3–31.

Pollock, S. (2009). Future Philology? The Fate of a Soft Science in a Hard World. *Critical Inquiry*, 35(4):931–961.

Pollock, S.I. (2008). The Real Classical Language Debate. *The Hindu* (newspaper).

Potter, K. and Bhattacharya, S. (2008). *Encyclopedia of Indian Philosophies: Indian Philosophical Analysis, Nyāya-Vaiśeṣika from Gaṅgeśa to Raghunatha Śiromaṇi*, volume IV. Motilal Banarsidass.

Potter, K.H. (1995). *Encyclopedia of Indian Philosophies: Bibliography*. Number v. 1-2 in Encyclopedia of Indian Philosophies: Bibliography. Motilal Banarsidass.

Pranesh, M.R. (2003). *Musical Composers During Wodeyar Dynasty, 1638-1947 A.D.* Vee Emm Publications, Bangalore.

Prasad, L. (2007). *Poetics of Conduct: Oral Narrative and Moral Being in a South Indian Town*. Columbia University Press, USA.

Purchas, S. (1625). *Purchas, His Pilgrimes*, volume 10. Haklyut Society, Facsimile Reprint of 1625 Edition.

Rai, S.P. (1985). Sariti: A 2000 year old bilingual Tulu-Greek play. *International Journal of Dravidian Linguistics*, 14:320–330.

Raja, C.K., editor (1968). *New Catalogus Catalogorum: An Alphabetical Register of Sanskrit and Allied Works and Authors*, volume i. University of Madras.

Rajagopalan, N. (1992). *Another Garland: Biographical Dictionary of Carnatic Musicians and Composers*. Carnatic Classicals, Indira Nagar, Madras.

Ramusack, B.N. (2004). *The Indian Princes and Their States*. The New Cambridge History of India. Cambridge University Press.

Ranade, M.G. (1992). *The Miscellaneous Writings of the Late Hon'ble Mr. Justice M.G. Ranade.* Sahitya Akademi, Delhi.

Rao, C.H. (1954). *History of Mysore, 1399–1799 A.D.; incorporating the latest epigraphical, literary, and historical researches*, volume 1–3. Superintendent, Government Press, Bangalore.

Rao, R.R.B.M.S. (1936a). *Modern Mysore: from the beginning to 1868.* Higginbothams, Bangalore.

Rao, R.R.B.M.S. (1936b). *Modern Mysore: from the coronation of Chamaraja Wodeyar X to the present time.* Higginbothams, Bangalore.

Rao, S.K.R. (1985). *Encyclopedia of Indian Medicine*, volume 1. Popular Prakashan, on behalf of Dr. V. Parameshwara Charitable Trust.

Reddy, D. (1995). Anekallu Paleyagarara Kaifiyath. *Itihasa Darshana.*

Revenue Board (1875). *Reports on the Settlements of The Land Revenue of The Provinces of The Madras Presidency for Fasli 1283 (1873-74).* The Board of Revenue, Madras.

Rice, B.L. (1868). *Report on Public Instruction in Mysore for the year 1867–1868.* Mysore Government Press, Bangalore.

Rice, B.L. (1877a). *Mysore and Coorg. A Gazetteer Compiled for the Government of India*, volume II, Mysore by Districts. Mysore Government Press, Bangalore.

Rice, B.L. (1877b). *Mysore and Coorg. A Gazetteer Compiled for the Government of India*, volume I, Mysore in General. Mysore Government Press, Bangalore.

Rice, B.L. (1884). *A Catalog of Sanskrit Manuscripts in Mysore and Coorg.* Mysore Government Press, Bangalore.

Rice, B.L. (1897a). *Mysore: A Gazetteer Compiled for Government*, volume 2: Mysore, by Districts. Archibald Constable and Company.

Rice, B.L. (1897b). *Mysore: A Gazetteer Compiled for Government*, volume 1: Mysore, in General. Archibald Constable and Company.

Rice, B.L. (1898). *Epigraphia Carnaṭica, Inscriptions in the Mysore District*, volume IV (Part II). Government of Mysore.

Rice, B.L. (1905). *Epigraphia Carnaṭica*, volume 5. Government of Mysore.

Rice, B.L. (1908). *Imperial Gazetteer of India: Mysore and Coorg*. Superintendent of Government Printing, Calcutta.

Rice, B.L. (2005). *Epigraphia Carnatica, CD Rom Version*. Indian Council of Historical Research, Bangalore.

Rice, L. (1879). *Mysore Inscriptions, Translated for Government*. Mysore Government Press, Bangalore.

Röer, D.E., editor (1850). *Division of the categories of Nyāya Philosopy, with a commentary by Viswanatha Panchanana*. Biblioteca India; A Collection of Oriental Works. The Directors of the East India Company, and the Aisatic Society of Bengal, Calcutta.

Roodermum, P.S. (2002). *Bhāmatī and Vivaraṇa Schools of Advaita Vedānta: A Critical Approach*. Motilal Banarsidass, Delhi.

Row, B.R. (1916). *Annals of the Mysore Royal Family*, volume I. His Highness Sri Krishnaraja Wodiyar IV, G.C.S.I., G.B.E., Mysore.

Row, B.R. (1922). *Annals of the Mysore Royal Family*, volume II. His Highness Sri Krishnaraja Wodiyar IV, G.C.S.I., G.B.E., Mysore.

Row, B.S. (1905). *A History of Vijayanagar: The Never To Be Forgotten Empire*. Asian Educational Services. Reissued in 1993.

Rāmaśāstri, C. (1997). *Mahāviduṣāṁ Çāmarājanagarābhijanānāṁ Rāmaśāstriṇāṁ Laghukṛtayaḥ*. Gargēśvarī Veṅkaṭasubbayya, Bangalore.

Salomon, R. (1993). Addenda to "Epigraphic Remains of Indian Traders in Egypt". *Journal of the American Oriental Society*, 113(4):593.

Saraswathi, A. (1957). Saintly Steerers of the Ship of Brahmadvaita of the Upanishaḍs. *T.T.D. Monthly Bulletin*, VIII(7).

Sarma, K.M.K. and Sarma, E.M.K. (1938–1939). The Date of the *Mahiṣaśatakavyākhyā*. *Annals of the Bhandarkar Oriental Research Institute*, 20(2):207–208.

Śāstri, A.K. (1937). *Advaitasiddhi, with the commentaries Gauḍabrahmānandī, Viṭṭhaleś'opādhyāyī, Siddhivyākhyā of Balabhadra, and a critical summary called Chaturgranthī by M.M. Ananta Kṛṣṇa Śāstri*. Pāṇḍurang Jāwājī, Bombay.

Sastri, A.K. (1951). *A Primer of Indian Logic*. The Kuppuswami Sastri Research Institute, Mylapore, Madras, 2nd edition.

Śāstri, B. (1949). *Karṇāṭaka Śākuntala Nāṭakam*. Basavappa Śāstri *Granthamālā*. Śrī Çāmuṇḍeśvarī Electric Press, Mysore.

Śāstri, C.V. (1917). Çāmarājanagarada Śrīkanṭha Śāstrigaḷa Çaritre. *Kādambarī Saṅgraha Granthamālā*, 36.

Śāstri, C.V. (1925a). Attiguppe Kṛṣṇaśastrigaḷa Çaritre. *Kādambari Saṅgraha Granthamālā*, 51.

Śāstri, C.V. (1925b). Karṇāṭaka Ratnadarpaṇa. *Kādambari Saṅgraha Granthamālā*.

Śāstri, C.V. (1927). Nālvaḍi Kṛṣṇarājābhyudaya. *Kādambarī Saṅgraha Granthamālā*.

Śāstri, C.V. (1934). Śrīkanṭha Smārākāṅka. *Kādambari Saṅgraha Granthamālā*.

Śāstri, K. (1946). Mahisha Satakam. In Aiyar, T.K.B., editor, *Srirangam Sri Sankaragurukula Series*. Sri Sankaragurukula, Srirangam.

Śāstri, K.L. (1928). *Guruvaṁśakāvya*, volume 1 of *Vāṇī Vilāsa Sanskrit Series*. Vani Vilas Press, Srirangam.

Sastri, K.N.V. (1932). *The Administration of Mysore Under Sir Mark Cubbon*. George Allen & Unwin, Ltd., London.

Sastri, R.S. (1927). A Greek farce with Old Kannada passages. *Annual Report of the Mysore Archeological Department for the Year 1926 (Mysore University)*.

Śāstri, S.G. (1891). *Çampūrāmayaṇa Yuddhakāṇḍa.* Sōsale Ayya Śāstri, printed at Maisūru Sadvidyāmandira Press.

Śāstri, T.V.V., editor (1999). *Mudrāmañjūṣa by Kempu Nārāyaṇa.* Sahitya Akademi, Delhi.

Śāstri, T.V.V. (2000). *Mulukunaḍu Brāhmaṇaru.* Mulukunāḍu Mahāsaṅgha, Bangalore.

Sāstri, T.V.V. (2002). Bhāgavata Subbarāv, in *Mārgadarśaka Mahanīyaru.* In *Śāstrīya*, volume 5, pages 3–15. Sapna Book House, Bangalore.

Sāstri, T.V.V. (2012). *Sāhitya Sandhāna.* Sapna Book House, Bangalore.

Sastry, K.A.N. and Venkataramanayya, N. (1946). *Further Sources of Vijayanagar History.* University of Madras, Madras.

Sastry, R.S., editor (1968). *South Indian Inscriptions: Miscellaneous Inscriptions in Kannada.* Archeological Survey of India.

Sastry, V.V. (1976). *Vedam Venkataraya Sastry.* Sahitya Akademi, New Delhi.

Sathyan, B.N.S., editor (1989). *Karnataka State Gazetteer, Bangalore Rural District.* Director of Print, Stationery, and Publications, Karnataka Government.

Satyanarayana, A. (1996). *History of the Wodeyars of Mysore.* Directorate of Archeology and Museums, Mysore.

Sewell, R. (1900). *A Forgotten Empire (Vijayanagar). A Contribution to the History of India.* Swan Sonnenschein & Co., Ltd., London.

Sharma, B.N.K. (1981). *History of the Dvaita School of Vedānta and its Literature.* Motilal Banarsidass.

Sharma, M.H.R. and Gopal, M.H. (1978). *The History of the Vijayanagar Empire*, volume 1. Popular Prakashan, Bombay.

Sharma, M.H.R. and Gopal, M.H. (1980). *The History of the Vijayanagar Empire*, volume 2. Popular Prakashan, Bombay.

Sharma, S.R. (1944). *Maratha History Re-examined.* Karnatak Publishing House, Chira Bazar, Bombay.

Sharp, H. and Richey, J.A. (1920). *Selections from Educational Records: 1781-1839, edited by H. Sharp.* Selections from Educational Records, Bureau of Education. Superintendent, Government Printing, India.

Siddhaliṅga, S. (1989). *Maḷeyarāja Çāritra.* Śrīgiri Prakāśana, Śrīgiri, 4/5A, Ali Āskar Road, Bangalore.

Simpson, W.J. (1905). *A Treatise on Plague dealing with the Historical, Epidemiological, Clinical, Therapeutic, and Preventive aspects of the Disease.* Cambridge University Press.

Sircar, D. (1966). *Indian Epigraphical Glossary.* Motilal Banarsidass, Delhi, Varanasi, Patna.

Sircar, D.C. (1971). *Studies in the Geography of Ancient and Medieval India.* Motilal Banarsidass, Delhi, Varanasi, Patna.

Sircar, D.C. (1996). *Indian Epigraphy.* Motilal Banarsidass, Delhi, Varanasi, Patna.

Skinner, Q. (2002). *Visions of Politics.* Number v.1 in Visions of Politics 3-Volume Set. Cambridge University Press.

Society, A. (1870). *Proceedings of the Asiatic Society of Bengal.* Asiatic Society of Bengal, Calcutta.

Śrīharṣa (1912). *Naishadhīyacharita.* Tukārām Jāvajī, Nirṇaya Sāgar Press, Śivadatta, editor, Bombay, 4th edition.

Srinivas, M.D. (1986). Indian Approach to Formal Logic and Methodology of Theory Construction. *PPST Bulletin,* (10):32–59.

Staal, F. (2001a). *Agni, the Vedic Ritual of the Fire Altar,* volume 1 of *Hinduism and Its Sources.* Motilal Banarsidass.

Staal, F. (2001b). *Agni, the Vedic Ritual of the Fire Altar,* volume 2 of *Hinduism and Its Sources.* Motilal Banarsidass.

Stanhope, E. (1878). *Copies or Extracts of Correspondence between the Secretary of State for India and the Governor General, regarding the Reestablishment of a Native Government in Mysore, by the time the Maharajah shall come of Age (in continuation of Parliamentary Papers, of Session 1867).* House of Commons.

Stein, B. (1985). Notes on 'Peasant Insurgency' in Colonial Mysore: Event and Process. *South Asia Research*, 5(11).

Stein, B. (1989). *Thomas Munro, The Origins of the Colonial State and His Visions of Empire.* Oxford University Press.

Subrahmanyam, S. and Shulman, D. (1990). The Men who Would be King? The Politics of Expansion in Early Seventeenth-Century Tamilnadu. *Modern Asian Studies*, 24(2).

Subramanian, K.S. (1985). An Introduction to the Vina. *Asian Music*, 16(2):7–82.

Sujātā, H.S. (2001). *M. S. Puṭṭaṇṇa.* Sahitya Akademi, New Delhi, India.

Sundaram, V. (2012). Get to know about Chentsal Rao Pantulu. In Rao, N.M.R., editor, *Feature Writing*. PHI Learning, New Delhi.

Svāmi, L.N. and Bhāratī, B.R. (2007). *Maisūru Saṁsthānada Pradhāna Veṅkappayyanavaru.* Śrī Ċinmaya Prakāśana, Ujire.

Swami Rama (2002). *Samadhi the Highest State of Wisdom: Yoga the Sacred Science*, volume 1 of *Yoga the Sacred Science*. Lotus Press, Himalayan Institute Hospital Trust, Dehra Dun, India.

Tavernier, J.B. (1889). *Travels in India.* MacMillan and Co., London and New York. (Translated by Valentine Ball).

Tripathi, G.C. (2004). *Communication with God: the Daily Puja Ceremony in the Jagannatha Temple.* Indira Gandhi National Centre for the Arts, Aryan Books International, Delhi, India.

Trivedi, P. and Bartholomeusz, D. (2005). *India's Shakespeare: Translation, Interpretation, and Performance.* International Studies in Shakespeare and his contemporaries. University of Delaware Press.

Utgikar, N.B., editor (1928). *Collected Works of Sir R.G. Bhandārkar*, volume II of *Government Oriental Series–Class B, No. II*. Bhandarkar Oriental Research Institute, Poona.

Varadachari, V. (1972). Contribution of Tamilnadu to Sanskrit—Srivaisnavism. In Raghavan, V. and Sharma, R.K., editors, *International Sanskrit Conference, New Delhi, March 26th-31st, 1972*, volume 1, part 1, pages 436–463. Indian Ministry of Education and Social Welfare.

Vāsudevāçārya, K. (1962). *Nenapugaḷu*. Kāvyālaya, Mysore.

Vasudevaçārya, M. (1994). *Nā Kaṇḍa Kalāvidaru*. V. R. Kulkarni, Directorate of Kannada and Culture, Bangalore.

Vedavalli, M.B. (1992). *Mysore as a Seat of Music*. CBH Publications, Trivandrum.

Venkaṭasubbayya, G. and Gītāçārya, N., editors (2000). *Sōsale Ayyāśāstrigaḷu*. B. M. Śrī. Smāraka Pratiṣṭhāna, Narasimharāja Colony, Bengaḷūru.

Veṅkāmātya (1954). Veṅkāmatya Rāmayaṇa, Ayodhyākāṇḍa (T. Chandrasekharan, editor). Number 36 in Madras Government Oriental Series.

Venkataramayya, D. (1905). *The Mysore Chief Court Reports*, volume IX.–1904. Government of His Highness The Maharaja of Mysore, Bangalore.

Venkatasubbayya, G. (1991). *Sammārjanī Śatakam of Āsūri Anantāçārya*. Yadugiri Yatirāja Maṭha and Akhila Karṇāṭaka Saṁskṛta Pariṣad.

Versaikar, V.B.G. (2013). *1857: The Real Story of the Great Uprising*. Harper Collins India.

Weidman, A.J. (2006). *Singing the Classical, Voicing the Modern: the Postcolonial Politics of Music in South India*. Duke University Press.

Whitehead, A.N. (1925). *Science and the Modern World. Lowell lectures*. The Macmillan Company, New York.

Whitehead, A.N. (1978). *Process and Reality: An Essay in Cosmology*. The Free Press, New York.

INDEX

Footnotes appear in italics, with the footnote number preceded by the character *f*.

Names of books and other works appear in italics, followed by the author's name in parentheses, if known.

Personal names appear in forms consistent with South Indian usage; *agnomina* appear first, with deference to the relative importance of the words in the name. Thus, we see "*Vīṇe* Śēṣaṇṇa, *Çikka*", not "*Çikka Vīṇe* Śēṣaṇṇa", as the *agnomen "Vīṇe"* is invariably used in this name, but *Çikka* is used only to disambiguate. Usage, however, dictates "*Çikka* Rāmappa", not "Rāmappa, *Çikka*", and "Jayarām Rāv", not "Rāv, Jayarām". Since standard usage can be a matter of judgment, it is best to look up a name under variant word orderings.

Compound personal names may witness elision of their first components in normal use, with *cognomina* such as "Śāstri" or "Bhaṭṭa" merged with the primary name. Thus "Lakṣmīnarasiṁha Śāstri" may have appeared as "Narasiṁhaśāstri" in the text.

Family relationships are abbreviated as follows: *b/o*: brother of, *bl/o*: brother-in-law of, *d/o*: daughter of, *dl/o*: daughter-in-law of, *f/o*: father of, *gd/o*: granddaughter of, *gf/o*: grandfather of, *ggd/o*: great-granddaughter of, *ggf/o*: great-grandfather of, *ggs/o*: great-grandson of, *gs/o*: grandson of, *h/o*: husband of, *m/o*: mother of, *s/o*: son of, *si/o*: sister of, *sl/o*: sister-in-law of, *w/o*: wife of.

A

C

D

S

W

Y

Z